OXFORD STUDIES IN EUROPEAN LAW

*Series Editors*

PAUL CRAIG

*Professor of English Law at St John's College, Oxford*

GRÁINNE DE BÚRCA

*Professor of Law at the European University Institute, and Florence Ellinwood Allen Professor of Law at New York University*

# The Law of EU Border Controls

# OXFORD STUDIES IN EUROPEAN LAW

*Series Editors*

Paul Craig, Professor of English Law at St John's College, Oxford
and Gráinne de Búrca, Professor of Law at the European University Institute,
and Florence Ellinwood Allen Professor of Law at New York University

The aim of this series is to publish important and original research on EU law. The focus is on scholarly monographs, with a particular emphasis on those which are interdisciplinary in nature. Edited collections of essays will also be included where they are appropriate. The series is wide in scope and aims to cover studies of particular areas of substantive and of institutional law, historical works, theoretical studies, and analyses of current debates, as well as questions of perennial interest such as the relationship between national and EU law and the novel forms of governance emerging in and beyond Europe. The fact that many of the works are interdisciplinary will make the series of interest to all those concerned with the governance and operation of the EU.

OTHER TITLES IN THIS SERIES

**Protecting EU Consumers in Internet of Things Ecosystems**
*The Intersection between Consumer, Competition, and Data*
Christof Koolen

**When Deportation Fails**
*Non-Removable Migrants in the European Union*
Diego Ginés Martín

**Legal Mobilization for Migrant Rights**
*Opportunities and Barriers at the European Court of Justice*
Virginia Passalacqua

**Saving the European Union from its Illiberal Member States**
András Jakab and Lando Kirchmair

**Constitutional Disintegration and Disruption**
*Withdrawal and Opt-Outs from the European Union*
Oliver Garner

**Business Freedoms and Fundamental Rights in European Union Law**
Niall O'Connor

**Compliance with European Consumer Law**
*The Case of E-Commerce*
Felix Pflücke

**Legislative Authority and Interpretation in the European Union**
Martijn van den Brink

**Secession and European Union Law**
*The Deferential Attitude*
Núria González Campañá

**Fiscal State Aid Law and Harmful Tax Competition in the European Union**
Dimitrios Kyriazis

**The Abuse of Constitutional Identity in the European Union**
Julian Scholtes

**Judging European Democracy**
*The Role and Legitimacy of National Constitutional Courts in the EU*
Nik de Boer

**EU Values Before the Court of Justice**
*Foundations, Potential, Risks*
Luke Dimitrios Spieker

**Postnational Constitutionalism**
*Europe and the Time of Law*
Paul Linden-Retek

**The Legislative Priority Rule and the EU Internal Market for Goods**
*A Constitutional Approach*
Eadaoin Ní Chaoimh

**The Jurisprudence of Constitutional Conflict in the European Union**
Ana Bobić

**Reflexive Governance in EU Equality Law**
Emma Lantschner

# The Law of EU Border Controls

## *Constitutional Compliance and Conditions for an Area without Internal Frontiers*

LEANDRO MANCANO, PHD
*Senior Lecturer, Edinburgh Law School, UK*

OXFORD
UNIVERSITY PRESS

OXFORD
UNIVERSITY PRESS

Great Clarendon Street, Oxford, OX2 6DP,
United Kingdom

Oxford University Press is a department of the University of Oxford.
It furthers the University's objective of excellence in research, scholarship,
and education by publishing worldwide. Oxford is a registered trade mark of
Oxford University Press in the UK and in certain other countries.



Published in the United States of America by Oxford University Press
198 Madison Avenue, New York, NY 10016, United States of America.

British Library Cataloguing in Publication Data
Data available

Library of Congress Control Number: 2025944218

ISBN 9780192869876

DOI: 10.1093/9780191966187.001.0001

Printed and bound by
CPI Group (UK) Ltd., Croydon, CR0 4YY

MIX
Paper | Supporting
responsible forestry
FSC® C013604

The manufacturer's authorised representative in the EU for product safety is
Oxford University Press España S.A. of Parque Empresarial San Fernando de Henares,
Avenida de Castilla, 2–28830 Madrid (www.oup.es/en or product.safety@oup.com).
OUP España S.A. also acts as importer into Spain of products made by the manufacturer.

*A Ruth e Federico. Noi ricominciamo da tre*

# Series Editors' Preface

Borders have traditionally been the sole preserve of the nation state, part and parcel of the very idea of state sovereignty. This is no longer so with the advent of the EU. Its very *raison d'être* was to render war between its member states both unthinkable in normative terms and economically problematic because of the interdependence of its economies.

Borders define the EU's very existence. This is so both physically and normatively. The borders of the EU are definitive of membership, with the plethora of rights and obligations that come with accession to the EU. They demarcate the outer boundaries of the EU, with all the attendant and controversial implications for asylum and migration. They shape its internal order, most notably in the provisions concerning free movement, Schengen, and the like. The very idea of the EU designed to secure peace and prosperity is captured in the idea of a polity without internal frontiers.

There is a dense network of EU rules relating to borders, based on Treaty articles, regulations, directives, and decisions, as well as multiple forms of soft law. This study explores both the internal and external dimensions of borders within the framework of the EU.

The author duly notes the 'three souls' that animate the law of EU border controls. One is constitutive of freedom by abolishing controls inside Schengen, and allowing that freedom to be enjoyed by those entitled to free movement. A second soul imposes constraints, principally by controlling the movement into and across Schengen of persons who do not meet certain criteria. The third acts to safeguard the different categories of the persons concerned, through rights and principles grounded in the EU's foundational values as enumerated in Article 2 TEU.

The book provides an insightful and informative guide to the complex world of the EU's borders. In Part I, the author discusses the interaction among the principal building blocks of the EU legal order, the main argument being the way in which principles of EU law function in this complex area. Parts II and III of the book deal respectively with external and internal EU border controls. Their structure is identical. There is consideration of the main values, objectives, and principles that inform the respective areas. This is followed in relation to external and internal borders with chapters on sources of controls, exercise of controls, and control of the controls.

The book is built around the flow of people. This is reflected in the main chapters on external border controls, which are concerned with three scenarios: before leaving, in transit, and at the EU's borders. By way of contrast, the discussion of internal borders is predicated on two main pillars, these being the absence of controls and exceptions to it; and compensatory actions implemented at, or close to, the EU's internal borders.

The study concludes by revealing the ways in which the law of EU border controls is not constitutionally compliant.

This book covers an important dimension of EU law that will be of interest to all those concerned with the subject.

Paul Craig
Gráinne de Búrca

# Acknowledgement

In writing this book, I have benefited enormously from discussions with many colleagues. They have challenged me and pushed my thinking further with respect to several key issues addressed in the volume. I am indebted to colleagues from my home institution, Edinburgh Law School, and particularly Stephen Coutts, Tim Jacob-Owens, Bob Lane, and Neil Walker. A special note of gratitude goes to Niamh Nic Shuibhne, who has patiently listened to my research 'blathering' for years (on this book before it was even a book proposal, and many other matters). Her encouragement and inspiration to think systemically have fundamentally shaped the approach developed in this monograph.

A heartfelt thanks goes to the several colleagues who kindly hosted me for 'test seminars' before the final submission of the manuscript: Christophe Hillon and Alessandro Petti from the University of Oslo, Ester Herlin-Karnell from the University of Gothenburg, Xavier Groussot and Alezini Loxa from the University of Lund, Sara Iglesias Sánchez from Universidad Complutense Madrid, Melanie Fink from the University of Leiden, Elise Muir from KU Leuven, and Lilian Tsourdi from the University of Maastricht. Their questions and comments, as well as those of the colleagues who attended my talks, significantly contributed to improving the final text of the book.

As the volume features a number of 'highlights' from certain member states, I must thank and mention my fantastic research assistants Roberta De Paolis, Adèle Kauffmann, Susanna Kerttula, and Rebekka Orskaug, who offered crucial help at an important stage of the research.

Thanks are also owed to the anonymous colleagues who took the time to carefully review the book proposal and the manuscript and who provided vital feedback to enhance the quality of this research.

Readying this research for publication was made much easier by my project editor, Paulina dos Santos Major, who was incredibly positive and responsive throughout: the best project editor an author could dream of.

This book is dedicated to my wife Ruth, who supported me every step of the way, and my son Federico, who has 'accompanied' me in the months of revision before making a spectacular arrival on Italy's Liberation Day.

# Contents

# Detailed Contents

## PART III. THE LAW OF EU INTERNAL BORDER CONTROLS

# Table of cases

## COURT OF JUSTICE OF THE EUROPEAN UNION

## EUROPEAN COURT OF HUMAN RIGHTS



## NATIONAL CASE LAW

### Italy



### France

**Norway**

# Table of Legislation

## INTERNATIONAL CONVENTION AND TREATIES



## EU TREATIES AND AGREEMENTS

## SECONDARY EU LAW

### Regulations

**Directives**

**Decisions**

### Norway

# Abbreviations

| | |
|---|---|
| AFSJ | Area of Freedom, Security and Justice |
| AMMR | Asylum and Migration Management Regulation |
| APD | Asylum Procedure Directive |
| API | advance passenger information |
| APR | Asylum Procedure Regulation |
| ATV | airport transit visa |
| CBSS | Copernicus Border Surveillance Service |
| CCI | Common Consular Instructions |
| CEAS | Common European Asylum System |
| CEPOL | European Union Agency for Law Enforcement Training |
| CFR | Charter of Fundamental Rights |
| CFSP | Common Foreign and Security Policy |
| CISA | Convention implementing the Schengen Agreement |
| CISE | Common Information Sharing Environment |
| CJ | EU Court of Justice |
| CNCDH | *Commission nationale consultative des droits de l'homme* |
| CO | coordinating officer |
| COSI | Committee on Operational Cooperation on Internal Security |
| CPIP | common pre-frontier intelligence picture |
| CPT | Committee for the Prevention of Torture |
| CSDP | Common Security and Defence Policy |
| DNPAF | Direction nationale de la police aux frontières |
| DoR | Defender of Rights |
| EASA | European Aviation Safety Agency |
| EAW | European Arrest Warrant |
| EBCG | European Border and Coast Guard |
| ECHR | European Convention of Human Rights |
| ECJ | EU Court of Justice |
| ECRE | European Council on Refugees and Exiles |
| ECRIS-TCN | European Criminal Record Information System for Third-Country Nationals |
| ECSC | European Coal and Steel Community |
| ECtHR | European Court of Human Rights |
| ED | Executive Director |
| EES | Entry/Exit System |
| EFCA | European Fisheries Control Agency |
| EFS | EUROSUR Fusion Services |
| EIBM | European Integrated Border Management |
| EJML | European Journal of Migration and Law |

| | |
|---|---|
| ELJ | European Law Journal |
| EMPACT | European Multidisciplinary Platform Against Criminal Threats |
| EMSA | European Maritime Safety Agency |
| EMU | Economic and Monetary Union |
| ENLETS | European Network of Law Enforcement Technology Services |
| ENP | European Neighbourhood Policy |
| EPL | European Public Law |
| EPPO | European Public Prosecutor's Office |
| ESP | European situational picture |
| ETIAS | European Travel Information and Authorisation System |
| EU | European Union |
| EUAA | European Union Agency for Asylum |
| EUMAM Ukraine | European Union Military Assistance Mission in support of Ukraine |
| EUROSUR | European Border Surveillance System |
| EU-STNA | EU Strategic Training Need Assessment |
| FOSS | Frontex One-Stop Shop |
| FRA | Fundamental Rights Agency |
| FRGB | Fundamental Rights Guidance Board |
| FRM | fundamental rights monitor |
| FRO | fundamental rights officer |
| FRTD | facilitated railway transit document |
| FTD | facilitated transit document |
| GC | General Court |
| GDPR | General Data Protection Regulation |
| ICC | International Coordination Centre |
| ICO | Inspection and Control Office |
| ILO | immigration liaison officer |
| ILON | Immigration Liaison Officers Network |
| IMO | International Maritime Organisation |
| ISPS Code | International Ship and Port Security Code |
| JHA | Justice and Home Affairs |
| JIT | Joint Investigation Team |
| JITs FD | Framework Decision on Joint Investigation Teams |
| LEW | Law Enforcement Working Party |
| LTV | limited territorial validity |
| MB | Management Board |
| MEEs | measures having an equivalent effect |
| MoU | Memoranda of Understanding |
| MRCC | Maritime Rescue Coordination Centre |
| MSC | Maritime Safety Committee |
| MSPC | Multiannual Strategic Policy Cycle |
| NCC | National Coordination Centre |
| NGO | non-governmental organizations |
| NIM | Norwegian National Human Rights Institution |
| NSP | national situational picture |
| OLAF | European Anti-Fraud Office |

| | |
|---|---|
| PAF | Police aux frontières |
| PCCC | Police and Customs Cooperation Centre |
| PNR | passenger name record |
| RBP | Return Border Procedure |
| RCC | Rescue Coordination Centre |
| SA | status agreement |
| SAR | Search and rescue |
| SBC | Schengen Borders Code |
| SEMM | Schengen Evaluation and Monitoring Mechanism |
| SESB | Surveillance of the External Sea Borders |
| SIR | Serious Incident Reporting |
| SIS | Schengen Information System |
| SLTD | Stolen and Lost Travel Document |
| SOLAS | Safety of Life at Sea |
| SOP | Standard Operating Procedure |
| SP | situational picture |
| TCN | third-country national |
| TDAWN | Travel Documents Associated with Notices |
| TFEU | Treaty on the Functioning of the EU |
| UNCLOS | UN Convention on the Law of the Sea |
| UoF | use of force |
| VIS | Visa Information System |
| WA | working arrangement |

# Introduction

## Searching for Order in a Borderless Europe

### People, Sovereignty, and Territory: The Border and Its Travel Companions

Borders demarcate and create[1] a sovereign space, where political power is exercised over a territory and the persons on it.[2] In doing so, borders define the boundaries of a community and are a vehicle of identity formation.[3] If they have historically been linked to warfare as a *cause of*, and *a way to settle*, conflicts, their role in controlling unwanted mobility[4] has mostly emerged in reaction to the mass population displacement that followed World War I.[5] Bordering—that is, examining[6] persons with the view to including them in, or excluding them from a sovereign space—has since become central to the view of borders as a litmus test for sovereignty.[7] As known, this development has gone hand in hand with the change in the meaning of security heralded by globalization and the end of the Cold War: as military aggression gave way to transnational phenomena, the relevance of the distinction between internal and external threats faded. A more personal connection between the individual (rather than the state as a whole) and the threat emerged, embodied by a more mundane and diffuse nature of the threat itself (eg the poor, the irregular migrant, or the terrorist): security became chiefly a matter of risk management and, therefore, prevention. In this context, borders are key to securitization through the application of 'selective permeability': movement of people across borders has been tightened through control, but not severed by it.[8]

[1] The multiplication of borders is therefore the multiplication of sovereignty—a process which increased significantly after the two world wars and the Cold War with the dissolution of the USSR and Yugoslavia.

[2] J Agnew, 'Mapping Political Power Beyond State Boundaries: Territory, Identity, and Movement in World Politics' (1999) Millennium 28.

[3] J Agnew, 'No Borders, No Nations: Making Greece in Macedonia' (2007) 97 Annals of the Association of American Geographers 398.

[4] MAH Van der Woude and P Van Berlo, 'Crimmigration at the Internal Borders of Europe? Examining the Schengen Governance Package' (2015) 11 Utrecht Law Review 61.

[5] T Hammar, 'Citizenship: Membership of a Nation and of a State' (1986) 24 International Migration 736–37.

[6] MB Salter, 'When the Exception Becomes the Rule: Borders, Sovereignty, and Citizenship' (2008) 12 Citizenship Studies 366.

[7] PE Villegas, 'Moments of Humiliation, Intimidation and Implied "Illegality": Encounters With Immigration Officials at the Border and the Performance of Sovereignty' (2015) 41 Journal of Ethnic and Migration Studies 2357.

[8] MB Sparke, 'A Neoliberal Nexus: Economy, Security and the Biopolitics of Citizenship on the Border' (2006) 25 Political Geography 151.

*The Law of EU Border Controls*. Leandro Mancano, Oxford University Press. © Leandro Mancano 2025.
DOI: 10.1093/9780191966187.003.0001

Against this background, the physical and figurative facilities of contemporary bordering have multiplied. The borderland reflects the social, economic, political, institutional, and cultural landscape created by the presence of the border.[9] The networked border spreads control across the sovereign space and beyond.[10] The network is outside,[11] in-between,[12] and within[13] the space of the state or other forms of territorial powers. It relies on technology as well as innovation in social practices.[14] It is also movement-friendly, unless the aspiring border-crosser fails to meet certain criteria and is then identified as an undesired visitor. Territorial borderlines have increased too,[15] and grown stronger through the use of technology.[16]

Therefore, the spectrum of functions associated with borders has translated into a range of activities related to their control. Far from losing importance, the physical protection of the borderline now works in conjunction with a diverse set of complementary measures covering the whole of the migratory process. Notwithstanding that paradigm shift, which reflects the change in threat targeted by bordering, border controls are still solidly anchored to their original mission: defending the effectiveness of sovereignty over the people on a certain territory, which includes deciding who can have access to it. All the trends described so far unfold very clearly in the supranationalization of border controls, as 'borderwork is no longer the exclusive preserve of the nation-state'.[17] In a context where the external threat to sovereignty is identified in migration rather than external aggressors, those presiding over the cross-border movement of people are often partners rather than antagonists.[18] This is, of course, unless and until migration itself becomes a weapon in warfare, alone or in conjunction with the violation of the territorial integrity of a sovereign power through military intervention.

## The Law of EU Border Controls: Marking the Conceptual Frontier

The sketch drawn in the previous section resembles a portrait of Europe—and of the EU in particular. The history of the Union, condensed in its overarching mission

[9] D Rumley and J Minghi, 'The Border Landscape Concept' in D Rumley and J Minghi, *The Geography of Border Landscapes* (Routledge 1991) 1.

[10] E Balibar, *We, the People of Europe? Reflections on Transnational Citizenship* (Princeton University Press 2004).

[11] Consulates and embassies deal with visa applications, while airlines and private carriers must check valid titles of those travelling on pain of dear penalties.

[12] A plethora of places such as surveillance areas, transit zones, and immigration centres govern and monitor the cross-border movement.

[13] Databases store biometrics information about potentially unwanted aliens, and private actors such as employers are co-opted in migration control.

[14] For example, via seconding liaison immigration officers in third countries.

[15] M Foucher, *L'obsession des frontiers* (Perrin 2007).

[16] For example, via the use of satellites and drones. J Brouwer, MAH Van der Woude, and J P Van der Leun, 'Border Policing, Procedural Justice and Belonging. The Legitimacy of (Cr)Immigration Controls in Border Areas' (2017) 58 British Journal of Criminology 624.

[17] C Rumford, 'Theorizing Borders' (2006) 9 European Journal of Social Theory 162.

[18] M Longo, 'A "21st Century Border"? Cooperative Border Controls in the US and EU after 9/11' (2016) 31 Journal of Borderlands Studies 187.

of promoting peace, its values, and the well-being of its people,[19] is a history of collapsing and erecting borders. Making war between its members 'not merely unthinkable, but materially impossible' has always been *the* fundamental underpinning of the EU, and peace within it was linked from the start to 'instrumental' goals such as the establishment of an integrated economic community.[20] On the one hand, the founders of a united Europe saw in the benefits that would flow from economic integration 'les premières assises d'une communauté plus large et plus profonde entre des peuples longtemps opposés par des divisions sanglantes, [pour] jeter les bases d'institutions capables d'orienter un destin désormais partagé'.[21] On the other hand, no shared destiny could exist without shared values, which the EU has identified over the decades and finally crystallized in its Treaties as the foundations of the Union itself.[22] Today, the peaceful coexistence of 450 million people embodies the 'European idea', where the interdependency of its economies goes hand in hand with the development of its common normative heritage. Although peace, prosperity, and values are the flesh and bones of this idea, no better image describes the ambition, trajectory, and essence of the EU as a polity than the creation and preservation of an area without internal frontiers.[23]

The spirit of the Schengen acquis[24] is embedded in the EU's pledge to offer its citizens 'an area of freedom, security and justice [AFSJ] without internal frontiers, in which the free movement of persons is ensured in conjunction with appropriate measures with respect to external border controls, asylum, immigration and the prevention and combating of crime'.[25] The acquis ensures free movement inside the EU, while establishing enhanced law enforcement cooperation from within and stronger controls at the Union's external borders. This picture, however, offers a deceptively simple characterization of what we will call the law of EU border controls. As a preliminary remark, 'border controls' cover those performed at the Schengen external borders as well as inside this area, and are defined as 'the activity carried out at a border . . . in response exclusively to an intention to cross or the act of crossing that border, regardless of any other consideration, consisting of border checks and border surveillance'.[26]

[19] While the idea of promoting those three concepts, as framed in Article 3(1) of Consolidated Version of the Treaty on European Union [2008] OJ C115/13 (TEU), betrays an external projection, it also presupposes laying that tripartite foundation inside the Union first.

[20] The original quote from the Schuman Declaration referred to France and Germany specifically. As known, the Declaration was the driving force behind the European Coal and Steel Community (ECSC), which turned out to be the embryo of what would then become the EU, https://european-union.europa.eu/principles-countries-history/history-eu/1945-59/schuman-declaration-may-1950_en.

[21] Preamble of the ECSC Treaty.

[22] TEU, Article 2. As shown in Chapter 1, this Article is substantiated by more specific provisions that make the EU legal order work.

[23] While 'borders' and 'frontiers' are used interchangeably in this book with reference to EU law, scholars see frontiers as a transitional buffering zone. This is supported by historic evidence on the nature of frontiers over the centuries. LKD Kristof, 'The Nature of Frontiers and Boundaries' (1959) 49 Annals of the Association of American Geographers 269.

[24] The expression is used to describe the 1984 homonymous agreement, abolishing controls between its original contracting parties, and all the measures adopted thereafter building upon it. Agreement between the Governments of the States of the Benelux Economic Union, the Federal Republic of Germany and the French Republic on the gradual abolition of checks at their common borders [2000] OJ L 239/13.

[25] TEU, Article 3(2).

[26] TEU, Article 2.

With this in mind, the EU has addressed borderland situations via measures on local border traffic at the EU external borders.[27] Secondly, the Union has built a system of networked borders, spanning from the EU's visa policy,[28] to different databases and the framework of interoperability between them,[29] through to agreements of different sorts with third countries,[30] the secondment of immigration liaison officers,[31] the co-opting of private actors into migration control by sanctions against employers[32] and carriers,[33] the provisions on external sea border surveillance,[34] the framework on the abolition of internal border controls and the exceptions to it,[35] and the mechanisms of law enforcement cooperation around frontier zones within Schengen.[36] The protection of the Schengen external borderline(s) is mainly ensured by the Schengen Borders Code (SBC) and the European Border and Coast Guard (EBCG) Regulation,[37] supported by the EU's return policy.[38] Asylum law forms an integral part of this framework, and the 2024 Pact has only increased the relevance of bordering to the reception of applicants for international protection and the processing of their claims.[39]

A closer inspection of the abovementioned measures and the constitutional framework in which they were enacted reveals certain structural features of the law of EU border controls. Firstly, the legislation in this area has grown enormously, particularly over the past decade. Such a vast body of law is only the tip of the iceberg. Beneath lies another world of documents fleshing out, substantively or procedurally, the exercise

[27] Regulation (EC) 1931/2006 laying down rules on local border traffic at the external land borders of the Member States [2006] OJ L 405/1.

[28] Regulation (EC) 810/2009 establishing a Community Code on Visas [2009] OJ L 243/1 (VISA Code).

[29] Regulation (EU) 2018/1861 on the establishment, operation and use of the Schengen Information System (SIS) in the field of border checks [2018] OJ L 312/14.

[30] As the book will show, the landscape of agreements co-opting third countries into EU border management is particularly complex. For a constitutional perspective on some of these agreements, see T Strik, 'EU External Cooperation on Migration: In Search of the Treaty Principles' (2023) 8 European Papers 905.

[31] Regulation (EU) 2019/1240 on the creation of a European network of immigration liaison officers [2019] OJ L 198/88 (ILON Regulation).

[32] Directive 2009/52/EC providing for minimum standards on sanctions and measures against employers of illegally staying third-country nationals [2009] OJ L 168/24.

[33] Directive 2001/51/EC supplementing the provisions of Article 26 of the Convention implementing the Schengen Agreement of 14 June 1985 [2001] OJ L 187/45.

[34] See inter alia Regulation (EU) No 656/2014 establishing rules for the surveillance of the external sea borders in the context of operational cooperation coordinated by the European Agency for the Management of Operational Cooperation at the External Borders of the Member States of the European Union [2014] OJ L 189/93 (SESB Regulation).

[35] This is defined in the SBC, Title III.

[36] For example, Articles 40 and 41 of the Convention implementing the Schengen Agreement of 14 June 1985 between the Governments of the States of the Benelux Economic Union, the Federal Republic of Germany and the French Republic on the gradual abolition of checks at their common borders OJ [2000] L 239/19, or Council Framework Decision on joint investigation teams 2002/465/JHA (JITs FD) [2002] OJ L 162/1.

[37] Regulation (EU) 2019/1896 on the European Border and Coast Guard [2019] OJ L 295/1 (EBCG Regulation).

[38] The EU's return policy barycentre lies in Directive 2008/115/EC on common standards and procedures in Member States for returning illegally staying third-country nationals [2008] OJ L 348/98 (or Return Directive), flanked by measures on: assistance in cases of transit for the purposes of removal by air; the organization of joint flights for removals from the territory of two or more Member States, of TCNs who are subjects of individual removal orders; and the mutual recognition of decisions on the expulsion of TCNs.

[39] See, for an overview, https://home-affairs.ec.europa.eu/policies/migration-and-asylum/pact-migration-and-asylum_en#:~:text=What%20is%20the%20Pact%20on%20Migration%20and%20Asylum%3F,results%20while%20remaining%20grounded%20in%20our%20European%20values.

of control inside the EU and at its external borders. Handbooks, working arrangements, status agreements, and administrative documents internal to EU agencies are only a few examples in this regard—all reflecting the complexity of actors involved in the making and implementation of this law. The phrase 'law of EU border controls', as opposed to 'the EU law of border controls', has not been chosen by accident. Border controls are an area of competence shared between the EU and the member states, and therefore subject to the principle of subsidiarity.[40] As a result, prerogatives and responsibilities are balanced in a delicate equilibrium.[41] While the Schengen acquis has granted the EU a greater say on member states' external and internal border controls, the Union is under an explicit obligation to respect the essential state functions.[42] There is more to this than meets the eye. For each of the two levels of governance involved, the legal framework brings a variety of actors around the table: different EU bodies and authorities in each member state act together in a game of three-dimensional chess.[43] Given the highly interactive nature of EU border controls, their proper functioning presupposes a strongly cooperative spirit of the actors in charge, embodied by mutual obligations of trust[44] and solidarity.[45] The expression 'law of EU border controls' aims to recognize precisely that multiplicity: control is 'of' as well as 'for' the EU as a whole, to the extent that it happens at its external borders or within it, but the law and its implementation are not—at least, not in their entirety. The multiplicity does not end there. Although the Schengen acquis forms an integral part of EU law,[46] the membership thereof and of the EU are not completely aligned. Most states are part of both the Union and Schengen. Some EU states are not in the borderless area,[47] whereas certain non-EU states are.[48] All these idiosyncrasies tie in with the manifold objectives pursued by the law of both external and internal border controls. We must facilitate the regular crossing of the Schengen external borders, but also oppose unauthorized entries into the EU and fight against cross-border crime, save lives, and identify vulnerable categories. Within Schengen, we want no border controls on anyone,[49] but also security—inter alia, via mechanisms preventing people from taking advantage of that freedom for non-commendable purposes.[50] Different objectives

[40] Consolidated Version of the Treaty on the Functioning of the European Union [2012] OJ C 326/47 (TFEU), Article 4(2)(j) and Title V and Article 5(3) TEU.

[41] See, for example, Article 7(1) EBCG Regulation: 'The European Border and Coast Guard shall implement European integrated border management as a shared responsibility of the Agency and of the national authorities responsible for border management... Member States shall retain primary responsibility for the management of their sections of the external borders.'

[42] TEU, Article 4(2).

[43] See EBCG Regulation, Article 8(6): 'in order to implement the multiannual strategic policy for European integrated border management, the Member States shall establish national strategies for European integrated border management through close cooperation between all national authorities responsible for the management of external borders and return.'

[44] See, by analogy, Joined Cases C-715/17, C-718/17, and C-719/17, *European Commission v Republic of Poland*, EU:C:2020:257, para 164.

[45] TFEU, Articles 67(2) and 80.

[46] For the sake of simplicity, and unless necessary otherwise, Schengen and EU will be used interchangeably, and so will the expressions 'member states' and 'Contracting Parties'.

[47] Ireland and Cyprus.

[48] Switzerland, Norway, Iceland, and Liechtenstein.

[49] Or, as the TFEU states, 'whatever their nationality' (Article 77(1)).

[50] These mechanisms can take different forms, such as the reintroduction of internal border controls in exceptional circumstances or the exercise of police powers for the purposes of security checks.

entail different types of addressees. We must facilitate the entry of EU citizens or bona fide travellers, but we need to stop the dinghies. In doing this, we must not assume that people who are on the same boat physically are also in the same boat metaphorically. Among those embarking on a perilous journey through unworthy means of transportation, we must identify the vulnerable, combat the criminal, and show the door to those who do not fit our criteria for entry. While the Union shall endeavour to ensure a high level of security, it must also constitute an AFSJ with respect for fundamental rights.[51] It must develop a policy on external borders, asylum, and immigration that is fair to third-country nationals (TCNs)[52] and ensure the absence of border controls inside Schengen.[53] As border controls entail the exercise of authority over different groups of persons for different purposes to different degrees, several key provisions of the EU constitution frame the law in the book and in action by safeguarding the persons concerned and constraining public powers. Many such safeguards and constraints can be found in the EU Charter of Fundamental Rights (CFR or Charter).[54] Some are of more general application, such as the principle of non-discrimination,[55] or the right to liberty,[56] whereas others relate to the specific type of targeted group, such as the right to seek asylum.[57]

## Heterogeneity, Compliance, and Conditions for an Area without Internal Frontiers

Three souls animate the law of EU border controls. One creates freedom by abolishing controls inside Schengen, which can be legitimately enjoyed by persons entitled to free movement. One imposes constraints, by controlling the movement into and across Schengen of persons who fail to meet certain criteria and, to a lesser extent, of those who do as well. One safeguards the different categories of the persons concerned, via a host of rights and principles rooted in the EU's foundational values enumerated in Article 2 TEU. Considering the number of persons that interact with this law every day and the impact it has on their lives, a balanced coexistence of these three souls is key to the health of the EU as a legal order wanting to promote peace, its values, and the well-being of its peoples. As the constraining soul of Schengen has progressively expanded to the detriment of the other two, this balance has been off for quite some time, both at the external and internal frontiers. Externally, the EBCG—better known as Frontex—has been described as the epicentre of the EU rule of law crisis[58] and part of a broader system of lawlessness.[59] This crisis touches upon different

[51] TFEU, Article 67(3) and (1), respectively.
[52] TFEU, Article 67(2).
[53] TFEU, Article 77(1)(a).
[54] Charter of Fundamental Rights of the European Union [2012] OJ C 326/391.
[55] CFR, Article 21(1).
[56] CFR, Article 6.
[57] CFR, Article 18.
[58] L Marin, 'Frontex at the Epicentre of a Rule of Law Crisis at the External Borders of the EU' (2024) 33 European Law Journal 11.
[59] D Kochenov and S Kochenov, 'EU Lawlessness Law: Europe's Passport Apartheid From Indifference To Torture and Killing' (2023), Jean Monnet Working Paper No 2/2022 (NYU Law School).

rights[60] and manifests itself in a number of ways—for example, the impunity and lack of accountability of actors involved in border controls,[61] the criminalization of solidarity via deterrence of search and rescue operations conducted by private parties,[62] and the dubious legality of soft law agreements with third countries.[63] Likewise, practices at the EU internal borders have drawn criticisms in many respects,[64] including vis-à-vis the democratic regression caused by the Schengen governance,[65] the inadequacy of the EU institutions' response to situations of crisis,[66] the drawbacks engendered by the 'contradictory driving forces for Schengen integration',[67] and the failures of interstate solidarity.[68] Considering how inextricably linked the systems of external and (no) internal controls are, the same issues will often straddle both domains, or at least experience a spillover effect from one into the other. Ultimately, the imbalance among the souls of Schengen is not merely part of a physiological process whereby a polity defines its policy priorities. To the contrary, it ends up pathologically undermining the spirit and principles meant to govern the legal framework and its implementation. All these stories, in one way or another, are stories of values, principles, and objectives of EU border controls. These stories raise intertwined questions of allocation of power, interinstitutional solidarity, and treatment of the persons concerned, but catch only fragments of a much bigger picture. In fact, these stories unfold not in a vacuum, but within the broader system to which border controls as an area of law and policy belong: the European Union.[69] In this sense, the structural features of the system shape the law of EU border controls. This is inevitable in any polity, and the Union is no exception. Border controls, as a specific legal phenomenon, contribute their own 'package' of idiosyncrasies too. Partly as a result of the system, partly because of its own nature, the law of EU border controls involves different levels of

[60] N Vavoula, *Immigration and Privacy in the Law of the European Union: The Case of Information Systems* (Brill 2021); R Mungianu, *Frontex and Non-Refoulement: The International Responsibility of the EU* (Cambridge University Press 2016).

[61] G Raimondo, *The European Integrated Border Management: Frontex, Human Rights, and International Responsibility* (Hart 2024); M Fink, *Frontex and Human Rights: Responsibility in 'Multi-Actor Situations' under the ECHR and EU Public Liability Law* (Oxford University Press 2018); S Ganty, A Ancite-Jepifánova, and D Kochenov, 'EU Lawlessness Law at the EU-Belarusian Border: Torture and Dehumanisation Excused by 'Instrumentalisation' (2023) 18 MOBILE Working Paper Series (University of Copenhagen).

[62] S Carrera and others, *Policing Humanitarianism: EU Policies Against Human Smuggling and Their Impact on Civil Society* (Hart 2019).

[63] V Moreno-Lax, 'EU Constitutional Dismantling Through Strategic Informalisation: Soft Readmission Governance as Concerted Dis-integration' (2024) 30 European Law Journal 29.

[64] CA Groenendijk, E Guild, and PE Minderhoud, *In Search of Europe's Borders* (Kluwer Law International 2003); D Bigo and E Guild, *Controlling Frontiers: Free Movement Into and Within Europe* (Ashgate 2005); E Guild and others, *What Is Happening to the Schengen Borders?*, CEPS, No 86/December 2015; and K Groenendijk, 'Reinstatement of Controls at the Internal Borders of Europe: Why and Against Whom?' (2004) 10 European Law Journal 150.

[65] D Curtin and H Meijers, 'The Principle of Open Government in Schengen and the EU: Democratic Retrogression?' (1995) 32 Common Market Law Review 403.

[66] D Thym and J Bornemann, 'Schengen and Free Movement Law During the First Phase of the Covid-19 Pandemic: Of Symbolism, Law and Politics' (2020) 5 European Papers 1143.

[67] G Cornelisse, 'What's Wrong with Schengen? Border Disputes and the Nature of Integration in the Area Without Internal Borders' (2014) 51 Common Market Law Review 741.

[68] S Carrera and others, *A Race Against Solidarity: The Schengen Regime and the Franco-Italian Affair*, CEPS Liberty and Security in Europe, April 2011.

[69] While recognizing that a distinction is sometimes drawn in scholarship between 'legal system' and 'legal order', this research uses the two terms interchangeably.

governance and, for each of those levels, different actors in the pursuit of different objectives, targeting different groups of people and resting on different sources of law (or quasi-law).

Can a conceptual category encapsulate the state of things outlined above? For example, 'complexity' is a familiar term in the debate on the EU legal system. It can be defined as a 'bilateral and active relationship between diversities' characterizing the interlaced legal orders in a multi-level situation.[70] Constitutional complexity 'has an explanatory value: it attempts to describe how the authority of EU law impacts on the domestic constitutional systems and how the constitutional systems react by challenging a complete unification'.[71] From the perspective of complexity, conflicts between levels are regarded as a driving force of constitutional development. These features separate complexity from other approaches to the functioning of the EU system, such as constitutional pluralism[72] and multi-level governance,[73] as these accounts seek to accommodate conflicts caused by the existence of competing claims of authority within the EU legal order. These accounts, and the vast range of valuable studies on the EU governance more broadly,[74] address only *some* of the abovementioned idiosyncrasies of EU border controls. Similar considerations apply to the contribution made by the discussion on the choice of the legal instrument[75] in EU law and the similar debate about the role of soft law in the Union's legal order.[76]

[70] G Martinico, 'The Tangled Complexity of the EU Constitutional Process: On Complexity as a Constitutional Theory of the EU' (2012) 31 Yearbook of European Law 207. More extensively, G Martinico, *The Tangled Complexity of the EU Constitutional Process: The Frustrating Knot of Europe* (Routledge 2024).

[71] Martinico, 'The Tangled Complexity' 221.

[72] See, in an incredibly vast literature, N MacCormick, 'Beyond the Sovereign State' (1993) 56 Modern Law Review 1; N Walker, 'The Idea of Constitutional Pluralism' (2002) 65 Modern Law Review 317; M Poiares Maduro, 'Three Claims of Constitutional Pluralism' in M Avbelj and J Komárek, *Constitutional Pluralism in the European Union and Beyond* (Hart 2012) 67; J Weiler, 'Federalism and Constitutionalism: Europe's Sonderweg', Harvard Jean Monnet Working Paper No 10/00 (2001); M Loughlin, 'Constitutional Pluralism: An Oxymoron?' (2014) 3 Global Constitutionalism 9; D Van Den Meerssche, 'European Perspectives on Constitutional Pluralism(s): An Ontological Roadmap' (2017) 9 Transnational Legal Theory 1; K Tuori, 'The Many Constitutions of Europe' in G A Caldeira, R D Kelemen, and K E Whittington, *Oxford Handbook Topics in Law* (Oxford University Press 2016); K Jaklic, *Constitutional Pluralism in the EU* (Oxford University Press 2014); and A Bobić, *The Jurisprudence of Constitutional Conflict in the European Union* (Oxford University Press 2022).

[73] L Hooghe, G Marks, and A Schakel, 'Multilevel Governance' in D Caramani (ed), *Comparative Politics* (Oxford University Press 2020) 193; I Pernice, 'Multilevel Constitutionalism and the Treaty of Amsterdam: European Constitution-Making Revisited?' (1999) 36 Common Market Law Review 703. For a critical view, see L Besselink, *A Composite European Constitution/Een Samengestelde Europese Constitutie* (Europa Law Publishing 2007) 6 onwards. See also HM Mamudu and DT Studlar, 'Multilevel Governance and Shared Sovereignty: European Union, Member States, and the FCTC' (2009) 22 Governance 73.

[74] See G De Búrca and J Scott, *Law and New Governance in the EU and the US* (Hart 2006), particularly the introduction and Neil Walker's chapter; K Armstrong, 'The Character of EU Law and Governance: From "Community Method" to New Modes of Governance' 64 Current Legal Problems 179. See also the concept of shared sovereignty, not infrequently associated with multi-level governance. C Freudlsperger, A Maricut-Akbik, and M Migliorati, 'Opening Pandora's Box? Joint Sovereignty and the Rise of EU Agencies with Operational Tasks' (2022) 55 Comparative Political Studies 1983.

[75] A von Bogdandy, F Arndt, and J Bast, 'Legal Instruments in European Union Law and their Reform: A Systematic Approach on an Empirical Basis' (2004) 23 Yearbook of European Law 91; S Hurka and Y Steinebach, 'Legal Instrument Choice in the European Union' (2021) 59 Journal of Common Market Studies 278.

[76] See, among many, M Eliantonio, E Korkea-a, and O Ştefan (eds), *EU Soft Law in the Member States: Theoretical Findings and Empirical Evidence* (Hart 2020); PL Láncos, N Xanthoulis, and L Arroyo

On the one hand, the specialized literature has not engaged with the systemic legal implications of the plurality of sources, levels of governance and actors, groups of persons concerned, and objectives characterizing EU border controls, nor with the interrelated questions of task allocation, interinstitutional cooperation, and treatment of the targeted individuals raised by those forms of plurality. The generalist scholarship, for its part, offers no analytical lens broad enough to deal with said questions in a holistic fashion. Against this background, this research introduces two concepts to fill the gap: heterogeneity and systemic appropriateness. 'Heterogeneity' can be defined as 'the quality or state of consisting of dissimilar or diverse elements'.[77] Heterogeneity is a matter of degree and is determined by either the quantity of the elements involved, by how different they are, or by a combination of both. We know that heterogeneity plays a role *a contrario* in EU–EEA relationships, which are based on the principle of homogeneity.[78] Heterogeneity in the sense proposed in this book has a distinct application. While heterogeneity is similar to complexity in that it has an exploratory value, it is also significantly different. Complexity focuses on the system as a whole, whereas heterogeneity helps us see certain structural features of more specific phenomena. Therefore, even though this book applies heterogeneity to EU border controls, it could be used potentially for many—if not all—areas of EU law. Given its flexible nature, the heuristic power of heterogeneity can be deployed with respect to any such structural aspect of a phenomenon that can be described as heterogeneous. In this research, the attention is on four main expressions of heterogeneity: sources, levels of governance and actors, addressees, and objectives of EU border controls. The observation of the law of EU border controls and the implementation thereof reveals not only the existence of these four types of heterogeneity, but also their mutual interaction. Furthermore, these aspects cover the fundamental questions around the exercise of power in a given legal area: who and against whom, why, how, and when. Heterogeneity enriches the vocabulary of EU law and offers a new way of thinking about legal phenomena in a composite polity like the EU. By providing an additional angle of analysis, looking beyond the issue of claims of authority, it incentivizes us to ask important legal questions from a theoretical and practical point of view. It brings together the systemic characteristics of the Union as a legal order and the peculiarities of the specific phenomenon under consideration—in this case, the law of EU border controls. Therefore, it can lead us to a better understanding of the field under consideration and potentially the system more broadly.

Given its revelatory value and flexibility, there is no predetermined question that heterogeneity could or should raise. Accounting for the four expressions of heterogeneity mentioned above, the holistic outlook entailed by the application of such a concept to EU border controls underpins the overarching question of this book: given its heterogeneity, is the law of EU border controls constitutionally compliant? Although the next chapters discuss in detail the meaning of both 'constitutional' and 'compliance'

Jiménez, *The Legal Effects of EU Soft Law: Theory, Language and Sectoral Insights* (Edward Elgar 2023); L Senden, *Soft Law in European Community Law* (Hart 2014).

[77] See https://www.merriam-webster.com/dictionary/heterogeneity.
[78] C Baudenbacher, *The Fundamental Principles of EEA Law: EEA-Ities* (Springer 2017).

espoused in this research, as well as the analytical framework more broadly, some introductory clarifications are in order. Unlike the super robot from 'Hitchhiker's Guide to the Galaxy', this book has no ambition to answer the ultimate question of life, the universe, and everything. More modestly, this is a doctrinal piece of research on EU constitutional law that focuses on a specific area of interest. The objective is to assess the compliance of EU border controls with the aspects of the EU constitutional framework deemed suitable and relevant to border controls *and* their heterogeneity. These two factors have guided the selection of the benchmarks of analysis.

And here enters the other main character of this short story: appropriateness. By observation, in border controls and beyond, EU law knows two main understandings of appropriateness. Appropriateness *stricto sensu* evokes an assessment of proportionality. This emerges particularly from the case law of the EU Court of Justice (CJ or the Court), indicating that a measure will comply with EU law if both appropriate and necessary to achieve its objectives.[79] The same use of appropriateness can be seen in the literature on proportionality.[80] As it emerges from the Treaty and the Court's case law, appropriateness *lato sensu* (or systemic appropriateness) is a byword for 'correct'. For example, the Union shall develop a common policy on international protection with a view to offering *appropriate* status to any requiring TCNs.[81] A member state can refuse to execute a European Arrest Warrant (EAW) following an *appropriate* examination of the risk of fundamental rights breach that would arise as a result of the surrender.[82] National courts are free to exercise the discretion to request a preliminary ruling 'at whatever stage of the proceedings they consider *appropriate*'.[83] As such, appropriateness *lato sensu* is much broader and nebulous. The two understandings are not mutually exclusive. The opposite is true: often, an assessment of proportionality is embedded into appropriateness *lato sensu*. A judicial authority must perform an overall assessment of the circumstances of the case to decide whether it is *appropriate* to refuse to execute an EAW.[84] Thereby, appropriateness *lato sensu* is a normative tool to carry out an overall assessment of whether a heterogeneous law is made and implemented 'correctly'. In this book, 'correct' (ie appropriate *lato sensu* or systemically) is understood *as* constitutionally compliant. As extensively explained in Part I, the structure of the EU legal system requires that the making and implementation of any area of Union law (including border controls) must comply with a specific set of legal parameters.

Unlike heterogeneity, appropriateness is already part and parcel of the EU law lexicon. Like heterogeneity, however, appropriateness is undertheorized. In this sense, heterogeneity is *functional* to appropriateness. The former is an analytical feature that

[79] Case 11/70, *Internationale Handelsgesellschaft, bH v Einfuhr- und Vorratsstelle für Getreide und Futtermittel*, EU:C:1970:114, paras 8, 12, 20, and 25.

[80] See, more broadly, R Alexy, *A Theory of Constitutional Rights* (Oxford University Press 2002) 210, stating that 'Constitutional judgments are only correct if they correspond to the outcome of an appropriate balancing of principles'. With specific regard to proportionality in EU law, W Sauter, 'Proportionality in EU Law: A Balancing Act?' (2013) 15 Cambridge Yearbook of European Legal Studies 439.

[81] TFEU, Article 78(1).

[82] Case C-158/21, *Puig Gordi and Others*, EU:C:2023:57, para 72.

[83] Case C-342/17, *Memoria and Dall'Antonia*, EU:C:2018:906, para 33 and the case law cited.

[84] Case C-318/24 PPU, *Breian*, EU:C:2024:658, para 61.

modulates the assessment of the latter as a constitutional benchmark, therefore being a variable to add to the equation in the appropriateness test. These two analytical tools add to our ability to assess constitutional compliance. On the one hand, heterogeneity allows us to uncover certain structural features of a legal phenomenon and jump-starts our analysis in a way we would not have done otherwise. On the other hand, appropriateness enables us to address the interconnected questions raised by heterogeneity in an integrated manner, by engaging different constitutional parameters and illuminating their mutual interaction with the view to achieving overarching conclusions about the compliance of the subject of our investigation.

The last keyword of this volume which must be introduced here defines the scope of the research: conditions. Even when assessed through the specific prism of heterogeneity and from the perspective of certain aspects of constitutional compliance, a systemic evaluation of the law of EU border controls warrants the adoption of further criteria to limit its scope. With this in mind, the assessment of constitutional compliance focuses on conditions for exercising controls, conditions imposed on the persons concerned, and the allowed or mandated conduct associated with both of the above. The choice ensures coherence and analytical rigour in this research endeavour. As shown throughout the book, 'conditions' as defined above are an aspect where the impact of heterogeneity on constitutional compliance emerges most prominently. 'Conditions' also has a wider meaning in the context of this book. By assessing the impact of heterogeneity on the constitutional compliance of EU border controls externally and internally, this book ultimately addresses the question of what the conditions are for an area without internal frontiers. The question is understood descriptively, as it evaluates the price being paid in constitutional terms for upholding such a borderless area. It is also approached normatively, since it explores concrete ways forward to make that area constitutionally sustainable.

## Roadmap: A Long and Winding Road

This book makes an original contribution to the debate on EU border controls. The concept of heterogeneity introduces a new perspective to grasp the complexity of one of the fastest-growing areas of EU law. The systemic understanding of appropriateness as constitutional compliance supports the creation of an innovative analytical framework to discuss the issues raised by this complexity in an integrated manner. The emphasis on conditions *for* control and *on* the persons concerned coherently frames this integrated assessment, which focuses on three intertwined macro-themes: allocation of power, mechanisms of interinstitutional cooperation, and treatment of the persons concerned. Most importantly, the book does all of the above via a conjoined analysis of external and internal border controls. The analysis is enriched by selected examples of bordering practices from certain member states. While these are not fully fledged case studies, which would warrant a standalone volume for each country, they allow us to gain a deeper understanding of the functioning of this area of law.

The holistic aspiration of this research informs the structure of the book, which consists of three Parts. In joining the systemic and the specific aspects of EU border controls, Part I starts by setting out the view of the EU legal order adopted in this volume. By keeping a close link with the subject of this research, Chapter 1 discusses the interaction among the three building blocks of the EU legal order: the main argument is that principles of EU law ensure that the pursuit of the EU's objectives is consistent with Union values. Against this background, Chapter 2 zooms in on the test of constitutional compliance. The test rests on a structured network of principles of EU law, selected based on their relevance to issues of heterogeneity in EU border controls. Parts II and III deal with external and internal EU border controls, respectively. Their structure is identical. A first chapter introduces the main values, objectives, and principles engaged in the field, as also framed by the policy discussion (Chapters 3 and 7), while also setting out in detail the structure of the next chapters and the materials analysed therein. Thereafter, three chapters follow on sources of controls (Chapters 4 and 8); exercise of controls (Chapters 5 and 9); and control of the controls (Chapters 6 and 10). The specific meaning and scope of each of these terms, such as 'source' and 'control of the controls', will be discussed in the relevant chapters.

The book follows the flow of people, rather than the flow of history. The analysis of external border controls precedes that on the abolition of controls inside Schengen, despite the former having emerged after the occurrence of the latter. Consistent with this logic, each of the three main chapters on external border controls revolves around three scenarios: before leaving, in transit, and at the EU's borders. In this Part, we look at some 'highlights' of the laws and practices of external border controls from Finland and Italy. The choice of these two countries aims to cover two different ratios of control: Italy represents a more traditional example in this regard, due to its geographical exposure to migratory flows. However, Finland offers an important case of 'back to the future': the external borders as a bulwark against a possible attack on sovereignty perpetrated by an external aggressor. Part III, instead, builds on two main pillars: the absence of controls and exceptions to it; compensatory actions implemented at, or in the vicinity of, the EU's internal borders. Here, we take a peek into the law and practices of France and Norway. The former is a founding member of Schengen and among the most active states in reintroducing internal controls. Norway has also made extensive use of controls over time, and provides an interesting example of a non-EU country which is part of the borderless area. The clear-cut organization of the content and the flow mentioned above are meant to facilitate the readers' navigation through an incredibly complex landscape. If lost, they will hopefully be able to find their way again by looking at the pole stars of this book: heterogeneity, compliance, and conditions. The conclusions reveal, perhaps unsurprisingly, that the law of EU border controls is not constitutionally compliant, and identify a series of important paths for future research.

The book creates an original analytical framework of EU constitutional law, built on the theorization of certain fundamental principles of Union law and their mutual interaction. This framework is applied to a specific policy area to discuss the normative and operational challenges caused by heterogeneity. Thereby, the volume speaks to both academics and practitioners. This research reveals the tensions between the increasing objectives and value commitments associated with European integration, and the challenges of reconciling those commitments with ongoing claims of national sovereignty. Ultimately, it highlights the impact of European legal integration on a key expression of sovereignty, and identifies solutions to the challenges caused by heterogeneity in a way suitable for the EU legal order. In so doing, this book significantly advances the understanding of this area of law and of the EU as a *sui generis* legal system.

All web links cited in this book were last accessed on 22 May 2025.

# PART I

# AN ANALYTICAL FRAMEWORK FOR THE LAW OF EU BORDER CONTROLS

# 1

# The Building Blocks of the EU Legal Order: Values, Principles, and Objectives

## 1.1 Introduction

This book addresses the following overarching question: does the heterogeneity of the law of EU border controls cause issues of constitutional compliance? The research focuses on four main expressions of heterogeneity, defined as 'the quality or state of consisting of dissimilar or diverse elements': sources, levels of governance and actors, objectives, and persons concerned. The scope of the analysis does not cover every aspect of the law, but it homes in on the conditions for exercising controls, the conditions imposed on the persons concerned, and the allowed or mandated conduct associated with both of the above. To assess the constitutional compliance of the law in light of its heterogeneity, Part I of the book creates a specific analytical framework which will be applied to the materials discussed in Parts II and III. Chapter 2 defines the meaning of 'constitutional compliance' adopted in this research. It also devises a legal test to evaluate this compliance, centred on a structured network of relevant principles of EU law.

The conception of the test of constitutional compliance is not a standalone exercise. Conversely, the test is developed in the context of a wider view of the EU legal order espoused here. This view, the test, and the analysis of the law are inextricably linked with one another. This chapter is the first step in the journey through the constitutional compliance of EU border controls. More specifically, the following pages set out a blueprint to understand the relationship between certain structural components of the EU legal architecture: values, principles, and objectives. Two preliminary remarks are necessary in this regard. The view of the legal order outlined below builds on the relevant law and literature, and provides a systemic way of looking at certain fundamental elements of EU law. In a sense, this chapter is an attempt at systematization. As such, we accept that it is inevitably exposed to objections and exceptions.[1] The central argument of this chapter is that values, principles, and objectives represent the three 'building blocks' of the EU legal order.[2] While the boundaries between these categories are not always straightforward,[3] their relation can be read as follows: the

[1] This is particularly the case for possible 'counterpoints' related to the abstract nature of the arguments developed in the next few pages. As shown throughout the chapter, one way to limit that risk is to consistently tie those arguments to concrete examples related to border controls.

[2] The role of actors and their actions would be to operationalize them, pursuant to the tasks assigned to them by EU and national law.

[3] For example, solidarity (among the EU peoples) is described as an objective in the preamble, and more broadly as a value in Article 2 TEU and a principle governing asylum, immigration, and border controls as

*The Law of EU Border Controls*. Leandro Mancano, Oxford University Press. © Leandro Mancano 2025.
DOI: 10.1093/9780191966187.003.0002

principles ensure that the EU and the member states pursue the Union's objectives in compliance with EU values. Although the discussion in this Part links to EU border controls, this analytical framework might help explain the functioning of the EU legal order beyond this area of law. The chapter is structured as follows. Firstly, we discuss the different ways in which Article 2 of the Treaty on EU (TEU) imbues the EU legal order, especially through obligations and mechanisms of enforcement. Here, we also introduce an overarching theme of the whole book: the connection between different values and interests, and the ensuing need for an assessment of how competing claims are accommodated in the making and implementation of the law. Secondly, we analyse the role of principles as tools of value-enforcement (broadly understood, as defined below). We show that the link between values and principles can vary in intensity and present the main modi operandi of principles as guardians of Article 2 TEU, including as regards the balancing between different principles as a reflection of different values and interests. Thirdly, and building on the previous sections, we consider the role of the EU objectives and their relationship with values and principles. The diversity of goals set in the Treaties reflects the different interests and understandings of EU values possibly held by the different actors involved in the law-making and implementation.

## 1.2 The Foundations of the EU Legal Order: Values, Enforcement, and Compliance

### 1.2.1 Setting the Scene: The EU Values as the Blood Vessels of the EU Legal Order

The building blocks of the EU legal order are at the forefront of the Treaties. The member states intend to deepen the solidarity between their peoples and enable the EU institutions to carry out their tasks. Competences are conferred upon the Union to attain the states' common objectives.[4] Against this background, Article 2 TEU stipulates:

> The Union is founded on the values of respect for human dignity, freedom, democracy, equality, the rule of law and respect for human rights, including the rights of persons belonging to minorities. These values are common to the Member States in a society in which pluralism, non-discrimination, tolerance, justice, solidarity and equality between women and men prevail.

This provision crystallizes decades of legal developments that started with the European Coal and Steel Community (ECSC) Treaty.[5] Over the years, European

per Article 80 of the Treaty on the Functioning of the EU (TFEU). See Consolidated Version of the TEU [2008] OJ C115/13, and the Consolidated Version of the TFEU [2012] OJ C 326/47.

[4] TEU, Article 1.

[5] D Kochenov, 'The Acquis and Its Principles: The Enforcement of the "Law" versus the Enforcement of "Values"' in A Jakab and D Kochenov, *The Enforcement of EU Law and Values* (Oxford University Press 2017) 12.

identity has been shaped around a group of concepts that have consistently included, inter alia, the rule of law and respect for human rights.[6] This core is now complemented by the second sentence of Article 2 TEU,[7] which has been described as having an 'obscure normative function'.[8] At the time of writing, the Treaties[9] and the case law of the EU Court of Justice (ECJ of the Court) still regard the terms in Article 2 TEU as values or principles, depending on the context in which they are referred to. Scholars deem the label of value or principle particularly important because of the different legal force attached to these two categories: unlike principles and rules, values are more akin to abstract aspirations than actual legal 'tools'.[10] Although values can constitute legal standards, they would differ from legally binding norms to be relied upon in a legal action.[11]

This definitional question is not particularly consequential in EU law, as several circumstances show the legal significance of the Union values. Article 2 TEU permeates the whole of the Union's legal order. The values listed in that provision are connected with one another,[12] with the EU objectives,[13] and with the principles that operationalize and give expression to them. Nowhere is this dynamic expressed more clearly than in the EU Charter of Fundamental Rights (CFR or the Charter). The preamble of the Charter largely mirrors Article 2 TEU, and so do the headings of its different Titles.[14] The legal structure of the EU is based on the premise that 'each Member State shares with all the other Member States, and recognises that they share with it, the common values'.[15] As the Union is *founded* on Article 2 TEU,[16] adherence to its values is a precondition for accession[17] and must persist

[6] Freedom, democracy, and liberty have also been part of this 'core' group. See the Declaration on the European Identity of the 1973 Copenhagen summit, EC Bull 12–1973 118–22 as well as, among a plethora of judgments, Case C-294/83, *Parti écologiste 'Les Verts' v European Parliament*, EU:C:1986:166, para 31.

[7] These stem from the recommendations of the Working Group on social Europe. CONV 516/1/03, Final Report of Working Group XI (n 104) [12]. See A Williams, *The Ethos of Europe: Values, Law and Justice in the EU* (Cambridge University Press 2010) 15.

[8] A von Bogdandy, 'Founding Principles' in J Bast and A von Bogdandy (eds), *Principles of European Constitutional Law* (Hart/Beck 2010) 22. Conversely, the authors consider the concepts enshrined in the first sentence as legal norms and founding principles.

[9] See, among several examples, Article 21(1) TEU.

[10] See in this sense E Wilfrid Thomas, *The Judicial Process: Realism, Pragmatism, Practical Reasoning, and Principles* (Cambridge University Press 2005) 344. A Jakab, 'Concept and Function of Principles' in M Borowski (ed), *On the Nature of Legal Principles* (Steiner 2009) 145. ML Fernandez Esteban, *The Rule of Law in the European Constitution* (Kluwer Law International 1999) 40–41. L Pech, '"A Union Founded on the Rule of Law": Meaning and Reality of the Rule of Law as a Constitutional Principle of EU Law' (2010) 6 EU Constitutional Law Review 367.

[11] E Dagilytė, 'Solidarity: A General Principle of EU Law? Two Variations on the Solidarity Theme' in E Dagilytė, A Biondi, and E Küçük (eds), *Solidarity in EU Law: Legal Principle in the Making* (Edward Elgar 2018) 72.

[12] See, for example, Case C-157/21 *Republic of Poland v European Parliament and Council of the European Union*, EU:C:2022:98, para 324.

[13] Article 3(1) TEU states that the Union's aim is to promote peace, its values, and well-being of its peoples.

[14] Case C-621/18, *Andy Wightman et al v Secretary of State for Exiting the European Union*, ECLI:EU:C:2018:999, para 63.

[15] Case C-156/21, *Hungary v European Parliament and Council of the European Union*, EU:C:2022:97, paras 125 and 147.

[16] *Opinion 1/91*, EU:C:1991:490, para 71.

[17] See Article 49 TEU and Joined Cases C-357/19, C-379/19, C-547/19, C-811/19, and C-840/19 *Euro Box Promotion and Others*, EU:C:2021:1034, para 162.

thereafter.[18] In this regard, EU law provides different mechanisms for enforcing those values, which are dependent on the gravity of the alleged infringement. Such mechanisms exist because primary and secondary EU law implement Article 2 TEU,[19] and 'grant the EU institutions the power to examine, determine the existence of and, where appropriate, impose penalties for breaches' thereof.[20] For example, in 2023, the European Commission brought an action against Hungary by using for the first time the infringement of Article 2 TEU as an 'autonomous' ground.[21] Accordingly, the scope for the enforcement of EU values is broad and is not limited to serious and persistent breaches.[22] Likewise, it does not require specific frameworks of the kind established by the Rule of Law Conditionality Regulation.[23] Conversely, enforcement can take place in a context as 'ordinary' as the infringement procedure under Article 258 TFEU.

EU law must be the law of EU values: the EU values are the blood vessels, with EU and national laws and practices acting as the blood of the Union legal order. The systemic consequences of a breach of Article 2 TEU can be particularly significant. Notably, a violation could affect a member state's enjoyment of its status as a fully fledged member of the Union. The Court sets this out very clearly in the *Rule of law conditionality* judgment:

> the Union budget is [an instrument] for giving practical effect . . . to the principle of solidarity, mentioned in Article 2 TEU, which is itself one of the fundamental principles of EU law . . . the implementation of that principle, through the Union budget, is based on mutual trust between the Member States . . . mutual trust is itself based . . . on the commitment of each Member State to comply with . . . the values contained in Article 2 TEU.[24]

Groussot, Zemskova, and Bungerfeldt argue that in said judgment, the Court created a link of interdependence between solidarity and the rule of law with the help of mutual trust.[25] The relation is, at least to an extent, circular. Since the values permeate EU law, a breach of a value (such as solidarity) through violation of norms meant to give effect to it (eg those budget-related) can affect mutual trust to the extent that, in certain cases, it can lead to the suspension of *other* measures expressing the same value which the member states in question had violated in the first place.

[18] Case C-896/19 *Repubblika v Il-Prim Ministru*, EU:C:2021:311, para 64.

[19] Purely by way of example and with no claim of completeness, see Articles 3(1), 8, 10, and 19(1) TEU, and Articles 80, 153(1)(i), and 157(1) TFEU.

[20] Case C-156/21, *Hungary v European Parliament and Council of the European Union*, EU:C:2022:98, para 159.

[21] Case C-769/22, *European Commission v Hungary* (2023/C 54/19).

[22] Article 7(2) TEU.

[23] Regulation (EU, Euratom) 2020/2092 on a general regime of conditionality for the protection of the Union budget [2020] OJ L 433I/1.

[24] Case C-157/21, *Republic of Poland v European Parliament and Council of the European Union*, para 147.

[25] X Groussot, A Zemskova, and K Bungerfeldt, 'Foundational Principles and the Rule of Law in the European Union: How to Adjudicate in a Rule-of-Law Crisis, and Why Solidarity Is Essential' (2022) 5 Nordic Journal of European Law 11.

Against this background, three observations on EU values and their relevance to border controls are warranted. Through different examples, we have seen that the whole of the Union's legal order channels the EU values and features mechanisms to ensure continuing adherence to them.[26] However, values do not exist in a vacuum. They are subject to external and internal pressures and tensions that lead to their constant 'reinvention' and reappropriation by different stakeholders. This holds true generally, and for EU border controls specifically. Scholars have highlighted that normative ideals and interests in this area—and on EU migration and asylum law more broadly—have changed over time. Such trends reflect the evolving impact of the actors involved, as well as the shifting attitude of the same actor diachronically. On the one hand, the more prominent role for interior ministers that accompanied the birth of Schengen was followed by a more rights-oriented approach in conjunction with increasing supranationalization of this area of law.[27] On the other hand, it has been argued that the greater powers granted by the Lisbon Treaty to the European Parliament (EP) have seen the latter moving from a liberal approach to a more 'mainstream' attitude to legislation in this field.[28] Values and interests are inextricably linked, but their relationship is far from linear. This is especially so as the heterogeneity of interests pursued by different stakeholders can reflect both a tension between different values and the different understanding of the same value held by different actors.

Secondly, several concepts mentioned in Article 2 TEU are relevant to EU border controls. Just to name a few, the rule of law matters in several ways: from the respect for the established prerogatives of the levels of governance involved in an area of shared competence, to the provision of an effective system of remedies, through to the requirement of legal certainty. Respect for human rights is an obvious protagonist, as border controls materialize in the exercise of public powers over the persons they target. Solidarity founds[29] and governs[30] the common policy on border control, and must be given effect by appropriate measures whenever necessary. The Union's common policy on asylum, immigration, and external border control must be fair towards third-country nationals (TCNs), which in turn evokes the value of justice.[31] Non-discrimination must inform the making, interpretation, and implementation of the law, as EU border controls aim to filter the movement into and across the Union of people from different nationalities and backgrounds.

Also, due to their foundational nature, the concepts mentioned in Article 2 TEU are highly versatile. The disputed nature and meaning of values, however, can directly

[26] The establishment by law of such mechanisms and their actual use are different if inextricably linked aspects. The reason lies, most obviously, in that the exercise of these mechanisms requires, in many cases, political will. This is apparent from the heavy criticisms of the European Commission's slow response to the rule of law crisis in Poland and Hungary.

[27] This phase also saw a more prominent influence of NGOs. See D Thym, *European Migration Law* (Oxford University Press 2023), sections 2.1 and 4.3 in particular and literature cited.

[28] D Thym, 'Institutional and Constitutional Framework' in E Tsourdi and P De Bruycker (eds), *Research Handbook on EU Migration and Asylum Law* (Edward Elgar 2022) 66. As the author observes at p 61, 'Increasing politicisation complicates the accommodation of countervailing interests and values on the basis of technical expertise'.

[29] TFEU, Article 67(2).

[30] TFEU, Article 80.

[31] TFEU, Article 67(2). See, among many, L Temkin, 'Equality as Comparative Fairness' (2017) 34 Journal of Applied Philosophy 43; J Rawls, 'Justice as Fairness' (1958) 67 Philosophical Review 164.

impact their capacity to be actioned. This point ties in with the two previous considerations. For example, a society founded on solidarity can be understood and pursued in endless ways. An approach to that principle as primarily favouring solidarity among member states and their peoples might be used to justify more restrictive measures—especially as immigration is increasingly linked to destabilization by hostile countries. The opposite might be true should a broader meaning of solidarity be adopted. The law of EU border controls involves a heterogeneous set of values and interests. This being the case, assessing the accommodation of different claims in line with the relevant legal standards will constitute a *fil rouge* through the whole book. With that in mind, the next section looks more closely at how values can be operationalized, regard being had to the two other building blocks of the EU legal order. For these purposes, we must introduce two key concepts: enforcement and compliance.[32]

### 1.2.2 Enforcement and Compliance: Operationalizing the EU Values

The building blocks of the EU legal order act together: the principles ensure the pursuit of the EU objectives in line with the EU values. Chiti has designed a rigorous and elegant account of the enforcement and compliance mechanisms of structural principles of EU external relations law.[33] His analysis of the interaction between the different components of EU law 'starts' with the principles. While agreeing with his approach overall, it is submitted that the dynamic he describes begins 'earlier'[34] and with the EU values. This is consistent with their role of the foundation of the EU legal order. Therefore, to paraphrase Chiti, enforcement is regarded as the set of processes that concern the execution of EU values and aim to achieve compliance, understood as obedience to legal norms.[35] In this book, compliance is used in a wide sense and covers not only the proper implementation of the law by the competent actor, but also the compatibility of, for example, EU legislation with primary law.[36] The values materialize into 'concretizing figures', which can be of a substantive or procedural nature. For example, one of the concretizing figures of the rule of law is the principle of effective judicial protection, which is in turn concretized, inter alia, by the right to an

[32] A crucial aspect of the debate about the values in Article 2 TEU concerns their enforceability.

[33] E Chiti, 'Enforcement of and Compliance with Structural Principles' in M Cremona (ed), *Structural Principles in EU External Relations Law* (Hart 2018).

[34] 'Earlier' is understood here both conceptually and chronologically. The argument put forward in this book builds on, rather than challenges or contradicts, Chiti's argument.

[35] Chiti, 'Enforcement of and Compliance with Structural Principles' 49. The author is aware of the extensive debate, especially in legal theory, on the differences between concepts such as obedience, compliance, and conformity. For the purposes of this book, these terms are used interchangeably.

[36] This use of the term 'compliant' can be found in instruments of EU law as well. For example, Article 2 of Council Regulation (EU) 2022/922 on the establishment and operation of an evaluation and monitoring mechanism to verify the application of the Schengen acquis, and repealing Regulation (EU) No 1053/2013 [2022] OJ L 160/1, defines 'non-compliant finding' as 'an assessment of a finding according to which national laws, regulations and administrative measures, or their implementation, do not comply with the legally binding provisions of the Schengen acquis'.

independent tribunal.[37] Solidarity as a value is concretized by the fundamental principle of solidarity, which founds and governs—among others—the EU law and policy of border controls. The EU budget, and the rules governing its adoption and implementation, are also a concretizing figure of solidarity. Different values may require different degrees of concretization.[38] How explicit or direct the connection between a concretizing figure and a value is may also vary.[39]

To function, the values and the concretizing figures must be 'operationalized' through procedures and regulatory frameworks. The procedures and frameworks, in many cases, structure the action of, and are implemented by, EU actors. In relation to EU law-making, for example, the rule of law expresses itself through, inter alia, the principle of conferral. This in turn unfolds through the establishment of specific legal bases in the Treaties, constraining the exercise of the EU competences. Concerns about the compliance of a legislative proposal with that principle, or about the choice of the correct legal basis, can be raised in the context of the legislative procedure.[40] These operationalizing frameworks can also—and sometimes simultaneously—target the member states as the ultimate implementers of EU law. This can happen less directly, or by leaving member states a certain margin of discretion, and/or by establishing 'obligations of result'. For example, Article 19(2) TEU prescribes that member states establish a system of effective remedies, without mandating them a specific method to achieve this. The main mechanisms of enforcement of EU values can come into play before or after a non-compliant measure or practice has deployed its effects. Proceduralization[41] is an example of the former scenario, whereas administrative control[42] and judicial scrutiny[43] would normally operate *ex post*. *Ex post* enforcement can, in turn, result in different outcomes such as restoring a state of compliance[44]

[37] See, among many, Case C-64/16, *Associação Sindical dos Juízes Portugueses*, EU:C:2018:117, paras 35–37.

[38] This can be in the seen in the values of the rule of law, on the one hand, and solidarity, on the other. The former has been developed to the extent that an instrument of secondary law identifies—presumably in a non-exhaustive way—the core components of that value. See Regulation 2020/2092, recital 3. By contrast, the next chapter shows that solidarity is much more elusive.

[39] For example, nobody would challenge the connection between the principle of non-discrimination and the value of equality. Whether that connection goes as far as justifying the legal existence and relevance of more detailed concretizing figures in EU law is, however, a different question. The Court stated that the principle of non-discrimination on grounds of age is a general principle of EU law and an expression of the broader principle of non-discrimination. See Case C-144/04, *Werner Mangold v Rüdiger Helm*, EU:C:2005:709. The same did not hold true with regard to the principle of equal treatment of minor shareholders. See Case C-101/08, *Audiolux SA and Others v Groupe Bruxelles Lambert SA (GBL)*, EU:C:2009:410.

[40] An example is Directive (EU) 2017/1371 on the fight against fraud to the Union's financial interests by means of criminal law [2017] OJ L 198/29. The Commission's proposal was based on Article 325(4) TFEU, but the EP secured a change to Article 83(2) TFEU. While the choice of the correct legal basis poses slightly different questions from the issue of whether the EU is competent to act at all, it is still nonetheless very important for the rule of law. For a comprehensive study on the legal basis in EU law, see A Engel, *The Choice of Legal Basis for Acts of the European Union: Competence Overlaps, Institutional Preferences, and Legal Basis Litigation* (Springer 2018).

[41] Once again, the subsidiarity control during the negotiation of EU legislation is a case in point.

[42] For example, infringement proceedings under Article 258 TFEU.

[43] This includes, for example, the preliminary rulings mechanism under Article 267 TFEU and the legality review governed by Article 263 TFEU.

[44] A typical example is the use of direct effect, on the basis of which the conflicting rule of national law must give way to EU law.

or redress.[45] This picture is consistent with the point made in the previous section that enforcement of EU values can occur via structural (infringement proceedings) or specific (rule of law conditionality) mechanisms.

This systematization must be nuanced as follows. Firstly, the values must inform EU law at the very least, or be actively promoted by specific measures if necessary (positive implementation). The review and setting aside of EU or national laws and practices contrary to the EU values is key as well (negative implementation). Positive and negative implementations are inextricably linked. The absence of an identifiable standard implementing EU values would make enforcement particularly difficult, if not impossible. The next chapter expands upon the relevance of the previous point to EU border controls, using the principles of solidarity and fairness as examples of the necessary link between definition and enforcement.[46] By the same token, the existence of specific concretizing figures giving effect to a value in a specific policy area could also prove ineffective, without mechanisms to guarantee compliance through an operationalizing framework.[47]

Secondly, and relatedly, a finding of a breach of Article 2 TEU requires, in principle, the violation of a more specific norm of EU law. The existence of provisions of secondary law giving expression to Article 2 TEU can be relevant, especially for triggering the application of the Charter, but is not always essential.[48] Furthermore, just as one cannot trace all norms of EU law back to the Union's values, not every breach of EU law would amount to an infringement of Article 2 TEU. There needs to be a sufficiently direct link between the provisions breached and the value(s) invoked. Depending on the circumstances of the case, the following criteria, in particular, should be relied on, either on their own or in combination, to determine the existence of such a link: quantity, scope, and seriousness of the violation. The first criterion would be relevant in cases of repeated violations, occurring over time or simultaneously, and irrespective of whether or not they concern the same provision. Repetition might not be necessary when the breach is particularly severe.[49] The scope of the infringement, for its part, could help establish a link where the nature or extent of the contested law or practice are such as to affect one or more groups of persons, or a system (the judiciary). Against this background, the next section moves on to the role of principles as vectors of values in the EU legal order.

[45] See, for example, the doctrine of EU or state non-contractual liability for damages caused by breach of EU law. As known, the leading case is Joined Cases C-6/90 and C-9/90, *Andrea Francovich and Danila Bonifaci and others v Italian Republic*, EU:C:1991:428, paras 31–37.

[46] Scholars have argued that solidarity alone cannot be used as a ground for review, because of its undetermined meaning. See Dagilytė, 'Solidarity: A General Principle of EU Law?' 61–90.

[47] The importance of the rule of law in the context of asylum law is an example of this. See E Tsourdi, 'Asylum in the EU: One of the Many Faces of Rule of Law Backsliding?' (2021) 17 European Constitutional Law Review 471.

[48] This is apparent from the case law on Article 19(1) TEU. See, among many, Case C-619/18, *European Commission v Republic of Poland*, EU:C:2019:531.

[49] Think of the impact of inhumane detention conditions on the absolute prohibition under Article 4 CFR. See Joined Cases C-404/15 and C-659/15 PPU, *Aranyosi and Căldăraru*, EU:C:2016:198. On this point see by analogy, A von Bogdandy, 'Principles of a Systemic Deficiencies Doctrine: How to Protect Checks and Balances in the Member States' (2020) 57 Common Market Law Review 718: 'an isolated phenomenon, such as breaking a taboo with a single case of torture, can indicate a systemic deficiency, especially when it is not met with an adequate institutional reaction'.

## 1.3 Principles of EU Law: Guardians of the EU Values?

### 1.3.1 Values and Principles: Protected Designation of Origin

In the previous section, we have seen that principles work as concretizing figures of the EU values. In this section, we zoom in on the connection of principles with the two other building blocks of the EU legal order (values and objectives), with the view to illuminating the functions and modus operandi of principles themselves. The link between values and principles in legal systems has been extensively debated,[50] including in the context of EU law.[51] As a preliminary remark, we must address the following distinction made in some scholarly accounts: the concepts contained in the first phrase of Article 2 TEU constitute traditional principles, whereas the second part of the provision consists of programmatic concepts.[52] The available evidence so far shows that such a distinction has no visible implications in practice, insofar as a concept is no less legally significant for the mere fact that it belongs to the second sentence of Article 2 TEU. Nonetheless, it should be observed that those programmatic concepts form a heterogeneous category, especially as regards the way they are relied on in practice. Solidarity and non-discrimination are acknowledged as values and principles that apply across EU law, whereas justice and tolerance do not necessarily have those two 'hats' (at least, not so obviously). This is not to say they are empty words. There are measures of EU law supporting the development of 'solidarity, mutual understanding and tolerance among young people and the society we live in',[53] or promoting the EU values and the combat of all forms of intolerance.[54] The reference to fair treatment of TCNs in the context of border controls is also evocative of the value of justice, even though that link has not explicitly translated into the legislation. However, some of the concepts in the second sentence of Article 2 TEU that are acknowledged as principles, such as solidarity, can present elusive meaning and scope. The degree and form of the value-concretizing function of principles, therefore, can vary, both in terms of degree and quality. That function can be substantial as much as procedural: principles shape the content of EU law, giving effect to EU values and contributing to operationalizing them. The next chapter focuses on the substance of the principles underpinning the test of constitutional compliance. Here, the emphasis is particularly on the different mechanisms of operationalization.[55]

[50] R Alexy, *A Theory of Constitutional Rights* (Oxford University Press 2002) 45; M Bódig, 'Rules, Principles, and the Problem of the Limits of Legal Reasoning' in M Borowski (ed), *On the Nature of Legal Principles: Proceedings of the Special Workshop 'The Principles Theory' Held at the 23rd World Congress of the International Association for Philosophy of Law and Social Philosophy (IVR), Kraków, 2007* (Franz Steiner Verlag 2010); J Habermas, *Between Facts and Norms: Contributions to a Discourse Theory of Law and Democracy* (MIT Press 1996).

[51] F Schorkopf, 'Value Constitutionalism in the European Union' (2020) 21 German Law Journal 956.

[52] M Klamert and D Kochenov, 'Article 2 TEU' in M Kellerbauer, M Klamert, and J Tomkin (eds), *The EU Treaties and the Charter of Fundamental Rights: A Commentary* (Oxford University Press 2019) 25.

[53] See Directive (EU) 2016/801 on the conditions of entry and residence of third-country nationals for the purposes of research, studies, training, voluntary service, pupil exchange schemes or educational projects and au pairing [2016] OJ L 132/21, recital 20.

[54] Regulation (EU) 2021/692 establishing the Citizens, Equality, Rights and Values Programme [2021] OJ L 156/1, Articles 2 and 4.

[55] The next chapter discusses the substance of certain principles used to test the constitutionality of EU border controls.

With this in mind, we must now zoom in on the role of principles as tools of values enforcement. Neuvonen observes that principles of EU law, and general principles in particular, are both influenced by and express normative considerations.[56] Even though she acknowledges that they 'are often seen as a legitimate means of opening judicial reasoning towards moral and political values', she voices concerns as to the suitability of general principles for securing the values of Article 2 TEU: 'The societal justification of the founding values indicates that they lay down a normative-ethical framework that is not necessarily confined to the general principles of EU law'.[57] This concern is understandable. As it was mentioned in the previous section and will be throughout the book, however, the enforcement of EU values—including through principles—seems possible only by means of more detailed legal constructs.[58] In this sense, the risk inherent in the Court 'substantiating the use of highly abstract values' might be overstated.[59]

Albeit EU law scholars widely agree on the presence of a connection between values and principles, dissenting voices exist. For example, von Arnaud distinguishes between formal and value-related principles,[60] suggesting that the former should not be rooted in values. Interestingly, he mentions *pacta sunt servanda* as an example of a formal principle.[61] A principle whose respect presupposes a party honouring their obligations might, however, be seen as value-based. This reflects the point made above: the intensity of the connection between a value, on the one hand, and a principle as a concretizing figure, on the other, can vary. Even principles that seem not to give effect to a specific value (e.g. effectiveness) are tied to the constitutional structure of the Union. The latter, in and of itself, builds on, expresses, or relates to the EU values (including the rule of law).[62] Or, as the Court put it, the

> essential characteristics of EU law [particularly primacy and direct effect] have given rise to a *structured network of principles*, rules and mutually interdependent legal relations linking the EU and its Member States, and its Member States with each other . . . This legal structure is based on the fundamental premiss that each

[56] PJ Neuvonen, 'The General Principle of Equality as a Value Commitment in EU Law: Scope, Limits, and Challenges' in KS Ziegler, PJ Neuvonen, and V Moreno-Lax (eds), *Research Handbook on General Principles in EU Law: Constructing Legal Orders in Europe* (Edward Elgar 2022) 281–82.

[57] Neuvonen, 'The General Principle of Equality as a Value Commitment in EU Law' 284–85.

[58] Examples in the next chapter show that this is not always the case.

[59] Schorkopf, 'Value Constitutionalism in the European Union' 965.

[60] Other accounts distinguish structural principles from those governing primarily the relations between individuals and authorities: M Wimmer, 'The Dinghy's Rudder: General Principles of European Union Law Through the Lens of Proportionality' (2014) 20 European Public Law 334. See, for further categorization, B de Witte, 'Institutional Principles: A Special Category of General Principles of EC Law' in U Bernitz and J Nergelius (eds), *General Principles of European Community Law* (Kluwer 2000) 143; A Arnull, 'What Is a General Principle of EU Law?' in R de la Feria and S Vogenauer (eds), *Prohibition of Abuse of Law: A New General Principle of EU Law?* (Hart 2011) 11; O Wiklund and J Bengoetxea, 'General Constitutional Principles of Community Law' in U Bernitz and J Nergelius (eds), *General Principles of European Community Law* (Kluwer 2000) 124.

[61] A von Arnauld, 'Harmonisation Through General Principles of Law' in Ziegler, Neuvonen, and Moreno-Lax (eds), *Research Handbook on General Principles in EU Law* 42–43.

[62] Take the principle of subsidiarity: establishing a constitutional criterion for law-making based on the assumption that decisions should be taken at the closest possible level to the citizens is, clearly, a value-driven choice.

> Member State shares with all the other Member States, and recognises that they share with it, a set of common values on which the EU is founded, as stated in Article2 TEU.[63]

A journey through the literature on the topic, which analyses forensically the law and especially the Court's approach, makes this apparent. Numerous categorizations of principles of EU law have emerged over the years, not infrequently accompanied by caveats concerning the limitations inherent in those efforts.[64] There is the distinction among different types of principles of EU law.[65] The Court itself uses different terminologies when referring to principles as 'general', 'fundamental' or 'very important' (just to name a few).[66] However, a recurring feature of academic accounts lies in the attempt to explain the differences between principles and other legal categories. Once again, this concerns the existence of different groups of principles in EU law. The terms of the debate about rules and principles,[67] for example, are not identical to those characterizing the discussion on rights and principles in the context of the Charter.[68]

Despite their multiform nature, finding a 'unifying' definition of principles is not impossible. Tridimas describes them as 'fundamental propositions of law which underlie a legal system and from which concrete rules or outcomes may be derived'.[69] He identifies principles that derive from the rule of law and are not specific to a legal order (eg proportionality and legal certainty) and systemic principles, which 'underlie the constitutional structure' of the Union and define its 'legal edifice'.[70] Other scholars regard systemic principles as '"bespoke" constructs. It does not matter that they do not find reflection in other international instruments or in the constitutional traditions common to the Member States; they are "of" the Union as much as they are "for" it'.[71] These 'umbrella' definitions answer—at least partly—not only the question of what principles in EU law are, but also where they come from and what functions they fulfil. Principles are connected to the legal system and the rules. They are expressions of that system. This connection must be understood in the sense that principles are 'anchored' to the system they belong to. In other words, they are rooted in its foundations: in EU law, this means the EU values and Article 2 TEU. However, principles find reflection in rules and may be used to produce specific 'outcomes'. This resonates with Chiti's view of structural principles mentioned

[63] *Opinion 2/13*, EU:C:2014:2454, paras 166–68.

[64] See C Semmelmann, 'General Principles in EU Law Between a Compensatory Role and an Intrinsic Value' (2013) 19 European Law Journal 460.

[65] S Besson, 'General Principles and Customary Law in the EU Legal Order' in S Vogenauer and S Weatherill (eds), *General Principles of Law: European and Comparative Perspectives* (Hart 2017) 111.

[66] See L Lourenço, '"A Matter of Principle": The Interaction of General Principles of EU Law With Other Legal Sources in the Case-Law of the CJEU' (DPhil thesis, European University Institute 2015) 51.

[67] See K Lenaerts and JA Gutiérrez-Fons, 'The Constitutional Allocation of Powers and General Principles of EU law' (2010) 47 Common Market Law Review 1629.

[68] See T Lock, 'Rights and Principles in the EU Charter of Fundamental Rights' (2019) 56 Common Market Law Review 1201.

[69] T Tridimas, *The General Principles of EU Law* (Oxford University Press 2006) 1.

[70] Tridimas, *The General Principles of EU Law* 1–4.

[71] Editorial comments, 'Is the "Indivisibility" of the Four Freedoms a Principle of EU Law?' (2019) 56 Common Market Law Review 1192.

in the previous section. Principles connect the values to the rules and the actions implementing them.

Such a deceptively straight line is curled by the heterogeneity of values and interests, as well as understandings thereof, involved in the making and implementation of the law. With this in mind, and consistent with the main argument of this chapter, it is argued that the values–principles connection can be better understood by considering the third building block of the EU legal order: the objectives.

Cremona's characterization of the principles of the EU external relations law is useful here. She distinguishes between structural principles and objective-oriented principles. Structural principles 'are both found in the Treaties and developed by the Court of Justice; they structure the system, functioning and exercise of EU ... competences and are designed to promote a smooth articulation of the ... system ... They regulate the relationships between the different actors in the complex EU system'.[72] They protect 'an institutional space within which policy may be formed, in which the different actors understand and work within their respective roles'. Structural principles, in turn, can be relational or systemic. Relational principles, such as conferral, govern the relationship between actors or legal subjects and relate to the constitutional structure of the EU, which is based on common values and mutual trust. Systemic principles are concerned with 'the operation of the system as a whole, with building the EU identity as a coherent, effective and autonomous actor in the world'. Objective-oriented principles, however, 'reflect the Union's foundational values and guide the policy direction' and are more concerned with the substantive content of the latter. While Cremona's analysis focuses on external relations law, she warns that 'the structure takes a different shape in the case of internal ... action, [so that] Structural principles in the internal context may be concerned primarily with the structure that it is the Union's mission to build'.[73] It should be highlighted that several principles that Cremona labels as 'structural' (as opposed to objective-oriented) have at least a close link to the EU objectives. Subsidiarity, proportionality, effectiveness, and sincere cooperation[74] are clear examples in this regard. Cremona's flexible systematization is enlightening. It articulates the variable connection between values and principles in EU law, and enriches it by drawing the objectives into the machinery of the EU legal order. Her hint at the specific nature of the internal structure seems to align with the view of the EU legal order put forward in this chapter. The values, principles, and objectives are bundled together in a mission to achieve the goals of the EU as a polity in accordance with its normative foundations. The next section discusses how principles can fulfil this function, specifically for the purposes of enforcement within the meaning of this research.

[72] M Cremona, 'Structural Principles and Their Role in EU External Relations Law' in M Cremona (ed), *Structural Principles in EU External Relations Law* 12.

[73] Cremona, 'Structural Principles' 16.

[74] Especially the third subparagraph of Article 4(3) TEU.

### 1.3.2 Beyond the Origins of Principles: Functions, Functioning, and Relationships

In EU law, the connection between values and principles is a two-way street. On the one hand, and consistently with the broader view of legal theorists, the (near) consensus among EU law scholars seems to be that principles are normatively 'charged'—or, at the very least, value-orientated. This connection is apparent from the 'multi-label' nature of concepts such as the rule of law or solidarity, which the Court of Justice has used and developed over the years. On the other hand, Article 2 TEU shows that compliance with EU values ultimately entails abidance by legal standards. The value of 'respect for human rights' is the starker example in this regard. In the approach to the EU legal order proposed in this book, principles fulfil a value-channelling function and interlock with the other building blocks mentioned above.[75]

Anchoring principles of EU law to EU values is important to clarify their roots, but it is no answer to some crucial questions around them. Firstly, there is the much-debated issue of identification. What makes a certain legal construct a principle is a question that has not yet found a clear answer.[76] Understanding their different functions and modus operandi is equally important, and warrants two preliminary observations. Certain principles find specific application(s) depending on the policy area involved, whereas others seem more 'content-neutral'. An example of the former is the principle of solidarity between member states in the context of EU border controls, whereas effectiveness and sincere cooperation would fall under the latter category.[77] Even more specifically, and as elaborated on in the next chapter, scholars have engaged with the question as to whether solidarity can be defined as a 'general principle'. The question is deemed relevant for two interrelated reasons: the label requires certain characteristics, and comes with a certain legal force.[78] However, there is no consensus in the literature about the use of the term 'general principles'.[79] Furthermore, the practice shows that, at least to an extent, principles can be used in ways that are considered reserved for general principles, without being necessarily qualified as such.[80] So much so that, according to some authors, the distinctive feature of a general principle would

[75] The Merriam Webster definition of 'interlock' explains the relation between building blocks clearly: an arrangement in which the operation of one part or mechanism automatically brings about or prevents the operation of another.

[76] On this aspect, see Besson, 'General Principles and Customary Law in the EU Legal Order' 112. It is held that principles are taken sometimes from the national systems, used at EU level, and 'returned' to the national level in a different shape. Tridimas, *The General Principles of EU Law* 6. See in a similar sense, Lenaerts and Gutiérrez-Fons, 'The Constitutional Allocation of Powers and General Principles of EU Law' 1630. Lourenço observes that 'they have served to transport the fundamental values of the legal systems adhering to the Union from the national level to this supranational, quasi-federalist, form of legal system'. Lourenço, *A Matter of Principle*, 31.

[77] The neutrality of these principles is relative, because they still work in combination with specific rules, principles, and objectives belonging to a specific area of law.

[78] It could be used as a ground for review, for example.

[79] See, for two examples of slightly different approaches to the category, the contribution of A Arnull's and M Dougan's in R de la Feria and S Vogenauer (eds), *Prohibition of Abuse of Law*.

[80] See the next chapter for the principle of solidarity.

be its independent application, rather than its general nature:[81] they 'confer on individuals a right which they may rely on as such in disputes between them in a field covered by EU law'. This would be so unless the principle in question requires further specification. The next chapter shows that this would be the case with the principle of fairness stated in Article 67 TFEU. While it is argued that a workable definition of such a principle can be provided, its operationalization presupposes reliance on more specific, and context-dependent, legal constructs.

How would that independent application materialize? Put differently, what are these important functions that make the attribution of a quality of 'general' so important, bearing in mind what was said above about the potentially overstated relevance of the 'general' label? A well-established view of general principles of EU law sees them as fulfilling a threefold role. Firstly, there is the gap-filling function, aimed at ensuring autonomy and coherence of EU law against fragmentation.[82] Secondly, they provide an aid to interpretation for the Court of Justice and the national courts. This is apparent from the duty of national courts to interpret EU and national law consistently with general principles of EU law—as long as the issue falls within the scope of application of EU law. To be sure, the same duty binds the Court vis-à-vis its interpretative task conferred by the Treaties.[83] Another manifestation of the aid-to-interpretation function consists of the use of general principles as directly effective norms to displace a conflicting national rule in the context of national proceedings. In this book, the focus is on the vertical direct effect of principles, the main theme being the action of public bodies and actors falling within the scope of 'emanation of the state doctrine'.[84] Thirdly, general principles can act as a benchmark for reviewing 'the legality of secondary EU law and the compatibility of national law falling within the scope of EU law with that law'.[85] The difference between principles and rules would be starker in this case.[86] Apart from presenting a lower degree of specificity, principles

[81] KS Ziegler and PJ Neuvonen, 'General Principles in the EU Legal Order: Past, Present and Future Directions' in Ziegler, Neuvonen, and Moreno-Lax (eds), *Research Handbook on General Principles in EU Law* 11–12.

[82] See, similarly, A von Arnauld, 'Harmonisation Through General Principles of Law' in Ziegler, Neuvonen, and Moreno-Lax (eds), *Research Handbook on General Principles in EU Law* 43–44. In the author's view, an example of a value-related principle generating a sub-principle would be legal certainty and res judicata, respectively. Other authors find that substantive coherence, produced by morally laden general legal principles, has become ever more vital for the functioning of the national legal order. See X Groussot, J Hettne, and G Thor Petursson, 'General Principles and the Many Faces of Coherence: Between Law and Ideology in the European Union' in Vogenauer and Weatherill (eds) *General Principles of Law European and Comparative Perspectives* 79. Other authors still point to the pluralism-preserving function of principles: S Besson, 'From European Integration to European Integrity: Should European Law Speak With Just One Voice?' (2004) 10 European Law Journal 257.

[83] The role played by general principles in this context is not without limits, but is constrained by their scope of application, the prohibition of an interpretation of national law *contra legem*, and the principle of legality in criminal law.

[84] While acknowledging the importance of the debate about the horizontal direct effect of general principles, the issue lies outwith the scope of this research.

[85] Lenaerts and Gutiérrez-Fons, 'The Constitutional Allocation of Powers' 1629.

[86] This account, and the one arguing for a blurred boundary between general principles and rules, are not mutually exclusive. Spotting rule-like qualities in general principles is not tantamount to dispensing with the distinction between the two categories. Furthermore, the emphasis on their independent application echoes, at least to an extent, their judicial review-related function. In other words, the independent application geared towards the enforcement of an individual right can explain the functioning only of some principles.

do not apply in an 'all-or-nothing' scenario,[87] 'leave more scope for judicial participation in law-making',[88] and require a greater level of accountability.[89] Principles guide the interpretation of the rule (which flows from, and must be consistent with, the former), are not placed in a hierarchical relationship and need to be balanced against each other in a step-by-step exercise.[90] The next chapter discusses how the principles forming the test can fulfil those functions, with a view to assessing the constitutional compliance of the law of EU border controls. It is clear that the heterogeneity of this law, and especially of the values and interests underpinning it, puts the issue of balancing front and centre in this research.

The absence of hierarchy between principles, when it comes to balancing, is not shared unanimously by scholars. As the balancing is guided by the values they protect, regard should be had to an axiological hierarchy – not legal, but still a hierarchy.[91] This is the case even when different principles stem from the same source.[92] According to some authors, a nucleus of absolute principles has emerged in recent years, which would not be subject to a balancing exercise in light of their superior value. While 'newer' principles such as autonomy and the indivisibility of the internal market[93] are used as examples, other more 'obvious' principles demonstrate this even more clearly. There seems to be no room for derogating from, or balancing, the principles of conferral or subsidiarity against other principles or interests. When it comes to the balancing, the objectives of Union norms under consideration, as well as the objectives of the wider legal context, play an important role.[94] The following section shows that the axiological and teleological orientation of the balancing, and of the interpretative exercise of the ECJ and national courts more broadly, are complementary.

In the EU legal order, principles reflect, and are linked to, the values under Article 2 TEU. The former 'channel' the latter through more specific principles or rules, which are actioned by the EU and member states and operationalized through dedicated frameworks and procedures. Principles often function together and are characterized by a complex network of relationship. They govern the interaction between actors and norms. Some make the system work by defining the respective roles of the different actors involved. Some others are more concerned with the content of a policy. They can find general application[95] or be area-specific,[96] or

[87] J Raz, 'Legal Principles and the Limits of Law' (1972) 81 Yale Law Journal 854.

[88] Some might say at the expense of legal certainty.

[89] A Von Bogdandy, 'Founding Principles of EU Law: A Theoretical and Doctrinal Sketch' (2010) 16 European Law Journal 103.

[90] See Lenaerts and Gutiérrez-Fons 'The Constitutional Allocation of Powers' 1652–53.

[91] For a classic study on balancing in the context of constitutional rights, see generally, R Alexy, *A Theory of Constitutional Rights* (Oxford University Press 2002).

[92] Besson, 'General Principles and Customary Law in the EU Legal Order' 113.

[93] N Nic Shuibhne, 'What Is the Autonomy of EU Law, and Why Does That Matter?' (2019) 88 Nordic Journal of International Law 9; Editorial comments, 'Is the "Indivisibility" of the Four Freedoms a Principle of EU Law?'. It is also true that, in order to claim that a principle may not be derogated from, its meaning and scope should be clearly identified. This is particularly difficult with concepts such as autonomy and the indivisibility of the internal market.

[94] M Poiares Maduro, 'Interpreting European Law: Judicial Adjudication in a Context of Constitutional Pluralism' (2007) 1 European Journal of Legal Studies 137.

[95] For example, sincere cooperation.

[96] See the retroactivity of more lenient criminal penalties.

both.[97] Regardless of their label as general principles or not, they can be so 'powerful' to act as a ground for review or cause the disapplication of a conflicting national rule.[98] As their overarching function is to ensure the pursuit of the EU objective is in line with its values, the heterogeneous understandings that can be adopted vis-à-vis the same or different values create the need for reconciling them where possible. The next section shows that objectives come into play especially, though not exclusively, in the context of balancing.

## 1.4 Objectives: Un(der)sung Heroes of European Integration?

### 1.4.1 A Systemic View of Objectives in the EU Legal Order

Objectives have been a protagonist in the process of European legal integration since its inception.[99] Their range has widened in line with the expansion of the EU project and the Union's competences.[100] Different views have been expressed on the relationship between values, principles, and objectives in EU law. Lourenço correctly notes that 'the relationship of synergy between the three concepts has [much] contributed to the harmonization of the system and integration of EU law'.[101] Finding a synergic relationship is not tantamount to suggesting that these three groups have the same legal meaning and modus operandi. In that regard, Rosas rightly observes that the values enshrined in Article 2 TEU form 'the ideological basis for the more precise objectives set forth in Article 3 TEU and the basic principles of the constitutional order enshrined in Articles 4 and 5 TEU'.[102] The key argument of this chapter reflects this view. The values found and pervade the EU as a polity, while the principles act as their vectors through the EU law 'machinery'. The objectives, for their part, are the driver of the EU action. The member states have agreed to limitations to their own sovereign rights[103] and confer competences upon the Union to attain their common objectives.[104] Looking at Article 3 TEU, scholars have argued that certain 'new entries among the EU objectives 'go in the direction of respecting human values

[97] Solidarity permeates the whole EU legal order, but is also explicitly referred to in specific Treaty chapters, such as under Articles 80 and 194 TFEU.

[98] The next chapter uses solidarity as an example of this.

[99] See J Larik, 'From Speciality to a Constitutional Sense of Purpose: On the Changing Role of the Objectives of the European Union' (2014) 63 International and Comparative Law Quarterly 1.

[100] 'In line' should not be read as 'linear'. In fact, the teleological interpretation of the Court has often led to an expansive interpretation of primary and secondary EU law, including those concerning the scope of EU competences.

[101] Lourenço, *A Matter of Principle* 97.

[102] A Rosas and L Armati, *EU Constitutional Law: An Introduction* (Hart 2012) 54.

[103] This expression was famously used for the first time by the Court of Justice in Case 26-62, *NV Algemene Transport-en Expeditie Onderneming van Gend & Loos v Netherlands Inland Revenue Administration*, EU:C:1963:1. While it is acknowledged that limitation of sovereign rights and transfer of competence are not to be used interchangeably, it is also equally undeniable that they are, at least in this context, inextricably linked.

[104] TEU, Article 1(1).

and caring for the well-being of the people'.[105] The movement of the Area of Freedom, Security and Justice (AFSJ) up the list, compared to previous Treaties, would certify its centrality to the Union's project.[106] In 'structural' terms, Article 3 TEU seems to be organized around 'primary' and 'derived' objectives. In its internal and external action, the EU aims to promote peace, its values, and the well-being of its peoples. Within this perimeter, each paragraph in turn enunciates objectives such as the establishment of the AFSJ, the internal market and the Economic and Monetary Union (EMU). Each of these derived objectives is organized, in turn, around an overarching goal and a series of more specific aims: take the AFSJ, where the absence of internal controls is flanked by measures on the external borders, asylum, immigration, and criminal law.[107] As Articles 2 and 3 TEU are closely connected,[108] the latter reflecting the former conceptually and normatively, the relation between 'primary' and 'derived' objectives is not a hierarchical one. Rather, it enshrines the idea that the objectives must be pursued in compliance with the values.[109] While the first paragraph of Article 3(1) TEU defines the boundaries of the playing field, the following provisions detail the mission of the Union as a polity (internally and externally) *within* that normative space. The concluding paragraph indicates the method and limits of the pursuit of the objectives—that is, the preconditions for any lawful EU action: conferral, subsidiarity, and proportionality. This threefold obligation is the starting point in the assessment of constitutional compliance of EU law and its implementation.

Therefore, the structure and content of Article 3 TEU reinforce the main claims of this chapter. Article 3(1) and (6) TEU reveals an understanding of the EU legal architecture where the founding values are the source of legal principles and objectives. If objectives 'trickle down' from values, the normative-oriented principles guide the pursuit of those objectives. As one would expect, the approaches in the scholarship to the relationship between the three building blocks—and between principles and objectives especially—vary. On the one hand, it is apparent that, at least in certain cases, objectives and principles overlap.[110] On the other hand, some scholars have opined that the objectives identify the domains of action and ends to achieve, and serve as a legal basis for action; whereas the principles operate in the sphere of said action, being intimately related to the notion of powers to be exercised.[111] The two ideas are not mutually exclusive. Article 80 TFEU states that solidarity is a principle that governs the law and policy of EU border controls, and constitutes the basis for the EU action

[105] See, for example, the references to full employment, social justice, solidarity between generations, respecting the Union's diversity, and ensuring the safeguard of Europe's cultural heritage. See in this sense J Piris, *The Lisbon Treaty: A Legal and Political Analysis* (Cambridge University Press 2010) 73.

[106] P Craig, *The Lisbon Treaty: Law, Politics, and Treaty Reform* (Oxford University Press 2010) 312.

[107] See also the reference to combating social exclusion and discrimination, or the promotion of social justice and equality between women and men, as well as the solidarity between generations, in the context of the objective of establishing the internal market.

[108] See in this sense F Dorssemont, 'Values and Objectives' in N Bruun, K Lörcher, and I Schömann (eds), *The Lisbon Treaty and Social Europe* (Hart 2012) 50.

[109] It would be absurd to set the objectives of promoting its values, and then pursue other targets potentially not aligned with Article 2 TEU.

[110] G Beck, *The Legal Reasoning of the Court of Justice of the EU* (Hart 2012) 323.

[111] C Blumann, 'Objectifs et Principes en droit communautaire' in *Le Droit de l'union en principes: Liber Amicorum Jean Raux* (Éditions Apogée 2006) 39 onwards.

via measures intended to give effect to that principle. This reflects the twofold path to implementation of EU values through law: positive, by means of measures (including principles-inspired) meant to actively promote them, and negative, with principles acting as the guardians of the EU values. The next chapters show that solidarity also orients the interpretation of EU law in this area beyond the solidarity—implementing measures specifically referred to in Article 80 TFEU. As a concretizing figure of the value of solidarity, the homonymous principle informs the content and guides the interpretation of EU law as well as the implementation thereof. There is, therefore, no contradiction between the ideas that principles are shaped by the objectives[112] *and* that they make 'the objectives operative'.[113] The heterogeneous nature of principles of EU law is incompatible with one-size-fits-all categorizations. The fact that one concept such as solidarity is referred to as a value, a principle, and an objective is not legal schizophrenia: quite the contrary, it perfectly embodies the idea that principles 'guard' the value-compliant pursuit of the EU objectives.

Against this background, we must consider the relationship between certain relevant principles and objectives in their legislative and judicial dimensions at EU and national level. This also entails considerations on how this relationship plays out in the making, interpretation, and implementation of secondary law. Once again, an assessment of the way different values and interests are accommodated is key. Balancing emerges as a fundamental exercise. This is especially true for EU border controls, where different and often competing objectives are involved. Balancing concerns not only judicial interpretation, but first and foremost the legislative process. Firstly, as a general observation, many important principles are linked to the EU objectives. The link can be inherent in the principle itself. The objectives are core parameters of an ex ante or ex post assessment of a piece of legislation in light of subsidiarity and proportionality pursuant to Article 5(3) and (4) TEU. A measure may well aim, in and of itself, to give effect to one or more principles (eg solidarity, as per Article 80 TFEU). This objective will have to be reconciled with other principles/objectives. For example, the imposition of solidaristic obligations on member states must be squared with the respect for their sovereignty (particularly through the principle of subsidiarity and proportionality).

Secondly, objective-related principles can also generate sub-principles, which in turn give rise to a complex relationship. Sincere cooperation, effectiveness, and mutual trust are a case in point. Both effectiveness and mutual trust are rooted in sincere cooperation as defined in Article 4(3) TEU. On the one hand, mutual trust is premised on, and justified by, the idea that member states comply with, and facilitate the fulfilment of, their obligations under the Treaties.[114] On the other hand, mutual trust is the cornerstone of mechanisms that aim to attain the Union's objectives and must orient the member states' implementation.[115] For example, mutual trust underpins

[112] C Semmelmann, 'Legal Principles as an Expression of a European Legal Culture Between Unity and Diversity' in G Helleringer and K Purnhagen (eds), *Towards A European Legal Culture* (Nomos/Hart 2014) 323.

[113] J Larik, 'Worldly Ambitions: Foreign Policy Objectives in European Constitutional Law' (Dphil thesis, European University Institute 2013) 195.

[114] And, ultimately, with Article 2 TEU and everything that flows from there (including the objectives). Case C-216/18 PPU, *Minister for Justice and Equality (Deficiencies in the system of justice)*, EU:C:2018:586, para 35.

[115] Inter alia, for the whole law of the AFSJ.

the regulatory framework established by the Dublin Regulation. As a result, member states must, save in exceptional circumstances, transfer an asylum seeker to the state identified as responsible for the examination of an application for international protection. To flip the perspective on its head, a challenge to the implementation of a measure built on mutual trust is a challenge to the effectiveness of EU law—that is, of the value-oriented objectives that the measure in question might pursue. The challenge can be justified for two main reasons. The measure itself and its objectives might not be compatible with EU values. Or else, the implementation of the instrument in question might pose a risk to *other* values—for example, where the transfer to the state responsible would endanger certain fundamental rights of the person concerned.[116] These examples reveal the importance of considering values, principles, and objectives holistically. Thirdly, as regulatory frameworks constitute the outcome of a balancing exercise (legally and politically), one instrument is likely to simultaneously pursue a diverse set of goals.[117] Measures of secondary law often lay down a framework without determining *a priori* how the balancing should be achieved when transposing or implementing the law. Questions arising in this sense might be answered in different fora—for example, by the European Commission in its capacity as guardian of the Treaties or, most likely, the ECJ and/or national courts.[118] To reconstruct the meaning of one or more provisions of EU law, and to assess their compatibility with the national laws and practices under consideration, the Court consistently relies on the wording, context, and objectives of those provisions.[119] In light of the integrated relationship between the building blocks of the EU legal order, such a tripartite exercise inevitably involves consideration of values and principles engaged by the specific instrument.

## 1.4.2 The Treaties and the Objectives of EU Border Controls

We have seen that, in the EU legal order, objectives are inextricably linked to principles and values. Due to their systemic role, objectives play a key part in the constitutional allocation of powers, as an aid to interpretation and for judicial review. The example of EU border controls illuminates the structural organization of objectives in the Union's legal edifice. The numerous objectives scattered throughout the policy areas composing the Treaties express the fundamental macro-objectives stated in Article 3 TEU—and, ultimately, the all-encompassing the EU supreme goals of promoting peace, its values, and the well-being of its people. More specifically, objectives are organized in concentric circles. While Article 3 TEU constitutes the overarching framework defining the objectives of the Union, Title V TFEU elaborates on the aims related to the creation of the AFSJ. The opening of the Title states that the Union shall

[116] The mind goes immediately to the non-execution of a Dublin transfer on the basis of the risk of inhuman treatment in the state responsible for the examination of the asylum claim. See Case C-578/16, *CK*, EU:C:2017:127 and case law cited.

[117] How well balanced the outcome is in each specific case, is a different question.

[118] This might not always be the case. The Court might shy away from ruling on issues that would be better left to the EU legislature or the member states.

[119] The context itself can also be set out by referring to the objectives of the measure.

constitute an area of freedom, security, and justice, with respect for fundamental rights and the different legal systems and traditions of the member states.[120] Also, it shall (a) ensure the absence of internal border controls and (b) frame a common policy on asylum immigration and external border control, based on solidarity between Member States which is fair to TCNs.[121] Against this background, Chapter 2 of Title V homes in on border checks, asylum, and immigration. Each of these areas has specific aims. As for border control, the Union shall: ensure the absence of any controls on persons, whatever their nationality, when crossing internal borders; carry out checks on persons and efficiently monitor the crossing of external borders; gradually introducing an integrated management system for external borders.[122] With regard to asylum, the Union's policy shall develop with a view to offering appropriate status to any TCN requiring international protection and ensuring compliance with the principle of non-refoulement.[123] The EU immigration policy must aim at the efficient management of migration flows, the fair treatment of TCNs residing legally in member states, and the prevention of, and enhanced measures to combat, illegal immigration and trafficking in human beings.[124] The chain of the EU objectives starts from Article 3 TEU; it continues through to the specific Treaty Title and Chapters; and, as detailed in Parts II and III, it ends with the secondary law enacted pursuant to those legal bases and the national implementation. The sequence unfolds hierarchically: the objectives set and pursued in each 'circle' must be consistent with those in the bigger circle that contains them. The way the objectives are pursued must comply with the value-driven principles. Thus, the policy area in question is based on solidarity, respect for fundamental rights and diversity of national legal systems, and the principle of fairness towards TCNs. In the background, there are principles related to the exercise of EU competence in these areas (primarily, but not exclusively, subsidiarity and proportionality) as well as other relevant components of the structured network of principles making EU law work. Throughout the book, the heterogeneity of EU border controls will raise questions of constitutional compliance and accommodation of different values and interests.

## 1.5 Conclusions

Values, objectives, and principles constitute the backbone of the EU as a legal order. Any area of EU law, to different extents and in different way, develops around this spine. Like bees in a hive, they all play a part in the life of EU law and its implementation. Their function can be properly understood only if their mutual relation is set out. Principles are concretizing figures of values, and are in turn concretized by more specific principles or rules, operationalized through frameworks and procedures. Compliance with them and through them is ensured via *ex ante* and *ex post*

[120] TFEU, Article 67(1).
[121] TFEU, Article 67(2).
[122] TFEU, Article 77(1).
[123] TFEU, Article 78(1).
[124] TFEU, Article 79(1).

mechanisms of enforcement. Objectives orient the function of the principles in different forms and must be guided by the values too. Given the different understandings that can underpin certain EU values, and the diverse interests pursued by the actors involved in the making and implementing of the law of EU border controls, we must assess whether competing claims are being accommodated in line with the relevant legal standards. Against this background, the next chapter sets out the test of constitutional compliance of the law of EU border controls.

# 2
# The Test of Constitutional Compliance

## 2.1 Introduction

The building blocks of the EU legal order (values, principles, and objectives) act together to make the system work. The values constitute the foundations of the Union. The principles channel those values and ensure that the objectives are pursued through EU and member state laws and practices consistently with Article 2 TEU. The objectives themselves flow from Article 2 TEU and often orient the functioning of the principles. Solidarity is one of the best showcases for this dynamic. It is a value under Article 2 TEU, a principle governing several areas of EU law, including border controls, and an objective—as inferred from Article 80 TFEU—that might warrant the adoption of specific rules to give effect to it. Values are concretized by principles, which are in turn concretized by sub-principles or rights, and operationalized through rules and procedures. The principles inform the procedures,[1] and find application through them.[2] This account is aspirational, and the reality is often much less harmonious and coherent. As EU border controls show, the making and implementation of laws and policies occur in a context where a heterogeneous set of values and interests are involved. The two 2015 Relocation Decisions,[3] enacted to give effect thereto, were not implemented by certain member states, which in turn led the Court of Justice to find those states in breach of EU law.[4] Therefore, the concepts of enforcement and compliance as defined in this chapter are particularly important to this research. In this regard, we have also clarified that values, principles, and objectives are not monolithic categories. Different values, principles, or objectives often pull in different directions. Examining how competing interests have been accommodated is crucial to the assessment of compliance.

As detailed in the following chapters, heterogeneity is a distinctive feature of the law of EU border controls. It involves different levels of governance and actors. It addresses different groups of people and pursues different objectives. This research aims to answer the question as to whether such heterogeneity creates issues of constitutional compliance, and devises a test for that specific purpose. Constitutional

[1] For example, effective judicial protection or the right to a good administration.

[2] Sometimes, this can be the result of the joint application of different principles, such as non-discrimination and direct effect.

[3] See, for example, Council Decision (EU) 2015/1523 establishing provisional measures in the area of international protection for the benefit of Italy and of Greece [2015] OJ L 239/146. The Decision set up a mechanism of compulsory relocation of applicants for international protection among member states, to relieve over-burdened states (Greece and Italy), and implement the principle of solidarity in the context of asylum law.

[4] Joined Cases C-715/17, C-718/17, and C-719/17, *European Commission v Republic of Poland and Others*, EU:C:2020:257.

*The Law of EU Border Controls*. Leandro Mancano, Oxford University Press. © Leandro Mancano 2025.
DOI: 10.1093/9780191966187.003.0003

compliance refers to legal obedience to the EU constitutional framework, and is defined by the Court as encompassing

> the founding values set out in Article 2 TEU . . . the general principles of EU law, the provisions of the Charter, and the provisions of the EU and FEU Treaties, which include, inter alia, rules on the conferral and division of powers, rules governing how the EU institutions and its judicial system are to operate, and fundamental rules in specific areas, structured in such a way as to contribute to the implementation of the process of integration described in the second paragraph of Article 1 TEU.[5]

This being the definition of constitutional compliance, the specific scope of this research is defined as follows. The test has no ambition to capture all the possibly relevant principles and rights that come into play in EU border controls. Since this book focuses on the heterogeneity of the law and its implementation, the benchmarks have been selected on the basis of their suitability for answering the overarching question of this research. Comprehensive as this volume aims to be, not all aspects related to EU border controls are considered in Parts II and III. Chapters 3 and 7 explain in detail the measures that are being analysed, and justify the choices made in this sense. However, at this stage of the book we must introduce the general criterion used to delimit the scope of the investigation. We focus on conditions for exercising border controls and conditions imposed on the persons concerned inside the EU and at its external borders. Lastly, the discussion in the following chapters also involves an analysis of the available mechanisms of enforcement as defined in this book, lest the assessment be incomplete.[6]

This chapter is structured as follows. Firstly, we unpack the research question. We explain the different steps of the analysis, by defining more specifically the perimeter of the research and introducing the parameters of constitutional compliance. We also account for the way those parameters have been categorized and presented in the following sections. Given the interactive nature of EU border controls and the fact that it is an area of shared competence,[7] the assessment of constitutional compliance develops along three main axes, each corresponding to a specific sub-question. In the EU–member states vertical axis, we consider whether the law allocates tasks in line with the principle of subsidiarity and respect for the essential state functions.[8] In the horizontal axis, we analyse the implications of the law for interstate cooperation, mainly from the perspective of solidarity.[9] In the EU/member state–individual vertical axis, we assess whether EU border controls are fair towards the persons concerned.[10]

[5] *Opinion 1/17*, EU:C:2016:656, para 110. The Treaties, the Charter, and the general principles make up the constitutional law of the Union. The specific reference to certain kinds of Treaties rules reveals their systemic relevance as concretizing figures of broader principles channelling the EU values.

[6] This question is inextricably linked to the discussion on the nature of a principle. For example, could solidarity be invoked and enforced in national proceedings?

[7] Consolidated Version of the Treaty on the Functioning of the EU (TFEU) [2012] OJ C 326/47, Article 4(2)(j).

[8] Consolidated Version of the Treaty on EU (TEU) [2012] OJ C 326/13, Articles 5(3) and 4(2) respectively.

[9] TFEU, Article 80.

[10] TFEU, Article 67(2).

The presentation of those parameters is preceded by the introduction of two principles: sincere cooperation and effectiveness. They 'come first' logically for three main reasons: they are 'transversal' principles, they form the basis of several of the principles discussed subsequently, and they are residual constructs (especially sincere cooperation), as they apply where no more specific legal tool is available. Importantly, the discussion shows how those parameters form a structured network of principles, relevant to answering the research question of this book consistently with its scope.

## 2.2 Constitutional Compliance as Appropriateness: Core Questions and Relevant Principles

The law of EU border controls embodies the supranationalization of an essential state function.[11] Its development has significant constitutional implications for the EU as a legal order. It unfolds through a wide range of interinstitutional activities and has a significant impact on the persons concerned. To discuss and understand the analytical framework, we must start with the research question raised in this book: is the law of EU border controls constitutionally compliant, despite the heterogeneity of sources, actors, objectives, and addressees of control ? The question can be framed more specifically as follows: is the appropriate action being taken at the appropriate level of governance and by the appropriate actor, on the basis of the appropriate source, for the appropriate purpose, vis-à-vis the appropriate group of persons? Despite the complexity of the overarching research question, the latter can be broken down into three main issues: allocation of a task to a given level of governance and actor; nature and mechanisms of interstate cooperation; and treatment of addressees of controls (primarily, but not exclusively, third-country nationals).

Secondly, on the basis of the definition of 'compliance' espoused in this research, the assessment revolves around:

I. The compatibility of the relevant instruments of secondary law with primary EU law;[12]
II. The compliance of the action of EU bodies with secondary and primary EU law;
III. The compliance of national laws and practices with secondary and primary EU law.

In Parts II and III, the assessment is conducted overall in the order as presented.[13] Such a multi-level evaluation cannot be treated as a mechanical or a form-filling

[11] Article 4(2) TEU defines essential state functions as including 'ensuring the territorial integrity of the State, maintaining law and order and safeguarding national security'. Even though border control is not explicitly mentioned here, it is widely acknowledged that one of the core sovereign rights of the state—or a territorial power—is to decide who can enter its territory, subject to a series of exceptions. See, in this sense, the European Court of Human Rights (ECtHR)'s judgment of 21 November 2019, *Ilias and Ahmed v Hungary*, App. no. 47287/15, para 12 , finding that states 'have the right, as a matter of well-established international law and subject to their treaty obligations, including the Convention, to control the entry, residence and expulsion of aliens'. On the concept of 'essential state function' in the case law of the Court of Justice, see T Boková, 'Exploring the Concept of Essential State Functions on the Basis of the CJEU's Decision on the Temporary Relocation Mechanism' (2022) 7 European Papers 773.

[12] Specifically, compatibility with certain principles that are relevant to issues of heterogeneity.

[13] This, it is argued, is the choice that makes most sense logically.

exercise, as both our benchmarks and subject of assessment can pose challenges of different kinds: in certain important respects, secondary law might be silent or ambiguous; doubts may exist about the capacity for certain principles to fill the gap left by the legislation; uncertainty could surround the possibility of using a principle as a ground for review.

Thirdly, the assessment starts with the objectives and proceeds in two steps:

1) Are the goals stated in measures of secondary law in line with those laid down in the Treaties?
2) Are the relevant rules of secondary law capable of *appropriately* achieving the objectives stated therein?

Achieving the objectives *appropriately* requires the attainment of those goals in line with the aspects of the EU constitutional framework relevant to the research question.

Fourthly, and coherently with the main themes involved in the research question, the scope of the investigation is limited to the conditions for exercising controls, the conditions imposed on the persons concerned, and the allowed or mandated conducts which the legal framework associates with those conditions (on the controller *and* the controlled).

Fifthly, how are we going to assess the appropriateness of the rules to the objectives? As a preliminary remark, the different types of heterogeneity characterizing EU border controls and the different elements of the scope of this research are inextricably linked. To provide a concrete example, the rules of the European Border and Coast Guard (EBCG) Regulation aim to facilitate regular entry, prevent cross-border crime, and identify vulnerable categories of people.[14] Different objectives are set for different groups of addressees, possibly pursued by different bodies.[15] This raises a series of questions. Is the allowed or mandated Union action in a given situation necessary, or would member states be better placed to act?[16] Is the empowerment of a certain body capable of achieving those different objectives in a way that is fair to third-country nationals ? Due to their interdependence, we cannot compartmentalize the different aspects of the research question and 'assign' a legal principle to the analysis of each of them. It is more rigorous to identify a suite of relevant principles and define their joint operation. The choice of this suite takes account of the interactive nature of EU border controls. The interaction occurs along two main axes: horizontal and vertical. The former concerns the interaction between member states, or between EU institutions and bodies. The latter looks at the interaction between the EU and the member states, or between EU/state bodies and the individual. While some principles are relevant to one specific axis of cooperation, others are more eclectic. For example, effectiveness must always be linked to a specific provision, which in turn could relate to any of those forms of interaction. The rest of this chapter discusses the meaning and

[14] Regulation (EU) 2019/1896 on the European Border and Coast Guard and repealing Regulations (EU) No 1052/2013 and (EU) 2016/1624 (EBCG Regulation) [2019] OJ L 295/1, Article 3(1)(a).

[15] For example, the EBCG is under an obligation to cooperate with a series of other EU agencies in certain circumstances.

[16] The law of EU border controls is characterized by cooperation between the EU and the member states, so the 'division of labour' between them is not always straightforward. The question remains; if anything, the uncertainty makes the identification of the right body even more relevant.

scope of the suite of principles, their mutual relationship, and their relevance to the research question.

We start with loyalty and effectiveness. These are 'transversal' principles insofar as they apply to both axes of interaction, and they are closely linked. They are the root (especially loyalty) or the pole star (effectiveness) of other relevant principles such as solidarity or mutual trust. They are geared towards the achievement of the EU objectives. As the assessment of appropriateness begins with the objectives, it makes sense to use those principles to open the presentation of the analytical framework. Relatedly, loyalty and effectiveness are 'neutral' principles: they say little or nothing as to how far the pursuit of the goals can go, or how to balance different objectives when a possible clash emerges. In the context of this specific research, they are also 'residual' benchmarks: more specific principles prove more relevant to answer the question raised in this book. This being said, discussing them is important to understanding the wider 'structured network' of legal constructs in which those more specific principles operate.

Against this background, the analysis is primarily conducted through three key principles: subsidiarity, solidarity between member states, and fairness. As mentioned, the implications of legal heterogeneity for the constitutional compliance of EU border controls can be understood by looking at three main themes: allocation of task, horizontal cooperation, and treatment of the persons concerned. Those three principles map onto the themes, with a view to developing an integrated approach to the study of EU border controls. The meaning of 'integrated' here is twofold. The book uses those core principles 'jointly' to show how the same aspect of the legal framework can have consequences on different levels, and considers how the numerous strands of the law of EU border controls work together. In this sense, the role of sincere cooperation and effectiveness is to support the compliance assessment carried out primarily through subsidiarity, solidarity, and fairness. There is no magic formula that can determine *a priori* how those different questions and principles should be reconciled. In defining the meaning of those principles and their interaction, this chapter aims to provide a blueprint that will be used for the substantive analysis in Parts II and III.

As for the 'EU–member states' axis of interaction, we must investigate whether a task has been allocated and performed at the appropriate level of governance. Beyond the evaluation concerning the level of governance, a more specific question may arise as to whether the appropriate actor has been put in charge. Furthermore, the allocation of a task related to the exercise of controls might require a degree of cooperation between the EU bodies, between member states, or both, in what we can call 'mixed allocation'. Is the allocation vis-à-vis the level of governance and the specific actor, and its implementation, in line with subsidiarity and solidarity? The question of allocation has implications not only from the viewpoint of the public powers, but also for the persons concerned. Both the institutional and individual perspectives must be part of the analysis. For example, a type of control might indeed be suitable for a certain group of persons, but would it be fairer to them if a different body or type of actor were entrusted with it? This question is different from that considering whether the kind of addressees and the conditions imposed on them are, in and of themselves, the appropriate target of a certain type of control or action. In both cases, an assessment of fairness is required. As will become apparent, the question of how to accommodate different values and interests arises from the discussion of most principles addressed below and will constitute a golden thread of the chapter and the book more broadly.

This having been clarified, the overarching research question can be reframed as follows: in the law of EU border controls, are the conditions for controls and on the persons concerned, considered together with the type of actors in charge and the group of addressees targeted, as established in the law and with regard being had to their implementation, capable of achieving its objectives in a way that is compatible with the principles of subsidiarity, solidarity, and fairness? A final note on mutual trust. This principle is not directly involved in the assessment of constitutional compliance. However, it is a fundamental component of the EU constitutional architecture and interlocks with the other principles mentioned above. For completeness, mutual trust is also discussed in this chapter to provide an essential element of the legal background to the law of EU border controls. By linking them to EU border controls, the chapter discusses these interrelated principles in turn, and specifically: their meaning and scope, their interplay, and conditions and limits of their use for enforcement.

## 2.3 Transversal Principles

### 2.3.1 *L'Origine du Monde*: The Principle of Loyalty

The discussion of the structured network of principles must start with loyalty, which represents the conceptual and legal root of most of the principles discussed below. Loyalty is one of the fundamental principles of EU law and is multidimensional: it acts in defence of many different interests and policy objectives, and is key to the harmonious working of the EU's complex system.[17] It is a centripetal force furthering integration, underpinning many fundamental chapters in the development of EU law, such as the duty of consistent interpretation,[18] or the direct effect of directives.[19] While the Treaties are dotted with provisions constituting a specification of loyalty—for example, establishing duties of abstention[20] or intervention[21]—the principle of sincere cooperation currently enshrined in Article 4(3) TEU is the golden child of loyalty.[22]

Based on Articles 4(3) and 13(2) TEU, we can distinguish between: horizontal loyalty among member states or EU institutions; vertical loyalty from the member states towards the EU; and reverse vertical loyalty from the EU to the member states.[23] On the one hand, the Union's institutions must act within their remit substantially and procedurally, horizontally[24] and vertically. On the other hand, member states must meet their obligations stemming from EU law. This includes facilitating the Union's

[17] M Klamert, *The Principle of Loyalty in EU Law* (Oxford University Press 2014) 34.

[18] Case C-14/83, *von Colson*, ECLI:EU:C: 1984:153, para 26; Case C-79/83, *Harz*, ECLI:EU:C:1984:155, para 26; Case C-129/96, *Inter-Environnement Wallonie*, ECLI:EU:C:1997:628, para 45.

[19] Case C-190/87, *Moormann*, ECLI:EU:C:1988:424, para 24.

[20] TFEU, Article 92. See Case C-195/90, *Commission v Germany*, ECLI:EU:C:1992:219, para 36.

[21] TFEU, Article 325. See Case C-186/98, *Nunes*, ECLI:EU:C:1999:376, para 13.

[22] Klamert, *The Principle of Loyalty in EU Law* 33.

[23] Case C-2/88, *JJ Zwartveld and Others*, EU:C:1990:440, para 10.

[24] Case C-5/16, *Republic of Poland v European Parliament and Council of the European Union*, EU:C:2018:483, para 84.

tasks and avoiding actions that might hamper the attainment of the EU objectives. The systemic location of Article 4(3) TEU is also key, as it follows the paragraphs on the principle of conferral[25] and the clause on national constitutional identity and essential state functions.[26] Those provisions, it might be argued, act as a guide for the use of Article 4(3) TEU in reverse loyalty scenarios.

Sincere cooperation achieves its mission through two main 'channels'. Firstly, it facilitates the enforcement of EU law directly in a number of ways. It serves as an aid to interpretation as well as a conflict resolution rule.[27] It is an autonomous basis for obligations under EU law[28] and a ground to find member states in breach thereof.[29] In what has been defined as a function of 'amplification', Article 4(3) TEU can work in combination with another provision of EU law to produce a result that would not have been possible without sincere cooperation itself.[30] Secondly, more indirectly, sincere cooperation is the root of important principles,[31] which in turn 'prop . . . up the enforcement of [EU law] instruments under the title of the principle of effectiveness'.[32] Alone or in conjunction with the latter principle, sincere cooperation creates legal doctrines such as state liability.[33] It is also closely connected to effective judicial protection and the rule of law.[34] Due to the highly interactive nature of EU border controls, its proper functioning presupposes compliance with the duties laid down in Article 4(3) TEU. Internally, it requires first and foremost that checks at the frontiers between two member states are only reintroduced consistently with the conditions established by EU law. Externally, it relies heavily on the interaction among different EU bodies, among the EU bodies and national authorities, and among the national authorities.

Nonetheless, sincere cooperation has a supporting role—rather than a protagonist role—in this research. Despite its apparent nature of super-principle, it has limits too. The different duties inherent in it can be given effect through provisions of secondary law: when that happens, and where Union law regulates a certain subject comprehensively, Article 4(3) TEU cannot be invoked to amplify its scope.[35] Parts II and

[25] TEU, Article 4(1).

[26] TEU, Article 4(2).

[27] Klamert, *The Principle of Loyalty in EU Law* 267.

[28] *Opinion 1/03*, EU:C:2006:81, para 119.

[29] Case C-22/20, *Commission v Sweden*, EU:C:2021:669, paras 144–49. At the same time, the earlier case law of the Court stated that the principle of sincere cooperation 'is worded so generally that there can be no question of applying it autonomously when the situation concerned is governed by a specific provision of the Treaty'. Case C-18/93, *Corsica Ferries*, EU:C:1994:195, para 18.

[30] In Case C-265/95, *Commission of the European Communities v French Republic*, EU:C:1997:595, para 39, the Court stated that Article 30 TEC therefore requires the member states not merely themselves to abstain from adopting measures or engaging in conduct liable to constitute an obstacle to trade but also, when read with Article 5 TEC, to take all necessary and appropriate measures to ensure that this fundamental freedom is respected on their territory.

[31] Case 33/76, *Rewe-Zentralfinanz eG and Rewe-Zentral AG v Landwirtschaftskammer für das Saarland*, EU:C:1976:188.

[32] Klamert, *The Principle of Loyalty in EU Law* 273.

[33] See Joined Cases C-6/90 and C-9/90, *Andrea Francovich and Danila Bonifaci and others v Italian Republic*, EU:C:1991:428, paras 31–37.

[34] M Klamert, 'Loyalty and Solidarity as General Principles' in P Neuvonen, K Ziegler, and V Moreno-Lax (eds), *Research Handbook on General Principles in EU Law* (Edward Elgar 2022) 124.

[35] For example, Article 1 of Regulation 2847/93 establishing a control system applicable to the common fisheries policy [1993] OJ L 261/1 calls on the member states to adopt appropriate measures to ensure the effectiveness of the Union system for conservation and management of fishery resources, and has been

III show that this is very often the case with legislative measures of border controls. Furthermore, sincere cooperation is the victim of its own success. Its 'principle-genic' capacity is the key reason why it constitutes a residual tool to assess the constitutional compliance of EU border controls. Not infrequently, sincere cooperation will play this role in conjunction with one of its most faithful travel companions: the principle of effectiveness.

### 2.3.2 Ensuring the Achievement of the EU's Objectives: Effectiveness

Just like loyalty, effectiveness evokes a concept wider than that used in EU law. Snyder defines effectiveness as meaning that 'law matters: it has effects . . . apart from simply the elaboration of legal doctrine'[36] and includes—inter alia—implementation, enforcement, and compliance.[37] These processes presuppose conditions that go well beyond the realm of the law. Effectiveness and compliance are inextricably linked, and it is not unusual to see them used interchangeably.[38] Effectiveness as a principle of EU law clearly possesses a narrower meaning, but is key to achieving effectiveness in the broader sense. As regards its origins, the principle of effectiveness is rooted in sincere cooperation,[39] although it has developed a story of its own. So much so that the two are often used jointly to create new and important doctrines of EU law, such as state liability and the duty of consistent interpretation.[40] Despite their 'genetic' connection, the functions and modus operandi of two principles should not be conflated. In this regard, it has been argued that loyalty would be (mainly) about the resolution and/or prevention of conflicts. Effectiveness would be a 'rule of construction', concerned with the nullification of the unlawful consequences of breaches of Union law, and geared towards the effective enforcement of EU law within member states. *Effet utile* is yet different: a rule of interpretation, which seeks to realize the maximum effect of Union law and cannot create new obligations.[41] We should be wary of overly

qualified by the Court as a specification of current Article 4(3) TEU. In these cases, Klamert argues that a failure to fulfil specific obligations under an act of secondary law cannot at the same time violate Article 4(3) TEU, which is subsidiary to Article 288 TFEU for directives, and to Article 291(1) TFEU with respect to all other binding legal acts. Klamert, *The Principle of Loyalty in EU Law* 293.

[36] F Snyder, *New Directions in European Community Law* (Weidenfeld & Nicolson 1990) 3.

[37] F Snyder, 'The Effectiveness of European Community Law: Institutions, Processes, Tools and Techniques' (1993) 56 Modern Law Review 19. These concepts are closely interrelated. We have seen in the previous chapter how enforcement is an essential instrument to achieve compliance.

[38] See, for example, L Mancano, *The European Union and Deprivation of Liberty: A Legislative and Judicial Analysis from the Perspective of the Individual* (Hart 2019) 56 onwards.

[39] The Court held that 'If the national court concludes that the application of the national provisions . . . has the effect that, in a considerable number of cases, the commission of serious fraud will escape criminal punishment . . . it would be necessary to find that the measures laid down by national law . . . could not be regarded as being effective and dissuasive, which would be incompatible with Article 325(1) TFEU . . . read in conjunction with Article 4(3) TEU'. Case C-105/14, *Taricco and Others*, EU:C:2015:555, para 47.

[40] 'Effectiveness can determine both the point at which [EU] law intervenes and the extent of remedial action required from the national court'. M Ross, 'Effectiveness in the European Legal Order: Beyond Supremacy to Constitutional Proportionality' (2006) 31 European Law Review 495.

[41] However, the Court created an obligation of consistent interpretation for third pillar measures on the basis of the *useful effect* doctrine, by arguing that its jurisdiction 'would be deprived of most of its useful effect if individuals were not entitled to invoke framework decisions in order to obtain a conforming

rigid characterizations, however, as examples from the case law could easily challenge them. Take, for example, the following excerpt from a Court's judgment: 'where a provision of [EU] law is open to several interpretations, preference must be given to that interpretation which ensures that the provision retains its effectiveness'[42] and 'in conformity with primary law as a whole'.[43]

With this in mind, we must consider how effectiveness can prove useful to our assessment of constitutional compliance. It has been noted that effectiveness has a subjective and objective side: the former relates to the effective protection of individual rights afforded by EU law, whereas the latter concerns more broadly the 'efficient operation of regimes created' by Union law.[44] Not too dissimilar is the distinction between procedural and substantive effectiveness. Procedural effectiveness refers to the protection of individual rights in the judicial context,[45] whereas substantial effectiveness concerns the achievement of the objectives of a given provision or measure.[46] A complementary view of effectiveness proposed here characterizes the principle as having two interlinked dimensions. One is objective-driven and used especially in the interpretation of secondary law.[47] Effectiveness also tells us that a rule or a principle is there for a reason: a cog in a wider mechanism that makes the system work. We can call this the 'existential' dimension of effectiveness, the underlying motive why it must be complied with.[48]

The principles tracing their origins back to effectiveness would have a common purpose: giving effect to EU norms before national courts.[49] Effectiveness itself, however, seems to have a broader mission. Firstly, and beyond being a basis for further doctrines, it is an aid to interpretation. This translates, most visibly, in the infamous

interpretation of national law before the courts of the Member States'. Case C-105/03, *Criminal proceedings against Maria Pupino*, EU:C:2005:386, para 38. Potacs and Mayer have distinguished *effet utile* in a narrow sense, which aims at ensuring a minimal effect of Union law, from *effet utile* in a broad sense, seeking to realize the maximum effect of Union law. See M Potacs and C Mayer, 'Effet Utile as a Method of Interpretation' in L Tichý, M Potacs, and T Dumbrovský (eds), *Effet Utile* (Charles University Prague 2014) 17.

[42] Case C-402/07 and C-432/07, *Sturgeon and Others*, EU:C:2009:716, para 47.

[43] Case C-12/11, *McDonagh*, EU:C:2013:43, para 44.

[44] D Leczykiewicz, 'Effectiveness of EU Law Before National Courts: Direct Effect, Effective Judicial Protection, and State Liability' in D Leczykiewicz, A Arnull, and D Chalmers (eds), *The Oxford Handbook of European Union Law* (Oxford University Press 2015), fn 8.

[45] Or, as it is sometimes referred to, the *Rewe* effectiveness, as established in Case 33/76, *Rewe-ZentralfinanzeG and Rewe-Zentral AG v Landwirtschaftskammerfür das Saarland*. For a discussion on the distinction between the *Rewe* effectiveness and effective judicial protection, see J Krommendijk, 'Is There Light on the Horizon? The Distinction Between "Rewe" Effectiveness and the Principle of Effective Judicial Protection in Article 47 of the Charter After Orizzonte' (2016) 53 Common Market Law Review 1395.

[46] See also P Mead, 'The Obligation to Apply European Law: Is Duke Dead?' (1991) 16 European Law Review 492–95.

[47] See, for example, the Court on Directive 2008/115/EC on common standards and procedures in Member States for returning illegally staying third-country nationals [2008] OJ L 348/98 (or Return Directive): 'States may not apply rules, even criminal law rules, which are liable to jeopardise the achievement of the objectives pursued by a directive and, therefore, deprive it of its effectiveness'. Case C-61/11 PPU, *Hassen El Dridi, alias Karim Soufi*, EU:C:2011:268, para 55.

[48] In other words, the effectiveness of Union law means that 'the authorities of the Member State must take the general or particular measures necessary to ensure that Community law is complied with within that state'. Joined cases C-231/06 to C-233/06, *Jonkman*, EU:C:2007:373, para 38.

[49] Leczykiewicz, 'Effectiveness of EU Law Before National Courts'.

three-step process whereby the Court reconstructs the meaning of a provision—or a set of provisions—having regard to their wording, context, and *objectives*.[50] Secondly, effectiveness can be used to review the compatibility of a national norm or practice with EU law,[51] possibly mandating, inter alia, the disapplication of the conflicting rule. Thirdly, it is a principle of law-making. Granting EU competences to adopt measures of criminal law to pursue the effective implementation of a Union policy[52] is one example in this regard. Since every measure has an objective, the provisions contained therein must create an effective framework to ensure those goals can be achieved.

Against this background, effectiveness would seem a natural centrepiece in a test of constitutional compliance, especially as regards the assessment of national law and practices. The nature and principle-genic function of effectiveness, combined with the structural features of EU border controls, make us consider more carefully its actual role in this research. As effectiveness aims to ensure compliance with EU law, the achievement of Union objectives and effective protection, it may well get caught between competing values.[53] When this happens, primary law—notably other principles and fundamental rights—can reinforce[54] or constrain[55] the effectiveness of the main provision(s) under consideration.[56] The Return Directive is a case in point. It states that clear and fair rules are necessary for an *effective* return policy,[57] while pointing to the importance of common safeguards to guarantee the *effective* protection of the person concerned.[58] This example also shows how little effectiveness on its own can do when dealing with different and possibly competing interests. As put eloquently by Ross, 'The most obvious problem with the ascendancy of effectiveness . . . is in resolving conflict with other principles recognised by the Court'.[59] Since effectiveness is always used together with another norm, a related question arises: how specific must that other legal construct be, for effectiveness to be successfully invoked? All these themes play out in the law of EU border controls, which is characterized by a heterogeneous set of objectives and is governed by different principles such as solidarity, fairness, and respect for member states' legal traditions. Could a national/EU law or

[50] See, among many, Case C-237/15 PPU, *Lanigan*, EU:C:2015:474, para 35. The last two steps are often closely linked: a look at the context of the provision(s) can help to reconstruct the objectives pursued by it.

[51] Ross, 'Effectiveness in the European Legal Order' 497.

[52] TFEU, Article 83(2).

[53] Snyder, 'The Effectiveness of European Community Law' 24.

[54] This in part echoes the suggestion that effectiveness of EU law depends not on the legal force of the norms invoked, but rather on the relationship between the different norms. For a more detailed discussion on the different combinations effect, see S Robin-Olivier, 'The Evolution of Direct Effect in the EU: Stocktaking, Problems, Projections' (2014) 12 International Journal of Constitutional Law 170 onwards.

[55] For example, the finding that the surrender of a person on the basis of a European Arrest Warrant might expose them to the risk of inhuman treatment 'cannot be weighed, for the purposes of deciding on that surrender, against considerations relating to the efficacy of judicial cooperation in criminal matters'. See Case C-128/18, *Dumitru-Tudor Dorobantu*, EU:C:2019:857, para 84. While the Court referred to efficacy rather than effectiveness, the context and the broader case law on the subject matter tell us that the difference in language on this occasion, while confusing, is not legally significant.

[56] Both types of interaction (constraining or reinforcing) could materialize in the context of effectiveness used as an aid to interpretation or ground for review.

[57] Return Directive, recital 4.

[58] Return Directive, recital 11.

[59] Ross, 'Effectiveness in the European Legal Order' 497.

practice be challenged because it would deprive the principle of fairness under Article 67 TFEU, or solidarity under Article 80 TFEU, of their effectiveness?

Read together, sincere cooperation and effectiveness possess an important interinstitutional flavour. They require, inter alia, different levels of governance and institutions to act within their respective remit and work together in a spirit of cooperation towards the Union's objectives. Their systemic importance cannot be overstated, because of the role they have in enforcement directly and through their principle-genic function. Nonetheless, the specific contribution they can bring to answering the research question raised in this book remains to be seen. EU border control is a highly interactive field, and it inevitably features provisions expressing duties of sincere co-operation. As mentioned above, in such situations, the more specific provision would override the principle. Effectiveness, for its part, might be of limited use where—as often happens with border controls—competing interests and objectives are at stake. These caveats are not to say that sincere cooperation and effectiveness are irrelevant to the assessment of constitutional compliance. However, these remarks add a note of nuance to the part those principles are likely to play. More 'tailored' constructs can better serve our purposes.

Against this background, we can zoom in on the first specific issue raised by the research question: namely, the allocation of tasks to the appropriate level of governance.

## 2.4 The Allocation of Tasks in Border Controls: Between Subsidiarity and Essential State Functions

### 2.4.1 Ratio and Scope of Application

The assessment of constitutional compliance is multidimensional. The law of EU border controls falls under an area of shared competence,[60] and involves a heterogeneity of levels of governance and actors. Therefore, the question of who should do what is key in several respects: more specifically, who is empowered to decide that controls should be exercised and how; and, who is tasked with the actual exercise of the controls, and under what conditions. These questions matter for consistency with the EU's and member states' areas of competence and responsibilities as set in the Treaties, and therefore have clear implications for the rule of law. Task allocation often has implications from the perspective of interaction between member states and fair treatment of TCNs. Here, we focus on the 'EU–member states' axis of cooperation. In this context, an analysis based on subsidiarity and proportionality seems a natural choice.[61] While proportionality informs the interpretation and review of EU law beyond the question

[60] TFEU, Article 4(2)(j).

[61] While the relevance of the principle of conferral in this area cannot be ruled out *a priori*, other principles are more likely to be engaged. See, on the principle of conferral post-Lisbon, I Govaere, 'To Give or to Grab: The Principle of Full, Crippled and Split Conferral of Powers Post-Lisbon' in M Cremona (ed), *Structural Principles in EU External Relations Law* (Hart 2018) 71. The issue of conferral is particularly prominent in the context of EU external relations law. See M Cremona, 'EU External Relations: Unity and Conferral of Powers' in L Azoulai (ed), *The Question of Competence in the European Union* (Oxford University Press 2014) 65.

of competence,[62] there is no consensus on whether the same holds true for subsidiarity. The principle of subsidiarity is built on a diverse set of normative foundations.[63] Scholars have argued that Article 5 TEU, as well as Protocols no 1 and 2 TFEU, should be read in light of Articles 2 and 3 TEU, and especially the respect for the rights of minorities, pluralism, and the Union's rich cultural and linguistic diversity and cultural heritage.[64] Preserving pluralism, enhancing the democratic legitimacy of decision-making, ensuring that actions take place at the closest possible level to citizens, and constraining the inroads into member states' sovereignty made by centralizing forces are seen as interrelated drivers of subsidiarity. Ultimately, the principle should be used to identify 'the *appropriate* locus of political and legal authority within a complex and multi-layered polity' (emphasis added).[65]

How is subsidiarity meant to achieve that, and how can we measure appropriateness in this context? Pursuant to the text of the Treaty, subsidiarity requires that the Union act *only if and in so far as* (a) the objectives of the proposed action cannot be sufficiently achieved by the member states, but can rather, by reason of the scale or effects of the proposed action, and (b) be better achieved at Union level.[66] These two steps of the test have been labelled as national insufficiency, and comparative efficiency, respectively.[67] It is not enough to show that member states are incapable of achieving certain objectives. There must be an added value in the EU's action, which offsets the encroachment upon member states' autonomy.[68] Article 5 TEU establishes the conditions for material subsidiarity, whereas the need for legal acts to state the reasons on which they are based embodies procedural subsidiarity.[69] The Edinburgh Guidelines on the application of subsidiarity refer to the following conditions, meeting which is necessary to comply with that principle: the issue under consideration has transnational aspects which cannot be satisfactorily regulated by the member states; action by member states alone or lack of EU action would conflict with the requirements of the Treaties or *would significantly damage member states' interests*; action at EU level would produce clear benefits by reason of its scale or effects compared with action at the level of the member states.[70] The link between subsidiarity and the member states'

[62] See, most prominently, Article 53 of the Charter of Fundamental Rights of the EU (CFR or the Charter) [2012] OJ C 326/391.

[63] P Craig, 'Subsidiarity: A Political and Legal Analysis' (2012) 50 Journal of Common Market Studies 72.

[64] D Edward, 'Subsidiarity as a Legal Concept' in A Rosas, P Cardonnel, and N Wahl (eds), *Constitutionalising the EU Judicial System: Essays in Honour of Pernilla Lindh* (Hart 2012) 96.

[65] G de Búrca, 'Reappraising Subsidiarity's Significance After Amsterdam' (1999) Harvard Jean Monnet Working Paper Series 7/99 43.

[66] TEU, Article 5(3).

[67] R Schütze, *From Dual to Cooperative Federalism: The Changing Structure of European Law* (Oxford University Press 2009) 250. AG Kokott refers to the negative and positive (or comparative efficiency) step of the test in Case C-358/14, *Republic of Poland v European Parliament and Council of the European Union*, EU:C:2015:848.

[68] Autonomy, understood as the main term of reference for an assessment of subsidiarity, is used by C Panara, 'Subsidiarity v. Autonomy in the EU' (2022) 28 European Public Law 293. Panara argues that the Court in particular considers both efficiency and autonomy in its assessment of subsidiarity, albeit efficiency would largely prevail.

[69] TFEU, Article 296. See A Estella de Noriega, *The EU Principle of Subsidiarity and Its Critique* (Oxford University Press 2002) 105.

[70] Edinburgh Guidelines 19. The guidelines were drafted at the time the principle of subsidiarity made its way into the Treaties for the first time in Maastricht.

interests gives us pause for thought. Firstly, the possibility of significant damage to such interests would certainly legitimize the EU's action as part of a subsidiarity assessment. That is very different from regarding the prospect of damage as *requiring* the Union to act, thus turning subsidiarity from a limit to the exercise of competences into an obligation to do so. Secondly, the Guidelines treat the member states' interests as a monolith, almost as a coherent *volonté général*. We know well that the law-making and implementation of EU law tell a very different story: member states often defend different and conflicting interests. Thirdly, and relatedly, a contextual analysis of those conditions reveals that this *volonté general*, consisting of the individual member states' interests, overlaps with that of the Union as a whole. This conceptual set-up poses a series of challenges in practice, particularly as regards the definition of the symbiotic interests across the member states, and between the member states and the EU. As shown below, these issues characterize the debate on solidarity as well.

The cumulative or alternative nature of the conditions stated in the Guidelines and their subsequent iterations is not the only reason for uncertainty concerning the operation of the principle.[71] The terms of its relation with the principle of proportionality have been debated too.[72] On the basis in particular of the Court's subsidiarity review, certain authors have argued that subsidiarity has been 'cannibalized' by proportionality, and that procedural subsidiarity has been heavily prioritized over material subsidiarity.[73] In a more nuanced account, the 'insofar as' clause has been seen as building *an element* of proportionality into the subsidiarity assessment.[74] Some other commentators regard the two as inextricably linked in a wider 'federal proportionality' test.[75] The proportionality component inherent in Article 5(3) TEU is undeniable. The proportionalities under this paragraph and Article 5(4) TEU have different scopes of application (the former only concerns shared competences) and protect different legal interests. Subsidiarity is a safeguard against excessive interference with member states' sovereignty, whereas proportionality is geared towards the protection of values under EU law.[76] With a slight twist on this view, it has been posited that 'subsidiarity protects the autonomy if and to the extent this is compatible with efficiency, and always giv[es] way to efficiency in case of a conflict between the two'.[77] This last qualification further nuances the weight of proportionality inherent in Article 5(3)

[71] Certain authors argue that the conditions must be met cumulatively (J Öberg, 'Subsidiarity as a Limit to the Exercise of EU Competences' (2017) 36 Yearbook of European Law 394), while some others take the view that meeting one or more of them would suffice (K Lenaerts, 'The Principle of Subsidiarity and the Environment in the European Union: Keeping the Balance of Federalism' (1994) 17 Fordham International Law Journal 846), and yet some others take no explicit position (K Granat, *The Principle of Subsidiarity and Its Enforcement in the EU Legal Order: The Role of National Parliaments in the Early Warning System* (Hart 2018) 23–24). The Edinburgh Guidelines use the word 'or' when enumerating certain conditions. In the Amsterdam protocol, modelled heavily on the guidelines, the 'or' has disappeared but has not been replaced by 'and' either. This is what—at least in part—causes uncertainty.

[72] While conferral concerns 'whether' the Union's action is possible in a policy area more generally, and can be thus more easily distinguished from the other principles in Article 5 TEU, the boundaries between subsidiarity and proportionality are more blurred.

[73] Schütze, *From Dual to Cooperative Federalism*.

[74] Lenaerts, 'The Principle of Subsidiarity and the Environment in the European Union' 875.

[75] X Groussot and S Bogojević, 'Subsidiarity as a Procedural Safeguard of Federalism' in L Azoulai (ed), *The Question of Competence in the European Union* (Oxford University Press 2014) 237.

[76] Lenaerts, 'The Principle of Subsidiarity and the Environment in the European Union' 884.

[77] Panara, 'Subsidiarity v. Autonomy in the EU' 270.

TEU. Allowing for a proportionality element in the subsidiarity test would not cannibalize the test. The question as to whether the EU's action in a given scenario is justified by qualitative and quantitative evidence (the 'specific whether' question) would still need an answer, and would be followed by the evaluation of *the extent to which* the proposed action is necessary to achieve the objectives which member states cannot achieve on their own.

The dilemmas around the modus operandi of subsidiarity go hand in hand with the uncertainty about its scope of application. According to Öberg, subsidiarity relates to the question of whether a measure falling under an area of shared competence should be adopted by the EU or the member states: the scope of the principle would, therefore, be limited to legislative proposals.[78] Although Article 5 TEU refers to 'action' more generally, it also stipulates that the EU institutions 'shall apply the principle of subsidiarity as laid down in the Protocol on the application of the principles of subsidiarity and proportionality', which in turn seems to confine the principle of subsidiarity to legislative proposals.[79] While the scholarship referenced so far seems to be implicitly on board with that, there are also authors who see the principle of subsidiarity as also applying to the implementation of EU law[80] as well as soft law.[81] Judge David Edward goes even further, arguing that subsidiarity should be treated as a general principle of law permeating all aspects of the life of the Union.[82] Similar to proportionality, its mention in Article 5 TEU should not be regarded as exhausting its possible uses in the context of the EU legal order more widely. This is an extremely fascinating argument. As the law stands at present, however, the core focus of subsidiarity seems to be on legislative action.

### 2.4.2 Acknowledging the Limits of Subsidiarity: The Role of the Essential State Functions

Discussing the existence of a wider understanding of subsidiarity, comprising a proportionality element and applying beyond the legislative function, is particularly relevant to the topic of this book. Assessing the constitutional compliance of EU border controls involves not only considerations of the enactment of a measure and its content, but also of its implementation. We may have situations where the legislation itself is unclear as to what level of governance or actor should be entrusted with the performance of a border control related task. Furthermore, the following chapters show that important operational details concerning the functioning of EU border controls are often referred to non-legislative sources. Beyond the legislative action itself, subsidiarity under Article 5 TEU might not be suitable for solving interpretative

[78] Öberg, 'Subsidiarity as a Limit to the Exercise of EU Competences' 392.

[79] See, for example, Protocol no 2 to the TFEU on the application of the principles of subsidiarity and proportionality, and Article 5 thereof especially.

[80] M Klamert, 'Article 5 TEU: Commentary' in M Kellerbauer, M Klamert, and J Tomkin (eds), *The EU Treaties and the Charter of Fundamental Rights: A Commentary* (Oxford University Press 2019) 70.

[81] C Molinari, 'The EU Readmission Policy to the Test of Subsidiarity and Institutional Balance: Framing the Exercise of a Peculiar Shared Competence' (2022) 7 European Papers 153.

[82] Edward, 'Subsidiarity as a Legal Concept' 103.

doubts, or assessing non-legislative sources as well as border control 'in action'. In this sense, Groussot and Bogojević use the expression 'covert subsidiarity' in respect of 'a broad understanding of judicial subsidiarity, which is encountered, in particular, when the ECJ relies on [inter alia] Article 4(2) TEU'.[83] The idea that Article 4(2) TEU might work better than subsidiarity to accommodate national specificities—at least in certain contexts—has found traction in the scholarship.[84] Millet observes that, due to its much broader scope, a joint use of the constitutional identity clause and proportionality 'looks more apt to be a political and judicial safeguard of a kind of federalism that would put more emphasis on diversity and respect for specificities rather than on the autonomy of the different political actors involved'.[85] Millet clarifies that Article 4(2) TEU would not be concerned with the allocation of competences, but it would rather act as 'an interpretative principle within the broad scope of application of EU law, requiring constructions of EU norms in conformity—or at least compatibility—with constitutional identity'.[86] Articles 4(2) and 5(3) TEU would be mobilized differently: the former, Miller opines, is an interpretative tool, much less likely to be used—or even invoked—than Article 5(3) TEU as a ground for review of EU legislation.

Traditionally, border controls conjure up the very idea of sovereignty.[87] Treaty provisions hint at the existence of a protected space, when it comes to the performance of certain tasks by member states that could relate to border controls. Beyond national constitutional identity, Article 4(2) TEU stipulates that the Union shall respect member states' 'essential state functions, including ensuring the territorial integrity of the State, maintaining law and order and safeguarding national security. In particular, national security remains the sole responsibility of each Member State'. Article 72 TFEU states that Title V thereof—which includes the provisions on border controls—'shall not affect the exercise of the responsibilities incumbent upon Member States with regard to the maintenance of law and order and the safeguarding of internal security'. The dissonance in terminology between the two provisions reveals their different scope and function. Subsidiarity speaks the language of competence, whereas Articles 4(2) TEU and 72 TFEU refer to *responsibility*. These Articles lend themselves to a more flexible use, and are probably better suited for the purposes of this research—at least, as regards their interpretation and implementation. As opined by AG Øe, 'the "respect" that the European Union must have for "essential State functions" does not limit the scope of EU law, but must be duly taken into account, especially in the adoption and the interpretation of instruments of secondary law . . . since the application of those instruments must, in accordance with Article 4(2) TEU, not prevent the smooth operation of those "essential . . . functions"'.[88] We also know that

[83] Groussot and Bogojević, 'Subsidiarity as a Procedural Safeguard of Federalism'.

[84] F Millet, 'The Respect for National Constitutional Identity in the European Legal Space' in L Azoulai (ed), *The Question of Competence in the European Union* (Oxford University Press 2014) 253.

[85] Millet, 'The Respect for National Constitutional Identity' 261.

[86] Millet, 'The Respect for National Constitutional Identity' 262–63.

[87] See M Longo, *The Politics of Borders: Sovereignty, Security, and the Citizen after 9/11* (Cambridge University Press 2017) 1.

[88] Case C-742/19, *BKV Republika Slovenija (Ministrstvo za obrambo)*, AG's Opinion, EU:C:2021:77, point 47.

Article 72 TFEU cannot be invoked by member states to derogate from EU law, where a specific provision of secondary law has taken into account and given expression to that Article. In the absence of such a 'concretizing provision', Articles 4(2) TEU and 72 TFEU might still play a role.[89]

In the quest for the correct legal construct(s) to decide on the appropriateness of task allocation in EU border control, and bearing in mind that each situation should also be considered in light of its context, we must therefore distinguish between different scenarios. We have the legislative action itself, and the specific choices about task allocation made in that instrument. Subsidiarity can serve to assess both aspects thanks to its 'if and insofar' clause (the 'insofar' covering the details of a measure). Articles 4(2) TEU and 72 TFEU would be useful in the phase of interpretation and implementation. It is also important to clarify that subsidiarity and essential state functions are not necessarily to be used in a mutually exclusive fashion. In this regard, AG Kokott correctly observes that, in the context of an assessment of subsidiarity, 'the situation of any particular Member State taken individually [could be relevant] where the action envisaged by the EU institutions affects the national identity of a Member State (Article 4(2) TEU) or its fundamental interests'.[90] This approach is constitutionally compliant, given the shared nature of EU competence in this area and the understanding of border controls as an essential state function. Articles 5(3) and 4(2) TEU can be useful to discuss questions about task allocation as regards the enactment, interpretation, and implementation of EU law, *regard being had to the objectives of the provision(s) under consideration and other relevant principles involved*. In other words, state sovereignty and essential state functions are not 'trump cards' taking precedence over any other interests at stake. Their role in shaping EU law is context-specific (at least to an extent) and must take account of the need to accommodate different claims as they might emerge in practice.

In the EU legal order, the principles ensure the pursuit of the EU's objectives in line with EU values. Those values may support different outcomes in law-making and implementation, which can translate into tension between competing objectives. In this context, the structured network of principles has two major parts to play. It offers us a method to try and balance those claims rationally (in principle), as is the case with proportionality. It also invites us to consider the implications of the same legal question from different perspectives, and reflect on whether and how they could be squared. In a multi-purpose legal framework like that governing EU border controls, the choice of task allocation is essential. To understand its implications more deeply, the assessment cannot be one-dimensional and focus exclusively on subsidiarity. Other parts of that network of principles might have something to say, especially as most measures of EU border controls pursue a heterogeneous set of objectives at once. Very important examples in this regard are the principles of sincere cooperation and effectiveness discussed above, but even more so solidarity and fairness. Solidarity is a fundamental principle of EU law, and governs the whole Treaty chapter on border

[89] This being said, the nature of a provision as a concrete expression of Article 72 TFEU might not always be straightforward.

[90] Case C-358/14, *Republic of Poland v European Parliament and Council of the European Union*, point 166.

controls, asylum, and immigration. The next section focuses on the horizontal axes of interaction between member states. Firstly, we discuss the principle of solidarity extensively. Secondly, we introduce the principle of mutual trust. While not directly relevant to the assessment of constitutional compliance, mutual trust is essential to the understanding of this area of law and the interaction between the different principles used in this research. As revealed, this principle can play a very important role beyond interstate cooperation, and help us with the constitutional compliance of the EU border controls in its internal and external dimensions.

## 2.5 The Foundations of Interaction between Member States: Mutual Trust and Solidarity

### 2.5.1 Solidarity within the EU: History, Meaning, and Legal Status

Solidarity is particularly helpful in discussing issues of constitutional compliance caused by the heterogeneity of EU border controls. It is a fundamental principle of EU law and explicitly governs border controls in accordance with Articles 67 and 80 TFEU. Coherently with the scope of this book, we evaluate the consistency of the existing legal framework with that principle. We also consider how solidarity could enhance the constitutional compliance of the law in the phase of interpretation and implementation. This section sets out the view of solidarity adopted in this book and makes the following arguments. Firstly, solidarity as a legal principle mostly governs the interaction between institutional actors: between member states, between EU bodies, and between member states and EU bodies. Solidarity is *directly* relevant for the analysis of two main decisions: what level of governance and actor should be allocated a certain border control related task, and what action should be taken by the empowered body in situations where they enjoy a margin of discretion. Therefore, we also need to clarify the relationship between solidarity and subsidiarity. This last point reflects very well the idea of the structured network of principles. It proves once again the importance of understanding the implications of the same legal question from different perspectives, and of analysing how to possibly reconcile them. Solidarity can also have an *indirect* impact on fairness to the addressees of control. These principles operate on different levels: one more institutionally, the other geared towards the persons concerned. Parts II and III show that, when considered together, they could produce a certain result in the making, interpreting, and implementing of the law of EU border controls.

#### 2.5.1.1 Setting the terms of the debate

The breadth of the discussion developed over the years concerning the principle of solidarity in EU law is directly proportional to its elusive nature. Solidarity is a hybrid concept, in that it can be used normatively or descriptively—as a *there ought to be* as well as *there is*.[91] It is also a relational concept, since it presupposes a connection

[91] J Viehoff and K Nicolaïdis, 'Social Justice in the European Union: The Puzzles of Solidarity, Reciprocity and Choice' in G de Búrca, D Kochenov, and A Williams (eds), *Europe's Justice Deficit* (Hart 2015) 283.

between two or more actors,[92] and has a strong link with morality.[93] In reconstructing the different trajectories characterizing the evolution of the concept of solidarity in history, Stjernø observes that solidarity presupposes both one's identification with others and a feeling of community. While his account seems to emphasize the inclusive nature of solidarity,[94] other authors see solidarity as characterized by struggle, mutuality, and exclusion,[95] with some scholars even considering reciprocity as a precondition for the proper functioning of solidarity.[96] Such an approach somehow resonates with more nuanced views of solidarity as linked to fairness for a group, thereby admitting an element of self-interest,[97] or as built on bonds and mutuality that achieve 'enhanced self-realisation by participation in collective action'.[98] As the example of the EU shows, solidarity can exist within *and* among communities.[99] The presence of a group is key to solidarity, although different angles have been explored to delineate a somewhat universal understanding thereof.[100] One of the possible issues with applying such a universal approach to EU law is that it risks collapsing together different—although closely related—concepts such as solidarity and fairness, or the universal application of certain fundamental rights.

Through a fascinating historical analysis, Karageorgiou and Noll outline two main understandings of solidarity: the one deriving from the Roman law tradition, where a creditor can claim the entirety of the sum owed to them from any of the debtors that are bound by the obligation *in solido*;[101] and the French positivist solidarity, premised on a contractual relationship 'between those taking a loss caused by an outsider'.[102] While the two forms of solidarity are rather different, they both presuppose a 'contractual' element that unites the parties 'against' an interlocutor—although, one might argue, a more threatening one in the case of the French tradition.[103] Therefore, the existence of a bond is essential to the existence of solidarity and can motivate

[92] Viehoff and Nicolaïdis, 'Social Justice in the European Union' 284.

[93] E Dagilytė, 'Solidarity: A General Principle of EU Law? Two Variations on the Solidarity Theme' in E Dagilytė, A Biondi, and E Küçük (eds), *Solidarity in EU Law: Legal Principle in the Making* (Edward Elgar 2018) 72.

[94] S Stjernø, *Solidarity in Europe: The History of an Idea* (Cambridge University Press 2005) 88–89.

[95] D Heyd, 'Justice and Solidarity: The Contractarian Case against Global Justice' (2007) 38 Journal of Social Philosophy 112.

[96] P Hilpold, 'Understanding Solidarity within EU Law' (2015) 34 Yearbook of European Law 274.

[97] M Baurmann, 'Solidarity as a Social Norm and as a Constitutional Norm' in K Bayertz (ed), *Solidarity* (Springer 1999) 243.

[98] M Ross, 'Solidarity: A New Constitutional Paradigm for the EU?' in M Ross and Y Borgmann-Prebil (eds), *Promoting Solidarity in the European Union* (Oxford University Press 2010) 35.

[99] J Bengoetxea, 'The Solidarity Constitution in the EU: Refugees and Asylum as Litmus Test' in A Hartzén, A Iossa, and E Karageorgiou (eds), *Law, Solidarity and the Limits of Social Europe: Constitutional Tensions for EU Integration* (Edward Elgar 2022) 118.

[100] For a very useful discussion on this topic, see V Moreno-Lax, 'Solidarity's Reach: Meaning, Dimensions and Implications for EU (External) Asylum Policy' (2017) 24 Maastricht Journal of European and Comparative Law 740.

[101] This form of obligation, which still exists today in civil law jurisdiction, can be translated in English as several and joint liability.

[102] E Karageorgiou and G Noll, 'What Is Wrong with Solidarity in EU Asylum and Migration Law?' (2022) 4 Jus Cogens 128–30.

[103] The principle of solidarity in French legal tradition is significant. See for more specific references, among many, X Groussot, A Zemskova, and K Bungerfeldt, 'Foundational Principles and the Rule of Law in the European Union: How to Adjudicate in a Rule-of-Law Crisis, and Why Solidarity Is Essential' (2022) 5 Nordic Journal of European Law 1.

solidarity-inspired actions. In an insightful exercise, Viehoff and Nicolaïdis place solidarity at the intersection between two continuums: one 'marked' at either end by self-interest and community, the other by political obligation and altruism. Although the interest of an actor is still distinguishable from that of the community to which they belong, their action is not motivated purely by self-interest.[104] Likewise, said action cannot be entirely altruistic, as solidarity cannot exist without any reciprocity.[105] At the same time, and unlike other sophisticated accounts in the literature, the authors argue that solidarity *as* fair reciprocity cannot be the sole ground for obligations of substantive justice—particularly in the context of the EU.[106]

#### 2.5.1.2 Solidarity in EU law

In most cases, solidarity arises in and/or among communities; it presupposes a degree of reciprocity but goes beyond that,[107] and guides the action of the group members in the performance of a task.[108] These elements are important to understand the meaning, scope, and application of solidarity in EU law. Solidarity is referred to in the preamble of the TEU as one of the objectives underlying the establishment of the Union, and as one of the features of the society founded on the EU values. Solidarity between member states is mentioned in relation to the objective related to the internal market,[109] with certain services being excluded from the Services Directive due to their importance for social cohesion.[110] Solidarity is a principle governing the EU's external action[111] as well as the common foreign and security policy.[112] The EU and member states must act jointly in a spirit of solidarity where a member state is the target of a terrorist attack or the victim of a disaster.[113] Solidarity is also the heading of Title IV of the EU Charter of Fundamental Rights. Solidarity is, therefore, at the basis of the whole EU system.[114] But who has, under EU law, an obligation of, and a right to, solidaristic conduct? The preamble of the TEU refers to the objectives of deepening solidarity among the peoples of the member states, and the several Treaty provisions in which the principle is mentioned implicitly frame it as applying to member states. In this sense, Bell observes that solidarity in EU law is reserved for EU citizens and, subject to limitations, legally resident TCNs.[115] Unsurprisingly, research has focused

[104] Viehoff and Nicolaïdis, 'Social Justice in the European Union'.

[105] Viehoff and Nicolaïdis, 'Social Justice in the European Union'285.

[106] Viehoff and Nicolaïdis, 'Social Justice in the European Union' 290, in relation to A Sangiovanni, 'Solidarity in the European Union' (2013) 33 Oxford Journal of Legal Studies 213.

[107] Reciprocity should not be understood as reciprocity in every single case of show of solidarity. In EU law, this systemic reciprocity is embodied by the mutual obligations to which member states and the EU are bound under the umbrella of mutual trust.

[108] This reflects a certain approach to solidarity in political philosophy, as a principle that can inspire and guide action. See H Arendt, *Sulla Rivoluzione* (Einaudi 2009) 94.

[109] TEU, Article 3(3).

[110] Case C-57/12, *Femarbel*, ECLI:EU:C:2013:517, paras 42–50.

[111] TEU, Article 21(1).

[112] TEU, Article 24(2) and (3).

[113] TFEU, Article 222. See M Fuchs-Drapier, 'The European Union's Solidarity Clause in the Event of a Terrorist Attack: Towards Solidarity or Maintaining Sovereignty?' (2011) 19 Journal of Contingencies and Crisis Management 184.

[114] Case 128/78, *Commission v United Kingdom*, EU:C:1979:32, para 12.

[115] M Bell, 'Irregular Migrants: Beyond the Limits of Solidarity?' in M Ross and Y Borgmann-Prebil (eds), *Promoting Solidarity in the European Union* (Oxford University Press 2010) 151–52.

considerably on solidarity in the period of the Eurozone crisis,[116] or the welfare state and EU citizenship law.[117] The latter, in fact, explicitly contemplates a certain degree of financial solidarity between EU nationals,[118] while member states can also 'protect the special relationship of solidarity and good faith between it and its nationals . . . which form the bedrock of the bond of nationality'.[119] That being said, Articles 2 and 3(5) TEU conjure up a more broadly applicable understanding of solidarity. The connection between this principle and other important values amplifies the universalistic aura. In this sense, the Court has found that discrimination based on racial or ethnic origin, or on sexual orientation, may undermine the achievement of the objectives of the Treaty, in particular solidarity, and may also undermine the objective of developing the EU as an Area of Freedom, Security, and Justice (AFSJ).[120] Solidaristic aspirations between the states and the peoples of the EU are not *a priori* irreconcilable with a wider reach of that principle. However, a not-so-latent tension has been brewing between the protection and promotion of the EU and its citizens' interests, on the one hand, and solidarity towards peoples 'outside' the Union, on the other.[121] Against this background, the member states and their citizens, as well as the common institutions, form the community on which solidarity in EU law primarily focuses. The motive of such solidarity, the *quid pluris* beyond self-interests, is the bond of membership of a community of values as established in Article 2 TEU.[122]

#### 2.5.1.3 Meaning, scope, and legal status

So far, and for the sake of simplicity, we have referred to *solidarity* (singular) in EU law. However, different types of solidarities seem to exist in the Treaties, even though their meaning and relationship are not so clear.[123] Scholars have categorized solidarity in EU law based on the actors of the relationship,[124] the objectives

[116] V Borger, 'How the Debt Crisis Exposes the Development of Solidarity in the Euro Area' (2013) 9 European Constitutional Law Review 7.

[117] D Thym, 'The Elusive Limits of Solidarity: Residence Rights of and Social Benefits for Economically Inactive Union Citizens' (2015) 52 Common Market Law Review 17; S Giubboni, 'Free Movement of Persons and European Solidarity' (2007) 13 European Law Journal 360; G De Búrca (ed), *EU Law and the Welfare State: In Search of Solidarity* (Oxford University Press 2005); S A Mantu and P E Minderhoud, 'EU Citizenship and Social Solidarity' (2017) 24 Maastricht Journal of European and Comparative Law 703.

[118] Case C-184/99, *Rudy Grzelczyk v Centre public d'aide sociale d'Ottignies-Louvain-la-Neuve*, EU:C:2001:458, para 44.

[119] Case C-135/08, *Janko Rottman v Freistaat Bayern*, EU:C:2010:104, para 51.

[120] Case C-83/14, *CHEZ Razpredelenie Bulgaria AD v Komisia za zashtita ot diskriminatsia*, EU:C:2015:480, para 74; Case C-507/18, *Associazione Avvocatura per i diritti LGBTI*, EU:C:2020:289, para 37.

[121] This means not only persons physically outside the EU, but also those TCNs who possess no 'enhanced' status, as that of long-term residents governed by Council Directive 2003/109/EC concerning the status of third-country nationals who are long-term residents [2004] OJ L 16/44. The status is no absolute shield, and the protection granted by it can be overridden if a member state considers it as a potential threat to public policy or security (assuming the conditions for doing so are met, of course).

[122] Or, as the Court forcefully put it, 'failure in the duty of solidarity accepted by Member States by the fact of their adherence to the Community strikes at the fundamental basis of the Community legal order'. Case 39/72, *Commission v Italy*, EU:C:1973:13, para 25.

[123] Ross makes the example of intergenerational solidarity. Ross, 'Solidarity: A New Constitutional Paradigm for the EU?' 44.

[124] See Sangiovanni, 'Solidarity in the European Union'. The author distinguishes between 'national solidarity', 'Member State solidarity', and 'transnational solidarity'.

thereof,[125] or the types of duties involved.[126] Overall, these different accounts build on the conceptual foundations of solidarity as discussed in the previous subsections. Thym and Tsourdi, for example, identify four dimensions of solidarity in the context of the EU: the transnational solidarity towards EU citizens living in a state other than that of nationality; the interstate dimension, key to border controls immigration and asylum; support among members of a group, which is at least partly based on an 'othering' process; the role for decision-making processes and the outlook of the actors involved, such as the case of visa procedures.[127] In relation to the issue of EU competences, Meloni identifies three visions of solidarity. Firstly, the functional vision aims to increase the effectiveness of common policies and the achievement of common objectives. This entails a shift of responsibility, which ties in with the previous discussion about subsidiarity. Secondly, the intergovernmental/voluntary notion of solidarity has characterized in particular the Common European Asylum System. Thirdly, the identity-driven vision focuses on the individual and purports a fundamental rights-oriented approach. The proposal of granting free movement rights for refugees is one possible expression of that vision.[128] These categorizations talk to each other. Especially in the context of border controls, interstate cooperation is also a vector for increasing solidarity between the peoples of the EU. It presupposes and fosters mutual support in dealing with a challenging task which, even if affecting some states more directly than others, ultimately impacts the Union as a whole. In this context, solidarity has a role to play in identifying both the appropriate locus of authority *and* the concrete course of action to take in a specific situation.

These approaches help us to understand the different dynamics characterizing the operation of the principle of solidarity. In more fundamental terms, it is useful to distinguish between vertical[129] and horizontal[130] obligations of solidarity.[131] To these two dimensions, Moreno-Lax adds a systemic one.[132] Embodied by the principle of sincere cooperation, this systemic dimension should work together with the other two dimensions to guide the creation and implementation of the EU policies with a view to achieving the

[125] For an objective-based categorization, see F De Witte, *Justice in the EU: The Emergence of Transnational Solidarity* (first edn, Oxford University Press 2015).

[126] Klamert distinguishes between negative and positive solidarity. The former refers to member states' duties of abstention from conducts defying the rules of EU law. The latter concerns the member states' obligation to provide financial mutual support, and is underpinned by an expectation of reciprocity over time as well as the understanding that the benefits for the EU as a whole also—if indirectly—would be felt by the supporting state. Klamert, 'Loyalty and Solidarity as General Principles' 125–26.

[127] D Thym and E Tsourdi, 'Searching for Solidarity in the EU Asylum and Border Policies: Constitutional and Operational Dimensions' (2017) 24 Maastricht Journal of European and Comparative Law 609.

[128] A Meloni, 'EU Visa Policy: What Kind of Solidarity?' (2017) 24 Maastricht Journal of European and Comparative Law 647–49.

[129] From the EU to the member states and vice versa.

[130] Between the member states and having regard to the common interests of the EU.

[131] Case T-883/16, *Republic of Poland v European Commission*, EU:T:2019:567, para 70. For a twist on this distinction, see Groussot, Zemskova, and Bungerfeldt, 'Foundational Principles and the Rule of Law in the European Union' 10. The article is very informative for the literature cited, and offers valuable insight into the French understanding of solidarity, including in legal terms.

[132] The primary focus of obligations of solidarity in border controls are public actors. However, as we mentioned, they are not the only agents bound by such obligations (or related ones) in the EU more widely, as shown by the example of the prohibition of discrimination for employers.

Union objectives.[133] This somehow resonates with the approach of the Court, which has found that solidarity is 'closely linked to'[134], and 'in accordance with', sincere cooperation, and implies mutual assistance in the case of a threat facing a member state.[135] It also echoes some of the reflections developed in the context of the sections on subsidiarity on the need to consider the question of task allocation in an integrated fashion, and not purely through the lens of a narrow understanding of subsidiarity.

Useful as it is, identifying the axes of operation of solidarity in EU law says little about its legal status. The question as to what are the modus operandi and the functions of solidarity in EU law has been extensively debated. The unobjectionable starting point is that solidarity constitutes a cornerstone of European integration as 'it connects peoples in networks of trust' and it transcends national interests.[136] A first strand of scholars argues that solidarity is neither a constitutional,[137] nor a general, principle, and possesses no direct effect: it 'cannot be relied upon as the basis of a concrete duty to give, or a right to receive assistance in Union law, unless such right or duty were operationalised by secondary law'.[138] European solidarity, therefore, would amount to a 'value as moral aspiration that underpins and shapes EU legal standards: it cannot be directly observed; it engages moral considerations; and it is a conception of the desirable (even though it may not always be achievable)'.[139] It would be an 'ordinary' (whatever that means), rather than a 'constitutional' principle.[140] It is not enforceable, it cannot be invoked as a ground for review and could only be used to orient judicial interpretation.[141] Another view of solidarity regards it as a systemic principle like direct effect and primacy, laying the foundation for the Union's institutional structure.[142] Even more strongly, other scholars have stated that solidarity has now been clearly anchored 'in the EU constitutional legal order as an existential principle that is non-regressive and absolute (non-flexible) in its meaning'.[143] While the specific meaning of non-regressive and non-flexible is not entirely clear, the said position seems to attribute significant legal force to solidarity. In this regard, Ross observed that solidarity can be the criterion to determine legal and constitutional outcomes and choose between priorities.[144] Solidarity would be a means to achieve

[133] Moreno-Lax, 'Solidarity's Reach' 747–50. Therefore, solidarity would imply a triple obligation of conduct, loyalty, and result.

[134] Case C-848/19 P, *Federal Republic of Germany v European Commission*, EU:C:2021:598, para 41.

[135] Case 6/69, *Commission v France*, EU:C:1969:68, para 16.

[136] Bengoetxea, 'The Solidarity Constitution in the EU' 120.

[137] J Monar, 'The AFSJ Two Decades After Tampere: Institutional Balance, Relation to Citizens and Solidarity' in S Carrera, D Curtin, and A Geddes (eds), *20 Year Anniversary of the Tampere Programme: Europeanisation Dynamics of the EU Area of Freedom, Security and Justice* (EUI 2020).

[138] Klamert, 'Loyalty and Solidarity as General Principles' 134.

[139] Dagilytė, 'Solidarity: A General Principle of EU law?' 74.

[140] C Hilson, 'Rights and Principles in EU Law: A Distinction without Foundation?' (2008) 15 *Maastricht Journal of European and Comparative Law* 196.

[141] Dagilytė, 'Solidarity: A General Principle of EU law?' 88.

[142] D Overgaauw, *A Polyphony of Principles: The Application and Classification of the Principles of European Union Law* (University of Groningen 2022) 124.

[143] Groussot, Zemskova, and Bungerfeldt, 'Foundational Principles and the Rule of Law in the European Union' 14. This would be the case especially following Case C-156/21, *Hungary v European Parliament and Council of the European Union*, EU:C:2022:97.

[144] Ross, 'Solidarity: A New Constitutional Paradigm for the EU?' 40. However, solidarity might find itself in competition with other paradigms such as market values or security.

effectiveness, and even a criterion to allocate competences between the EU and member states.[145] Somehow similarly, Moreno-Lax argues that solidarity is closely linked to fairness and can optimize effectiveness. It cannot be regarded as purely an ex post, reactive mechanism, but it entails an 'institutional, procedural, and material duty of shared responsibility that is fair ab initio'.[146] Or else, as Bengoetxea puts it, solidarity 'feeds into the law in the form of (i) a legal value or general principle of law, aiding legal construction and systemic interpretation, generating legal standards and directly informing norms; or (ii) concrete legal rules, as in Articles 78(3) and 80 TFEU, providing for fair sharing of responsibilities relating to refugee protection'.[147] These accounts in the literature are based on the observation of the law, and develop further the understanding of solidarity discussed here. Solidarity is at the centre of a structured network of principles featuring inter alia sincere cooperation, effectiveness, subsidiarity, and fairness. In relation to subsidiarity, and subject to the principle of proportionality, solidarity might facilitate the attainment of the EU objectives. In this capacity, it can tilt the balance in favour of a common action at EU level. This concerns not only the exercise of competence itself, but also the way in which responsibilities and burdens are distributed through legislative action. The same approach applies to the interpretation and implementation of the law, with solidarity orienting the action of the responsible actor—once again, bearing in mind the possible existence of other interests and the need for balancing. It can serve as an aid to interpretation and ground for review.

Arguing in favour of or against the enforceability of a principle goes only so far. Enforceability is contingent upon the definition, with a minimum level of precision, of the core meaning of a legal construct. This is one of the most difficult issues related to solidarity in EU law. Since solidarity can be implemented in different ways, it is difficult to enforce and grant the actors involved a wide margin of discretion.[148] A look at the Court's case law tells us that in some cases, solidarity requires that certain actors accept greater sacrifices than others.[149] For example, producers might have to bear the consequences of the EU actions when pursuing the objective of responding to the risk of market imbalance in specific areas.[150] This resonates with the redistributive dimension of solidarity,[151] which can materialize, for example, in compulsory contributions.[152] The principle founds not only mechanisms aimed to overcome situations of crisis, but also preventative measures.[153] As elaborated on below, these are all elements that we also find in solidarity as applicable in EU migration and asylum law.

[145] Ross, 'Solidarity: A New Constitutional Paradigm for the EU?' 42–43. In this regard, Ross raises the issue of the complex relationship between solidarity and subsidiarity.

[146] Moreno-Lax, 'Solidarity's Reach' 754.

[147] Bengoetxea, 'The Solidarity Constitution in the EU' 122–23.

[148] Thym and Tsourdi, 'Searching for Solidarity in the EU Asylum and Border Policies 609–12.

[149] Case 154/78, *Valsabbia v Commission*, EU:C:1980:81, paras 57, 71, and 87. See also Case 26/79, *Thy-Marcinelle and Monceau v Commission*, EU:C:1980:82, para 10.

[150] Case C-56/99, *Gascogne Limousin Viandes SA and Office National Interprofessionnel des Viandes de l'Élevage et de l'Aviculture (Ofival)*, para 40.

[151] Case C-375/96, *Galileo Zaninoto*, EU:C:1998:517, para 45.

[152] Case C-238/94, *José García and Others and Mutuelle de Prévoyance Sociale d'Aquitaine and Others*, EU:C:1996:132.

[153] Case C-848/19 P, *Federal Republic of Germany v European Commission*, EU:C:2021:598, para 69.

#### 2.5.1.4 Solidarity in EU migration and asylum law

EU asylum and immigration law are areas where the principle of solidarity has been debated significantly over the last few years. As mentioned, solidarity explicitly governs the Treaty Chapter on border controls, immigration, and asylum. Article 67 TFEU refers to the solidarity among member states, whereas Article 80 TFEU flanks that principle with fair sharing of responsibility. In the previous subsections, we have uncovered the link between solidarity and the EU objectives, manifesting especially in its interaction with subsidiarity and effectiveness. This link poses a series of challenges. Karageorgiou rightly points to the different objectives pursued by the policy areas covered by Articles 67 and 80 TFEU: solidaristic obligations in border controls and asylum law might be difficult to reconcile with each other.[154] Secondary law compounds this observation. Parts II and III reveal that such heterogeneity of objectives is apparent from EU border controls across the board, as well as each legislative measure taken individually.

Building on the key features of solidarity introduced in the previous subsections, three aspects of the principle in border controls must be dealt with: operationalization, personal scope, and legal scope. As to the first aspect, Noll identifies four ways of operationalizing 'solidarity through sharing': legally (via approximation), financially, operationally, and physically (by relocation).[155] While this account focuses on asylum law, it works for border controls too. As shown in Part II in particular, asylum and border controls are inextricably linked. As regards the scope of the principle *ratione personae*, Mitsilegas defined the EU's approach to solidarity in the context of asylum law as state-centred, securitized, and exclusionary, which kicks in as a response to a perceived threat.[156] In a similar way, it has been observed that 'Article 80 TFEU should be understood as an alliance clause against the external threat that irregular migration, including that of asylum seekers, is perceived to be'.[157] To the contrary, other scholars have argued that asylum is itself a form of solidarity,[158] and that therefore TCNs would benefit from member states' obligations ensuing from the Common European Asylum System (CEAS).[159] While we agree that asylum is a form of solidarity broadly speaking, we reiterate the argument made above that the principle in this context focuses on institutional interaction.

As for its legal force, and consistent with some of the accounts referred to above, Bast opines that solidarity and fairness would provide only broad guidelines for the EU legislature.[160] Of a very different view is Moreno-Lax, who, other than making a case for a 'pervasive' solidarity in law-making and implementation, also sees this principle

[154] E Karageorgiou, 'The Distribution of Asylum Responsibilities in the EU: Dublin, Partnerships With Third Countries and the Question of Solidarity' (2019) 88 Nordic Journal of International Law 333.

[155] G Noll, *Negotiating Asylum: The EU Acquis, Extraterritorial Protection, and the Common Market of Deflection* (Nijhoff 2000) 263.

[156] V Mitsilegas, 'Humanizing solidarity in European Refugee Law: The Promise of Mutual Recognition' (2017) 24 Maastricht Journal of European and Comparative Law 722.

[157] Karageorgiou and Noll, 'What Is Wrong With Solidarity in EU Asylum and Migration Law?' 147.

[158] J Bast, 'Deepening Supranational Integration: Interstate Solidarity in EU Migration Law' in A Biondi, E Dagilytė, and E Küçük (eds), *Solidarity in EU Law* 115–16. See in this sense also Karageorgiou, 'The Distribution of Asylum Responsibilities in the EU' 319.

[159] Whether the system as it is on paper and in action is satisfying are different questions.

[160] Bast, 'Deepening supranational integration' 117.

as inseparable from the obligation(s) of fair sharing. Interestingly, Karageorgiou and Noll distinguish between the two: solidarity would relate to the ordinary, daily operation of the CEAS, while the fair sharing of responsibility addresses extraordinary situations of crisis.[161] The next subsection and Parts II and III provide some clarity on the previous points. Firstly, solidarity can indeed work as an aid to interpretation and ground for review, thus going beyond the role of mere guidelines. Secondly, solidarity entails a core obligation of taking into account the common interest in decision-making processes. This confirms one of the main arguments on solidarity made in this section, and illuminates the relationship between solidarity and fair sharing. The two are undeniably linked: it is difficult to see how a legal framework could respect the principle of solidarity without distributing responsibilities fairly. However, there is life for solidarity beyond the 'sharing' (including responsibilities). The reason for the coupling of solidarity and fair sharing might be much less sophisticated than we think. Considering how elusive the contours and implications of solidarity are, the Treaty drafters might have wanted to add a more specific clause—the obligation of fair sharing—to which the whole policy area could be anchored.[162] A detailed assessment of whether the law of EU border controls distributes responsibilities among member states fairly falls outside the scope of this research.[163] The attention is instead on the role of solidarity in orienting decision-making processes, in allocating competences, and especially during the implementation and interpretation of the law. The final two subsections discuss an important judicial saga addressing several questions around the functioning of solidarity in the context of the common energy policy, and draw lessons for EU border controls.

#### 2.5.1.5 The dawn of a new era? Operationalizing solidarity

The debate about the meaning and operationalization of the principle of solidarity is partly explained by the relatively scarce legal developments around it, especially in comparison to some of the principles covered above. An important judicial saga, concerning the common energy policy, might provide some helpful indications on the questions addressed so far. The parts of the ruling directly related to solidarity revolved around the interpretation of Article 194(1) TFEU. This provision enumerates the objectives of that policy, stating that they must be pursued 'in a spirit of solidarity between Member States'.[164] The judgments focused on a European Commission decision. Poland contested the decision, inter alia on the ground that it jeopardized the energy security of certain member states and thus breached the principle of solidarity under Article 194(1) TFEU. The General Court (GC) found in favour of Poland. It stated that the principle entails rights and obligations for the EU and member states

[161] Karageorgiou and Noll, 'What Is Wrong with Solidarity in EU Asylum and Migration Law?' 137. The authors also observe, however, that such a distinction has blurred due to the perpetual state of emergency in which the CEAS finds itself.

[162] Whether or not they have succeeded is another question. As emerged from the section on fairness, defining 'fair' distribution—including the identification of the criteria behind it—is as challenging as defining fairness itself.

[163] It is argued that a proper investigation would require an in-depth state-by-state analysis of the system of allocation of financial, human, and material resources.

[164] Such objectives include ensuring the functioning of the energy market as well as the security of energy supply in the Union, or promoting energy efficiency and energy saving.

going beyond mutual assistance and the legislative action in extraordinary situations. Solidarity 'also implies a *general obligation* for the EU and the member states, *in the exercise of their respective competences*, to consider the interests of the other stakeholders, and to *endeavour* to avoid "measures liable to affect the interests of the European Union and the other member states . . . and to do so in order to take account of their interdependence and de facto solidarity"' (emphasis added).[165]

The implications of these passages are significant. Firstly, obligation(s) of solidarity are of a general nature, and therefore permeate the whole of the EU legal order, and the EU and member states actions. Secondly, solidarity is inextricably linked to the issue of competence. The question of where an obligation falls depends on the type of action at stake, and whether said action is a matter entrusted to the EU or the member states, or both. Thirdly, compliance with solidarity does not prevent a measure from negatively impacting the interests of a member state. Rather, it requires that the implementation of the policy takes account of those interests and balances them against those of the EU and other member states.[166] Since the Commission's decision did not contain any examination of the decision's effect on the energy security of Poland, nor balance those effects against the increased security of supply it found at the EU level,[167] the GC annulled the contested decision as having been adopted in breach of the principle of energy solidarity under Article 194(1) TFEU.[168] The Court of Justice upheld the GC's findings in the appeal.[169] The spirit of solidarity referred to in Article 194 TFEU constitutes a specific expression of the fundamental principle of solidarity. It can, *as such*, produce binding legal effects on the member states and the EU, and 'form the basis' of the objective of that policy, 'serving as the thread that brings them together and gives them coherence'.[170] The acts adopted by the EU institutions under this policy, therefore, 'must be interpreted, and their legality assessed, in the light of the principle of energy solidarity'.[171] This principle, *like* general principles of EU law, constitutes a criterion for assessing the legality of measures adopted by the EU institutions.[172] The Court also rejected the argument that only provisions of secondary law giving specific expression to the principle could be relied on to review the legality of the Commission's decision.[173] Furthermore, these provisions cannot be used to limit the scope of the principle of solidarity, which according to Article 194(1) TFEU governs the whole EU energy policy.[174] The fact that the principle of solidarity governs a policy area has also another important implication: the absence, in legislative instruments adopted under this policy area, of references to the principle of solidarity does not 'relieve the Commission of the need to examine the effect of that principle on the derogating measures adopted by' its decision.[175] Furthermore, the principle must

[165] Case T-883/16, *Republic of Poland v European Commission*, EU:T:2019:567, paras 72–73.
[166] Case T-883/16, *Republic of Poland v European Commission*, EU:T:2019:567, para 79.
[167] Case T-883/16, *Republic of Poland v European Commission*, EU:T:2019:567, paras 79–82. Specifically, as regards the consequences for the energy policy of Poland.
[168] Case T-883/16, *Republic of Poland v European Commission*, EU:T:2019:567, paras 83–85.
[169] Case C-848/19 P, *Federal Republic of Germany v European Commission*, EU:C:2021:598.
[170] Case C-848/19 P, *Federal Republic of Germany v European Commission*, EU:C:2021:598, para 43.
[171] Case C-848/19 P, *Federal Republic of Germany v European Commission*, EU:C:2021:598, para 44.
[172] Case C-848/19 P, *Federal Republic of Germany v European Commission*, EU:C:2021:598, para 45.
[173] Case C-848/19 P, *Federal Republic of Germany v European Commission*, EU:C:2021:598, para 46.
[174] Case C-848/19 P, *Federal Republic of Germany v European Commission*, EU:C:2021:598, para 47.
[175] Case C-848/19 P, *Federal Republic of Germany v European Commission*, EU:C:2021:598, para 48.

be taken into account in a decision-making process regardless of whether information is provided or a point is raised by the member state(s) concerned.[176] The principle of solidarity requires that the EU institutions conduct an analysis of the interests involved in the light of this principle, taking into account the interests both of the member states and of the EU as a whole.[177]

#### 2.5.1.6 A general obligation of solidarity: In whose name?

The judgments crystallize in primary law a series of key features of solidarity. The principle applies across the board, not only in specific situations. It must inform and can orient the decision-making processes of both the EU and the member states. It goes beyond burden-sharing and requires that actors subject to it take into account the EU's and other states' interests. The extent of this obligation depends on the issue of competence. The saga also raises further questions, however. It has been argued that such a broad interpretation of solidarity can lead to unpredictable results.[178] More specifically, the Court has not explained 'how the principle should be applied as between different energy policy objectives'.[179] This observation, made in relation to Article 194(1) TFEU, resonates with one of the points made in the previous subsection concerning Chapter II, Title TFEU. We agree with Münchmeyer that such an understanding of solidarity 'could make it more difficult for Member States to justify not following a Commission recommendation if this has the potential to jeopardize the attainment of pan-European targets', but it could also work as a catalyst for member states to defend their own competences and functions on the basis of a vertical solidarity.[180] This is even more so as solidarity—in energy policy as in border controls—has a strong connection with security.

In light of the foregoing, we must address two key questions about solidarity and the scope of this research: what is the relationship between solidarity and other relevant components of the structured network of principles? How should we balance solidarity across objectives, and decide what interest should take the driving seat (the EU as a whole and/or other member states)? Clearly, solidarity has a more specific nature than sincere cooperation, although it is rooted in it. Parts II and III uncover the situations in which solidarity would be more relevant, and those where sincere cooperation can still be helpful. Similarly, consideration of fairness and redistributive justice are part of solidarity, but this book focuses specifically on the more 'procedural' side of this principle. This being said, we must distinguish between the scenarios of law-making, interpretation, and implementation of the law of EU border controls. In law-making, solidarity interacts with effectiveness, subsidiarity, and proportionality. Solidarity can justify the adoption of a measure under the subsidiarity test as well as

[176] Case C-848/19 P, *Federal Republic of Germany v European Commission*, EU:C:2021:598, paras 50–51.

[177] Case C-848/19 P, *Federal Republic of Germany v European Commission*, EU:C:2021:598, para 53.

[178] K Huhta and L Reins, 'Solidarity in European Union Law and Its Application in the Energy Sector' (2023) 72 International and Comparative Law Quarterly 781.

[179] Huhta and Reins, 'Solidarity in European Union Law' 791.

[180] M Münchmeyer, 'The Principle of Energy Solidarity: Germany v Poland' (2022) 59 Common Market Law Review 928–29; see also A Boute, 'The Principle of Solidarity and the Geopolitics of Energy: Poland v. Commission (OPAL Pipeline)' (2020) 57 Common Market Law Review 889.

its content, where that would contribute to better achieving the EU objectives. Such objective-oriented use of solidarity in a subsidiarity context can be explained by an explicit reference in the Treaty (as in Articles 194(1) or 80 TFEU), or be implicit: as shown by the literature, several instruments of secondary law hint at the need for solidarity in order to improve, for example, the functioning of the internal market.[181] Solidarity should not be flattened over effectiveness, however. The Edinburgh Guidelines mention the possible damage to the member states' interests as a condition legitimizing the EU action. This is a solidarity-oriented requirement which is not linked to effectiveness (not directly, at least). After all, the ratio of the EU as a polity and legal order is that states are stronger together: it can only function properly if that spirit imbues everything the EU does. As we mentioned above, solidarity must be accommodated with other possible principles and objectives too. This is particularly the case in an area of shared competences and is as sensitive to national interests as border controls.

The phases of interpretation and implementation of the law also feature a link among different levels of analysis, and in particular: the question of how to identify the common and/or member states' interests; the question of which one should prevail in the case of conflict; the issue of competence; and effectiveness. The interest(s) involved can be identified by looking at the relevant provisions of primary or secondary law under consideration, or be stated by the relevant stakeholders in the context of political discussion or litigation. What interest(s) should take precedence, where the law pursues different objectives, or where the common interest and that of member state(s) are not aligned? To recall, our focus is specifically on solidarity as a criterion orienting decision-making processes in interpreting or implementing the law of EU border controls. The member states and the EU are under an obligation to take into account the common and other states' interests *in the exercise of their respective competences*. Therefore, a balancing method must start from the consideration that border controls are an area of shared competence: unless stated otherwise, competence in that field will remain with the member states. As Parts II and III show, this is reflected in the set-up of the law. Overall, the harmonization of procedures and the increasing powers of EU bodies in this field are flanked by a decentralized system of decision-making—for example, the processing of visa and asylum applications. In most cases, member states are still the masters of their own destiny. The effects of a duty of taking into account the EU and states' interests depend on the context. In EU border controls, such an obligation matters particularly in cases where the competent body enjoys a certain margin of discretion. Against this background, the question of whether and how solidarity can orient the decision-making processes should be answered by applying the following test:

[181] See Huhta and Reins, 'Solidarity in European Union Law'. For more on the connection between solidarity and subsidiarity, see L Marin and E Pistoia, 'Captured Between Subsidiarity and Solidarity: Any European Added Value for the Pact on Migration and Asylum?' (2021) 2 Freedom, Security & Justice 167; M Balboni, 'Subsidiarity Versus Solidarity? EU Asylum and Immigration Policy' in G Walzenbach and R Alleweldt (eds), *Varieties of European Subsidiarity: A Multidisciplinary Approach* (E-International Relations 2021).

- is the Union or the member state empowered with decision-making?
- does the relevant provision(s) allow the responsible actor to introduce a derogation from EU law (eg reintroduction of internal border controls)? *or*,
- does it simply leave discretion to that actor as part of the general legal set-up (as with the member states' power to revoke a Schengen visa issued by another member state)?
- do the provision(s) lay down an explicit obligation of 'taking into account', and of what sort?

We cannot answer all the questions in advance, as we will apply this test to the sources in Parts II and III. As shown in Figure 2.1, however, we can establish a series of guiding criteria. If (a) the provision governs a derogation and/or (b) contains an explicit duty of taking into account, solidarity will be at its most powerful, and the review of the actor's conduct must be strict, to the extent that particularly cogent reasons will justify disregarding the interests involved. This will be particularly the case where both (a) and (b) are present. At the opposite end of the spectrum, we have situations imposing no such obligation, and allowing a certain margin for manoeuvre *not* in the context of a derogation. These are situations where the shared nature of the competence and the understanding of border controls as an essential state function can underpin a less strict review of the action of the responsible actor. This being said, a fundamental factor that must be considered in all scenarios, and especially the abovementioned ones, must always be part of the assessment: the consequences of the competent actor's exercise of discretion, particularly in relation to the objectives of the relevant measure.

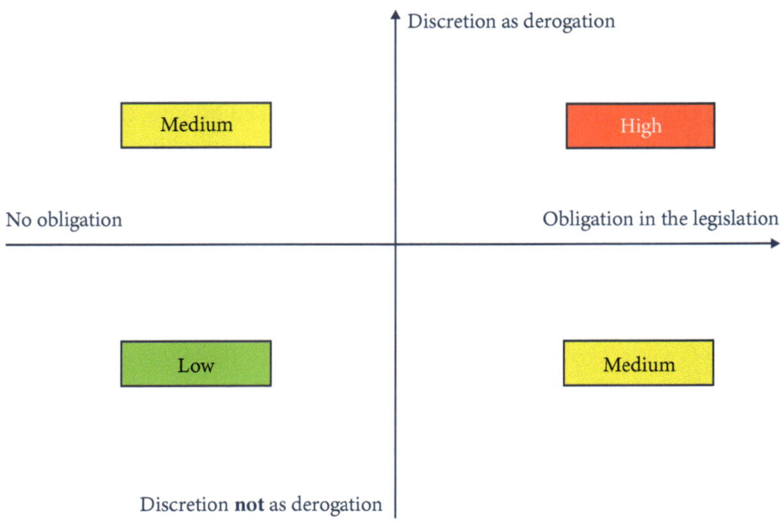


**Figure 2.1** Solidarity Review of the Actor's Conduct—Scale of Intensity

### 2.5.2 Between Effectiveness and Solidarity: The Principle of Mutual Trust

Mutual trust is inextricably linked to solidarity and the structured network of principles we are discussing in this chapter. Broadly, trust is an important tool to deal with social complexity.[182] On the one hand, trust is facilitated by the existence of certain values shared within a community, and helps to create expectations of regular and honest behaviour. On the other, trust entails a risk-based decision-making process. It rests on a presumptive element, possibly as the outcome of a rational calculation and consideration of previous experience.[183] The proper functioning of a complex system relies, furthermore, on the balance between trust and distrust.[184] In EU law, trust plays a role primarily through the principle of *mutual* trust. This mutual trust is not one of the foundational doctrines of EU law such as primacy and direct effect, but has ascended to the rank of principle of 'fundamental importance in EU law',[185] and underlies the '*raison d'être* of the European Union'.[186] Neither the TEU nor the TFEU offer an explanation of what mutual trust is,[187] but in the 'umbrella' definition provided by the Court of Justice, mutual trust is regarded as the rebuttable presumption that member states comply with EU law and particularly with fundamental rights.[188] The very legal structure of the EU 'is based on the fundamental premiss that each Member State shares with all the other Member States, and recognises that they share with it, a set of common values on which the EU is founded, as stated in Article 2 TEU. That premiss implies and justifies the existence of mutual trust between the Member States that those values will be recognised and, therefore, that the law of the EU that implements them will be respected'.[189] The states' status as EU members underpins the presumption that they respect the EU values stated in Article 2 TEU: they have signed up to a pact, meaning they are committed to act systemically in line with the Union's guiding light of Article 2 TEU. The two key legal implications flowing from such an understanding of mutual trust are that: member states may not normally demand higher standards from another member state than that provided by EU law; nor check, save in exceptional circumstances, whether that other member state has actually, in a specific case, observed the standards guaranteed by EU law.[190] The principle of mutual trust is rooted in the principle of equality between member states[191]

[182] F Fukuyama, *Trust: The Social Virtues and the Creation of Prosperity* (Penguin 1995); G Majone (ed), *Regulating Europe* (Routledge 1996). Trust has also been studied in the context of international relations. See, for example, A Hoffman, 'A Conceptualization of Trust in International Relations' (2002) 8 European Journal of International Relations 375.

[183] N Luhmann 'Familiarity, Confidence, Trust: Problems and Alternatives' in D Gambetta (ed) *Trust: Making and Breaking Cooperative Relations* (Blackwell 1988) 100.

[184] Luhmann 'Familiarity, Confidence, Trust'.

[185] *Opinion 2/13*, EU:C:2014:2454, para 191.

[186] Joined Cases C-411 and 493/10, *NS and Others*, EU:C:2011:865, para 83.

[187] This definitional gap notwithstanding, there are references to mutual trust in the Treaties that can reveal, in certain areas of EU law at least, some of its structural functions. See, for example, Article 82 TFEU.

[188] *Opinion 2/13*, para 191.

[189] *Opinion 2/13*, para 168; see also Case C-216/18 PPU, *LM*, EU:C:2018:586, para 35.

[190] In a sense, this reflects the origins of mutual trust much earlier in mutual recognition, where the idea of 'except for good reason' developed. See *Opinion 2/13*, paras 191–92.

[191] TEU, Article 4(2) TEU. K Lenaerts, 'La Vie Après l'Avis: Exploring the Principle of Mutual (Yet Not Blind) Trust' (2017) 54 Common Market Law Review 805.

and the threefold obligation associated with sincere cooperation:[192] mutual assistance (between the EU and the states) in carrying out their respective tasks; (for the states specifically) taking the appropriate measures to fulfil their obligation under EU law; facilitating the attainment of the Union's objectives and refraining from measures which could jeopardize this. We have also seen that mutual trust is often coupled with the principle of solidarity. The match between the two is inevitable. Mutual trust possesses the element of reciprocity that is required for solidarity to exist, and they both operate in the context of a community.

Despite its relevance, the status, contours, and application of mutual trust in EU law are contested.[193] The two main areas where the full power of mutual trust has unfolded are the internal market[194] and the AFSJ.[195] It has been noted that, apart from a '*core*, recognisable content' identifiable through a high level of abstraction, mutual trust is a particularly manifold and multi-layered concept, which is applied very differently depending on the specific context in which it is relied upon.[196] An attempt at such an abstraction exercise, based on the use of mutual trust in different areas of EU law, reveals that the principle plays a key role of facilitator in the EU legal order: that is, facilitating the application of EU law and, through that, the achievement of the Union objectives. In fact, the presumption of mutual trust is a precondition for, and an aspiration of, measures of secondary EU law.[197] On the one hand, the principle is closely connected to (though goes beyond) mutual recognition of member states' standards. This link materializes into specific instruments governing (in very different ways) mutual recognition in the internal market and the AFSJ. On the other hand, mutual trust finds expression in[198]—and is enhanced by—approximation of rules at the EU level. Not only because 'a sufficient degree of functional equivalence or approximation is essential as precondition for mutual recognition', but the establishment of a level playing field can also foster mutual trust.[199] The different frameworks introduced by secondary law establish a presumption of adequacy of those standards.[200] This is visible in the context of the internal market,[201] as well as in civil justice.[202] The approximating rules based on mutual trust allow each state to interpret and apply them with the same

[192] See M Fichera, 'Implementation of the European Arrest Warrant in the European Union: Law, Policy and Practice' (2009) University of Edinburgh 191.

[193] Among many, see M Schwarz, 'Let's Talk About Trust, Baby! Theorizing Trust and Mutual Recognition in the EU Area of Freedom, Security and Justice' (2018) 24 European Law Journal 124; E Xanthopoulou, 'Mutual Trust and Rights in EU Criminal and Asylum Law: Three Phases of Evolution and the Uncharted Territory Beyond Blind Trust' (2018) 55 Common Market Law Review 489.

[194] See N Cambien, 'Mutual Recognition and Mutual Trust in the Internal Market' (2017) 2 European Papers 93.

[195] TFEU, Title V.

[196] F Maiani and S Migliorini, 'One Principle to Rule Them All? Anatomy of Mutual Trust in the Law of the Area of Freedom, Security and Justice' (2020) 57 Common Market Law Review 9.

[197] See Cambien, 'Mutual Recognition and Mutual Trust in the Internal Market' 101.

[198] Case C-536/13, *Gazprom*, EU:C:2015:316, para 37.

[199] M Möstl, 'Preconditions and Limits of Mutual Recognition' (2010) 47 Common Market Law Review 418. Once again, the extent to which this connection exists and operates varies significantly from one policy area to another.

[200] Case C-286/06, *Commission v Spain*, EU:C:2008:586, para 65.

[201] See, among many, Case C-175/12, *Sandler AG*, EU:C:2013:681, para 49; Case C-286/06, *Commission v Spain*, para 65.

[202] Case C-527/10, *ERSTE Bank Hungary*, EU:C:2012:417, para 34.

authority across the Union.[203] The integrated system of judicial remedies of the EU—consisting of the combination of the EU's and the states'—reinforces the presumption that individual rights are sufficiently protected even if breaches do occur.[204]

If mutual trust amounts to the presumption of commitment to the EU values based on states' membership, approximation through a sector-by-sector approach in turn builds on and fosters that presumption, and organizes in greater detail the interaction between member states.[205] Such a dynamic streamlines the operation of EU law and enhances its effectiveness. Differences across the Union are reduced and diversities are arranged to achieve the objectives of the EU as a polity. The rules are thus an emanation of those values, and both of them lie at the core of trust. This commonality of values, interests, and rules creates a situation of high legal proximity between member states. It goes without saying that mutual trust is only sustainable if the shared values and the agreed rules are effectively abided by. A breakdown in mutual trust can impact the solidarity and the effectiveness of EU law. Precisely because solidarity requires the reciprocity embodied by mutual trust, if the latter collapses, so will the former. The practical manifestations of this vicious circle can be manifold. Successfully challenging the presumption of mutual trust can halt the operation of infra-Union mechanisms of cooperation, such as in judicial cooperation in criminal matters, as well as asylum law. As EU border controls straddle different policy areas, the role of international law must not be underestimated. As Article 78(1) TFEU requires compliance with the Refugee Convention and other relevant conventions, interinstitutional solidarity is also based on mutual trust that each member state will fulfil its international duties to refugees arriving at its borders. The domino effect can unfold outwith transnational processes too. Solidarity-based allocation of EU funding can be affected if a member state's commitment to the EU values—and specifically the rule of law—can be seriously questioned.[206] The foregoing picture must be qualified as follows. The discussion has primarily revolved around the role mutual trust plays in the context of horizontal cooperation between member states. As mutual trust and solidarity are inextricably linked, and solidarity applies to vertical interactions too, the same holds true for mutual trust. This is particularly the case in an area such as border controls, where EU agencies have been conferred greater powers over the years. Parts II and III consider how the breakdown in the circle of trust–solidarity–effectiveness might play out in state–EU cooperation. Secondly, mutual trust is not *a priori* irreconcilable with the effective protection of EU values in general and in border controls more specifically. In this regard, the fundamental issue lies in the threshold set to challenge that presumption and the practice of applying it. In other words, how stringent are the mechanisms in place to verify the subsistence of the conditions justifying trust?

[203] Case C-159/02, *Turner*, EU:C:2004:228, para 25.

[204] Case 294/83, *Parti écologiste 'Les Verts' v European Parliament*, EU:C:1986:166, para 23. More recently, and as a reaction to the authoritarian reforms of the judiciary carried out by the Polish government, the Court of Justice has used Article 19 TEU to strengthen the role of national judges in the EU system of judicial protection. See, among many, Case C-64/16, *Associação Sindical dos Juízes Portugueses*, EU:C:2018:117.

[205] There may be different levels of approximation underpinning mutual recognition. At the very minimum, for example in the case of EU criminal law, approximation concerns purely the rules governing mutual recognition itself. See Möstl, 'Preconditions and Limits of Mutual Recognition' 414.

[206] See in particular Case C-156/21, *Hungary v European Parliament and Council of the European Union*.

Complex enough when discussed in the context of EU member states only, the existence and operation of mutual trust require an even more articulated analysis when the Union's neighbours and partners enter the picture. In many cases, the *internal presumption* of trust has been balanced by a presumption of distrust vis-à-vis third countries: 'whilst EU Member States are, in principle, to be considered equals before the law of the EU by virtue of the set of common values that they share, the same does not hold true as regards an EU Member State and a third country. An EU Member State and a third country may be equals before international law, but they are *not equals* before the law of the EU as only the former is part of the EU, understood as a *Union of values*'.[207] Mutual trust, as defined in the Court's case law, would thus not be applicable to non-EU member states.[208] This holds true, for example, for the importation of goods and the requirement of health inspections thereof.[209] The same goes for the Council's adoption of restrictive measures which are based on decisions of third countries whose level of procedural safeguards cannot be presumed equivalent to that of the EU.[210] The issue is, once again, one of standards: anything 'imported' into the EU from the 'outside' must comply with the Union's canons, which in turn requires a preliminary check as to whether this is indeed the case. As the EU has evolved internally and in its relationships with the rest of the world, however, so have the two equations of 'EU state = trust' and 'non-EU countries = distrust'.

The existence of, and compliance with, common values directly impact the law and the nature of the legal relationship within member states, and between the EU and the outside world. Trust in third countries, and in the EU's neighbours especially, is key. While the Union, 'in its relations with the wider world, shall uphold and promote its values and interests and contribute to the protection of its citizens',[211] it is with neighbouring countries that the EU shall develop special relations, 'aiming to establish an area of prosperity and good neighbourliness, founded on the values of the Union and characterized by close and peaceful relations based on cooperation'.[212] The different wordings of Articles 3(5) and 8 TEU are without prejudice to strong partnerships between the Union and non-neighbouring countries.[213] It is with neighbouring states, however, that the EU has the specific objective to build value-based and trustworthy relationships. When it comes to EU external relations, proximity is

[207] Lenaerts, 'La Vie Après l'Avis' 809.

[208] *Opinion 1/17*, EU:C:2019:341.

[209] See Case 138/77, *Firma Hermann Ludwig*, EU:C:1978:151, at 1650.

[210] See Case C-599/14, *Council of the European Union v Liberation Tigers of Tamil Eelam (LTTE)*, EU:C:2017:583, paras 22–38, as well as the Opinion of AG Sharpston (points 62–67) in the same case; see also Case C-530/17, *Mykola Yanovych Azarov v Council of the European Union*, EU:C:2018:1031, paras 35–36. For an enlightening reflection on structural principles of EU external relations law, including on mutual trust, see M Cremona 'Structural Principles and Their Role in EU External Relations Law' in M Cremona (ed), *Structural Principles in EU External Relations Law* 3.

[211] TEU, Article 3(5).

[212] TEU, Article 8. See C Hillion, 'Anatomy of EU Norms Export Towards the Neighbourhood: The Impact of Article 8 TEU' in R Petrov and P Van Elsuwege (eds), *Legislative Approximation and Application of EU Law in the Eastern Neighbourhood of the European Union: Towards a Common Regulatory Space?* (Routledge 2014) 13–20.

[213] See, for example, the Agreement on extradition between the European Union and the United States of America [2003] OJ L 181/27.

an important concept.[214] A 'proximity policy',[215] whose name has evolved over time and is now referred to as the European Neighbourhood Policy (ENP),[216] is the policy whereby 'the EU offers its neighbours a privileged relationship, building on a mutual commitment to common values'.[217] While 'proximity' is often used geographically in this context,[218] the term also seems to describe a broader closeness going beyond mere territorial vicinity. Legal proximity is more specific still. It describes a situation where two or more parties share, to variable degrees, legal standards in one or more policy areas, which in turn fosters cooperation. Facilitated by normative alignment, the EU's aspiration of special relations with neighbouring countries is where geographical and legal proximity (should) meet.[219]

The variable geometries of mutual trust in its external projection are particularly visible in the context of EU border controls. As known, four non-EU countries apply the Schengen acquis in full: Switzerland,[220] Liechtenstein,[221] Iceland, and Norway.[222] Their participation is predicated on mutual trust and commitment to common values. They are all Parties to the ECHR, but they are not bound by the Charter or the EU system of judicial remedies. Divergences in the implementation of the acquis—including when caused by those states' highest courts—are dealt with by an intergovernmental committee.[223] Examples in Parts II and III show how this legal set-up can create heterogeneity of applicable standards in the law of EU border controls. This issue, however important, is not the main cause of controversy around the extension of the presumption of trust to non-EU countries. As discussed in detail in the following Parts, certain EU–third-country partnerships on matters of border controls

[214] Proximity broadly understood should not be confused with the principle of proximity, which also exists in various guises in EU law. The principle of proximity expresses the idea that 'decisions are taken as closely as possible to the citizen' (Article 1 TEU). Other examples of this principle can be found in EU waste law and policy and competition law. See, respectively, Article 191(2) TFEU and implementing legislation, and C Volpin, 'The Ball Is in Your Court: Evidential Burden of Proof and the Proof-Proximity Principle in EU Competition Law' (2014) 51 Common Market Law Review 1159. Proximity is also important in the context of jurisdiction agreements and cooperation in civil justice. See M Winkler, 'Understanding Claim Proximity in the EU Regime of Jurisdiction Agreements' (2020) 69 International and Comparative Law Quarterly 431.

[215] R. Prodi, 'A Wider Europe: A Proximity Policy as the Key to Stability', 'Peace, Security and Stability International Dialogue and the Role of the EU', Sixth ECSA–World Conference, Jean Monnet Project. December 5–6, Brussels. Speech 02/619.

[216] K E Smith, 'The Outsiders: The European Neighbourhood Policy' (2005) 81 International Affairs 757, fn 3 in particular; S Ganzle, 'EU Governance and the European Neighbourhood Policy: A Framework for Analysis' (2009) 61 Europe-Asia Studies 1715.

[217] See COM(2004)0373 final 3.

[218] See, for example, COM(2003) 104 final 3 and 6.

[219] In its 2015 review of the ENP, the Commission refers to the objective of pursuing regulatory approximation with neighbours in areas of mutual interest. See JOIN(2015) 50 final 12.

[220] Agreement between the European Union, the European Community and the Swiss Confederation on the Swiss Confederation's association with the implementation, application and development of the Schengen acquis [2008] OJ L 53/52.

[221] Protocol between the European Union, the European Community, the Swiss Confederation and the Principality of Liechtenstein on the accession of the Principality of Liechtenstein to the Agreement between the European Union, the European Community and the Swiss Confederation on the Swiss Confederation's association with the implementation, application and development of the Schengen acquis [2011] L 160/21.

[222] Agreement concluded by the Council of the European Union and the Republic of Iceland and the Kingdom of Norway concerning the latters' association with the implementation, application and development of the Schengen acquis [1999] OJ L 176/36.

[223] See, for example, [1999] OJ L 176/36, Articles 10 and 11.

have proved particularly problematic. Arrangements which would form the basis for impinging upon individual rights have not been preceded by a proper assessment of legal proximity with the third country in question, and have been concluded in very flexible forms which raise concerns of judicial protection (such as Memoranda of Understanding).

Against this background, the internal and external dimensions of mutual trust do not map onto the internal and external dimensions of the law of EU border controls. The internal dimension of mutual trust—that is, internal to the EU and between member states especially—is important for the operation of the law of internal and external border controls. It requires primarily that member states abide by the twofold obligation of trust stated above—that is, they do not demand (higher standards than the EU's from other states) and do not check (other states' compliance with EU law, save in exceptional circumstances). Within the EU and at the Union's outer borders, trust is key as it underpins the proper functioning of the compensatory measures that make the area without internal frontiers sustainable.[224] If each state does not do its fair share of protecting the external borders and internal security *in compliance with EU values*, that area cannot survive. In its external dimension, mutual trust and the partnerships based on it can arise only following an assessment of a legal proximity. Two questions guide our discussion: what evidence is required (quantitatively and qualitatively) before such proximity between the EU and a non-EU country can be said to exist, and therefore some sort of presumption can be established?[225] What threshold must be met to rebut that presumption? These questions have acquired growing salience, given the controversial EU–third-country agreements in this area. In light of the nature and function of mutual trust as outlined here, its use to deal with issues caused by the heterogeneity of border controls might not be obvious. As Parts II and III show, however, mutual trust is one of the golden threads running through the different components of the legal framework. Furthermore, that principle can prove particularly helpful to analyse the constitutional compliance of EU border control internally and externally—especially, though not exclusively, where that law or its implementation might be unfair to the persons concerned and therefore in breach of primary law.

## 2.6 Treatment of Third-Country Nationals: The Role for Fairness

Fairness is the main parameter to assess the constitutional compliance of EU border controls vis-à-vis the treatment of the persons concerned. As we define a coherent and comprehensive notion of fairness, and apply it to the specific context of this research, we lie at the intersection between two important debates: the role of fairness in the EU legal order and the assessment of EU laws and policies in migration and asylum. As to the former, questions of fairness have been raised in relation to different areas of

[224] This trust, as shown particularly in Part III, is increasingly to do with member states' effective exercise of their responsibilities in addressing threats to public policy and internal security.

[225] Beyond broad normative alignment between the EU and the third country, the more specific subject of the presumption partly depends on the area(s) covered by the agreement.

EU law, such as competition law,[226] social rights and citizenship,[227] data protection,[228] and consumer protection.[229] The variety of the research reveals how extensively fairness permeates the EU as a whole. Despite not being mentioned among the Union values, fairness is inextricably linked to most—if not all—the concepts enumerated in Article 2 TEU.[230] Subject-specific analyses revolve around provisions of primary and secondary EU law which, expressly or by implication, engage with fairness on different levels and to different degrees. For example, one of the preconditions for a member state's compliance with the rule of law lies in the protection, by that member state, of judicial independence and the individual right to a fair trial.[231] The connection of fairness with the EU values and the law that implements them[232] explains its ubiquitous nature in EU law. Victim of its own success, however, the ubiquitous nature of fairness has occasioned two distortions in the attempts to study it: discussions on fairness in EU law tend to be restricted to the area they focus on, and broader theorizations that are directly concerned with fairness often have their centre of gravity in some other concepts. Solidarity is a case in point.[233] Those distortions affect EU migration and asylum law too, and border controls in particular. Among the studies mentioned above, for example, fairness as such barely figures. At best, questions of fairness in EU migration and asylum law have been addressed from the back door of solidarity.[234] Therefore, there exists a clear gap in the literature as regards both a systemic understanding of fairness in the EU legal order and its application in the context of migration and asylum law.

Against this background, assessing the constitutional compliance of EU border controls also entails addressing the question of whether this law is fair to (mostly) TCNs. This question is particularly important for two reasons. As the principle of fairness pervades EU law across the board, we must put that concept centre stage and attempt to develop an overarching framework to discuss issues related to it. Also, pursuant to the TFEU, the Union 'shall ensure the absence of internal border controls for persons and shall frame a common policy on asylum, immigration and external border control, based on solidarity between Member States, which is fair towards third-country

[226] A Lamadrid de Pablo, 'Competition Law as Fairness' (2017) 8 Journal of European Competition Law and Practice 147.

[227] See, for example, Viehoff and Nicolaïdis, 'Social Justice in the European Union'.

[228] G Malgieri, 'The Concept of Fairness in the GDPR: A Linguistic and Contextual Interpretation' (2020) Proceedings of FAT* 20, 27–30 January 5.

[229] I Graef, D Clifford, and P Valcke, 'Fairness and Enforcement: Bridging Competition, Data Protection, and Consumer Law' (2018) 8 International Data Privacy Law 200.

[230] To recall, Article 2 TEU reads as follows: 'The Union is founded on the values of respect for human dignity, freedom, democracy, equality, the rule of law and respect for human rights, including the rights of persons belonging to minorities. These values are common to the Member States in a society in which pluralism, non-discrimination, tolerance, justice, solidarity and equality between women and men prevail'.

[231] See Article 47 CFR.

[232] See Case C-284/16, *Achmea*, EU:C:2018:158, para 34: 'EU law is based on the fundamental premiss that each Member State shares with all the other Member States, and recognises that they share with it, a set of common values on which the European Union is founded, as stated in Article 2 TEU. That premiss implies and justifies the existence of mutual trust between the Member States that those values will be recognised, and therefore that the EU law that implements them will be respected'.

[233] A Sangiovanni, 'Solidarity in the European Union' 213.

[234] E Küçük, 'The Principle of Solidarity and Fairness in Sharing Responsibility: More Than Window Dressing?' (2016) 22 European Law Journal 456; V Moreno-Lax, 'Solidarity's Reach' 761.

nationals'.[235] The connection between fairness and the EU's *policy* must not be read as leaving the law out of the equation. There would be little point in devising a fair policy if that fairness was not reflected in the law substantiating it.[236] The existence of an *explicit* obligation of fairness in primary law makes the assessment of those legal areas particularly relevant.

To answer the question raised above, we must define how the fairness of a legal framework should be assessed and how this principle could be operationalized. First, we need to engage with the philosophical and legal debate on fairness, and coherently combine different literatures into a new framework that is suitable for the structural features of the EU as a polity. This book proposes an original approach to discussing the legal meaning and scope of fairness in the EU, and adapts that definition to the characteristics of the area analysed in this research. By setting out a blueprint for understanding what fairness entails legally, and by showing how to adjust it to the specific polity and field under consideration, this research can also be relevant to actors and policies beyond the EU and migration and asylum.

### 2.6.1 Defining Fairness: Introducing (Some) Terms of the Debate

Fairness has been the subject of extensive debate in political philosophy,[237] legal theory, and many substantive areas of policy.[238] It has different values in different cultures,[239] and there probably is no persuasive way of 'tidying up the many considerations that we ordinarily adduce when discussing' it.[240] Like other principles often referred to in the context of both EU and international law, such as trust or solidarity, it represents an overarching idea, applicable in different domains[241] and across them.[242] It informs the structure of a society and the interaction between societal actors along different axes,[243] and is fundamentally aspirational in nature.[244] To start with a dictionary definition of 'fair', this adjective is described as 'marked by impartiality and honesty',[245] or 'the quality of treating people in the same way'.[246] In this understanding

[235] TFEU, Article 67(2).

[236] The question concerning the distinction between law and policy is different, and falls outside the scope of this research. Among a plethora of contributions on the relationship between law, principles, and policy, see S Waddams, 'Principle and Policy in Contract Law: Competing or Complementary Concepts?' (Cambridge University Press 2011); FAR Bennion, 'Legal Policy' in FAR Bennion (ed), *Understanding Common Law Legislation: Drafting and Interpretation* (Oxford University Press 2009); N MacCormick, *Legal Reasoning and Legal Theory* (Oxford University Press 1994).

[237] J Broome, 'Fairness' (1990) 91 Proceedings of the Aristotelian Society 87; A Ryan, 'Fairness and Philosophy' (2006) 73 Social Research 597.

[238] D Kahneman, JL Knetsch, and RH Thaler, 'Fairness and the Assumptions of Economics' (1986) 59 Journal of Business 285; HE Arnett, 'The Concept of Fairness' (1967) 42 Accounting Review 291.

[239] See E Porter ('Globalization and Fairness', p. 33) and S Inayatullah ('Culture and Fairness: The Idea of Civilization Fairness', p. 31) in J Dator, R Pratt, and Y Seo, *Fairness, Globalization, and Public Institutions: East Asia and Beyond* (University of Hawai'i Press 2006).

[240] A Ryan, 'Fairness and Philosophy' 602.

[241] Economics, law, or sport.

[242] Contract law, competition law, or administrative law.

[243] Among institutions, among the institutions and the individuals, and among individuals.

[244] It tells how a society should work, as opposed to describing how it currently operates.

[245] See https://www.merriam-webster.com/dictionary/fair#.

[246] See https://dictionary.cambridge.org/dictionary/english-italian/fair.

of fair treatment, fairness is seen as requiring non-arbitrariness and that like situations be dealt with alike. This approach resonates with many philosophical accounts[247] as well as with EU law across the board. Such a definition of fairness evokes the values of the rule of law, justice, non-discrimination, and equality, and is reflected in the numerous provisions of primary and secondary law that give effect to them. Only to mention the most obvious examples, we can refer to the principle of non-discrimination and the legislative instruments implementing it,[248] or the protection against arbitrary detention enshrined in the right to liberty.[249]

Another, non-mutually exclusive, perspective on fairness focuses on how claims are accommodated,[250] with authors equating it to 'appropriate concession in the context of a mutually beneficial cooperative arrangement'.[251] To frame issues of fairness in a way that, at least in part, maps onto the *summa divisio* between its substantive and procedural versions, we can identify two main scenarios: fair division of something, where the fairness is embodied by the outcome and/or the act of dividing itself, and fair response, which could be negative or positive, depending on the conduct of the interlocutor.[252] The EU's budget is an area where the complementarity between those two aspects is most visible in the Union, as the allocation of resources to member states can now be affected by their compliance with the rule of law.[253] Other examples of the systemic importance of a response and the required features thereof can be found in provisions on penalties for violations of EU law (including competition rules).[254] Questions of redistributive justice and allocation, therefore, lie at the core of the debate on the meaning and scope of fairness. As known, however, the choice of the 'right' criterion for division constitutes one of the most contentious aspects of the discussion. Distributing burdens and benefits on 'good reasons'—for example, effectiveness or efficiency—might not be fair in and of itself. Likewise, there are situations—like lotteries—that are not concerned with fairness and yet, we would not necessarily label their outcomes as unfair.[255] In certain contexts, the link between fairness and justice brings consideration of solidarity into the conversation. This is apparent from Union law, as shown inter alia by the rules on budget, as well as the requirement that the EU policies on migration and asylum be

[247] See for this, J Wolff, 'Fairness, Respect, and the Egalitarian Ethos' (1998) 27 Philosophy and Public Affairs 97; TM Scanlon, *What We Owe to Each Other* (Harvard University Press 1998).

[248] Non-discrimination is both a fundamental objective of the EU (see Articles 3(3) TEU and 10 TFEU) and a general principle running through the entirety of the EU legal system, as apparent from Articles 18, 19, 36, 37, 40, 45, 95, 107, 157, 200, and 214 TFEU. Among the many examples of legislative measures in this area, see Council Directive 2000/78/EC establishing a general framework for equal treatment in employment and occupation [2000] OJ L 303/16.

[249] Article 6 CFR.

[250] J Broome, 'Fairness' (1990–1991) 91 Proceedings of the Aristotelian Society, New Series 87; B Hooker, 'Fairness' (2005) 8 Ethical Theory and Moral Practice 329; P Tomlin, 'On Fairness and Claims' (2012) 24 Utilitas 200.

[251] C McMahon, *Reasonableness and Fairness: A Historical Theory* (Cambridge University Press 2016) 22.

[252] J Elster, 'Fairness and Norms' (2006) 73 Social Research 365–66.

[253] Regulation (EU, Euratom) 2020/2092 on a general regime of conditionality for the protection of the Union budget [2020] OJ L 433I/1 (Rule of Law Conditionality Regulation) and Case C-156/21, *Hungary v European Parliament and Council of the European Union.*

[254] Articles 103(2) and 260(2) TFEU.

[255] A Ryan, 'Fairness and Philosophy' 602.

governed by the principle of solidarity and fair sharing of responsibility between the member states.[256]

Rawls is one of the scholars who has made the connection between fairness and justice most explicit, as he famously devised an account of justice *as* fairness.[257] Rawls' focus is on the justice of social institutions and their practices, and specifically the distribution of primary goods understood as not only wealth, but also rights and liberties.[258] Several aspects of his account evoke the terms of the debate introduced so far. In his view, questions of fairness are likely to emerge when conflicting claims 'are made upon the design of a practice'.[259] Rawls' approach builds on 'the elimination of arbitrary distinction' and the establishment 'of a proper balance between competing claims'.[260] His idea of fairness 'involves the mutual acceptance . . . of the principles on which a practice is founded, and . . . the exclusion from consideration of claims violating the principles of justice'.[261] He argues that 'acting unfairly is but taking advantage of loop-holes or ambiguities . . . insisting that rules be enforced to one's advantage when they should be suspended [and] acting contrary to the intention of a practice'.[262] Therefore, fairness is also ensured through the appropriate response against unfair behaviour—identified primarily by the perversion of the objectives of a 'practice' and the disregard for the principles underpinning it. The mutual acceptance of principles governing a practice, and the importance of balancing competing claims *appropriately* when designing it, presupposes the existence of some sort of group of reference within which such claims emerge. Who are the subjects of the interaction?—or alternatively, what is the group of reference? Although Rawls uses the ambiguous and widely defined term 'persons', in other works he consistently talks about 'citizens'. Furthermore, his understanding of justice as fairness governs the interaction—via cooperation or competition—of free 'persons' that have no authority over one another.[263]

Rawls' framework of fairness has been applied in areas as different as contract law,[264] international criminal law,[265] environmental law,[266] international negotiations,[267] and

[256] Article 80 TFEU.

[257] See, primarily, J Rawls, 'Justice as Fairness' (1958) 67 Philosophical Review 164; J Rawls, *A Theory of Justice* (Harvard University Press 1999). In reflecting on some of the criticisms raised by other scholars on his account, Rawls refined and expanded on certain aspects thereof over the years. See in particular J Rawls, *Political Liberalism* (Columbia University Press 2005).

[258] Rawls, *A Theory of Justice* 6; Rawls, *Political Liberalism* 258.

[259] Rawls, 'Justice as Fairness' 172.

[260] ibid 165. The two fundamental tenets of Rawls' theory read as follows: First, each person participating in a practice, or affected by it, has an equal right to the most extensive liberty compatible with a like liberty for all; and second, inequalities are arbitrary unless it is reasonable to expect that they will work out to everyone's advantage, and provided the positions and offices to which they are attached, or from which they may be gained, are open to all. Inequality is allowed only if there is reason to believe that the practice with the inequality, or resulting in it, will work for the advantage of every party engaging in it. Rawls himself admits his ambiguous use of the term 'person', intended as not only individuals but also nations or firms.

[261] Rawls, 'Justice as Fairness' 193.

[262] Rawls, 'Justice as Fairness' 180.

[263] Rawls, 'Justice as Fairness' 178 and 183.

[264] J Klijnsma, 'Contract Law as Fairness' (2015) 28 Ratio Juris 68.

[265] LN Sadat, 'A Rawlsian Approach to International Criminal Justice and the International Criminal Court' (2010) 19 Tulane Journal of International and Comparative Law 261.

[266] S Hsu, 'Fairness Versus Efficiency in Environmental Law' (2004) 31 Ecology Law Quarterly 303.

[267] C Albin, *Justice and Fairness in International Negotiation* (Cambridge University Press 2001).

international law[268]—to name a few. In devising a Rawlsian theory of international law, Franck argued that the fairness of 'any . . . legal system, will be judged, first by the degree to which the rules satisfy the participants expectations of justifiable distribution of costs and benefits, and secondly by the extent to which the rules are made and applied in accordance with what the participants perceive as right process'.[269] Franck posits that a debate about fairness presupposes two elements: moderate scarcity and community. Without the moderate scarcity, there would be no need to engage in a discussion of the mechanisms of distribution of the 'fair share' of goods and the allocation of rights and duties. Without community, there cannot be such a discussion: any meaningful discourse about fairness presupposes the identification of an 'irreducible core of shared assumptions about fairness'.[270] In Rawls' wake, Franck's approach presupposes the existence of a community—if a global one—in which the applicable rules are assessed against a benchmark of fairness. Franck's framework is enlightening, particularly because it connects the debate on fairness to law as a societal tool to achieve a negotiated balance between order and change—or, to put it differently, between a view of legitimacy as process fairness (the agreed rules will be respected and enforced) and distributive justice as moral fairness.[271] These two dimensions seem to come together in the EU, where every area of law and policy must be consistent with its value-laden legal foundations enumerated in Article 2 TEU.

The previous discussion is particularly relevant to understanding questions of fairness in 'social institutions and their practices'—that is, a polity like the EU, its laws and policies and particularly asylum and migration. More specifically, we are concerned here with the questions of how to fairly allocate rights, how to fairly restrict them, and according to what procedures. In order to do this, we must first distinguish between different levels of analysis. Investigating the fairness of a polity,[272] for example, deals with different questions from those concerning the legal system as a whole or the justice system more narrowly.[273] When the focus is on an area of law in particular, fairness can be assessed in different scenarios, although it is inevitably linked to said systemic aspects. The fairness of the law-making process is distinct from the fairness of the content of a given measure, but the two cannot be compartmentalized entirely. The specific measure might, in turn, establish procedures to achieve a certain result,[274] and/or set out substantive conditions for those purposes,[275] or yield it directly.[276]

[268] T Franck, *Fairness in International Law and Institutions* (Oxford University Press 1997).

[269] Franck, *Fairness in International Law and Institutions* 9.

[270] Franck, *Fairness in International Law and Institutions* 16.

[271] Franck, *Fairness in International Law and Institutions* 22–23.

[272] See, among many, S Verba, 'Fairness, Equality, and Democracy: Three Big Words' (2006) 73 Social Research 499. The author argues that a polity is fair when citizens' voices—as defined in the article—are equal.

[273] F Wilmot-Smith, *Equal Justice: Fair Legal Systems in an Unfair World* (Harvard University Press 2019).

[274] As discussed in the following chapters, EU law establishes different sets of procedures for TCNs wanting to enter EU territory, from those concerning the acquisition of a visa, to those related to application for international protection made at a member state's border.

[275] As known, a visa can be granted, just like international protection or entry clearance for holiday purposes, if the person concerned fulfils certain requirements.

[276] For example, the EBCG Regulation establishes directly, state-by-state, the annual contribution to the Guard in terms of standing corps through long-term (Annex II) or short-term (Annex III) secondment, or reserve for rapid reaction (Annex IV).

These situations map onto some of the themes discussed above, such as fair play/fair outcomes or procedural/substantive fairness. Fairness can also play a decisive role in judicial reasoning. This is not only concerned, as is often mentioned in the literature, with courts embedding policy considerations in their judgments. It also concerns the interpretation and application of the law consistently with its spirit.[277] The assessment of fairness of a polity, of law-making, of a specific measure, or of judicial reasoning must not be conflated. This is not to say that these levels of analysis should be treated as watertight compartments. The fairness of law-making is likely to impact the fairness of the area to which that law will apply. Likewise, the overall fairness in a certain law or policy field can tell us something about the fairness of a polity where those laws and policies are being developed. The judicial interpretation and application of the relevant rules and principles can also play a major role in an evaluation of fairness of a legal phenomenon and/or the system more broadly.

Against this background, a workable definition of fairness comprises at the very least the following elements. Firstly, it entails the non-arbitrary accommodation of claims emerging *during* the designing of a practice by equal persons in a community *as well as* from its implementation by the competent authorities. Secondly, it requires compliance with the intentions of a practice and the mutually accepted principles underlying it. Thirdly, it presupposes a response to unfair behaviour, defined as violations of those principles and intentions. It is important to clarify that, consistent with Rawls' theory, the approach to fairness defined in this research focuses on the 'equal basic liberties', which include the freedoms specified by liberty, the integrity of the person, and the rights and liberties covered by the rule of law.[278] The priority of liberty—required under 'reasonably favourable conditions'—implies 'that a basic liberty can be limited or denied solely for the sake of one or more other basic liberties, and never . . . for reasons of public good'.[279] This is, of course, without prejudice to the extension of the proposed approach beyond the scope of this book. It is argued that these three (minimum) requirements of fairness have the advantage of being applicable to the different levels of analysis of fairness outlined above.

How would that definition apply to the EU as a polity, and to the subject of this book more specifically? Firstly, the competing claims (different views) are those of the 'equal persons' (decision-makers) involved in the designing of its practices (including the law and policy of EU border controls). Under the Treaties, the principle of equality applies to both the member states and their citizens.[280] The different bodies of EU law-making—and, through them, EU citizens—are also in a position of equal footing, with the member states having accepted the primacy of EU law and Treaty-based counterpoints to this.[281] Consistent with its founding values, the accommodation of competing claims in the EU must be non-arbitrary, non-discriminatory (unless otherwise

[277] See, on these issues, FAR Bennion, 'Legal Policy'; S Waddams, *Principle and Policy in Contract Law: Competing or Complementary Concepts?* (Cambridge University Press 2011), ch 1; TRS Alla, 'Justice and Fairness in Law's Empire' (1993) 52 Cambridge Law Journal 64; R Dworkin, *Law's Empire* (Fontana 1986); CR Sunstein, 'Two Conceptions of Procedural Fairness' (2006) 73 Social Research 619.

[278] Rawls, *Political Liberalism* 291.

[279] Rawls, *Political Liberalism* 295–97.

[280] Articles 4(2) and 9 TEU.

[281] See, for example, Article 4(2) TEU.

justified), and solidarity-oriented. Secondly, in the Union, the EU values constitute the mutually accepted principles on which its 'practices' (laws and policies) must build. Thirdly, as hinted above, effective mechanisms to react to unfair behaviour must be provided and deployed. These three requirements must be respected, *within their mandates*, by the 'persons'—institutions, bodies, and agencies—in charge of making, interpreting, and implementing the law. The Court of Justice's judgment on the legality of the Rule of Law Conditionality Regulation is a perfect showcase for fairness in EU law as conceptualized in this book, as it brings together the accommodation of claims, the role for compliance, and the importance of a response: 'the Union budget is [an instrument] for giving practical effect . . . to the principle of solidarity, mentioned in Article 2 TEU, which is itself one of the fundamental principles of EU law . . . the implementation of that principle, through the Union budget, is based on mutual trust between the Member States . . . mutual trust is itself based . . . on the commitment of each Member State to comply with . . . the values contained in Article 2 TEU'.[282] As the values permeate EU law, a breach of a value (such as solidarity) through violation of norms meant to give effect to it (eg those budget-related) can affect mutual trust to the extent that, in certain cases, it can lead to the suspension of *other* measures expressing the same value which the member states in question had violated in the first place.

The challenge, when assessing fairness in the context of border controls, is that in many cases it affects especially persons who are not—unlike citizens—considered part of the community strictly speaking, and who are often excluded from most questions about allocation of benefits (but not duties). This consideration is inextricably linked to, and compounded by, every polity's sovereign right to decide who can access its territory and under which conditions. An assessment of fairness in this area is not impossible, but the specific features of the legal framework under consideration must be borne in mind.[283] Against this background, this research proposes an integrated approach to the use of fairness—that is, evaluating the consistency of the details of a 'practice' (the system of border procedures) with its intentions (the objectives), and the compatibility of both with the mutually accepted principles underlying it (the EU values). To be sure, gauging the fairness of the substantive and procedural conditions for exercising control, or the conditions imposed on the control subject, will not always be a straightforward task. This is even more so as the law of EU border controls builds on a wide spectrum of sources, pursues different objectives, targets a diverse range of TCNs, and involves different levels of governance and actors. Two main allies can come to our rescue. Firstly, there is the wider 'structured network of principles' discussed in this chapter.[284] For example, proportionality is particularly

[282] Case C-157/21, *Republic of Poland v European Parliament and Council of the European Union*, para 147.

[283] 'Specific' must not be understood as 'unique'.

[284] The 'essential characteristics of EU law [particularly primacy and direct effect] have given rise to a *structured network of principles*, rules and mutually interdependent legal relations linking the EU and its Member States, and its Member States with each other . . . This legal structure is based on the fundamental premiss that each Member State shares with all the other Member States, and recognises that they share with it, a set of common values on which the EU is founded, as stated in Article2 TEU'. *Opinion 2/13*, paras 166–68.

helpful, as the same framework simultaneously pursues different—and possibly conflicting—objectives. Secondly, as further specified below, the principles that constrain the sovereign right mentioned above will be key, and especially what we can call 'universal principles'—that is, those applicable regardless of the fact that the person invoking and potentially benefiting from them belongs to the 'community', such as non-refoulement.

In this section, we have seen how many of the themes characterizing the philosophical debate on fairness resonate with systemic features of the EU legal order. We have attempted a workable definition of legal fairness, identified the relevant levels of analysis, and related them to the specific context of the EU and border controls. We must now zoom in on the different types of fairness existing in EU law. The following (brief) taxonomy focuses on examples where fairness is explicitly referred to in the relevant provision of primary or secondary law. By understanding the nature of these different kinds of fairness featured in the EU legal order, we can learn lessons for the purposes of the discussion carried out in this book.

### 2.6.2 Fairness in EU Law

The different manifestations of fairness in EU law are not restricted to EU citizens and can protect persons as well as systems or structures such as markets. Broadly, we can identify three main applications of fairness in EU law. Firstly, the systemic dimension of fairness manifests itself in competition law,[285] with this law linking closely to the prevention of abuse and the achievement of a fairer society.[286] At the same time, it is also important that the enforcement of rules of competition is fair, regard being had to procedural safeguards and the right to a good administration. Secondly, fairness plays a part horizontally in relations between private parties—and particularly so in situations marked by an imbalance of contractual power. For example, personal data must be processed fairly.[287] In the context of employment relationships, the right to fair and just working conditions—rooted in human dignity[288]—is protected, especially in the form of conditions that respect workers' health, safety, and dignity, as well as the establishment of maximum working hours, rest periods, and paid leave.[289] Thirdly, the vertical dimension concerns the interaction between public authorities and the individual. Everyone has the right to fair compensation being paid in good time for their loss in the case of dispossession of their property on grounds of public interest.[290]

[285] TFEU, Article 101(3). As regards the common agricultural policy, Article 39 TFEU states that the objectives of the latter shall be to 'increase agricultural productivity by promoting technical progress and by ensuring the rational development of agricultural production and the optimum utilisation of the factors of production, in particular labour' and 'thus to ensure a fair standard of living for the agricultural community, in particular by increasing the individual earnings of persons engaged in agriculture'.

[286] P Akman, *The Concept of Abuse in EU Competition Law: Law and Economic Approaches* (Hart 2012); A Lamadrid de Pablo, 'Competition Law as Fairness'.

[287] CFR, Article 8(2).

[288] S Peers and others (eds), *The EU Charter of Fundamental Rights: A Commentary* (Hart 2021), Article 31 889.

[289] CFR, Article 31.

[290] CFR, Article 17(1).

The right to property, which constitutes the logical *prius* of the right to fair compensation, requires that the dispossession achieves a fair (ie proportionate) balance between the individual rights and the interest of the community.[291] Of different sorts, but still within the vertical scenario, there are procedural rights. As regards the right to a good administration at the EU level, every person has the right to have their affairs handled impartially, fairly, and within a reasonable time.[292] The duty to act fairly consists of, inter alia, the obligation to give careful consideration to the factual and legal elements of the claimant's case.[293] Furthermore, everyone has the right to a fair trial held by an independent and impartial tribunal established by law.[294] That right is the cornerstone of any system based on the rule of law, and includes aspects such as the principle of equality of arms and adversarial proceedings.[295]

Before going any further with closer consideration of some of these examples, we must resist the temptation to take any of the understandings of fairness mentioned above and transplant them, *sic et simpliciter*, to the law of EU border controls. The extreme opposite position should not be espoused either. Looking at how fairness unfolds in other fields of EU law might provide useful insight. This is true especially in light of the existence of certain universal rights that constrain polities' sovereign rights related to border controls.

These reflections find great resonance in the horizontal application of fairness. This scenario is structurally different from border controls, because the types of relationship between the parties involved in either situation are not comparable. There are interesting elements, however, that can be drawn from the meaning of fairness in contractual relationships. For example, the Unfair Terms Directive imposes certain obligations of good faith and transparency in contracts concluded between a seller or supplier and a consumer, with a view to addressing the significant imbalance between such parties in a contractual relationship.[296] The Unfair Commercial Practices Directive defines commercial practices as unfair if they are contrary to the requirements of professional diligence and materially distort economic behaviour of the average consumer:[297] in particular, through misleading[298] and aggressive practice[299] affecting the consumer's freedom of choice. This would be the case of factually incorrect information, which was however presented in a way that led the consumer to make a decision they would not have otherwise made.[300]

As regards data processing by controllers and processors in particular, two concepts are worth mentioning: procedural fairness and fair balancing between different

[291] See Peers and others, *The EU Charter of Fundamental Rights*, Article 17(1) 508–11. Case C-112/00, *Eugen Schmidberger, Internationale Transporte und Planzüge v Republik Österreich*, EU:C:2003:333.
[292] CFR, Article 41(1).
[293] Peers and others, *The EU Charter of Fundamental Rights*, Article 41. Article 41(2) CFR also lists, in a non-exhaustive manner, what kind of specific rights would be covered by the right to a good administration.
[294] CFR, Article 47.
[295] See S Trechsel and S Summers, *Human Rights in Criminal Proceedings* (Oxford University Press 2006), particularly ch 4.
[296] Council Directive 93/13/EEC on unfair terms in consumer contracts [1993] OJ L 95/29, Articles 3–5.
[297] Directive 2005/29/EC concerning unfair business-to-consumer commercial practices in the internal market ('Unfair Commercial Practices Directive') [2005] OJ L 149/22, Article 5.
[298] Directive 2005/29/EC, Article 6.
[299] Directive 2005/29/EC, Article 8.
[300] See I Graef, D Clifford, and P Valcke, 'Fairness and Enforcement'.

(conflicting) interests. The former consists of transparency, timeliness, and burden of care, whereas the latter comprises proportionality and necessity. According to Malgieri, the difference between 'mere' transparency or lawfulness and 'fair' transparency or lawfulness is the adoption of additional safeguards that can effectively re-balance the unfair imbalance between the data controller and the subject in specific circumstances.[301] Fairness also entails consideration of 'the substantial circumstances at stake', such as expectations of the individuals, effects on the data subjects, and actual interests of the parties.[302] Valcke and others also highlight the relationship between the implementation of fairness by controllers and processors and the trust of data subjects.[303] From these examples, fairness plays the role of 'enhancer' of other principles to inject greater balance in an asymmetric relationship. Fair processing also entails that a data subject should not be misled in concluding a contract which authorizes the processing of certain personal data which the control subject might have refused to agree to—in other words, the data controller must demonstrate that the data subject had 'information relating to all the circumstances surrounding that processing, in an intelligible and easily accessible form, using clear and plain language, allowing that person easily to understand the consequences of that consent, so that it is given with full knowledge of the facts'.[304] This, to the contrary, echoes Rawls' view of unfairness as exploiting loopholes or ambiguities to defeat the purposes of a practice. At the intersection between copyright law and data protection, the Court has also stated that EU law must be transposed and interpreted by member states in a way that ensures a *fair* balance between different fundamental rights protected by the EU legal order.[305]

How could the foregoing analysis relate to EU border controls? Firstly, fairness requires compliance with the agreed principles underpinning a 'practice', as well as the intentions thereof. As we can presume that the objectives stated in the Treaties align with the EU values, we must consider whether: the objectives pursued by the relevant measures governing border procedures are consistent with those set in primary law; and, whether the details of the legal framework and its implementation are capable of achieving those objectives in compliance with the EU's values. As regards the parameters of that assessment, fairness can work to balance an asymmetrical relationship such as that between public authorities and the individual. While border controls are an expression of a core sovereign right, it is also true that states and the EU collectively have accepted universally applicable constraints on that right (such as non-refoulement). Secondly, and relatedly, an assessment of fairness entails consideration of how competing claims are balanced. The structured network of principles moving EU law, and particularly the principle of proportionality, can be particularly

[301] G Malgieri, 'The Concept of Fairness in the GDPR'.

[302] Malgieri, 'The Concept of Fairness in the GDPR' 6 and 10.

[303] D Clifford and J Ausloos, 'Data Protection and the Role of Fairness' (3 August 2017) 29/2017 CiTiP Working Paper 42.

[304] Case C-61/19, *Orange Romania*, ECLI:EU:C:2020:901, para 52. For a judgment on the (un)fairness of the balance struck by the national legislation on the period of time for which the data subject could access information about the recipients of their own data, on the one hand, and the interest of the controller of not being imposed an disproportionate burden, see Case C-553/07, *Rijkeboer*, ECLI:EU:C:2009:293.

[305] Case C-275/06, *Promusicae*, ECLI:EU:C:2008:54, para 70; Case C-101/01, *Lindqvist*, ECLI:EU:C:2003:596, para 72.

helpful to assess the accommodation of competing claims. Thirdly, fairness presupposes an effective response to violations of the principles and intentions of the practice. In the context of EU law and border procedures, this amounts in particular to a system of effective legal protection. We have argued that, beyond a certain level of abstraction, what is fair depends—at least to an extent—on the specific question under consideration. The assessment of fairness relies on the parameters—the 'constraints' mentioned above—deemed most relevant to each of those scenarios, with a view to drawing conclusions on the overall fairness of this law. For example, the discussion on sources pays particular attention to legal certainty and accessibility to the legal information, understood both as accessibility to the source itself and to the substantive content thereof. When it comes to mechanisms of scrutiny, the book investigates the effects of the new legislative measures in terms of accountability and effective judicial protection. As regards the conditions for the performance of the border procedures, the research considers the implications of the law of EU border controls, especially for the right to seek asylum and non-refoulement, non-discrimination, and the right to liberty.

## 2.7 Conclusions

This book assesses the constitutional compliance of EU border controls in light of its heterogeneity of levels of governance and actors, objectives, addressees of control, and sources. Given the breadth of the legal framework, the focus of the research is on the conditions for exercising controls, the conditions on the persons concerned, and allowed/mandated conduct associated with both. This innovative angle warrants a new framework, which builds on the view of the EU legal order presented in the previous chapter: a structured network of principles ensures that the Union's objectives are pursued in line with EU values. Parts II and III assess whether a border-control related task has been allocated to and performed by the appropriate level of governance and actor, on the basis of the appropriate source, for the appropriate purpose, and vis-à-vis the appropriate group of persons. This evaluation in terms of constitutional compliance/appropriateness is carried out through selected aspects of the structured network of principles chosen for their suitability to answer the research question and consistency with the scope of this book. The image of the network conveys perfectly the idea of the joint operation of the selected principles, and especially subsidiarity, solidarity, and fairness. To achieve a more rounded understanding of this complex area of law, this book proposes the integrated use of those principles to address the three macro-themes covered by the research question: allocation of task, nature of interstate cooperation, and treatment of the persons concerned.

# PART II
# THE LAW OF EU EXTERNAL BORDER CONTROLS

# 3
# Setting the Context: Objectives, Values, and Principles

## 3.1 Introduction

In the EU legal order, a structured network of principles ensures that the Union's objectives are pursued in compliance with the values enumerated in Article 2 of the Treaty on EU.[1] Those values are no monolith. Their meaning and scope are not set in stone, nor are the interests associated with them which shape the EU laws and policies. This is particularly visible in EU border controls, where the existence of competing priorities has often impacted the making and implementation of the law. These observations are compounded by the structural heterogeneity characterizing EU border controls: the latter do not only pursue a variety of objectives (often within the same regulatory framework) vis-à-vis a heterogeneous range of people. As an area of shared competence,[2] they involve different levels of governance and, at each of those levels, a plurality of actors. Implementation occurs based on a complex system of sources, going beyond the traditional legislative measures listed in Article 289 TFEU. Against this background, this book asks whether EU border controls are constitutionally compliant.[3] To answer that question, we rely on a structured network of relevant principles to assess the constitutionality of the law and its implementation in three interrelated areas: allocation of task, interstate cooperation, and treatment of the persons concerned. It is important to recall that the analysis focuses on issues possibly caused by the heterogeneity as described above. Furthermore, the scope of this research is limited to the following aspects: conditions for exercising controls; conditions imposed on the persons concerned; allowed or mandated conducts associated with both of the above. The primary—if not exclusive—benchmarks are the principles of subsidiarity,[4] solidarity,[5] and fairness.[6] As announced in Chapter 2, the assessment consists of two steps: are the goals stated in secondary law

[1] Or, as the Court put it: the 'essential characteristics of EU law [particularly primacy and direct effect] have given rise to a *structured network of principles*, rules and mutually interdependent legal relations linking the EU and its Member States, and its Member States with each other . . . This legal structure is based on the fundamental premiss that each Member State shares with all the other Member States, and recognises that they share with it, a set of common values on which the EU is founded, as stated in Article 2 TEU'. *Opinion 2/13*, EU:C:2014:2454, paras 166–68.

[2] Consolidated Version of the Treaty on the Functioning of the EU (TFEU) [2012] OJ C 326/47, Article 4(2)(j).

[3] In this research, the concept of compliance covers: the compatibility of the relevant instruments of secondary law with primary EU law; the compliance of the action of EU bodies with secondary and primary EU law; the compliance of national laws and practices with secondary and primary EU law.

[4] TFEU, Article 5(3).

[5] TFEU, Article 80.

[6] TFEU, Article 67(2).

*The Law of EU Border Controls*. Leandro Mancano, Oxford University Press. © Leandro Mancano 2025.
DOI: 10.1093/9780191966187.003.0004

in line with those laid down in the Treaties? Are the relevant rules of secondary law capable of appropriately achieving the objectives stated therein?

The book follows the flow of people, and therefore we begin our discussion with an investigation into EU external border controls. This scene-setting chapter addresses the first step of the assessment and is divided into five sections. Firstly, we outline the background to the birth and initial development of the law and policy of EU external border controls. Attention is paid in particular to the main drivers behind the emergence of this field, and the impact they have had on the architecture of Treaties governing external border controls. Secondly, we zoom in on the concept of European Integrated Border Management (EIBM), which is essential to understand the evolution and current state of EU external border controls. Here, we consider in particular the policy context in which the EIBM has come into being. In line with the scene-setting nature of this chapter and the scope of this book, this section is not concerned with every aspect of the debate around the EIBM. Rather, it homes in on the conceptual heterogeneity of the EIBM featuring in the policymaking. As shown, that heterogeneity underlies several of the questions of constitutional compliance analysed throughout this Part. Thirdly, the chapter uncovers the heterogeneity of the objectives pursued by the EU policy on external border controls and compares such objectives with those established in the TFEU. This section reveals the strong law enforcement-oriented approach espoused by the Commission and the Council in particular, and highlights the thin normative foundations underneath the variety of policy interests in this area. Fourthly, the chapter considers the policy approach to certain fundamental principles that should inform the functioning of EU external border controls: inter alia, sincere cooperation, solidarity, mutual trust, and fairness. The depth of conceptual development of those principles varies, and the lack of elaboration is particularly visible in the case of fair treatment of third-country nationals (TCNs). Against this background, the last substantive section moves on to the objectives stated in the relevant measures of secondary law. This section has different purposes. We examine the consistency between the goals set in the legislation and the corresponding objectives identified by the TFEU. In doing so, we introduce the main primary sources that will be assessed in the following three chapters. We categorize those sources, explaining the reasons behind the inclusion or exclusion of certain materials from the scope of this book. Furthermore, we present the structure of the next three chapters and justify its articulation.

## 3.2 The External Borders of the EU: Genesis

The idea of common external borders has underpinned European integration since its inception.[7] This was perhaps not evident at first, although it certainly accompanied the coming into being of the common market as well as the establishment of a customs union.[8] A single tariff applicable to all goods entering this bounded

[7] For the sake of simplicity, and unless necessary otherwise, the term 'EU' is used throughout and also to refer to the European Communities as well as the European Community.

[8] See P Hobbing, *Customs Cooperation in the Area of Freedom, Security and Justice: The Role of Customs in the Management of the EU's External Border* (CEPS 2011).

area—geographically and legally—was the first step towards building a territory where its members share values and responsibilities. Only decades after the creation of the European Communities, however, did the member states start to think more decisively about a common approach to the outer borders for 'filtering' people wanting to access the EU.[9] Attributing such a new role to the external borders was not a standalone initiative. Following the principle that every hero needs a sidekick, a common legal framework governing the movement of persons *into* the EU emerged to compensate for the abolition of border controls between member states.

From the start, there was something Schrödinger-like about the creation of a borderless area in Western Europe and the so-called flanking measures:[10] they were EU projects, and they were not. The 1985 Schengen Agreement[11] and the 1990 Implementing Convention (CISA)[12] were signed by *some* member states, but outwith the institutional edifice of the Communities. The Titles composing the CISA revealed the Contracting Parties' priorities: rules on the abolition of checks at the internal borders and movement within the Schengen area; common provisions on the crossing of the external borders, visas, and asylum; and law enforcement co-operation and data protection. Somehow simultaneously, the abolition of controls inside the EU was pursued by its institutions as well, particularly—albeit not exclusively—in connection with the internal market.[13] The 1984 European Council of Fontainebleau promoted the abolition of police and customs formalities for people crossing intra-EU frontiers and the introduction of a common passport, with the view to responding to 'the expectations of the people of Europe'.[14] A series of documents ensued. The two 1985 Adonnino Reports,[15] the 1985 European Commission White Paper on completing the internal market,[16] the 1986 Single European Act,[17]

[9] With few and collateral exceptions, such as Council Directive 64/221/EEC on the co-ordination of special measures concerning the movement and residence of foreign nationals which are justified on grounds of public policy, public security or public health [1964] OJ 56/850 and related instruments, concerning the entry, movement, and residence of family members of Community citizens.

[10] The Treaty of Amsterdam itself uses the term 'flanking measures', and connects them to the aim of ensuring free movement within the EU. Treaty of Amsterdam amending the Treaty on European Union, the Treaties establishing the European Communities and certain related acts [1997] OJ C 340/1, Title IIIa, Article 73i(a).

[11] Agreement between the Governments of the States of the Benelux Economic Union, the Federal Republic of Germany and the French Republic on the gradual abolition of checks at their common borders [2000] OJ L 239/13. The agreement was, in turn, based on the Saarbrücken Agreement, signed in July 1984 between France and Germany.

[12] Convention implementing the Schengen Agreement of 14 June 1985 between the Governments of the States of the Benelux Economic Union, the Federal Republic of Germany and the French Republic on the gradual abolition of checks at their common borders [2000] OJ L 239/19 (CISA).

[13] See White Paper from the Commission to the European Council on Completing the Internal Market, COM(85) 310.

[14] See the conclusions of this European Council, under the heading 'A People's Europe' 8.

[15] P Adonnino, *A People's Europe: Reports from the Ad Hoc Committee. Bulletin of the European Communities*, Supplement 7/85.

[16] COM(85) 310.

[17] [1987] OJ L 169/1. The impact of the Adonnino report on the SEA is considered by some to have been rather underwhelming, specifically on issues of EU citizenship. See P Mindus, *European Citizenship After Brexit: Freedom of Movement and Rights of Residence* (Palgrave Macmillan 2017) 9. See also the European Parliament Briefing, *The European Parliament and the Development of European Citizenship from Fontainebleau to Maastricht (1984–1992)* (October 2024) 4.

and the 1989 Palma Report addressed, to different extents, the issues of free movement of people within the Union, and flanking measures to offset the unintended consequences of removing internal checks.[18] As the Commission put it in its infamous 1985 White Paper on the completion of the internal market, controls between member states could 'only be abolished as part of a legislative and administrative process' which included the approximation on arms and drugs legislation, the coordination on rules of entry and residence for TCNs, asylum-related measures, a common visa policy, the redeployment of resources to strengthen controls at the external frontiers, and enhanced police cooperation.[19] The abolition of internal border controls emerged as the epicentre of several seismic shifts: around this project, new ideas such as the EU external borders and unprecedented legal frameworks started to coalesce. The key genetic traits of EU external border controls were clear from those early days, particularly as regards their ratio and modus operandi. Firstly, there is the integrated approach to different strands of competences related to movement into and across the Union. Strengthening the EU external borders was not—and could not have been—understood as a discrete mission. Conversely, it was regarded as an 'umbrella' covering, inter alia, law enforcement activities strictly speaking, rules on entry, visas, and asylum. The need to develop a holistic approach to border controls, asylum, and migration has been from the start at the forefront of the policy discussion.[20] Secondly, the principles inspiring the creation of these laws and policies have influenced their subsequent development. When preparing for the lifting of internal controls, it was stated that external checks must be 'highly effective', carried out 'in a spirit of mutual trust' and must 'allow to face risks or threats'.[21] Given the filtering function of borders, acting as the boundary of a distinct legal space comes with great responsibilities: '[E]ach country needs to take into account the interests of all contracting parties when conducting controls at the external borders'.[22] This statement resonates with the approach to solidarity developed by the EU Court of Justice (ECJ or the Court) discussed in the previous chapter. It also signals the ambiguities around the nature of states' borders and territories: to what extent do they fall within the exclusive responsibility of the state itself? When could the common interest prevail over the state's own decision-making, if at all? Effectiveness, trust, and solidarity

[18] R Zaiotti, 'Revisiting Schengen: Europe and the Emergence of a New Culture of Border Control' (2007) 8 Perspectives on European Politics and Society 31.

[19] COM(85) 310, 15–16.

[20] Council of the European Union, Ad hoc Group on Immigration, 'Report from the Ministers responsible for immigration to the European Council meeting in Maastricht on immigration and asylum policy' (SN 4038/91 [WGI 930] 3 December 1991). See also the 1992 European Council declaration on the principles governing external aspects of migration policy where the emphasis was also on respect for human rights. This comprehensive approach already features references to the need to develop an external dimension and tackling the root causes of migration.

[21] R Zaiotti, *Cultures of Border Control: Schengen and the Evolution of European Frontiers* (University of Chicago Press 2011) 88 and 94.

[22] CISA, Article 6(1).

emerge from the start as fundamental principles underpinning the EU stance on its external borders.

Against this background, the Maastricht Treaty conferred on the EU certain competences on external border crossing and related areas under the so-called Third Pillar, which governed issues of Justice and Home Affairs (JHA).[23] At the same time, the Schengen acquis continued to develop outside the Union's institutional structure, and especially through the decisions of the Schengen Executive Committee.[24] These intra- and extra-EU paths met upon the signing of the Treaty of Amsterdam: the Union established the creation of an Area of Freedom, Security and Justice (AFSJ) as one of its objectives; the competences on borders, asylum, and migration moved away from the intergovernmentalism of the Third Pillar to the supranational First Pillar;[25] the Schengen acquis was integrated into the EU legal framework via a dedicated protocol.[26] The 'incomplete'[27] supranationalization carried out by the Treaty of Amsterdam was finalized by the Treaty of Lisbon.[28] As detailed throughout this Part, the described process has not eliminated the asymmetry that characterized the birth of the borderless area-plus-flanking measures. In fact, the asymmetry—or heterogeneity—of Schengen endures to this day in other forms. The most obvious example is the non-alignment between the membership of Schengen and that of the EU.[29] Nonetheless, such gradual supranationalization did mean that the EU law and policy on external borders really started to take off at the end of the last century.[30] So much so that authors have argued that those born as flanking measures soon acquired their own independent *raison d'être* (ie assuaging national concerns over immigration).[31]

[23] As known, the third pillar of the Maastricht Treaty was characterized by intergovernmental rule-making and escaped the jurisdiction of the Court of Justice. On the basis of these competences, a number of non-binding measures were adopted. See E Guild, *Immigration Law in the European Community* (Kluwer 2001) 255 onwards.

[24] For a list of those decisions until communitarization, see Council Decision 1999/435/EC concerning the definition of the Schengen acquis for the purpose of determining, in conformity with the relevant provisions of the Treaty establishing the European Community and the Treaty on European Union, the legal basis for each of the provisions or decisions which constitute the acquis [1999] OJ L 176/1.

[25] TEC, Title IV TEC.

[26] For an overview, see S Peers, *EU Justice and Home Affairs Law* (Oxford University Press 2023) vol I, 13 onwards.

[27] D Thym, *European Migration Law* (Oxford University Press) 27 onwards.

[28] One of the main signs of full integration of the Schengen acquis into the EU framework lies in the abolition of the Schengen Executive Committee and the attribution of its tasks to the Council. See TFEU, Protocol 19, Article 2. More generally, the legislative procedure governing borders, asylum, and migration and the jurisdiction of the Court are the same as any other areas of EU law—with certain exceptions, such as the Common Foreign and Security Policy.

[29] Ireland is in the EU and the single market, but not in Schengen: travelling from/into Ireland into/from the EU means, to an extent, crossing the external border of the Union. Based on association agreements, Switzerland, Liechtenstein, Iceland, and Norway apply the Schengen acquis in full, despite not being member states of the EU.

[30] For an overview of the evolution of the institutional frameworks through the different Treaty changes, see S Peers, *EU Justice and Home Affairs Law*.

[31] G Cornelisse, 'What's Wrong with Schengen? Border Disputes and the Nature of Integration in the Area Without Internal Borders' (2014) 51 Common Market Law Review 741.

## 3.3 External Border Control and Its Friends: Introducing the European Integrated Border Management

A diachronic analysis of the EU policy priorities on external border controls shows that they have evolved over time while remaining true to themselves. Inspired by the 'security deficit' caused by the abolition of border controls inside the Union,[32] a heterogeneous range of rules relevant to the protection of external borders has emerged over the last three decades. Such a range covers areas as diverse as visas, police cooperation, asylum, as well as controls strictly understood. The centre of gravity of the EU strategy lies in the concept of European integrated border management (EIBM),[33] which started to appear regularly in policy documents—and subsequently in the Treaties—from the beginning of this century.[34] The drivers behind the conception of the EIBM and its constitutive elements are consistent with the picture sketched above. On the one hand, the EIBM should cover measures applicable in the country of departure, in transit, at the external borders, and inside the Union. On the other hand, from the start such a policy has aimed primarily at safeguarding internal security.[35] Border controls have been *one* tile in the bigger mosaic of the EIBM. The policy approach to the scope of border controls and their relationship with other components of integrated border management have changed over the years—and so have the ingredients of the EIBM itself. For example, in defining the EIBM, the Council has placed border controls *next to* numerous other components (including some concerning the fight against crime).[36] With time, some of those aspects have been 'cannibalized':[37] prevention of cross-border crime, crime intelligence, and inter-agency and interinstitutional cooperation are now considered as falling squarely within the scope of border controls. The Council definition of border controls itself exudes heterogeneity: they are 'a *multi-disciplinary law enforcement* activity and a shared interest among the Member States',[38] which can boost EU citizens' 'sense of belonging to a shared area

[32] C Kaunert and S Léonard, 'The Development of the EU Asylum Policy: Venue-Shopping in Perspective' (2012) 19 Journal of European Public Policy 1396–413.

[33] The adjective European constitutes a more recent addition. In fact, even Article 77(1)(b) TFEU still uses the expression 'integrated border management'.

[34] Communication from the Commission to the Council and the European Parliament on a Common Policy on Illegal Immigration, COM(2001) 672 final 17.

[35] G Raimondo, *The European Integrated Border Management: Frontex, Human Rights, and International Responsibility* (Hart 2024) 21 onwards.

[36] Border control—including relevant risk analysis and crime intelligence—would act alongside: detection and investigation of cross-border crime; the four-tier access control model (measures in third countries, cooperation with neighbouring countries, border control, control measures within the area of free movement, including return); inter-agency cooperation for border management and international cooperation; and coordination and coherence of the activities of member states and institutions and other bodies of the Union. See Council of the European Union, 7864/09 8. Legally speaking, such an encompassing definition would create an issue in terms of using Article 77 TFEU for adopting measures of criminal law, for example. For this reason, some scholars see this chiefly as a political—rather than legal—definition. See R Mungianu, *Frontex and Non-Refoulement: The International Responsibility of the EU* (Cambridge University Press 2016).

[37] For an initial definition of EIBM, see Council of the European Union, 15801/06 27.

[38] Council of the European Union, 7864/09 12. While not going as far as describing border control as a law enforcement activity, the Commission acknowledges that the competent authorities might find themselves in a situation where they must carry out different tasks simultaneously. See Communication from the Commission to the Council and the European Parliament, 'Towards Integrated Management of the External Borders of the Member States of the European Union', COM(2002) 233 final 2.

and destiny'.[39] The European Border and Coast Guard (EBCG) Regulation now crystallizes in secondary law a similarly broad definition of the EIBM,[40] and names border control at the top of the list. At the same time, the Regulation clarifies that the EIBM is 'based on' a four-tier access control model, comprising measures in third countries, measures with neighbouring third countries, border controls at the external borders, and risk analysis and measures within the Schengen area and return.[41]

This book focuses on border controls. These are central to the EIBM, but the EIBM has a wider scope which goes beyond the remit of this research.[42] This being said, different items of the EIBM featuring in Article 3 EBCG Regulation *alongside* border controls are also considered in the following chapters, depending on their relevance to border controls themselves. Search and rescue (SAR) activities, cooperation with third countries, and measures within Schengen are some examples in this regard.

On a broader level, the policy and legal approach to the definition of the EIBM and the role of border controls within it is confusing and problematic. It juxtaposes activities of border management (eg border surveillance) and activities that should facilitate the performance of this management (coordination between different authorities). Moreover, the never-ending scope of external border controls paves the way for the blurring of boundaries between migration control and criminal law. Viewing those controls as an instrument to forge the EU identity is prone to fostering an 'us' and 'them' logic.[43] This is particularly the case when border controls are conceived of as a law enforcement activity *tout court*. As posited by several authors, the ubiquitous system of control poses significant challenges to numerous provisions of EU and international law, particularly as regards access to asylum.[44] In continuity with its origins, we also see how the implicit element of solidarity remains firmly in the background through the reference to the shared interest. It is a security-oriented solidarity though, which resonates with the idea that the Union and its states should close ranks against an external threat.[45]

The Commission has not been oblivious to the challenges inherent in pulling together in one framework different areas such as migration, crime, and customs. To the contrary, acknowledging the heterogeneity of border controls has correspondingly resulted in a quest for homogeneity as regards the implementation of the Schengen acquis at the external borders,[46] as well as across its internal and external

[39] COM(2002) 233 final 2.

[40] Regulation (EU) 2019/1896 on the European Border and Coast Guard [2019] OJ L 295/1 (EBCG Regulation), Article 3(1).

[41] EBCG Regulation, recital 11.

[42] For example, the volume does not cover returns—at least not in detail or as the primary focus of the analysis.

[43] M Van der Woude, 'The Crimmigrant "Other" at Europe's Intra-Schengen Borders: The "Others" Amongst "Us"' in J Moritz (ed), *The 'Others' Amongst 'Us'* (Cambridge University Press 2021).

[44] E Guild, 'The Border Abroad: Visas and Border Controls' in K Groenendijk and others (eds), *In Search of Europe's Borders* (Kluwer 2003) 87; S Carrera, *Whose Mare? Rule of Law Challenges in the Field of European Border Surveillance in the Mediterranean* (Centre for European Policy Studies 2015); N Markard, 'The Right to Leave by Sea: Legal Limits on EU Migration Control by Third Countries' (2016) 27 European Journal of International Law 591.

[45] Mitsilegas defined the EU's approach to solidarity in the context of asylum law as state-centred, securitized, and exclusionary. See V Mitsilegas, 'Humanizing Solidarity in European Refugee Law: The Promise of Mutual Recognition' (2017) 24 Maastricht Journal of European and Comparative Law 722.

[46] COM(2002) 233 final 9.

dimensions.[47] The Commission highlights the multifaceted nature of heterogeneity as concerning not only the different legal frameworks on EU border controls at national level, but also the range of actors in charge. However, from the dawn of the EU external border policy, the need to achieve uniformity in the implementation thereof was linked directly to the level of security that the former would be able to provide for the whole Union.[48] Over the last 20 years, EU border controls have undergone a gradual and seemingly ineluctable process of legal harmonization and centralization. Paradoxically, the complexity of the policy and legal framework permeating the EU external border controls has only grown. As recently as in 2023, when setting out the multiannual strategic policy cycle for the EIBM,[49] the Commission recognized that a 'wide array of authorities' cooperates towards its effective implementation.[50] This could lead to 'a fragmented and uncoordinated approach', and a duplication 'of efforts and loopholes that can be exploited by criminal networks'.[51] Heterogeneity is thus acknowledged as an issue, but through rather narrow lenses: only as regards the actors in charge, and only for its possible security implications. Other forms of heterogeneity—apparent, yet unspoken—are either seen as unproblematic, or are not seen at all. The objectives pursued by EU external border controls and the categories of persons concerned are also heterogeneous. As elaborated on in the following chapters, this blindness poses significant challenges to the constitutional compliance of EU border controls. The lack of awareness leads to an imbalanced pursuit of the Union's objectives in this area. As a result, the legal framework itself or its implementation might prove inappropriate for achieving those objectives in accordance with EU values.

## 3.4 Values and Objectives behind EIBM

The diverse objectives of border controls reflect the comprehensive definition of EIBM. As shown in this Part, attributing a heterogeneous range of goals to a single function, as is the case of border controls, is bound to create tensions and require some difficult balancing. In this context, we can also observe the underwhelming role played by values in shaping the policy approach. Coherently with the Treaty structure, the policy objectives of the EIBM are organized into concentric circles. The overarching goal is a high level of internal security within the Union, in a manner that fully respects fundamental rights and safeguards the free movement of persons.[52]

[47] COM(2002) 233 final 10.

[48] This had to be achieved by taking account of 'the multiplicity of aspects to the management of the external borders', COM(2002) 233 final 3–5.

[49] On the basis of Article 8(5) EBCG Regulation, the strategy steers the technical and operational activities of the EBCG.

[50] See Commission Policy document developing a multiannual strategic policy for European integrated border management in accordance with Article 8(4) of Regulation (EU) 2019/1896, COM(2022) 303 final 6. See also EUCO 1/23, 9 February 2023 and Letter from the Chairman of the Committee on Civil Liberties, Justice and Home Affairs of the European Parliament, 17 January 2023, IPOL-COM-LIBE D(2023) 1361.

[51] Communication from the Communication from the Commission to the European Parliament and the Council establishing the multiannual strategic policy for European integrated border management, COM(2023) 146 final 3.

[52] COM(2023) 146 final 3.

The EIBM must be implemented in full compliance with EU and international law,[53] and must be based on respect for all people. In particular, it would be 'in contradiction with Europe's traditions' to deny access to the EU to '*those with a legitimate interest*' (emphasis added) in it—including people in need of international protection.[54] This framing resonates with the phrasing of Article 3(2) TEU and Article 67 TFEU. On this basis, the Union shall develop a policy to establish an EIBM and adopt any measures necessary for that purpose.[55]

Within the EIBM, what does the 'inner circle' of EU external border controls tell us about their objectives? The Treaties provide no details beyond what is stated above and in the previous chapters. The relevant policy documents and secondary law do, however. EU external border controls aim to: facilitate legal border crossing; prevent irregular entry and cross-border crime; identify and provide first assistance to victims of crime, vulnerable persons, and unaccompanied minors, as well as persons in need of international protection or who wish to apply for such protection;[56] and effectively counter unauthorized secondary movements.[57] These are the core objectives also set out in the legal framework, against which we will test the appropriateness of the rules. They express either the freedom, security, or justice spirit of the Treaty title to which they belong.[58] Three remarks are in order in this regard. The approach to the concept of vulnerability is not used in a particularly coherent manner. This translates into a certain terminological inconsistency, which will emerge from the analysis of the legislation.[59] Secondly, even though external border controls, asylum, and migration are understandably covered by discrete Articles in the TFEU, border controls have become a way of ensuring the implementation of certain fundamental aspects of the other two areas of law and policy as well. The relation among these three policy subareas is consistent with the holistic approach to the strengthening of the internal borders proposed by the Commission in the 1980s and developed thereafter. Relatedly, said objectives span *across* the law of EU border controls. While certain measures focus primarily or exclusively on certain goals, several instruments pursue most, if not

[53] COM(2022) 303 final 28.

[54] European Council, Presidency Conclusions, Tampere, SN 200/99, 15–16 October 1999, para 3. Considering the legal and policy context in which the conclusions were adopted, it is not implausible to read 'traditions' here as a hint at EU values. On the relationship between legal integration in Europe and evolution of values and (legal) traditions, see N Bodiroga-Vukobrat, S Rodin, and G Sander (eds) *New Europe—Old Values? Reform and Perseverance* (Springer 2016).

[55] Among the types of measures for which the EU has legislative competence, the TFEU separately mentions rules on the common policy on visas and the checks on persons crossing the external borders. Since the reference to EIBM comes at the end of the list of measures indicated in Article 77(2) TFEU, this can be read as 'any other' measure beyond the more specific ones mentioned above.

[56] COM(2022) 303 final 12–15.

[57] COM(2022) 303 final 24; Proposal for a Regulation of the European Parliament and of the Council introducing a screening of third country nationals at the external borders and amending Regulations (EC) No 767/2008, (EU) 2017/2226, (EU) 2018/1240 and (EU) 2019/817, COM(2020) 612 final 4–5.

[58] Justice is not understood strictly as judicial cooperation, but in a broader sense and closer to the scope of the value mentioned in Consolidated Version of the Treaty on EU (TEU) [2012] OJ C 326/13, Article 2.

[59] For a systematic study on the vulnerable groups in the EU, see F Ippolito and S Iglesias Sánchez, *Protecting Vulnerable Groups: The European Human Rights Framework* (Hart 2015). On vulnerability in EU asylum law, see specifically L Jakulevičienė, 'Vulnerable Persons in EU Asylum Legislation: Central Feature or Necessity on the Outskirts?' in L Tsourdi and P De Bruycker (eds), *Research Handbook on EU Migration and Asylum Law* (Edward Elgar 2022) 225.

all, those objectives simultaneously. This requires careful consideration of how well they have been accommodated within the same regulatory framework.[60]

In bringing together this heterogeneous range of objectives, the Commission stresses the importance of eliminating 'loopholes between border protection, security, return and migration', including abuses of the asylum system.[61] Beyond the uncertain meaning and scope of the different areas named therein, it is worth dwelling on the use of the word 'loophole', which can be described 'as a means of living to the letter of the law while simultaneously violating its spirit, or as an elevation of legal form over substance'.[62] While this beautifully crafted definition vaguely resonates with Rawls' understanding of unfair behaviour and might be seen as evoking a sense of justice, the use of the term in this context serves to throw asylum seekers into the all-encompassing cauldron of border security. On the one hand, the need to close loopholes reveals the EU emphasis on the effective pursuit of the objectives of external border controls. On the other hand, the heed paid to the prevention of abuses betrays the actual EU priority among the manifold objectives of border controls—that is, denying entry to potentially undesirable persons. Against that background, the policy approach to the successful accommodation of the heterogeneous set of goals pursued by border controls can be summarized with the maxim 'each to their own'.[63] Each actor must act in line with their responsibilities, and each group of persons concerned must be directed towards the appropriate procedure. While the maxim might be seen as advocating for fair treatment of TCNs, the broader context outlined above and the detailed analysis in the following chapters challenge that first impression. Solidarity is visible also in the background, as the institutional division of labour is centred on cooperation and coordination between EU bodies,[64] within the member states[65] as well as between them[66] and, most obviously, between the Union's and national authorities.[67]

[60] The quest for balance among the different 'souls' of the AFSJ more widely emerged from the start as a very difficult, yet important, task. See M Anderson and J Apap, *Striking a Balance Between Freedom, Security and Justice* (CEPS 2002).

[61] Communication from the Commission to the European Parliament and the Council, 'A strategy towards a fully functioning and resilient Schengen area', COM(2021) 277 final 5; Amended proposal for a Regulation of the European Parliament and of the Council establishing a common procedure for international protection in the Union and repealing Directive 2013/32/EU, COM(2020) 611 final 5. Those macro-objectives then find expression in more specific goals such as to respond to all border incidents and threats of a hybrid nature, to apprehend individuals and intercept transportation, and to contribute to ensuring the protection and saving of lives at sea in all weather conditions.

[62] D Ostas, 'Legal Loopholes and Underenforced Laws: Examining the Ethical Dimensions of Corporate Legal Strategy' (2009) 46 American Business Law Journal 509.

[63] A distinctive feature of the 2024 reforms is the quick referral of TCNs to the 'appropriate procedure'. This also implies that certain groups of TCNs at high risk must be granted protection on a quick (immediate) basis. COM(2020) 612 final 2 and 10.

[64] COM(2022) 303 final 21.

[65] More specifically, there should be 'a well-defined division of work'. COM(2023) 146 final 7.

[66] The reference here is particularly to the SAR activities that have developed in recent years with the regular involvement of private actors. Communication from the Commission to the European Parliament, the Council, the European Economic and Social Committee, and the Committee of the Regions on a New Pact on Migration and Asylum, COM(2020) 609 final 13.

[67] For example, Frontex should provide increased operational and technical support within EU competence. This includes the deployment of maritime assets to member states, with the view to improving the states' capabilities and thus contributing to saving lives at sea. COM(2020) 609 final 13. See also COM(2023) 146 final 9.

The policy approach to EU external border controls is characterized by a very broadly scoped definition. This translates into the involvement of a plurality of authorities from the member states and the EU, pursuing fundamentally a triad of objectives: facilitating regular entry, combating irregular migration and cross-border crime, and identifying vulnerable groups. To those objectives correspond a series of stereotyped categories of persons subject to control, the contours of which are rather unclear—especially the understanding of vulnerability. Beyond the vague and occasional reference to compliance with fundamental rights, the normative foundations of the policy are almost non-existent, and the emphasis is very much on the prevention of entry. Such multifaceted heterogeneity should be dealt with solidarity as regards interinstitutional cooperation, and fair treatment of the persons concerned. These two principles do not operate in a vacuum, but function in the wider context of a structured network of principles.

## 3.5 A Structured Network of Principles for EU External Border Controls

If the policy framework is very 'generous' in identifying the objectives of external border controls, the same may not hold true for the principles that should govern or inform their pursuit. To an extent, this is a reflection of the thin normative foundations characterizing this area, as shown in the previous section. Solidarity and fairness are relevant in particular to achieve the objectives in a balanced manner. With that in mind, two questions must be addressed: what are their meaning and scope? What role can be played by other important principles, particularly those that are part of the test of constitutional compliance developed in Chapter 2? The EIBM and external border controls should be 'robust and fair',[68] efficient, coordinated, and safe.[69] In the adjectives used to describe a desirable EIBM, the muscularity of the language (robust) goes hand in hand with a protective and justice-oriented tone (fair and safe).[70] Those qualities, combined with consistent implementation,[71] are key to ensuring trust between member states, which in turn is necessary to achieve 'open but well controlled and secure borders'. The importance of coordination draws sincere cooperation into the fray. The connection between the feature of the external border control policy and the principles that should govern it is apparent from the other adjectives as well. Apart from the obvious example of fairness, efficient and robust border controls evoke the effectiveness of certain objectives mentioned in the previous section. The combined operation of these qualities, and the structured network of principles that underpin them, ensure the proper functioning of the EIBM. The latter is a precondition for the thriving of Schengen and the Union *raison d'être*.

[68] COM(2020) 609 final 2.

[69] COM(2023) 146 final 2.

[70] As rightly argued, we should not assume that a 'protective' language will play to the advantage of the persons concerned as it can also justify restrictive measures. See D Thym, *European Migration Law* 22 onwards.

[71] COM(2020) 609 final 5–6. Digitalized visa procedures are also referred to as a factor that could improve trust in Schengen.

In this context, it is worth reflecting on the role of mutual trust. Trust in a robust EIBM is normally linked to the existence of Schengen because it is believed that, if trust exists, member states would be willing to keep their internal borders open.[72] Trust for the sake of external border management itself is a slightly less explored line of argument. Furthermore, and differently from the approach we have seen upheld in areas such as law enforcement cooperation, here trust is very much evidence-based. The emphasis is not on encouraging member states to *presume* that they abide by their obligations under EU law, but to make sure that they actually fulfil them. Trust, therefore, is treated more as a means towards a greater good, rather than a principle that should govern this area of law.[73] It also challenges the purely instrumental nature of external border controls. The way those controls work is as much a showcase for the EU identity as the area without internal frontiers. This impression is reinforced by the conceptual horizon trust is geared towards: open and secure borders.

Clearly, several principles underpinning the EU external border control policy resonate with those of the test of constitutional compliance.[74] Identifying the relevant principles governing this area goes only so far, if their meaning and scope are unclear. For example, solidarity traditionally features as a protagonist of policy documents in this area.[75] What this entails is not straightforward, however. Beyond the definition of Frontex as an instrument of European solidarity,[76] the often-cursory references to this principle concern the use of specific EU funds,[77] or the development of certain forms of cooperation (including with third countries).[78] That being said, the EU institutions have deepened the meaning and role of solidarity in recent years. More specifically, the Commission has advocated for a wider concept of solidarity: compulsory (if need be), applied 'on a constant basis', and 'stronger in situation of crisis'[79] across a wide range of situations—including SAR operations.[80] This is to respond predictably and effectively to the changing realities with an increasing share of mixed migration flows towards the Union,[81] and to ensure a fair sharing of responsibility in line with the Treaty. Those qualities align with the features of solidarity as a legal principle discussed in the previous chapter. The approach to solidarity described here resonates with the idea of the principle as entailing a general obligation, for the EU and the member states in their respective areas of competence, to take account of

[72] COM(2021) 277 final 4.

[73] The two understandings are not mutually exclusive. Trust is also a protagonist in the Commission proposal for a new pact on asylum and migration, underpinning some of the concrete measures featured therein. For example, it is argued that the pre-screening will increase transparency for people and build trust in the system. COM(2020) 609 final 4.

[74] Inter alia, shared responsibility, duty to cooperate in good faith, high level of professionalism, and functional integrity. Functional integrity and professionalism are clearly something that have an impact in the way controls are exercised and therefore on the principle of fairness towards the persons concerned.

[75] From the very early days of EIBM, it was stated that solidarity should 'figure prominently', [1999] OJ C 19/8.

[76] EUCO 79/14, CO EUR 4 CONCL 2 19.

[77] COM(2022) 303 final 27.

[78] For example, the Council mentioned the development of the European Patrol Network, of a network of ILOs, capacity building, and practical cooperation more broadly. COM(2006) 733 final 3–4.

[79] COM(2020) 609 final 10.

[80] COM(2020) 609 final 2, 5–6; COM(2020) 610 final 12.

[81] This reflects the view of EIBM as being driven by risk analysis and built on, inter alia, constant surveillance.

other states' interests and the common interest in their decision-making processes.[82] The call for stronger solidarity in situations of crisis is particularly important for two reasons. Firstly, it confirms that solidarity does not operate purely in exceptional circumstances. Secondly, it suggests that, in such a situation of crisis, it could steer more forcefully the discretion normally left to the competent actor. There, the review of the responsible actor's conduct based on the duty of 'taking into account' might be stricter than it otherwise would. Conversely, there is next to no detail on fair treatment of the different groups of addressees of control beyond the generic reference to respect for fundamental rights. The 2024 migration and asylum pact contains several references to fair treatment of TCNs, and substantiates that concept specifically vis-à-vis the right to asylum.[83] Interestingly, each instrument of the pact focuses on a different set of safeguards.[84] This reflects the approach to fairness proposed in this book—particularly as regards the importance of setting the specific parameters of fairness based on the context of our analysis.

From a preliminary observation, the policy objectives of EU external border controls broadly align with those established in the Treaties. As in the Treaties, the different layers of objectives span from wider to progressively more specific goals. Also as in the Treaties, they point towards the protection of the Union as an area without internal frontiers. While the appeal to security-oriented targets is accompanied by references to respect for fundamental rights, the accent is very much on preventing entry, closing loopholes, and avoiding abuses of the system. The overarching theme of heterogeneity emerges clearly. The EU institutions seem to acknowledge this as an issue only in part. Heterogeneity concerns the actors and levels of governance of EU external border controls, but also their objectives and addressees. There are interesting elements in the EU approach to how those different forms of heterogeneity should be dealt with. On the one hand, each actor should play their part, acting within their remit in a spirit of solidarity. The problem with this seemingly uncontroversial approach is twofold. Firstly, the boundaries of this remit might not always be clear in any given situation: what principles should guide the allocation of a task in uncertain situations? Secondly, the nature of border controls as an area of shared competence and essential state function underpin a legal framework where member states often enjoy significant discretion in operational decision-making. Respecting that discretion fully might, on certain occasions, sit at odds with other principles such as fair treatment of TCNs, solidarity, or both. On the other hand, there is the related question of how to ensure the fair treatment of all the different persons addressed by the law and policy of EU external border controls. The idea that fundamental rights should always be respected is vague and offers little help—especially when it comes to defining what the principle of fairness might require in this context. A rather specific response comes from one of the recently adopted measures, stating that the person should be immediately directed to the appropriate procedure. The answer presupposes previous identification of the relevant criteria enabling an assessment of appropriateness. The

[82] See section 2.5.

[83] Regulation (EU) 2024/1348 establishing a common procedure for international protection (Asylum Procedure Regulation or APR), inter alia recitals 56, 68, and 96.

[84] This being said, some rights recur more regularly. See the APR, recital 108; Regulation 2024/1351 on asylum and migration management (AMMR), recital 87.

last substantive section considers how the objectives stated in the relevant measures of secondary law fit in with the legal policy and legal framework discussed so far, and draws a roadmap of the scope and structure of the next three chapters.

## 3.6 The Objectives of EU External Border Controls in the Legislative Framework

### 3.6.1 A Roadmap for Assessing the Constitutional Compliance of EU External Border Controls

The EU model of integrated border management, and of border controls more specifically, is a continuum aimed to ensure that every step of the migratory process is closely monitored—from the country of departure through to the Schengen area itself. Heterogeneity is a structural feature of the policy framework. As to the multitude of authorities involved in external border controls, the EU approach betrays awareness of this heterogeneity and regards coordination and cooperation as ways of managing it. In other respects, the policymaking only increases this heterogeneity by bringing very different objectives and groups of persons concerned under the same regulatory framework. The challenges created by these features are amplified by the shallow conceptual elaboration of the principles that should support the operation of external border controls.

With that in mind, this section takes the first step in our assessment of constitutional compliance and addresses the following question: How do the relevant measures of secondary law map onto the policy and, most importantly, the objectives set in the Treaties? Before we engage with this question, we must set out the structure, scope, and rationale of the next three chapters. To recall, the analysis focuses on issues possibly caused by the interrelated heterogeneity of sources, levels of governance and actors, persons concerned, and objectives. It looks at conditions for establishing controls *and* conditions imposed on persons concerned. The next three chapters revolve around the following areas: the system of sources, the exercise of controls, and the pathways to scrutiny. There are different reasons for starting with a discrete chapter on the sources. Firstly, the procedures behind the creation of the law and the specific forms it can take must come *before* the evaluation of the substantive conditions for the actual performance of controls. Secondly, EU border controls are an area of shared competence. Not infrequently, measures of secondary law often leave the member states free to decide 'if and how' controls should be exercised. Thirdly, EU border controls are an area where the operation of the law builds on an increasingly complex system of sources.[85] This heterogeneous system raises questions of constitutional compliance along different axes of interaction and warrants a dedicated discussion. The need for a chapter on conditions related to the exercise of controls in a narrower sense is self-explanatory. The last chapter, on pathways to scrutiny, is consistent with the scope of

[85] For one of the latest contributions on the topic, see V Moreno-Lax, 'EU Constitutional Dismantling Through Strategic Informalisation: Soft Readmission Governance as Concerted Dis-integration' (2024) 30 European Law Journal 29.

this book. An assessment of constitutional compliance that disregards mechanisms of enforcement would be incomplete.[86] This is particularly the case as regards the test of fair treatment of the persons concerned, as designed in Chapter 2. That test requires, inter alia, an analysis of what ways are afforded and deployed, in the legal system and field of law under consideration, to react to 'unfairness'.[87] To facilitate the navigation of this Part, the three chapters have an identical skeleton. The discussion of the materials is organized around three scenarios: before leaving, in transit, and at the EU external borders. The focus is on the activities of public authorities. Therefore, the outsourcing of controls to private actors falls outside the scope of this book.[88]

Against this background, the scope of the chapters has been defined by starting from the definition of 'border controls' provided for in the Schengen Borders Code (SBC): namely, the activity carried out at a border, in accordance with and for the purposes of this Regulation, in response exclusively to an intention to cross or the act of crossing that border, regardless of any other consideration, consisting of border checks and border surveillance.[89] Strictly speaking, measures applicable before leaving (ie in the country of departure) go beyond that definition of border controls. There exist, however, certain 'before leaving' instruments that are worth considering—especially visas requirements and the European Travel Information and Authorisation System (ETIAS),[90] and provisions on the tasks of immigration liaison officers (ILOs). Said scenarios lie at different levels of proximity to the definition of border controls adopted in EU law, and there are also different reasons for discussing them. The possession of a valid title of entry is a precondition for accessing the Union's territory—unless specific exceptions apply. The SBC sees border control as an activity carried out at a border 'in response exclusively to an intention to cross or the act of crossing that border'. It also considers airports as borders—internal or external, depending on the nature of the flight—and 'border checks' as aimed to ensure that persons may be authorized to enter or leave the territory.[91] Conceptually, the 'before leaving' measures resonate at least with the spirit of control[92]—or, as they

[86] For the meaning of compliance and enforcement adopted in the book, see section 1.2. For the link between scrutiny and enforcement, see section 6.1.

[87] For an extensive discussion of fairness, see section 2.6.

[88] See CISA, Article 26(1)(a) and (b). Secondary law focuses on sea and air carriers. In the maritime sector, the EU has established a complex legal framework consisting of obligations for carriers, a monitoring system, and mechanisms of liability. Similarly, we must mention Directive 2004/82 on communication of advance passenger information [2004] OJ L 261/24 (API Directive). The API system has been recently revised by the EU legislature. See https://www.europarl.europa.eu/thinktank/en/document/EPRS_ATA(2024)760430. As far as land carriers are concerned, EU law provides for no specific obligations in terms of the collection and transfer of passenger data. For a comprehensive overview of these measures, see the study by N Vavoula and V Mitsilegas, *Advance Passenger Information (API): An Analysis of the European Commission's Proposals to Reform the API Legal Framework*, June 2023, available at https://www.europarl.europa.eu/RegData/etudes/STUD/2023/745768/IPOL_STU(2023)745768_EN.pdf.

[89] Regulation (EU) 2016/399 establishing a Schengen Borders Code [2016] OJ L 77/1 (SBC), Article 2.

[90] Regulation (EU) 2018/1240 establishing a European Travel Information and Authorisation System (ETIAS) [2018] OJ L 236/1 (ETIAS Regulation).

[91] The Court stated that 'crossing the external borders of the Member States . . . refers, *in the case of an airport*, to the crossing of those borders at a border control point, permitting the holder of the visa to enter and to move within the internal market'. See Case C-170/96, *Commission of the European Communities v Council of the European Union*, EU:C:1998:219, paras 21–26 (emphasis added).

[92] This is very different from arguing that those measures fall within the scope of the SBC. In fact, the SBC is clear in stating that it applies to persons crossing the internal or external borders of member states.

have also been referred to, 'remote control'.[93] As regards the common visa policy, the main sources discussed are: the VISA Code,[94] the Visa Information System,[95] the Visa Reciprocity Regulation,[96] as well as the relevant operational handbooks and Common Consular Instructions. As shown in the following chapters, different aspects of the visa policy are closely related to readmission agreements and cooperation with third countries.[97] While the relevance of this connection is acknowledged and explained, an in-depth analysis of such agreements is beyond the scope of this book.

The activities of ILOs, on the other hand, provide an example of 'home affairs diplomacy' which can potentially feed into the EU exercise of external border controls.[98] While we are aware that such diplomacy goes way beyond the ILOs, including as far as EU border controls are concerned, it is argued that the ILOs constitute a case of the EU legislating—vaguely—in this area with direct relevance to the scope of this research.

The 'in transit' scenario focuses on two main areas: surveillance of the EU external borders, particularly through Frontex-coordinated joint operations and the use of the European Border Surveillance System (EUROSUR), and agreements with third countries.[99] With regard to the former, the discussion mostly revolves around: the relevant provisions of the EBCG Regulation, the EUROSUR Implementing Regulation[100] and operational handbook, and the Regulation on Surveillance of the External Sea Borders (SESB);[101] the SBC; and soft law documents in areas directly linked to external border

[93] The creation of this expression has been attributed to A R Zolberg, 'The Great Wall Against China' in J Lucassen and L Lucassen (eds), *Migration, Migration History, and History: New Perspectives* (Peter Lang 1997). For a more recent contribution, among many, see D S FitzGerald, 'Remote Control of Migration: Theorising Territoriality, Shared Coercion, and Deterrence' (2020) 46 Journal of Ethnic and Migration Studies 4.

[94] Regulation (EC) No 810/2009 establishing a Community Code on Visas [2009] OJ L 243/1 (VISA Code).

[95] Regulation (EC) No 767/2008 on the Visa Information System (VIS) and the exchange of data between Member States on short-stay visas [2008] OJ L 218/60 (VIS Regulation).

[96] Regulation (EU) 2018/1806 listing the third countries whose nationals must be in possession of visas when crossing the external borders and those whose nationals are exempt from that requirement [2018] OJ L 303/39 (Visa Reciprocity Regulation).

[97] P Stutz and F Trauner, 'The EU's 'Return Rate' With Third Countries: Why EU Readmission Agreements Do Not Make Much Difference' (2022) 60 International Migration 154; H O Ariner and K Yigit, 'On the Removal of Asylum Seekers to Third Countries and the Scope of the 'EU-Turkey Readmission Agreement' (2022) 34 International Journal of Refugee Law 416; S. Carrera, *Implementation of EU Readmission Agreements: Identity Determination Dilemmas and the Blurring of Rights* (Springer 2016); F Trauner and K Imke, 'EC Visa Facilitation and Readmission Agreements: A New Standard EU Foreign Policy Tool?' (2008) 10 European Journal of Migration and Law 411.

[98] Regulation (EU) 2019/1240 on the creation of a European network of immigration liaison officers [2019] OJ L 198/88 (ILON Regulation). See more broadly on the topic T Emiliani and A Linck, 'The External Dimension of EU Immigration Policies: Reacting to External Events?' in C Damro, S Gsteohl, and S Schunz (eds), *The European Union's Evolving External Engagement: Towards New Sectoral Diplomacies?* (Routledge 2018).

[99] S F Nicolosi, 'Externalisation of Migration Controls: A Taxonomy of Practices and Their Implications in International and European Law' (2024) 71 Netherlands International Law Review 1; S Cobarrubias and P Novak, 'Embedding Externalisation: How Bordering Practices Transform Places' (2024) 30 Geopolitics 1.

[100] Commission Implementing Regulation (EU) 2021/581 on the situational pictures of the European Border Surveillance System [2021] OJ L 124/3 (EUROSUR Implementing Regulation).

[101] Regulation (EU) No 656/2014 establishing rules for the surveillance of the external sea borders in the context of operational cooperation coordinated by the European Agency for the Management of Operational Cooperation at the External Borders of the Member States of the European Union [2014] OJ L 189/93 (SESB Regulation).

surveillance, such as SAR and humanitarian assistance. As for the last category, only agreements with neighbouring third countries are considered. This is to retain a degree of geographical and conceptual proximity to the scope of the research. In fact, the specific sources considered here enable the joint performance of tasks directly linked to border controls or the exercise of those functions in the third-country territory. Depending on the concrete aspects analysed in this scenario, the discussion of provisions of EU asylum law might prove relevant to the assessment of constitutional compliance. As regards instruments applicable at the external borders proper, we focus on: the SBC; the EBCG Regulation as appropriate; the Entry/Exit System (EES);[102] and the relevant instruments of the 2024 Asylum and Migration, whose combined operation creates a complex system of borders procedures. These are: the Screening Regulation;[103] the Asylum Procedure Regulation; the Return Border Procedure (RBP) Regulation;[104] and the Crisis Regulation.[105] The following issues or characteristics cut across the 'before leaving', 'in transit', and 'at the borders' scenarios. Thematically, the large use of information systems[106] and reliance on partnerships with third countries will emerge as constant features in all those different situations—if to a variable degree. In terms of sources, the analysis of the legislative materials is complemented by the case law of the Court of Justice and sources emanating from other relevant EU bodies (such as the European Ombudsman), as well as the literature as appropriate. Also, certain insights from Finland and Italy will enrich the discussion.[107] These countries were chosen because of their relevance to the research question and consistency with the scope of the book.[108] That being the roadmap for the next three chapters, the next subsection focuses on the objectives of the mentioned measures and their consistency with primary law.

### 3.6.2 Objectives of Border Controls in Secondary Law and Their Consistency with Primary Law

As mentioned in the previous subsection, the reinforcement of checks against large information systems and their interoperability has emerged especially over the last few years as a cross-cutting feature of EU external border controls. Such checks are regarded as a stronghold of the borderless area and the long-term security of the Union

[102] Regulation (EU) 2017/2226 establishing an Entry/Exit System (EES) to register entry and exit data and refusal of entry data of third-country nationals crossing the external borders of the Member States and determining the conditions for access to the EES for law enforcement purposes [2017] OJ 327/20 (EES Regulation).

[103] Regulation (EU) 2024/1356 introducing the screening of third-country nationals at the external borders (or Screening Regulation).

[104] Regulation (EU) 2024/1349 establishing a return border procedure (or RBP Regulation).

[105] Regulation (EU) 2024/1359 addressing situations of crisis and force majeure in the field of migration and asylum (or Crisis Regulation).

[106] N Vavoula, *Immigration and Privacy in the Law of the European Union* (Brill 2022).

[107] For more on the reasons for selecting these two countries, see the Introduction at section 'Roadmap: A Long and Winding Road'.

[108] A last note on the financial instruments. While acknowledging the increasing relevance of such instruments for EU border controls (including as regards cooperation with third countries), this research focuses on conditions for controls and on the persons concerned. Therefore, this issue lies outwith the remit of this book.

and its citizens.[109] One of the purposes of such checks is to prevent any threat to the internal security and public policy of the member states, including where such a threat derives from Union citizens.[110] Interoperability between the EES, the VIS, the ETIAS, the Schengen Information System (SIS),[111] Eurodac,[112] and the European Criminal Record Information System for TCNs (ECRIS-TCN)[113] is established so that they can complement each other while respecting individual rights, and particularly the right to protection of personal data.[114] The aim of interoperability is the correct identification of persons within the Schengen area for the dual purpose of facilitating identity checks for bona fide travellers and combating identity fraud.[115] This is also pursued by allowing law enforcement authorities access to IT systems not established for those purposes.[116] On the one hand, measures such as the interoperability of IT systems are a broadly scoped tool, so their objectives should not be equated with those of EU external border policy. On the other hand, they are used specifically in the context of EU external border policy and most of them are inextricably linked to border checks.

Against this background, it is worth looking closely at the main objectives of the measures falling within the three scenarios outlined above. As for the measures applicable before leaving, these mostly concern the different systems of travel authorizations and the tasks of the ILOs. As to the former, we must distinguish between rules on the common visa policy and the ETIAS. The common visa policy is one of the fundamental components of a multi-layered system aimed at facilitating legitimate travel and tackling illegal immigration.[117] Its implementation is supported by the VIS Regulation and intends to prevent 'visa shopping', contributing to the fight against fraud and checks at external borders as well as within the EU.[118] It supports the application of the Dublin Regulation and contributes to the prevention of threats to the internal security of the member states.[119] The Visa Reciprocity Regulation aims to prevent and counter abuses of visa exemptions by TCNs posing a threat to the public policy (ordre

[109] Regulation (EU) 2017/458 amending Regulation (EU) 2016/399 as regards the reinforcement of checks against relevant databases at external borders [2017] OJ L 74/1, recital 17.

[110] This is related in particular to the phenomenon of foreign fighters. Regulation (EU) 2017/458, recitals 1 and 2.

[111] Regulation (EU) 2018/1861 on the establishment, operation and use of the Schengen Information System (SIS) in the field of border checks [2018] OJ L 312/14.

[112] Regulation (EU) No 603/2013 on the establishment of 'Eurodac' for the comparison of fingerprints for the effective application of Regulation (EU) No 604/2013 and on requests for the comparison with Eurodac data by Member States' law enforcement authorities and Europol for law enforcement purposes [2013] OJ L 180/1.

[113] Regulation (EU) 2019/816 establishing a centralised system for the identification of Member States holding conviction information on third-country nationals and stateless persons (ECRIS-TCN) to supplement the European Criminal Records Information System [2019] OJ L 135/1.

[114] Regulation (EU) 2019/817 on establishing a framework for interoperability between EU information systems in the field of borders and visa [2019] OJ L 135/27 (Interoperability Regulation), recital 9.

[115] Regulation (EU) 2019/817 (Interoperability Regulation), recital 24.

[116] Regulation (EU) 2019/817, recital 25. See same Regulation, Article 2. This is apparent from the objectives of the Interoperability Regulation, which are: improved efficiency and effectiveness of external border checks; prevention and counter of illegal immigration; contribution to a high level of security within the Union; improved implementation of the visa policy; assistance in the examination of applications for international protection; and contribution to the prevention of serious crime.

[117] VISA Code, recital 3.

[118] Especially with a view to identifying those who may no longer fulfil the conditions of entry and stay as established in the SBC.

[119] VIS Regulation, recital 5.

public) and the internal security of the member state concerned.[120] The ETIAS, on the other hand, establishes a mechanism requiring visa-exempt TCNs to acquire a travel authorization to enter the EU for short stays. ETIAS should contribute to a high level of security, to the prevention of illegal immigration, and to the protection of public health by providing an assessment of visitors prior to their arrival at the external borders.[121] It should also contribute to the facilitation of border checks by reducing the number of refusals of entry.[122] The EU has also established rules to better coordinate the use of the network of ILOs deployed to third countries, in order to respond more effectively to the Union priorities on illegal immigration and cross-border criminality, returns, and readmission and reintegration activities.[123] From this brief overview, we can conclude that the provisions relevant before leaving are primarily concerned with internal security threats that could be caused by irregular entry—understood as security internal to the member states.[124] The facilitation of regular travel also features among the objectives—especially of the Visa Code—whereas aspects of international protection are absent from the legal framework. The next chapters show that the provisions of the abovementioned instruments are not concerned at all with such issues as humanitarian visas. The fact that the VISA Code leaves the member states free to grant such visas on certain conditions is without prejudice to the previous observation. The member states' leeway adds no intentions to the legislation beyond the objectives explicitly stated therein, and this distinction proves key to determining the margin of manoeuvre left to the member states in this area.

The 'in transit' scenario focuses primarily on measures involving surveillance of the external borders. The SEBS Regulation applies to border surveillance operations carried out by member states at their external sea borders in the context of operational cooperation coordinated by Frontex.[125] The main objective is to ensure the efficient monitoring of the crossing of the external borders, prevent unauthorized entry, and counter cross-border criminality, while contributing to the protection and saving of lives.[126] Very similar objectives are pursued by controls at the external borders proper. These are described as a necessary corollary to the free movement of persons,[127] essential to safeguard the functioning of the Schengen area and respecting the overarching principle of solidarity.[128] Contributing to reducing the loss of lives of migrants is also a fundamental objective of external border controls.[129] From a systemic point of view, controls should not hinder trade and social interchange.[130] Border checks should be carried out in a way that fully respects human dignity, professionally, respectfully, and proportionately to its objectives.[131] As mentioned, checks at the external borders will

[120] Visa Reciprocity Regulation, recital 20.
[121] ETIAS Regulation, recital 10.
[122] ETIAS Regulation, recital 11.
[123] ILON Regulation, recital 10.
[124] While internal security and irregular migration are cited as separate concepts, they are also constantly mentioned together.
[125] SESB Regulation, Article 1.
[126] SESB Regulation, recital 1. These include interception of vessels trying to enter the EU irregularly.
[127] EBCG Regulation, recital 1.
[128] EBCG Regulation, recital 9.
[129] EBCG Regulation, recital 38.
[130] SBC Regulation, recital 17.
[131] SBC Regulation, recital 7.

be enhanced by the establishment of the EES, which aims to improve the management of external borders, prevent irregular immigration, and facilitate the management of migration flows as well as law enforcement.[132]

Last but not least, 2024 hailed the enactment of the asylum and migration pact reform. Several legislative instruments interacted with one another to create a complex system of border procedures. Firstly, the Screening Regulation establishes a screening mechanism, with the view to facilitating the proper identification of TCNs and their efficient referral to the appropriate procedures.[133] In doing this, the Regulation should contribute to identifying vulnerable persons, countering secondary irregular movement within the Union, and achieving the objectives of border controls more broadly (including reducing illegal migration and combating crime).[134] When performing border controls and screening procedures, member states must act in compliance with relevant Union and international law, and in particular: the rights of applicants for international protection (especially non-refoulement), the best interest of the child enshrined in Article 24(2) CFR, and human dignity and non-discrimination.[135] Secondly, a humane, fair, and efficient asylum policy is a complementary component of the EU AFSJ.[136] The Asylum Procedure Regulation (APR) aims to ensure timeliness and effectiveness of the asylum procedures, equity and equality in treatment, and clarity and legal certainty for applicants. A more consistent system applied across the Union has also the objective of reducing secondary movement.[137] Interestingly, the APR clearly identifies a series of conditions for asylum procedures to be fair: effective access to the procedure; an effective opportunity to present all elements available to the applicant; an effective right to a personal interview (subject to limited exceptions) with time to prepare and consult a legal advisor and access to free legal assistance;[138] and a rigorous examination of the application, taken impartially and objectively based on relevant, precise and up-to-date information.[139] Effective access to the examination procedure should also be available to persons at border crossing points and in detention facilities.[140] As regards asylum border procedures more specifically, these aim to quickly assess 'whether applications are unfounded or inadmissible and to swiftly return those with no right to stay, in a manner that fully respects the principle of non-refoulement, while ensuring that those with well-founded claims are channelled into the regular procedure and provided quick access to international protection'.[141] As apparent from the preamble of the APR, the fairness of the procedures rests, for the most part, on the effectiveness of its constitutive components. This aspect is highly relevant for the detailed analysis of the framework developed in the next chapters and fits in with the approach to fairness proposed in this book. In fact, effectiveness is essential to ensure that the intentions and underlying principles of a practice are respected. When the same instrument (or set of

132 EES Regulation, recital 15.
133 Screening Regulation, recital 2.
134 Screening Regulation, recitals 7, 6, and 3 respectively.
135 Screening Regulation, recitals 5, 25, and 26 respectively.
136 APR, recital 4.
137 APR, recitals 3 and 5.
138 APR, recitals 13–16.
139 APR, recital 38.
140 APR, recital 33.
141 APR, recital 58.

instruments) pursues different objectives, and in the absence of any information on implementation due to their recent nature, the details of the framework are key to understanding how those different objectives have been accommodated.

The RBP Regulation takes a similar tone to that of the Screening and AP Regulations. It establishes procedures applicable to TCNs whose application for international protection has been rejected in accordance with asylum border procedures, while also reiterating that member states are bound by international law instruments and provisions on fundamental rights (particularly as regards the best interest of the child).[142] The same holds true for the Crisis Regulation, which sets out procedures for the adoption of emergency measures in exceptional situations (including derogations from provisions of asylum law). As such, the Regulation upholds the respect for the fundamental rights of TCNs and the principles recognized by the Charter.[143] The extent to which this statement of intent is reflected in the provisions of the Regulation is discussed in the following chapters. Overall, this subsection has shown that the objectives pursued by instruments governing external border controls do not depart from those stated in the Treaties or in policy documents. Consistent with the integrated approach to migration proposed by the Commission, several measures straddle the scope of the different provisions of the TFEU mentioned above and cover or touch upon issues of asylum, irregular migration, and external border controls simultaneously. Given the diversity of goals pursued by these sources, a careful assessment of how different claims are accommodated is key to the overall assessment of constitutional compliance carried out in this book.

## 3.7 Conclusions

This chapter has introduced some key elements of the discussion on EU external border controls. The heterogeneity of objectives goes hand in hand with that of types of persons concerned: preventing irregular migration and cross-border crime, facilitating regular entry, and identifying and protecting the vulnerable correspond to stereotyped actors of cross-border movement. However, the heterogeneity is expressly recognized by the EU as an issue exclusively with regard to the authorities involved. As substantiated in the following chapters, this limited view can hinder constitutional compliance. When considered together, the different forms of heterogeneity inherent in the law of EU border controls require a multi-layered assessment of systemic appropriateness, based on a structured network of relevant principles. The principles mentioned by the policy documents and legal instruments covered in the previous pages reflect those discussed in Chapter 2. Sincere cooperation and effectiveness are always in the background. Solidarity, supported by mutual trust, has been increasingly fleshed out over the years, whereas fairness remains nebulous while constantly figuring in the relevant sources. This structured network of principles is supposed to hold together a complex landscape, fraught with tensions between different values and interests. The next three chapters explore to what extent that mission is realistic or even possible at all.

142 RBP Regulation, recitals 4–5.
143 Crisis Regulation, recital 8.

# 4
# Preparing Controls

## 4.1 Introduction

Border controls, defined in the Schengen Borders Code (SBC) as checks-plus-surveillance,[1] are the barycentre of the European Integrated Border Management system (EIBM). This system closely monitors every step of the migratory process into and across the EU, and is increasingly reliant on two tools across the board: the use of interoperable databases and partnership with third countries. Within the analytical framework proposed in this book, the previous chapter took the first step in the assessment of constitutional compliance. It considered the consistency of the objectives stated in the relevant instruments of secondary law with those set in the Treaties. While no major incompatibilities were found, the following caveats are in order. The Commission, in particular in its role of policy-setter, has emphasized the need to manage the heterogeneity of the responsible actors for the negative effects it could have on border security. The impact on individual rights possibly caused by the heterogeneity of objectives, and the stereotyped addressees of control that map onto those goals, has been overall neglected. These features have emerged on the back of a policy framework showing weak normative foundations. Mostly, values appear in generic references to the need to respect fundamental rights, or via appeals to a security-oriented solidarity among the bodies competent for border control related tasks. Since the multifaceted heterogeneity of EU border controls and the policy might have repercussions on the details of the applicable measures, we must analyse whether the rules are *appropriate* to achieve those objectives. We do so in the context of an analytical framework which regards the structured network of principles making the EU legal order work as a tool to ensure that the Union's objectives are pursued in line with its values.[2]

In this chapter, we address a type of heterogeneity that has not emerged from the previous discussion, but which constitutes an increasingly important trait of the law of EU border control: namely, the heterogeneity of its sources. The centre of gravity of this law lies in instruments adopted pursuant to Article 289 of the Treaty of the Functioning of the EU.[3] However, a deeper understanding thereof requires consideration of other sources, to which those measures often refer and which add (much) flesh onto the bones of the legislation. The wide range of documents spans from delegated and implementing acts to operational handbooks, through to status agreements (SAs) and working arrangements (WAs). Can such a system of sources appropriately

[1] Regulation (EU) 2016/399 establishing a Schengen Borders Code [2016] OJ L 77/1 (SBC), Article 2.
[2] Consolidated Version of the Treaty on EU (TEU) [2012] OJ C 326/13, Article 2.
[3] Consolidated Version of the Treaty on the Functioning of the EU (TFEU) [2012] OJ C 326/47.

*The Law of EU Border Controls*. Leandro Mancano, Oxford University Press. © Leandro Mancano 2025.
DOI: 10.1093/9780191966187.003.0005

achieve its objectives, despite its heterogeneity? To answer this question, the chapter focuses on: the different types of sources establishing the conditions for the exercise of controls, the actors tasked with their enactment or adoption, and the procedures for doing so.[4] We adopt a broad meaning of 'source' and 'law'. Sources are here regarded as 'facts that a law-applying institution is legally required to [use] in order to identify the law' and discharge its duties,[5] where failing to do so would attract legal consequences.[6] The focus is on 'codified sources'—that is, those which are conferred such status, expressly or by implication, by another source which mentions them.[7]

The chapter evaluates the choice of 'allocation of power' concerning the adoption of a certain source from the perspective of subsidiarity, solidarity, and fairness. The discussion related to this last principle considers the implications of the heterogeneity of sources, especially for legal certainty and transparency. Other principles mentioned in Chapter 2, such as effectiveness, sincere cooperation, and mutual trust, will also make their regular appearance in the discussion. They can help us understand the logic behind the system of sources (or part of it) and can guide the interpretation of unresolved questions arising from the legal analysis. Their concrete relevance will vary, depending on the specific question discussed in the chapter.

Consistent with the ratio, scope, and structure of this Part,[8] the discussed materials are organized into three main scenarios. Firstly, there are the sources concerning the establishment of conditions for control in the country of departure and mostly provisions on visas and travel authorizations and the role of the Immigration Liaison Officers (ILOs). Secondly, certain sources are relevant in situations after the person has left but before they have reached the EU external frontiers. This is the so-called 'in transit' scenario, which primarily addresses: surveillance of the EU external borders, particularly through Frontex-coordinated joint operations and the use of EUROSUR; agreements with neighbouring third countries enabling the joint performance of border control related tasks, or the exercise of those functions in those countries' territory. Lastly, there are the sources that find application at the EU outer frontiers. For each scenario, the chapter identifies three main types of sources. Firstly, there are EU institutional sources, which are attributable to one of the bodies listed under Article 13(1) TEU (but mostly the European Commission and the Council). Secondly, we find sources concerning matters left to the member states. The analysis links to the following structural aspects of the legal framework. On the one hand, the heterogeneity of the levels of governance is apparent from the member states' attempt to 'slot into' the gaps explicitly or implicitly left by EU law. On the other hand, the member state oriented decentralization inherent in the law creates a heterogeneity of decision-making centres. Thirdly, we discuss operational sources. These in particular constitute no homogeneous category, but share a number of traits. They are based

4 The next chapter assesses the substantive conditions necessary for the exercise of controls, as well as the conducts associated therewith.

5 G Pino, 'Sources of Law' in J Gardner, L Green, and B Leiter (eds), *Oxford Studies in Philosophy of Law*, vol 4 (Oxford University Press 2021) 67–68. This insightful chapter engages extensively with the classic literature on sources of law.

6 Pino, 'Sources of Law' 69.

7 Pino, 'Sources of Law' 71.

8 See section 3.6.1.

on sources belonging to either of the two previous categories. They are produced 'closer to the field' by an EU body (eg Frontex) or the member states. They tend to be non-structured and/or barely regulated in nature. In line with the objectives of this research, the focus is on sources deciding that border controls should be performed. Given the interdependence of these sources, and for the purposes of a better systemic understanding, this section also refers to sources having an *indirect* impact on the establishment of the conditions for exercising controls. Last but not least, the different scenarios cover certain laws and practices of two member states (Finland and Italy). We consider selected examples of such laws and practices from those countries to provide insight into their use of the discretion left by EU law in cases of particular relevance to the scope of this research.

## 4.2 Before Leaving

### 4.2.1 EU Institutional Sources

As mentioned, the three sections of this scenario revolve around two main groups of sources: those related to visas and travel authorizations and those concerning the ILOs. This section homes in on the former group. It reveals the EU increasing use of implementing and delegated acts to establish: whether the third-country national (TCN) will require such titles of entry and the person's eligibility for those purposes. This trend is linked to two main structural features of the law of EU external border controls: co-opting of third countries in cooperation on readmission of their own nationals; reliance on databases and statistics to decide on the TCN's worthiness to be granted a visa/travel authorization.

#### 4.2.1.1 Visa policy and lack of cooperation by third countries

The EU has exercised its competence to enact several measures in these areas.[9] The VISA Code[10] is the main instrument governing conditions and procedures for issuing the following types of visas:[11] uniform visas, allowing the TCN to travel across the Schengen area; visa with limited territorial validity (LTV), to enter only one or more Schengen states; and airport transit visas, to transit through a Schengen airport. The VISA Code delegates powers to the Commission vis-à-vis a range of different situations, such as: the adoption of the Common Consular Instructions (CCI), to ensure a harmonized application of the VISA Code;[12] a harmonized list of supporting documents for each jurisdiction, when this is necessary to take account of local circumstances.[13] Occasionally, throughout the law of border controls, implementing powers

[9] The competence is conferred by Article 77(2)(a) TFEU. Member states remain competent for long-term visas.

[10] Regulation (EC) No 810/2009 establishing a Community Code on Visas [2009] OJ L 243/1(VISA Code). 'Short-term' is normally understood as any (maximum) 90-day stay in a 180-day period.

[11] For the origins of the EU visa policy, see F Infantino, *Schengen Visa Implementation and Transnational Policymaking* (Springer 2019), part I in particular.

[12] VISA Code, recital 22 and Article 51.

[13] VISA Code, Article 14(5a). Importantly, this provision refers to Article 48 VISA Code, but this Code merely states that consulate and Union delegated acts shall cooperate to take account of local circumstances.

are conferred upon the Council.[14] The European Border and Coast Guard (EBCG) Regulation explains why that might be the case: namely, 'because of the potentially politically sensitive nature of the measures to be decided, which are likely to touch on national executive and enforcement powers'.[15] As seen through numerous examples in the book, the Council's role as guarantor of member states' prerogatives is a key element in the delicate balance of responsibilities in this policy area.

Beyond the general framework established by the VISA Code, the EU has also adopted a list of countries whose nationals either require, or are exempt from, the possession of a visa to enter the Schengen area.[16] For context, the decision about which country falls within which list shows the interplay of the EU visa policy and questions of external relations.[17] On the one hand, the listing of a country as visa-free often follows the signing of a visa waiver agreement between that country and the EU.[18] The Union can also conclude, as an intermediate step, visa facilitation agreements.[19] On the other hand, EU law provides for a visa suspension mechanism[20] and a visa reciprocity mechanism for countries which are/were visa-exempt.[21] Third-country co-operation, especially on readmission of their own nationals, has acquired a growing importance in the EU decision-making in this area. Readmissions are normally supported by standalone agreements,[22] or by broader negotiating frameworks linking co-operation on this specific issue to benefits and incentives in other fields.[23] In different ways, the VISA Code and the Visa Reciprocity Regulation tie the conditions to obtain a visa, or even the existence of a visa requirement itself, to the success rate of the third country in readmitting its own nationals (or the EU state's ability to return them). This approach has been heavily criticized as counterproductive[24] and defined as a form of

[14] In such cases, the Commission can at best recommend that the Council adopt the act—for example, to suspend the application of a number of provisions to certain categories of TCNs, when their country does not cooperate on readmission. VISA Code, Article 25a. The Commission is also empowered to adopt delegated acts in a number of cases, including as regards the revision of the amount of the visa fees set out in Article 16(9) VISA Code. See, for a dispute on the empowered institution to adopt an implementing decision pursuant to the Comitology Regulation, Case C-257/01, *Commission of the European Communities v Council of the European Union*, EU:C:2005:25.

[15] Regulation (EU) 2019/1896 on the European Border and Coast Guard [2019] OJ L 295/1 (EBCG Regulation), recital 57.

[16] Regulation (EU) 2018/1806 listing the third countries whose nationals must be in possession of visas when crossing the external borders and those whose nationals are exempt from that requirement [2018] OJ L 303/39 (Visa Reciprocity Regulation).

[17] P Koutrakos, 'Visa-Free Travel: Foreign Policy in the Making' (2009) 34 European Law Review 669.

[18] For a list of such agreements, https://eur-lex.europa.eu/EN/legal-content/summary/visa-waiver-agreements.html.

[19] See, for example, Agreement between the European Union and the Republic of Armenia on the facilitation of the issuance of visa [2013] OJ L 289/2.

[20] Visa suspension aims to address the abuse of visa-free travel, whereas visa reciprocity is a 'retaliation' against visa-exempt countries that have (re)introduced visa requirements for EU citizens.

[21] Visa Reciprocity Regulation, Articles 8 and 7, respectively.

[22] See, among several examples, Agreement between the European Community and the Islamic Republic of Pakistan on the readmission of persons residing without authorisation [2010] OJ L 287/52.

[23] For comments on some of such agreements, see J Silga, 'Assessing the Consistency of EU Development Co-operation with Readmission in the "EU-Philippines Agreement" Case: A Balancing Exercise' (2015) 40 European Law Review 439; S Wolff, 'The Politics of Negotiating EU Readmission Agreements: Insights from Morocco and Turkey' (2014) 16 European Journal of Migration and Law 69.

[24] M Czaika and M Hobolth, 'Do Restrictive Asylum and Visa Policies Increase Irregular Migration into Europe?' (2016) 17 European Union Politics 345.

collective punishment,[25] breaching the principle of non-discrimination on grounds of nationality.[26]

These themes emerge clearly from the framework on the (re)introduction of visa requirements provided in the Visa Reciprocity Regulation, which shows how the EU uses different sources to retaliate against non-cooperation by certain third countries. This decision will in turn have an impact on the exercise of controls towards those TCNs. Non-cooperation, broadly defined, can concern two different issues: the third country has (re)introduced a visa requirement for at least one member state; the third country has failed to cooperate on issues of readmission. For our purposes, the emphasis is on the type of sources whereby the EU response can take place. To recall, the Regulation

> determines the third countries whose nationals are subject to, or exempt from, the visa requirement, on the basis of a case-by-case assessment of a variety of criteria relating, inter alia, to illegal immigration, public policy and security, economic benefit, in particular in terms of tourism and foreign trade, and the Union's external relations with the relevant third countries, including, in particular, considerations of human rights and fundamental freedoms, as well as the implications of regional coherence and reciprocity.[27]

Generally, several aspects concerning the decision on visa exemptions/restrictions are delegated to either the Council or most commonly the Commission, empowering them to adopt delegated or implementing acts.[28] Firstly, as mentioned, there are cases where a country listed as 'visa-free' introduces a visa requirement for one or more member states. In such a scenario, the Commission may either adopt an implementing act to suspend the exemption for certain categories of nationals from that country, or explain to the assisting committee why it has decided not to do so.[29] The final decision, therefore, lies with the Commission and there is no obligation to act. Or else, such an obligation kicks in if the visa requirement imposed by the third country has persisted for at least two years. Only then, and through a delegated act, *must* the Commission suspend the visa exemption. The third country, however, would not be moved to the list of non-exempt states. Such a change requires a legislative amendment, which can be proposed by the Commission following a certain period of time after the suspension. Until this happens, the country will remain on the list of visa-free countries, with

[25] E Guild, 'Amending the Visa Code: Collective Punishment of Visa Nationals?' (EU Immigration and Asylum Law and Policy: Blog of the Odysseus Academic Network, 10 May 2019) accessed 21 December 2021.

[26] M. den Heijer, 'Visas and Non-discrimination' (2018) 20 European Journal of Migration and Law 470.

[27] Visa Reciprocity Regulation, Article 1.

[28] As for implementing acts specifically, the Commission is always assisted by a specific committee as provided for in Regulation (EU) No 182/2011 on the rules and general principles concerning mechanisms for control by Member States of the Commission's exercise of implementing powers [2011] OJ L 55/13 (Comitology Regulation).

[29] This step can be taken in the case where the requirement has not been lifted for some time. The introduction of such a visa requirement must initially be notified by the member states concerned to the European Parliament, the Council, and the Commission, and the information must be published in the Official Journal.

a footnote added next to its name on the list, explaining they are no longer (for the time being) visa-exempt. If the requirement is subsequently lifted by the Commission, this information must be published in the OJ, and the implementing or delegated act that had reimposed the visa requirement will expire seven days *after* publication. The fact that the Commission is the body in charge of adopting the act in question is not problematic from the perspective of the principle of subsidiarity. It is consistent with the overall set-up and the degree of centralization reached in this area. The same may not hold true for the person's accessibility to the relevant information, and more broadly for legal certainty, as doubts may arise about the applicable provision in the interim period.[30]

Secondly, we have situations where the EU might reintroduce visa requirements following the third country's non-cooperation on matters of irregular migration. The Commission *may* adopt an implementing act to suspend the visa waiver for nine months for certain categories of TCNs, when a member state has informed the Commission—an action that is not mandatory either—of for example a substantial increase in the rate of nationals from a third country who are refused entry, the number of asylum applications for which the recognition rate is low, or a decrease in cooperation on readmission by that third country.[31] The Commission must take account of information such as the 'overall question' of public policy and internal security, and can decide, on the basis of an open-ended list of criteria, for which categories of TCNs the visa waiver is suspended.[32] Such categories must be identified having regard to the circumstances which the act aims to remedy, and must be framed in a way that is 'broad enough' to achieve the objective while respecting the principle of proportionality. If the circumstances persist, the Commission *must* adopt a delegated act suspending the visa-free travel for all nationals of the country concerned.[33]

The Regulation identifies delegated acts as the source of law to be used for these purposes. This choice raises questions. Firstly, as stated above, the procedures governing the adoption of delegated acts are not exactly transparent. Their nature of 'executive acts' explains their use in the Visa Reciprocity Regulation. In both cases of retaliation by the EU discussed in this subsection, the obligation for the Commission to act requires a certain level of severity and passage of time, which is accompanied by the need for diplomatic work with the third country to solve the issue in a less confrontational manner. Given the absence of urgency, a legal act allowing for more open consideration of the evidence underpinning the decision would ensure stronger constitutional compliance. The argument makes even more sense when we look at the broader framework of the Commission's decision. Such retaliatory steps can be taken on extremely broad grounds, as apparent from expressions such as 'the overall

[30] Issues of solidarity possibly arising from the Commission's (in)action are considered in the next chapter. Here, we focus on the appropriateness of the source, rather than on the actual exercise of competence/power.

[31] Visa Reciprocity Regulation, Article 8(2).

[32] Visa Reciprocity Regulation, Article 8(6)(a), stipulates that the suspension shall apply to certain categories of nationals 'by reference to the relevant types of travel documents and, where appropriate, to additional criteria'.

[33] See the broader context of Articles 7 and 8, Visa Reciprocity Regulation.

situation of public policy', the possibility of relying on 'additional criteria',[34] and the fact that the Commission's action can (must) target 'broad enough' groups of people. The breadth of both the grounds justifying the delegated act *and* the range of addressees makes the use of delegated acts particularly problematic. As a note of nuance, we should observe that a visa requirement is not an automatic refusal to grant a travel authorization. The next subsection reveals that the growing reliance on delegated acts in this area can, in certain circumstances, lead to a negative decision on the TCN's application.

#### 4.2.1.2 Databases, visas, and travel authorizations

As further detailed below and in the next chapter, a fundamental aspect of a member state's examination of a visa application lies in the risk posed by the TCN in terms of public security, illegal immigration, or public health. The interoperability of databases changes the way such risks are determined. In this regard, the EU visa policy is primarily supported by the Visa Information System (VIS).[35] The Commission adopts implementing acts on a series of aspects concerning the functioning and use thereof.[36] Most notably, the Commission has adopted a delegated act to *further* define the risks of security, illegal immigration, or high epidemic associated with specific groups of visa holders, but the measure is not publicly accessible.[37] Such a risk-definition exercise is based on a series of criteria and information, which include: statistics generated by the Entry/Exit System (EES)[38] or the VIS indicating *abnormal* rates of overstaying, refusals of entry or of visa applications[39] for a specific group of visa holders; and statistics generated by the VIS and the EES, indicating correlations between information collected through the application form and overstaying by visa holders or refusals of entry.[40] The Commission must adopt an implementing act to specify the risks on which the risk indicators mentioned above are based.[41]

These provisions take the concerns about accessibility and transparency expressed above to a whole new level. The combination of the type of sources, the type of information underlying them, and their impact on the person concerned is particularly worrying. As before, the main questions of constitutional compliance concern not the principle of subsidiarity or solidarity, but the fair treatment of the persons concerned, understood as inter alia: non-arbitrary accommodation of claims emerging

[34] See J Mendes, 'Delegated and Implementing Rule Making: Proceduralisation and Constitutional Design' (2013) 19 European Law Journal 22; S Peers and M Costa, 'Accountability for Delegated and Implementing Acts after the Treaty of Lisbon' (2012) 18 European Law Journal 427.

[35] Regulation (EC) No 767/2008 on the Visa Information System (VIS) and the exchange of data between Member States on short-stay visas [2008] OJ L 218/60 (VIS Regulation), Article 6(3).

[36] See, for example, VIS Regulation, Article 6(5); Article 9h; Article 29(2)(a); and Article 45(3).

[37] See the European Data Protection Supervisor Formal comments on the draft Commission Delegated Decision on further defining the risks related to security or illegal immigration or a high epidemic risk of 14 October 2022.

[38] Regulation (EU) 2017/2226 establishing an Entry/Exit System (EES) to register entry and exit data and refusal of entry data of third-country nationals crossing the external borders of the Member States and determining the conditions for access to the EES for law enforcement purposes [2017] OJ 327/20 (EES Regulation).

[39] In this specific case, the refusal must be due to a security, illegal immigration, or high epidemic risk.

[40] VIS Regulation, Article 9j(2).

[41] VIS Regulation, Article 9j(3).

during the designing and implementation of a 'practice'; and compliance with the intentions of a practice and the mutually accepted principles behind it. While it is true that the main objective of the VIS is to contribute to the prevention of threats to the internal security of the member states,[42] the VISA Code—and the EU visa policy more broadly—aims to facilitate legitimate travel *and* tackle illegal immigration.[43] The VIS clearly supports the latter objective, including via its interoperability with the EES. Scholars have rightly pointed to the effects of interoperability for migration control, including from the perspective of the non-discrimination-data protection nexus,[44] as well as privacy.[45] More 'systemic' consequences should also be highlighted. The interplay of the VIS and the VISA Code creates, in itself, an imbalance in the pursuit of the different goals of the EU visa policy. The imbalance is compounded by the details of the framework. Firstly, there is the choice of the source of law itself: once again, we observe an inversely proportional relationship between the impact of such sources on the visa application and their level of transparency. The sources-underpinning-the-sources, to coin a phrase, are even more problematic. The statistics and correlation mentioned in the VIS Regulation are likely to undermine the individualized nature of visa decisions. As further detailed below, general information about the country, or the specific group to which the applicant belongs, already plays a role in the EU visa policy. These provisions, however, challenge to a much greater extent the spirit of the VISA Code: namely, that each application should be examined on the basis of its own merit. Two more points are worth making, which relate more specifically to the information substantiating the risk indicators. Firstly, the type of correlation between the information in the form and the rate of overstay could potentially cover everything and lead to an arbitrary result. If, by chance, the statistics showed a high rate of overstay by TCNs named Ajeje Brazorv, would that be sufficient ground to consider the application worth rejecting? Secondly, and relatedly, the weight each of those risks and risk indicators will carry in legal terms is unclear and the Commission will ultimately enjoy the broadest discretion in that regard.

The same legislative pattern emerges from the framework governing the other main set of travel authorizations to enter the EU: the European Travel Information and Authorisation System (ETIAS), which is supposed to start its operations in 2025.[46] The system has been established for non-EU nationals from visa-exempt countries, who will need a travel authorization, rather than a visa, to enter the EU. The visa and the travel authorization are, therefore, mutually exclusive. The procedure and the conditions for obtaining the latter are much simpler than the former, as they mostly aim to ascertain whether the presence of the person in the EU would pose a security, illegal immigration, or high epidemic risk.[47] Not dissimilar to the visa-related

[42] VIS Regulation, recital 5.
[43] VISA Code, recital 3.
[44] E Brouwer, 'Large-Scale Databases and Interoperability in Migration and Border Policies: The Non-Discriminatory Approach of Data Protection' (2020) 26 European Public Law 71.
[45] N Vavoula, 'Interoperability of EU Information Systems: The Deathblow to the Rights to Privacy and Personal Data Protection of Third-Country Nationals?' (2020) 26 European Public Law 131.
[46] Regulation (EU) 2018/1240 establishing a European Travel Information and Authorisation System (ETIAS) [2018] OJ L 236/1 (ETIAS Regulation).
[47] ETIAS Regulation, Article 1(1).

measures, the Commission is empowered to adopt implementing[48] and delegated[49] acts on a series of technical features.[50] In this case as well, delegated acts are the source of choice for regulating important aspects of the ETIAS. While the procedures around their adoption remain the same as other instruments, the difference lies in their use and the significance of the issues they are meant to govern.[51] Crucially, they will further define the risks related to security or illegal immigration or a high epidemic risk. Similarly to the VIS, the delegated act must be based on statistics generated by the EES or ETIAS, or information provided by member states, related to inter alia: security, epidemic, illegal immigration risk for a specific group of travellers; specific security risk or threats identified by a member state; and correlations between information collected through the application form and overstaying by travellers or refusals of entry.[52] The Commission has also adopted an implementing act to 'specify the risks ... on which the specific risks indicators ... shall be based'.[53] Different from the VIS Regulation, however, the risk indicators established by the ETIAS Central Unit consist of a combination of data, including a series of information such as age, sex, nationality, education, and occupation.[54] Therefore, while the ETIAS Regulation makes explicit reference to the information on which the risk indicators must be based, the VIS indicates no such criteria. This leaves the latter exposed to the risk of even more arbitrary decisions.[55]

The EU Court of Justice (ECJ or the Court) has, on previous occasions, struck down an implementing decision concerning border controls because it supplemented or changed essential elements of the main act.[56] While such a main act stated the objectives of the provision allowing delegation (preventing unauthorized border crossings, countering cross-border criminality), it offered no details on the possible measures that border guards could take in the fulfilment of their duties.[57] The implementing

[48] For example, on the operation of the website and the app. ETIAS Regulation, Article 16(10); or for the purposes of adopting a standard form for refusal, annulment or revocation of a travel authorization. See ETIAS Regulation, Article 38(3).

[49] See, for example, ETIAS Regulation, Article 18(4).

[50] As those acts must be adopted under the examination procedure, in case of no opinion provided by the committee on the proposed implementing act, the act must not be implemented. ETIAS Regulation, Article 90(2). While this provision mirrors the VISA Code, no such clause is provided in the Visa Reciprocity Regulation.

[51] The delegation can be revoked by the European Parliament or the Council at any time, and those institutions must be notified of a delegated act as soon as adopted. Acts enter into force if no objection has been expressed by either institution within two months or if they agree expressly before then.

[52] ETIAS Regulation, Article 33(2).

[53] Commission Implementing Decision on specifying risks related to security, illegal immigration or high epidemic risk C(2021) 4980 final; Commission Delegated Decision on further defining security, illegal immigration or high epidemic risks C(2021) 4981 final.

[54] ETIAS Regulation, Article 33(4).

[55] For insightful analysis of the challenges posed by the ETIAS to individual rights, see inter alia: A Eklund, 'Rule of Law Challenges of "Algorithmic Discretion" Automation in EU Border Control: A Case Study of ETIAS Through the Lens of Legality' (2023) 25 European Journal of Migration and Law 249; L Gugliotta and A Elbi, 'Will AI "Subtly" Take Over Decision-Making in the EU Migration Context? Warnings and Lessons from ETIAS and VIS' (2024) European Papers 1018.

[56] Case C-355/10, *European Parliament v Council*, EU:C:2012:516. For a comment, see M Chamon, 'How the Concept of Essential Elements of a Legislative Act Continues to Elude the Court: Parliament v. Council' (2013) 50 Common Market Law Review 849.

[57] Case C-355/10, *European Parliament v Council*, para 76.

act, for its part, conferred powers of public authority on border guards such as stopping apprehended persons, seizing vessels, and conducting persons apprehended to a specific location. Two core principles led the Court to its finding of illegality: aspects which presuppose political choices fall within the responsibility of the legislature and cannot be delegated;[58] the possible interference with fundamental rights caused by the exercise of those powers could be such as to require the involvement of the EU legislature.[59] The legal background in the case under consideration, and the ETIAS/VIS frameworks, are objectively different. The principles established by the Court, however, might still prove relevant. While there is no right to be granted a visa, the person is certainly entitled to a fair processing of their application in line with the principle of non-discrimination, and the delegated and implementing acts might interfere with those rights to the extent that they would warrant a democratically legitimated decision.

### 4.2.2 Delegation to Member States

We have observed a degree of centralization of decision-making towards the Commission and the latter's reliance on different sources in the following areas: the application of visa requirements to certain third countries; and the establishment of criteria that might impact the decision on applications for travel authorizations. It is not only the heterogeneity of sources itself—and especially delegated acts—that might negatively impact the fair treatment of applicants, but also the wider legal framework in which the use of such sources occurs. In this section, we move to another structural feature of the legal framework, where the heterogeneity of sources is the result of the heterogeneity of decision-making centres. Visas and travel authorizations show that member states remain at the centre of the implementation process of EU border controls, as each of them is responsible for the processing of the application. While member states enjoy a certain discretion in this regard, EU law by definition strives for uniformity. How should member states stay 'united in diversity', as far as sources of controls 'before leaving' are concerned? Primarily, through three types of 'duties' of mutual cooperation: cooperation *stricto sensu*, consultation, and encouragement. As a preliminary observation, the decentralization of decision-making and the heterogeneity it creates are only the first example of a delicate equilibrium which characterizes the law of EU border controls. Harmonization in an area of shared competence which also corresponds to an essential state function is achieved by leaving most tasks to the member states. While this makes sense from the perspective of subsidiarity, we must consider the impact of such a set-up on interstate cooperation and the persons concerned.

Broadly, member states' consulates and delegations (ie those in charge of deciding on visa applications) must cooperate with each other to ensure the harmonized application of the common visa policy while taking into account local circumstances. More specifically, member states must exchange information in a number of areas,

[58] Case C-355/10, *European Parliament v Council*, paras 64–65.
[59] Case C-355/10, *European Parliament v Council*, para 77.

such as the assessment of migratory and security risks concerning document fraud or irregular immigration routes.[60] Such duties are not accompanied by prescribed forms or procedures,[61] and they constitute obligations of means rather than of result. Intelligence-gathering and sharing is an important source of border controls, and starts in the country of departure. Such cooperation has no defined structure and seems quite opaque, but is key to decisions about visa applications. Two main issues of constitutional compliance might arise in practice. To start, there is the possible lack of cooperation from a member state. The principle of solidarity entails, inter alia, a general obligation for both the EU and the member states, in their respective areas of competence, to endeavour to avoid 'measures liable to affect the interests of the European Union and the other member states . . . and to do so in order to take account of their interdependence and de facto solidarity' (emphasis added).[62] This procedural obligation could support the assessment of the member state's conduct: there might be circumstances where the lack of cooperation would be justified. A member state might worry that sharing intelligence with the requesting member state might lead to a violation of the fundamental rights of the person concerned. The concerns might relate, for example, to the type of information or the specific groups of persons concerned, and be based on updated, objective, specific, and reliable information on the requesting state's laws or practices. Admittedly, it seems difficult to devise a test applicable by the requesting state by dealing in hypotheticals. It is even less likely that such circumstances would be brought to the attention of the Court of Justice, given their informal nature. Nonetheless, it is important to stress the relevance of the interaction—and possibly tension—between different principles of EU law in this area, and points to the types of circumstances that should be taken into account by the member states concerned.

Secondly, there are duties of consultation. On the grounds of a threat to public policy, internal security, international relations, or public health, a member state may require other member states to consult with it during the examination of applications submitted by nationals of specific third countries, or by specific categories of such nationals. This information must be communicated in the jurisdiction concerned.[63] Similarly, a member state may require to be informed when a visa has been issued by another member state to nationals of specific third countries or to specific categories of such nationals.[64] While these provisions do not empower a member state to decide how another member state should assess a visa application, they do provide the legal basis for a legal obligation of information and consultation. The dynamic painted by the VISA Code is quite peculiar here. Beyond the absence of any indication on the form which the requirement of information/consultation should take, two main questions arise. Firstly, the Code allows one member state to introduce a requirement of consultation or information on another member state. If that, supposedly, were to

[60] VISA Code, Article 48.

[61] Cooperation duties exist also between the Commission and the member states, in particular as regards the preparation of the list of supporting documents required of the applicant. VISA Code, Article 48(1a)(a).

[62] Case T-883/16, *Republic of Poland v European Commission*, EU:T:2019:567, paras 72–73.

[63] This is, presumably, the jurisdiction of the relevant third country.

[64] In both cases, the introduction of such a requirement must be communicated to the Commission, which must inform the member states. VISA Code, Article 31.

materialize into a legal provision under the law of the requiring member state, it is not clear how that unilateral action would bind the other member states concerned. A question of substance can also arise, and concerns the role of the principle of solidarity as described above. Two main situations can be envisaged here: the member state responsible for the visa application might decide against the other state's opinion, having either taken that opinion into account, or not. The latter situation seems more difficult to square with solidarity obligations—just as the failure to inform the state without legitimate justification would be. Were the opinion to be taken into account, however, a breach of the principle of solidarity would be much harder to find. Consistent with the test for the solidarity review set out in this book, the finding of a violation would require that the deciding state had overlooked the likely occurrence of seriously adverse consequences as a result of their decision (see Figure 2.1.).

Thirdly, the legal framework on visas can address the member states in the form of an operational encouragement. If a member state has no consulate in a third country, it shall *endeavour to* conclude representation arrangements with a member state that does so.[65] As we will see in the next two chapters, the representation arrangements could entail a shift in responsibility for the examination of the application itself. If a member state is neither present nor represented in the third country where the applicant is to lodge the application, it shall *endeavour* to cooperate with an external service provider in that third country, in compliance with public procurement and competition rules.[66] The decision about the involvement of the external service provider is also left to the member states, with few constraints on form or procedures.[67] However, the VISA Code does require that cooperation be established in a legal instrument containing a series of mandatory provisions.[68] Among those, there is the indication of the tasks of the provider, or the requirement that its staff respect the human dignity of the applicants without discriminating against them on grounds of sex, racial or ethnic origin, religion or belief, disability, age, or sexual orientation.[69] While the list of the provider's tasks that must be referred to in the legal instrument is left open, the same may not hold true for the grounds of prohibited forms of discrimination. Although this seems particularly problematic, the wider requirement of respect for the applicant's dignity and integrity *should* guarantee the necessary legal basis for protection. Member states may also cooperate with commercial intermediaries for the lodging of applications, except for the collection of biometric identifiers, and on the basis of accreditation granted by the member state.[70] Member states' cooperation with commercial intermediaries knows, even more than that with external service providers, almost no constraints on form or procedures. As with the previous types of duties, issues of form and substance can arise. A look at a member state's practice in this area shows how inaccessible such agreements can be. For example, Finland is represented[71] and

[65] VISA Code, Article 8.

[66] VISA Code, Article 8(10).

[67] For an early analysis of the EU strategy of outsourcing, see G Beaudu, 'L'externalisation dans le domaine des visas Schengen (2009) 74 Cultures et Conflits 111.

[68] VISA Code, Article 43.

[69] VISA Code, Annex X.

[70] VISA Code, Article 45.

[71] See https://um.fi/finland-represents-another-schengen-member-state.

represents[72] different member states as regards Schengen visa applications, but the texts thereof are generally not available. The lack of accessibility has no clear justification, and prevents any scrutiny as to the compliance of such agreements with the requirements established in EU law. Secondly, and relatedly, the member states' obligation to *closely* monitor the activities of the service providers should not be underestimated. Importantly, the Commission mentioned precisely the lack of member states' monitoring as a shortcoming in the implementation of the legal framework,[73] and named Austria's imposition of penalties for the non-compliant providers among the best practices to be followed in this respect.[74] It is argued that an excessively lax approach by member states on this issue might affect the fair treatment of the persons concerned, and in turn undermine the effective achievement of the objectives of the legal framework in this specific aspect.

#### 4.2.2.1 Restrictions on the issuing of tourist visas to Russian citizens: The example of Finland

Having looked at the broader framework of EU law on tasks left to member states, it is now worth looking more closely at the example of a member state's practice in this area to uncover some of the challenges that might arise from the exercise of discretion at national level. Like other states on the EU eastern flank,[75] Finland has tightened control, especially over tourist visas issued to Russian citizens following the start of the war with Ukraine.[76] While no legislative amendment was introduced, the national government adopted a so-called decision-in-principle to guide national authorities in their consideration of whether to issue a visa and the conditions for authorizing entry. Therefore, as further explained below, the decision also covers the assessment carried out by the border guards at the external borders. On the one hand, Finland's policy refers to halting the travel of Russian citizens to Finland for non-essential reasons 'altogether'. In doing so, the policy relies on the grounds for refusing a visa stated in the VISA Code—and specifically the threat to public policy, security, or international relations.[77] On the other hand, the decision exempts certain groups from the scope of those visa restrictions.[78] More broadly, and beyond the enumerated exemptions, the new policy may not be used to prevent travel that is necessary for humanitarian reasons, national interest, or international obligations. Furthermore, it does not affect the right to apply for international protection.[79]

[72] See https://um.fi/finland-is-represented-by-another-schengen-member-state.

[73] State of Schengen Report 2023, Annex 1 3.

[74] State of Schengen Report 2023, Annex 2 6.

[75] See in particular the measures taken by Poland and the Baltic states: https://www.lemonde.fr/en/international/article/2022/09/09/poland-baltic-states-join-european-visa-restrictions-for-russians_5996360_4.html.

[76] These are political statements that give the government instructions and guidelines on how to prepare matters. They are by nature preparatory decisions. Final decisions are taken by the authority dealing with and preparing the matter. Decisions of principle do not have direct legal effects. They are binding to the government that has approved one. See Government Decision in Principle UM/2022/199 and Press Release by the Ministry for Foreign Affairs 29 September 2022.

[77] Visa Code, Article 32(1).

[78] See the list of groups exempts from the restrictions.

[79] Government Decision in Principle UM/2022/199 3.

The restrictions on visa-issuing have been strongly criticized by scholars, particularly because of their alleged 'blanket ban' nature and breach of the principle that each application should be assessed on a case-by-case basis.[80] Admittedly, the approach entails that, unless a person falls under one of the exceptions, a visa application from a Russian citizen will be rejected. This would turn the logic of the VISA Code on its head, since a travel authorization should in principle be issued unless one of the grounds for refusal applies. Is that sufficient to claim that, in such circumstances, a member state has misused its discretion and the policy is incompatible with EU law? The answer is in the negative. To recall, the case under consideration concerns only a change in approach to the treatment of visa applications from a third country which is *already* subject to visa requirements. The member state's new policy entails no change of the third country's 'status' in that regard, which would indeed raise issues of compliance with EU law.[81] Furthermore, the spirit of the Finnish government's decision is not dissimilar to the communication, issued around the same time by the European Commission, providing common guidelines on visa issuance to Russian applicants.[82] The political and legal convergence of the initiatives taken at national and EU levels has prevented the emergence of tensions in this regard. This convergence should not be seen as accidental. To the contrary, it is the consequence of the content of the decision-in-principle itself. This is apparent from the three main features thereof. Firstly, the principle of individual assessment has not been abandoned by the government policy. In fact, it is expressly referred to in it.[83] Secondly, the decision reiterates the commitment to the member state's obligations under international law, and specifically the right to apply for international protection. Thirdly, the list of exemptions is, in and of itself, a sign that we are not dealing with a blanket ban. As set out in the Introduction, the interplay of the sovereign right to decide on entry and the individual rights constraining the former provides a useful angle of analysis: not only to assess the specific example of Finland, but also to understand more broadly the limits of member states' action in this area. When it comes to visa issuing specifically, EU law establishes specific obligations on examining each application on its own merit and complying with international law. A policy such as that adopted by Finland reconciles these aspects—at least in principle. It is perfectly possible that a visa application

[80] S Ganty, D Kochenov, and S Roy, 'Unlawful Nationality-Based Bans from the Schengen Zone: Poland, Finland, and the Baltic States against Russian Citizens and EU Law' (2023) 48 Yale Journal of International Law 1.

[81] This would be a decision for the European Commission. See Visa Reciprocity Regulation, Articles 7 and 8.

[82] Communication from the Commission Providing guidelines on general visa issuance in relation to Russian applicants following Council Decision (EU) 2022/1500 of 9 September 2022 on the suspension in whole of the application of the Agreement between the European Community and the Russian Federation on the facilitation of the issuance of visas to the citizens of the European Union and the Russian Federation, C(2022) 6596 final.

[83] Certain groups can enter Finland, and in particular: persons travelling with residence permits issued by Finland, a member state of the European Union, and a country belonging to the European Economic Area or Switzerland, and with national long-stay visas (D visas) of Schengen countries. While the government refers to entry rather than granting a visa, it can be inferred from the government policy that both aspects cover those categories: 'By decision-in-principle, the Government will adopt guidelines that will be taken into account when assessing the conditions for entry of Russian citizens, issuing visas and assessing the conditions for the validity of visas'.

(eg for tourism purposes) will be individually examined *and* rejected because—in the absence of a cogent reason—its acceptance would endanger Finland's international relations. Given the wide discretion states have in this domain, and as long as they act within the framework of principles and procedures established by law, it seems also unlikely that a judicial challenge would be successful.[84] The conclusion would be different in the case of a true blanket ban, doing away with the need for individual assessment required by secondary EU law or having the effect, in practice, of overriding the absolute obligation of non-refoulement: in other words, situations that would be difficult to square with the limits on the sovereign right to decide on who can access a polity's territory.

This being said, initiatives of the kind discussed here are not risk-free. Such risks relate particularly to the system of task allocation set up by the legal framework. As mentioned, the decision-in-principle also covers the border guards' assessment at the external border. In the case of a border guard's decision to refuse entry during the period of validity of the restriction, the visa will be revoked (in principle). If the visa was issued by a Schengen state other than Finland, the border guard will consider the revocation on a case-by-case basis and will inform the authorities of the issuing state of the possible revocation of the visa. This is, once again, not inconsistent with the VISA Code, to the extent that the Code authorizes a member state to revoke a visa issued by another member state, and the person would still have a right of appeal against the decision.[85] The member state which had issued the visa in the first place might have even adopted a policy similar to Finland's, but it might have come to a different conclusion in the specific circumstances of the case. To reiterate, the (possibility of) tensions are first and foremost the product of the legal set-up, but they are compounded by individual states' initiatives of the kind discussed here. In such cases, it is argued that exercising discretion in line with EU law would require compliance with the principle of solidarity as discussed earlier in this section.

### 4.2.3 Operational Sources

The range of operational sources concerning the 'before leaving' scenario is not as extensive as other areas, but is still worth discussing. As regards the visa policy, operational instructions for the application of the VISA Code are further specified in two handbooks. These focus on the processing of visa applications and the modification of issued visas,[86] as well as the administrative management of visa processing and local Schengen cooperation.[87] Such sources contain information and guidance concerning the cases in which applications should be treated as inadmissible, how to assess the

[84] We refer here to the challenge against the visa decision specifically, rather than the policy more broadly.

[85] VISA Code, Article 34(2).

[86] Commission Implementing Decision amending Decision C(2010) 1620 final as regards the replacement of the Handbook for the processing of visa applications and the modification of issued visas (Visa Code Handbook I) and its ANNEX C(2020) 395 final.

[87] Commission Implementing Decision establishing the Handbook for the administrative management of visa processing and local Schengen cooperation (Visa Code Handbook II) and repealing Commission Decision C(2010) 3667 and its ANNEX C(2020) 1764 final.

security and health risk, or the visa applied for at the external borders.[88] Broadly, the Common Consular Instructions (CCI) encourage diplomatic missions and consular posts to harmonize working practices, procedures and criteria for monitoring the proper functioning of private administrative agencies.[89] Consular cooperation, more specifically, can be resorted to for different objectives. The CCI refers to the possibility of 'on the spot consular cooperation' to assess the existence of security or illegal immigration risks, which could in turn be decisive to the outcome of a visa application. Clearly, this cooperation is conceived of as informal and non-structured.[90] Consular cooperation—through exchange of information in particular—can also be used to 'facilitate the assessment of the applicant's good faith', in accordance with national legislation and on the basis of arrangements concluded at a local level.[91] Exchange of information can home in on cooperation with private agencies as well.[92] These examples confirm a key feature which characterizes the sources applicable 'before leaving': their informal, non-structured, or otherwise non-transparent nature, which makes them very difficult to challenge or question.

Opacity and intelligence gathering figure in the other relevant example of operational sources 'before leaving': namely, those related to the Immigration Liaison Officers Network (ILON).[93] The ILON Regulation describes an 'immigration liaison officer' as an officer designated and deployed abroad, by the competent authorities of a member State, or by the Commission or by a Union agency, in accordance with the respective legal basis, to deal with immigration-related issues.[94] Their responsibilities are determined by the deploying authorities, although the Regulation does not specify what form this allocation should take.[95] Information about deployment—be it by the member state or a Union body—must be communicated to the ILON Steering Board and made available through a secure platform set up and managed by the Commission. Therefore, such information is not accessible.[96] The ILON Steering Board carries out a number of vaguely defined tasks on the basis of 'a comprehensive situational picture and on analyses provided by the relevant Union agencies', and 'considering the Union's priorities on immigration'. Among these, the Board establishes priorities and plans activities, and adopts a biannual report.[97] Considering the operational needs of the Union, the Steering Board should also agree on ad hoc actions.[98] While the Regulation is clear that no strictly confidential information related to law enforcement should be exchanged on the platform, the type of information that can be uploaded is

[88] On the role for solidarity in local Schengen cooperation, see A Meloni, 'EU Visa Policy: What Kind of Solidarity?' (2017) 24 Maastricht Journal of European and Comparative Law 660 onwards.
[89] Common Consular Instructions VIII.5.2.
[90] Common Consular Instructions 27.
[91] Common Consular Instructions 28.
[92] Common Consular Instructions 30.
[93] Regulation (EU) 2019/1240 on the creation of a European network of immigration liaison officers [2019] OJ L 198/88 (ILON Regulation).
[94] ILON Regulation, Article 2.
[95] For analysis of the previous version of the Regulation, see F Mc Namara, 'Member State Responsibility for Migration Control Within Third States: Externalisation Revisited' (2013) 15 European Journal of Migration and Law 319
[96] ILON Regulation, Article 4(2).
[97] ILON Regulation, Article 9.
[98] ILON Regulation, Article 8.

defined generically: other than a list of ILOs deployed, there is a reference to 'relevant' documents.[99] The lack of detail is even more striking when the Commission itself acknowledged that one of the purposes of ILOs concerns the prevention of irregular migration and cross-border crimes[100]—presumably, as Moreno-Lax argued, through intelligence-gathering.[101]

### 4.2.4 Interim Conclusions

Measures applicable before leaving, and particularly the visa policy and the ETIAS, aim to strike a balance between facilitation of legitimate travel and security concerns. The analysis of the heterogeneous system of sources in this area has raised doubts about the appropriateness of that system to achieving those objectives. In terms of task allocation, the instruments attempt to balance centralization of certain decisions towards the Commission and empower the member states to implement most aspects of the legal framework. The set-up raises no serious questions in terms of subsidiarity. The heterogeneity of decision-making centres, however, might create tensions between different member states. While further centralization is not necessarily the answer, it is argued that a rigorous application of the principle of solidarity might be conducive to the sound management of that heterogeneity. The heterogeneity of sources can seriously affect the fair treatment of the persons concerned too. On a systemic level, we notice a concerning combination of non-transparent sources and/or informal cooperation, use of correlations and statistics drawn from interoperable databases, and vague grounds possibly leading to restrictions on entry. This, in itself, challenges the idea of an individualized decision on applications for visa or travel authorization. When combined with the very strong emphasis placed by the plethora of different measures and frameworks on the prevention of irregular migration, the facilitation of regular entry might be easily undermined and so would the effectiveness of the legal framework.

## 4.3 In Transit

### 4.3.1 EU Institutional Sources

EU law governs different situations of border controls in 'transit'—that is, between the country of origin and the arrival at the Union's outer frontiers. Discussing them all

[99] ILON Regulation, Article 9(2)(a).

[100] See https://home-affairs.ec.europa.eu/policies/migration-and-asylum/irregular-migration-and-return/migrant-smuggling_ens.

[101] V Moreno Lax, *Accessing Asylum in Europe: Extraterritorial Border Controls and Refugee Rights under EU Law* (Oxford University Press 2017), ch 5 in particular. On the under-researched role of ILOs from a British perspective, see N Ostrand, 'Overseas Immigration Liaison Officers: "Knowledge Brokers" and Transnational Spaces of Mid-Level Negotiations Shaping Extraterritorial Migration Control Practices' (2022) 10 Migration Studies 41; N Ostrand and P Statham, 'Liaison Officers as Influential "Immigration Risk" Brokers in Visa Policy Implementation: Intermediaries across Institutional and National Borders' (2022) 48 Journal of Ethnic and Migration Studies 3985.

would fall outside the remit of this research, which assesses the impact of the heterogeneity of EU border controls on its constitutional compliance, and revolves around conditions for controls and on the persons concerned. Two main areas are considered in this scenario: external border surveillance and arrangements with neighbouring third countries. These areas overlap in part, to the extent that partnership with a neighbouring third country can *also* focus on surveillance. As with 'before leaving' situations, two transversal themes will emerge from the analysis of the framework: the reliance on information systems (and technology more broadly),[102] and the co-opting of third countries in the control of the EU external borders.[103] As with the previous scenario, we can distinguish between EU 'institutional',[104] member state-driven, and operational sources. When assessing the appropriateness of the system of sources, we should not conflate two different, if related, levels of analysis. On the one hand, we assess the appropriateness of the overall legal framework for achieving the threefold objectives of external border controls stated in the policy and the legislation: namely, facilitating regular entry, preventing illegal migration and cross-border crime, and identifying vulnerable persons. On the other hand, we consider the consistency of the rules of a measure with its objectives more specifically.

To begin with the external border surveillance, this covers a wide range of actions, through several means and by the involvement of a multitude of actors.[105] Broadly, it mostly materializes into information exchange and operational cooperation. As for the EU institutional sources, the starting point is the EBCG Regulation and the Regulation on Surveillance of the External Sea Border Regulation (SESB Regulation).[106] Before we move on to a closer inspection of the heterogeneity of sources in this area, we must address a definitional issue. The SBC describes border surveillance as the surveillance of, and between, border crossing points. It provides no definition, however, of what surveillance itself is. The EBCG Regulation does so, at least in part, by mentioning the 'monitoring, detection, identification, tracking, prevention and interception of unauthorised border crossings'.[107] This is a remarkably broad definition of surveillance. Not only is the list of actions not exhaustive, but it also encompasses active and intrusive tasks such as interception. While it is inevitable that activities of surveillance

[102] The increase of technology in external border surveillance has been well-documented. See, inter alia, P Loukinas, 'Drones for Border Surveillance: Multipurpose Use, Uncertainty and Challenges at EU Borders' (2022) 27 Geopolitics 89; MG Jumbert, 'Control or Rescue at Sea? Aims and Limits of Border Surveillance Technologies in the Mediterranean Sea' (2018) 42 Disasters 674; GJ Huber, *Power, Policies, and Algorithms: Technologies of Surveillance in the European Border Surveillance Regime* (KIT 2022).

[103] As shown below, these arrangements and agreements can also entail operations in third countries and include the prevention of irregular departures among their objectives—be that expressly stated or not. These sources could, arguably, be placed under the 'before leaving' umbrella as well. Some of the countries with which the EU or the member states cooperate, however, are at least *also*—if not primarily—countries of transit.

[104] Namely, those enacted on the basis of direct involvement of an EU institution and primarily the Commission and the Council.

[105] See, for a non-exhaustive list of examples, the EUROSUR Handbook 19. To give an idea, there are four different systems for ship reporting only.

[106] Regulation (EU) No 656/2014 establishing rules for the surveillance of the external sea borders in the context of operational cooperation coordinated by the European Agency for the Management of Operational Cooperation at the External Borders of the Member States of the European Union [2014] OJ L 189/93 (SESB Regulation).

[107] EBCG Regulation, Article 19(1).

(such as monitoring and tracking) will be used for the purposes of interception, conflating the two is conceptually adventurous.

Against this background, the heterogeneity of sources is apparent from both areas of surveillance activities. As regards the exchange of information, EUROSUR (the EU system of external border surveillance) takes centre stage. EUROSUR is an integrated framework for the exchange of information and operational cooperation in border controls, with a view to improving the member states' and the EU situational awareness and reaction capability.[108] One of the fundamental functions of EUROSUR, as the name suggests, is the surveillance of the EU external borders. The member states and Frontex are under an obligation to use EUROSUR, *taking into account existing information exchange and cooperation mechanisms.* This duty expresses well the heterogeneity of the sources of EU external border controls. The obligation to take into account vaguely defined systems and mechanisms is not a point that favours legal certainty. While it is possible that working arrangements with certain EU bodies discussed below could slightly substantiate this provision, its scope remains particularly nebulous, and so are its implications.

The SESB Regulation is *the* EU institutional source governing operational activities, by establishing a framework for sea border surveillance. The Regulation mentions a series of other relevant sources, which show the relevance of international law in this scenario. Such references concern the definition of 'contiguous zone',[109] and the need for the EU and the member states to comply with the Protocol Against the Smuggling of Migrants. External border surveillance, broadly understood, is also characterized by the *absence* of (certain) sources of EU law. This is particularly the case for search and rescue (SAR), which is governed by the SESB Regulation only within the limits of its scope (ie Frontex-coordinated operation). In this context, we must distinguish between different issues. On a more general level, there is the question of whether the EU would be competent to adopt common rules in this area beyond what it has already done. A more specific question concerns the criminalization of humanitarian assistance and SAR activities performed by private vessels. The intersection between border surveillance, the fight against smuggling and trafficking, and the protection of vulnerable groups has proved particularly delicate. This is especially so in relation to the policies of some member states' governments, like Italy, which have attempted to deter non-governmental organizations (NGOs) from taking life-saving actions at sea. The Commission has adopted two documents dealing with these issues in whole or in part: a recommendation on cooperation among member states concerning operations carried out by vessels owned or operated by private entities for the purpose of SAR activities;[110] and a communication on the implementation of EU rules on the

[108] EBCG Regulation, Article 18.

[109] This is a zone contiguous to a State's territorial sea, where the State may exercise the control necessary to, inter alia, prevent infringement of its immigration laws and may not extend beyond 24 nautical miles from the baselines from which the breadth of the territorial sea is measured. United Nations Convention on the Law of the Sea, Article 33.

[110] Commission Recommendation (EU) 2020/1365 on cooperation among Member States concerning operations carried out by vessels owned or operated by private entities for the purpose of search and rescue activities [2020] OJ L 317/23. The choice of an instrument of soft law in this area is not unique to the EU legislature, but can be seen at the level of certain member states. For example, Italy has adopted a Code of Conduct for NGOs engaging in SAR. For a critical discussion, see L Masera, 'Il d.l. Piantedosi sulle operazioni di soccorso in mare: l'ennesimo tentativo di impedire ciò che il diritto internazionale

definition and prevention of the facilitation of unauthorized entry, transit, and residence.[111] We can observe a similarity between the heterogeneous use of sources in 'before leaving' and 'in transit' scenarios. In both cases, the heterogeneity weakens the pursuit of objectives favourable to the persons concerned for the benefit of more restrictive goals.

Despite or perhaps *because of* these initiatives, the question remains as to whether the EU could legislate on SAR beyond Frontex-coordinated operations. Would the EU legislature be the *appropriate* locus of political and legal authority? As known, member states are very reluctant to see any binding rules adopted at EU level in this area, as they consider SAR issues as falling outwith the scope of the Union's legislative competence.[112] Two observations must be made in this regard. Firstly, it is argued that no provision in the Treaties expressly prevents the Union from action in this area. Invoking Articles 4(2) TEU or 72 TFEU *sic et simpliciter* might be unsuccessful, since the impact on the functions and responsibilities protected by those provisions would concretely depend on the specifics of the common rules adopted in this area. Secondly, the effectiveness-oriented side of solidarity might justify the Union's legislation in terms of subsidiarity.[113] Granted, we cannot presume that the adoption of binding rules would ensure the better achievement of the EU objective, which includes saving lives at sea and identification of vulnerable people. The interaction between member states, and between member states and EU bodies in this area, can have a direct impact on the protection of the persons concerned. A more structured mechanism of cooperation and sharing of responsibilities between states, and between member states and EU bodies, could facilitate the achievement of those objectives. Furthermore, in creating a system for sharing responsibilities (including in the phase of disembarkation post-SAR), it could alleviate the pressure on over-burdened states, mitigate the risk of their systems becoming dysfunctional, and lead to a more accurate identification of the persons concerned and their referral to the appropriate procedures. Therefore, solidarity-based legislation in this area would increase protection of the persons concerned while also enhancing border security through more effective contrast to irregular migration and cross-border crime.

Turning to partnership with neighbouring countries in transit *as relevant to the scope of this research*,[114] institutional sources mostly relate to operational activities

impone e il problema della depenalizzazione come fuga dalla giurisdizione' (2023) 2 Sistema Penale 83 onwards.

[111] Communication from the Commission Guidance on the implementation of EU rules on definition and prevention of the facilitation of unauthorized entry, transit, and residence [2020] OJ C 323/01. The EU and especially the member states' approach is being tested—at least to an extent—before the Court of Justice, thanks to a reference from the Bologna Tribunal. Case C-460/23, *Kinshasa*. On this, and the proposal for the reform of the 'facilitators package' in November 2023 more broadly, see V Mitsilegas, 'Reforming the EU "Facilitators' Package"', School of Law and Social Justice, University of Liverpool.

[112] See European Parliament Briefing, *Search and Rescue in the Mediterranean*, January 2021.

[113] See section 2.5.1.6.

[114] As explained in section 3.6.1, the remit of the analysis focuses only on certain types of agreements. For a broader discussion of the EU externalization strategy in this area, see SF Nicolosi, 'Externalisation of Migration Controls: A Taxonomy of Practices and Their Implications in International and European Law' (2024) 71 Netherlands International Law Review 1; T Strik, 'EU External Cooperation on Migration: In Search of the Treaty Principles' (2023) 8 European Papers 905.

and materialize in: status agreements on operations carried out by Frontex in third countries; Memoranda of Understanding (MoU).[115] Status agreements are based on a model adopted by the Commission through a communication,[116] and are concluded on the basis of Article 73(3) EBCG Regulation. They govern the deployment of border management teams with executive powers to a third country, and must cover all aspects necessary for performing those actions. The EBCG Regulation stipulates what provisions the agreements must contain *in particular*: inter alia, the scope of the operation, rules on civil and criminal liability, the tasks and powers of the members of the teams, and practical measures related to the respect of fundamental rights including a complaint mechanism. Unfortunately, the EBCG Regulation states only in the preamble—thus not in the text—that the Commission must assess the fundamental rights situations in the third country and inform the European Parliament (EP) before concluding such agreements.[117] The MoU is the newest source in town, as shown by the Memorandum signed by the European Commission with Tunisia in 2023. These sources tend to be broader in scope, but migration plays a crucial role insofar as the third country is co-opted in EU external border control in exchange for benefits.[118]

Leaving aside their specific content and implementation, these sources raise two important issues of constitutional compliance. Firstly, there is the issue of effective judicial protection. Status agreements are formally adopted through a Council decision and are therefore amenable to judicial review, but MoUs are not, at least in principle. The recently agreed MoU with Tunisia indicates that the parties 'share the priorities of combating irregular migration in order to avoid loss of human lives' and that their approach must be based on respect for human rights. Given the informal nature of the source underpinning the partnership, which enables the avoidance of scrutiny and justiciability of rights violation, serious doubts arise as to its appropriateness to achieve the goals established therein.[119] Secondly, both sources are affected by a flaw in the procedure leading to their adoption—more specifically, they do not comply with the external dimension of the principle of mutual trust.[120] Neither source seems to be anchored to a rigorous assessment of the third country's legal proximity to the EU and compliance by the former with agreed standards.[121] This issue is crucial to

[115] For completeness, we must also mention the Common Foreign and Security Policymissions, which however fall outwith the scope of this research. See, inter alia, Council Decision (CFSP) 2020/472 on a European Union military operation in the Mediterranean (EUNAVFOR MED IRINI) [2020] OJ 101/4; Council Decision (CFSP) 2022/1968 on a European Union Military Assistance Mission in support of Ukraine (EUMAM Ukraine) [2022] OJ L 270/85; Council Decision (CFSP) 2015/778 on a European Union military operation in the Southern Central Mediterranean (EUNAVFOR MED) [2015] OJ L 122/31.

[116] Communication from the Commission to the European Parliament and the Council on Model status agreement as referred to in Regulation (EU) 2019/1896 of the European Parliament and of the Council of 13 November 2019 on the European Border and Coast Guard and repealing Regulations (EU) No 1052/2013 and (EU) 2016/1624, COM(2021) 829 final.

[117] EBCG Regulation, recital 88.

[118] Memorandum of Understanding between the EU and Tunisia.

[119] For a detailed assessment of the MoU, see T Strik and R Robbesom, 'Compliance or Complicity? An Analysis of the EU-Tunisia Deal in the Context of the Externalisation of Migration Control' (2024) 71 Netherlands International Law Review 199.

[120] See section 2.5.2.

[121] See L Mancano, 'Trust Thy neighbour? Compliance and Proximity to the EU Through the Lens of Extradition' (2021) 40 Yearbook of European Law 475.

the constitutional compliance of EU border controls, as confirmed by the European Ombudsman's decision to open an inquiry into how the Commission intends to guarantee respect for human rights in the context of the EU–Tunisia MoU, and even more by the recommendations contained in the Ombudsman's final decisions.[122]

### 4.3.2 Delegation to Member States and the Example of the Italy–Albania MoU

The system of sources of EU border controls 'in transit' knows explicit and implicit 'delegation'. As to the former, and in the context of external border surveillance, the competent authorities of each member state are given a fundamental role. To this end, each member state must have a national coordination centre (NCC) for the purposes of EUROSUR, in charge of coordinating the exchange of information among all the national authorities competent for border control, and with Frontex as well as other NCCs. The relevance of NCCs is apparent from the SESB Regulation too. Pursuant to the latter, the NCC can delegate certain functions to regional, local, or other authorities. There are two main conditions for this: such bodies must be *in a position* to take operational decisions in relation to situational awareness and reaction capability *in their respective areas of competence*;[123] and such a delegation must not affect the tasks of the NCC. Only in certain scenarios, however, does EU law prescribe that delegation be underpinned by national provisions which predefine the cases in which delegation can happen. For example, this requirement would apply where the NCC would like to entrust those authorities with communication and information exchange with authorities of another member state or third country.[124] Other than this, however, the framework of delegation to member states for deciding about the exercise of control is rather vague, and the organization of the NCC is entirely referred to the member states.

Implicit delegation has been explored to a lesser extent, but it is equally relevant. With this expression, we refer to initiatives taken by member states in the absence of EU action—and particularly as regards partnerships with neighbouring third countries. In this regard, member states are expressly allowed to cooperate with third countries via agreements or *other forms of arrangement*, provided that their establishment and implementation comply with the EU and international law. To this end, member states must assess and take into account the third-country situation on a regular basis.[125] Beyond its long-standing and very controversial partnership with Libya,[126] Italy has recently signed a Protocol with Albania (Protocol or MoU). The Protocol

[122] See Case OI/2/2024/MHZ. See more detail on this in Chapter 6, section 6.3.1.2.
[123] EBCG Regulation, Article19(4).
[124] EBCG Regulation, Article 19(6). This is subject to regular information to the NCC.
[125] EBCG Regulation, Article 72.
[126] For some background and a link to the original version of the MoU, see https://www.osservatoriosullefonti.it/archivi/archivio-rubriche/archivio-rubriche-2017/419-fonti-dell-unione-europea-e-internazionali/1840-osf-3-2017-int-3.

The Italy–Lybia MoU was signed in 2017 and renewed for a further three years in February 2023. https://www.hrw.org/it/news/2023/02/01/italy-reups-funding-force-migrants-back-libya.

was ratified by Law no 14/2024, which adds flesh to the bones of the former. The MoU will remain in force for five years and will be automatically renewed unless either Party wishes not to do so,[127] and any dispute concerning the interpretation or application thereof will be settled amicably through consultations.[128] In essence, the MoU enables the transfer to Albania of migrants intercepted by Italian authorities on the high seas, in order to carry out 'border and return procedures' in centres built in this third country specifically for those purposes.[129] In doing so, the Protocol introduces a new—at least in the EU—way of addressing the management of migration flows after the persons have left their country of origin and before they have reached the EU borders. This being a solo endeavour in an area of shared competence, it is worth considering whether, and to what extent, the text and implementation interact with existing provisions of EU law. This section addresses three main legal issues arising from the Protocol, in the chronological order in which they would emerge from its application: interception and disembarkation; territoriality and performance of the relevant procedures; and effective protection of procedural rights.

The personal scope of the Memorandum concerns 'migrants', and specifically non-EU nationals, who: must be subject to a verification concerning their fulfilment of the conditions for entry and stay in Italy; and have already been subject to that verification, and been found not to meet those requirements.[130] Law no 14/2024 further clarifies that the persons who can be taken to the facilities are: persons embarked on vehicles of the Italian authorities outside the territorial sea of the Republic or of other Member States of the European Union, including as a result of rescue operations; persons subject to a detention order issued on the basis of Italian migration law.[131] In order to understand the relationship between sources of EU, international, and national law, we must first distinguish between situations where Italian authorities will be acting on their own, and situations where the interception will be performed by those vessels in the framework of an operation of surveillance of the external sea borders coordinated by Frontex.

To start with the latter, such operations are governed by the SESB Regulation. They provide for the possibility of disembarkation in a third country, and make it conditional upon the assessment of the situation therein.[132] In giving expression to a broader principle of international law, the Regulation also requires that disembarkation be carried out without delay.[133] This is accompanied by a more general obligation, for the units participating in the operation, to address the special needs of certain

[127] Italy–Albania Protocol, Article 13.
[128] Italy–Albania Protocol, Article 14.
[129] Italy–Albania Protocol, Article 4(2).
[130] Italy–Albania Protocol, Article 1.
[131] Law no 14/2024, Article 3(2).
[132] SESB Regulation, Article 4(2).
[133] See SESB Regulation, Article 10(1)(c). See also the International Maritime Organization's MSC.167(78)—Guidelines on the Treatment of Persons Rescued at Sea (hereafter MSC.167(78)), para 6.9, stating that 'Responsible State authorities should make every effort to expedite arrangements to disembark survivors from the ship'; para 6.20, stipulating that 'Any operations and procedures such as screening and status assessment of rescued persons that go beyond rendering assistance to persons in distress should not be allowed to hinder the provision of such assistance or unduly delay disembarkation of survivors from the assisting ship(s)'.

categories of people in a situation of vulnerability.[134] The Protocol and the Law can clearly 'interact' with said provisions, which raises a number of questions. Firstly, the national rules offer no clear indication of when the Italian authorities might want to resort to the transfer to Albania following an interception. Given that the MoU sets a limit on the number of persons that can be held (ie detained) at the centres, recourse to such an option will have to be made parsimoniously. Secondly, the Regulation provides for a limited possibility of disembarkation in third countries. In the case of interception on the high seas, the persons can be disembarked in a third country if the vessel is assumed to have departed from there; otherwise, the state of disembarkation will have to be the host state.[135] Disembarkation following a SAR operation is the only situation where the Protocol could be applied in the context of a Frontex-coordinated operation, as it must be carried out at a place of safety designated by the Rescue Coordination Centre rapidly and effectively.[136] While a place of safety need not be a member state, thus making the application of the Protocol consistent with the Regulation, the obligation of rapid and effective disembarkation might limit its geographical scope.[137] Depending on where the SAR will take place, the transfer to Albania might not allow for a rapid disembarkation where a closer place of safety is available.[138] A detail of high practical relevance concerns the procedure for the transfer of migrants to and from Albanian territory. This will be carried out on the basis of a separate agreement, to be signed by the Parties.[139] It remains to be seen what form this agreement will take and how accessible it will be. The impact on legal certainty and effective judicial protection might be significant. The case could be made, however, that the period of the transfer should count towards the overall limit of detention when assessing the proportionality of its duration, either in the context of EU asylum law or the Return Directive.[140]

Once landed in Albania, the persons will be taken to the centres. Albanian authorities will be responsible for the security of the outer perimeter of the facilities[141] and during the transfer of the persons to the area.[142] Italian authorities will be responsible for security inside the centres, but can authorize Albanian personnel to enter.[143] As regards actions performed during the discharging of their duties, Italian authorities will be subject to Italian jurisdiction.[144] For the purposes of implementing the Protocol,

[134] SEBS Regulation, Article 4(4).

[135] SESB Regulation, Article 10(1)(b).

[136] SESB Regulation, Article 10(1)(c).

[137] For an integrated interpretation of 'place of safety' in light of migrants' vulnerability, see A Campàs Velasco, 'Vulnerability and Marginalisation at Sea: Maritime Search and Rescue, and the Meaning of "Place of Safety"' (2022) 18 International Journal of Law in Context 85.

[138] The principle of rapid disembarkation would also apply, as a matter of international law, to interceptions occurring outwith the framework of an operation governed by the Regulation.

[139] Italy–Albania Protocol, Article 8(2).

[140] Directive 2008/115/EC on common standards and procedures in Member States for returning illegally staying third-country nationals [2008] OJ L 348/98 (or Return Directive).

[141] Italy–Albania Protocol, Article 5(2).

[142] Italy–Albania Protocol, Article 6(2).

[143] Italy–Albania Protocol, Article 6(3).

[144] Italy–Albania Protocol, Article 7(4). The actual wording of this provision states that the personnel will not be subject to Albanian jurisdiction, rather than expressly establishing Italian jurisdiction for it. This is unfortunate phrasing, but existing provisions of national criminal law should prevent the emergence of

the centres will be treated as border or transit areas.[145] Italian and European law will apply to the persons held in the centres, and specifically the provisions relating to the entry and stay of third-country nationals.[146] These include rules on asylum procedures and reception conditions, the Return Directive, and the relevant case law of the Court of Justice. Therefore, the approach of the MoU is consistent with accounts in the literature which convincingly argue that the MoU falls within the scope of EU law and will thus have to be implemented consistently with this law.[147]

In this context, identifying the benchmark of EU law is important for two main reasons: to assess the procedural safeguards embedded in the Protocol; and, most importantly, to understand what role EU law can play *in the absence of such safeguards* in respect of issues arising from the practical implementation of the MoU. As to assessing the procedural safeguards, Italian authorities are under an obligation to take the necessary measures to ensure the timely and full exercise of the right of defence.[148] To this end, access to the areas must be guaranteed to counsels, and international and EU bodies, 'within the limits provided for by the applicable Italian, European and Albanian legislation'.[149] An important provision relates to the necessary healthcare in the centres, which must be arranged by Italian authorities. Where this is not possible, Albanian authorities must cooperate to ensure essential and non-deferrable medical care for the persons in the centres.[150] Once again, the idea that access to the centres will also be governed by European standards seem to raise no issue of compatibility between the Protocol and EU law. Obviously, this compatibility in principle must be followed by compliance in practice. The extent to which the effectiveness of the procedural rights can be guaranteed in the circumstances governed by the Protocol remains to be seen.[151] Not knowing the detail on Albanian legislation, there should be no presumption that the latter will be incompatible with Italian and European standards. There is potential for legal uncertainty, however, with regard to the respective scope of application of those frameworks, which in turn might impact the accessibility to the centres by the relevant stakeholders.

Stronger questions of compatibility arise from the obligation, for Italian authorities, to prevent the person held in the centres from leaving, including once the relevant procedures have come to an end and regardless of their outcome.[152] The implicit consequence is that the facilities will be places of deprivation of liberty.[153] The Protocol

pockets of impunity. See in particular the Articles of the Italian Criminal Code on the offence committed abroad by public officials.

[145] Law no 14/2024, Article 3(3).

[146] Italy–Albania Protocol, Article 4(1).

[147] E Celoria and A De Leo, 'Il Protocollo Italia-Albania e il diritto dell'Unione Europea: una relazione complicata' (2024) Diritto, Immigrazione e Cittadinanza 1.

[148] Law no 14/2024, Article 4(2) and (3).

[149] Italy–Albania Protocol, Article 9(2).

[150] Italy–Albania Protocol, Article 4(6) and (8).

[151] See C Siccardi, 'La legge di ratifica ed esecuzione del Protocollo Italia-Albania per il rafforzamento della collaborazione in materia migratoria: problematiche costituzionali' (2024) Osservatorio Costituzionale 112.

[152] Italy–Albania Protocol, Article 6(5).

[153] On the definition of detention in frontier and transit zones, see the very important judgment in Joined Cases C-924/19 PPU and C-925/19 PPU, *FMS, FNZ SA, SA junior v Országos Idegenrendészeti Főigazgatóság Dél-alföldi Regionális Igazgatóság, Országos Idegenrendészeti Főigazgatóság*, EU:C:2020:367.

covers the processing of returns and asylum applications. The rules governing both—that is, the Return Directive and instruments of EU asylum law—establish very clearly the principle that detention can only be resorted to as an *extrema ratio*, in compliance with the principle of proportionality and necessity and on the grounds established in the relevant legislation. The Italy–Albania deal constitutes a new entry into the landscape of the debate on EU migration and asylum management. Controversial as it might be, it is not in open contradiction with EU law. It takes a reconciling tone instead, insofar as it upholds Italy's obligations under national, European, and international law. Given the Protocol and the Law as they stand, Italy is exercising its discretion in line with Union law. There is more to it than meets the eye, however. In practice, several aspects of its implementation will bring the action of the competent authorities within the scope of EU law. Two main conclusions can be drawn in this regard, at this stage. Firstly, the TCNs' effective access to procedural rights protected by EU law will be the area where ensuring compliance will be most challenging. Secondly, EU law is capable of orienting the conduct of national authorities and the interpretation of the relevant provisions of national law. However, the example of the SESB Regulation shows that the overlap between the Union and national frameworks is rather 'patchy'.

### 4.3.3 Operational Sources

There exist different streams of operational sources of border controls 'in transit', falling either within border surveillance or partnership with third countries. The narrative developed so far continues here, and particularly as regards the emphasis on data and statistics, the informal nature of cooperation, and the wide operational discretion left to the competent authorities. As regards border surveillance, it is once again useful to distinguish between operational activities and the exchange of information centred on EUROSUR. As to the former, the SESB Regulation stipulates that the operational plan of Frontex-coordinated sea surveillance operations must contain an assessment of the general situation in the third country where disembarkation is being considered.[154] The assessment is based on a *broad range of sources*, emanating for example from Union and international bodies, and may take into account the existence of agreements with that country on migration and asylum.[155] This provision could prove particularly problematic for different reasons. A generous interpretation thereof might see it as an encouragement to conduct a rigorous assessment of the situation in a third country—hence the reference to the broad range of sources. The broader and the more heterogeneous the range, however, the more likely the sources will not lead to the same conclusion. From the wording of it, it is also clear that the existence of an agreement with a third country should (could) be read as an indication that this country is suitable for disembarkation. This interpretation would be grossly misplaced. Granted, those agreements must be 'carried out

[154] The operational plan must also contain specific information on SAR. Needless to say, the plan must comply with the relevant measures of international law. SEBS Regulation, Article 9(2).

[155] SEBS Regulation, Article 4(2).

in accordance with Union law and through Union funds'. Who ascertains the non-accordance of the agreement or the programme with EU law, though? It is difficult to see how the Council or Commission could do so, having probably greenlighted the use of Union funding for those purposes in the first place. That Frontex could challenge the lawfulness of an existing agreement appears highly unlikely, especially in cases where it was directly involved in the signing and/or the implementation thereof. The Court's reluctance to take a firm stance on the EU action at the external borders—including as regards the specific question on sources—offers little reassurance.[156] The lack of a proper fundamental rights-compliance assessment before the conclusion of the EU–Tunisia MoU further confirms that existing cooperation is an inappropriate source/safeguard, when considering the level of safety of the third country of disembarkation.

As for surveillance and the exchange of information, important operational sources of the law 'in transit' can be found in the Commission Implementing Regulation on the European situational picture of EUROSUR[157] and the Commission Recommendation on the EUROSUR Handbook.[158] As above, a prominent aspect of this area is its flexibility—or, its over-reliance on informal arrangements and non-structured co-operation. The EUROSUR Handbook details the framework established in the EBCG Regulation.[159] It also adds elements that are not referred to it therein, such as the *common pre-frontier intelligence picture* (CPIP). The EUROSUR Handbook defines the national situational picture (NSP) as 'the sum of all information provided by that Member State to EUROSUR'. National authorities exchange information among themselves via the NSP. The European situational picture (ESP) is based on NSPs and 'other surveillance tools', whereas the CPIP 'relates to information and intelligence on the areas beyond the external borders'. The ESP and the CPIP should, therefore, cover the same thematic areas, and together provide geographic continuity. Both pictures are shared among the member states and are available to Frontex.[160] A situational picture (SP) comprises different sets of information called layers, and in particular: the event layer, the operational layer, and the analysis layer.[161] Each layer

[156] See the controversial EU–Turkey statement saga in Case T-192/16, *NF v European Council*, EU:T:2017:128 and Joined Cases C-208/17 P to C-210/17 P, *NF and Others v European Council*, EU:C:2018:705.

[157] Commission Implementing Regulation (EU) 2021/581 on the situational pictures of the European Border Surveillance System [2021] OJ L 124/3 (EUROSUR Implementing Regulation).

[158] ANNEX to the Commission Recommendation adopting the Practical Handbook for implementing and managing the European Border Surveillance System (EUROSUR Handbook) C(2015) 9206 final. The Commission apparently adopted a new Handbook in January 2025 (Commission Recommendation of 17.1.2025 establishing the practical handbook for the implementation and management of EUROSUR ('EUROSUR Handbook'), C(2025) 117 final), but the document is not available through research in eurLex.

[159] For a detailed analysis of the development of EUROSUR, see S Ellebrecht, *Mediated Bordering: Eurosur, the Refugee Boat, and the Construction of an External EU Border* (Bielefeld 2020) 81 onwards.

[160] EUROSUR Handbook 17. EUROSUR has been the focus of an important judgment of the Court in Case C-44/14, *Spain v European Parliament and Council of the European Union (Eurosur)*, EU:C:2015:554, concerning the coherence of the Schengen acquis. For a comment, see D Hanf, 'Balancing Openness and Coherence of Enhanced Cooperation: The Principle of Coherence Affirmed by Drawing Its Outer Limits—Spain v. Parliament and Council (Eurosur)' (2017) 54 Common Market Law Review 873.

[161] This last layer covers products (not delivered on demand and including reports delivered by the EU Satellite Centre) and services (all on demand and shared through the EUROSUR Fusion service, which include pre-frontier monitoring reports). See also Council Decision 2014/401/CFSP on the European Union

of an SP contains sub-layers—for example, the events layer features a sub-layer on crisis situations, which covers any situations that might have a significant impact on the border.[162] Through the EUROSUR Fusion Service, Frontex combines information gathered through different surveillance tools and can provide NCCs with a multi-layered situational picture.[163] Other than providing deeper insight into the workings of EUROSUR, the Handbook offers examples of non- or little-regulated forms of co-operation within the systems. Two instances are worth highlighting. Firstly, users of EUROSUR can form communities of interest, which are not formally established and can 'reach beyond the scope of EUROSUR'. This aspect is not mentioned in the legislation and is left without any specific formal or procedural constraints. The second example of a scarcely regulated system of surveillance is the Common Information Sharing Environment (CISE), which is referred to in the EUROSUR Handbook but has not been established through a proper instrument and operates within the EU Maritime Safety Agency.[164] Its role, therefore, is not clear.[165]

The EUROSUR Implementing Regulation, for its part, lays down more specific rules about the use of the surveillance system. There are a number of categories of reporting and obligations related thereto, which lie at the core of the framework: in particular, events reporting and risk analysis reporting. These duties are important for the establishment of the SP, risk analysis, and reaction capability. As to events reporting, the NCCs must ensure that authorities responsible for border management report an event in the relevant situational picture. Frontex and the International Coordination Centres have the same tasks. The NCC must report indicators about the events. For example, in reporting the number of irregular entries or stays detected over the previous month, the figures should be broken down into sub-indicators. These include information such as nationality, age, and gender of the persons concerned. In particular, 'the data corresponding to the indicators may be derived from information and statistics available to national authorities including through searches of relevant Union databases and large-scale information systems, in accordance with the legal framework applicable to those databases and systems'.[166] From a

Satellite Centre and repealing Joint Action 2001/555/CFSP on the establishment of a European Union Satellite Centre [2014] OJ L 188/73.

[162] EUROSUR Handbook 20. This type of impact is understood as 'as affecting conditions at the border to such an extent that additional measures or special intervention need to be taken, including the need for reinforcements and urgent decision-making and response'. This definition might prove helpful for a systemic interpretation of the notion of impact, which, as shown further below, is relevant to determine certain obligations for member states. Being able to define impact, therefore, is particularly important.

[163] Combining, for example, imagery related to an accident with that related to weather conditions and vessel traffic.

[164] See also Communication from the Commission to the European Parliament and the Council—Better situational awareness by enhanced cooperation across maritime surveillance authorities: next steps within the Common Information Sharing Environment for the EU maritime domain COM(2014) 451 final and Joint Communication to the European Parliament and the Council on the update of the EU Maritime Security Strategy and its Action Plan "An enhanced EU Maritime Security Strategy for evolving maritime threats" JOIN(2023) 8 final.

[165] We can find a definition of CISE in a piece of legislation as 'an environment of systems developed to support the exchange of information between authorities involved in maritime surveillance, across sectors and borders, in order to improve their awareness of activities at sea'. Regulation (EU) 2021/1139 establishing the European Maritime, Fisheries and Aquaculture Fund [2021] OJ L 247/1, Article 2(2).

[166] EUROSUR Implementing Regulation, Article 8(2).

cross-cutting analysis, it is difficult to know what purposes these indicators and statistics could serve. The flexibility of the legal framework would, however, certainly leave scope for their use in many different ways related to migration control broadly understood. They also resonate with the increasing—and increasingly disturbing—reliance on statistics that we have unveiled through the discussion on the ETIAS and the VIS. The NCC and Frontex reporting duties on risk analysis must cover a series of sources, including reports from third countries. These reports can be useful to understand border events and incidents, as well as for planning and carrying out border control operations.[167] Risk analysis also entails holding a watchlist—which is presumably different from the watchlist referred to in the ETIAS Regulation. Watchlists *must* include, inter alia, profiles and behaviours which might be connected to one of the pillars of border controls (irregular migration, cross-border crime, saving life at sea) and *may* comprise, among other things, suspected vessels, aircraft, places of origin, and operators.[168] There is, therefore, a clear emphasis on the profiling of 'suspected' troublemakers.

With regard to the other strand of sources in transit, Frontex and member states have a broader obligation to cooperate with third countries,[169] with the view to promoting EIBM standards.[170] This duty can manifest itself through different sources. For example, Frontex can act within the framework of working arrangements concluded with the authorities of third countries.[171] These arrangements must specify the scope, nature, and purpose of the cooperation and concern the management of operational cooperation.[172] Furthermore, we have operational 'sources' adopted on the basis of status agreements between the EU and third countries. As Frontex is responsible for the implementation of such agreements, it is also empowered to flesh out important aspects of such cooperation (eg through MoUs). Examples in this regard are the MoU establishing complaint mechanisms in the context of such SAs, or those establishing the initiation of first-line border checks outside the EU.[173] Such a chain of operational delegation increases the depth of the law of EU border controls, but raises further questions about the control subject's access to effective legal protection and makes the exercise of executive powers by EU bodies even less transparent.

[167] EUROSUR Implementing Regulation, Article 13.

[168] EUROSUR Implementing Regulation, Article 15.

[169] Frontex must facilitate operational cooperation between the member states and Ireland and the UK. Exchange of information with those countries can take place on the basis of agreements with neighbouring member states, but must be limited to the exchange of information between NCCs. EBCG Regulation, Article 70. A Frontex–UK WA was signed on 24 February 2024 and is available on the Frontex website.

[170] EBCG Regulation, Article 71. As for Frontex's cooperation with other Union's bodies and agencies, this must take place on the basis of specific WAs, subject to the Commission's prior approval. These arrangements are concluded on the basis of Article 73(4) EBCG Regulation.

[171] See Management Board Decision 25/2023 authorising the Executive Director to negotiate working arrangements with selected EU entities and third countries.

[172] EBCG Regulation, Article 73. For an early analysis of WAs, see M Fink, 'Frontex Working Arrangements: Legitimacy and Human Rights Concerns Regarding "Technical Relationships"' (2012) 28 Utrecht Journal of International and European Law 20.

[173] See https://www.frontex.europa.eu/media-centre/news/news-release/frontex-initiates-first-line-border-checks-outside-eu-nXm2OJ#:~:text=Frontex%20marked%20a%20significant%20milestone%20in%20international%20border,checks%20at%20a%20border%20outside%20the%20European%20Union.

### 4.3.4 Interim Conclusions

The heterogeneous range of sources governing situations 'in transit' shows similarities to those applicable before the TCN's departure. The analysis has cast serious doubts on the capacity of that system of sources to achieve its objective appropriately. The heterogeneity of sources is inextricably linked to inadequate protection of individual rights. On the one hand, the adoption of measures of soft law on criminalization of humanitarian assistance betrays the member states' stance on the lack of Union competence on this matter. In this regard, we argued that an effectiveness-oriented understanding of solidarity would offer a solid legal argument to justify the enactment of common rules. On the other hand, the forms taken by agreements with third countries raise questions of constitutional compliance. The adoption of such agreements, be they SAs or MoUs, must be preceded by a rigorous assessment of legal proximity with the partner country. MoUs prove even more inadequate, due to their generic nature and the associated difficulties in challenging them. Operational sources, and particularly WAs adopted by EU agencies, only take the exercise of public powers further away from scrutiny. The heterogeneity of sources increases when we look at the practices of certain member states—especially where those states identify a gap in the existing legal framework and exploit the ambiguities that derive from it. The Italy–Albania deal is a case in point. Here, questions of constitutional compliance concern both the compatibility of such initiatives with EU law, as they might undermine the objectives of a measure of EU law they are closely linked to, and the strain on legal certainty and effective legal protection caused by the range of relevant sources used at national level. Border controls in transit also confirm the systemic use of statistics and correlation, with the vocabulary of the relevant sources being strikingly similar to the previous section (eg indicators, watchlist). Despite the difference in meaning of such words across these two different scenarios, the concern remains the same: the greater reliance on such data, the higher the chances of inaccuracy caused by the reduced margin for an individualized assessment. In the wake of the previous scenario, the discussion of border controls in transit has fundamentally questioned the idea that fairer treatment of the persons concerned—and thus greater constitutional compliance—would undermine the effective achievement of other core objectives of EU border controls, such as preventing cross-border crime and illegal migration.

## 4.4 At the Border

Once arrived at the EU borders, several different types of sources will apply. Many of them link to legislative measures 'in transit', and their application can straddle the two scenarios.[174] Consistent with the previous two sections, we can find examples of sources that map onto the main objectives of EU external border controls. There are instruments aimed at facilitating—albeit to different extents—bona fide travellers

[174] This scenario includes the arrival at border crossing points as well as, for example, presence in the territorial waters.

such as highly qualified employees,[175] researchers,[176] persons that possess a residence permit from certain Schengen countries,[177] and the local border traffic regime, to avoid EU external borders with its neighbours becoming a barrier to trade, interchange, or cooperation.[178] Most sources, however, are concerned with presiding over the external borders from a securitized perspective, with a view to preventing irregular entry and fighting cross-border crime. As with the two previous sections, reliance on information systems and engagement with third countries are two distinctive (if interrelated) features of EU border controls.

### 4.4.1 EU Institutional Sources

When it comes to EU institutional sources, we must draw a preliminary distinction between those directly related to the implementation of the EIBM, and the specific set of sources governing the new complex system of external border procedures established by the 2024 migration and asylum pact.

Let us start with the former. At a systemic level, the Commission establishes the multiannual strategic policy cycle (MSPC) to identify the challenges related to EIBM. On the basis of Frontex's risk analysis, the Commission prepares a policy document for submission to the EP and Council. Following discussion with such institutions, it adopts a communication to that effect. Within this broader framework, three main categories of more targeted documents are worth mentioning. Firstly, there are those necessary to ensure uniform conditions for the implementation of EIBM. We have observed that operational handbooks, normally adopted through a Commission recommendation or decision, feature across the board in the system of sources of external border controls.[179] This is also the case for situations unfolding at the border, and particularly as regards the exercise of border guard[180] and border coast guard functions.[181]

[175] Directive (EU) 2021/1883 on the conditions of entry and residence of third-country nationals for the purpose of highly qualified employment [2021] OJ L 382/1.

[176] Directive (EU) 2016/801 on the conditions of entry and residence of third-country nationals for the purposes of research, studies, training, voluntary service, pupil exchange schemes or educational projects and au pairing [2016] OJ L 132/21.

[177] Decision 896/2006/EC establishing a simplified regime for the control of persons at the external borders based on the unilateral recognition by the Member States of certain residence permits issued by Switzerland and Liechtenstein for the purpose of transit through their territory [2006] OJ L 167/8. See Case C-139/08, *Rafet Kqiku*, EU:C:2009:230.

[178] Regulation (EC) No 1931/2006 laying down rules on local border traffic at the external land borders of the Member States [2006] OJ L 405/1 (LBT Regulation), recital 2. For a constructivist perspective on the LBT Regulation, see K Żęgota, 'How to Construct Cross-Border Cooperation? Local Border Traffic as a Mechanism of Shaping the External Relations of the European Union and Schengen Area from the Perspective of Constructivism: The Case of the Baltic Sea Region' (2021) 52 Journal of Baltic Studies 397.

[179] Some of them have not been adopted yet, but the main legal act imposes an obligation on the Commission to do so. See, for example, the EES Regulation, Article 71.

[180] ANNEX to the Commission Recommendation establishing a common "Practical Handbook for Border Guards (Schengen Handbook)" to be used by Member States' competent authorities when carrying out the border control of persons and replacing Recommendation (C (2019) 7131 final), C(2022) 7591 final.

[181] Commission Recommendation 2021/1222 establishing a 'Practical Handbook' on European cooperation on coast guard functions [2021] OJ L 268/3.

Secondly, there are the documents related to the external dimension of border controls (and specifically the relation with third countries). In this respect, the Commission draws up:[182]

- the model status agreement for actions in third countries, *after consulting* the member states, Frontex, the Fundamental Rights Agency, and the European Data Protection Supervisor (EDPS);
- the model provisions for the exchange of information in the framework of EUROSUR *in cooperation with* the member states and Frontex;[183]
- the model for the working arrangements between Frontex and third countries.

In the previous scenario, we highlighted some of the issues of constitutional compliance arising especially from this second group of sources: primarily, the lack of an assessment of legal proximity before concluding SAs, and the deepening of the chain of delegation of executive powers carried out by working arrangements. In this scenario, we must highlight the peculiarities of the EU institutional sources at the borders when addressing a specific—and at times urgent—situation. Where a member state failed to adopt measures recommended on the basis of a vulnerability assessment, or when a member state under pressure has not requested or implemented measures concerning a joint operation or a rapid border intervention, the Council *may* adopt an implementing act based on a Commission proposal. The decision would provide for measures such as rapid border intervention, or coordination of activities between member states and third countries, including through joint operations. The Executive Director (ED) determines the specific actions to be taken and draws up the operational plan, to be agreed with the member state concerned. The member state must comply with the implementing decision,[184] otherwise the Commission can propose that the Council recommends that a member state reintroduces internal border controls.[185] The Commission *may* adopt an implementing act to recommend that the member state takes certain measures to address serious deficiencies at its external borders, such as initiating the deployment of European border guard teams, and/or submitting its strategic plans to Frontex.[186] Importantly, the Commission can also adopt delegated acts concerning *additional* measures on surveillance.[187]

The dynamic set-up of these sources is rather curious. If your stomach aches, you might hit yourself on the head with a hammer to shift your focus somewhere else. You are not really tackling the main problem directly, though. By the same token, recommending that *another* member state reintroduces internal border controls reveals the impotent enforcement of certain decisions on the external borders management against the member state. This chapter is not suggesting that Frontex should take over

[182] EBCG Regulation, Article 76.

[183] For a critical discussion of this issue, see L Marin, 'The Cooperation Between Frontex and Third Countries in Information Sharing: Practices, Law and Challenges in Externalizing Border Control Functions' (2020) 26 European Public Law 157.

[184] EBCG Regulation, Article 42.

[185] This is the procedure laid down in Article 29 SBC.

[186] SBC, Article 21. The recommendation is adopted in the case where these deficiencies are identified in an evaluation report drawn up pursuant to the Schengen Evaluation.

[187] SBC, Article 13(5).

the control of the specific border section under the responsibility of the non-compliant member state. It is, however, important to understand these idiosyncrasies in order to gain a better systemic understanding of this area of law. In this regard, the heterogeneity of institutional sources in the strands discussed so far does not raise issues of constitutional compliance to the same extent as the two previous scenarios. There are, however, two structural elements in these sources 'at the borders' that are consistent with those analysed 'before leaving' and 'in transit'. Firstly, we observe a link between the variety of sources used and the sensitive nature of border controls, as also apparent from the allocation of power to the Council. As with the regulation of SAR and private vessels, reliance on 'weaker' measures aims to prompt member states' compliance while leaving them the last word on the exercise of an essential state function.[188] Once again, the principle of solidarity might contribute to higher constitutional compliance. Consistent with the test for a solidarity review set out in Chapter 2 (see Figure 2.1.), the discretion left to the member states in the circumstances constitutes no derogation from a general rule of EU law; likewise, there is no explicit obligation to 'take into account' the common interest in these cases. These two circumstances would call for a low level of intensity of the solidarity review. As with examples discussed in the two previous scenarios, however, there is another variable to be factored in: did the member state consider the impact of foreseeable consequences of its inaction? Did they outweigh the impact on the interests it meant to protect with its own decisions? If both questions are answered negatively, a case could plausibly be made that the member state did not comply with the principle of solidarity. The second element of continuity concerns the type of sources used and the lack of certainty concerning the exercise of such law-making power. The introduction of supplementary rules of surveillance can happen, once again, via delegated acts. There is, however, no detail on what those rules would add to, on what grounds, and for what purposes.[189]

Moving on to the second set of sources considered in this subsection, the recently agreed migration and asylum pact has significantly changed the legal landscape of migration and asylum law. The following measures operate together to establish a complex system of border procedures: the Screening Regulation;[190] the Asylum Procedure Regulation (APR);[191] the Return Border Procedure (RBP) Regulation;[192] and the Crisis Regulation.[193] The focus of this chapter is on sources 'internal' to the measures considered.[194] In the new system of border procedures created by the pact, the Screening Regulation comes first logically and chronologically. The Regulation governs the screening of TCNs who have crossed the external borders illegally, have

[188] The fact that the example of SAR concerned the exercise of EU competence, and this related to the implementation of the law, does not undermine the main argument made here.

[189] The Commission is also empowered to adopt delegated acts on the Annexes to the SBC. Article 36. Specifically in relation to Annexes III, IV, and VIII.

[190] Regulation (EU) 2024/1356 introducing the screening of third-country nationals at the external borders (or Screening Regulation).

[191] Regulation (EU) 2024/1348 establishing a common procedure for international protection (Asylum Procedure Regulation or APR).

[192] Regulation (EU) 2024/1349 establishing a return border procedure (or RBP Regulation).

[193] Regulation (EU) 2024/1359 addressing situations of crisis and force majeure in the field of migration and asylum (or Crisis Regulation).

[194] For the purposes of this section, some measures are more relevant than others. Specifically, the discussion here does not cover the APR.

applied for international protection during border checks, or have been disembarked after a SAR operation.[195] The screening takes place before entry and aims to facilitate the referral of the TCN to the appropriate procedure. More specifically, the competent authorities must carry out a preliminary health check, and they must check for indications that the person is stateless, vulnerable, a victim of torture or inhuman treatment, or has special needs within the meaning of the Return Directive, Article 25 Reception Conditions Directive[196] and Article 20 APR.[197] Under the Return Directive, the category 'vulnerable persons' covers minors, disabled people, elderly people, pregnant women, single parents with minor children, and persons who have been subjected to torture, rape, or other serious forms of psychological, physical, or sexual violence.[198] While the Reception Conditions Directive merely refers back to the APR, the latter only mentions applicants who might have been victims of torture, rape, or another serious form of psychological, physical, sexual, or gender-based violence.[199] The definitions provided for in those instruments do not exactly overlap, which can create issues of legal certainty and gaps in protection. One of the objectives of the Regulation is to identify vulnerable persons, so that their special needs are fully taken into account in the determination of the applicable procedure.[200] To ensure the widest possible scope of protection and pursue that objective more effectively, the different scopes of the concept of 'vulnerable persons' should be interpreted 'cumulatively'.

While this example refers to a specific (however important) aspect of interaction between sources within the Screening Regulation, more structural questions emerge from the sources relevant to the application of the Crisis Regulation. The latter sets out rules for the adoption of exceptional measures in situations of crisis or force majeure, consisting essentially of derogations from certain provisions of EU asylum law and/or solidarity measures for the management of the situation. The first step in the framework governed by the Regulation is the reasoned request for such measures, sent by the member state(s) concerned to the Commission.[201] In the request, the member states must include a number of sources (ie information) which vary depending on whether they claim to be experiencing a situation of crisis, instrumentalization, or force majeure. The way we interpret the nature and role of these sources is key to the assessment of fairness: a successful request from a member state will lead to derogations from provisions of asylum law (as detailed below), which will in turn impact the position of the TCNs concerned. As such, a fairness-oriented construction of these provisions would warrant a restrictive interpretation of the grounds on which such derogations could be invoked. This is particularly the case when it comes to situations of crisis. In its request, the member state must describe how, as a result of the situation, its asylum and reception system has become non-functional. It also must describe the measures it has taken to address the situation and a justification that, although

[195] Or, who have been found to stay illegally in the EU and there are no indications that they have been subject to border controls.

[196] Directive (EU) 2024/1346 laying down standards for the reception of applicants for international protection (or Reception Conditions Directive).

[197] Screening Regulation, Article 12.

[198] Return Directive, Article 3.

[199] APR, Article 20(4).

[200] Screening Regulation, recital 7.

[201] Crisis Regulation, Article 2.

well-prepared, their system is unable to address the situation.[202] To determine the level of fairness of the law in action, we will have to assess how the Commission will interpret these requirements, and how it will 'weigh' the information provided by the member state. We must also acknowledge that the assessment cannot be one-dimensional and consider exclusively the implications for fairness to TCNs. An excessively restrictive interpretation of the described legal requirements would undermine the effectiveness of the Regulation, which would also be legally unsound. It is argued, however, that fairness would require a rigorous upholding of the conditions stated in the Regulation, and particularly the need for the state to have been well-prepared, and the cumulative nature of the impact on the asylum *and* the reception system.

In this regard, the sources relied on by the Commission to decide on the state's request include information and data contained in its annual asylum and migration report.[203] If the Commission deems the situation under consideration as constituting a case of crisis or force majeure, it will adopt an implementing decision for those purposes. Alongside this, the Commission will propose that the Council itself adopts an implementing decision, which must state the grounds on which it is based and the time frame for its application, and identify the specific provisions from which the member state is allowed to derogate. We must highlight the lack of any details concerning the methodology of the assessment, which leaves the Commission the widest discretion in the use of the data.[204] While the provisions of a margin of manoeuvre in this regard are understandable, the absence of constraints stands out. Such implementing decisions can significantly impact the right to asylum, which is a principle binding the Union as well as the member states, and which constrains their sovereign right to decide on the entry of TCNs. The mentioned provisions raise issues of clarity. Excessively vague concepts and procedures are unsuitable grounds for restricting individual rights. They can result in situations of arbitrariness, which would in turn be difficult to reconcile with fairness itself. This being said, both the Commission proposal and the Council implementing decision must respect the principles of necessity and proportionality. Once again, the assessment of the implementation will be key. While some of the questions around legal certainty can potentially be addressed by means of a fairness-oriented interpretation as proposed above, the broad discretion left to the Commission in its assessment might be harder to scrutinize.

### 4.4.2 Delegation to Member States

The system of sources 'at the borders' leaves, of course, several decisions to the member states.[205] Broadly, the guiding principle is that the member states will assist

[202] Crisis Regulation, Article 2(2)(a)(i).

[203] See Regulation (EU) 2024/1351 on asylum and migration management (AMM Regulation), Article 9.

[204] With specific regard to instrumentalization, the Commission must indicate in an implementing decision why measures under Article 6(3) AMM Regulation are not sufficient to address the situation. Crisis Regulation, Article 3.

[205] A recent amendment to the SBC has introduced the national facilitation programmes, which would allow (certain) TCNs who do not enjoy free movement rights not to be subject to thorough checks for certain aspects. SBC, Article 8d. These are set in in Article 8(3)(a)(iv) and (v) SBC, and particularly: 'verification

and cooperate constantly and closely with each other to implement border control *effectively*—through, primarily, exchange of information and operational cooperation.[206] While this would normally be coordinated by Frontex, there can be instances where member states—between each other or with a third country—continue pre-existing cooperation, including via the exchange of liaison officers. In general, member states must refrain from activities which could jeopardize the functioning of Frontex or the attainment of its objectives. These provisions are an almost perfect *replica* of the principle of sincere cooperation in the context of external border controls, and frame the more specific obligations stated in the relevant instruments of secondary law.[207] This being said, two factors must be highlighted that could foster constitutional compliance. As with other situations discussed so far, the role for the principle of solidarity should not be understated—and particularly as a general obligation for the member states to take account of the other states' and the common interests. More specifically, and relatedly, two of Frontex's main objectives consist of identifying vulnerable people and contributing to saving lives at sea. Any such agreement that could undermine the pursuit of those objectives would not be compatible with EU law.

Against this background, there are four main scenarios where the member states enjoy a certain discretion concerning the decision as to whether and how to exercise control. Firstly, they can add to the provisions stated by EU law. For example, the SBC features a non-exhaustive list of supporting documents that the border guards *may* request from the TCN to ascertain that they meet the entry requirements.[208] This open-ended list might create uncertainty and issues of accessibility, especially if not accompanied by an obligation of notification and further publication in the Official Journal.[209] Secondly, they can depart from the established rule. In exceptional and unforeseen circumstances, member states can relax checks at their external borders where the waiting time caused by the intense traffic becomes excessive and all member states' resources have been exhausted.[210] From the wording of this provision, it would seem that the latter only applies to land borders. We cannot be sure about what such a relaxation would entail, and what the criteria to establish the excessive nature of the traffic would be. In the absence of further guidance or coordination mechanisms,

regarding the point of departure and the destination of the third-country national concerned and the purpose of the intended stay, checking, if necessary, the corresponding supporting documents; verification that the third-country national concerned has sufficient means of subsistence for the duration and purpose of the intended stay, for his or her return to the country of origin or transit to a third country into which he or she is certain to be admitted, or that he or she is in a position to acquire such means lawfully'. The controls to which the TCN would be subject, including by means of the procedure leading to the acceptance on the programme, cast doubt on the actual benefit of it.

[206] In this regard, it is worth noting that Finland has recently intensified border cooperation with neighbouring countries—especially Estonia, Norway, Latvia, Lithuania, and Poland—'with the aim of advancing active information exchange as well as joint preparedness and bilateral support in case of different disturbances within border security'. There is, however, no specific information or details available about this co-operation beyond what is stated on the Finnish government's website.

[207] On the basis of what was stated in Chapter 3, therefore, Article 4(3) TEU could not be relied on in these cases.

[208] SBC, Article 6(3).

[209] See also SBC, Article 6(4).

[210] SBC, Article 9.

such a power will inevitably be applied differently by different member states. It is also noteworthy that, in such circumstances, the EU would simply allow a member state to relax checks, rather than providing for the possibility of receiving operational assistance from Frontex or other member states. Thirdly, member states are under an 'obligation of waiver'. They must perform only random checks on frequent border-crossers, to verify that they meet the necessary entry requirements—and particularly, that they are not subject to an alert in the Schengen Information System (SIS).[211] The same may apply to other categories of regular cross-border commuters.[212] Doubts remain, however, on the difference between those kinds of checks and the thorough checks that will be carried out on those frequent border-crossers from time to time.[213] Fourthly, and perhaps most importantly, member states can conclude bilateral agreements for different purposes. Member states can conclude bilateral agreements with third countries establishing shared border-crossing points located on the territory of either country. In both cases, the agreement must authorize the authorities of one party to perform checks on the territory of the 'host' state. The two scenarios are not treated identically, however. In the case of a shared-border crossing point in the third country, checks carried out by the member state must be regarded as having been performed in the member state concerned.[214] A person who has passed the exit control and has asked the member state's guards for international protection while still in the third country's territory, will be given access to the relevant procedure in line with the member state and EU law. If the member state's border guards believe there are reasons to arrest a person or place them under protection, the third country will accept the transfer of the person concerned to the member state. When the shared border-crossing point is in the member state, the third country's authorities must ensure that a person wanting to ask for international protection is given access to the relevant procedures. If the third country's authorities believe there are reasons to arrest or place a person under protection, or to deny a person enjoying free movement and exit from the third country, they must inform the competent authorities of the host EU state. The member state will follow up appropriately.

The provisions on these bilateral agreements raise a number of questions. What would happen were an agreement to be concluded in spite of the Commission's negative opinion? The most likely outcome is that the agreement would be considered as non-existent due to a procedural flaw. As for the 'direct' obligation for the third country to accept the transfer to the EU state, it might be plausibly argued that that obligation should be included in the agreement. An agreement not containing this or any other clauses referred to in the SBC would be found incompatible with EU law.

We have come to realize how the heterogeneity of sources and decision-making centres is a structure and an ineluctable feature of EU external border controls. Their nature of essential state function and the principle of subsidiarity underpin a high degree of decentralization within a legal framework that has, admittedly, taken forward

[211] Regulation (EU) 2018/1861 on the establishment, operation and use of the Schengen Information System (SIS) in the field of border checks [2018] OJ L 312/14.

[212] SBC, Annex VI, 5.3.

[213] SBC, Annex VI, 5.2.

[214] SBC, Annex VI, 1.1.4.3.

legal integration in this area over the years. On closer inspection, the interaction between EU and the member state levels of governance can potentially cause issues of legal certainty and solidarity. More homogeneity is not necessarily the answer to these two issues. However, better mechanisms of coordination and/or making relevant information publicly accessible could contribute to enhancing constitutional compliance. A rigorous application of the principle of sincere cooperation, and even more so the specific obligation of solidarity in the sense proposed in this book, would ensure that the EU objectives are pursued in line with the Union's values as stated in Article 2 TEU.

### 4.4.3 Operational Sources

The operational sources related to activities unfolding at the EU borders are mostly covered by the EBCG Regulation, and in many cases are also relevant to 'in transit' activities. At the top of the system of operational sources sits, as mentioned, the Commission's MSPC. The EBCG should use the MSPC to prepare its technical and operational strategy. This strategy, in turn, must inform the member states' national strategies, which must align with the MSPC as well as the technical and operational strategy.[215] Within this framework, a number of operational sources provided in the EBCG are worth highlighting. In this subsection, we can also distinguish between two main groups of sources: the operational sources stricto sensu and those focusing on safeguards for the person affected by Frontex activities.

Starting with the former category, there are the sources related to plans and planning processes. Each specific operational activity must have an operational plan.[216] This is drawn up by, and binds, Frontex and the participating member states.[217] We have seen in the previous section that the plan comes into play in the context of border surveillance as well. Risk analysis[218] and vulnerability assessment are also important sources to determine the exercise of border controls. They are the basis for Frontex's attribution, in agreement with the member state concerned, of 'impact levels' to sections of the external borders. Those levels are categorized on the basis of the impact of an incident concerning illegal migration or cross-border crime on border security: low, equating to insignificant impact; medium, if the impact is moderate; high, where the impact is significant; and critical, to swiftly address a crisis situation caused by incidents having a decisive impact to the extent that they risk jeopardizing the functioning of the Schengen area.[219] However, none of the relevant concepts, such as 'decisive' or 'border security', are defined. There is more to this, however. An incident is defined as 'a situation relating to illegal immigration, cross-border crime, or a risk to the lives of migrants at, along or in the proximity of, the external borders', and must

[215] EBCG Regulation, Article 8.

[216] EBCG Regulation, Article 9(2).

[217] EBCG Regulation, Article 38.

[218] Using the Common Integrated Risk Analysis Model (CIRAM). EBCG Regulation, Article 29. Risk analysis must be carried out before approving a member state's request for launching a joint operation or rapid border intervention.

[219] It is also odd that only as regards the last scenario does the Regulation stipulate that the level is attributed 'temporarily' and when the risk analysis shows the level of risk.

be categorized by each NCC as 'low', 'medium', 'high', or 'very high'.[220] Beyond the absence of criteria to determine the level of impact of an incident, the impact levels of the incident do not match the impact levels attributable to the external border section. The inconsistency is not only terminological, but also substantive. An incident can also concern the risk for migrant's lives, whereas the impact levels of the border section are exclusively concerned with border security—whatever that means. Crucially, and as a further example of the centralization–decentralization dynamic, the previous impact level attributed to a border section will remain applicable if the member state disagrees with Frontex's proposal.[221] The link between risk analysis and vulnerability assessments, the attributed level of impact and exercise of control is significant: this level determines what kind of action member states must take in response.

This aspect is addressed in more detail in the next chapter. To mention just one example, the operational plans of member states concerning border sections with high and critical impact levels must be coordinated with neighbouring member states and Frontex. The impact level on a given external border section must also be taken into account when deciding about the launching of a joint operation or a rapid border intervention at the request of a member state.[222] The decision is made by the ED, although the sources underpinning it are not clearly stated. As regards rapid interventions, the decision about launching them takes account of risk analyses, the ESP, the vulnerability assessment, and any other relevant information provided by the member states.[223] The linguistic variance of the sources goes hand in hand with the connection between them and the decision: 'preceded by', 'taken into account', 'based on' all set different thresholds, rendering the criteria and procedures for operational decision-making particularly vague and uncertain. Furthermore, in the specific case of a joint operation, the ED is under no obligation to state the reason for their decision to start it (or not). Except for the cases stated in Article 42 EBCG Regulation, taking action must be preceded by a request from the member state. At best, Frontex can recommend that the member state submits a request to that effect in certain cases.[224]

The heterogeneity of the terminology makes it very difficult to identify the conditions under which a decision about the exercise of control should be taken. What is very clear, however, is that once again, the member states have the last word on the control of their external borders. This is certainly compliant with the principle of subsidiarity and Article 4(2) TEU. It is argued that the principle of solidarity can make a dent in what looks like an ironclad protected space of sovereignty. The pursuit of the objectives stated in the EBCG Regulation, which include identifying vulnerable people and contributing to saving lives at sea, express the common interest of the Union. The strengthening of controls at the external borders brought about by the asylum and migration pact reinforces the argument that the protection of lives should not come at the expense of preventing irregular migration and cross-border criminality. With this in mind, where the member state's refusal to follow the given

[220] EBCG Regulation, Article 2.
[221] EBCG Regulation, Article 34.
[222] EBCG Regulation, Article 37(3).
[223] EBCG Regulation, Article 39.
[224] See also EBCG Regulation, Article 41.

recommendation could undermine or has undermined a fundamental objective of the Regulation without a cogent justification, finding a breach of the principle of solidarity seems not so implausible.

Turning to the safeguarding sources, these are issued following a specific provision in the EBCG Regulation[225] by a decision of either the Management Board (MB) or the ED and relate to: the establishment of a supervisory mechanism to monitor the application of the provisions on the use of force by Frontex statutory staff;[226] adopting implementing rules concerning the tasks, duties, and powers of the Data Protection Officer;[227] internal rules concerning restrictions of certain data subject rights in relation to the processing of personal data in the framework of activities carried out by Frontex;[228] rules on the complaint mechanism;[229] the establishment of a Standard Operating Procedure (SOP) for Serious Incident Reporting (SIR);[230] Policy on Identification and Management of Frontex Sensitive Functions;[231] and the Frontex code of conduct.[232] The next two chapters unpack some of these sources in more detail. However, it is clear that delegating the regulation of such important to acts internal to an administrative agency can potentially raise serious concerns with regard to the transparency and justiciability.

## 4.5 Conclusions

The law of EU external border controls rests on a heterogeneous system of sources. Underneath the many sources adopted pursuant to Article 289 TFEU lies another world of measures which contribute significantly to shaping the functioning of border controls. The analysis has uncovered the existence of a series of common themes across the different steps of the migratory process governed by EU law. Situations before leaving, in transit, or at the borders have revealed the presence of a substantial body of measures that may be EU-originated, member states-driven, or chiefly operational. Partnerships with third countries and reliance on databases have emerged as two of the main protagonists of the discussion. Overall, this chapter has raised serious questions on the appropriateness of the system of sources for achieving its objectives. This holds true if our parameters are the overarching goals of this area, and if we consider the appropriateness of the rules to the objective in each individual measure. The assessment of appropriateness is one of constitutional compliance, centred on a structured network of relevant principles. Consistent with the integrated approach proposed in this book, we have explored the implications of the different scenarios for the three main macro-themes of this research: task allocation, interinstitutional cooperation, and treatment of the persons concerned. Generally, the overall set-up

225 See, for example, EBCG Regulation, Article 55(4), Article 80(1), and Article 81(1).
226 MB Decision 7/2021.
227 MB Decision, 9/2023.
228 MB Decision, 28/22.
229 MB Decision, 19/22.
230 Decision of the Executive Director No R-ED-2021-51.
231 MB Decision, 1/24.
232 This is accessible on the Frontex website and dated 4 April 2024.

of the law is based on a delicate balance between centralization, via establishment of common rules and the empowerment of EU institutions or bodies, and decentralization, with member states in charge of implementation and left with the final say on the most crucial issues of external border control. Within this framework, EU institutional sources mostly consist of acts adopted by the Commission where a decision applicable to the Union as a whole is deemed necessary. Here, the heterogeneity concerns not the number of decision-making centres, but the range of sources used by the same rule-making body.

Two main overarching conclusions can be drawn from the analysis. On the one hand, we have seen a reliance on very 'executive' sources used for intrusive purposes. This range of sources, among which delegated acts feature prominently, is often linked to the adoption of measures that would negatively affect the person concerned and overall create an imbalance between the pursuit of different objectives. The imbalance between objectives matters legally. In certain cases, the excessive emphasis on one goal (prevention of illegal migration and cross-border crime) may come at the expense of the other (identifying vulnerable people and saving lives at sea), therefore undermining the effectiveness of the relevant measure(s). A comprehensive look at the measures of external border controls shows that the opposite is not true: the idea that rebalancing the pursuit towards non-restrictive measures would affect the achievement of other objectives *a priori* is wrong and should be rejected. The lack of transparency of these sources is compounded by the fact that they are built on correlation and statistics, which can be particularly problematic in areas where the framework requires an individualized decision.

On the other hand, we have observed the use of very 'innocuous sources', such as recommendations, to respect member states' prerogatives and sensitivities. This is the case with the criminalization of humanitarian assistance and SAR operations carried out by private vessels. In its external dimension, the sources underpinning partnerships with neighbouring third countries are not preceded by an assessment of legal proximity. In doing so, they are in contradiction with the principle of mutual trust and the rule of law. Through different routes, the results produced by both delegated acts and recommendations are to the detriment of the person concerned.

In terms of task allocation, the quest for homogeneity never seems to cross the line of subsidiarity and respect for essential state functions. Delegation to member states—understood in a wider sense—is key to achieving this delicate balance between centralization and member state autonomy. The heterogeneity of decision-making centres provided by EU law itself (eg processing of visa applications) lives alongside the heterogeneity of approaches that could be taken by the member states in areas possibly not entirely covered by EU law (eg the Italy–Albania deal) and the different kinds of sources used by member states in these solo endeavours (eg visa restrictions in Finland via a decision-in-principle, and the different non-legislative sources related to the implementation of the Italy–Albania agreement). The possible tension caused by these forms of heterogeneity in interinstitutional cooperation (between member states, or between the EU and member states) is not just a matter of subsidiarity, sincere cooperation, or solidarity. It can have an impact on the fair treatment of the persons concerned. It has been argued that a rigorous interpretation of the principle of solidarity, as a duty to take into account the common interest, can support the management of this form of heterogeneity.

External border controls would not work without operational sources. Be they placed at EU or national level, the exercise of law-making power often materializes into non-binding documents and is framed very flexibly, or links directly to non-structured forms of cooperation. Many of these sources underlie the establishment of profiles of the persons concerned through non-transparent measures, which raises concerns in terms of democratic legitimacy, transparency, and legal certainty, as well as accessibility to the legal information. They create a system heavily unbalanced, which neglects facilitating legitimate travel and saving lives, and ultimately alters the spirit of the law and questions the principles on which such practices should be built. These core features combined make us seriously question the capacity of the system of sources of the law of EU border controls to achieve its manifold objectives appropriately.

# 5
# Exercising Control

## 5.1 Introduction

A closer look at the heterogeneous fabric of EU external border controls, and specifically its sources of law, has revealed a series of interwoven threads. Consistent with the scope of this book, we have assessed the impact of that heterogeneity on constitutional compliance and considered whether the system of sources is appropriate to achieve the objectives of the legal framework. To answer this question, our evaluation has relied on a structured network of principles. Based on the view of the EU legal order espoused in this book, the principles are regarded as the tools to ensure that the Union and its states pursue the common objectives in line with their common values.[1] The assessment has unfolded through three interrelated sub-questions/themes: allocation of law-making tasks on border controls to the appropriate level of governance and actor; provision and application of appropriate mechanisms of interinstitutional cooperation (between member states, between the EU and the member states, and between both the above and third countries);[2] and the fair treatment of the persons concerned.[3] In answering the question of who decides when controls should be exercised, and how, the legal framework sets up a delicate balance between the need for centralization and respect for subsidiarity and essential state functions. Through the integrated approach adopted in this book, we have shown that this arrangement might be appropriate from the perspective of the EU use of competences, but it also poses challenges in terms of solidarity and fairness. On the one hand, the Commission increasingly expresses its executive role through the use of sources which are not appropriate to achieve the objectives of EU external border controls. The adoption of delegated acts for certain key decisions is characterized by a lack of transparency and democratic scrutiny, while negatively impacting persons trying to legitimately access the EU territory. Similar considerations apply to sources underpinning partnerships with neighbouring third countries. As shown in more detail in this chapter, the nature of these arrangements presupposes a certain level of mutual trust. However, their adoption has not been preceded by an adequate assessment of legal proximity between the EU and the partner third country. On the other hand, the member states themselves have proven partial to reliance on sources challenging legal certainty and effective legal protection. On a systemic level, the decentralization of border controls creates a heterogeneity of decision-making centres. This could put a strain on the principle

[1] Consolidated Version of the Treaty on EU (TEU) [2012] OJ C 326/13, Article 2.
[2] Consolidated Version of the Treaty on the Functioning of the EU (TFEU) [2012] OJ C 326/47, Article 80.
[3] TFEU, Article 67(2).

*The Law of EU Border Controls*. Leandro Mancano, Oxford University Press. © Leandro Mancano 2025.
DOI: 10.1093/9780191966187.003.0006

of interinstitutional solidarity, understood as a duty to take account of the interest of other states and the Union as a whole. On several occasions, the law allows the EU and its states (not) to act. Depending on the specific circumstances of the case and the way in which the competent actor comes to a certain decision, such formally allowed conduct might be incompatible with the mentioned obligations of solidarity. Ultimately, the excessive emphasis on preventing irregular migration and cross-border crime can come at the expense of facilitating regular entry, identifying vulnerable persons, and saving lives, thereby undermining the effectiveness of the law and, more broadly, its spirit and underlying principles. Read together, the sources of EU external border controls seem inappropriate for achieving their objectives.

This chapter expands upon those themes, as the assessment of appropriateness moves onto the actual exercise of controls and specifically: the conditions for that exercise, the conditions imposed on the persons concerned, and the allowed or mandated conduct associated with both of the these conditions. By looking at these aspects, we consider what issues of constitutional compliance can arise from the heterogeneity of actors, objectives, and addressees of control. The analysis revolves around the materials set out in section 3.6.1 and covers three scenarios: 'before leaving', focusing on visas, travel authorizations, and the role for Immigration Liaison Officers (ILOs); 'in transit', homing in on operational cooperation and the exchange of information for border surveillance; and 'at the borders', looking at controls in reaction to an emerging situation, as part of ordinary checks on people entering the Schengen area, or within the framework of border procedures established by the 2024 migration and asylum pact. As with the previous chapter, the use of databases and partnerships with third countries will be two cross-cutting themes of the discussion. In further uncovering the heterogeneity of the law, this chapter tests this heterogeneity against the three main parameters of constitutional compliance adopted in this research: Are the levels of governance and actors entrusted with the exercise of control in any given situation appropriate vis-à-vis subsidiarity and respect for essential state functions?[4] To what extent do the law and practice take account of the principle of solidarity? Is the law and its implementation fair to the persons concerned (and particularly in terms of non-discrimination, the right to liberty, access to asylum procedures, and non-refoulement)? Overall, is the system of conditions, actors, and addressees of control appropriate to achieve the objectives of the law of EU border controls?

## 5.2 Before Leaving

This scenario revolves around the visa policy and the system of travel authorization established by the European Travel Information and Authorisation System (ETIAS). Concerning the visa policy, we discuss the role of the competent authorities in relation to the performance of the risk assessment at the core of the processing of visa applications. We also highlight the dynamic of inter-institutional cooperation designed by the VISA Code and the Visa Reciprocity Regulation. The sections on the ETIAS

[4] TEU, Articles 5(3) and 4(2).

follow a similar structure. There, we assess the conditions for the processing of travel authorizations and the distribution of tasks among the different levels of governance and actors involved in the legal framework. Overall, this scenario shows that data and intelligence can be used for unfair fishing expeditions with a view to finding reasons to refuse the TCN a title of entry. Furthermore, it shows how the heterogeneity of decision-making centres can create tensions in terms of interinstitutional solidarity.

## 5.2.1 The Visa Policy

### 5.2.1.1 Competent authorities and risk assessment: An unfair fishing expedition?

When it comes to visas, the examination of the relevant conditions and procedures must be preceded by a fundamental question: on what grounds can a visa requirement be imposed on a third country in the first place? To recall, EU law governs the issuing of three types of short-term visas for one, two, or multiple entries:[5] uniform (allowing the person to travel across the Schengen area),[6] limited territorial validity (LTV),[7] and airport transit (ATV).[8] The provisions of the VISA Code are without prejudice to the derived rights of free movement enjoyed by family members of citizens of the EU and of countries whose nationals enjoy free movement rights equivalent to those of the EU or Schengen-associated countries.[9] The Visa Reciprocity Regulation allows the EU to impose a visa requirement on the basis of a heterogeneous list of criteria, ranging from economic benefit to countering illegal immigration.[10] As a specific expression of the role for irregular migration in the visa policy, a low readmission rate of certain categories of third-country nationals (TCNs) allows the Commission to tighten the procedures and conditions for acquiring a visa set in the VISA Code[11] and reintroduce a visa requirement on visa exempt countries/groups of people.[12] The law and practice of this link have proven contentious. The evidence of irregular migration behind the decision has been questioned, and so has been the consistency with which the Commission has applied such a criterion.[13] Furthermore, it has been argued that the connection between readmission and visa

[5] Short-term here means allowing to stay for a maximum of 90 days in every 180-day period. The regulation of longer-term visas remains within the competence of the member states.

[6] Regulation (EC) No 810/2009 establishing a Community Code on Visas [2009] OJ L 243/1 (VISA Code), Article 24.

[7] VISA Code, Article 25.

[8] VISA Code, Article 26. TCNs of certain states are required to have an ATV, whereas some are exempt, and member states can always introduce a requirement to hold an ATV in urgent cases of mass influx of migrants from countries that are not on the list. They must inform the Commission when they do so and when they withdraw such a requirement. VISA Code, Article 3(2).

[9] VISA Code, Article 1(2).

[10] Regulation (EU) 2018/1806 listing the third countries whose nationals must be in possession of visas when crossing the external borders and those whose nationals are exempt from that requirement [2018] OJ L 303/39 (Visa Reciprocity Regulation), Article 1.

[11] VISA Code, Article 25a.

[12] Visa Reciprocity Regulation, Article 8.

[13] E Guild and M Grunder, 'The EU Visa Policy: To Deter and to Facilitate' in L Tsourdi and P De Bruycker (eds), *Research Handbook on EU Migration and Asylum Law* (Edward Elgar 2022) 390.

requirements not only breaches the principle of non-discrimination,[14] but is also ineffective[15] if not counterproductive.[16]

Against this background, a heterogeneous range of actors can play a role—directly or indirectly—in the decision on a visa application. The conditions and procedures governing the substantive examination thereof illustrate well the combined operation of the three types of sources discussed in the previous chapter. To start with the identification of the competent authority, the member state responsible for the examination of an application is that of the sole or main destination, or the first or main state of transit.[17] Once established which member state is responsible, the following question concerns what kind of bodies can decide on the applications. As a rule, these are normally dealt with by consulates or central authorities.[18] However, the VISA Code states that 'other authorities' may be required to become involved in the examination and decision-making process. What these other authorities could be, whether they need to meet certain minimum requirements, and the extent to which they can become involved and influence the decision-making process are all questions left unanswered.[19] If the admissibility criteria are met,[20] two broad principles will apply at the stage of the substantive examination of the application. Member states' personnel must act in full respect of human dignity and should not discriminate on any of the grounds stated therein.[21] Secondly, an application should not be automatically refused because a previous application from the same person was refused in the past.[22]

Within this framework, the VISA Code identifies a series of verifications to be performed by the competent authority. At its core, the examination constitutes an assessment of the risk posed by the TNC to the member states in terms of illegal immigration, public policy, public health, public security, or international relations.[23] This assessment, centred on the verification that the person meets certain criteria established in the Schengen Borders Code (SBC),[24] is based on a number of factors (such as financial self-sufficiency) and is supported by the consultation of the VIS,[25]

[14] M den Heijer, 'Visas and Non-discrimination' (2018) 20(4) European Journal of Migration and Law 470.

[15] P Stutz and F Florian, 'The EU's 'Return Rate' With Third Countries: Why EU Readmission Agreements Do Not Make Much Difference' (2022) 60 International Migration 154.

[16] M Czaika and M Hobolth, 'Do Restrictive Asylum and Visa Policies Increase Irregular Migration into Europe?' (2016) 17 European Union Politics 345.

[17] VISA Code, Article 5.

[18] VISA Code, Article 4.

[19] As mentioned in the last chapter, member states can also entrust external service providers or commercial intermediaries with certain tasks related to visa applications. While the tasks of the external providers are more clearly stated in the legislation, we only know that commercial intermediaries cannot collect biometrics. See VISA Code, Article 43(6)(c) and Article 45.

[20] For the specific conditions, see Article 19(1) of the VISA Code.

[21] VISA Code, Article 39. These grounds are sex, racial or ethnic origin, religion or belief, disability, age, or sexual orientation.

[22] VISA Code, Article 21. If this is the case, however, the consulate should contact the member state that refused the visa to learn about the specific circumstances behind the decision. See C(2019) 3464 final 55.

[23] VISA Code, Article 21.

[24] Regulation (EU) 2016/399 on the Schengen Border Code [2016] OJ L 77/1 (SBC).

[25] Regulation (EC) No 767/2008 on the Visa Information System (VIS) and the exchange of data between Member States on short-stay visas [2008] OJ L 218/60 (VIS Regulation).

as well as the second generation of the Schengen Information System (SIS II).[26] A look underneath the surface of these provisions reveals the heterogeneity of authorities that can influence the assessment and the criteria that can contribute to determining the risk(s). Two main areas are at play here: the use of interoperable databases and co-operation on the ground. In the previous chapter, we mentioned the link between the VIS and the Entry/Exit System (EES).[27] Although the legislation stipulates that direct consultation between the two is possible only if the relevant Regulations so provide, those measures allow visa authorities to access the EES any time a visa application is being processed. The full force of interoperability goes way beyond those two information systems, however. In itself, interoperability allows information systems to 'speak to each other' and is 'an evolutionary tool that enables further uses through the aggregation of data from different sources'.[28] Two different Regulations[29] allow for such aggregation of data from a wide range of databases: the VIS, SIS II, Eurodac,[30] the EES,[31] the ETIAS,[32] and the European Criminal Record Information System for TCNs (ECRIS-TCN).[33] Ultimately, the interoperability infrastructure enables migration and law enforcement authorities with access to one database to check information about a person across all the other systems.[34] As convincingly argued by different authors, this approach is hardly constitutionally compliant. In the specific context of

[26] Three Regulations govern the use of SIS II in three domains: checks, returns, and law enforcement. See, respectively: Regulation (EU) 2018/1861 on the establishment, operation and use of the Schengen Information System (SIS) in the field of border checks [2018] OJ L 312/14; Regulation (EU) 2018/1860 on the use of the Schengen Information System for the return of illegally staying third-country nationals [2018] OJ L 312/1; and Regulation (EU) 2018/1862 on the establishment, operation and use of the Schengen Information System (SIS) in the field of police cooperation and judicial cooperation in criminal matters [2018]OJ L 312/56. In the case of a hit, the competent authority should analyse the results. C(2019) 3464 final 60.

[27] Regulation (EU) 2017/2226 establishing an Entry/Exit System (EES) to register entry and exit data and refusal of entry data of third-country nationals crossing the external borders of the Member States and determining the conditions for access to the EES for law enforcement purposes [2017] OJ 327/20 (EES Regulation).

[28] N Vavoula, 'Interoperability of EU Information Systems: The Deathblow to the Rights to Privacy and Personal Data Protection of Third-Country Nationals?' (2020) 26 European Public Law 139.

[29] Regulation (EU) 2019/817 on establishing a framework for interoperability between EU information systems in the field of borders and visa [2019] OJ L 135/27 and Regulation (EU) 2019/818 on establishing a framework for interoperability between EU information systems in the field of police and judicial cooperation, asylum and migration [2019] OJ L 135/85. The adoption of two distinct Regulations depends on the legal basis on which they were enacted, and respectively: Article 16(2), Article 74, Article 78(2)(e), Article 79(2)(c), Article 82(1)(d), Article 85(1), Article 87(2)(a), and Article 88(2) TFEU; and Article 16(2), Article 74, and Article 77(2)(a), (b), (d), and (e) TFEU.

[30] Regulation (EU) No 603/2013 on the establishment of 'Eurodac' for the comparison of fingerprints for the effective application of Regulation (EU) No 604/2013 establishing the criteria and mechanisms for determining the Member State responsible for examining an application for international protection lodged in one of the Member States by a third-country national or a stateless person and on requests for the comparison with Eurodac data by Member States' law enforcement authorities and Europol for law enforcement purposes, and [2013] OJ L 180/1 (Eurodac Regulation).

[31] EES Regulation, Article 8(3) and Article 17a VIS Regulation.

[32] Regulation (EU) 2018/1240 establishing a European Travel Information and Authorisation System (ETIAS) [2018] OJ L 236/1 (ETIAS Regulation), Article 3(1).

[33] Regulation (EU) 2019/816 establishing a centralised system for the identification of Member States holding conviction information on third-country nationals and stateless persons (ECRIS-TCN) to supplement the European Criminal Records Information System [2019] OJ L 135/1.

[34] For a detailed and comprehensive explanation of the interoperability of such databases, see N Vavoula, *Immigration and Privacy in the Law of the European Union* (Brill 2022).

the VISA Code, it might enable a more effective achievement of *one* of its objectives (risk prevention) at the expense of proportionate and non-discriminatory application of the principle of purpose limitation.[35] Secondly, the effectiveness of interoperability itself cannot be taken for granted, given some of the issues around data quality that have emerged in the past and particularly as regards the VIS.[36]

Information acquired and exchanged on the ground is also vital to the risk assessment. In this regard, the VISA Handbook states: 'The depth of the examination [of an application] depends on the risk presented by the applicant according to . . . nationality, local circumstances . . . profile and personal history'.[37] To assess the risk of illegal migration, consulates should define profiles of applicants that might present a specific risk based on the local circumstances, without prejudice to the principle of the individual assessment of the application. Such a profile could be based on the stability of the person's situation, regard being had, for example, to their social status in the country of residence. Aspects that should be considered as part of the assessment are the previous abuse of social welfare in the member states or a succession of different visa applications (short-stay or long-stay visas) presented for different and unrelated purposes.[38] The importance of being 'particularly vigilant when dealing with risk categories' is emphasized, with specific references to unemployed persons or people with no regular income. Subject to verification with the national data protection authorities, the use of local warning lists containing data on certain persons—rather than profiles—is also possible. The opposite approach is taken vis-à-vis the known bona fide traveller. The requirements usually imposed on applicants in terms of supporting documents, particularly to enable an assessment of their intention to leave the member state within the period of validity of the visa,[39] can be waived for a person 'known to the consulate or the central authorities for his integrity and reliability'. Member states can presume the insurance requirement will be met, based on the applicant's professional situation.[40] In a very different fashion, the ILOs might also be relevant to cooperation on the ground. Their tasks are defined quite vaguely. ILOs should collect information on a number of issues—but not, as a rule, personal data—including European Integrated Border Management (EIBM) at the external borders, migratory flows and routes, ways and means to assist the authorities in third countries in preventing illegal immigration flows, facilitating readmission, and effective access to protection in the third country.[41] Importantly, ILOs may also assist with the identification of TCNs to facilitate their return, information-sharing with relevant authorities concerning illegal migration and cross-border crime, and identifying a person in need of international protection with a view to their resettlement in the Union.[42] ILOs

[35] E Brouwer, 'Large-Scale Databases and Interoperability in Migration and Border Policies: The Non-Discriminatory Approach of Data Protection' (2020) 26 European Public Law 86 onwards.
[36] N Vavoula, 'Interoperability of EU Information Systems' 152 onwards.
[37] C(2019) 3464 final 55.
[38] C(2019) 3464 final 67–69.
[39] See VISA Code, Articles 14(1)(d) and 31(1)(b).
[40] VISA Code, Article 15(6).
[41] Regulation (EU) 2019/1240 on the creation of a European network of immigration liaison officers (ILON Regulation) [2019] OJ L 198/88 (ILON Regulation), Article 3(4).
[42] ILON Regulation, Article 3(6).

may process personal data in relation to the activities in which they may provide assistance (identification of TCNs for different purposes). This can include data to confirm the identity of TCNs for the purposes of return and prevention of cross-border crime.[43]

The activities carried out in the country of the applicant's nationality could be problematic. Despite the principles stated on paper, and depending on the circumstances, the emphasis on the creation of profiles can be difficult to square with the principle of non-discrimination and risks seriously undermining the individualized nature of the application. This is even more so as these activities are particularly difficult—if not impossible–to scrutinize. The combination of informal cooperation, very broadly-worded grounds for establishing the risk, and the difficulty in challenging this decision may de facto place the burden of proof on the applicant. The VISA Handbook also suggests the creation of warning lists, without providing any details as to what their scope should be. Furthermore, their compilation is subject to consultation with national data protection authorities, who must be the authorities of the examining member state, lest the limits of EU data protection law be easily circumvented. Overall, the heterogeneity of criteria and factors to be considered by the competent authorities turns the risk assessment into a fishing expedition. Just as a broken clock marks the correct time twice a day, the more heterogeneous and wider the criteria to 'box' TCNs in different categories, the easier it will be to find a reason why a certain person might be at risk of irregular migration or might cause concerns in terms of public policy. It can lead to the over-pursuit of one objective at the expense of the effectiveness of facilitating regular travel. Ultimately, the way competing interests are accommodated in the legal framework verges on arbitrariness and seems to contradict the spirit and underlying principles of this 'practice'. These observations make the framework hardly compatible with the approach to fair treatment proposed in this book.

#### 5.2.1.2 Refusal and revocation of a visa: Challenges for interinstitutional cooperation

The heterogeneity of actors, procedures, and criteria involved in the risk assessment exposes the unfairness of the visa processing. Refusal and revocation of a visa are two areas where tensions with the principle of subsidiarity and solidarity are most likely to arise, due to the heterogeneity of levels of governance and decision-making centres. To recall, the assessment performed by a member state's authority must take account of the risk posed by the person to *any* of the member states. This provision expresses very clearly the general obligation of mutual trust and solidarity in the context of visa procedures, and stresses the role of each member state as the guardian of the whole Schengen area. The VISA Code provides an exhaustive list of grounds for refusing a visa, thus leaving no possibility for member states to introduce additional reasons in that respect.[44] This being said, member states enjoy some leeway on other related

[43] ILON Regulation, Article 10.

[44] Case C-84/12, *Koushkaki*, EU:C:2013:862, paras 45 and 47.

aspects. Firstly, a visa can be granted in the case of an inadmissible application for reasons of national interest, because of international obligations or on humanitarian grounds.[45] Secondly, an LTV will be issued, despite the person's non-compliance with the entry requirements,[46] when the member state considers it necessary on humanitarian grounds, for reasons of national interest, or because of international obligations. The same applies when the consulted member state has given a negative opinion on that visa application.[47] The phrasing of this exception is rather curious. Member states have a certain discretion when assessing the opportunity to issue a visa. However, they must do so once they have concluded that it might be necessary on one of the grounds stated.

However, the leeway seemingly left to the member states by these provisions has been significantly narrowed by the interpretation of the Court of Justice (Court or CJ). In particular, we must consider the example of a visa application on humanitarian grounds, submitted at the embassy of a member state (Belgium) in a third country (Lebanon) with a view to applying for asylum once in the EU and being granted a residence permit. The Court found that the VISA Code was not applicable to such an application, which fell solely within the remit of national law. Relatedly, the Court concluded that the Belgian authorities should not have regarded these applications as applications for short-term visas.[48] The CJ's reasoning was based on the following factors. Firstly, the definition of a visa under the Code as an authorization for, inter alia, an intended stay of 90 days maximum could not apply to the circumstances of the application.[49] Secondly, Article 25 of the VISA Code must not be taken as establishing common rules on humanitarian visas. The opposite interpretation would entail that member states must allow TCNs to apply for international protection through their representations in third countries, whereas the Asylum Procedure Regulation (APR) excludes these situations from its geographical scope.[50] Of a completely different nature was the conclusion of Advocate General Mengozzi. The AG opined that Article 25(1)(a) VISA Code would require a member state to issue an LTV, if there were 'substantial grounds to believe that a refusal to issue that document will have the direct consequence of exposing that national to treatment prohibited by Article 4' of the EU Charter of Fundamental Rights (CFR or the Charter).[51] The idea that the intention of the visa application placed that application outside the scope of EU law underpinned the Court's judgment. As the AG rightly noted, the applicant's intention to leave the member state constituted an explicit ground for refusal under Article 32 VISA Code, and the latter provision clarifies that it applies *without prejudice to* Article 25 of the

[45] VISA Code, Article 19(4).

[46] These are the entry requirements stated in the SBC and referred to in the VISA Code, Article 21.

[47] VISA Code, Article 25.

[48] Case C-638/16 PPU, *X and X v État belge*, EU:C:2017:173. For a comment on this case, see S Morgades-Gil, 'Humanitarian Visas and EU Law: Do States Have Limits to Their Discretionary Power to Issue Humanitarian Visas?' (2017) 2 European Papers 1005.

[49] Case C-638/16 PPU, *X and X v État belge*, paras 42–47.

[50] Case C-638/16 PPU, *X and X v État belge*, para 49. See also Regulation (EU) 2024/1348 establishing a common procedure for international protection in the Union (APR), Article 2(1).

[51] Case C-638/16 PPU, AG's Opinion, EU:C:2017:93

Code (the provision on LTV on humanitarian grounds).[52] This ground for refusal confirms that, in the circumstances under consideration, the VISA Code *does* apply, and so would Article 25 thereof. The interpretation proposed by the AG is truer to the wording and the spirit and context of the relevant provisions of the VISA Code, and would ensure a fairer implementation of the legal framework. It would also respect the autonomy of the member state in an area where the law has clearly accorded them a certain margin for manoeuvre.

Decisions on visas can also create 'horizontal' tensions (ie between member states). The previous chapter discussed how a member state might be in breach of the principle of solidarity, should it issue a visa despite another state's negative opinion or in the case where it ignored the other state's request to be informed.[53] Furthermore, a member state can annul[54] or revoke[55] a visa issued by another member state. In these two cases, the responsible member state is only subject to an obligation of information—rather than consultation—towards the issuing member state.[56] Therefore, the scope for a solidarity review in such situations would be narrower. A last note on possible issues of vertical and horizontal solidarity concerns the Visa Reciprocity Regulation. Such issues might emerge in the case of the Commission's inaction where a third country has decided to reintroduce a visa requirement for at least one member state.[57] As mentioned, the Commission has an explicit obligation to act once a series of procedures and negotiations have proved unsuccessful.[58] Arguably, a solidarity review of the Commission's conduct would be more meaningful in the phase that preceded the arising of such an obligation, since the Regulation already lays down that obligation explicitly.[59] We have also seen that member states are under no obligation to notify the arising of one of the factors which could, if reported, result in the suspension of the visa waiver.[60] If one of those factors was quantitatively or qualitatively significant, and the member state did not report it to the Commission, questions about compliance with solidarity would equally emerge. That principle would come into play when a member state's misuse of discretion left by the legislation had undermined the effectiveness and achievements of the objectives of the visa reciprocity mechanism. A member states inertia might affect the interests of other member states and the EU as a whole.

[52] Case C-638/16 PPU, AG's Opinion, point 51.

[53] See section 4.2.2.

[54] A visa must be annulled where the conditions for issuing it were not met at the time it was granted.

[55] A visa must be revoked where the conditions are no longer met. Article VISA Code, Article 34(2)

[56] VISA Code, Article 34(1). This was the factual background in Case C-83/12 PPU, *Minh Khoa Vo*, EU:C:2012:202.

[57] Visa Reciprocity Regulation, Article 7.

[58] Before this obligation kicks in, the Commission will enjoy discretion in its assessment of the opportunity to introduce a visa requirement against the third country in question. Case C-137/21, *European Parliament v European Commission*, EU:C:2023:625, where the Court found that the Commission had lawfully exercised this discretion in the case of the USA's imposition of visa requirements on Bulgarian, Croatian, Cypriot, and Romanian nationals.

[59] The finding could still be supported by solidarity.

[60] Low readmission rate, abnormal rate of overstay, or low recognition of asylum applications.

### 5.2.2 The European Travel Information and Authorisation System

#### 5.2.2.1 Risk indicators, watchlist, and profiling: Fishing expeditions against visa-exempt nationals?

The ETIAS is the other main channel of travel authorizations required of TCNs who wish to enter the EU.[61] The ETIAS and the VISA Code have mutually exclusive scope, since the former only applies to TCNs of visa-exempt countries. The ETIAS lays down 'lighter' procedures than those provided in the VISA Code. Such procedures mostly aim to ascertain that the applicant poses no security, illegal immigration, or high epidemic risk to the member states. The implications of the ETIAS for fundamental rights have been studied from different perspectives.[62] Here, we assess the impact of heterogeneity of actors, persons concerned, and objectives of the legal framework on constitutional compliance, by focusing on conditions for control and on the persons concerned. We will consider both the different sets of information underlying the risk assessment, and the processing of applications. While both are relevant to questions of fairness towards the persons concerned, it is particularly in the processing of applications that tensions in terms of interinstitutional cooperation can occur.

As with visa procedures, the concept of risk assessment lies at the core of the ETIAS. In this regard, the Regulation adopts a disturbingly expansive definition of security risk as covering threats to public policy, internal security, or international relations of any of the member states.[63] This notion, covering a heterogeneous range of grounds, introduces an all-encompassing understanding of security which departs from the approach traditionally espoused by the Court of Justice or the legislation itself.[64] Within this framework, the processing of the risk assessment ultimately aims to find—or exclude—genuine 'hits'. The hit is a correspondence resulting from the comparison between the personal data in an application file of the ETIAS Central System and one or more of the following: the specific risk indicators in the ETIAS Central System, the SIS, the EES, the VIS, Eurodac, Europol data, and Interpol's Stolen and Lost Travel Documents database (SLTD) and Travel Documents Associated with Notices database (TDAWN).[65] Here, we must introduce a distinction between the two main

[61] For a comprehensive study on the Regulation, see J Jeandesboz, S Alegre, and N Vavoula, *European Travel Information and Authorisation System (ETIAS): Border Management, Fundamental Rights and Data Protection* (Study for the European Parliament, PE 583.148, 2017).

[62] Among the plethora of contributions on the subject, see A Musco Eklund, 'Rule of Law Challenges of "Algorithmic Discretion" & Automation in EU Border Control: A Case Study of ETIAS Through the Lens of Legality' (2023) 25 European Journal of Migration and Law 249; T Zandstra and E Brouwer, 'Fundamental Rights at the Digital Border: ETIAS, the Right to Data Protection, and the CJEU's PNR Judgment' VerfassungBlog, 24 June 2022; C Derave, N Genicot, and N Hetmanska, 'The Risks of Trustworthy Artificial Intelligence: The Case of the European Travel Information and Authorisation System' (2022) 13 European Journal of Risk Regulation 389; C Blasi Casagran, 'Fundamental Rights Implications of Interconnecting Migration and Policing Databases in the EU' (2021) 21 Human Rights Law Review 433.

[63] ETIAS Regulation, Article 3(1).

[64] See, for a discussion of this conflation in another but somehow related area, L Azoulai and S Coutts, 'Restricting Union Citizens' Residence on Grounds of Public Security: Where Union Citizenship and the AFSJ Meet' (2013) 50 Common Market Law Review 553.

[65] ETIAS Regulation, Article 3.

categories of people covered by ETIAS: visa-exempt TCNs; and family members of EU citizens/TCNs who enjoy free movement rights because of an agreement between the EU and their state of nationality, who do not hold a residence card or a Single Residence Permit.[66] The second category enjoys a more favourable status in different respects. For example, their application is not checked by the ETIAS Central System against the EES or Eurodac. The ETIAS National Unit must verify the reasons for entering the alert in the SIS which triggered a hit in the context of the automated processing. The alert will not be taken into account in the decision on the application if related to a risk of illegal immigration.[67]

We have already pointed to the opacity of law-making underpinning the risk indicators, as well as the challenges caused by interoperability of databases in terms of constitutional compliance. These concerns are compounded by two tools introduced by the Regulation: the watchlist and the screening rules. The ETIAS watchlist contains data, entered by Europol or member states, 'related to' persons suspected of having committed or taken part in a criminal offence, or persons 'regarding whom there are factual indications or reasonable grounds, based on an overall assessment of the person, to believe that they will commit' a serious criminal offence.[68] The conditions for entering data into the watchlist are framed quite broadly, especially when considering that the link with the past or future commission of a crime is ultimately based on an open-ended 'overall assessment' of the person. The screening rules, for their part, fall under the responsibility of Frontex. They are defined as an algorithm for profiling, registered in the ETIAS Central System, which works through comparison of the data in the ETIAS application with the specific risk indicators established by the ETIAS Central Unit, *pointing to* security, illegal immigration, or high epidemic risks.[69] The screening rules perform profiling within the meaning of the General Data Protection Regulation (GDPR), defined as 'automated processing of personal data consisting of the use of personal data to evaluate certain personal aspects relating to a natural person, in particular to analyse or predict aspects concerning that natural person's performance at work, economic situation, health, personal preferences, interests, reliability, behaviour, location or movements'.[70] The system of fishing expeditions established by the ETIAS Regulation will likely deliver an unfair mechanism of control which disproportionately restricts the scope for an individualized examination of the application. The issues raised by the opaque and widely defined risk indicators are amplified by the predictive nature of the automated processing. Furthermore, the fact that such profiling is expected to *point to* one of the very broad risks the Regulation aims to prevent constitutes another element of flexibility in the legal framework and makes the latter prone to leading to arbitrary results.

[66] ETIAS Regulation, Article 2(1)(c).

[67] ETIAS Regulation, Article 24. All that glitters is not gold, however. Among other things, a person belonging to this category can only enter if accompanied by or joining the primary right-holder.

[68] ETIAS Regulation, Articles 35 and 36.

[69] ETIAS Regulation, Article 33.

[70] 'Profiling' here is used within the meaning of Article 4 of Regulation (EU) 2016/679 on the protection of natural persons with regard to the processing of personal data and on the free movement of such data [2016] OJ L 119/1 (GDPR).

#### 5.2.2.2 Data processing and risk assessment

The distribution of tasks featured in the ETIAS Regulation appears significantly more complex than the VISA Code. As mentioned, the main purpose of the system is to spot possible 'hits' for the risk assessment. To this end, all applications are automatically processed by the ETIAS Central System. The automated processing, which compares the applicant's data with the comparators mentioned in the previous section, aims to verify in particular whether the applicant: is subject to an alert in the SIS or a European Arrest Warrant; was reported in the EES as an overstayer or as having been refused entry, or in the VIS as having a short-term visa refused, annulled, or revoked; or, is registered in Eurodac.[71] While the processing of personal data under the ETIAS Regulation must comply with fundamental rights, and fully respect human dignity and integrity,[72] concerns have been voiced about the compliance of such provisions with the GDPR.[73] Furthermore, since the Regulation refers to *a* correspondence and makes no mention of a minimum threshold, *a* correspondence might be taken to mean *any* correspondence. For example, the comparison between an application by someone of a certain nationality might result in a hit with applications from the same nationality.[74] If the automated processing has reported a hit, the ETIAS Central Unit, established within the European Border and Coast Guard (EBCG), will compare the applicant's data with that of the person who has caused a hit. The range of the possible 'terms of comparison' is the same as with the automated processing.[75] In the absence of correspondence, the Central Unit must delete the false hit. If the correspondence is confirmed, or doubts persist about the identity of the applicant, the ETIAS Central Unit must inform the competent ETIAS National Unit, which must manually process the application and assess the illegal immigration, security, or epidemic risk.[76] The fact that the Regulation provides no element concerning what type of correspondence the ETIAS Units are supposed to look for, and how they differ from that found by the Central System (if at all), adds another layer of potential arbitrariness in the processing of travel authorizations. Furthermore, the specific criteria whereby such a risk assessment should be carried out seem to be left entirely to the member states, with no further specification in the Regulation.

When it comes to refusal of the application, the margin left by the ETIAS Regulation to the member states is tighter than that afforded under the VISA Code, at least in certain respects. In most cases, the authorization will have to be refused if the person is

[71] ETIAS Regulation, Article 20(2).

[72] ETIAS Regulation, Article 41.

[73] L Gugliotta and A Elbi, 'Will AI "Subtly" Take Over Decision-Making in the EU Migration Context? Warnings and Lessons from ETIAS and VIS' (2024) 9 European Papers 1018.

[74] More noteworthy still is the automatic comparison between the applicant's name (including the parents' name), date and place of birth, nationality, sex, education, and current occupation with the specific risk indicators. In the case of comparison with the data in the watchlist, further data concerning the applicant are involved, such as the member state of intended stay and the applicant's IP address. The comparison can also involve minors. ETIAS Regulation, Article 17(2)(a), (b), (c), (d), (f), (g), (j), (k), and (m), and Article 17(8).

[75] ETIAS Regulation, Article 7(2)(a).

[76] The member state responsible for manually processing an application in the case of a hit with an alert is the one which entered an alert that caused the hit or, if more member states are identified, the one that supplied the most recent data on the alert. ETIAS Regulation, Articles 25 and 26(2). The ETIAS National Units are in charge of the annulling and revoking of an authorization. ETIAS Regulation, Articles 40 and 41.

deemed to pose one of the risks the Regulation intends to prevent.[77] Therefore, an obligation of refusal arises as a result of the member state's discretionary assessment. This leeway disappears in other contexts, however. Specifically, the ETIAS National Unit(s) of the member state(s) which entered the data that caused the hit must be consulted and give their reasoned opinion about the application. While silence is taken as acceptance of the application,[78] a negative opinion by the consulted member state will bind the examining member state to refuse the travel authorization.[79] This mechanism establishes a particularly forceful system of mutual recognition and potentially reduces the likelihood of interinstitutional tensions. A final and particularly unfortunate note concerns cases where the member state does retain a margin of discretion. If the travel authorization was issued after a verification that a hit was in fact a false hit, the responsible National Unit *shall have the possibility* to add a flag for the benefit of border authorities and other bodies with access rights.[80] The absence of an obligation is difficult to explain. It would not have affected the member state's competences or responsibilities in terms of internal security, and is only likely to negatively impact the performance of border checks for no good reason.

### 5.2.3 Interim Conclusions

In the 'before leaving' scenario, the way tasks are allocated seems, overall, to respect the principle of subsidiarity and the essential state functions. The heterogeneity of different aspects of the legal framework has implications for solidarity and fairness. Firstly, the heterogeneity of the decision-making centres may lead to tensions between different member states' views on the granting of a visa or a travel authorization. Here, the principle of sincere cooperation and especially solidarity should be applied rigorously by the member states involved to minimize the risk caused by such decentralized systems. While solidarity is not an insurance policy against any adverse consequence or greater contribution possibly borne by a member state, it does require that other states' and the EU interests be taken into account when making the decision. The heterogeneity of decision-making centres can also create issues of equality of treatment—especially when combined with the vagueness of the criteria and the wide discretion left to national authorities. The extent of this discretion is broadened by the heterogeneity of the factors informing a decision authorizing a person to enter the EU (eg risk of irregular migration v humanitarian grounds). The contradiction might be an optical illusion, however. The humanitarian element seems to be rather weak in the bigger scheme of the legal framework. This weakness is compounded by the case-law based constraints on the autonomy of member states concerning the issuance of travel authorizations on humanitarian grounds. The more or less structured forms to assess risks of different kinds, the heterogeneity and vagueness of criteria underpinning

[77] ETIAS Regulation, Article 37.

[78] ETIAS Regulation, Articles 28 and 29

[79] ETIAS Regulation, Article 28(7). If the data that caused the hit was supplied by Europol and Europol provides a negative opinion, the member state may still grant the travel authorization, subject to justification and recording thereof in the application file. ETIAS Regulation, Article 29.

[80] ETIAS Regulation, Article 36(3).

this assessment, combined with the focus on irregular migration, significantly tilt the overall balance of the EU approach towards prevention—rather than facilitation—of entry. Read together, all these factors take the law away from the individual assessment, which raises serious questions about the fairness of the law of EU border controls. The lack of transparency, the broadly worded grounds, and the shortage of constraints on both these aspects increase the chances that regular entry will not be facilitated, thus perverting the intention of the practice of EU border controls.

## 5.3 In Transit

The analysis of EU border controls in transit focuses on two interrelated areas: surveillance through operational cooperation and information sharing; and partnership with neighbouring third countries, particularly those enabling the joint performance of tasks directly linked to border controls or the exercise of those functions in the third country's territory. The policy framework and secondary law on surveillance activities aim at preventing irregular entry as well as saving lives at sea and identifying vulnerable people. The previous chapter has shown that the heterogeneity of levels of governance and actors has led to the emergence of a heterogeneity of a system of sources which is much more effective in preventing entry than saving lives. This creates a situation of unfairness, as the 'practice' designed is not true to its spirit and objectives. By focusing on the conditions for exercising control and imposition on the persons concerned, this chapter assesses the appropriateness of the specific rules to achieve the objectives of the legal framework, regard being had to the heterogeneity of the objectives themselves, and the actors and the persons concerned. In order to do so, we must first understand the approach to the concept of surveillance taken by the legislation. Then we move on to the main strands of activities governed by EU law: sharing of information via EUROSUR, and operational activities (with a focus on sea border surveillance). Finally, we analyse the possible implications of agreements with neighbouring third countries.

### 5.3.1 Introducing the EU Border Surveillance: Definitions and Context

Surveillance activities at the EU external borders have increased exponentially over the years, through the use of technologies[81] as well as physical infrastructure.[82] These activities can be driven by member states (in isolation or via interparty agreements[83]), coordinated by Frontex,[84] and often receive the support of EU

[81] See https://ecre.org/mediterranean-disagreement-about-funding-for-new-fence-and-concerns-about-surveillance-on-greece-turkiye-border-%e2%80%95-investigation-into-migrant-death-in-greek-police-station-%e2%80%95-italy-consi/.

[82] See, for example, https://borderviolence.eu/reports/surveillance-technologies-at-european-borders-evros/.

[83] See https://www.agenzianova.com/en/news/migrants-italy-slovenia-and-croatia-sign-memorandum-for-joint-patrols-at-eu-border/.

[84] See https://www.statewatch.org/news/2024/september/frontex-flights-and-fatalities-in-the-channel/.

funding.[85] It is not possible to cover all such examples and legal issues they raise. Therefore, the discussion focuses on the research question and develops within the analytical framework of this book.

We can start answering this question by looking at how EU law approaches the concept of surveillance. In this sense, the legislation provides no 'hard-and-fast' definition thereof. The SBC defines it as 'the surveillance of borders between border crossing points and the surveillance of border crossing points outside the fixed opening hours, in order to prevent or detect unauthorised border crossing or the circumvention of border checks, to contribute to raising of situational awareness, to counter cross-border criminality and to take measures against persons who have crossed the border illegally'.[86] However, this provides no useful indications on the material scope of surveillance itself, other than teleologically they have a preventative nature vis-à-vis the irregular border crossing, be it related to a criminal activity or not. Conversely, the EBCG Regulation stipulates that EUROSUR must be used for 'external land, sea and air border surveillance, *including* the monitoring, detection, identification, tracking, prevention and interception of unauthorised border crossings for the purpose of detecting, preventing and combating illegal immigration and cross-border crime and contributing to ensuring the protection and saving the lives of migrants' (emphasis added).[87] The 'including' might be interpreted as establishing either a closed or an open list.[88] A look at the EUROSUR Handbook favours the first option, since it enumerates those activities—and only those—as 'in scope'.[89] The objectives of EUROSUR, one of the main instruments of EU border surveillance, thus map onto the objectives of EU border controls more widely. Both the list and the objectives are consistent with the preventative approach mentioned a few lines above. Curiously, the Regulation on Surveillance of the External Sea Borders (SESB Regulation) offers no explicit definition of surveillance either. It does, however, govern areas that fall—directly or indirectly—within the scope of that concept.[90] More generally, the EU approach is remarkably expansive, as it also covers activities more proactive in nature, such as interception, that would better fit the broader notion of prevention.[91]

Surveillance rests on, and aims to enhance, two qualities of both member states and the EU: situational awareness and reaction capability. These concepts have the same territorial scope, as they focus on activities at, along, or in the proximity of the

[85] See https://www.statewatch.org/news/2023/october/eu-more-surveillance-funding-and-operational-cooperation-to-fight-migrant-smuggling/.

[86] SBC Regulation, Article 2, point 12.

[87] Regulation (EU) 2019/1896 on the European Border and Coast Guard [2019] OJ L 295/1 (EBCG Regulation), Article 20(1).

[88] This might be read as signalling that these—and only these—are the activities forming part of the concept of surveillance. However, it might implicitly signify that surveillance includes those concepts, albeit not exhaustively.

[89] EUROSUR Handbook 7. At page 8, the Handbook further defines each of those concepts in turn. The Commission apparently adopted a new Handbook in January 2025 (Commission Recommendation of 17.1.2025 establishing the practical handbook for the implementation and management of EUROSUR ('EUROSUR Handbook'), C(2025) 117 final), but the document is not available through research in eurLex.

[90] The main example is SAR, which is not, arguably, part of the concept of the surveillance but rather a related activity.

[91] Instead, the legislation reverses the conceptual relationship between the two, and portrays prevention as an integral part *and* objective of surveillance.

external borders. However, their material scope is slightly different. Situational awareness is described as the ability to 'understand illegal cross-border activities', with a view to finding 'reasoned grounds' for reaction measures and reducing the loss of lives, whereas reaction capability relates to the actions aimed at countering illegal cross-border activities.[92] The legislation itself crystallizes the overemphasis of border surveillance on prevention of entry, potentially at the expense of the fair treatment of TCNs. This resonates with the relevant provisions of the SBC on border surveillance, where the saving of lives at sea reads like an afterthought.[93] With this in mind, we can now focus on the specific provisions of the exchange of information and operational cooperation.

### 5.3.2 EUROSUR: The Centrepiece of EU External Border Surveillance

The *constant monitoring* of the EU external borders is the *pièce de résistance* of the Union's system of surveillance,[94] which translates primarily into a series of information-gathering and reporting duties. These, in turn, can result in different types of operational activities.[95] Exchange of information and operational cooperation are, therefore, complementary. Before we zoom in on the rules concerning the functioning of EUROSUR, we must place the latter in the wider context of EU-related information systems relevant to this aspect of the legal framework. While EUROSUR is the main tool for the exchange of information and cooperation on surveillance for the purposes of border controls, with Frontex and competent national authorities primarily involved in it, the landscape of EU surveillance tools and relevant actors is much more complex. The heterogeneity of actors and tools of surveillance should be conducive to the achievements of its numerous objectives, but also increases the risk of uncertainty. Frontex in particular works in partnership with different bodies. It signed a tripartite agreement with the European Maritime Safety Agency (EMSA) and the European Fisheries Control Agency (EFCA) to cooperate on coast guard functions, including through surveillance mechanisms.[96] On this basis, the exchange of information takes place within different frameworks, depending on the objective at stake: if related to combating illegal immigration and cross-border crime and protecting lives of migrants, the Agencies will cooperate within EUROSUR; information exchange for maritime safety will instead take place within the framework of SafeSeaNet. It is plain to see how the scope of the two systems might overlap, with no clear criteria to identify which one should take precedence over the other in 'hybrid' situations. The Agencies also contribute to the development of the Common Information Sharing Environment (CISE).[97] Arrangements are in place with the

[92] EBCG Regulation, Article 2.

[93] SBC, Article 12(3).

[94] Article 25 EBCG Regulation betrays the variety of sources that can feed information into the national situational picture, spanning from stationary and mobile sensors to patrols through to ship reporting systems.

[95] Such as interception or SAR.

[96] See the Tripartite Working Arrangement between Frontex, EMSA, and EFCA.

[97] Tripartite Working Arrangement, Article 8.

European Aviation Safety Agency (EASA)[98] and the EU Satellite Centre.[99] Frontex and EASA cooperate within EUROSUR, particularly through the establishment of a specific situational picture (SP) related to air border surveillance, whose rules are set out in a specific arrangement detailing its content and scope.[100] Beyond EUROSUR, Frontex plays an important role in the context of the Copernicus programme. More specifically, Frontex is the 'entrusted entity' for the provision of the Copernicus Border Surveillance Service (CBSS).[101] Copernicus is the Earth observation component of the EU Space Programme, and offers services taken from Earth observation and non-space data. The Border Surveillance Component of the Copernicus Security Services is described as complementing the services provided by Frontex through EUROSUR.[102] These examples form an integral part of a much broader and articulated system of interagency cooperation in this area, which also and most prominently involves cooperation among Area of Freedom, Security and Justice (AFSJ) bodies.[103] To conclude this quick overview, we must mention Frontex One-Stop Shop (FOSS). This is the Agency's platform for sharing information with member states, Schengen-associated countries, and other designated partners.[104] It facilitates the cooperation between Frontex and its partners by making information accessible 24/7, according to defined standards and among predefined users. Other than such a laconic description, published on Frontex's website, the EBCG Regulation makes no reference to FOSS at all—including, most notably, to its relation with EUROSUR itself.[105]

In the context of this heterogeneity-driven uncertainty, EUROSUR remains the cornerstone of the system among the different EU surveillance tools for the purposes of border controls—a *primus inter pares*—including with regard to cooperation with third countries.[106] The conditions for the use of EUROSUR and the dynamic governing the interaction between the actors involved show that the system is based on a balance between centralization and decentralization. Therefore, at least in this sense, its set-up is consistent with that of the other strands of the law of external border controls considered so far. With this in mind, two principal questions of constitutional compliance arise: do the rules create the possibility of tensions in terms of interinstitutional solidarity, and how can they be resolved? Does EUROSUR perpetuate the imbalance towards the prevention of entry, at the expense of saving lives? To start with, EUROSUR

[98] See the working arrangement between Frontex and the European Aviation Safety Agency.

[99] See the working arrangement between Frontex and the EU Satellite Centre.

[100] Frontex-EASA Working Arrangement, Section 4. The arrangement describes cooperation between the two agencies as aimed more broadly at contributing to the EUROSUR Fusion Services and the European situational picture.

[101] This is under the Copernicus Contribution Agreement (2021–28). Frontex and EU SatCen have cooperated since 2015 on the basis of a service level agreement for the provision of border surveillance services.

[102] See https://www.frontex.europa.eu/what-we-do/beyond-eu-borders/copernicus-programme/.

[103] For further details, see https://www.frontex.europa.eu/our-partners/eu-agencies/eu-agencies/. This goes beyond the scope of the book, and has been extensively researched and discussed in D Fernández-Rojo, *EU Migration Agencies: The Operation and Cooperation of FRONTEX, EASO and EUROPOL* (Edward Elgar 2021).

[104] See https://foss.frontex.europa.eu/.

[105] FOSS is also mentioned in Frontex's operational plans.

[106] As stated in the 2025 State of Schengen report, Frontex is currently negotiating working arrangements with almost 20 third countries, which could cover information sharing via EUROSUR and risk analysis arrangements.

consists of different components, but the only actors that figure among them are the National Coordination Centres (NCCs).[107] The other constitutive elements are the different types of SPs,[108] the EUROSUR Fusion Services (EFS) and the integrated planning. Within the scope of this research, three interrelated aspects are relevant to assess the appropriateness of the rules to the objectives: the sources, the division of labour, and the system of reporting duties. The importance of the provisions on sources of surveillance is self-explanatory. The different pieces of information fed into the different SPs play a major role in determining the action at the EU external border. Remarkably, such information can be collected from an open-ended list of sources. It can be drawn from national border surveillance systems, other relevant national authorities and systems as regards the national situational picture (NSP), and for both the NSP and the European situational picture (ESP) from any 'other sources'.[109] Liaison officers, staff from missions, and delegations also provide intelligence for the purpose of the analysis layer of EUROSUR.[110]

Secondly, there is the issue of the distribution of tasks between the heterogeneous range of levels of governance and actors involved. Here, we must highlight an apparent divergence between the EBCG Regulation and the EUROSUR Implementing Regulation. On the basis of the former, Frontex is in charge of maintaining the ESP and coordinating the EFS, whereby the Agency provides the NCCs with information on the external borders and on the pre-frontier area.[111] Each NCC is, for its part, entrusted with a corresponding duty vis-à-vis its NSP,[112] and must transmit information about the relevant SP to Frontex.[113] The EUROSUR Implementing Regulation establishes a somewhat different framework of division of labour; different is not to be taken as contradictory. The heterogeneity of the different components of the legal landscape does impact its understanding, however. The Implementing Regulation distinguishes between the originator of the reports and the owners of the situational picture.[114] The originator of a report is described as the one *managing* the specific SP, who will transmit reports in EUROSUR. Such an entity could be the NCC, Frontex, or any other 'entities' in charge of this. The owner of the SP is the recipient of a report and must be responsible for processing it. This being said, another provision of the same instrument defines the owner as the entity managing the SP and the corresponding reports.[115] Furthermore, none of the abovementioned provisions lays down any requirements that the bodies in charge of the various SPs should possess.

The sources of surveillance are open-ended; the allocation of tasks is at times unclear, and the scope of bodies or systems of surveillance overlaps on certain occasions. While this creates no major issue in terms of subsidiarity, the question does arise as to whether interstate tension in cooperation might emerge, and most importantly

[107] EBCG Regulation, Article 20(1)

[108] See the previous chapter for further discussion of the details.

[109] See EBCG Regulation, Articles 25(1) and (2), and 26(2).

[110] EUROSUR Handbook 25.

[111] EBCG Regulation, Article 28(1) and (2).

[112] EBCG Regulation, Articles 25(1) and 26(1).

[113] EBCG Regulation, Article 20.

[114] Commission Implementing Regulation (EU) 2021/581 on the situational pictures of the European Border Surveillance System [2021] OJ L 124/3 (EUROSUR Implementing Regulation), Article 5.

[115] EUROSUR Implementing Regulation, Article 3.

whether the framework can appropriately pursue the main objectives of border controls. To better illustrate this point, let us take a closer look at the third relevant aspect of our analysis: the series of reporting duties that EU law imposes on member states and Frontex. Three types of such duties must be considered here. Firstly, there are the event reporting duties. The NCC must ensure that national authorities responsible for border management report all events detected while performing their tasks. The same applies to Frontex and the International Coordination Centre (ICC).[116] The NCC must report single events to Frontex and in EUROSUR whenever a timely reaction is needed or when the impact on the external borders is high or very high.[117] It is not clear whether the two requirements are cumulative. An effectiveness and fairness oriented interpretation of the Implementing Regulation suggests that they should not be, lest the achievement of the objectives of border surveillance—which includes taking life-saving action at sea—be jeopardized. If needed, the entity managing the specific SP might request further reports on a specific event from one of the sources of the NSP or the ESP.[118] The provision offers no indication as to what this request for information should be needed for, leaving the duty of cooperation on the other state's authorities rather nebulous. Presumably, there must be a connection to the objectives of border surveillance. Furthermore, the owner of the SP may close the event when it is believed, inter alia, that the estimated impact of the event does not justify the reporting.[119] This could, in turn, express a different position from that of the authority that reported the event.

Secondly, there are operational reporting duties. While the NCC must ensure that the participating units report their plan on the NSP more generally, the NCC must report on the plan on the ESP where the impact level at a border section is high or critical, or where there is a joint operation underway.[120] The extent of this obligation (eg when and how often the reporting should occur) is left undetermined. Certain provisions apply to different layers of the situational picture. In particular, the originator of an event or a risk analysis report must attribute a level of confidence to it by assessing its reliability. The owner must take this into account when updating the situational picture.[121] The originator must also attribute an impact level to each of these reports, based on its impact on the three main objectives of border surveillance (detection, prevention, and combating of irregular migration, cross-border crime, and saving lives at sea). The owner must attribute a level of impact based on information received and on its own risk analysis.[122] The obligation of merely taking into account makes sense, to the extent that anything stronger might not work from an operational point of view. We must highlight, however, the inevitable risk of tension between different

[116] EUROSUR Implementing Regulation, Article 7.

[117] EUROSUR Implementing Regulation, Article 9. A single event must also be reported in the case where it is covered by the list in Annex 2 of the Implementing Regulation. That is, inter alia: any event related to SAR; any event related to unauthorized border crossing; cross-border crime, or suspicion of attempted cross-border crime; or the hit in the database has an impact on border control measures.

[118] EUROSUR Implementing Regulation, Article 14.

[119] EUROSUR Implementing Regulation, Article 9(7).

[120] EUROSUR Implementing Regulation, Article 11.

[121] EUROSUR Implementing Regulation, Article 16.

[122] EUROSUR Implementing Regulation, Article 17.

reports, which in turn might result in a 'sliding doors' scenario as regards the actions taken based on one or another level of confidence or impact.

Last but not least, the EUROSUR Implementing Regulation features a chapter on the reporting of specific border control activities. Each NCC must ensure that the units under its control and participating in maritime border surveillance report on suspect vessels, or in the case where there might be a risk to migrants' lives.[123] Similar provisions apply to air border surveillance.[124] In the context of maritime border surveillance, and when rendering assistance to a vessel in distress at sea, the intervening authorities must 'take account of' and forward all relevant information 'related to a potential [search and rescue] incident' to the Maritime Rescue Coordination Centre (MRCC) and inform the NCC. There is no such duty of informing the NCC if the authorities 'clearly establish' that the incident is not related to saving lives or cross-border crime. It would seem that the obligation of involving the MRCC and the NCC arises only in more extreme situations, given the link to the assistance of a vessel in distress. The absence of an obligation to report requires an assessment of no risk to life. The danger, however, is that such an obligation would kick in only when the situation has become particularly serious or even irreversible. These requirements embody a relatively 'relaxed' approach to the risk of deaths at sea, when compared to the strongly preventative stance generally taken in relation to the prospect of irregular migration. The tragic failures in the implementation of border surveillance and the resulting loss of lives that have occurred over the years have been well documented. As revealed by the foregoing analysis, the legal framework embeds the imbalance in focus between the different objectives of external border controls and is inappropriate for achieving its objectives.

The debate around EUROSUR and border surveillance in certain member states aligns with some of the themes discussed above. For example, the Finnish Parliament passed a law on the implementation of EUROSUR into national legislation,[125] which has been met with mixed opinions by experts.[126] Interestingly, some of these remarks resonate with the issues of heterogeneity highlighted in relation to the relevant measures of EU law. For example, the Finnish Chancellor of Justice[127] emphasized the importance of defining ex ante and monitoring ex post the boundaries of competence and division of duties between the authorities involved, and pointed to the possible need for sharper regulation in light of the practical experience gained during the implementation of the Regulation. The Deputy Parliamentary Ombudsman stressed the need to ensure that officers from Finland and other EU countries know their powers 'accurately', particularly when operating in Finnish territory. The Deputy

[123] EUROSUR Implementing Regulation, Article 19.

[124] EUROSUR Implementing Regulation, Article 21.

[125] See Finnish Government proposal to Parliament for supplementary legislation concerning the European Border and Coast Guard. The amendment was finally adopted on 30 December 2020.

[126] Summary of opinions; Draft Government proposal for supplementary legislation on the European Border and Coast Guard.

[127] The Chancellor of Justice of the Government of Finland serves as the supreme guardian of the law, overseeing the legality of the activities of the Government and the President of the Republic. They also ensure that the authorities comply with the law and fulfil their duties. Citizens can file complaints with the Chancellor of Justice about an authority's activities that they suspect to be illegal. See the Act on the Chancellor of Justice of the Government.

Ombudsman also highlighted the risk of conflict between powers arising from nationally applicable legislation (especially the SBC and the Border Guard Act) and operation-specific executive powers. In particular, it should be specified whether the monitoring of fundamental rights compliance refers to national fundamental rights or only to those enshrined in the CFR. While acknowledging the similarity between the two standards, the Deputy Ombudsman deemed such a terminological clarification particularly important for the purposes of establishing what control mechanism would apply—whether the national one, or that internal to Frontex.[128]

### 5.3.3 Operational Activities: Focus on Sea Border Surveillance

The provisions governing EUROSUR reinforce the idea that the prevention of irregular migration and cross-border crime is *the* priority of EU border surveillance. This occurs as a result of four interrelated factors: the open-ended nature of sources feeding into the system; uncertainty around the distribution of tasks; the decentralized nature of EUROSUR and the heterogeneity of decision-making centres; and the conditions for the use of that system. Saving life is, to put it mildly, placed on the back burner.

Operational activities are inextricably linked to the exchange of information, and show the same priority. Before we move on to the specific focus of this section, we must set out the wider context in which the debate on border surveillance has developed. Surveillance activities can take place by air, sea, or land,[129] and are increasingly supported by different types of technology. As the focus of the EU and member states is on the prevention of entry,[130] their actions have caused controversy in several respects. Without aiming to be exhaustive, three main threads can be identified in this respect. Firstly, member states have criminalized humanitarian assistance in different fora. While this issue has often been discussed in relation to surveillance at sea, the increasing tensions at the EU Eastern borders have widened its geographical scope. Different member states have taken measures to prevent entry under the banner of the fight against the instrumentalization of migration.[131] The new measures of EU

[128] Some of these remarks, which were raised in the context of legislative negotiations, were addressed by the final text. This is the case specifically for aspects concerning the Chancellor's comments on the division of duties (see Articles 15a, 15b, and 35a) and competences (Article 35a and 35i). However, nothing on ex post monitoring was mentioned in the approved law. As regards the observations made by the Deputy Parliamentary Ombudsman, no consequential change was made in respect of the officer's knowing their powers accurately. The same holds true for the conflict between powers and the terminological uncertainty, except for the following statement made in the final document approving the legislation: 'The Deputy Parliamentary Ombudsman considered that the proposal should clarify the supervision of compliance with fundamental rights from the perspective of national and internal monitoring arrangements of fundamental rights and the Border and Coast Guard Agency. Based on the statement, the justifications for the proposal have been refined with a description of the EU Charter of Fundamental Rights'. In the Government proposal to Parliament for supplementary legislation concerning the European Border and Coast Guard, it is also stated that, based on Article 82(3) of Regulation 2019/1896, the legality oversight by the Chancellor of Justice and the Parliamentary Ombudsman extends also to the members of the standing corps groups operating in Finland.

[129] These types are often interconnected and support one another.

[130] See, for example, https://www.statewatch.org/news/2024/september/frontex-flights-and-fatalities-in-the-channel/.

[131] See the discussion below in sections 5.4.3.4 and 5.4.4.

law governing instrumentalization state only in the preamble that 'humanitarian assistance should not be considered as instrumentalisation of migrants when there is no aim to destabilise'.[132] This is consistent with the stand taken by EU law more generally and beyond instrumentalization, the emphasis having consistently been on criminalizing the facilitation of irregular entry.[133] In this regard, the Commission's recent proposal for a reform of the facilitator package fails to introduce a mandatory humanitarian exception to criminalization,[134] thereby making no progress in comparison to the existing legislation.[135] As observed,[136] this approach contradicts international law but has been very effective in allowing different forms of criminalization of humanitarian assistance to prosper across the EU.[137] This issue partly overlaps with a second theme characterizing the debate on EU border surveillance: SAR operations. Different questions have been addressed in the scholarship and at an institutional level. In the wake of the previous point, the laws and policies of certain member states have deterred NGOs from conducting life-saving operations at sea.[138] In this specific domain as well, the EU has acted through non-binding provisions.[139] More broadly, the alleged lack of EU competence in this area has meant that no common rules on SAR could be enacted beyond those laid down in the SESB Regulation.[140] The absence of a single piece of legislation must not be taken for Union inaction. To the contrary, the EU has developed a multi-layered strategy[141] on SAR that follows a paradigm of 'rescue-through-interdiction'/'rescue-without-protection'.[142] A third theme on external border surveillance has homed in on the responsibility of public[143]

[132] SBC, recital 12; Regulation (EU) 2024/1359 addressing situations of crisis and force majeure in the field of migration and asylum (or Crisis Regulation), recital 16.

[133] See the study for the EP, 'Fit for Purpose? The Facilitation Directive and the Criminalisation of Humanitarian Assistance to Irregular Migrants'.

[134] Proposal for a Directive of the European Parliament and of the Council laying down minimum rules to prevent and counter the facilitation of unauthorised entry, transit and stay in the Union, and replacing Council Directive 2002/90/EC and Council Framework Decision 2002/946 JHA, COM(2023) 755 final, recital 7.

[135] See Council Directive 2002/90/EC defining the facilitation of unauthorised entry, transit and residence [2002] OJ L 328/17, Article 1(2).

[136] See V Mitsilegas, 'Reforming the EU "Facilitators' Package"', School of Law and Social Justice, University of Liverpool.

[137] For an overview of such practices, see International Commission of Jurists, *Criminalization of Humanitarian and Other Support and Assistance to Migrants and the Defence of Their Human Rights in the EU*, April 2022.

[138] S Carrera and others, *Policing Humanitarianism: EU Policies Against Human Smuggling and Their Impact on Civil Society* (Hart 2020).

[139] Commission Recommendation (EU) 2020/1365 on cooperation among Member States concerning operations carried out by vessels owned or operated by private entities for the purpose of search and rescue activities [2020] OJ L 317/23; [2020] OJ C 323/01.

[140] Regulation (EU) No 656/2014 establishing rules for the surveillance of the external sea borders in the context of operational cooperation coordinated by the European Agency for the Management of Operational Cooperation at the External Borders of the Member States of the European Union [2014] OJ L 189/93 (SESB Regulation), Article 1. See previous chapter on solidarity.

[141] V Moreno-Lax, 'A New Common European Approach to Search and Rescue? Entrenching Proactive Containment' EU Immigration and Asylum Law and Policy Blog, 3 February 2021.

[142] V Moreno-Lax, 'The EU Humanitarian Border and the Securitization of Human Rights: The 'Rescue-Through-Interdiction/Rescue-Without-Protection' Paradigm (2018) 56 Journal of Common Market Studies 119.

[143] M Fink, *Frontex and Human Rights: Responsibility in 'Multi-Actor Situations' under the ECHR and EU Public Liability Law* (Oxford University Press 2018); G Raimondo, *The European Integrated Border Management: Frontex, Human Rights, and International Responsibility* (Hart 2024); F Mc Namara.

and private actors[144] involved in the implementation of the EIBM. Among the several controversial issues, we must mention the activities of the EU aerial surveillance enabling interception by Libyan authorities.[145]

Against this background, the scope of this section is much more specific and limited to issues of constitutional compliance caused by the heterogeneity of the legal framework. Sea border surveillance sees the involvement of different actors and levels of governance, but the SESB Regulation is not always straightforward as to where the responsibility for a certain action lies. The Regulation concerns surveillance operations carried out by member states and coordinated by Frontex. As we aim to assess the appropriateness of the rules to their objective, we must note that the Regulation aims to efficiently monitor the crossing of external borders as well as ensure the protection and saving of lives. As with the previous sections, we look at the conditions for exercising control and consider the issues arising from the different expressions of heterogeneity addressed in this book. Let us first introduce the main actors involved in such operations. In the context of the Regulation, the host member state is the one where the operation takes place or from where it is launched, while the participating member states provide support in terms of equipment or personnel. Both states engage in the operation through their participating units, which act under the responsibility of each country.[146] The International Coordination Centre (ICC), established within the host member state, is the structure coordinating the sea operation[147]—despite the title of the Regulation itself, according to which such a coordination would be performed by Frontex.[148] The Rescue Coordination Centre (RCC), for its part, is the unit responsible for *efficiently* organizing and conducting SAR operations within a SAR region. The RCC can play a particularly important role, as it must be promptly informed by a participating unit when they might be facing a situation of uncertainty, alert, or distress,[149] and provide instructions in reaction to that.[150]

The Regulation governs four different scenarios: detection; interception (in territorial waters, contiguous zone, and high seas); SAR; and disembarkation. For the purposes of our discussion, we must focus on the system of authorization to act in these situations. Such a system is a perfect showcase for the interdependence between the choices on task allocation, the nature of interinstitutional cooperation, and the

Externalised and Privatised Procedures of EU Migration Control and Border Management: A Study of EU Member State Control and Legal Responsibility (DPhil thesis, European University Institute 2017).

[144] See on this issue more broadly M Sagal Ambroso, 'Offshoring and Outsourcing Border Control: The EU use of Private Military and Security Companies', Migration Policy Centre, Migration Policy Centre Blog, 22 March 2022; A Pacciardi and J Berndtsson, 'EU Border Externalisation and Security Outsourcing: Exploring the Migration Industry in Libya' (2022) 48 Journal of Ethnic and Migration Studies 4010.

[145] See https://www.hrw.org/news/2022/12/12/eu-frontex-complicit-abuse-libya.

[146] The unit can be aerial, maritime, or land.

[147] SESB Regulation, Article 2.

[148] This ambiguity epitomizes a more systemic issue, which concerns the identification of the correct locus of legal responsibility for activities related to EU external border controls.

[149] Pursuant to Article 9 SEBS Regulation, the participating unit must also inform the ICC of any contact with the RCC.

[150] Depending on the circumstances, however, the instructing actor might also be the host member state or the third country responsible for the SAR operations.

impact on the persons concerned. More specifically, the analysis below makes it clear once again that a solidarity-oriented interpretation of the legal framework can result in fairer treatment of the addressees of control (understood as treatment truer to the spirit and principles underlying the law), despite the constitutional constraints on division of competences.

We start with the different types of interception covered in the Regulation. If a stateless vessel has been intercepted in the territorial waters of a host or participating state, and there are reasonable grounds to suspect that it intends to engage in smuggling or circumvention of checks,[151] that state *must* authorize the participating unit to take certain measures.[152] The same state *can* allow further action if the suspicion is confirmed.[153] When interception occurs in the water of a non-participating member state, however, any activities must be carried out *in accordance with* its authorization. A comparable dynamic emerges from the analysis of interception on the high seas.[154] Any action requires the agreement of the flag state, which is under no obligation to allow the measure. If a non-participating flag state refuses to react against smuggling as requested by the participating unit, a request to the same state must follow, to allow an action by one of the participating states. The only measures that the participating unit can take, in such circumstances, are 'those necessary to relieve imminent danger to the lives of persons or those measures which derive from relevant bilateral or multilateral agreements'.[155] Thirdly, action must or may be taken against a vessel intercepted in the contiguous zone of the host or a participating member state on the same conditions established for interception in territorial waters.[156] However, only measures to prevent infringement of laws and regulations within that member state's territory (including its waters) may be authorized. If the measures are to be taken in the contiguous zone of a non-participating member state, this state must provide its authorization.

In situations governed by EU law, a vessel can clearly experience a very different fate, depending on whether or not it enters the territorial waters of a state that is participating in an operation. If it does, the state is under an obligation to authorize *certain* measures, whereas if it doesn't, any action taken must be subject to the authorization of the state concerned and the specific scope thereof. The need to obtain authorization before acting in territorial waters, or with regard to a vessel flying the flag of a non-participating state, makes sense from the perspective of respecting its essential state functions. The same holds true for the discretion left to the participating member states with regard to the adoption of measures such as seizing the vessel or

[151] SEBS Regulation, Article 6.

[152] Such as stopping, boarding, and searching the vessels.

[153] For example, seizing the vessel and apprehending the persons, or altering the vessel's course to somewhere else. SESB Regulation, Article 6.

[154] The standard of proof, the suspected activities, and the possible measures are the same as for interception in territorial waters. The actions that can be taken if the suspicion is confirmed are also almost identical, with some further options added to the list.

[155] SEBS Regulation, Article 7(10). This clause should be taken to cover, for example, the SAR Convention and the Safety of Life at Sea (SOLAS) Convention. The issue of authorization would not arise with regard to a stateless vessel, which the participating unit may board and search in case of suspicion and, if confirmed, inform the host state for a decision on the appropriate action. Monitoring of the vessel should continue, if the suspicion of smuggling proved unfounded or if the participating unit cannot act for lack of jurisdiction.

[156] SEBS Regulation, Article 8.

apprehending the persons. Is a purely formalistic approach to the interpretation of these provisions constitutionally compliant? To determine the extent of the state's obligations and responsibilities, we must pay attention to the specific circumstances of the case and rely on the structured network of principles of EU law. The authorities that are supposed to authorize an action must, at the very least, comply with the principle of solidarity as defined in this book. Have those authorities, in their decision-making process, respected the procedural obligation to take account of the common interest? Or have they simply exercised their (legitimate) discretion, without consideration of the impact of their conduct on the objectives of the Regulation? As the discretion is neither linked to a derogation from EU law nor to any express obligation of solidarity, this principle could be meaningfully deployed in most serious cases—particularly, where the member state should be, or should have been, aware of the real risk that its conduct could have undermined a fundamental objective of the Regulation (see Figure 2.1).

These themes recur in the framework governing SAR.[157] Member states have an obligation to ensure that their participating units comply with the obligation to render assistance to any vessel or person in the context a sea operation 'in accordance with international law and respect for fundamental rights'.[158] The participating unit must inform the RCC responsible for the region where there is a vessel that is suspected to be in a state of uncertainty, alert, or distress.[159] While the Regulation lays down a series of criteria to determine the state of the vessel,[160] it is not entirely clear which actor is supposed to establish it. It seems only logical that the RCC's opinion would (and should) prevail. Furthermore, there is no mention in the Regulation of what course of action should be taken in cases where the vessel is in the SAR region of a non-participating state. The practice confirms that issues of allocation of tasks and compliance therewith are key to saving lives in the context of sea surveillance operations. Importantly, the EU Ombudsman conducted an own-initiative inquiry on Frontex's compliance with fundamental rights in this area[161] and issued strong recommendations to improve the performance of such operations. It was stated that Frontex should adopt and publish guidelines on how to deal with maritime emergencies. In this regard, the operation plan should contain specific provisions on a number of aspects, and particularly what course of action a participating unit should take pending instructions from the RCC and the allocation of responsibilities between Frontex and the participating member states. Also, more stringent conditions should be imposed on member states when using the services of aerial surveillance. Such conditions might include the member state's provision of timely updates in cases of maritime emergencies and an explanation for refusing Frontex's assistance. The recommendations show once again the impact of heterogeneity on constitutional compliance. This holds true on a very practical level, as regards the clear allocation of tasks and the establishment of adequate

[157] SEBS Regulation, Article 9.

[158] SESB Regulation, Article 9(1).

[159] In the absence of further detail, we can presume the participating unit is the one detecting the vessel or receiving a report about it.

[160] Such as the seaworthiness of the vessel, the number of persons on board or the presence of qualified crew, and the weather and sea conditions.

[161] Decision in Case OI/5/2020/MHZ.

procedures where a plurality of actors is involved. However, the link between assistance and cooperation made by the EU Ombudsman also matters on a systemic level, and particularly for the interaction between principles. To endure, solidarity requires solidarity: in this specific case, operational support cannot be unconditional, especially where a member state is requesting such support while also refusing assistance/provision of vital information and, in so doing, disregards the common interest and undermines the objectives of the legal framework. The interplay of the heterogeneity of actors and the possibility of deadly consequences also emerges at the national level. This is apparent from the indictment submitted by the Crotone Prosecutor's Office against four officers of the Guardia di Finanza and two members of the Italian Coastguard in relation to the Cutro shipwreck of 26 February 2023, in which 94 migrants died, including 35 children. Notably, the indictment linked the cause of the tragedy to a dereliction of duty as a result of a lack of proper coordination between the different national authorities responsible for external border controls.[162]

Interception and SAR operations are normally followed by disembarkation, which is the fourth macro-area governed by the SESB Regulation.[163] The different components of the legal framework are inextricably linked, so that some of the controversial issues raised above 'spill over' into this scenario. In case of interception in the territorial sea or the contiguous zone, disembarkation should take place in the coastal member state,[164] without prejudice to the order that might have been given to the vessel to alter its course.[165] Where interception has occurred on the high seas, disembarkation must happen in the host country if it cannot take place in the third country from which the vessel is assumed to have departed. In the context of SAR, the host and the participating states must cooperate with the responsible RCC to identify a place of safety[166] and, once that happens, disembark the persons rapidly and effectively. The heterogeneity of the actors involved in the phase of disembarkation creates two interconnected issues of constitutional compliance: one of solidarity between member states due to, for example, the unwillingness of a state or local authorities to provide authorization to disembark;[167] and one of respect for standards of asylum law and the principle of non-refoulement, in cases of disembarkation in third countries.

[162] See https://www.rainews.it/articoli/2024/07/strage-a-cutro-chiusa-inchiesta-della-procura-indagati-gdf-guardia-costiera-d82184a1-a336-45a2-8bcb-22d70ca684db.html.

[163] At some point, the EU had explored the possibility of regional disembarkation platforms. For comment, see F Maiani, '"Regional Disembarkation Platforms" and "Controlled Centers": Lifting the Drawbridge, Reaching Out Across the Mediterranean, or Going Nowhere?', RefLaw (14 September 2018).

[164] This is defined as the member state in whose territorial sea or contiguous zone an interception takes place. SESB Regulation, Article 2.

[165] Disembarkation seems difficult to reconcile with the order in question, so the 'without prejudice' clause can be explained in the sense that disembarkation would have to take place when the course-altering order has proved impossible to implement for any reasons.

[166] This is 'a location where rescue operations are considered to terminate and where the survivors' safety of life is not threatened, where their basic human needs can be met and from which transportation arrangements can be made for the survivors' next destination or final destination, taking into account the protection of their fundamental rights in compliance with the principle of non-refoulement'. SESB Regulation, Article 2.

[167] For reports on stand-offs between member states, see https://ecre.org/mediterranean-stand-off-over-disembarkations-of-survivors-rescued-by-civilian-search-and-rescue-operators-leaves-italian-government-on-collision-course-with-france-ngos-and-international-law/; https://ecre.org/mediterranean-italy-delays-malta-ignores-tunisia-and-libya-pull-back-and-abuse-people-on-the-move-suffer/.

As to the former, the Regulation makes no distinction between participating and non-participating states. In the case where a non-participating member state can provide the closest place of safety available and refuses to do so in the absence of valid justification, this state may be found in breach of the principle of solidarity, based on the test for a solidarity review proposed in this book. As to the disembarkation in a third country, the wide discretion granted by the 'assumed' nature of the vessel's country of origin is mitigated by the general principle that no person should be disembarked where the member states are aware—or they ought to be—that that third country engages in practices contrary to direct or indirect non-refoulement.[168] This provision goes hand in hand with the obligation, for the participating member states and Frontex, to coordinate and take account of the general situation in that country. However, the heterogeneity of the decision-makers involved is not accompanied by a proper mechanism of cross-scrutiny between them, nor criteria or procedure to orient the assessment of suitability for disembarking. Such concerns are compounded by the fact that, while the operational plan should contain details on this aspect, some of those published on Frontex's website feature little more than formulaic references to the SEBS Regulation.[169]

The analysis of the detailed rules on sea border surveillance echoes, to an extent, the reflections developed vis-à-vis the previous subsection. In the pursuit of a heterogeneous set of objectives, measures of secondary EU law try to balance the respect for essential state functions, interstate solidarity, and compliance with fundamental rights in a delicate equilibrium. Centralized coordination goes hand in hand with a heterogeneity of decision-making centres and a series of important 'sovereignty clauses' on the authorization of certain actions in a state territory. In this sense, heterogeneity opens our eyes to the functioning of a legal phenomenon, without automatically advocating for further homogeneity. Heterogeneity of decision-making centres as well as objectives is not *mala in se*, but we must identify possible issues occasioned by them as well as avenues for managing them. One way to do this is by improving the quality of the law outlining the division of labour as to the performance of certain tasks. In other contexts, and especially where member states are left a significant margin of discretion, the role of principles as enforcers of EU values within the meaning of this book is key. This includes, inter alia, taking account of other states' and the EU common interest when exercising that discretion.

### 5.3.4 Surveillance in Action: Agreements and Arrangements

The landscape of EU–third country cooperation on external border surveillance is complex. This section does not address all the possible forms of externalization or EU partnerships with third countries that might fall within this area.[170] Moreover, it does not cover the Common Security and Defence Policy (CSDP) missions

[168] SEBS Regulation, Article 4(2).

[169] This is the case for Operations Indalo, Poseidon, and Themis.

[170] SF Nicolosi, 'Externalisation of Migration Controls: A Taxonomy of Practices and Their Implications in International and European Law' (2024) 71 Netherlands International Law Review 1.

(including where they see the participation of non-EU states).[171] Consistent with the scope of the 'homologous' section to this one developed in the previous chapter, we must mention status agreements (SAs) and working arrangements (WAs) concerning cooperation with third countries or EU missions. The previous chapter highlighted the problematic aspects inherent in the choice of sources such as MoUs or working arrangements. Those concerns are compounded by the way decision-making powers are allocated. Frontex has signed a number of WAs, including with the UK in 2024.[172] Frontex also has WAs with missions such as EUNAVFORMED Irini and EUCAP Sahel Niger. All these arrangements feature a clause stating that the WAs do not constitute a legally binding international agreement. On closer inspection, there is more to them than meets the eye. The main purpose of these WAs is information sharing and joint risk analysis. They also allow the third country concerned to appoint a national contact point, with a view to participating as an observer in meetings of the Frontex Risk Analysis Network.[173] This, in itself, might pose challenges in terms of transparency, accountability, and privacy.[174] Certain WAs provide for the use of the third country's seaports and airports as Frontex's logistical bases for implementing cooperation,[175] whereas certain others pursue elaboration and coordination of joint operational measures.[176] Two aspects in particular are worth highlighting, beyond those addressed in the previous and the following chapter. Firstly, the SAs delegate the definition of certain conditions for control to future sources. For example, Frontex and Montenegro will make the arrangements for the fulfilment of the tasks assigned to the antenna offices. Such details will be set out in a separate arrangement,[177] but there are no traces of any such arrangements. Another example is the initiation of first-line checks in Moldova, which started at the end of 2023.[178] This is on the basis of the EU–Moldova SA, but the document has not been published online.[179] The use of such forms of (quasi)law creates a situation of high impact and low scrutiny as the administrative and judicial avenues of review are paved with hurdles.

[171] J Andersson, *INTO THE BREACH! EU Military CSDP Missions and Operations* (EUISS 2024); M Dobrescu, 'Explaining Third-Country Participation in CSDP Missions: The Case of the Association Trio—Ukraine, Georgia and Moldova' (2023) 32 European Security 539; SØ Johansen, 'Accountability Mechanisms for Human Rights Violations by CSDP Missions: Available and Sufficient? (2017) 66 International and Comparative Law Quarterly 181.

[172] This latest WA is much more detailed than those established in the past.

[173] A similar provision features in the WA with Georgia.

[174] See L Marin, 'The Cooperation Between Frontex and Third Countries in Information Sharing: Practices, Law and Challenges in Externalizing Border Control Functions' (2020) 26 European Public Law 157.

[175] See Frontex–Albania WA, https://prd.frontex.europa.eu/document/albania-working-arrangement/wa_with_azerbaijan.pdf.

[176] Frontex–Azerbaijan WA, Point 3(iv), https://prd.frontex.europa.eu/document/albania-working-arrangement/wa_with_azerbaijan.pdf.

[177] EU–Montenegro SA, Article 6(5) and (6), https://op.europa.eu/en/publication-detail/-/publication/86d86e24-edce-11ed-a05c-01aa75ed71a1/language-en.

[178] See https://www.frontex.europa.eu/media-centre/news/news-release/frontex-initiates-first-line-border-checks-outside-eu-nXm2OJ.

[179] See https://www.frontex.europa.eu/media-centre/news/news-release/frontex-initiates-first-line-border-checks-outside-eu-nXm2OJ.

### 5.3.5 Flexible Arrangements, Surveillance, and Off-Shore Processing: The Example of the Italy–Albania Deal

The different heterogeneity-related themes, discussed so far primarily in relation to EU law, can unfold powerfully at the level of member states too. In this regard, we must take a closer look at the substance of the Italy–Albania deal, which allows Italy to process returns and certain asylum claims in centres built in Albania, where Italian and EU law will apply.[180] The Protocol and the Law subject the centres, and the treatment of the persons held therein, to national and European law. Therefore, the relevant provisions of the new asylum and migration pact will apply, once they enter into force. It is thus important to consider, moving forward, how those measures might enhance—or weaken further—the position of the persons concerned. Three main procedures would apply: screening, asylum, and return. The Screening Regulation will apply first, logically and chronologically.[181] It will regulate the performance of screening procedures vis-à-vis TCNs who, inter alia, have applied for international protection during border checks, or have been disembarked after a SAR operation.[182] These two situations might 'match' the scope of the Protocol. This is particularly the case for post-SAR disembarkation. The question arises as to whether the other category—TCNs applying for protection during border checks—might cover the situation of migrants who were disembarked but *not* following a SAR operation. The Protocol and the Law treat the centres as frontier and transit areas. The new APR sees 'crossing points' as also covering transit zones,[183] and the SBC considers checks performed at border crossing points as 'border checks'.[184] Therefore, there should be correspondence between the Protocol and the Screening Regulation. It may well be the case, however, that TCNs will apply for international protection *when intercepted*. They might, therefore, be subject directly to border asylum procedures, as shown below.

There is an unfortunate similarity between the Protocol and the Regulation, insofar as both mandate the member states to prevent the entry of TCNs into the EU until and unless prescribed otherwise by EU law. However, the Regulation does provide for more specific obligations. Firstly, competent authorities must carry out a preliminary health check, and must check for indications that the person is stateless, vulnerable, a victim of torture, or inhuman treatment, or has special needs.[185] Secondly, they must ensure that minors are accompanied and assisted by a representative or a person trained for those purposes, who acts independently from the screening authorities.[186]

[180] For further context, see 4.3.2.

[181] Regulation (EU) 2024/1356 introducing the screening of third-country nationals (Screening Regulation).

[182] Or, who have been found to be staying illegally in the EU and there is no indication that they have been subject to border controls.

[183] Regulation (EU) 2024/1348 establishing a common procedure for international protection (Asylum Procedure Regulation or APR), Article 30(1).

[184] SBC, Article 2.

[185] Screening Regulation, Article 12. The reference here is to within the meaning of Directive 2008/115/EC on common standards and procedures in Member States for returning illegally staying third-country nationals [2008] OJ L 348/98 (Return Directive), Article 25 of Directive (EU) 2024/1346 laying down standards for the reception of applicants for international protection and Article 20 APR.

[186] Screening Regulation, Article 13.

Thirdly, while member states can, in certain cases, limit the access of persons providing assistance and counselling to the screening,[187] those restrictions will not apply to the UN High Commissioner for Refugees.[188] The Screening Regulation also obliges the member states to introduce an independent fundamental rights monitoring mechanism, although it imposes no formal requirements on them as regards its establishment.[189]

A particularly controversial aspect of the reform package concerns the much wider use of asylum border procedures.[190] Such a procedure will apply where an application has been made at the border, or post-SAR disembarkation, or following apprehension *in connection with* an unauthorized crossing. The last scenario might apply to TCNs who have applied for protection at the moment of the interception, as mentioned above. The APR defines the expression 'intercepted in connection with unauthorised crossing' as implying interception 'at the very time of the irregular crossing of the external border or near that external border after it has been crossed, or by persons disembarked following a search and rescue operation'.[191]

The expression 'third-country nationals intercepted in connection with unauthorised crossing' also features in Article 2(2)(a) Return Directive, and allows member states not to apply the Directive in such cases. The Court has interpreted this expression restrictively, and as implying 'a direct temporal and spatial link' with that crossing of the border. That situation therefore concerns third-country nationals who have been apprehended or intercepted by the competent authorities at the very time of the irregular crossing of the border or near that border after it has been so crossed'.[192] Not all the interceptions referred to in the Protocol will fall within this definition, however—for example, interceptions not carried out in the immediate vicinity of the borders and not related to a SAR. The question remains open, therefore, as to what framework would apply in the case where a TCN does apply for international protection at the moment of interception.

The application of asylum border procedures will have significant consequences. The person must not be authorized to enter the territory, and measures taken to prevent this will have to comply with the Reception Conditions Directive.[193] The terms for registration and examination will be much shorter than standard procedures.[194] This will be a double-edged sword: it will mean less time spent in detention, but also less time to examine the application and thus, potentially, a negative impact on the fairness of the procedure. This being said, the applicant must be granted leave to enter the member state, unless the return border procedure is applicable (ie the application

[187] Screening Regulation, Article 8(6).
[188] APR, Article 6(1).
[189] Screening Regulation, Article 10.
[190] APR, Articles 42 and following.
[191] APR, recital 57.
[192] Case C-47/15, *Sélina Affum v Préfet du Pas-de-Calais, Procureur général de la cour d'appel de Douai*, EU:C:2016:408, para 72.
[193] APR, Article 43(1).
[194] Border procedure applications must be lodged no later than five days from registration, as opposed to the 21 days for the ordinary procedures under Article 28 APR. The border procedures can last for 12 weeks maximum, starting from the registration of the application, in contrast to the much longer term provided for in Article 35 APR.

has been rejected).[195] Furthermore, two important safeguards are laid down in the APR which would be particularly relevant to the Protocol. Firstly, if the Commission has reasons to believe that a member state is not complying with obligations on reception standards of vulnerable people and especially families with minors,[196] it must issue a recommendation to suspend the border procedures and the member state must take 'utmost account' of that.[197] Secondly, the determining authority must cease to apply border procedures if it considers that necessary support cannot be offered in the circumstances, paying particular attention to victims of torture, rape, or other serious forms of psychological, physical, sexual violence, or gender-based violence.[198] Also, the Return Border Procedure (RBP) Regulation will apply to TCNs whose application for international protection has been rejected in accordance with asylum border procedures.[199] The RBP Regulation allows member states' extensive use of detention until the person leaves—voluntarily or not—EU territory, which adds to the periods already spent in detention on the basis of the screening and asylum border procedures.[200] To be sure, this is a result of the pact, rather than the Protocol itself. It is, however, helpful to understand how this new policy—assuming it will remain unchanged—will interact with the new system of EU asylum and migration law. In restricting individual protection as far as legally possible prima facie, the pact is consistent with the approach of certain member states. The two risk mutually reinforcing each other in a race to the bottom. Overall, this forward-looking analysis has left us with mixed results. While certain safeguards are contained in the new measures which should benefit the TCNs concerned, the pact on the whole has its barycentre in the member states' obligation to prevent most TCNs from entering the EU. This is very likely to result in prolonged periods of detention at the borders, which might compound the concerns on effective access to procedural rights caused by the Protocol and the Law discussed above. In certain respects, EU law is going to further constrain national discretion at the expense of the persons concerned; in others, national authorities are being granted much wider leeway in comparison to the existing measures of EU asylum and migration law. The *fil rouge* in these deceptively contradictory trends is the restriction on individual rights of the persons concerned.

### 5.3.6 Interim Conclusions

Consistent with the previous scenario, the law of EU border controls in transit pursues its different objectives in an unbalanced manner. While the different actions aimed to prevent entry are underpinned by a robust legal framework, supported by a strong preventative dimension, the same cannot be said vis-à-vis the protection of lives and rights of TCNs. Heterogeneity, in its different forms, is the *fil rouge* running through the different themes touched upon in this section. The system of distribution of tasks,

[195] APR, Article 51.
[196] APR, Articles 53(2)(b) and 54(2).
[197] APR, Article 45(4).
[198] APR, Article 21(2).
[199] Regulation (EU) 2024/1349 establishing a return border procedure (RBP).
[200] See in particular the RBP Regulation, Articles 4 and 5.

in part built to respect essential state functions, is prone to creating legal incongruities and tensions between the EU and the member states, as well as among the member states. Furthermore, the strongly preventative approach applied to irregular migration is not matched by a similar working method when it comes to saving lives at sea. The connection between allocation of power and solidarity emerges not only from EU law as it is, but also from how it is *not*. The heterogeneity caused by the absence of a common minimum framework on SAR beyond the Frontex-coordinated operation, the lack of a prohibition to criminalize humanitarian assistance, and sharing responsibilities on addressing post-disembarkation situations are all connected in a picture that comes at the expense of the lives and rights of TCNs. Innovative approaches developed by certain member states, exemplified by the Italy–Albania deal, contribute further to devoid the law in action of its spirit and undermine the principles on which it should be built, ultimately compromising its fairness.

## 5.4 At the Borders

The exercise of controls at the EU external borders is governed by a variety of instruments.[201] As we know by now, controls are regarded as including: measures to facilitate legitimate border crossings; where *appropriate*, measures related to the prevention and detection of cross-border crime; identification and referral to the appropriate procedures of vulnerable persons, including those in need of, or wishing to apply for, international protection.[202] The prevention of entry has emerged as a priority in EU law, to such an extent that it undermines the effectiveness of the legal framework and the fair treatment of the persons concerned.

While border controls are normally thought of as checks on persons to ensure they meet the required entry conditions, this section discusses a wider range of control-related tasks and associated conduct. More specifically, we can distinguish between three macro-scenarios. Firstly, we have the rules governing the EBCG's reaction to an emerging situation—for example, via a SAR mission or a joint operation (or 'reactive controls'). Secondly, there are the 'ordinary' controls performed in respect of the thousands of people who present themselves every day at the EU external borders seeking entry, whether on the basis of a valid title or not. Thirdly, there are hybrid situations. These essentially consist of the system of border procedures established by certain measures of the 2024 asylum and migration pact. Such procedures do not necessarily require the involvement of Frontex, nor do they correspond to the ordinary border crossing. The scenarios are not watertight. The EBGC tends to become involved particularly in reactive controls, whereas ordinary and hybrid checks are normally performed exclusively by member state authorities competent for these purposes. Be that as it may, all these scenarios fall within the EIBM. Legal issues arising from the conduct of Frontex and member states at the EU external borders and violation of migrants' fundamental rights have extensively been covered in the policy[203]

[201] For context, the external borders are the same as those defined by the SBC. EBCG Regulation, recital 118.

[202] EBCG Regulation, Article 3.

[203] T Strik, 'Pushbacks in the EU: How to End Impunity?' European Policy Centre, 16 December 2020.

and legal debate,[204] by NGOs,[205] and at an institutional level as well.[206] The analysis is developed within the scope of this research, and therefore focuses on the impact of heterogeneity on constitutional compliance.

### 5.4.1 Reactive Controls: Conditions for Assistance

Consistent with the definition of reactive controls provided above, these involve close cooperation between two levels of governance (the EU and the member states) and a number of different actors from either of them. This cooperation generally materializes in the assistance provided by EU bodies to one or more member states. As with other scenarios discussed so far, a heterogeneous range of actors is tasked with pursuing a heterogeneous range of objectives, while addressing a heterogeneous range of persons. Against this background, the appropriateness of the legal framework is best assessed by considering the principles underlying this cooperation and these activities, and also the conditions for requesting, granting, and terminating assistance.

Generally, the effective implementation of the EIBM rests on cooperation and good faith between Frontex and the member states,[207] and it is a shared responsibility between the two. However, the member states retain primary responsibility for the management of their sections of the external borders, with Frontex 'reinforcing, assessing and coordinating' the actions of member states and providing technical and operational assistance.[208] The emphasis on member states' responsibilities is without prejudice to a major role for Frontex in terms of decision-making concerning the exercise of control. The question of ultimate liability, which remains difficult to answer, will be addressed in the following chapter.[209] For context, the EBCG consists of member state authorities responsible for border management and returns *and* the EBCG stricto sensu—or Frontex.[210] The EBCG operational staff is composed of the staff forming part of the EBCG standing corps who act as members of the teams having executive powers[211] and the staff responsible for the functioning of the ETIAS.[212] The EBCG standing corps, in turn, is composed of four categories of operational staff.[213]

[204] I Kalpouzos, 'International Criminal Law and the Violence Against Migrants' (2020) 21 German Law Journal 571; M Moraru, 'Generalised Push-Back Practices in Europe: The Right to Seek Asylum Is a Fundamental Right' (2022) 1 Quaderns IEE 154; E Guild, 'The Frontex Push-Back Controversy: Lessons on Oversight (Part I)—EU Immigration and Asylum Law and Policy', Blog of the Odysseus Network, 19 April 2021; 'The Frontex Push-Back Controversy: What Oversight for Frontex?' (Part II)—EU Immigration and Asylum Law and Policy, Blog of the Odysseus Network, 22 April 2021.

[205] See https://www.europarl.europa.eu/RegData/etudes/BRIE/2021/698816/EPRS_BRI(2021)698816_EN.pdf.

[206] See, for example, this comprehensive overview at https://www.europarl.europa.eu/RegData/etudes/BRIE/2021/698816/EPRS_BRI(2021)698816_EN.pdf.

[207] EBCG Regulation, recital 25.

[208] EBCG Regulation, Article 7(1) and (4).

[209] See, for the most recent development, Case T-600/21, *WS v European Border and Coast Guard Agency (Frontex)*, EU:T:2023:492.

[210] EBCG Regulation, Article 4.

[211] Border management teams are deployed during joint operations or rapid border interventions, while the migration management support teams provide reinforcement to member states. These can be drawn from the operational staff, from the EUAA, Europol, the FRA, or other Union bodies and member states.

[212] EBCG Regulation, Article 2.

[213] EBCG Regulation, Article 54.

The statutory staff in particular[214] can be authorized by the Executive Director (ED) to carry and use weapons.[215] All persons participating in Frontex operational activities must comply with its code of conduct.[216] In all activities, members of the teams must fully respect fundamental rights and pay particular attention to vulnerable persons. Any measures taken shall be proportionate to the objectives pursued.[217] Statutory staff deployed as members of the teams must observe the rules on the use of force.[218] They are generally competent to perform verification of the identity of the person, authorize or refuse entry, issue or refuse visas at the border, register the fingerprints of persons apprehended in connection with the irregular crossing of an external border in Eurodac, and liaise with third countries to identify and obtain travel documents for returnees.[219] The preamble of the EBCG Regulation suggests that executive powers should be set out in the relevant national law or in this Regulation,[220] but the Regulation itself offers very little on what those executive powers could be. Having clarified that Frontex's staff can be directly involved in actions related to the actual exercise of control, it is important to set out the 'chain of command' of such activities. As a rule, Frontex-coordinated activities see the host state in charge of issuing instructions, in line with the operational plan, to the members of the teams,[221] who must normally act in the presence of staff from the host state.[222] Similarly, staff can only carry and use weapons during operations in compliance with the law of and in the presence of the border guards from the host state—unless the latter agrees otherwise.[223] Interestingly, the host state can only prohibit the carrying of weapons where the same prohibition applies to its own border guard when involved in return-related tasks.[224] This is a remarkable provision, as it applies a principle of equivalence to a very sensitive area related to an essential state function. The use of force by statutory staff must respect fundamental rights, and specifically the principles of necessity,[225] proportionality,[226] and precaution.[227] This brief sketch is relevant to understanding

[214] This is staff deployed as an operational team in an operational area.

[215] This must be in accordance with Article 82 and Annex V EBCG Regulation.

[216] This is available at https://prd.frontex.europa.eu/document/code-of-conduct-for-all-persons-participating-in-frontex-operational-activities/.

[217] EBCG Regulation, Article 43(4).

[218] EBCG Regulation, Annex V EBCG.

[219] EBCG Regulation, Article 55.

[220] EBCG Regulation, recital 59.

[221] EBCG Regulation, Article 43(1). In the case of an activity implementing a status agreement with a third country, the third country's authorities might also be tasked with giving instructions.

[222] EBCG Regulation, Article 82(2) and 82(4).

[223] The conditions for carrying and using weapons must be detailed in the operational plan.

[224] EBCG Regulation, Article 82(8).

[225] This entails its use in exceptional and strictly necessary circumstances, as a last resort after every reasonable effort has proved ineffective, to discharge Frontex's duties or in self-defence, and never to be arbitrary or abusive.

[226] Relatedly, the use of force must be unavoidable, and be used in proportion to the seriousness of the situation and the objectives. Proportionality must inform the nature and the extent of force used.

[227] This requires that staff give clear warning of their intention, unless this were to cause risk of death or serious harm to others, or be clearly ineffective or inappropriate. Specifically, the objectives justifying the use of firearms are to deal with extreme emergencies, to defend themselves or others from an imminent threat of death or serious injury (including preventatively), or to repel or prevent an impending dangerous attack on essential services or facilities. Other means of forces, such as baton, lachrymatory agents, and handcuffs follows the same or very similar principles. Interestingly, lachrymatory agents can be used to avert an attack, whereas the use of the baton requires that the attack be on property specifically.

the complex organization of the division of labour within activities at the external borders, but should not convey the idea that Frontex's staff are mere executors of the host member state's instructions and therefore shielded from responsibility. The next chapter shows that the different monitoring officers and mechanisms built into the EBCG Regulation make such a claim disingenuous.

With this in mind, we must take a look at the conditions under which activities at the external borders can take place. In the two previous scenarios, we have seen that the heterogeneity of levels of governance involved in external border controls is managed through balancing centralization and decentralization. As we have learnt from the scenario 'in transit', a fundamental feature associated with this approach is that any forms of assistance provided by Frontex in this regard must—at the very least—have the agreement of the member state concerned.[228] This is consistent with the spirit of the whole framework. In the previous chapter, we highlighted that the attribution of an impact level to an external border section is key to deciding what action to take. Member states must organize regular, appropriate, or reinforced border controls depending on the low, medium, or high level of impact attributed to a section of their borders. The level must also be agreed upon by the member state concerned. In the case of high impact, a member state *may* also request support from Frontex. When the impact level is critical, Frontex must notify the Commission, and the ED must recommend that the member state requests one of the relevant actions, such as a joint operation or rapid border intervention. The member state concerned must respond to the recommendation, stating the reason for refusing to issue a request.[229] The decision on the impact level as well as the acceptance of Frontex's assistance embody the connection between choices of task allocation, interinstitutional cooperation, and the fair treatment of the persons concerned. We have consistently argued that the current set-up respects subsidiarity and the essential state functions, but creates tensions on the two other levels of analysis addressed in this research. While within its prerogatives, a member state's decision to refuse assistance could impact constitutional compliance. In the absence of any considerations for other states and the common interest and/or a justified reason to refuse assistance, the member state's conduct could be difficult to square with the principle of solidarity. As discussed above, the EU Ombudsman recommended that Frontex 'link' the provision of assistance to the cooperative conduct from the requesting member state. Relatedly, and depending on the circumstances of the case, it might undermine the effectiveness of the legal framework and jeopardize the *appropriate* achievement of the EU objectives. A member state refusing assistance when confronted with pressure on its external borders might be very effective in preventing entry, but also increase the possibility of violations of the right to asylum and the principle of non-refoulement.[230] The evidence tells us that, at the moment, the involvement of Frontex is not a guarantee of fair treatment of the persons concerned. The point made here is systemic, however. Beyond the importance of not resigning

[228] EBCG Regulation, Article 7.
[229] EBCG Regulation, Article 35(1).
[230] See https://ecre.org/eu-eastern-borders-poland-ignores-commission-pressure-for-frontex-deployment-eastern-states-move-to-legalise-pushbacks-belarus-suspends-return-agreement/#:~:text=Poland%20refuses%20European%20Commission%20push%20for%20a%20Frontex,pushbacks%20at%20the%20EU%20level%20in%20%E2%80%9Cextreme%E2%80%9D%20situations.

to the idea that the EBCG will *always* be a vector for fundamental rights violations, the argument emphasizes the operational manifestation of the structured network of principles, and highlights the role that solidarity can play to achieve higher constitutional compliance.

In a different scenario of a request for assistance *from* a member state, Frontex *must* provide it *appropriately*.[231] This is not the same as being under an obligation to assist in the specific way requested. In fact, certain measures can be taken if specific conditions are met. The threshold to request the launch of a joint operation, for instance, is relatively low and can also be made to obtain increased technical and operational assistance in relation to an upcoming challenge. A rapid border intervention, on the other hand, requires a specific and disproportionate challenge. In both cases, there seems to be no obligation for Frontex to grant the request.[232] Obligations of solidarity apply to Frontex too. As solidarity features an element of reciprocity, as also hinted at by the EU Ombudsman in her recommendations, a crucial question arises: how, if at all, should such a reciprocity condition be 'enforced'? If the provision of assistance must be linked to the cooperation of a member state, what threshold would legitimize the Agency withholding such assistance?

A discrete sort of request for assistance can be submitted by a member state facing disproportionate migratory challenges in particular hotspot areas characterized by large inward mixed migratory flows. In such a case, the member state may request reinforcement from migration management support teams. The request is made to the Commission, which coordinates the whole process in cooperation with the relevant actors.[233] This is one of the few occasions where the Commission intervenes directly in the operational stage of external border controls, which is probably related to the seriousness of the situation. This is the only form of assistance that expressly provides for the participation of personnel from the European Union Agency for Asylum (EUAA; formerly the European Asylum Support Office) and, where appropriate, the Fundamental Rights Agency (FRA).[234] Once again, however, the process is unequivocally bottom-up and can be triggered exclusively at the initiative of the member state. Once again, we are confronted with the dilemma concerning the limits of the exercise of the state's discretion and the meaning of the *appropriate* pursuit of the EU objectives. Is it 'more' constitutionally compliant to seemingly redesign the boundaries of a state's discretion hermeneutically, with the help of principles such as solidarity, in order to increase the chances of achieving the goals of the legal framework (preventing irregular entry as well as identifying vulnerable persons)?

Any of the activities described above must be terminated by the ED if the conditions are no longer met.[235] More precisely, the ED may withdraw the financing if the host state is not complying with the operational plan, and must do so if they believe there are serious—or likely to persist—violations of fundamental rights.[236] Similarly,

[231] EBCG Regulation, Article 36(2).
[232] EBCG Regulation, Article 37.
[233] Depending on the circumstances, these could be Frontex or the EUAA, or both. The reinforcement may consist of assistance in screening TCNs, providing information to persons wanting to apply for international protection, and referral to the competent national authorities. EBCG Regulation, Article 40.
[234] EBCG Regulation, Articles 2 and 40.
[235] EBCG Regulation, Article 46(1) and (2).
[236] EBCG Regulation, Article 46(3) and (4).

the ED must not launch any activities if they believe there would be serious reasons to suspend the activity at the beginning.[237] The obligation to withdraw financing or not launch activities must be based on duly justified grounds, regard being had to a series of factors: the number and substance of registered and non-resolved complaints; reports of serious incidents; and reports from coordinating officers, international organizations, and Union bodies.[238] The following chapter addresses in more detail the questions related to the threshold for suspending or terminating activities, and the issues caused by the lack of legal avenues to flesh out the bare bones of the Regulation in this area.

### 5.4.2 Ordinary Controls: Actors, Subjects, and Conditions

Reactive control can result in activities falling under the broader category of 'ordinary controls'. For example, if TCNs on a vessel have been disembarked in the territory of a member state following an interception or a SAR, procedures for the identification of the persons concerned will follow. In many cases, these procedures are linked to the submission of an application for international protection. These types of activities also unfold through diplomatic or consular channels of cooperation with the possible countries of origin, and can involve the ILOs. The next section focuses on the system of border procedures established by the 2024 pact. Here, we deal with 'routine' checks at the EU external borders. Through several examples, we highlight how the legal set-up in this context leaves considerable discretion to border guards on the final decision of granting or refusing entry, and creates opportunities for tensions between different member states.

The main instrument governing ordinary checks is the SBC, which has been significantly amended on different occasions over the past few years. All persons crossing the external borders are subject to border checks, but the type of control varies depending on the category of control subject. Generally, border checks must always be performed in compliance with fundamental rights, particularly by fully respecting the person's dignity and the principle of non-discrimination.[239] Databases play a crucial role in controls at the borders, and their use will be significantly enhanced by interoperability. The start of the operation of the EES will herald a new era of automated border controls, consisting of the combination of the self-service system and the e-gate. The self-service system is the automated system performing—entirely or partly—border checks and may be used for pre-enrolling data in the EES. The e-gate, already commonly in place in airports, is the infrastructure 'where the border is crossed'.[240] The EES adds a further layer of control for certain categories of TCNs,[241]

[237] EBCG Regulation, Article 46(5).

[238] EBCG Regulation, Article 46(6).

[239] SBC, Article 7.

[240] SBC, Article 2. By this definition, we might take it to mean that a person will not be regarded as having irregularly entered the EU before they have crossed the e-gate. They would still be in that state's territory and subject to their jurisdiction, however. As per Article 2(2) Return Directive, in this situation member states would be allowed to apply different procedures from those set out in the Directive.

[241] TCNs admitted for a short-stay and TCNs' family members who are EU citizens/nationals of Schengen-associated countries who are not in possession of a residence card or a residence permit.

who will have to register their data (including biometrics) in the system on entry and exit through the EES self-service system.[242] Self-service systems must be used under the supervision of a border guard, who decides, on the basis of the results of the checks through self-service, whether to allow the entry or exit, or to refer the person to a border guard. Essentially, the person can be referred to a border guard on any grounds or situations,[243] including when they have successfully used the self-service system and want to use an e-gate.[244]

Through the VIS/VISA Code, the ETIAS, and the EES, EU law now pervasively controls access to the Union for short-stays by TCNs needing a visa, as well as visa-exempt TCNs. The VIS and the ETIAS, combined, aim to close gaps in the monitoring of different categories of TCNs travelling to the EU for short periods. The EES complements the system. It allows the automated monitoring of entry and exit of those categories of TCNs to and from the EU, with a view to streamlining checks at the borders and ensuring continuing control over the TCNs' fulfilment of entry and stay requirements. In fact, by recording such data at the point of entry and exit, the EES will automatically generate alerts in cases where there is no exit recorded for a person at the moment that their title of stay has expired.[245] These databases will work together to verify the identity of the person as well as the validity of their title of entry and travelling documents.[246] The EES Regulation stipulates that certain categories of TCNs must have their data recorded in the EES once they get to the external borders, so that an individual file in that system can be created. Absent such a file on a TCN present in the EU, or where the entry/exit record contains no exit date following the expiry of their authorized stay, the member state *may* presume the person does not fulfil the conditions for staying. The presumption does not apply to TCNs who provide credible evidence that they enjoy free movement rights or possess a residence card or a residence permit. The presumption may also be rebutted where the person provides credible evidence that they are not an overstayer. If the presumption is not rebutted, however, the Return Directive or the Citizenship Directive will apply as appropriate.[247] The provision leaves a great degree of administrative discretion to the member state authorities, with no further guidance whatsoever as to what kind of evidence might be regarded as suitable for rebutting the presumption, what threshold

[242] Their data, and those of a number of other categories (eg holders of a long-stay visa) should not, however, be entered into the EES when they are refused entry. The TCNs who must record their data and create a file in the EES can use its self-service pre-enrolment. The system must verify the identity of the person and whether they are already registered, possibly followed by checks on their fingerprints. If the data are not recorded in the system, the person must pre-enrol themselves through the self-service and subsequently get checked by a border guard. Such checks can involve the correspondence between the facial image and fingerprints of the document used at the self-service system and those of the person in front of them.

[243] Even though the SBC enumerates a series of grounds for referral—including 'in case of doubt'—it also stipulates that the person can be subject to further checks 'based on other reasons'.

[244] SBC, Article 8a. TCNs subject to a second line of checks must be informed, in writing and in a language they may reasonably be presumed to understand, of the objectives and procedure of such verification. The information must include the fact that the person can request the name or service identification number of the border guards carrying out the check, the name of the border crossing point, and the date on which the border was crossed.

[245] Interestingly, some of the TCNs to whom the EES applies are not subject to the automatic calculator, which indicates a period of overstay on exit, for example. See EES Regulation, Article 11.

[246] EES Regulation, Article 23 and ff.

[247] SBC, Article 12.

should be reached for those purposes, and according to what procedures. The risk inherent in this potential heterogeneity of approaches across the Union, and the ensuing danger of forum shopping and inequality of treatment, are only part of the problem. Legal certainty is another illustrious victim of such broadly-scoped provisions.

The data being recorded into the EES and the associated checks concern only certain categories of TCNs. However, the checks in databases more broadly apply to every person crossing the border and focus on certain essential entry requirements: the identity of the person seeking entry; the existence of threats, posed by the person concerned to one of the interests stated in the SBC; and the existence and validity of a short-stay visa or travel authorization as well as their travel document.[248] While this last condition is not applicable to a person enjoying free movement rights, they are still subject to verification of identity and security checks.[249] The 'thorough checks' applicable to TCNs[250] must focus on the fulfilment of the entry requirements. Firstly, as discussed above, a fundamental condition is the possession of a valid title of entry, such as a visa or a travel authorization.[251] Other than short-stay visas granted under the VISA Code, a person can be allowed entry and stay in the EU on the basis of a national long-stay visa or a residence permit.[252] Visas and travel authorizations are normally applied for and issued in advance. In some cases, however, they can be issued at the borders. This being said, a visa can be issued at the borders only in exceptional circumstances and if certain conditions are met.[253] In the specific case where the person is of a nationality for which prior consultation is required by another member state, the visa should not be issued at the borders unless humanitarian grounds, reasons of national interest, or international obligations exist.[254] This provision raises once again issues about the possible tension between different decision-making centres mentioned in previous parts of the book. Failure of the visa holder to produce, at the border, one or more of the supporting documents mentioned in

[248] SBC, Article 8(3)(a)(i), (iii), (iv). See also Article 8(3)(g)(iii) and (iv).

[249] SBC, Article 8(5) stipulates that checks on persons enjoying the right of free movement are carried out in accordance with the Citizenship Directive. See Citizenship Directive, Article 5.

[250] SBC, Article 8(3).

[251] Specific rules apply to TCN family members of either EU citizens or TCNs enjoying free movement rights equivalent to EU citizens. See, for example, the EES Regulation, Article 2(3)(b). Such TCN family members must be granted leave to entry with a valid passport and must possess a visa only when they are not in possession of a 'family member' residence card. This card can be issued if a previous card for family members of EU citizens has been obtained. If this is the case, and they arrive at the borders without having applied for a visa, they must be given 'every reasonable opportunity' to obtain all the relevant documents within a 'reasonable period of time' to demonstrate that they enjoy free movement rights. See C(2019) 3464 final, p. 111.

[252] Other documents for these purposes are the facilitated transit documents (FTD), as per Council Regulation (EC) No 693/2003 establishing a specific Facilitated Transit Document (FTD), a Facilitated Rail Transit Document (FRTD) [2003] OJ L 99/8; and the facilitated railway transit documents (FRTD) as per Council Regulation (EC) No 694/2003 on uniform formats for Facilitated Transit Documents (FTD) and Facilitated Rail Transit Documents (FRTD) provided for in Regulation (EC) No 693/2003, OJ L 99/15.

[253] VISA Code, Article 35. The applicant fulfils the conditions laid down in the SBC, ie Article 5(1)(a), (c), (d), and (e); the person could not apply for a visa in advance and present evidence of unforeseeable and imperative reasons for entry; and the applicant's return to the country of origin or residence is assessed as certain. In such circumstances, the requirement of having travel medical insurance can be waived if such insurance is not available at the borders, or for humanitarian reasons. Such a visa must be for a stay of a maximum of 15 days. If these conditions in the SBC are not met, the responsible authorities can issue an LTV.

[254] The reference is, more broadly, to the grounds stated in Article 25 VISA Code.

the VISA Code,[255] should not automatically lead to a decision to annul or revoke the visa.[256] While this is a provision that aims to avoid unnecessary disruptions to legitimate travel, it also offers another example of the incredibly wide discretion left to border guards of each member state. As regards travel authorizations specifically, the mandatory consultation in the ETIAS system might show the existence of a flag attached to the authorization.[257] In particular, a flag can be added when the authorities are unsure that sufficient reasons exist to reject the travel authorization, and thus recommend a second line of checks.[258] If that is the case, the person at the border *must* be subject to such checks. If a flag was added because the hit triggered during the processing turned out to be a false one,[259] and an additional verification is needed, the authority *may* access the system for further information.[260] The power to carry out a second line of checks is left very open, and there are no constraints or guidance on when this could be imposed on the person concerned.

Secondly, the TCN must justify the purpose and conditions of their trip, showing that they have the means of subsistence for the duration of their stay.[261] A fundamental entry condition is that the person is not subject to an alert in the SIS and does not pose a threat to internal security, public policy or public health, or the international relations of any member states.[262] In this context, it must be highlighted that EU law has different understandings of public policy and policy security, whose meaning and scope depend on the context in which they are referred to. The requirement of 'present, genuine and sufficiently serious threat' applies to persons enjoying the right to free movement[263] and to certain—but not all–TCNs.[264] The SBC, however, requires no such threshold. Border authorities have a much wider discretion in this regard. The 'concept of "threat to public policy or public security" [as referred to in the context of the entry requirements by the SBC is] appreciably different from' those mentioned above.[265] However, the authorities must still comply with the principle of proportionality. This also requires that, in the absence of a conviction, a visa-exempt TCN present in the EU for a short stay can be returned for no longer fulfilling the SBC entry requirements on public policy grounds 'only if there is consistent, objective and specific evidence' for suspecting that the TCN has committed an offence.[266]

[255] See in particular VISA Code, Article 14(3).

[256] VISA Code, Article 34(4).

[257] ETIAS Regulation, Article 47.

[258] ETIAS Regulation, Article 36(2).

[259] ETIAS Regulation, Article 36(3).

[260] ETIAS Regulation, Article 48.

[261] The assessment of sufficient means of subsistence may be based on the cash, travellers' cheques, and credit cards in the TCN's possession.

[262] TCNs who do not fulfil the conditions, but hold a residence permit or a visa of a member state, must be allowed to transit through the member state whose external border they wish to cross to the state of residence/permit, unless the TCN is on the list of alerts of the state of crossing and that alert specifies that the person should be refused entry.

[263] Directive 2004/38/EC on the right of citizens of the Union and their family members to move and reside freely within the territory of the Member States [2004] OJ L 158/77 (Citizenship Directive), Article 27(2).

[264] Contrast Case C-554/13, *Zh and O*, EU:C:2015:377, para 60 with Case C-544/15, *Fahimian*, EU:C:2017:255, para 40.

[265] Case C-380/18, *Staatssecretaris van Justitie en Veiligheid v EP*, EU:C:2019:1071, para 42.

[266] Case C-380/18, *Staatssecretaris van Justitie en Veiligheid v EP*, paras 46–49.

Furthermore, entry cannot be refused because of practical difficulties experienced by border guards in checking the TCN.[267] As the entry requirements are exhaustive, allowing member states to refuse entry on additional grounds would undermine the objective of facilitating legitimate travel, and justifying the refusal of entry on practical difficulties would go against the proportionality of checks.[268] Especially in light of the heterogeneity of the IT systems on which external border controls now rely, we cannot ignore the risk inherent in individual rights violation, possibly caused by the inaccuracy of data processing and/or storing. A person can also be allowed entry into the EU on humanitarian or public interest grounds, despite not meeting one or more entry requirements. This being said, if the person is subject to an alert, however, the other member states must be informed.[269] The member state deciding on entry has no obligation to follow the view of the other member state, which, depending on the specific circumstances of the case, might lead to questions of compliance with sincere cooperation and solidarity.

Checks against databases can be reduced to targeted checks in case of disproportionate impact of traffic flow, on the basis of an assessment of the risks mentioned above.[270] Even when controls are targeted, the databases should be checked if 'there are indications that such a person could represent a threat to the public policy, internal security, public health or international relations' of the member states.[271] The member state pivoting to targeted checks must inform the Commission and also the other member states, who can notify the member state of their concerns, which must be taken into account. As in many other examples discussed in this and the previous chapter, the conduct of member states should be informed by solidarity and sincere cooperation, even though the Regulation only establishes an obligation to take into account the comments from other member states.

### 5.4.3 In between: The 2024 Asylum and Migration Pact and the Complex Landscape of Border Procedures

The reform of EU asylum and migration law has established a complex system of border procedures, with the different instruments of the pact interacting with each other. These measures also interact with certain major amendments to the SBC, formally approved in 2024 as well. Two such amendments are relevant to our discussion, both of them introducing new grounds for restricting entry at the external borders of the EU. Firstly, member states may take the necessary measures to preserve security, law, and order where a large number of migrants attempt to cross the external border

[267] Case C-575/12, *Air Baltic Corporation AS v Valsts robežsardze*, EU:C:2014:2155. The case concerned an Indian national travelling from Russia to Latvia with a valid passport without visa affixed, and a cancelled passport by Russian authorities with a valid visa affixed.

[268] Case C-575/12, *Air Baltic Corporation*, paras 67–70. This is even more so as nothing in the VISA Code or the SBC suggests that, in such a situation, a visa should be annulled and/or entry should be refused.

[269] SBC, Article 6.

[270] At the very least, the identity of the person should be established by consultation of their documentation.

[271] SBC, Article 8(2a) and (2b).

in an unauthorized manner, en masse, and using force.[272] *In particular* in a situation of instrumentalization of migrants, member states can temporarily close specific border crossing points or limit their opening hours. Measures taken to this effect must be applied in compliance with the principle of proportionality and 'taking full account' of the rights of persons entitled to free movement, long-term residents under the relevant Directive, persons with a right to reside on the basis of EU or national law or long-stay visa and their family members, and applicants for international protection.[273] As further unpacked below, the concept of instrumentalization is destined to ascend to the role of protagonist of external borders management. For the time being, we must note the *carte blanche* given by the SBC to member states to address situations such as those observed at the Poland–Belarus border. The SBC has also introduced a further restriction on travel to the EU in the event of large-scale public health emergencies.[274] These restrictions must be based on a Council implementing regulation at the Commission's proposal. They may entail restrictions on entry, or other measures such as quarantine and self-isolation, and must be applied proportionately and in a non-discriminatory manner. Restrictions on entry must not apply to persons entitled to free movement, long-term residents under the homonymous Directive, persons with a right to reside on the basis of EU or national law or long-stay visa holders and their family members, or applicants for international protection. However, health-related measures must be compatible with the Citizenship Directive. The Council regulation will also determine the categories of people undertaking essential travel and exempted from restrictions on entry. If a decision is made in the sense of applying such restrictions to persons undertaking essential travel, they may only be imposed exceptionally, for a strictly limited period, until sufficient information about the emergency is available and until other health-related restrictions are identified and adopted by the Council on a proposal by the Commission. This may present a significant example of the incoherence in the way such restrictions apply, as a direct result of the heterogeneity of membership of Schengen and of the EU. On the one hand, the provisions refer to persons entitled to free movement, which include the nationals of Schengen-associated countries. On the other hand, the SBC prescribes that such restrictions be imposed compatibly with the Citizenship Directive, which by definition covers only EU citizens. Turning to the migration and asylum pact, this consists of several legislative instruments. The Asylum and Migration Management Regulation (AMMR) gives concrete effect to the principle of solidarity and fair sharing of responsibility. This is especially regarded as the need to take account of the member states' shared interest in the effective functioning of the EU asylum and migration system. Solidarity entails an obligation to cooperate closely, as well as a more specific obligation concerning the allocation of sufficient resources and effective management to the national systems, and the provisions of support to other member states in the form of solidarity contributions.[275] While measures of solidarity on asylum and migration management are

[272] SBC, Article 5(3).
[273] SBC, Article 5(4).
[274] SBC, Article 21a.
[275] Regulation 2024/1351 on asylum and migration management (AMMR or AMM Regulation), Article 6. The provision also refers to a series of measures that can serve to support member states in the framework of the Permanent EU Migration Support Toolbox.

closely linked to border controls, the scope of this section matches that of its 'homologous' section in Chapter 4: namely, the complex system of border procedures established by the new pact. There, we discussed the system of sources governing border procedures, whereas below we assess the conditions for controls.[276]

#### 5.4.3.1 Step 1: The screening

As mentioned in the previous chapter, the system of border procedures established by the pact starts with the screening. To assess the consistency of the rules with the intentions and underlying principles of this 'practice', it is worth reminding ourselves of the objectives of the measures: facilitating the identification of TCNs (and vulnerable persons in particular) to refer them efficiently to the appropriate procedures, as well as contributing to achieving the objectives of border control in compliance with Union and international law. There are certain aspects of the framework that might jeopardize the proper identification and referral to the appropriate procedure. The two goals are inextricably linked, as the correct referral can only follow proper identification. Closer consideration of the undermining factors must be prefaced by an important observation. Pursuant to the Screening Regulation, the categories of TCNs subject to the screening must not be allowed to enter the member state. The member states must ensure that the TCN 'remains available' for the screening, which must take place at an adequate and appropriate location designated by them. In practice, this is very likely to result in a generalized use of detention of TCNs, including most applicants for international protection. Consistent with the right to liberty as enshrined in the Charter and the European Convention of Human Rights (ECHR),[277] EU asylum law as it currently stands also allows for the detention of asylum seekers for the purpose of identification. However, it subjects deprivation of liberty to the principles of necessity and proportionality,[278] and presupposes an individual assessment.[279] Realistically, it is unlikely that this provision of the pact will be found in breach of Article 6 CFR.[280] The fact that the procedures must be completed within seven days probably mitigates in favour of its legality as well.[281] This being said, the mandatory and generalized nature of the 'holding' raises questions of compatibility with proportionality and necessity, and therefore with fairness more broadly.

Against this background, three main elements can undermine the proper identification and referral of TCNs. Firstly, the Regulation establishes a strong presumption against entry, even when a member state has favourably assessed the situation of the TCN concerned. In fact, the screening must also apply to the persons falling under Article 6(5)(c) SBC who have made such an application. These are TCNs who do not

[276] See G Cornelisse and M Reneman, 'Border Procedures in the European Union: How the Pact Ignored the Compacts' (2022) 11 Laws 38; V Apatzidou, 'The Complex Landscape of Asylum Border Procedures in the New Asylum Procedures Regulation', European Law Blog, 25 June 2024.

[277] See also Article 5(1)(f) ECHR, which allows detention of a person to prevent their effecting an unauthorized entry into the country.

[278] See the current Reception Conditions Directive, recital 15 and Article 8. This reflects the test for restrictions of Charter rights established in Article 52(1) CFR.

[279] Reception Condition Directive, Article 8(2).

[280] See Case C-601/15 PPU, *JN*, EU:C:2016:84, where the Court found that the possibility to detain an asylum seeker on security grounds did *not* make the Reception Condition Directive in breach of 52(1) CFR.

[281] Screening Regulation, Article 8(3).

fulfil the conditions of entry but *may be* authorized to enter on humanitarian or public interest grounds.[282] Despite the person having already been granted leave to enter by the member state on one of these grounds, the Screening Regulation mandates that the state apply the screening procedure to that person nonetheless. This clause is particularly unfortunate, as it overrides a decision already made by a member state, which presumably had already taken into account the implications of that authorization of entry, including on humanitarian grounds. To the contrary, the provisions on assistance provided by the EU Asylum Agency or the EBCG are under-prescriptive. These agencies *can* assist the member states with the screening,[283] but they are under no obligation to do so under any circumstances. The lack of more forceful wording is probably explained by the intention to avoid unwelcome inroads into member states' autonomy, but the TCNs may pay the price for this (especially in situations where a member state is under particular pressure). Such consequences could impact the quality of the conditions of 'holding' pending the screening, as well as the quality and accuracy of the screening itself.

Secondly, beyond the health and vulnerability checks mentioned above, the screening consists of searches in databases for verification of identity and security.[284] Therefore, a decision will rely significantly on the interoperability of these databases, as the competent authorities will be able to access the VIS, the EES, and the ETIAS. The Regulation, however, is not clear as to what the screening authorities should be specifically looking for. In this regard, it must be emphasized that a new character has recently entered the scene of immigration-related databases: the risk indicators. Pursuant to a recent amendment to the VIS Regulation, the Commission must adopt delegated acts to *further* define the risks of security, illegal immigration, or high epidemic, which must inform the decision-making of visa authorities. Such a risk-definition exercise is based on a series of criteria and information, which include: statistics generated by the EES or the VIS indicating *abnormal* rates of overstaying; refusals of entry or of visa applications[285] for a specific group of visa holders; and statistics generated by the VIS and the EES indicating correlations between information collected through the application form and overstaying by visa holders or refusals of entry.[286] The Commission must adopt an implementing act to specify the risks on which the specific risk indicators mentioned above are based.[287] An almost identical legal framework applies to the ETIAS. The Commission must adopt delegated acts to further define the risks related to security, illegal immigration, or a high epidemic risk. Different from the VIS Regulation, however, the risk indicators established by the ETIAS Central Unit consist of a combination of data, including a series of information such as age, gender, nationality, education, and occupation.[288]

282 Screening Regulation, Article 6.
283 Screening Regulation, Article 8(9).
284 Screening Regulation, Article 14 and Articles 20–23. The Screening Regulation provides for other types of purpose limitations. For example, the data from the ECRIS-TCN can only be retrieved on convictions related to terrorist offences and other serious criminal offences.
285 In this specific case, the refusal must be due to a security, illegal immigration, or high epidemic risk.
286 VIS Regulation, Article 9j(2).
287 VIS Regulation, Article 9j(3).
288 ETIAS Regulation, Article 33(4).

The role that such risk indicators might play in the screening is unclear. Even though they were not *directly* relied on by the competent authorities, they might still impact the outcome of the process. They might have previously led to a refusal of a visa or a travel authorization, and been used to attach a label to the person concerned. The combination of the type of non-transparent sources such as delegated acts, the type of information underlying it, and their impact on the person concerned is likely to affect the fairness of the screening procedure. Such (un)defined statistics and correlations are tools for profiling, which in turn will orient the decision-makers on the applications for visas and, as shown below, travel authorizations. Furthermore, the legal framework grants incredibly broad executive discretion to the Commission.

Thirdly, the TCNs must be provided with information about their rights and obligations under EU law. However, member states must provide information *where appropriate* about the conditions for entry and stay within the SBC, the obligations under the Return Directive, and the conditions for relocation or other existing solidarity mechanism.[289] The difference between the two obligations to provide information is not insignificant. The 'where appropriate' is probably to be read as 'where applicable'. However, the meaning of the actual text leaves a considerably wider discretion to the national authorities, without a justifiable rationale behind it. In creating an unnecessary distinction in the type of information shared with the TCN, it might in certain cases affect the information provided by the person concerned and affect the accuracy of the referral. Lastly, when the screening is completed or the deadline expires, the TCN will be referred to the competent authorities.[290] Where the screening ends at the expiry of the deadline, the referral will likely be made on the basis of incomplete information, which might in turn undermine the person's right to access asylum procedure.

#### 5.4.3.2 Step 2: Asylum border procedures

The new APR allows member states to make much wider use of asylum border procedures. This expresses a core feature of the pact, consisting of mandatory (for the member states) and systematic prevention of entry of TCNs. Let us remember that the APR identifies a series of requirements characterizing the fairness of asylum procedures, predicated upon compliance with Union law more broadly. The questions of fairness arising in relation to these procedures resonate with those discussed in the previous sections and concern more specifically: legal certainty, the right to liberty, and the fairness of the procedures themselves. Firstly, the APR provides for a mandatory accelerated procedure in a large number of cases, but there are no provisions on how that procedure should be conducted and how it would be different from border procedures.[291] Secondly, a member state can apply border procedures following the screening of certain categories of applicant.[292] In some cases, the member state *must* apply the border procedures.[293] The consequences of applying such procedures are

[289] Screening Regulation, Article 11.

[290] Screening Regulation, Article 18.

[291] APR, Article 42. For example, where an applicant does not fulfil the conditions for entry set in the SBC and has not been otherwise allowed to access the state's territory.

[292] APR, Article 43(1).

[293] This is particularly the case if the TCN comes from a country for which the rate of acceptance of applications is 20% or lower, or there are reasonable grounds to consider the person a danger to national security

not insignificant. The border procedure should be as short as possible, without prejudice to its fairness. We should not generally presume that the lengthier the examination, the fairer the procedure, and vice versa. In practice, however, the relation between time and fairness can be important, and constitutes a decisive aspect of the assessment of the member states' compliance with that principle. The person subject to such procedures must not be authorized to enter the territory. This obligation, which follows the obligation of the same kind established in the context of the screening, will likely result in a seamless and extended period of deprivation of liberty. The border procedures can last for 12 weeks maximum, which can be prolonged to 16 weeks if the member state to which the person is relocated is applying the border procedure.[294] The quasi-indiscriminate use of detention, its maximum length, and the overall duration thereof resulting from the combined operation of the different instruments of the asylum pact negatively impact the fairness of the legal framework.

To be sure, the member states have specific obligations when it comes to the reception standards of vulnerable people and especially families with minors.[295] If the Commission has reason to believe a member state is not complying with such obligations, it must issue a recommendation to suspend the border procedures, and the member state must take 'utmost account' of that.[296] The member state will still be subject to the obligation of standards of reception, and must report to the Commission on the measures taken to give effect to the recommendation. It is plain to see, however, that an obligation to take into account is no obligation to cease to apply the procedure, and will leave the member states free to continue to implement it in situations where it would not be suitable for the circumstances of the applicant.

#### 5.4.3.3 Step 3: Return border procedures

The Return Border Procedure (RBP) Regulation applies to TCNs whose application for international protection has been rejected in accordance with asylum border procedures. In this context, the TCNs must reside in the proximity of the external borders for a period of up to 12 weeks, with calculation starting from the moment when the TCN will no longer be allowed to remain. The person must be given a period of voluntary departure unless they are at risk of absconding or pose a threat to public policy, or public or national security.[297] Otherwise, the person can be placed in detention for the whole duration of the RBP. This can add to the period of detention that the person might have already spent during screening and asylum border procedures. The grounds of detention change slightly, depending on whether or not the person was detained during the asylum border procedures: in the first case, they can

or public order of the member state. See APR, Article 42(1)(c), (f), (j). The last ground mentioned in the text is also one of the scenarios where the accelerated procedure can be applied to minors. See APR, Article 42(3)(b). APR, Article 44 establishes a series of groups, among those mentioned above, to whom the border procedure should be applied as a matter of priority. There are exceptions to the member states' obligation to apply such procedures. See APR, Articles 47 and 48.

[294] APR, Article 51.
[295] APR, Articles 53(2)(b) and 54(2).
[296] APR, Article 45(4).
[297] RBP Regulation, Article 4.

be deprived of liberty for preventing entry or preparing return; in the second case, detention can be ordered if the person is at risk of absconding, obstructs the return process, or poses a risk to public policy, or public or national security.[298] While the second case resonates with the grounds stated in the Return Directive,[299] the first case is particularly problematic as it potentially allows for a three-month detention period on the basis of administrative convenience. That ground is also difficult to square with the requirement that a period of voluntary departure must be given, except for the cases mentioned above. In principle, a TCN could find themselves in a situation where they have been granted a period of voluntary departure but they are being detained, since Articles 4(5) and 5(2) RBP Regulation do not dovetail. What is more, the relevant provisions of the Return Directive apply to the RBP, including where a return decision cannot be enforced within the time limits set in the RBP Regulation. This means that the 18-month maximum period of detention established in the Return Directive could then apply, on top of the 12 weeks of deprivation of liberty already applied in the context of the asylum border procedures. As for TCNs whose application has been rejected under the asylum border procedure and who have no right to remain,[300] member states can prolong the maximum duration of holding or detention by a further six weeks.[301] In addition, member states can derogate from certain important provisions of the RBP if they are found to be in a situation of crisis. This legal framework must be read jointly with the Screening and AP Regulations. The assessment of these measures taken individually raises serious questions of compliance with the requirement of necessity, proportionality, and legal certainty inherent in the right to liberty.[302] Their integrated analysis compounds those concerns further and casts doubt on the fairness of the legal framework.

#### 5.4.3.4 The wild card: The Crisis Regulation

The Crisis Regulation can alter the picture drawn in the previous sections, as it lays down rules for the adoption of measures—including those of a temporary nature—in exceptional situations of crisis and force majeure. A preliminary observation is in order, with regard to the personal scope of the derogations applicable in a case of instrumentalization. Such a situation would arise where a third country or a hostile non-state actor encourages or facilitates the movement of TCNs to the EU external borders, with the aim of destabilizing the EU or a member state, and where such actions are liable to put at risk essential functions of a member state. Importantly, a member state can *only* apply for derogations in relation to instrumentalized TCNs apprehended at the external borders in connection with an unauthorized crossing.

[298] RBP Regulation, Article 5.

[299] Return Directive, Article 15.

[300] RBP Regulation, Article 6. This category includes applicants whose application has been rejected before the adoption of the Council Implementing Decision referred to in Article 4(3) of Regulation (EU) 2024/1359.

[301] Detention must be included in the calculation of the maximum period under the Return Directive. Where a procedure to obtain a derogation has already been initiated pursuant to Article 2 Crisis Regulation, the member states can submit a request to apply the derogations provided for in Article 6 of the RBP Regulation in the context of that procedure. See RBP Regulation, Article 7.

[302] Case C-241/21, *IL v Politsei- ja Piirivalveamet*, EU:C:2022:753, paras 47–48.

The extent to which a member state will be able—or willing—to distinguish between TCNs who are being instrumentalized and those who are not remains to be seen. Therefore, should the Commission find a case of instrumentalization and the Council follows suit with an implementing decision, the derogations are likely to be generally applied to the TCNs concerned.[303]

Beyond the adoption of solidarity measures that can be requested by the member state,[304] the most controversial part of the Crisis Regulation concerns the possibility of derogating from certain provisions of EU asylum law. There are four main types of such derogations. Firstly, in a situation of crisis or force majeure, the state can register the claim up to four weeks after the application was made.[305] The persons concerned must still be able to access and exercise their rights under EU asylum law effectively.[306] Secondly, in a situation of crisis or force majeure, member states can extend the maximum duration of border procedures for the examination of the application by a further six weeks.[307] Thirdly, in a situation of crisis that is not instrumentalization-driven, a member state can apply border procedures to TCNs from a country whose rate of acceptance of asylum application is 50% or lower (compared to the 20% normally established by the AP Regulation).[308] Fourthly, in a case of crisis caused by instrumentalization of migrants, the member state can apply border procedures to decide on the merit of *all* the TCNs concerned, as opposed to specific categories stated in Article 44(1)(b) APR.[309] In the wake of the point made above, this derogation will likely apply to all the TCNs arriving at the border when a finding of instrumentalization is made, as a result of the difficulty in distinguishing in practice between instrumentalized and non-instrumentalized migrants.[310] The member states must not use this extended application of border procedures where there are

[303] Generally, the derogations and solidarity measures apply for three months, and can be extended once by three months following confirmation by the Commission that the situation persists. Furthermore, a member state can request that the Commission proposes an extension or amendment for a further period of three months, which can be extended by a further three months following Commission confirmation as stated above. In total, the derogations and solidarity measures can apply for a maximum duration of 12 months. See Crisis Regulation, Article 5. Similarly, the Commission must submit a proposal to the Council to repeal the implementing decision if it considers that the situation of crisis or force majeure no longer exist. See Crisis Regulation, Article 6(3).

[304] See Crisis Regulation, Articles 7 and 8.

[305] When submitting the reasoned opinion, the member state can declare that it considers it necessary to apply this derogation before receiving authorization to do so, but in any event it cannot for longer than 10 days—unless receiving explicit authorization from the Council in this sense.

[306] Crisis Regulation, Article 10.

[307] However, the period must not be used in addition to the period under Article 51(2), third subparagraph APR.

[308] This figure is based on the latest available yearly Union-wide average Eurostat data.

[309] This asylum border procedure can be extended so the applications are registered in the period during which the derogation is applicable.

[310] However, and based on the indication contained in the Council implementing decision, member states must either: exclude from border procedures minors under 12 and their family members as well as person procedural or reception needs; or cease to apply those procedures when those persons—and vulnerable TCNs—are likely to have submitted a well-founded application. Interestingly, Article 11(7) Crisis Regulation stipulates: 'This paragraph shall be without prejudice to the mandatory nature of the border procedure as referred to in Article 46 of Regulation (EU) 2024/1348'. The latter provision, however, is nothing to do with that but it rather concerns the number of adequate capacity at Union's level.

medical reasons, or where the necessary support for people with special needs cannot be provided.[311]

The derogations from asylum law allowed in a situation of crisis or force majeure amplify the problematic aspects of the recently enacted reforms. Alongside the uncertainty related to how strictly the Commission will assess the member states' fulfilment of the criteria required by the Regulation, the types of derogations have serious implications for fairness. Firstly, the much more extensive use of border procedures will likely lead to a wider use of detention. This will add to periods of deprivation of liberty 'ordinarily' allowed under the measures discussed above, which are themselves difficult to reconcile with the principles of proportionality and necessity. Secondly, the extended application of border procedures widens the possible restriction on the applicants' access to legal assistance and information, which may jeopardize the fair examination of their asylum claim. Even when the procedures do not apply indiscriminately, as is the case for derogations based on instrumentalization, member states will be allowed to resort to them vis-à-vis TCNs coming from a country where one person out of two is granted international protection.

However problematic, the system of border procedures probably accommodates the conflicting claims in a non-discriminatory and non-arbitrary manner. In the legal framework, the EU and state interest in preventing entry is often used to justify restrictions on individual rights without sidelining them entirely. This is not to say, however, that the law is consistent with its objectives and underlying principles, and therefore fair. Certain structural features emerging from the analysis point to the contrary. In several respects, the system of border procedures introduces mechanisms of general and indiscriminate application and thus drastically reduces the role for individualized examination of the specific circumstances of the case. This is particularly true for the use of detention, which might be enforced for years due to the interaction between the instruments discussed above. As the different steps of this new system work together, it is important to consider its overall fairness. The discussed issues of appropriate identification and referral occurring in the context of the screening, for example, could have an impact on the effective enjoyment of the right to asylum, considered in its different components, and ultimately affect compliance with the principle of non-refoulement.

### 5.4.4 Stories from the Eastern Front: Finland's Reaction to the War

In the previous chapter, we considered Finland's reaction to the Russian invasion of Ukraine via its new visa policy. This chapter continues along this path and discusses a very controversial reform adopted by that member state in 2024.

[311] Crisis Regulation, Article 11. Other derogations are stipulated in Articles 12 and 13 Crisis Regulation, but their link with external border controls is fainter. Further, the member state can derogate from the obligation to take back an applicant in a situation of extraordinary mass arrivals—including in situations where the derogating state is identified as responsible pursuant to the AP Regulation. The arrival must be of such a scale and intensity that it could create a serious risk of serious deficiencies in the treatment of applicants, thereby creating a serious risk that the Common European Asylum System (CEAS) is rendered non-functional. This derogation is not applicable to situations of instrumentalization.

#### 5.4.4.1 Foreign influence, instrumentalization, and asylum: Introducing the recent reforms in Finland and the EU

Alongside changes in visa policy, the Russian invasion of Ukraine has sparked member states-driven initiatives on border controls strictly understood. For context, towards the end of 2023, the Finnish authorities registered an unusually high number of asylum seekers arriving at the border of Southeast Finland without required travel documents.[312] Following cases of illegal entry in the area of the Southeast Finland Border Guard District,[313] Finland's entire Eastern border was closed,[314] and still remains closed until further notice.[315] In order to deal with this trend, a first set of legislative amendments to the Border Guard Act was approved. These empower the Government—the decision lying primarily with the Ministry of the Interior—to close a border crossing point or to restrict border crossing traffic for an indefinite period, if necessary to prevent a serious threat to public order, national security, or public health.[316] On the same grounds, the Government can centralize applications for international protection at one or more border crossing points at Finland's border. Such a decision can also be taken in the case of an 'exceptionally large number of migrants arriving within a short period of time', or where there is 'information or reasonable suspicion that the entry is due to the influence of a foreign state or other actor'. When this happens, the application must be made only at the identified points, with exceptions possibly allowed on individual cases based on the vulnerability of the TCN.[317] These measures must remain in place only for as long as necessary to prevent the threat, and should be revoked when no longer necessary. They must, furthermore, be implemented in compliance with EU law and particularly with free movement and asylum law.

The second reform on foreign influence through migration, enacted by the Finnish Parliament on 12 July 2024, has taken those measures significantly further.[318] The new law focuses specifically on preventing foreign influence on Finland through the exploitation of migrants.[319] The Government will be allowed to restrict the reception of applications for international protection in a limited part of the Finnish border and in its immediate vicinity for a maximum period of one month at a time. In order to take such a measure, the President of the Republic and the Government will have to be in agreement that the following criteria are met: there is information or reasonable suspicion that a third country is attempting to influence Finland by exploiting incoming migrants; the influence seriously endangers Finland's sovereignty or national

[312] See the information from the Finnish Government at https://raja.fi/-/kaakkois-suomen-rajalle-on-saapunut-tavallista-enemman-turvapaikkaa-hakeneita-henkiloita-puutteellisin-matkustusasiakirjoin?languageId=en_US.

[313] See https://raja.fi/en/-/phenomenon-of-illegal-entry-in-the-area-of-southeast-finland-border-guard-district.

[314] See https://raja.fi/en/-/government-finland-s-entire-eastern-border-closed-again.

[315] See https://raja.fi/en/-/finland-s-eastern-border-to-remain-closed-until-further-notice.

[316] Border Guard Act, Article 16.

[317] Beyond a more generic reference to vulnerable persons, the Border Guard Act mentions children and person with disabilities.

[318] See https://api.hankeikkuna.fi/asiakirjat/c1846832-bfdc-4115-8b17-85dfaedf450a/d08119c3-40f4-44e3-86a7-1f7b19fc17cc/LAUSUNTOPYYNTO_20240315113602.PDF?gsid=ae1939a3-b4a0-40c0-b87a-fc68376d40e5.

[319] Law on instrumentalized immigration, Article 1.

security; and the restrictions are necessary to protect those interests, and no other means can sufficiently achieve that. The Ministry of the Interior should provide sufficient information on the decision.[320]

The legal implications are significant. Firstly, entry into the country would be denied to any person used as a means of influence in the specific area covered by the governmental decision. The person would be immediately removed from the country and 'directed to move' to the place where applications for international protection are received. The grounds for removal must be communicated in writing to the person concerned, who can request a reassessment of the removal. Such a request has, however, no suspensive effect and can be processed without hearing the TCNs. The new law also features certain safeguards, even though questions may be raised as to their suitability for adequately mitigating the effects of the reform. The reception of applications for international protection may not be more widely restricted or kept in place for longer than necessary to prevent serious danger to Finland's sovereignty or security. An application for international protection will be accepted despite having been made outwith the area covered by the decision, on the basis of an individual assessment carried out by the border guard. This would be the case, for example, if the guard considers that accepting to assess the application is necessary to safeguard the rights of a child or a vulnerable person,[321] or that the person is in real danger of being subjected to inhumane or degrading treatment in the country they have come from.[322] For the purposes of the assessment, the border guard must ensure that the person is sufficiently understood.[323] As a modest improvement added to the final version of the law, only suitably trained border guards can make decisions about accepting to assess the application for international protection. However, and this is probably the most controversial aspect of all, entry by violence or the exploitation of a large number of persons may be prevented immediately at the border without carrying out a case-by-case assessment, if this is necessary to ensure the life and health of persons and if the procedure as a whole can be considered defensible.[324]

Finland's new laws explicitly aim to protect its sovereignty and essential state functions. The changes to Finnish law resonate with the overhaul of the EU asylum and migration legal framework recently approved by the Union legislature, without mirroring it entirely. The questions raised by both these sets of instruments are relatively new—at least as far as the Union is concerned—but they are also here to stay. One concept in particular connects the law on foreign influence to the EU reforms,

[320] Law on instrumentalized immigration, Article 3. Applications for international protection may still be accepted normally outside the area to which the restriction applies.

[321] The assessment must take into account the best interests of the child, and the danger posed by the removal to the person's life or health.

[322] The assessment must consider in particular material presented by the person, externally observable facts concerning the person, and up-to-date information obtained from various sources on the security of the country. Other grounds are, obviously, danger of death penalty, torture, or other treatment violating human dignity.

[323] Law on instrumentalized entry, Article 5.

[324] Law on instrumentalized entry, Article 6. Or 'Intrusion into the country using violence or a large number of people can be immediately prevented at the national border without conducting the case-by-case assessment referred to in section 5, if it is necessary to ensure the safety and health of persons and if the overall procedure can be deemed defensible'.

and particularly to the SBC: instrumentalization of migration. The term has featured regularly in the European debate lately. Instrumentalization has gained the spotlight, particularly following the arrival of large numbers of applicants for international protection at the Polish and Lithuanian borders, orchestrated by Belarus with a view to destabilizing the EU.[325] Poland and neighbouring EU countries have reacted with a host of measures that have been described as undermining the right to asylum and the principle of non-refoulement.[326] Against this background, instrumentalization has also made its way into EU law through the recent recast of the SBC. On this basis, member states may now take the 'necessary measures' to preserve security, law, and order where a large number of migrants attempt to cross the external border in an unauthorized manner, *en masse* and using force.[327] *In particular* in a situation of instrumentalization of migrants, member states can temporarily close specific border crossing points or limit their opening hours. Measures taken to this effect must be applied in compliance with the principle of proportionality and 'taking full account' of the rights of, inter alia, applicants for international protection.[328] On a general level, the scope of application of these provisions is quite flexible. On the one hand, borders can be closed particularly (ie not exclusively) in cases of instrumentalization. On the other hand, the necessary measures can be taken in the situations described therein, which include instrumentalization but are by no means limited to this. Therefore, the existence of a case of instrumentalization is not a precondition for the member states' lawful reliance on the most broadly-worded clause of Article 5 SBC. This being said, it is important to carefully consider the requirements established in that provision. The 'general' clause is rather vague, as it allows member states to take essentially *any* measures. However, it also establishes three cumulative conditions for those purposes. The attempted entry into the member state must be in breach of the conditions laid down in the SBC. It must be characterized by violence, and be carried out *en masse*. The use of the latter expression is rather peculiar. The *levée en masse* is probably the most prominent example of the term being relied on in a (very different) legal context. A concept dating back to the French Revolution and borrowed from the law of armed conflict, it 'occurs when inhabitants of a non-occupied territory, without time to form into a regular armed unit, spontaneously take up arms to resist an invading force'.[329] It is safe to say that *en masse*, therefore, presupposes an action being perpetrated not only as a group, but also by a large number of persons. Zooming in on the concept of 'instrumentalization', the SBC offers no definition thereof, but it cross-references the

[325] Instrumentalization of migration is not a new phenomenon at all. See in this sense, N Vavoula and V Apatzidou, 'The EU Response to the Instrumentalisation of Migration: Towards Normalised Derogations, Intensified Border Surveillance and Flexible Responsibility?' in L Lonardo (ed), *Addressing Hybrid Threats* (Edward Elgar 2024) 105. The EU itself covered the issue in its security strategy in 2016. See, inter alia, JOIN (2016) 18 final. On hybrid threats more generally, see M Regan and A Sari (eds), *Hybrid Threats and Grey Zone Conflict: The Challenge to Liberal Democracies* (Oxford University Press 2024).

[326] See A Ancite-Jepifánova, 'Migrant Instrumentalisation: Facts and Fictions—Realities On the Ground at the EU-Belarus Border', VerfBlog, 21 September 2023, https://verfassungsblog.de/migrant-instrumentalisation-facts-and-fictions/.

[327] SBC, Article 5(3).

[328] SBC, Article 5(4).

[329] See D Wallace and S Reeves, 'The Law of Armed Conflict's "Wicked" Problem: Levée en Masse in Cyber Warfare' (2013) 89 International Law Studies 646, in relation to the Convention Relative to the Treatment of Prisoners of War, Article 4(A)(6), 12 August 1949, 6 UST 3316, 75 UNTS 135.

Crisis Regulation. Pursuant to the latter, instrumentalization must be understood as a situation where a third country or a hostile non-state actor encourages or facilitates the movement of TCNs to the EU external borders, with the aim of destabilizing the EU or a member state, and where such actions are liable to put at risk essential functions of a member state.[330]

From the juxtaposition between Finland and the EU framework, we can draw two preliminary conclusions. Firstly, the new national laws fall clearly within the scope of recently introduced provisions of Union law, and particularly the SBC and the Crisis Regulation. Secondly, they both empower states' authorities to derogate from existing provisions of EU law—especially asylum law—in order to react to situations and protect interests centred on similar concepts: the instrumentalization (EU)/exploitation (Finland) of migrants, to destabilize (EU)/influence (Finland) and threatening essential state functions (EU)/sovereignty and security (Finland).

Against this background, the next subsection considers more closely the potential impact of these reforms on the persons concerned. With references to the relevant case law of the Court of Justice, we highlight how these new laws make the most of existing legal *vacua* to restrict individual rights as much as possible.

#### 5.4.4.2 Compliance assessment of Finland's reform

Finland's reform on foreign influence resembles the example of the change in its visa policy. It shows a clear link to, and falls within the scope of, initiatives taken in parallel by the EU. It is also different, as it is much more forceful in making the most of ambiguities and grey areas characterizing the applicable standards. Two aspects of this reform are particularly worth considering. Firstly, there is the power to deny entry to any person used as a means of influence in the specific area covered by the governmental decision, and the need for that person to move to the place where applications for international protection are received. A related issue concerns the possibility for national authorities to reassess the removal without hearing the third-country national. We have also mentioned that the law features certain safeguards, such as: the need that the restrictions comply with the principle of proportionality; and the possibility for the border guard to grant certain categories on the basis of a case-by-case assessment, to receive applications for international protection even when they have been made in an area subject to restrictions. The Border Guard Act provides for the possibility of restricting the reception of asylum claims at certain border crossing points. The provision seems to concern the manifestation of the intention to apply itself, rather than the formal lodging of the application.[331] The 'reception' of the application,

[330] Crisis Regulation, Article 1(4)(b). For further definition of instrumentalization in EU policy documents, see Joint Communication of the European Commission and the High Representative of the Union for Foreign Affairs and Security Policy to the European Parliament and the Council 'Joint Framework on countering hybrid threats a European Union response', JOIN(2016) 18 final and Joint Communication of the European Commission and the High Representative of the Union for Foreign Affairs and Security Policy to the European Parliament, the Council, the European Economic and Social Committee and the Committee of the Regions, 'Responding to state-sponsored instrumentalisation of migrants at the EU external border', JOIN (2021) 32 final. In the literature, see Vavoula and Apatzidou, 'The EU Response to the Instrumentalisation of Migration'.

[331] There seems to be no distinction, in Finnish law, between the making and the lodging of an application. See the explanatory notes to especially Articles 6 and of Government's Proposal to Parliament for an Act to Amend the Aliens Act (HE 218/2014).

and the acceptance of the reception thereof, would thus refer to both the making and the submission of it. The same would apply to the law on instrumentalization. If this was the case, questions could be raised about the compatibility between the measure and the Court of Justice's ruling *in Commission v Hungary (Accueil des demandeurs de protection internationale)*. The judgment found Hungary in breach of the Asylum Procedure Directive (APD),[332] as that state required third-country nationals to make applications for international protection only in two transit zones, 'while adopting a *consistent and generalised* administrative practice drastically limiting the number of applicants authorised to enter those transit zones daily' (emphasis added).[333]

Firstly, the Court noted that while the APD allowed member states to require the lodging of applications at a designated place,[334] no corresponding provision existed with regard to the making of the application.[335] Secondly, pursuant to the APD, an application is deemed to have been made, and the person to have become an applicant, as soon as they have declared, to one of the competent authorities, their wish to receive protection and without the declaration being subject to administrative formalities.[336] The person has, therefore, the right to make such an application to one of the designated authorities,[337] to which corresponds the obligation for the member state to register the application and ensure that the person has an effective opportunity to lodge it as soon as possible.[338] From the date on which the application for international protection is made, the time limit for the registration of the application will start to run, which in turn triggers the running of the time limit related to the decision on the application itself.[339] *Unjustifiably* delaying the opportunity for the person to make their application would undermine the effectiveness of the ADP and the right to asylum more broadly.[340] From the Court's judgment, it is not entirely clear what impact the limitation on the number of applicants (or the absence thereof) would have on the assessment of compliance with the national measure. On the one hand, Finland seems not to have adopted an administrative practice comparable to Hungary's. This is corroborated by the possibility of exempting certain categories from the obligation to make the application at a designated place, which by definition would exclude a practice of a generalized nature. Furthermore, it might be argued that, if the requirements set in the national legislation were met, we would be dealing with circumstances that might justify the delay caused by the centralized reception of applications. On the other hand, the principles set by the Court seem to draw a clear distinction between the making and the lodging of the application. This distinction may have an impact on the limits of member states' discretion. In the end, the practice is likely to be

[332] Directive 2013/32/EU on common procedures for granting and withdrawing international protection [2013] OJ L180/60 (APD).

[333] Case C-808/18, *European Commission v Hungary*, EU:C:2020:1029, para 128.

[334] APD, Article 6(3).

[335] Case C-808/18, *European Commission v Hungary*, para 96.

[336] Case C-36/20 PPU, *Ministerio Fiscal (Authority likely to receive an application for international protection)*, EU:C:2020:495, paras 93 and 94.

[337] Case C-808/18, *European Commission v Hungary*, para 98 and Case C-36/20 PPU, *Ministerio Fiscal*, para 92.

[338] Case C-808/18, *European Commission v Hungary*, para 93.

[339] Case C-808/18, *European Commission v Hungary*, para 101.

[340] Case C-808/18, *European Commission v Hungary*, paras 102–103.

the decisive element in cases where a member state decides to centralize the reception of applications. It is undeniable, however, that such a centralization delays the beginning of the asylum procedures, which may be difficult to reconcile with the spirit of the legislation and the Court's interpretation.

A related aspect worth considering is the possibility of reassessing the removal without hearing the person challenging it. In this case as well, neither the legislation nor the existing case law provides a straightforward answer. The Court has developed its interpretation of the right to be heard in the context of the Return Directive as well as the APD, but in rather different situations—for example, concerning the possible infringement of that right in relation to a decision on the extension of pre-removal detention, or in the context of the examination of an asylum claim. The fact that the national legislation allows the assessment without the hearing, rather than preventing the hearing itself, probably shelters Finnish law from a finding of incompatibility. This is without prejudice to the possibility that certain of those case law-based principles might be extended to the situation discussed here. For example, it is well established that a decision could be reversed—in this case, the removal—if the competent authority 'considers, in the light of all of the factual and legal circumstances of each case, that the infringement at issue actually deprived the party relying thereon of the possibility of arguing his defence better, to the extent that the outcome of that administrative procedure could have been different'.[341] There seems to be no convincing reason why this principle could not apply to our example. This is even more so when we consider that the removal links to a right protected by EU law—that is, the right to make an application to one of the authorities established in the ADP. Secondly, the Court has indicated that, in certain circumstances, the national authority *must* hear the person.[342] This principle was stated in relation to the examination of the application itself, which might make the possibility of interpretation by analogy less tenable. However, since the person has a right to make the application, there might be cases where the hearing might be important to make a decision with full knowledge of the facts in relation to a right protected by EU law.[343]

Most controversial of all is the possibility that potential applicants for international protection be pushed back without examination of their application, if the procedure as a whole is considered defensible. One such case is the exploitation of—attempt to enter by—a large number of persons. The explanatory note to the proposal seems to balance the protection against non-refoulement and the right to security and the life of other persons. However, any balancing act would be incompatible with the absolute nature of the non-refoulement. This is apparent from the scope of Article 15 of the European Convention of Human Rights (ECHR), which includes Article 3 thereof among the provisions that cannot be derogated from by the contracting parties in times of a public emergency threatening the life of the nation. As known, the principle

[341] Case C-383/13 PPU, *G and R*, EU:C:2013:533, para 45.

[342] Case C-560/14, *M v Minister for Justice and Equality, Ireland, Attorney General*, EU:C:2017:101.

[343] The proposal has been widely criticized. Koskennemiv observed that the proposal would be incompatible with EU law and the Finnish Constitution, and would violate more specifically the right to life, the prohibition of torture, the right to an effective remedy, the right of asylum, and the prohibition of collective expulsion, as well as measures of EU asylum law. Among the many expert opinions on the proposal, see the Comment by the Chancellor of Justice.

of non-refoulement has also been codified in EU law, specifically via Article 19 of the Charter. In order for the reform to be lawful, the provisions in question should be interpreted and implemented in a way that does not result in non-refoulement *tout court*. The essential state functions clause is without prejudice to that argument. Beyond the absolute nature of non-refoulement, Article 4(2) TEU has been 'concretized' by specific provisions of the reformed SBC and the new asylum and migration pact. As mentioned above, the SBC now allows member states to take the necessary measures in a situation such as that governed by Finnish law on foreign influence. However, it also links any such actions to compliance with EU and international law. Under the Screening Regulation, member states must not authorize the entry of persons apprehended in connection with an unauthorized crossing of the external border.[344] However, the same instrument requires that the screening be conducted at an adequate and appropriate location designated by each member state, be carried out without delay, and completed within seven days from the apprehension.[345] Pursuant to the Crisis Regulation, a member state found by the Commission to be facing a situation of instrumentalization can be authorized by the Council to derogate from certain provisions of EU asylum law. None of such derogations can be construed as allowing straight pushbacks, without any examination at any point of an application for international protection. Admittedly, the measures provided for in the law on foreign influence might apply only to certain portions of the Finnish Eastern border. Once again, a constitutionally oriented application of such provisions would require that the TCNs be directed to the location where they can exercise their right to seek asylum. A practice of pushback resulting in sending potential applicants to a third country where they might face persecution would be incompatible with non-refoulement.[346] It would also have systemic implications for intra-EU cooperation. This is shown by a CJ's ruling concerning the impact, on the Dublin Regulation, of similar practices implemented by Polish authorities at their external borders. The Court found that a member state might refuse to transfer an asylum seeker to the state that would be responsible for examining the application pursuant to the Dublin Regulation, where a real risk exists that the receiving state will engage in practices contrary to the principle of non-refoulement.[347]

Member states can adopt wide-ranging measures at different stages of the migration process. A state's decision on who can enter their territory lies at the core of their sovereignty, which explains the broad discretion they enjoy in this regard. This discretion is not limitless, particularly as a result of the member states' commitment to a host of instruments of international and Union law. However, states still have plenty of room to act within areas of legal uncertainty, especially where they aim to address new challenges and introduce new methods of migration control. In so doing, they

[344] Screening Regulation, Art 6.

[345] Screening Regulation, Articles 8(1) and (3). The new instruments will apply from 2026. However, Finland is still bound by the previous generation of EU law measures, which is arguably much stricter in terms of derogations from standard procedures and reception of asylum seekers.

[346] On the prohibition of collective pushbacks without examination of asylum claims, see the ECtHR's judgment of 7 January 2025 in *ARE v Greece*, App no 15783/21.

[347] Case C-392/22, *X v Staatssecretaris van Justitie en Veiligheid*, EU:C:2024:195. See also ECtHR, judgment of 23 July 2020, *MK and Others v Poland*, App nos 40503/17, 42902/17 and 43643/17.

can trigger complex questions about the limits of the lawful exercise of their discretion. Through an exploration of the existing legal framework, we have sought answers to some of these dilemmas. Such a compliance assessment is particularly important where, as with foreign influence/instrumentalization, the measures clearly express a shift in the approach to migration control. While no definitive answers to such questions have been provided in this section, a series of possible legal standards have been identified for these purposes.

### 5.4.5 Interim Conclusions

The heterogeneity of the legal framework impacts the constitutional compliance of the exercise of controls at the borders. We have observed heterogeneity at play in reactive controls (to deal with emerging situations), ordinary controls as governed by the SBC, and hybrid controls (embodied by the system of border procedures established by the migration and asylum pact). In continuity with the two previous scenarios, we have seen that the delicate balance on which the system of allocation of tasks is built respects subsidiarity and essential state functions. Unless supported by a rigorous application of the procedural duties associated with obligations of solidarity, this balance can negatively affect principles governing interinstitutional cooperation as well as the treatment of the persons concerned. As member states have the last say on requesting assistance or deciding the impact level on a section of the external border, their view will be key to identifying the action to take and ultimately to appropriately implement the legal framework. Similarly, the decentralized system of border checks prioritizes the defusing of threats to member states through reliance on the interoperability of databases. Beyond the concerns expressed above with regard to the systemic use of large information systems, this chapter has revealed the plethora of large pockets of discretion afforded to border guards and the impact these might have on solidarity and the uniform application of EU law. Hybrid controls put all those features on steroids. The combined operation of several new Regulations, which is centred on the prevention of entry via disproportionate detention at the border, stretches legal fairness to its absolute limits—if not beyond. Central to this system is the concept of instrumentalization of migration, allowing derogations from the already more restrictive norms of EU asylum law introduced by the pact. As the proverbial nail in the coffin, the practice of certain member states (Finland) has shown how effectively instrumentalization can be operationalized to exploit legally the grey areas between the breach of non-refoulement and the legitimate control of the borders, ultimately undermining the fairness of the legal framework through perversion of its objectives and underlying principles.

## 5.5 Conclusions

The analysis of conditions for exercising controls, and conditions imposed on the control subject, confirmed the heterogeneity of the legal framework as regards the decision-making centres involved in its implementation, as well as the criteria for the performance of checks or surveillance. While the details of the assessment change, depending on the specificities of the scenario under consideration, common threads have appeared very clearly. These conditions lean heavily towards the prevention of entry at the expense of both fair treatment of TCNs and—potentially—solidarity and sincere cooperation between member states. The unfairness of the treatment can have different sources: it might lie in how databases are used in each step of the border control chain (from the country of departure to the EU borders), or it might be caused by the blind spots of the legal framework and its application concerning the saving of lives at sea; or else, it might be occasioned by the extremely broad discretion left to border guards, the high risk of disproportionate use of detention in the context of the new system of border procedures, or the undermining of fair examination of a person's asylum claim. The stories from the member states are even less encouraging. Paradoxically, the EU asylum and migration reforms might somehow contribute to constraining initiatives at the level of national law which are difficult—or in certain cases impossible—to reconcile with EU and international law. Against this background, the next chapter concludes this part of the book and explores what mechanisms of scrutiny are available over activities taking place at the EU external borders.

# 6
# Controlling Controls

## 6.1 Introduction

In the previous chapters, we have addressed the following question: how does the heterogeneity of EU external border controls impact its constitutional compliance? We have considered four expressions of heterogeneity: sources, levels of governance and actors, objectives, and persons concerned. By focusing on conditions for controls and on the addressees of control, we have assessed the *appropriateness* of the rules to the objectives of the legal framework; or, put differently, we have assessed whether the rules and their implementation pursue their objectives in line with the EU values.[1] Such systemic appropriateness, understood as constitutional compliance, has been evaluated through a structured network of relevant principles of EU law and notably subsidiarity, interinstitutional solidarity,[2] and fairness towards the persons concerned.[3] We have not only analysed the compatibility of the rules with those principles *in abstracto*, but also explored how the principles could be 'enforced' *in concreto* and thus ensure greater constitutional compliance.[4]

We have highlighted that the heterogeneity of the law does undermine constitutional compliance. The heterogeneous system of sources often lacks transparency and legal certainty, while relying increasingly on statistics and correlation, which stereotypes the persons subject to control.[5] The allocation of tasks and responsibility in the maze of decision-making centres is not always clear-cut (to put it mildly), and considerable discretion—verging on arbitrariness—is left to the competent authorities. Insight into certain member states' practices, and the recent reform of EU asylum and migration law, will likely amplify those shortcomings. As a result of this set-up, the law is structurally unbalanced towards the prevention of cross-border crime and irregular entry. This issue cannot be dismissed as a matter of policy discretion. If the same regulatory framework aims to achieve a heterogeneous range of objectives, a significant imbalance in the pursuit thereof can come at the expense of effectiveness—especially as regards identifying vulnerable persons, guaranteeing access to fair asylum procedures, and preventing the loss of lives.

[1] See Consolidated Version of the Treaty on EU [2008] OJ C115/13 (TEU), Article 2.

[2] Consolidated Version of the Treaty on the Functioning of the EU [2012] OJ C 326/47 (TFEU), Article 80.

[3] TFEU, Article 67(2).

[4] Consistent with the scope of this book, 'enforcement' is understood broadly as 'as the set of processes that concern the execution of EU values and aim to achieve compliance, understood as obedience to legal norms'. See section 1.2.2.

[5] This lack of transparency is twofold, as it can regard procedure leading up to the adoption of the relevant source and/or its content.

*The Law of EU Border Controls*. Leandro Mancano, Oxford University Press. © Leandro Mancano 2025.
DOI: 10.1093/9780191966187.003.0007

Against this background, we now expand upon the forms of heterogeneity developed in the previous chapters, and connect them to the heterogeneity of what we will call 'pathways to scrutiny'.[6] The chapter follows the same trail trodden so far and develops along three scenarios: before leaving, in transit, and at the border. In each of them, three main types of pathways to scrutiny emerge: individual control, scrutiny at the level of the EU, and scrutiny of member states. To better understand the reasons behind this structure and how this fits in with the scope and approach of this research, we must introduce some key concepts underpinning the chapter. More specifically, we must set out the relationship between transparency and openness, scrutiny, and accountability.

Schmidt and Wood draw a clear distinction between openness and transparency. Openness would consist of 'the extent of opportunities for non-state organizations and individuals to become involved in EU consultations and civil society umbrella groups', whereas transparency, specifically in the context of the EU, would refer to its institutions and bodies making available information about their internal processes.[7] However, Kostadinova states that '[t]ransparency, understood as the openness of the EU institutions, implies on one hand the right of citizens to have access to information about the activities of EU institutions, and on the other these institutions' responsibility to provide such access and information'.[8] This resonates with Hoffman and Leino-Sandberg, who see transparency and openness of Union decision-making procedures as 'foundational values of the EU and essential to a system under the rule of law'.[9] These last two definitions are particularly useful, as they highlight the legal importance of transparency in EU constitutional law. It matters to the rule of law, first and foremost, but also to representative democracy[10] and good governance,[11] as well as to the more specific fundamental rights specified below. For the purposes of this chapter, transparency is key as it enables the scrutiny of the EU activities. When discussing *parliamentary* scrutiny, Holzhacker defines this as 'the exercise of power by the legislative branch to control, influence, or monitor government decision-making'.[12] This definition is helpful for two reasons. It implicitly introduces a distinction between different kinds of scrutiny. Scrutiny in courts, for example, is obviously very different from that described by Holzhacker. This being said, the broader understanding of scrutiny as a

[6] This chapter is not concerned with the Schengen Evaluation and Monitoring Mechanism (SEMM). While relevant to the instruments considered here *ratione materiae*, it will be discussed more extensively in Part III.

[7] V Schmidt and M Wood, 'Conceptualizing Throughput Legitimacy: Procedural Mechanisms of Accountability, Transparency, Inclusiveness and Openness in EU Governance' (2019) 97 Public Administration 731–33. It is directly linked to the influencing of policymaking and, as such, overlaps with input legitimacy.

[8] P Kostadinova, 'Improving the Transparency and Accountability of EU Institutions: The Impact of the Office of the European Ombudsman' (2015) 53 Journal of Common Market Studies 1080.

[9] H Hofmann and P Leino-Sandberg, 'An Agenda for Transparency in the EU', European Law Blog, October 2019, https://doi.org/10.21428/9885764c.a8cd3c26.

[10] TEU, Article 11.

[11] TFEU, Article 15(3).

[12] R Holzhacker, 'National Parliamentary Scrutiny Over EU Issues: Comparing the Goals and Methods of Governing and Opposition Parties' (2002) 3 European Union Politics 462. On this topic, see also D Finke and T Dannwolf, 'Who Let the Dogs Out? The Effect of Parliamentary Scrutiny on Compliance with EU Law' (2015) 22 Journal of European Public Policy 1127.

way to control, influence, or monitor the EU activities can be adopted *beyond* the role of parliament(s). Scrutiny is, in turn, vital to ensure accountability (in itself an important vector of enforcement of the EU values and constitutional compliance).

In this regard, different types of scrutiny entail different types of accountability.[13] Broadly, Bovens defines accountability as 'a relationship between an actor and a forum, in which the actor has an obligation to explain and to justify his or her conduct',[14] possibly under the pain of a 'sanction' (widely understood).[15] Accountability to law (or legal accountability) presupposes 'the judicial enforcement of constitutional standards of fair or just treatment [and, above all] compliance with the rule of law'.[16] Accountability for elected officials is linked to representation *and* post-electoral evaluation and control.[17] However, we must distinguish between 'political actors being "held accountable" by citizens through elections (input legitimacy) and by their reason-giving in public forums (throughput legitimacy)'.[18] Accountability in public forums is 'the ex post complement to the ex ante mechanisms of democratic election or authorization through which executive actors are initially appointed'.[19] Alongside the democratic scrutiny embodied by the duty of explanation in a public forum, mechanisms of administrative scrutiny offer 'post hoc answerability of administrators [and not only of elected officials] during the policy implementation'. Such mechanisms, exemplified by the individual right to file a complaint to the EU Ombudsman, constitute a form of 'government *with* the people',[20] as they enable 'direct individual citizen participation in the EU institutions and processes, outside of elections for the EP', and bear 'great potential for strengthening supranational democracy'.[21] These forms of legal, democratic, and administrative accountability can be accessed via a series of pathways to legal, democratic and administrative scrutiny, which in turn allow the monitoring, influencing, and control of the EU and member states' activities in EU external border controls. The labels should not mislead the reader, though. The degree of available democratic and administrative scrutiny is of great legal relevance—not least, as mentioned above, for a polity's compliance with the rule of law.

With this in mind, this chapter discusses the existing mechanisms of EU and national law for scrutinizing the constitutional compliance of EU external border controls. The analysis maps onto the themes and materials covered in the previous two chapters. Consistent with the scope of this research, these are the mechanisms to

[13] For a 'classic' on EU accountability, see C Harlow, *Accountability in the European Union* (Oxford University Press 2002).

[14] M Bovens, 'New Forms of Accountability and EU Governance' (2007) 5 Comparative European Politics 107.

[15] See M Busuioc, *European Agencies: Law and Practices of Accountability* (Oxford University Press 2013).

[16] TRS Allan, 'Accountability to Law' in N Bamforth and P Leyland (eds), *Accountability in the Contemporary Constitution* (Oxford University Press 2013) 77.

[17] RB Andeweg, 'Beyond Representativeness? Trends in Political Representation' (2003) 11 European Review 147.

[18] Schmidt and Wood, 'Conceptualizing Throughput Legitimacy' 730.

[19] B Crum and D Curtin 'The Challenge of Making European Union Executive Power Accountable' in S Piattoni (ed), *The European Union: Democratic Principles and Institutional Architectures in Times of Crisis* (Oxford University Press 2015) 64–66.

[20] V Schmidt, *Democracy in Europe: The EU and National Polities* (Oxford University Press 2006).

[21] Kostadinova, 'Improving the Transparency and Accountability of EU Institutions' 1079.

assess the compatibility of the conditions for controls and on the persons concerned with the core principles of the analytical framework. This chapter shows that the legal framework poses serious challenges to the fair treatment of the person concerned, regard being had in particular to the following provisions of the Charter:[22] the right to a good administration, especially the right of every person to access their file and be heard before any adverse individual measure is taken, as well the obligation of the administration to give reasons for its decisions;[23] the right to access documents, granting a right of access to documents of the institutions, bodies, offices, and agencies of the Union to EU citizens and persons residing or having its registered office in a Member State;[24] and the right to an effective remedy and to a fair trial.[25] The materials have been clustered into individual-led scrutiny and scrutiny at the level of the EU and the member state. These 'scrutinizers' are the actors who make and implement the rules, or the addresses of the law. Beyond specific legislative provisions, their role is rooted in EU constitutional law. This is apparent from the example of certain fundamental rights mentioned above, but also for EU institutions and the member states: from the Commission as 'guardian of the Treaty'[26] to the role of the European[27] and national parliaments,[28] to the different provisions on direct action[29] or failure to act.[30] As shown below, the relevance of democratic, administrative, or legal scrutiny varies depending on the scenario (before leaving, in transit, or at the border) and the cluster under examination.

## 6.2 Before Leaving

In the previous two chapters, we highlighted certain problematic features of the law of EU external border control 'before leaving'. The emphasis on preventing entry and creating profiles, the wide discretion granted to the competent bodies to introduce and implement restrictions on movement into the EU, and the possible tension between different decision-making centres are the overarching themes emerging from the discussion of visas and the European Travel Information and Authorisation System (ETIAS),[31] as well as the Immigration Liaison Officers (ILOs). Against this background, we now investigate the available mechanisms of scrutiny provided in the legal framework and by the EU system more broadly. Firstly, we deal with individual scrutiny. We look at the different procedures enabling an applicant for a visa or a travel authorization to challenge adverse decisions made by the competent authorities, and

[22] Charter of Fundamental Rights of the European Union [2012] OJ C 326/391.
[23] CFR, Article 40.
[24] CFR, Article 41.
[25] CFR, Article 47.
[26] TFEU, Article 258.
[27] TEU, Article 14(1).
[28] TFEU, Protocol nos 1 and 2.
[29] TFEU, Article 263.
[30] TFEU, Article 265.
[31] Regulation (EU) 2018/1240 establishing a European Travel Information and Authorisation System (ETIAS) [2018] OJ L 236/1 (or ETIAS Regulation).

the right to access information.[32] Secondly, we consider the different pathways to scrutiny at different levels, by paying particular attention to the role of the European Parliament and the mechanism of internal monitoring established in the ETIAS system. Thirdly, we analyse the existing pathways to scrutiny within each member state and across them.

## 6.2.1 Individual Scrutiny

### 6.2.1.1 Effective legal protection in decision-making on visas and travel authorizations

The previous two chapters discussed several issues concerning the conditions for issuing visas and travel authorizations. The first relevant decision—for visa applications and, indirectly, for the ETIAS—concerns the introduction of a visa requirement. To recall, such a requirement can be imposed by the Commission on certain TCNs based on certain criteria (eg the risk of irregular migration), including as a retaliation against: a visa-exempt third country introducing a visa requirement on one or more member states;[33] and a visa-exempt third country whose nationals are deemed to pose a risk of irregular migration or a security threat more broadly.[34] Given the wide discretion enjoyed by the Commission in this area and the very broad grounds on which such decisions could be taken, the scope for individual scrutiny is very restricted. The restriction concerns the unlikely success of a challenge to the merit of the decision, as well as access to scrutiny itself. Legal scrutiny illustrates the point clearly. This pathway would be taken primarily via Article 263(4) TFEU, but the conditions for standing would not be satisfied *except*, perhaps, in situations where the decision to suspend the visa exemption is limited for certain categories of people.[35] Depending on the circumstances, the person(s) affected might claim to be part of a 'closed group' and therefore meet the requirement of 'individual concern' under the *Plaumann* test.[36]

Beyond the decision on the visa requirement itself, we must consider pathways to administrative and legal scrutiny vis-à-vis the decision on an application for a visa or a travel authorization. These are governed by the procedures laid down in the VISA

[32] Sometimes, this corresponds to, or is expressed as, an obligation on an EU or national body or institution. Other times, the wording of a provision raises the question as to whether the legislation confers an actual right, or a vaguer 'entitlement' falling short of this quality. See also Regulation (EC) No 767/2008 on the Visa Information System (VIS) and the exchange of data between Member States on short-stay visas [2008] OJ L 218/60 (VIS Regulation), Article 25(3).

[33] Regulation (EU) 2018/1806 listing the third countries whose nationals must be in possession of visas when crossing the external borders and those whose nationals are exempt from that requirement (codification) [2018] OJ L 303/39 (Visa Reciprocity Regulation), Article 7.

[34] This could be on the basis of different circumstances, such as: the third country is not cooperating on readmission of its own nationals; a substantial increase in the number of TCNs refused entry or overstaying; or a substantial increase in the number of asylum applications from TCNs for which the recognition rate is low. Visa Reciprocity Regulation, Article 8.

[35] Visa Reciprocity Regulation, Article 7(c) and (i) and Article 8(6)(a).

[36] Case 25-62, *Plaumann & Co v Commission of the European Economic Community*, EU:C:1963:17; see Joined Cases C-182/03 and C-217/03, *Belgium and Forum 187 v Commission*, 2006, paras 60–64. See K Lenaerts, K Gutman, and JT Nowak, *EU Procedural Law* (Oxford University Press 2023) 331 onwards.

Code[37] and the ETIAS Regulation, respectively. Firstly, we will familiarize ourselves with the general framework set in the two systems. In this context, we consider key principles established by the Court with regard to the VISA Code and explore their applicability to the new, and thus underdeveloped, ETIAS Regulation. Thereafter, we discuss the issues arising from the use of data in decision-making. To start with visas, the refusal to issue a visa and the reasons for it must be communicated to the applicant through the standard form, in the language of the member state responsible and another official language of the institutions of the Union, alongside information concerning the appeal procedures.[38] The appeal must be brought against the member state responsible pursuant to its national law.[39] Similar provisions apply where the visa has been annulled or revoked,[40] and to negative decisions on visa applications made at the border.[41] The principles also hold in the case of representation agreements.[42] Comparable rules apply to the ETIAS National Units, which must provide applicants with information on the appeal procedure to challenge the rejection,[43] annulment,[44] and revocation[45] of the travel authorization.[46]

If the legislation establishes common procedures for the issuing of short-term visas and travel authorizations, it says next to nothing on appeal procedures beyond what we have just mentioned. However, certain important principles have been developed by the Court when interpreting the VISA Code. Generally, member states must use their national autonomy in compliance with effectiveness and equivalence and, more broadly, the Charter and the general principles of EU law.[47] These include the right to a good administration and the right to an effective remedy. As to the former, which includes a person's right to be informed of the reasons behind the decision on their application, the Court has ruled that Article 41 CFR gives expression to a broader general principle binding the member states when they are implementing EU law. In

[37] Regulation (EC) No 810/2009 establishing a Community Code on Visas [2009] OJ L 243/1 (VISA Code).

[38] In cases where the application was submitted by a representative, this representative cannot be the person lodging the appeal. Case C-680/17, *Vethanayagam and Others*, EU:C:2019:627, para 57.

[39] VISA Code, Article 32(2) and (3).

[40] VISA Code, Article 34(7).

[41] VISA Code, Article 35(7).

[42] If the Netherlands had no consular representation in Sri Lanka and signed a representation agreement with Switzerland entrusting the latter to decide on the merit of the application, it would be Switzerland that would hear the appeal. See Article 8 VISA Code and Case C-680/17, *Vethanayagam and Others*, para 77. The representation might also be a lighter touch, with the representing state only gathering the information to pass on to the represented state; or, while examining the application in the merit, referring the final decision on rejection to the represented state.

[43] ETIAS Regulation, Article 37(3).

[44] ETIAS Regulation, Article 40(3).

[45] ETIAS Regulation, Article 41(7).

[46] Annulment entails that the conditions for the issuing of a travel authorization were not met when it was either applied for or granted. The ETIAS does not specify which one it is, although logic should possibly make us lean towards the latter. Revocation, instead, concerns situations where the conditions are no longer met. The end result might look the same—or very similar—but the possible ramifications are rather different, not least because normally annulment implies invalidity *ex tunc*, rather than *ex nunc*. Think, for example, of a case where either scenario arises once the person is in the EU and the person was or might have been aware that the conditions were not met *ab initio*. The way in which a member state would deal with this, including the consequences faced by the person concerned, would be left to national procedural autonomy.

[47] As long as, of course, the visa in question is of a kind governed by EU law.

other words, even though Article 41 CFR only applies to EU institutions and agencies, the right to a good administration under the guise of a general principle applies to member states too.[48] Article 47 CFR, for its part, requires that a number of conditions be met. The person must be able 'to ascertain the reasons upon which the decision [was] taken'[49] and to challenge the decision before a court, especially when the previous decision was not rendered by a judicial body.[50] The right to an effective remedy is respected where the judicial review of that decision is not limited 'to a formal examination of the grounds set out in [the legislation, but covers also] the legality of that decision, taking into account all of the elements in the file, both factual and legal, on which the competent national authority based that decision'.[51] More specifically, the competent court must check whether such a decision was based on a sufficiently solid factual basis and was not vitiated by a manifest error.[52] The applicant must be granted the 'practical possibility' to exercise their rights, failing which the appeal cannot be dismissed.[53] Where the refusal was based on an objection from another member state, the judicial review in the state that made the final decision must concern the compliance with the relevant safeguards. The procedure of prior consultation under Article 22 VISA Code must have been properly followed, regard being had to the correct identification of the applicant as the addressee of the member state's objection.[54] While some of these principles relate to a member state objecting to the issuing of a visa, most are amenable to broader application as expressions of effective judicial protection. As regards Schengen-associated countries, these are not bound by the Charter. However, the agreement whereby they are associated with the Schengen acquis requires that they respect the rule of law and fundamental rights as guaranteed in particular by the ECHR.[55] As shown, the heterogeneity of decision-making centres can potentially impact access to administrative and legal scrutiny in the context of visa appeal procedures. The Court has attempted to mitigate that impact. Firstly, it has developed 'concretizing figures' of effectiveness and equivalence to manage the possible side effects of procedural autonomy: see, respectively, the reference to the *practical* possibility of exercising one's rights under Article 47 CFR, and the member states' obligation to respect the right to a good administration as a general principle. Secondly, the heterogeneity of decision-making centres links to the heterogeneity of the membership of Schengen. This, in turn, materializes in the heterogeneity of legal standards going beyond the 'ordinary' diversity occasioned by the procedural autonomy mentioned above.

The relevance of the foregoing discussion is twofold. On a more general level, the implementation of the ETIAS Regulation should be subject to the abovementioned

[48] Case C-230/18, *PI*, EU:C:2019:383, para 57 and case law. The Court stated that Article 41 CFR, which only applies to EU bodies, 'reflects a general principle of EU law, which is applicable to member states when they are implementing that law'.

[49] Joined Cases C-225/19 and C-226/19, *RNNS and KAA v Minister van Buitenlandse Zaken*, EU:C:2020:951, para 43.

[50] Case C-403/16, *Soufiane El Hassani v Minister Spraw Zagranicznych*, EU:C:2017:960.

[51] Joined Cases C-225/19 and C-226/19, *RNNS and KAA*, para 48.

[52] See, by analogy, Case C-544/15, *Fahimian*, EU:C:2017:255, paras 45 and 46.

[53] Joined Cases C-225/19 and C-226/19, *RNNS and KAA*, para 54.

[54] Joined Cases C-225/19 and C-226/19, *RNNS and KAA*, para 51.

[55] See, with regard to Switzerland specifically, Case C-680/17, *Vethanayagam and Others*, para 86.

principles *mutatis mutandis* (and no provision in that Regulation would prevent such an extension).[56] It also reveals the inextricable link between procedural safeguards and substantive reasons for refusal. The link is particularly visible in the specific context of data-based decision making, which is where these principles can deploy their full potential. We have seen that the processing of both visa and ETIAS applications entails assessing the risk posed by the person concerned on different levels. Often, and particularly as regards visas, this risk assessment is based on the creation of profiles through intelligence gathering and sharing, which is in itself almost impossible to challenge. The automated processing (performed by the VIS and the ETIAS, at least in the initial stages) and the interoperability of databases add another thick barrier to scrutiny. To recall, the ETIAS National Units produce analysis on security or illegal migration risks posed by a specific group of travellers with a certain set of characteristics. On this basis, the ETIAS Central Unit will specify the risk in a standard format, including: a description of the risk in free text, referencing the sets of characteristics and the size of the specific group considered; and guidance for ETIAS National Units to consider when assessing a hit.[57] To be sure, the VIS and ETIAS Regulations must be implemented in compliance with EU data protection law, the latter providing a series of important safeguards, particularly as regards the automated processing of the data.[58]

This notwithstanding, a systemic view reveals that individual access to scrutiny *across* the chain of processing can be seriously hindered. Firstly, the decisions that actually matter are not publicly available. We know that the Central and National Units will shape these risk indicators, but there will be no access to any relevant data underpinning the analysis. The lack of information concerns both the statistics and correlations, as well as the relevant sets of characteristics, which are a fundamental element of the risk assessment. However, we know nothing about what these characteristics could be, how they would be identified, and whether they would all 'weigh' the same. The set-up undermines the intelligibility of decision-making,[59] in itself essential to the rule of law.[60] Drawing from the Court's existing case law,[61] authors have questioned the compliance of the systems with data protection law. The proper functioning of both the VIS and ETIAS requires meaningful human processing, which will indeed occur in the case of a hit, but the reliability of this processing cannot be taken

[56] Significantly, the ETIAS Regulation stipulates that, subject to the consent given by the person, and with the view to facilitating new applications, the personal data can be retained in the ETIAS Central System for three years following the expiry of the previous application. Requests for consent should be presented 'in an intelligible and easily accessible form and using clear and plain language'. The Commission must adopt a delegated act 'to further define the tool to be used by the applicants to give and withdraw their consent' enabling the retention of data for three years after the expiry of their previous travel authorization for the purposes of facilitating new applications. ETIAS Regulation, Article 54(2).

[57] Commission Implementing Decision on specifying risks related to security, illegal immigration or high epidemic risk, C(2021) 4980 final, Article 3; see also the Commission Delegated Decision on further defining security, illegal immigration or high epidemic risks, C(2021) 4981 final.

[58] Regulation (EU) 2016/679 on the protection of natural persons with regard to the processing of personal data and on the free movement of such data [2016] OJ L 119/1 (GDPR), Articles 21 and 22.

[59] H Hofmann and P Leino-Sandberg, 'An Agenda for Transparency in the EU'.

[60] This is even truer as regards the VIS, since the implementing decisions on specifying the relevant risks are not publicly available unlike those concerning the ETIAS.

[61] Case C-817/19, *Ligue des droits humains v Conseil des ministres*, EU:C:2022:491, para 124.

for granted.[62] There can be no doubt that both the automated and non-automated processing must be open to review by the competent supervisory and judicial authorities.[63] The extent to which such processing could be challenged *effectively* ultimately depends on the possibility of understanding the factual and legal basis underlying the decision, and the risk exists that the competent authorities will entrench themselves behind generic grounds such as public security.[64] This being the case, it is argued that the degree of constitutional compliance in this area will depend on how rigorously the requirement of substantive judicial review will be applied. The need to go beyond a formalistic box-ticking exercise will play a decisive role in guaranteeing the necessary pathways to scrutiny and ensuring respect for the rule of law.

Concerns about procedures extend to the effective protection guaranteed by substantive conditions of control, and especially the prohibition of discriminatory data processing. Beyond the procedural challenges to compliance with this prohibition resulting from the foregoing discussion,[65] we must highlight a certain inconsistency between the VISA Code and the ETIAS Regulation. The processing of data within the ETIAS *must not result in discrimination on grounds of* sex, race, colour, ethnic or social origin, genetic features, language, religion or belief, political or any other opinion, membership of a national minority, property, birth, disability, age or sexual orientation, and must respect the fundamental rights of the person, including their dignity and integrity.[66] However, the VIS stipulates that '[e]ach competent authority shall ensure that in using the VIS, it does not discriminate against applicants and visa holders on grounds of sex, racial or ethnic origin, religion or belief, disability, age or sexual orientation'.[67] The same grounds of non-discrimination apply to consular staff in the performance of their duties more generally.[68] The ETIAS Regulation sets out a more comprehensive list, and requires that the processing 'must not result in discrimination'. This is slightly different from the phrasing of the VIS Regulation—for example, that the competent authorities do not discriminate when using the VIS. This, it might be argued, is preferable because of the wider scope, focusing as much on the 'process' as it does on the result.

#### 6.2.1.2 Right to information

The previous section has shown how important access to information is for the purposes of scrutinizing decisions on visa and ETIAS applications. What do the relevant instruments provide in this regard? Broadly, the general public must *have access to* a series of information concerning *in particular* the criteria, conditions, and procedures for applying for a visa.[69] A comparable legal framework is set up by the ETIAS

[62] L Gugliotta and A Elbi, 'Will AI "Subtly" Take Over Decision-Making in the EU Migration Context? Warnings and Lessons from ETIAS and VIS' (2024) 9 European Papers 1018.

[63] ETIAS Regulation, recital 57.

[64] On the use of AI tools in ETIAS, see N Vavoula, 'Algorithmic Accountability Through the "Human over the Loop" in Interoperable and EU AI-Reliant Large-Scale IT Systems for Migration and Security' (2024) 3 European Papers 1228.

[65] See also in the literature.

[66] ETIAS Regulation, Article 14.

[67] VIS Regulation, Article 7(2).

[68] VISA Code, Article 39(3).

[69] VISA Code, Article 47. These include information on admissibility, deadlines, and appeal, as well as the place and addressee of the application. It also entails an obligation to give access to information on

Regulation. ETIAS Central Units must provide the general public with the relevant information concerning the application for a travel authorization.[70] The must-be-accessible information comprises that mentioned in Article 38(5) VISA Code. This relates to a procedure which member states must put in place, allowing applicants to submit complaints against the conduct of staff of consulates or service providers and/or the application process. That same provision stipulates that member states must *make information on such procedures available to the public*.[71] The wording of the two provisions is similar enough, although not identical, and their interpretation should in principle align. It is not entirely clear, however, whether the right to have access to the information—or the corresponding member states' obligation to make the same information available—means that such information must be published, or that it must be made available at the public's request, or whether either would be compatible with the Regulation. Furthermore, neither the minimum content of such information nor the timeframe for responding is specified.

With specific regard to data processing, the person must be provided by the member state 'responsible' (presumably the one entering the data) with important information,[72] which must be communicated in a clear, concise, and intelligible way.[73] If the member state disagrees with the alleged inaccuracy of the data or the unlawfulness of its recording, it must 'without delay' adopt a reasoned administrative decision and transmit it to the person.[74] The member state can decide not to provide the information, however, if this constitutes a proportionate restriction to inter alia protect national or public security, or the rights and freedom of others.[75] While the decision must contain information about the right to appeal and relevant procedures,[76] the broad grounds contained in the clause are capable of restricting further access to scrutiny.

## 6.2.2 Scrutiny at EU Level

### 6.2.2.1 The role of the European Parliament

Scrutiny at the EU level of activities 'before leaving' materializes in two main systems of control: the European Parliament and the monitoring mechanism internal

representation arrangements, before its entry into force, for both the represented and the representing member states. Interestingly, the accessible information must also cover the categories of nationals whose application for a visa triggers a duty of consultation with or information from another member state.

[70] In particular, see the possibility to report abuses by commercial intermediaries. See also ETIAS Regulation, Article 71.

[71] Consulates or central authorities must also keep a record of complaints and the follow-up given. VISA Code, Article 38(5).

[72] This includes the identity of the controller, the reasons for processing it, as well as the right to access the data and request rectification or erasing thereof if necessary.

[73] VIS Regulation, Article 37(1).

[74] VIS Regulation, Article 38(3) and ETIAS Regulation, Article 64(3).

[75] VIS Regulation, Article 38(7).

[76] Records of such requests must be kept. The Visa Handbook on the processing of visa applications encourages member states to store in national IT systems all the relevant documents to the decision-making, so that the reasons for this can be retrieved. See C(2019) 3464 final ANNEX 70.

to the ETIAS system. Parliamentary scrutiny is key to the pursuit of accountability and constitutional compliance, especially given the heterogeneous system of sources and the widespread 'delegation' of powers discussed in Chapters 3 and 4. Generally, the Commission's exercise of law-making powers by the adoption of implementing acts is governed by the procedures established in Regulation (EU) No 182/2011 (Comitology Regulation)[77], and particularly the examination procedure. Pursuant to the latter, the European Parliament should have access to the documents kept in a register related to the committee proceedings. These include a 'summary record', which can be accessed 'in accordance with the relevant rules'.[78] While the summary nature of the record and lack of clarity concerning the specific procedure to access the documents are worth highlighting, the obligation to keep a list of the member states' representatives on the committee can at least allow some scrutiny on the possible interference or influence in the proceedings. However, there does not seem to be a constraint on who the member states can nominate,[79] or an institutionalized mechanism of challenge or scrutiny on this.

Beyond the specifics of committee procedures, the monitoring powers enjoyed by the European Parliament over 'before leaving' decisions leave much to be desired. Three examples can be offered in this regard. With decisions on visa reciprocity, the Commission must publish in the Official Journal the member state's notification concerning the introduction of a visa requirement by a visa-exempt third country. The Commission must keep the Council and the EP apprised of any steps taken in reaction to this requirement. The Council and the EP must be informed by the member state of a request made to the Commission that the visa exemption be suspended, as well as a Commission decision not to suspend it. While there is no obligation for the Commission to submit the report on its negative decision to the two institutions, the latter may have a discussion 'on the basis of the report'. Paradoxically, there is no obligation of notification either when the mandatory suspension kicks in for the Commission, which arises two years following the introduction of the visa requirement by the third country.[80] When it comes to the suspension of the exemption due to non-cooperation on readmission or other reasons related to the risk of illegal immigration or security, the Commission has a similar duty towards the EP and the Council. This means that there is an obligation of notification at earlier stages, but not at the more meaningful moment where the Commission has decided to adopt an implementing or a delegated act to that effect.[81] The second example concerns member states' representation arrangements with other countries or service providers. Following a mandatory notification from the member state(s) concerned, the Commission should make information about representation arrangements available

[77] Regulation (EU) No 182/2011 on the rules and general principles concerning mechanisms for control by Member States of the Commission's exercise of implementing powers (Comitology Regulation) [2011] OJ L 55/13.

[78] Comitology Regulation, Article 10.

[79] Article 10(1)(c) Comitology Regulation, refers to 'the lists of the authorities and organisations to which the persons designated by the Member States to represent them belong', implicitly leaving such list open.

[80] Visa Reciprocity Regulation, Article 7(f).

[81] Visa Reciprocity Regulation, Article 8. The implementing act is adopted to suspend the visa exemption only for certain groups of nationals from a third country, whereas the delegated act is directed at all nationals from the same state.

to the member states and the public via electronic publication. There is, however, no obligation to publish them in the Official Journal, nor to make them available to the EP.[82] Examples from Italy confirm this impression, as those member states have barely published any information about representation agreements with other states or external service providers, let alone about the existing mechanisms of monitoring thereof. Thirdly, and consistently with the picture drawn in the previous chapters, transparency is not exactly a trademark of the Immigration Liaison Officer Network (ILON) either. The ILON Steering Board establishes priorities and plans activities, and adopts a biannual report. These documents must be submitted to the European Parliament. There is no obligation to make them publicly available. The EP should be given access to certain parts of the secure web-based information exchange platform, as determined by the Steering Board in its rules of procedure *and in accordance with the applicable Union and national rules and legislation*.[83]

#### 6.2.2.2 Internal monitoring before leaving: The example of the ETIAS

The establishment of an 'internal' monitoring and evaluation mechanism is one of the most relevant innovations introduced by the ETIAS Regulation.[84] In a way, it aligns part of the law 'before leaving' to 'in transit' and 'at the border', as the mechanism of scrutiny internal to Frontex will show. This is not a positive development for transparency and accountability. The ETIAS Regulation establishes reporting duties on ETIAS Central Units, including on abuses by commercial intermediaries.[85] Within the ETIAS, a Fundamental Rights Guidance Board (FRGB) must be established, which will regularly appraise applications and their processing.[86] The risk indicators and the watchlist will be an important test bed for the scrutinizing powers of the Board. In this regard, the ETIAS Regulation also establishes a Screening Board, composed of a representative of each ETIAS National Unit, of the EBCG, and of Europol.[87] The Screening Board must be consulted by the Central Unit on the definition, establishment, assessment *ex ante* and *ex post* of the risk indicators, and by member states and Europol on the implementation of the watchlist. The cost and servicing of the meetings for both Boards will be borne by Frontex, which will also provide the premises and the secretariat for the FRGB meetings.[88] A representative of the FRGB will have the right to sit on the Screening Board in an advisory capacity, and the FRGB will assist the Screening Board in the performance of its tasks. The Screening Board must take into consideration recommendations by the FRG Board, but consultation of the latter by the former is only optional.[89] To be sure, the FRGB will monitor the implementation of the provisions on the risk indicators (including via access to the audits

82 VISA Code, Article 53.

83 Regulation (EU) 2019/1240 on the creation of a European network of immigration liaison officers [2019] OJ L 198/88 (ILON Regulation), Article 9.

84 ETIAS Regulation, Article 92.

85 ETIAS Regulation, Article 7.

86 ETIAS Regulation, Article 10. The members of the Board are the fundamental rights officer of Frontex, and a representative each from the consultative forums on fundamental rights of Frontex, the European Data Protection Supervisor, the European Data Protection Board, and the FRA.

87 ETIAS Regulation, Article 9.

88 ETIAS Regulation, Articles 9(4) and 10(3).

89 ETIAS Regulation, Article 9(5).

of the Central Unit). It will also publish a report once a year on this matter, which will have to be made publicly available. However, three structural weaknesses cast doubt on the effectiveness of the FRGB and its scrutinizing powers. Firstly, the risk indicators will ultimately be reviewed by the ETIAS Central Unit after consultation with the Screening Board, and the FRGB will have no involvement in the watchlist. Europol and the member states will review the accuracy of the data entered therein.[90] Secondly, consultation of the FRGB Board is not mandatory in any circumstances. Thirdly, the scrutiny of a crucial component of the functioning of ETIAS, potentially affecting a very large number of people, is internalized by Frontex. This also raises serious questions about its effectiveness, as the discussion of the next two scenarios will show.

### 6.2.3 Scrutiny by the Member States

The member states monitor the constitutional compliance of border controls 'before leaving' along different axes. The control can be 'internal' to the same member state and focus on public authorities or private parties, or it can concern activities by other member states. As to the former, we can identify three main types of internal monitoring duties. Firstly, in the context of local Schengen cooperation, consulates must assess the implementation of the conditions related to the documents that must be submitted by the applicant when applying for a uniform visa, with a view to taking account of local circumstances, and of migratory and security risks.[91] This obligation is very obscure. In a way, the non-structured nature of cooperation concerning the establishment of conditions of control and their actual performance characterizes the compliance monitoring as well. Secondly, there are obligations related to the use of external service providers and commercial intermediaries.[92] On the one hand, a member state must *closely* monitor the implementation of the legal instrument. The range of monitoring obligations includes the carrying out of spot checks on the premises of the external service provider. The requirement to monitor *closely* must not be underestimated, as apparent from the Commission reproaching several member states' lack of monitoring of service providers. Thirdly, we must mention the provisions concerning the use and misuse of databases. The VIS Regulation provides for specific rules on the role of national[93] and EU[94] data protection supervisory authorities, as well as cooperation between them.[95] Member states can be held liable for, and obliged to compensate for, damages suffered by a person or a member state caused by any act incompatible with the VIS Regulation, unless the member state proves that it is not responsible for the event resulting in the damage. Member states are also under an obligation to ensure that national authorities entitled to access the VIS cooperate with the National Supervisory Authority,[96] and that misuses of data are punished.[97] Since

[90] ETIAS Regulation, Article 35(5).
[91] VISA Code, Article 14(5).
[92] VISA Code, Articles 43 and 45.
[93] VIS Regulation, Article 41.
[94] VIS Regulation, Article 42.
[95] VIS Regulation, Article 43.
[96] VIS Regulation, Article 35.
[97] VIS Regulation, Article 36.

this is presumably left to member states' procedural autonomy, there is a serious risk of divergence depending on the state concerned.

The use of databases is also the most relevant area of interstate scrutiny 'before leaving'.[98] Some of the relevant provisions fall under the category of interstate monitoring. As a rule, member states are responsible for ensuring the security of data they receive and enter into the VIS.[99] If a member state has reason to believe that data have been entered incorrectly or that they were processed in contravention of the governing Regulation, it must inform the member state responsible. The latter must then check the accuracy and compliance with the VIS Regulation, and, if necessary, amend the data.[100] The ETIAS Regulation has provisions comparable to the VIS as regards the security of processing,[101] self-monitoring,[102] penalties,[103] and liability.[104] There is a very important difference between the VIS and the ETIAS, however, as the VIS features no rules on security incidents.[105] Furthermore, the specific provisions in the ETIAS Regulation on interstate data scrutiny are problematic in two main respects. Firstly, there is no explicit requirement concerning the threshold or the required quality that the evidence must possess. This might raise issues of legal protection, especially where the amendment would be at the detriment of the applicant. Secondly, the deadlines indicated therein are probably not as tight as they should be. If the ETIAS Central Unit is in possession of such evidence, it must contact the National Unit within 14 days, which shall in turn check the accuracy within a month. The procedure lengthens further if another member state has evidence, in which case they must contact the Central Unit within 14 days so that the process just mentioned can take place.

### 6.2.4 Interim Conclusions

The heterogeneity of border controls before leaving impacts the existing mechanisms of scrutiny on multiple levels. The Court has attempted to manage the heterogeneity of standards arising from the heterogeneity of decision-making centres, by establishing concretizing figures of effectiveness and equivalence with a view to reining in national procedural autonomy. This heterogeneity is not only the result of different member states applying different levels of protection, but also exists within and across the legal framework itself. The example of the different grounds and standards for non-discrimination in data processing demonstrates this powerfully. On a systemic level, the effects of heterogeneity on pathways to scrutiny is not met with appropriate

[98] The main instruments are the VIS and the ETIAS Regulations, as well as Regulation (EU) 2019/817 on establishing a framework for interoperability between EU information systems in the field of borders and visa [2019] OJ L 135/27; and Regulation (EU) 2019/818 on establishing a framework for interoperability between EU information systems in the field of police and judicial cooperation, asylum and migration [2019] OJ L 135/85.

[99] VIS Regulation, Article 32.

[100] VIS Regulation, Article 24(2).

[101] ETIAS Regulation, Article 59.

[102] ETIAS Regulation, Article 61.

[103] ETIAS Regulation, Article 62.

[104] ETIAS Regulation, Article 63.

[105] See ETIAS Regulation, Article 60.

counterpoints as the law stands at present. Firstly, the heterogeneity of sources affects the intelligibility of decision-making on applications for visas and travel authorizations and the persons' opportunity to challenge such decisions effectively. Relatedly, the heterogeneity of levels of governance links to a mechanism of human scrutiny of automated processing, but serious doubts exist about how meaningful this will be. Secondly, the existence of a heterogeneity of centres of scrutiny suffers from serious limitations, as shown by the example of interstate scrutiny or the role of the European Parliament. Thirdly, some of such centres of scrutiny might be inherently inadequate. The new mechanism of monitoring internal to ETIAS follows the non-promising example of Frontex. Internalizing scrutiny can only be compatible with effective judicial protection if other pathways of control, and particularly access to documents and/or judicial review, remain accessible.

## 6.3 In Transit

Consistent with the previous chapters, we assess pathways to scrutiny of EU border controls 'in transit' by focusing on surveillance (mostly, exchange of information and operational activities) and cooperation with third countries. To better understand the scope of scrutiny over such activities, we need to first understand where the responsibility lies. Therefore, in this section we reverse the order followed so far and start with the EU and member state mechanisms of controlling the controls. To facilitate the navigation of this chapter, we must introduce a brief taxonomy. As shown over the following pages, individual scrutiny can be performed through two main channels: complaint mechanisms broadly understood (encompassing judicial and administrative procedures) and access to information.[106] The main avenues for individual control under the first category can be internal to the relevant EU body (like Frontex), or structural (ie proper to the Union's legal order, such as complaints to the Ombudsman,[107] legality review,[108] and proceedings for failure to act before the Court of Justice).[109] EU-driven scrutiny (not prompted by the person concerned) is not too dissimilar. Among the types of scrutiny internal to Frontex, we must mention: the system of fundamental rights monitoring; the monitoring of the use of force; and the Standard Operating Procedure (SOP) for Serious Incident Reporting (SIR). Examples of structural scrutiny relate to the role played by the Court of Auditors,[110] the EU Ombudsman's own-initiative inquiries, and the different venues provided to different institutions and bodies,[111] as well as the legality review or action for failure to

[106] This is governed by Regulation (EC) No 1049/2001 regarding public access to European Parliament, Council and Commission documents [2001] OJ L 145/43, to which Frontex is subject pursuant to Article 114(1) of Regulation (EU) 2019/1896 on the European Border and Coast Guard [2019] OJ L 295/1 (EBCG Regulation). The two are not watertight. Certain documents could potentially be the subject of both a request for access by the public and of some form of 'challenge' as explained below.

[107] TFEU, Article 228(1).

[108] TFEU, Article 263(4).

[109] TFEU, Article 265.

[110] TFEU, Article 285 onwards.

[111] See the European Parliament working group on Frontex.

act. Likewise, member states can scrutinize certain aspects of border controls through specific provisions of the legal framework, and can rely on the structural systems provided for in the Treaties. Categorized as *rationae materiae*, pathways of scrutiny concern the activities and sources discussed so far and include: border surveillance (including detection, interception, SAR operations, and disembarkation); operational activities that may not be purely about surveillance (such as joint operations, rapid border intervention, and returns); and exchange of information, within or outwith the framework of EUROSUR. The main sources, related to those activities, are: Frontex's operational plans, status agreements (SAs) and working arrangements (WAs), as well as those which might themselves constitute a mechanism of scrutiny. For example, the question can arise as to whether the procedures governing the complaint mechanism within Frontex are appropriate to achieve their objectives. Furthermore, especially as far as individual control is concerned, the EU level can interact with the national system of 'remedies' *lato sensu*. There is thus a degree of permeability between: the 'in transit' and 'at the border' scenarios; the different macro-areas of scrutiny (individual, EU, or member states), as well as within each of their sub-components; between the national and the EU systems; and each of these 'fora' with one another.

### 6.3.1 Scrutiny at EU Level

Surveillance and operational cooperation in third countries constitute the main areas of control in transit. As mentioned, much of the discussion on scrutiny at EU level 'at the borders' is applicable 'in transit' as well, especially as regards Frontex's activities. With this in mind, the analysis here focuses on issues that are more specific to this scenario and possess a lesser degree of 'permeability'. Before we delve into such specific themes, we must mention certain important pathways to political and administrative scrutiny. As shown more extensively in the next section, there are several obligations of notification and/or reporting to the EU institutions. For example, Frontex must submit an annual report on the application of the SESB,[112] and particularly as regards cases of disembarkation in third countries.[113] Beyond communication with the EU institutions, other and less obvious forms of structural scrutiny have come to the fore over the years. The Court of Auditors[114] and the EU Ombudsman[115] have performed an important role in this regard. Consistent with the scope of the research, the two sections below assess pathways to scrutiny of conditions for the exercise of controls, which materialize through the exchange of information and operational cooperation (including with third countries).

[112] Regulation (EU) No 656/2014 establishing rules for the surveillance of the external sea borders in the context of operational cooperation coordinated by the European Agency for the Management of Operational Cooperation at the External Borders of the Member States of the European Union (SESB Regulation) [2014] OJ L 189/93, Article 13.

[113] SESB Regulation, Article 4(3).

[114] See, for example, https://www.eca.europa.eu/Lists/ECADocuments/SR21_08/SR_Frontex_EN.pdf.

[115] Decision in Case OI/5/2020/MHZ.

#### 6.3.1.1 External border surveillance: Exchange of information and operational cooperation

As regards exchange of information, the EBCG Regulation stipulates that Frontex and the member states must ensure that procedures are in place to monitor the functioning of EUROSUR against the objectives of achieving situational awareness and reaction capabilities.[116] It is not entirely clear how this monitoring takes place, but the EUROSUR Handbook provides some examples.[117] The Handbook states that Frontex and partner organizations evaluate the outputs produced in the framework of EUROSUR. The EUROSUR Expert Group acts as an advisory body to the Senior Business Owner by providing opinions and recommendations from end users.[118] It ensures the exchange of experiences gained at a practical level and improves coordination between internal and external stakeholders.[119] The EUROSUR Change Advisory Board is a consultative and decision-making forum managed by Frontex, which inter alia monitors and makes use of the EUROSUR change register and feedback system.[120] The EUROSUR Implementing Regulation, for its part, lays down provisions on the monitoring of data quality entered into the system EUROSUR,[121] as well as on data security.[122] The system of internal scrutiny of EUROSUR seems to involve a heterogeneity of actors, each with unclear tasks, and remains fundamentally a mystery.

If we exclude scrutiny that is individual-led, or carried out within the broader framework discussed 'at the border', control at EU level over activities of surveillance is very limited. Disembarkation in third countries, occurring in the context of Frontex-coordinated operations, is the main case worth mentioning. This can happen only (a) following interception on the high seas, (b) in the country from which the vessel is assumed to have departed, and (c) where the assessment of the situation in that country excluded a risk of direct or indirect *refoulement*.[123] Two main factors hinder access to scrutiny. While details on disembarkation procedures should be established in the operational plan, the relevant provisions contained in certain operational plans available on Frontex's website either merely mirror the SEBS Regulation or are rather generic in nature. Secondly, disembarkation exemplifies the negative impact of the heterogeneity of actors and sources on accountability—a theme that will be developed more extensively 'at the borders'. The host state, in coordination with participating states and Frontex, must take into account the general situation in this third country when planning the operation. The heterogeneity of the decision-makers involved is not accompanied by a proper mechanism of cross-scrutiny between them. The host

[116] EBCG Regulation, Article 23(1).

[117] The Commission has apparently adopted a new Handbook in January 2025 (Commission Recommendation of 17.1.2025 establishing the practical handbook for the implementation and management of EUROSUR ('EUROSUR Handbook'), C(2025) 117 final), but the document is not available through research in eurLex.

[118] EUROSUR Handbook 45.

[119] EUROSUR Handbook 50.

[120] EUROSUR Handbook 45–46.

[121] Commission Implementing Regulation (EU) 2021/581 on the situational pictures of the European Border Surveillance System [2021] OJ L 124/3 (EUROSUR Implementing Regulation), Article 22.

[122] EUROSUR Implementing Regulation, Article 23.

[123] SESB Regulation, Article 10(1)(b).

state seems to be given the final say, with neither Frontex nor the participating states being granted meaningful 'swaying' power in any legal sense. Furthermore, the assessment may take into account the existence of agreements with that country on migration and asylum 'carried out in accordance with Union law and through Union funds'.[124] Who ascertains the non-accordance of the agreement or the programme with EU law, though? It is difficult to see how the Council or Commission could, having probably greenlighted the use of Union funding for those purposes in the first place. That Frontex could challenge the lawfulness of an existing agreement appears highly unlikely, especially in cases where it was directly involved in the signing and/or the implementation thereof. In conclusion, the analysis of EU scrutiny 'in transit' reveals a fundamental lack of clear allocation of monitoring responsibility—if not, in certain cases, the absence of any monitoring at all.[125]

#### 6.3.1.2 Cooperation with third countries

In the previous two chapters, we have covered cooperation with neighbouring third countries enabling the joint performance of border control-related tasks or the EU exercise of such tasks in the third country's territory. We have primarily focused on WAs and SAs, but we have also mentioned how the EU is more broadly exploring partnerships through less transparent sources, such as the MoU with Tunisia. Beyond the issues discussed in Chapters 4 and 5, these sources raise concern for the types of monitoring mechanisms they establish (or not, in certain cases) and for the lack of transparency around their adoption and implementation.

To start with the first issue, the EU has entered into SAs with several third countries, some of which were already party to a WA with Frontex (ie Albania and North Macedonia). All the SAs are implemented by Frontex, which has also signed a number of WAs, including with Albania, Azerbaijan, Bosnia and Herzegovina, Georgia, North Macedonia, and the UK. It also signed WAs for EU missions, specifically EUNAVFORMED Irini and EUCAP Sahel Niger. Therefore, Frontex is a protagonist of both SAs and WAs. These two types of agreements are interesting to consider on their own, but especially when we compare them with each other. SAs tend to be much 'younger', and this shows through their form (an agreement formally concluded by the EU) as well as their content. However, WAs are very loosely structured and self-proclaimed as non-legally binding, even though they clearly underpin significant forms of cooperation. The SAs and WAs involving Albania and North Macedonia are not necessarily in contradiction. They are certainly complementary and might overlap in part, and there is no doubt that the SA is the 'prevailing' source in this regard.

[124] SEBS Regulation, Article 4(2).

[125] There is a vast literature on the connection between EU activities at sea, particularly in relation to the right to asylum. Just to cite a few, see E Cusumano, 'Migrant Rescue as Organized Hypocrisy: EU Maritime Missions Offshore Libya Between Humanitarianism and Border Control' (2019) 54 Cooperation and Conflict 3; E Guild's blogposts on the blog of the Odysseus network: The Frontex Push-Back Controversy: Lessons on Oversight (Part I), EU Immigration and Asylum Law and Policy; The Frontex Push-Back Controversy: What Oversight for Frontex? (Part II), EU Immigration and Asylum Law and Policy; and V Moreno-Lax, 'The EU Humanitarian Border and the Securitization of Human Rights: The "Rescue-Through-Interdiction/Rescue-Without-Protection" Paradigm' (2018) 56 Journal of Common Market Studies 119.

The mechanisms of scrutiny are one of the key elements separating the WAs from the SAs. In fact, WAs tend to feature no form of scrutiny whatsoever. The control mechanisms provided in SAs present shortcomings as well. Firstly, the Executive Director (ED) may withdraw financing of the relevant operational activity, and/or suspend or terminate it, if the SA or the operational plan are not respected. The host state *may* also—but is under no obligation to—report to Frontex *incidents related to non-compliance* with the operational plan, including in relation to fundamental rights.[126] More shockingly, the ED has no duty to suspend or terminate the relevant operational activity or aspects thereof if the security of any participant of an operational activity cannot be guaranteed.[127] Secondly, Frontex and the third country must each have an incident reporting mechanism, and they must assist each other in investigating the incident through their respective mechanisms, including by collecting and producing evidence.[128] This is presumably on the basis that each mechanism would deal with complaints or incidents involving their respective staff. Thirdly, all SAs stipulate that disputes on the interpretation and application of the SA are examined jointly by the parties' representatives, and in the absence of a settlement, the dispute on interpretation and translation is settled *exclusively* by negotiation.[129] The SAs extend provisions contained in the EBCG Regulation, which are underpinned by mutual trust justified by the state's membership of the Union. In its role as implementer of SAs, Frontex has also signed different MoUs on a complaint mechanism, aimed 'to address any allegations of breaches of fundamental rights during operational activities'.[130] This relates to the SAs mentioned above. However, the legal basis relied on to conclude such an MoU concluded by Frontex is not clear. The use of such forms of (quasi)law creates a situation of high impact-low scrutiny as the administrative and especially judicial avenues of review are paved with hurdles.[131] More broadly, these partnerships appear to be established in the absence of a fundamental rights impact assessment, showing that the extension of such trust-based provisions to a third country is justified. These structural flaws in the EU approach were brought to the fore by the Ombudsman's own-initiative inquiry on the EU–Tunisia MoU, which investigated how the European Commission intended to guarantee respect for human rights in the context of the MoU.[132] The Ombudsman's final decision contained a series of important recommendations for the Commission, which include: publishing a summary of the risk management exercise conducted for Tunisia before signing the MoU; regularly updating and publishing information on the outcome of the human rights monitoring by the partners that implement projects started after the MoU; making public the criteria behind the suspension of contracts due to violations of human rights in the implementation of EU-funded projects in Tunisia; and encouraging the

[126] EBCG Regulation, Article 82(5).

[127] EU–North Macedonia SA, Article 18.

[128] EU–Albania SA, Article 5.

[129] EU–Montenegro SA, Article 21.

[130] See the following example of the MoU with Moldova.

[131] On the justiciability of EU soft law measures before the Court of Justice, see G Gentile, 'Ensuring Effective Judicial Review of EU Soft Law via the Action for Annulment before the EU Courts: A Plea for a Liberal-Constitutional Approach (2020) 16 European Constitutional Law Review 466.

[132] Case OI/2/2024/MHZ.

implementing partners to set up complaint mechanisms for individuals to report alleged violations of their human rights in the implementation of EU-funded projects and programmes in Tunisia.[133]

### 6.3.2 Scrutiny by Member States

In Chapter 5, we discussed two key features of interaction between member states on activities 'in transit'. We highlighted the role of the consent of the flag or coastal state during sea surveillance, and the possibility of disagreement between the originator of a report in EUROSUR and the owner of a situational picture on impact and confidence levels. Especially the latter can be seen, somehow, as a form of interstate control. Beyond this, EU law provides almost no provision on 'cross-examination' between states. There is no parallel provision to those featured in the VIS and ETIAS, according to which member states can inform each other about the possible inaccuracy of the information provided or the lawfulness of the processing.

On a closer inspection, the SESB Regulation might offer some facilities for interstate scrutiny. This is especially the case for disembarkation in a third country and the assessment of the situation therein. Here, we must distinguish between two such assessments. The first one, performed by the host state when planning a sea operation in coordination with the participating states and Frontex (or 'planned disembarkation'); and a second one, at the moment of disembarkation proper, assuming the action itself could be carried out by a country other than the host state ('actual disembarkation'). As regards the former, the previous section cast doubts on the participating states' meaningful power of influencing the planned disembarkation. As for actual disembarkation, the participating units should assess the personal circumstances of the persons before disembarking and give them an opportunity to express reasons for believing that disembarkation would constitute *refoulement*.[134] Furthermore, disembarkation in a third country must not take place where the participating states are aware or ought to be aware of a risk of direct or indirect *refoulement*.[135] Two questions arise concerning the scrutinizing role of the participating member states. Firstly, in what circumstances and on what grounds could a member state be thought to have been unaware of the situation in the third country and thus to have acted in compliance with EU law? At the very least, the concerns raised by a person intercepted should be treated as the manifestation of intention to apply for international protection, which would prevent disembarkation from going further as far as those persons are concerned. Secondly, the legal relevance of interstate scrutiny can be seen from the absence of its impact. It is the host state which instructs the participating units. The latter, presumably, would have to follow the instruction on the basis of the chain of command at the basis of the surveillance operation. The legal consequences of a

[133] For an earlier study on Frontex and the role of the EU Ombudsman, see N Vogiatzis, 'Frontex: Human Rights Obligations and the Role of the European Ombudsman' in A Karatzogianni, D Nguyen, and E Serafinelli (eds), *The Digital Transformation of the Public Sphere* (Palgrave Macmillan 2016) 303.
[134] SESB Regulation, Article 4(3).
[135] SESB Regulation, Article 4(2) and (3).

possible disembarkation in breach of *non-refoulement* would then become primarily a matter of national proceedings. As shown by the example of Italy discussed below, this could lead to the imposition of criminal penalties and call into play the specific rules on criminal liability laid down in the EBCG Regulation.[136]

## 6.3.3 Individual Control

As mentioned, individual-led scrutiny can be pursued mainly through 'complaint' mechanisms broadly understood and access to information. This scenario shows the permeability between these different pathways to scrutiny. Regulation 1049/2001 governs public access to documents of, inter alia, the European Commission and Frontex.[137] A decision to grant or refuse access can, in turn, result in a complaint to the EU Ombudsman or an action before the Court of Justice.[138] Like the two other types of scrutiny 'in transit' discussed above, heterogeneity has an important role to play in constitutional compliance. The first subsection addresses two main issues. The heterogeneity of objectives of border surveillance and of corresponding tasks attributed to Frontex impacts the individual scrutiny for activities in this area.[139] The second subsection, however, shows a positive example related to such heterogeneity. A line of case law developed by the Italian Supreme Court on illegal pushbacks following interception on the high seas reveals the potential for national criminal proceedings to enhance individual protection through accountability of the responsible actors.

### 6.3.3.1 Surveillance, access to documents, and (certain) direct actions

Surveillance, especially at sea, has been an area of controversy for activities by the member states and Frontex, and one where access to documents has been consistently pursued by private actors over the years.[140] However, Frontex's approach to such requests has been significantly restrictive.[141] In this regard, the Regulation on access to documents imposes an obligation to refuse access where the disclosure would undermine the protection of one or more of the interests enumerated therein, which include public security and the integrity of the individual.[142] Such an approach has led to the quest for alternative pathways to scrutiny, and especially through the Court and the

[136] This issue links decisively to the debate about the concept of the safe third country in EU law. While important, this issue falls outside the scope of this research. See B Nur Osso, 'Unpacking the Safe Third Country Concept in the European Union: B/orders, Legal Spaces, and Asylum in the Shadow of Externalization' (2023) 35 International Journal of Refugee Law 272.

[137] Frontex is subject to these rules pursuant to the EBCG Regulation, Article 114.

[138] See Article 228 and 263 TFEU, respectively.

[139] For an in-depth analysis of Frontex's approach to access to documents, see M Fink and M Hillebrandt, 'Access to Documents and the EU Agency Frontex: Growing Pains or Outright Obstruction?' in M Hillebrandt, P Leino-Sandberg, and I Koivisto (eds), *(In)visible European Government: Critical Approaches to Transparency as an Ideal and a Practice* (Routledge 2023). See also L Salzano and M Gkliati, 'Mysteriousness by Design: the Case of Frontex and the Regulation on Public Access to Documents', ADiM Blog, April 2022.

[140] Frontex has adopted practical arrangements regarding public access to documents in its possession in April 2024. MB Decision 19/2024.

[141] See in this sense Fink and Hillebrandt, 'Access to Documents and the EU agency Frontex'.

[142] Regulation No 1049/2001, Article 4.

EU Ombudsman. On different occasions, the Ombudsman has played an important role in this regard. This is apparent from examples of systematic refusal to provide lists of documents identified as falling within the scope of requests for access.[143] Other times, the Ombudsman has proposed that Frontex revise its initial refusal, at least in part.[144] Or else, the Ombudsman has pointed to the excessive redacting by Frontex on serious incident reporting and insufficient explanation for this.[145] This pathway to scrutiny has, in turn, paved the way for positive changes in the practice.[146]

However, the multi-purpose nature of Frontex, and of border surveillance more broadly, has inevitably entailed the management of competing interests. In *Izuzquiza*, two applicants contested Frontex's decision to refuse access to documents containing information on the name, type, and flag of every vessel deployed between 1 June and 30 August 2017 in the central Mediterranean under Joint Operation Triton.[147] Frontex refused access on the basis of the fact that, if granted, that information would allow traffickers to locate the patrolling vessels and avoid control. The Court found such an exception to the rule of giving the widest possible access must be interpreted strictly.[148] The body concerned must, in principle, explain how disclosure could *specifically* and *actually* undermine the interest protected in a way that is reasonably foreseeable and not purely hypothetical.[149] It also stated that the relevant body enjoys wide discretion, which is not in itself incompatible with the principle of strict construction. In its judicial review, the Court is not to engage with the merit of the decision. Instead, it must focus on the compliance with the relevant procedural rules—including the duty to state reasons—and whether there have been errors in fact or in the assessment or misuse of powers.[150] Non-compliance with these requirements (such as stating reasons for refusal) can also ensue from the non-disclosure of certain documents that fall within the scope of the request. Sea-Watch eV had requested access to a series of documents concerning Operation Themis.[151] Frontex identified 73 documents in its possession related to the areas of interest referred to in the request for access, but it refused disclosure on either public interest, or privacy and integrity grounds. However, in a following submission from Frontex to the General Court (GC), it emerged that the Agency was in possession of many more pictures related to the aerial operation in question than it had identified in its response to the applicant.[152] Frontex, therefore, had failed to mention these documents in its decision and breached the obligation to state the reason for the refusal to give access in those cases.[153]

[143] Case 1129/2023/OAM.
[144] Case 652/2023/VB.
[145] Decision in case 1616/2016/MDC.
[146] See https://www.statewatch.org/observatories/frontex/legal-and-administrative-complaints/complaints-to-the-european-ombudsman-on-europol-frontex-and-access-to-documents-documentation/.
[147] Case T-31/18, *Luisa Izuzquiza and Arne Semsrott*, EU:T:2019:815.
[148] Case C-266/05 P, *Sison* v *Council*, EU:C:2007:75, para 63.
[149] Case C-350/12 P, *Council* v *in't Veld*, EU:C:2014:2039, para 52.
[150] Case C-266/05 P, *Sison* v *Council*, para 64.
[151] Case T-205/22, *Naass and Sea-Watch v Frontex*, EU:T:2024:266.
[152] This submission occurred following the measure of inquiry adopted on the basis of Article 91(c) of the Rule of Procedure of the Court.
[153] Case T-205/22, *Naass and Sea-Watch v Frontex*, paras 75–79.

The heterogeneity of objectives of border surveillance poses a clear challenge to scrutiny. It might be difficult to ascertain that the body concerned has satisfied the 'specifically and actually' components of the procedural requirements, without either the body revealing details that should not be disclosed, or the Court looking at least to an extent into the substance of the decision. Access to documents is inevitably subject to certain exceptions, and assessing the appropriateness of such restriction is fact-dependent. General grounds that might be prone to being invoked for those purposes, such as public interest in limiting access, can often mitigate in favour of openness. This is apparent from an important decision by the EU Ombudsman, who found maladministration by the Commission insofar as the latter refused to give wider public access to documents concerning human rights monitoring of EU-funded projects in Libya.[154] In quoting the Court's case law, she observed that 'the mere fact that certain documents contain information or negative statements about the political situation, or the protection of human rights, in a third country does not necessarily mean that access to them may be denied on the basis that there is a risk that the public interest may be undermined'.[155]

Limitations on successful scrutiny of controls 'in transit' are not unique to the issue of access to documents. These have also emerged from the pursuit of legal scrutiny through Articles 263 and 265 TFEU, and more specifically from actions against Frontex's surveillance activities in the Aegean Sea. Such actions sought a declaration to the effect that: Frontex had failed to act, insofar as it had not suspended or ceased its activities despite the applicant's request and the alleged commission of serious fundamental rights violations occurred during those activities;[156] or, alternatively, that Frontex's decision *not* to suspend or terminate the activities be annulled. In the proceedings before the GC, the actions were dismissed on procedural grounds. In a first case, which focused primarily on Article 265 TFEU, Frontex successfully claimed to have fulfilled the requirement to act as it had defined its position in a letter of response to the applicant.[157] In a second line of cases, the GC and the Court of Justice in appeal addressed the question related to Article 263 TFEU as well. The GC ruled that the person had no vested and present interest in the annulment of the decision, since they claimed 'in an abstract and general manner [that the annulment was] liable to have a positive effect on his situation, since it [would reduce] his risk of exposure, at the time of his imminent and inevitable further attempt to cross the Aegean Sea, to fundamental rights violations committed jointly by the Hellenic Republic and Frontex'.[158] However, the GC noted that the annulment of the decision would only lead to Frontex reconsidering its decision, not to an automatic suspension of the activities. The Court of Justice confirmed the findings of the GC in appeal.[159] Given the discretion enjoyed by the ED under Article 46(4) EBCG Regulation, there could be no presumption that a new examination of the applicant's request would end up with a suspension or termination of its activities. The unfavourable outcome should be contextualized.

[154] Case 2089/2023/ACB.
[155] Case T-211/00, *Aldo Kuijer v Council*, EU:T:2002:30, para 60.
[156] See, in this sense, Article 46(4) EBCG Regulation.
[157] Case T-282/21, *SS and ST v Frontex*, EU:T:2022:235, paras 21–23 and case law cited.
[158] Case T-600/22, *ST v European Border and Coast Guard Agency (Frontex)*, EU:T:2023:776, para 27.
[159] Case C-62/24 P, *ST v European Border and Coast Guard Agency (Frontex)*, EU:C:2024:882.

The reasoning in the rulings is broadly consistent with the principles governing actions for failure to act and for annulment. Furthermore, the persons concerned were able to access scrutiny, even though they did not achieve compliance through enforcement—that is, ensuring that the ED uses the discretion under Article 46(4) EBCG Regulation appropriately, which might not have been the case under consideration.[160] Heterogeneity seems to play no major role either. What the judgments reveal, however, is that there are structural limitations on the extent to which the persons concerned can achieve through legal scrutiny of surveillance. On the one hand, and as long as the ED denies the existence of fundamental rights violations that occurred during Frontex's activities, the successful pursuit of an action for failure to act seems precluded. On the other hand, an examination of the merit of such a decision seems prevented by the need to demonstrate a current interest in acting. It is very difficult to envisage a situation where this requirement might be met, as regards surveillance activities. The discussion of controls 'at the borders' covered further limitations of the legal framework, directly related to the heterogeneity of the levels of governance and actors.

#### 6.3.3.2 Non-refoulement and criminal proceedings at national level: Two tales from Italy

This section highlights the significant limitations of the mechanisms of liability established by the EBCG Regulation. A fundamental flaw is linked to the way responsibilities are divided between Frontex and national authorities. The former seems shielded from liability, as only the latter are deemed to be formally responsible for control-related actions. Scrutiny and accountability should, therefore, be pursued through civil or criminal proceedings within the state concerned, which in practice often proves to be very difficult. Experience tells us that this is not always the case, however. In this regard, the Italian Supreme Court rendered an important judgment which convicted the captain of the private vessel *Asso28*.[161] The vessel rescued a small boat with 101 migrants around 57 miles off the Libyan coast,[162] to subsequently disembark them in Tripoli. The captain acted upon the instructions of a supposed Libyan customs official, without having previously identified him. Beyond the specific provisions of the Italian criminal code engaged in this case,[163] the Supreme Court found the captain's conduct in breach of the procedures laid down in the Convention on Safety of Life at Sea (SOLAS) as well as the directives of the International Maritime Organisation (IMO).[164] The lack of identification was in breach of the Technical Regulations, International Ship and Port Security Code (ISPS Code), introduced by the SOLAS

[160] From the rulings, it appears that the applicants had submitted evidence of the alleged fundamental rights violations, including from the European Anti-Fraud Office and the United Nations High Commissioner for Refugees. Case C-62/24 P, *ST v European Border and Coast Guard Agency (Frontex)*, para 23.

[161] Corte di Cassazione, Sez V, judgment 4557/2023. For a comment, see S Zirulia, 'Refoulement as a Crime: Insights from the Asso28 Push-Back Case', VerfassungBlog (2 February 2024).

[162] The point fell within the territorial scope of Libya's SAR region.

[163] In particular, Articles 591 (arbitrary disembarkation and abandonment of people) and 1155 of the Maritime Code.

[164] Corte di Cassazione, Sez V, judgment 4557/2023, para 2.2.

Convention.[165] Secondly, while the captain rescued and boarded the persons, he did not inform the competent Rescue Coordination Centres, either before or after having performed the SAR operation, as prescribed by said instruments of international law. Thirdly, he failed to prompt the coordination of the competent SAR authorities and comply with the information obligations stated by the relevant resolutions of the Maritime Safety Committee (MSC).[166] Fourthly, he was in breach of the ISPS Code as he did not identify the rescued persons, in order to obtain information on their origin and nationality, their health conditions, their intention to apply for international protection, and the possible presence of unaccompanied minors. Finally, in taking the rescued persons back to Tripoli, he violated the prohibition of collective expulsion and refoulement. The Italian Supreme Court built this last finding on the nature of Libya as an unsafe port, which was in turn justified by the fact that that third country was not a Party to the Geneva Convention, and the 'high risk' existed that the persons would suffer from inhumane and degrading treatment as well as the violation of their rights of effective legal protection. In this specific regard, the Supreme Court referred to several provisions from different sources of international and EU law which are part of Italian law, including the ECHR,[167] the Geneva Convention,[168] the CFR,[169] and the abovementioned SOLAS and SAR Conventions and related directives.

The judgment is significant for a number of reasons, as it joins international, EU, and national law to enhance respect for individual rights in different ways. Most importantly, it does so in a way that could potentially be used by other national courts. To be sure, the idea that the captain of a vessel flying the flag of a state Party to a Convention must abide by the obligations stated therein might not sound particularly earth-shattering. There is more to these references to international law than meets the eye, however. The link between the responsibility of the captain of a private vessel and the obligations to which the state is subject (eg the ECHR and the Geneva Convention) is significantly less obvious than that involving instruments of maritime security. The latter expressly point to the responsibility of the captain, whereas the former binds the states and their officials. In this sense, the Supreme Court addressed in depth the applicability of the latter type of Conventions to private persons. As known, the ECtHR in *Hirsi v Italy* established the applicability of the ECHR in a situation where public officials of an Italian military vessel intercepted on the high seas and took back to Libya a group of migrants without examining their applications for international protection.[170] The *Asso28* judgment extends this case law to private

[165] SOLAS Convention, Chapter XI, Article 7(A) and Articles 8 and 9(B).

[166] MSC resolution 167/168, Article 5.

[167] European Convention of Human Rights, Articles 3 (prohibition of inhumane and degrading treatment) and 14 (prohibition of discrimination) as well as Article 4 of the Additional Protocol (prohibition of refoulement of foreigners to countries where they may be subject to inhuman or degrading treatment or where the exercise of fundamental rights is in any case impeded).

[168] Convention Relating to the Status of Refugees (adopted 28 July 1951, entered into force 22 April 1954) 189 UNTS 137, Article 33, which prohibits the expulsion or refoulement of a refugee to the borders of territories where his life or freedom would be threatened because of his race, religion, nationality, membership of a social group, or political opinion.

[169] CFR, Article 19.

[170] European Court of Human Rights (ECtHR), *Hirsi Jamaa and Others v Italy*, judgment of 23 February 2012, App no 27765/09.

vessels,[171] attributing the role of what can be loosely translated as 'public official' to the captain of such vessels, as far as their SAR-related obligations are concerned.[172] The captain is a state agent (including when operating in international waters), and is therefore bound by the ECHR and the Geneva Convention when exercising authority and control over rescued persons.[173] This obligation includes, inter alia, the duty to respect the rights of the persons subject to their jurisdiction as guaranteed by the ECHR.[174] What is particularly striking is that, in reaching such a conclusion, the Supreme Court relied not only on the specific features of Italian law, but also—once again—on international law, and specifically the provisions prescribing certain conduct to the captain (directly or indirectly).[175]

An aspect closely related to the finding of violation concerns the scope of the risk assessment that must be carried out before bringing the rescued persons back to the point of departure or to the identified place of safety. The Supreme Court emphasized the importance of ascertaining the safety of the place of destination *in concreto*, and particularly so in situations where it might be presumed that the fundamental rights of the persons will not be effectively guaranteed. This is even more the case where the identification of such a place of safety is not performed by the authorities competent for the SAR region concerned. It is worth noting that, on this point, the Supreme Court refers to a rather specific—and for this reason important—circumstance. At the time the events behind the judgment occurred—in fact, at the time the judgment was rendered as well—the establishment of a SAR region for Libya had been notified to the IMO, but the latter was not yet operative.[176]

The definition of a captain of a private vessel as a stage agent, the necessary qualities of the actor identifying the place of safety, and the required depth of the risk assessment are all inextricably linked aspects of a powerful point of law established by the Italian Supreme Court. There is one more significant consequence to the extension of the *Hirsi* case law to private vessels. In *Asso28*, the breach was very obvious because the captain had failed to identify the persons and gave them no opportunity to make an application for international protection. Had he done this, the captain of *Asso28* may not have been entirely exempt from responsibility anyway. The ECtHR stated in *Hirsi* that the officials concerned were not qualified, nor were they assisted adequately, to properly assess the individual situation of the intercepted persons. This detail seems to have played a role in the finding of a violation of the prohibition of collective expulsion.[177] The intervention of such qualified personnel is therefore

[171] Corte di Cassazione, Sez V, judgment 4557/2023, para 5.4.

[172] The actual expression used by the Supreme Court is 'incaricato di pubblico servizio'. In Italian law, the 'incaricato di pubblico servizio' is under the obligations and enjoys certain safeguards of the public official without having their powers. For other specific functions performed by the captain, however, the Supreme Court expressly attributes them the quality of public officials.

[173] Corte di Cassazione, Sez V, judgment 4557/2023, para 5.5.

[174] Corte di Cassazione, Sez V, judgment 4557/2023, para 5.6.

[175] More specifically, Article 98 of the United Nations Convention on the Law of the Sea (adopted 10 December 1982, entered into force 16 November 1994) 1833 UNTS 3 and Article 10 of International Convention on Maritime Search and Rescue (adopted 27 April 1979, entered into force 22 June 1985) 1405 UNTS 97.

SAR Convention.

[176] Corte di Cassazione, Sez V, judgment 4557/2023, para 5.7.

[177] ECtHR, *Hirsi and Others v Italy*, para 185.

necessary.[178]

The judgment is part of a broader line of cases in which the Supreme Court has combined international and criminal law either to punish or to absolve, but in any event to enhance respect for the rule of law. In *Asso28*, the conviction was not based directly on the violation of these obligations under international and EU law. All these actions were subsumed under the offences of arbitrary disembarkation and abandonment of people in a state of danger, governed by specific provisions of the Italian Criminal Code. Not long before the ruling under discussion here, the Italian Supreme Court had acquitted a group of TCNs who, after having been rescued by the private vessel *Vos Thalassa*, had used threats and violence to avoid being brought back to Libya.[179] The acquittal was based on the relevant provision of the Italian Criminal Code on self-defence,[180] which presupposes that the person has committed the offence in a state of necessity, with a view to defending a right of theirs or of others against the present danger of an unlawful or unjustified behaviour. The unlawful behaviour—under customary and conventional international law—in this specific case being the *refoulement*, to which corresponds the individual right against it.

The question, then, arises as to what could be the broader implications of such judgments beyond the specific circumstances of the case. EU member states are generally tied to the ECHR and the conventions referred to in the ruling. Many, if not all of them, are likely to feature provisions in their criminal law which are comparable to those used by the Italian Supreme Court. Therefore, it is not implausible that the principles stated by the Supreme Court—or at least the spirit thereof—could *in abstracto* be espoused by courts from other member states, to the extent that they have not already developed principles of the sort. This is certainly the case for situations comparable to those discussed in *Asso28* or *Vos Thalassa*.

### 6.3.4 Interim Conclusions

The analysis of pathways to scrutiny of controls in transit has amplified some key issues discussed in the 'before leaving' scenario, but has also added a further layer of complexity to the picture. Similarly to what we observed with regard to scrutiny before leaving, the heterogeneity of levels of governance and decision-making centres is not matched by effective mechanisms of interinstitutional scrutiny. The choice about disembarkation in a third country is a case in point. As for individual scrutiny, the heterogeneity of sources entails delegation of decision-making for crucial aspects of the framework. This, combined with the heterogeneity of objectives of surveillance activities, can hinder scrutiny both in terms of access to documents and legal certainty. Furthermore, the recent case law of the Court of Justice has revealed the existence of structural hurdles to legal scrutiny caused by *locus standi* and lack of interest to act. While Emily O'Reilly's tenure as EU Ombudsman has brought to the fore the

[178] This principle is important beyond the specific case of pushbacks to Libya, given its nature of unsafe country.

[179] Corte di Cassazione, Sez VI, judgment 15869/2021.

[180] Italian Criminal Code, Article 52.

potential for heterogeneity of actors of scrutiny, this body can 'only' refer a finding of maladministration and any recommendations they might have to the European Parliament and the institution/office concerned.

## 6.4 At the Borders

To a large extent, the scrutiny of activities carried out at the borders overlaps with the themes raised in the previous scenario. Since the analysis below critically discusses the suitability of pathways to scrutiny of Frontex's activities, those considerations are applicable to surveillance-related actions as well. The first part of the discussion focuses on scrutiny at EU level, to then move on to scrutiny of member states and individual-led scrutiny.

### 6.4.1 Control at EU Level

As mentioned above, EU-driven scrutiny can be structural or internal to Frontex. The two pathways do not live in isolation. To grasp the actual accessibility of structural scrutiny for activities at the borders, we must familiarize ourselves with the existing forms of administrative control within the Agency. Furthermore, we must set out the allocation of responsibilities and liability established by the EBCG Regulation. Before we delve into those areas, it is worth mentioning, on a more general level, different kinds of democratic and administrative scrutiny provided for in the relevant instruments of secondary law. Unsurprisingly, the Commission has a central role in monitoring, reporting, and disseminating to the public information related to external border controls.[181] It also has a right to be informed—and sometimes to veto—different types of agreement. More specifically:

- it must be notified of, and approve, Frontex–third-country working arrangements;
- it must be notified of the operational plans for operations on the territory of a third country;
- it must be notified of bilateral agreements and arrangements between member states—for example, when establishing rules for the control of a common border;[182]
- it must be consulted by member states on agreements with third countries which establish a shared border crossing point, and notify these states if it considers their agreement incompatible with Union law. The member state must then take steps to make the agreement compatible following the Commission's remarks.[183]

[181] See, for example, Regulation (EU) 2016/399 establishing a Schengen Borders Code [2016] OJ L 77/1 (SBC), Articles 21 and 42.
[182] SBC Regulation, Article 18.
[183] SBC Regulation, Annex VI, 1.1.4.4.

The European Parliament must be kept fully informed of these activities.[184] Furthermore, the Commission must be informed by Frontex's ED of the risk that a member state will not implement a measure recommended on the basis of the vulnerability assessment. If the member state fails to implement the measure, the management board can decide what measure must be taken by the member state. The measure is binding, and failure to comply will be followed by a notification to the Council and the Commission (but not the European Parliament).[185] Frontex itself is accountable to the European Parliament and the Council,[186] and must make public the agreements, WAs, and projects with third countries.[187] Frontex should allow the Committee for the Prevention of Torture (CPT) of the Council of Europe to carry out visits in the context of return operations. This is established in a recital, and is anyway subject to the agreement of the member state concerned.[188] Frontex is subject to a series of instruments, such as the Regulation on the European Anti-Fraud Office (OLAF),[189] the European Public Prosecutor's Office (EPPO),[190] and rules on access to documents.[191] Frontex activities are also subject to different types of scrutiny, especially concerning fraud. The Agency's WA with third countries must contain provisions empowering said bodies to perform such investigative activities.[192] Against this background, the core of EU scrutiny focuses on two main aspects: the different mechanisms of fundamental rights monitoring laid down in the EBCG Regulation,[193] and the monitoring of the use of force in the activities of Frontex and the member states.

#### 6.4.1.1 Monitoring of fundamental rights compliance during Frontex's activities

The EBCG Regulation provides for a diffuse system of fundamental rights monitoring over Frontex's and member states' activities. In this subsection, we cover the following offices and related tasks: the EDs, Frontex liaison officers (FLOs), coordinating officers (COs), fundamental right monitors (FRMs), and fundamental rights officers (FROs). The ED must evaluate the results of all Frontex operational activities through reports sent to the MB after the activity has ended, alongside observations from the FRO. The analysis is geared towards an improvement of the *quality, coherence, and effectiveness* of those activities.[194] Crucially, the ED must also assess, '*prior* to any operational activity' of Frontex, whether there are fundamental rights violations of a serious nature or likely to persist 'in accordance with Article 46(4) and (5)'. However, only Article 46(5) refers to a situation where an activity might not be launched due

[184] EBCG Regulation, Article 76(4).
[185] EBCG Regulation, Article 32(9) and (10).
[186] EBCG Regulation, Article 6.
[187] EBCG Regulation, Article 73.
[188] EBCG Regulation, recital 82.
[189] Regulation (EU, Euratom) No 883/2013 on investigations conducted by the European Anti-Fraud Office (OLAF) [2013] OJ L 248/1. See recital 113 of the EBCG Regulation. See M Gigli, 'Financial Scrutiny of Frontex as a Political Accountability Tool', VerfassungBlog, 8 September 2022.
[190] Regulation (EU) 2017/1939 establishing the European Public Prosecutor's Office [2017] OJ L 283/1. See recital 114 of the EBCG Regulation.
[191] EBCG Regulation, recital 115.
[192] EBCG Regulation, Article 117.
[193] This is an expression of a more general obligation for Frontex to monitor compliance with fundamental rights as part of its mandate. EBCG Regulation, Article 10(1)(g).
[194] EBCG Regulation, Article 47.

to serious concerns related to *future* fundamental rights compliance. Article 46(4), however, refers to the ED's obligation to withdraw financing and suspend or terminate the activity if they consider that there are serious or likely to persist breaches of fundamental rights *related to* the activity.[195] In other words, if the activity is already ongoing, how can the ED's assessment happen *prior* to that?

Beyond this logical inconsistency, the ED's power to suspend or terminate an activity on fundamental rights grounds is key to assessing the appropriateness of Frontex's scrutiny. The requirement that the breach be *related* to the activity is, in theory, a safeguard against an overly restrictive interpretation of the scope of Article 46(4) of the EBCG Regulation. Likewise, the seriousness of a violation might be caused either by its nature *or* its enduring character. The non-cumulative nature of those conditions also has a protective potential. However, several limitations affect the proper use of the EDs. Some of them are inherent in the wording of the provision and its context. The absence of any provisions governing the follow-up of a suspension of the activity is a serious shortcoming of the legal framework. Even more fundamentally, questions arise as to: what type of violations might warrant the use of the ED's power, and how 'close' the violation should be to Frontex's action in order to trigger Article 46(4), bearing in mind that the ED enjoys some discretion in assessing whether such conditions are met. The uncertainty here is caused, at least in part, by the lack of substantive legal scrutiny of Frontex's activities, which is in turn occasioned by procedural hurdles, as the case law on Article 263 and 265 TFEU discussed in the previous scenario has shown. In the absence of any jurisprudential development of such provisions, the uncertainty is bound to persist. The analysis of scrutiny at the borders only corroborates the argument. To better get a sense of this argument, it might be useful to take a look at the Court's case law on the rebuttal of mutual trust for the purposes of refusing the execution of a European Arrest Warrant (EAW)[196] or an intra-EU transfer under the Dublin Regulation.[197] Cooperation under these mechanisms can be refused if there is a real risk that transferring the person will result in a violation of an absolute right[198]—including, but not limited to, the cases of possible detention in inhumane or degrading conditions. As for relative rights, the Court of Justice requires that the risk in the individual case be linked to the existence of deficiencies which might be systemic, or affect certain places or groups of people.[199] For example, a risk of violation of Article 47 CFR might arise from deficiencies in the justice systems caused by a lack of independence of the judiciary, or by an ineffective system of remedies in the specific context under consideration.[200] This case law shows how important the refinement of the interpretation of the legislation has been. It also offers, implicitly, a term of comparison in identifying the threshold for the exercise of the ED's powers. The wording

[195] EBCG Regulation, Article 106(4)(m). See also Article 46(4) and (5) thereof.

[196] Council Framework Decision 2002/584/JHA on the European arrest warrant and the surrender procedures between Member States [2002] OJ L 190/1.

[197] Regulation (EU) No 604/2013 establishing the criteria and mechanisms for determining the Member State responsible for examining an application for international protection lodged in one of the Member States by a third-country national or a stateless person [2013] OJ L 180/31.

[198] Joined Cases C-404/15 and C-659/15 PPU, *Aranyosi and Căldăraru*, EU:C:2016:198.

[199] Case C-158/21, *Puig Gordi*, EU:C:2023:57.

[200] To stick with the example of the EAW, an issue would arise if there were no effective possibility of challenging a decision of execution based on the fact that the executing court lacked jurisdiction.

of Article 46(4) of the EBCG Regulation is clearly less exacting. It requires no systemic deficiencies, and it can be either backward- or forward-looking: reliable information about violations of Article 4 CFR would meet the threshold, even in the absence of a likely repetition thereof.

The other, and perhaps more decisive, issue lies in the necessary degree of proximity between Frontex's activities and the violations. Frontex's activities need only be *related to* the violations. The threshold is very clearly lower than that necessary to establish liability. Would this degree of proximity be met if Frontex assisted a member state with interception and disembarkation where reliable information existed that TCNs were detained by that state in inhumane and degrading conditions? Would it be met if evidence existed that the member state is not providing TCNs with an effective system of remedy against alleged violations of their fundamental rights? Even if the threshold for termination and the degree of proximity were interpreted favourably to the person concerned, the elephant in the room would remain: namely, the lack of effective exercise of the power by the ED. Decisions by the EU Ombudsman,[201] and the case law on direct actions mentioned above, confirm the pattern of failure to act by Frontex's leadership and the difficulty in activating structural pathways to scrutiny to remedy this.

Beyond the role of the ED, the EBCG Regulation establishes a series of officers with monitoring tasks. Firstly, Frontex liaison officers contribute to the application of the Union acquis (including as regards fundamental rights), monitor the member states' management of the external borders, and can raise issues of concern with the ED, who in turn informs the member state.[202] Secondly, a coordinating officer (CO) appointed by the ED from the statutory staff acts on behalf of Frontex to foster cooperation and coordination among the member states involved in an operation. The CO must monitor the correct implementation of the operational plan, also in relation to respect for fundamental rights.[203] At least one FRM must assist and advise the coordinating officer.[204] Thirdly, antenna offices can be established in the host state or the host third country to monitor the activities of the teams, supporting the CO and FRMs, as well as the liaison officers.[205] Fourthly, as mentioned, there are officers specifically tasked with the monitoring of fundamental rights compliance.[206] The fundamental rights officers (FROs) are the main actors in this regard. They perform their role through a series of activities: they conduct investigations, advise Frontex, provide opinions on WAs or operational plans, carry out spot visits, and appoint the FRMs and assign them to different operations and activities. The MB must ensure that it takes action with regard to recommendations from the FRO.[207] Fifthly, the FRMs are statutory staff who must constantly assess, advise, and assist vis-à-vis the compliance of operational activities with fundamental rights.[208] The FRMs must, in particular, follow the

[201] Decision in Case OI/5/2020/MHZ.
[202] EBCG Regulation, Article 31.
[203] EBCG Regulation, Article 44.
[204] EBCG Regulation, Article 44(3)(b).
[205] EBCG Regulation, Article 60.
[206] Frontex has developed a fundamental rights strategy on the basis of Article 80 EBCG Regulation as well as an action plan to implement it.
[207] EBCG Regulation, Articles 109 and 110.
[208] EBCG Regulation, Article 110.

preparation of the operational plan and report to the FRO. Strictly speaking, there seems to be no obligation for the FRO to issue an opinion on each activity plan. The FRMs also conduct visits and liaise with both the CO and the FRO. There must be an FRM assigned to each operation, who *can* be assigned to any activity the FRO deems relevant. Pursuant to the EBCG Regulation, Frontex has also established a consultative forum to advise on fundamental rights matters.[209] The forum must be consulted on, inter alia, the complaint mechanisms and the code of conduct. It must report annually on its activities and must be given access to matters and information relevant to fundamental rights. On-spot visits, however, are subject to the consent of the host state, which can object as long as it justifies its refusal.[210]

This overview offers an important element in the overall analysis of the existing pathways to scrutiny of border controls *related to* Frontex's activities—that is, activities performed by the Agency itself or the member states in connection with Frontex's fulfilment of its tasks. Needless to say, the degree of Frontex's involvement in border control activities varies, depending on whether, for example, it is merely providing assistance and operational support, or it is coordinating a joint operation or rapid border intervention. The EBCG Regulation provides for a heterogeneous system of administrative scrutiny. A plurality of officers is involved, more or less directly, in the monitoring of compliance with fundamental rights. The set-up established in the Regulation is a double-edged sword. The heterogeneity creates overlapping remits, and there is no clear distinction between the respective mandates of competent officers. This is likely to lead to tensions and diverging views on operational matters, which is aggravated by the absence of explicit criteria for decision-making should divergence arise. Such shortcomings affect the transparency as well as the effectiveness of the legal framework.[211] The substantive powers endowed to those officers are not particularly incisive, which raises further questions about the effectiveness of the system. It is only the ED who can, by exercising a significant degree of discretion, make a consequential decision that is fundamental rights-driven. These concerns are compounded by the lack of independence of such a framework, which is entirely internal to the Agency. This bleak picture must be nuanced in two ways. Firstly, a more rounded conclusion on the appropriateness of the overall system of scrutiny of activities at the external borders requires an assessment of other existing mechanisms, especially legal scrutiny. Secondly, while the several officers mentioned above might not look particularly forceful, they open several channels for feeding concerns on fundamental rights compliance into the leadership of the Agency. The legal framework offers more than adequate tools to make sure that non-compliant action by member states or Frontex personnel is either prevented or addressed. This last point proves particularly important to the discussion of Frontex's liability.[212]

[209] EBCG Regulation, Article 108.

[210] EBCG Regulation, Article 108(5).

[211] The practice shows that Frontex's control over its handling of data can also be a sore point, as apparent from the European Data Protection Supervisor's reprimand EDPS/2022/09.

[212] Some authors rightly note, however, that on a systemic level the framework of accountability is fragmented and needs resetting. See M Gkliati, 'Decoding Frontex's Fragmented Accountability Mosaic and Introducing Systemic Accountability—System Reset' (2024) 30 European Law Journal 197.

### 6.4.1.2 Monitoring on the use of force

A more specific monitoring framework internal to the Agency focuses on the use of force by Frontex's statutory staff. This framework consists of the 'ground rules' laid down in the EBCG Regulation[213] and the relevant decision of the MB. Pursuant to Annex V EBCG, incidents concerning the use of force must be immediately reported, including to the FRO and the ED, with the statutory staff and any other participants being under an obligation to cooperate in fact-gathering. Without prejudice to rules on criminal liability, the ED must take adequate measures (including the immediate recall of the member) and disciplinary measures where Frontex has established that a statutory staff member has breached any applicable rules. The FRO must ensure that incidents related to the use of force and use of weapons are thoroughly investigated and reported without delay to the ED. The results of such investigations must be transmitted to the consultative forum.

The MB's Decision fleshes out the content of the Regulation.[214] According to the Decision, any events involving the use of force (UoF) must be reported and subject to an initial assessment to verify whether an incident has occurred. An incident covers, inter alia, situations where it is reasonable to believe that UoF was contrary to the operational plan, fundamental rights, or the code of conduct.[215] Should an incident occur, an administrative inquiry can be conducted, possibly followed by pre-disciplinary and disciplinary proceedings.[216] The CO carries out the initial assessment and reports on the outcome thereof, whereas the duty officer takes the assessment forward and reports in turn to the ED and the FRO.[217] The duty officer can also seek an opinion from Frontex's Head of Inspection and Control Office (ICO). The FRO, for their part, investigates the incident and shares the results with the ED, the consultative forum, and the MB. For these purposes, the FRO must have access to all areas and documents related to the operational activity.[218] The ED decides on precautionary and suspensive measures, initiation of administrative enquiries, pre-disciplinary and disciplinary proceedings, and transmission of information to the FRO.[219] The Advisor Committee on the UoF, appointed by the ED, assists the latter by issuing recommendations on the supervisory mechanism.[220] In the case where an inquiry is opened, the inquiry team can carry out visits of joint operations and rapid border intervention. The ED can close the case without further action, and mandate the opening of pre-disciplinary proceedings or, on the basis of a decision of an MB, disciplinary proceedings.[221]

Frontex's monitoring mechanism on the UoF shares a number of problematic aspects with the system of fundamental rights monitoring discussed in the previous

[213] EBCG Regulation, Article 55(5)(a). The decision establishing the mechanism and the amendment thereto are available respectively at Frontex decision on supervisory mechanism to monitor the application of provision on the use of force and Amendment to Frontex decision on supervisory mechanism to monitor the application of provision on the use of force.

[214] MB Decision 7/2021.

[215] MB Decision 7/2021, Article 2.

[216] MB Decision 7/2021, Article 4.

[217] MB Decision 7/2021, Articles 6 and 7.

[218] MB Decision 7/2021, Article 9.

[219] MB Decision 7/2021, Article 5.

[220] MB Decision 7/2021, Article 8.

[221] MB Decision 7/2021, Articles 30, 35, and 36.

section. Firstly, the administrative scrutiny is kept entirely within the Agency. Secondly, responsibility for monitoring is allocated to a heterogeneous range of actors. In this regard, the framework established by the MB's Decision is not entirely consistent with the intent clearly pursued by the Regulation, that the FRO take a leading role in the investigation in monitoring of incidents related to the use of force. It is far from clear how the tasks of the FRO square with the role of the duty officer, the ICO, or the inquiry team, and who is in charge of appointing this team. The Decision stipulates that the MB and the ED must be informed by the FRO 'about any diverging conclusions of the investigation of the [FRO] and the conclusion of the verification by the duty officer'.[222] As a matter of fact, the Decision establishes a detailed monitoring mechanism empowering different officers to carry out the internal investigation, while simply paying lip service to the FRO's duty of investigating without any further indication. Thirdly, the ultimate authority lies with the ED, who is also empowered to appoint an advisory committee. The combination of these features considerably undermines accountability and democratic legitimacy. In what seems to be a 'divide and conquer' strategy, the legal framework identifies a multitude of centres of scrutiny, which increases the chances of conflicting views and in turn broadens the discretion of the office having the final say (ie the ED). The heterogeneity is increased by the fact that the monitoring of the UoF exists alongside the SOP for SIR.[223] While the two mechanisms are supposed to have different scopes, as the SOP–SIR mechanism has a wider remit, the potential overlap is evident, and is in fact mentioned by the SOP–SIR mechanism itself.

### 6.4.2 Control by Member States and Beyond: Focus on the Migration and Asylum Pact

As seen with the 'in transit' scenario, which shares many features with the scenario 'at the border', the scope for a scrutiny of member states which is not individual-led, is relatively limited. The main point of interest lies in the new framework of border procedures established by the 2024 pact, discussed in the previous chapters, which lays down a series of pathways to scrutiny.[224] They can be 'institutional', in the sense that they are engaged at the initiative of an EU or a member state, or 'individual', when they are activated by a natural person or an organization. The 'institutional' pathway comprises a series of monitoring obligations that are established in the context of the Crisis Regulation. While both the Commission and the Council monitor the persistence of a situation of crisis or force majeure, the Commission specifically must focus on the compliance with fundamental rights and humanitarian standards. It can also

[222] MB Decision 7/2021, Article 9(4) MD.

[223] Decision of the Executive Director No R-ED-2021-51. The SOP–SIR references the Executive Director Decision No R-ED-2021-38 of 6 March 2021 on Standard Operating Procedure (SOP)—Use of force and incidents involving the use of force reporting (UFR/IFR), but this decision is not available on Frontex's website.

[224] See T Molnár, 'Monitoring Fundamental Rights Compliance in the Context of Screening and the Asylum Border Procedure: Putting Bricks Back into the EU House of Rule of Law?' EU Asylum Law and Policy Blog, 19 September 2024.

ask the EU Asylum Agency to initiate monitoring.[225] The Commission must also report to the EP and the Council every three months on the application of the decision and the effectiveness of the measures, and the continuing respect for the principles of proportionality and necessity.[226]

The Screening Regulation features the most important provisions in relation to institutional scrutiny. Each member state must establish an independent monitoring mechanism, focusing on the activities of national authorities. The mechanism must oversee the compliance of the screening authorities with the right of access to asylum procedures, non-refoulement, the best interest of the child, and the relevant rules on detention, as well as ensure that allegations of fundamental rights breaches are dealt with effectively. To this end, member states must establish a system for investigating allegations of violations. The mechanism will consist of on-the-spot checks and random and unannounced checks, and its members must have access to the relevant locations and documents *insofar as necessary*.

In the absence of implementation (especially at the national level), three main remarks are worth making at this stage on the fairness of the monitoring framework. The first consideration concerns legal certainty. As stated in the Screening Regulation, the future monitoring mechanism must live together with other existing monitoring mechanisms, such as those established within the EU Asylum Agency or the EBCG Regulations.[227] Coordination among them on the ground will be key to avoiding conflicts and inconsistencies in approaches. Such coordination should also aim to ensure that TCNs are clear as to what pathway of scrutiny is the most suitable for their specific situation or grievance.

Secondly, the Asylum Procedure Regulation (APR) states that member states must provide for monitoring of fundamental rights of border procedures which meet the standards of the monitoring mechanisms under the Screening Regulation. However, a comparable obligation is not established vis-à-vis return border procedures. This is particularly disappointing, as the pact leaves an unjustified hole in the system of responses to legal unfairness. Thirdly, one of the obligations related to the establishment of the monitoring consists of ensuring its independence. In this regard, the FRA will issue general guidance on the establishment of the mechanism, and can assist for those purposes at the request of the member states.[228] Since the independence of the monitoring will be a precondition for its fairness, the member states' set-up thereof will have to be closely monitored (pun intended).

The provisions on non-institutional pathways to scrutiny are no less problematic. Under the Screening Regulation, persons providing assistance and counselling must be given access to the screening. Member states can limit—but not severely restrict—such access when objectively necessary for the security, public order or administrative

[225] This takes place pursuant to Article 15(2) of Regulation (EU) 2021/2303.

[226] Regulation (EU) 2024/1359 addressing situations of crisis and force majeure in the field of migration and asylum (or Crisis Regulation), Article 6. See also Article 17(6).

[227] Regulation (EU) 2024/1356 introducing the screening of third-country nationals (Screening Regulation), Article 10.

[228] Screening Regulation, Article 10(2). See the guidance issued by the FRA in September 2024 on https://fra.europa.eu/sites/default/files/fra_uploads/fra-2024-independent-border-monitoring-mechanisms_en.pdf.

management of the facility where the screening is performed.[229] The same provision applies to access to applicants in detention[230] or at border transit zones,[231] as well as to cases where the member states are derogating from certain provisions of EU asylum law on the basis of the Crisis Regulation.[232] While public security or public order seem legitimate—if broad—grounds on which access can be limited, the same may not hold true for the management of the facility. If anything, it explicitly allows limitations for a very broadly worded reason based on matters of administrative convenience. To be sure, these restrictions do not apply to the UN High Commissioner for Refugees' access to applicants, including at the borders and in transit zones.[233] The limitations on scrutiny in practice might still be significant, as the High Commissioner alone might not be able to ensure the same 'coverage' as that resulting from granting access to other bodies (alongside the High Commissioner themselves).

When it comes to pathways to scrutiny afforded to the person concerned, the pact features a series of provisions on 'traditional' remedy—that is, against decisions strictly related to international protection[234] or intra-EU transfer.[235] However, there is no possibility of appealing against the outcome of the screening, the use of asylum border procedures, or the decision not to be granted entry. Strictly speaking, this aspect of the framework is not in *direct* conflict with the right to an effective remedy, to the extent that there is no established right to a specific type of asylum procedure—as long as it is fair—or to be granted entry.[236] To borrow from the ECtHR's approach to Article 6 ECHR, one might also argue that the assessment should focus on the overall fairness of the procedure: such fairness would be ensured if a wrong occurred at a certain stage and was subsequently 'corrected'. Given the highly interdependent nature of the different steps of border procedures, questions can be raised about the suitability of such an interpretation by analogy. On a more specific note, the information indicated in the initial screening form must be recorded 'in a way that is amenable to administrative or judicial review' during asylum or return procedures. However, this obligation does not concern information such as the reason for irregular arrival or entry, any comments and other relevant information, or information on routes travelled or suspected smuggling or trafficking in human beings.[237] There seem to be no justifiable grounds for leaving this information out of potential challenges or requests for revision. Quite the contrary, it might provide important material to define the individual situation of the person undergoing the screening.

The system of response to unfairness arising from the implementation of border procedures is rather 'patchy'. At the very least, we can safely say that the introduction

[229] Screening Regulation, Article 8(6).

[230] Regulation (EU) 2024/1349 establishing a return border procedure (RBP), Article 6(3).

[231] Regulation (EU) 2024/1348 establishing a common procedure for international protection in the Union (APR), Article 30(3).

[232] Crisis Regulation, Article 11(10) second subparagraph.

[233] APR, Article 6(1).

[234] APR, Section III and Chapter V.

[235] Regulation 2024/1351 on asylum and migration management (AMMR or AMM Regulation), Article 43.

[236] Unless there were cogent reasons to do so (eg in case of vulnerable persons). The different instruments provide for exceptions in this regard.

[237] Screening Regulation, Article 17.

of such procedures is not matched by a power of scrutiny attributed to the person concerned. Apart from certain aspects of the framework which will be fleshed out by the national implementation, the different measures themselves leave gaps in protection that seem not to be sufficiently justified and thus border on arbitrariness, or might appear disproportionate. Whether or not these elements would survive a test of legality before the Court of Justice is difficult to say. The integrated analysis of the Regulations, however, leaves the impression that the legal framework has limited the response to unfairness to the greatest possible extent of the legally defensible.

## 6.4.3 Individual Control

So far, we have shown that the heterogeneity of actors, levels of governance, and objectives can hinder access to scrutiny. The heterogeneity concerns not only the actors performing border controls, but also the actors of scrutiny themselves. The analysis of individual-led scrutiny is consistent with this broader observation. In this section, we focus on two main issues: the complaint mechanism, and the allocation of responsibility and liability of actors of controls. The framework, as mentioned, also applies to activities 'in transit'.

### 6.4.3.1 The complaint mechanism

The provisions in the EBCG Regulation[238] on the complaint mechanism must be read jointly with those in the relevant MB's decision.[239] The EBCG Regulation states that procedures to receive and transmit complaints to Frontex must be included in the operational plan.[240] Presumably, this provision makes no reference to the handling or processing of the complaint because these aspects are governed by the rule on the complaint mechanism. Anyone directly affected by Frontex's action or failure to act, and who considers that their fundamental rights have been breached as a result thereof, can submit a complaint. The FRO must handle the complaint in accordance with the right to a good administration. The FRO must decide whether the complaint is admissible and, if so, forward it to the ED and to the competent body of the seconding state (if the complaint concerns a deployed member of the teams). All decisions must be in writing and reasoned. The FRO must recommend an appropriate follow-up, on which the main addressee must report.[241] The relevant member state—presumably, the one to which the complaint was forwarded—must report back 'as to the findings and follow-up to the complaint'. If the member state does not report back or reports inconclusively, the FRO must inform the ED and the MB, and Frontex must follow up on the matter. Frontex must ensure that the form and information about the complaint mechanism are available and that further guidance and assistance on the procedure are provided.[242]

[238] EBCG Regulation, Article 111.
[239] MB Decision 19/2022, available at Frontex rules on complaints mechanism.
[240] EBCG Regulation, Article 38(3)(n).
[241] This could be the ED, the host state, or a participating state, depending on whether the complaint concerns a staff member from Frontex or the state to which the members of the team belongs.
[242] EBCG Regulation, Article 111.

From an observation of the ground rules on the complaint mechanism established in the Regulation, we can identify a series of features characterizing this pathway to administrative scrutiny. These features are consistent with the picture that emerged from the analysis of Frontex's different monitoring systems. On a broader level, the complaint mechanism is entirely internalized[243] and envisages no forms of external accountability whatsoever.[244] Secondly, the division of labour between the FRO and the responsible national authorities—or the ED—is far from clear. On what basis does the FRO recommend a certain follow-up, and how does the scope of their investigation compare to that of the ED or the relevant member state? Thirdly, the FRO seems to have no power vis-à-vis the inaction of the ED or the addressees of the complaint. The effectiveness of this mechanism of monitoring is also entirely dependent on how well the subject of the complaint will mark their own homework. Fourthly, the relevant actors involved (be they the investigators or the investigated) enjoy the widest possible discretion, specifically on crucial aspects of the whole process—for example, the timeline for the follow-up, or the range of options available to the FRO for the recommended actions. The only, and relatively narrow in scope, exception would apply should a member of the team be found to have violated fundamental rights or international protection obligations. In such a scenario, Frontex must request that the member state immediately remove the responsible member of the team from the activity of Frontex *or* the standing corps.[245] The two alternatives are rather different, and only reinforce the significant leeway left to the addressee of a complaint.

The MB Decision details the rules established in the Regulation. A complaint can be submitted by a person 'directly affected by actions or failure to act' by staff involved in Frontex's activity, including where this results in an alleged breach of fundamental rights. Importantly, submitting a complaint to Frontex is without prejudice to the seeking of other judicial or administrative remedies.[246] The mechanism is structured into three stages: receipt and admissibility review, handling of admissible complaints by the FRO, and action by the ED or home member state.[247] Once the FRO considers that the conditions for admissibility laid down in the rules are met, which might entail liaising with other 'entities' within Frontex, the complaint is forwarded to the ED. The FRO must ascertain the accuracy of the complaint and the underlying facts 'in close cooperation with other entities' within Frontex, including by relying on information provided by the relevant FRMs. If the facts amount to a fundamental rights violation, the FRO drafts a report by setting out the legal analysis behind the findings and recommends an appropriate follow-up.[248] The FRO must transmit all

[243] See the proposal in M Stefan and L den Hertog, 'Frontex: Great Powers But No Appeals' in M Chamon, A Volpato, and M Eliantonio (eds), *Boards of Appeal of EU Agencies* (Oxford University Press 2022) 151.

[244] Broader forms of scrutiny of the mechanisms exist, such as that performed by the EU Ombudsman—see, for example, https://www.ombudsman.europa.eu/en/news-document/en/151372. To be sure, the subject of this scrutiny is the mechanism itself or the way Frontex might have handled it. It is not a facility for reviewing Frontex's decision.

[245] EBCG Regulation, Article 111(8).

[246] MB Decision 19/2022, Article 3.

[247] MB Decision 19/2022, Article 4.

[248] MB Decision 19/2022, Article 7.

complaints to the host and home state.[249] The ED deals with complaints concerning Frontex's staff.[250] Incredible as it might seem, the Decision deepens the trench of discretion and unaccountability protecting the EBCG's personnel. Beyond the shortcomings mentioned vis-à-vis the provisions of the Regulation, the internal rules offer little detail about what the relevant entities might be, for the purpose of the investigation and confer an unbounded power to the ED. The MB's Decision refers to other measures which might be relevant, such as MB Decision 26/2018 adopting general implementing provisions on the conduct of administrative inquiries and disciplinary procedures. Decision 26/2018 also allows for complete internalization of scrutiny. While it provides for a series of possible penalties, the choice of the sanction is not connected to a range of violations and therefore still leaves significant discretion to the body in charge.[251]

These observations are compounded by the very weak provisions of the complaint mechanisms in situations of emergency. If there is an imminent risk of irreparable harm to the complainant or Frontex, the latter must *consider* taking immediate action. In the same situation, the FRO *may* recommend an *appropriate* action to the ED.[252] These provisions show a striking chasm between the seriousness of the situation they govern (the risk of irreparable harm) and what they mandate/empower Frontex to do (only considering action, or the possibility of recommending an action). Democratic scrutiny, and particularly through the Frontex Scrutiny Working Group of the European Parliament, has cast light on how these shortcomings of the law translate into, and are compounded by, poor implementation.[253]

#### 6.4.3.2 Allocation of responsibility and rules on liability

In the previous sections, we have uncovered several shortcomings of the mechanisms of administrative scrutiny for activities at the borders, be they established within Frontex or left to the member states in the context of the new pact. With specific regard to the former, the decisions taken by the manifold actors of scrutiny are not subject to any forms of external check. Against this background, we must now consider the legal framework on the liability of the actors performing border controls. This aspect is complementary to those discussed so far: it could alleviate or aggravate the concerns raised in the previous sections.

In order to better understand the level of accessibility to this type of scrutiny, we must first identify the locus of legal responsibility for the performance of actions at the external borders. Generally, Frontex and national authorities implement border control as a shared responsibility, but member states retain *primary*—so not exclusive—responsibility for the management of their sections of the external borders.[254] This provision concerns the responsibility for the implementation of the EIBM (including

[249] MB Decision 19/2022, Articles 5(2) and 8(1). Specifically, the National Frontex Point of Contact and the relevant competent authorities
[250] MB Decision 19/2022, Article 10.
[251] MB Decision 26/2018, Articles 17 and 18.
[252] MB Decision 19/2022, Article 11.
[253] T Strik, 'European Oversight on Frontex: How to Strengthen Democratic Accountability', VerfassungBlog, 8 September 2022.
[254] EBCG Regulation, Article 7(1).

border controls) rather than liability for damages and losses caused by Frontex or member states' action.[255] Frontex is fully responsible and accountable for any decision it takes and for any activity for which it is *solely* responsible under this Regulation.[256] The wording of this provision is ambiguous. Firstly, we must clarify the relationship between responsibility and accountability. Responsibility, we argue, refers to the possibility of attributing consequences of an event to an actor; whereas accountability, as outlined in the introduction, implies a relationship between an actor and a forum, and the duty for the former to respond to the latter. The two concepts are therefore distinct, but inextricably linked. In terms of their respective scope, accountability has a political dimension as well,[257] but that does not exclude legal accountability from it. Furthermore, 'responsibility' within the meaning of this provision should not be treated as a byword for 'liability'. There are specific Articles in the Regulation that use the term 'liability', and there is no reason to presume they are interchangeable. *Ratione materiae*, the provision refers to two scenarios: the decisions taken by Frontex *and* the activity for which the Agency is solely responsible. The two situations are obviously different. On the one hand, the former is much larger in scope and might also concern decisions not to act, such as the ED's decision not to suspend or terminate an activity despite evidence that the conditions of Article 46(4) EBCG Regulation have been met. On the other hand, the activities for which Frontex will be *fully* responsible and accountable are only those where the Agency has *sole* responsibility. If we combine this clause with the statement that border controls are a shared responsibility, the legal framework seems bound to create pockets of impunity. However, we should not underestimate the connection between the 'full' nature of the responsibility and the 'sole' responsibility for the activity. This might be seen, in fact, as leaving the door open to the possibility of joint liability.[258]

The rules on legal scrutiny are less evasive.[259] Broadly, proceedings may be brought before the Court of Justice for the annulment of acts of Frontex that are intended to produce legal effects vis-à-vis third parties, for failure to act, and for non-contractual liability in accordance with the respective provisions of the TFEU.[260] In the previous sections, we have shown that the person's successful reliance on Articles 263 or 265 TFEU is hindered by a significant procedural hurdle—that is, the applicant's

[255] On Frontex and action for damages, see M Fink, 'The Action for Damages as a Fundamental Rights Remedy: Holding Frontex Liable' (2020) 21 German Law Journal 532.

[256] EBCG Regulation, Article 7(4).

[257] This is also confirmed by the principle that Frontex is accountable to the EP and the Council, EBCG Regulation, Article 6.

[258] This type of liability exists in other areas of EU law, however. See the example of Europol and member states in the case of unlawful data processing, as stated in Case C-755/21 P, *Kočner v EUROPOL*, EU:C:2024:202. See on this, J de Coninck and S Tas, 'Investigating Five Dimensions of the EU's Liability Regime: Marián Kočner' (2025) 62 Common Market Law Review 195.

[259] The issue of the responsibility/liability of Frontex has been studied extensively. Just to name a few, see M Fink, *Frontex and Human Rights: Responsibility in 'Multi-Actor Situations' under the ECHR and EU Public Liability Law* (Oxford University Press 2018); G Raimondo, *The European Integrated Border Management: Frontex, Human Rights, and International Responsibility* (Hart 2024); F Mc Namara. *Externalised and Privatised Procedures of EU Migration Control and Border Management: A Study of EU Member State Control and Legal Responsibility* (PhilD thesis, European Union Institute 2017); J de Coninck, *The EU's Human Rights Responsibility Gap: Deconstructing Human Rights Impunity of International Organisations* (Hart 2024).

[260] These are Articles 263, 265, and 340 TFEU, respectively. EBCG Regulation, Article 98.

interest to act or, to put it differently, the difficulty in identifying in practice a concrete advantage, rather than a future and hypothetical one, that would result from the annulment of an act or the omission behind the use of Article 265 TFEU. This difficulty exists both for actions of surveillance and those taken at the borders. As regards liability, Frontex must be liable for activities undertaken in accordance with its governing Regulation.[261] Frontex is also obliged, in accordance with the general principles common to the laws of the member states, to make good the losses caused by it in the performance of its duties, with the Court of Justice having jurisdiction for compensation disputes arising from the occurrence of such damages.[262] The mentioned provisions are 'without prejudice' to the civil and criminal liability of the members of the teams. For damage caused by members of the teams operating in the host state, the host state must be liable in accordance with its national law.[263] In relation to criminal offences committed by or against deployed members of the team or statutory staff, the latter must be treated as officials of the host state under its national law.[264] The scope of the provisions on civil and criminal liability seems limited to the damages that occurred in the territory of the host state. It is not clear what law would apply if the damage occurred at sea or in the territory of a third country. In this regard, however, and especially in relation to the former, the operational plan must include rules about the applicable jurisdiction.[265] It seems, therefore, that the rules on civil and criminal liability are *lex specialis* to Article 97 EBCG Regulation. Against this background, the fundamental question is: In what cases could Frontex's staff be found liable? Or, where could we find the existence of a causal link between the performance of staff's duties and the damage caused by the breach of a person's right, as required by the *Francovich* doctrine? The answer to the question is inextricably linked to the issue of allocation of responsibility established by the EBCG Regulation. Generally, it is the host member state—or a third country, in accordance with the relevant status agreement—that issues instructions to deployed members of the team.[266] The specific and general instructions are contained in the operational plan for joint operations, which is drawn up by the ED with the host member state.[267] Technically, it is only the liaison officers who take instructions from Frontex.[268] These provisions seem to exclude the possibility of a direct causal link between Frontex's (in)activity and damage that occurred as a violation suffered by the person concerned. The EBCG Regulation paints a more nuanced picture. On a general level, we have seen in the sections above that several officers within Frontex have an explicit obligation to monitor legal compliance during activities where the Agency is involved. One example of this would be that the

[261] See, for a thought-provoking contribution on the possibility of introducing criminal liability for Frontex's members of staff, A di Martino, 'Does the European Union's Rule of Law Require the Criminalisation of EU Public Officials? A First Appraisal' (2024) 30 European Law Journal 181.

[262] EBCG Regulation, Article 97.

[263] The host state can request that the home state or Frontex reimburse any sums paid to injured parties when the damage was caused by gross negligence or wilful misconduct by either a deployed member of the team or a statutory staff. EBCG Regulation, Article 84(1) and (2).

[264] EBCG Regulation, Article 85.

[265] EBCG, Article 38(3)(j).

[266] EBCG Regulation, Article 43(1).

[267] EBCG Regulation, Article 38.

[268] EBCG Regulation, Article 31(7).

coordinating officer *may* communicate their views on the instructions, which must be followed *to the extent possible* by the host state.[269] Furthermore, the ED can withdraw the financing or suspend or terminate the activities if informed by the coordinating officer that the instructions are not in compliance with the operational plan.[270]

The question under discussion has been given an answer for the first time by the GC in the *WS* judgment (under appeal before the CJ at the time of writing).[271] The case concerned Syrian nationals who arrived in Greece and wished to apply for international protection. On the basis of a joint return operation, they were transferred to Türkiye. The applicants lodged a complaint against their return there. The first complaint was forwarded to Frontex's ED and the Greek Ombudsman, and then to the Greek police. The applicants lodged a second complaint against the handling of the first one, with the two being subsequently joined. The Greek police closed their internal investigation and refused to share their report as it was classified as 'confidential'. The FRO sent the applicants his final report and closed the procedure. In response to the applicants' claim that the final report did not address Frontex's role in the return operation or the second complaint, the FRO responded that Frontex had complied with its obligations. The applicants' main line of argument consisted of Frontex's infringements of its obligations, specifically in relation to the principle of non-refoulement, the right to asylum, the prohibition of collective expulsion, the right to good administration, and the right to an effective remedy. If they had been granted international protection, to which they were entitled as Syrians in 2016, they would not have been returned to Türkiye and would not have suffered the material and non-material damage they did. The GC replied that Frontex's role was merely to provide assistance in the return operation, and that the decisions on asylum applications and returns lie exclusively with the member states.[272] Therefore, the direct causal link between the damage suffered and the conduct of Frontex could not be established. In her expert opinion on the case, Fink argues that the monitoring obligations imposed on Frontex by the Regulation raise questions about its liability in parallel to that of the member state concerned.[273] The ruling, however, does not address this aspect. It is difficult to see how Frontex's staff assisting with the operation on the ground were not aware of the applicants' nationality, which in turn gives a very strong impression that those staff turned a blind eye to it. Imagine a famous Russian dissident and vocal opponent of the state regime was found to be staying illegally in a member state and was subject to a forced return procedure, with Frontex assisting in the operation.

[269] EBCG Regulation, Article 43(2).

[270] EBCG Regulation, Article 46(3). However, the EU Ombudsman has recently found that the ED is not making effective use of the possibility of withdrawing financing, or suspending or terminating its activities in a member state. Furthermore, she recommended that a better system of fundamental rights monitoring in such circumstances be introduced. In particular, the Ombudsman recommended that an FRM should be present in the European Surveillance Room in the case of a serious maritime incident. See Case OI/3/2023/MHZ.

[271] Case T-600/21, *WS v European Border and Coast Guard Agency (Frontex)*, EU:C:2022:970. The case revolved around the previous version of the EBCG Regulation. See M Gkliati, 'Shaping the Joint Liability Landscape? The Broader Consequences of WS v Frontex for EU Law' (2024) 9 European Paper 69; J De Coninck, 'Shielding Frontex: On the EU General Court's "WS and others v Frontex"', VerfassungBlog, 9 September 2023.

[272] Case T-600/21, *WS*, paras 64—65.

[273] See M Fink, Expert Opinion: Case T-600/21 WS and Others v Frontex (3 February 2022).

Would the GC hold the same line of argument in such a case too? It should also be noted that the judgment does not address the issue of Frontex's handling of the complaint, which might have been subsumed under the plea that the applicants' right to a good administration and effective remedy had been breached. Overall, the judgment marks a missed opportunity insofar as it keeps a firmly closed door on the possibility of holding Frontex liable for damages. The post-*WS* case law only compounds those concerns, with the GC dismissing an action for damages by imposing an exceedingly high evidentiary threshold which departs from the practice of the ECt HR.[274]

#### 6.4.3.3 Interim conclusions

Consistent with the previous scenarios, the heterogeneity of the legal framework has revealed its impact on pathways to scrutiny of activities performed at the borders. Here, the heterogeneity of the sources concerns the mechanisms of administrative scrutiny. Several of such sources, governing the supervision of the use of force or complaints lodged by the persons concerned, are documents internal to Frontex and empower a heterogeneous range of actors with overlapping and/or extremely broad mandates. The heterogeneity of actors of administrative scrutiny also emerges from the legal framework proper, with a plethora of Frontex officers featuring functions related to fundamental rights monitoring, but none of them 'with teeth' (except for the ED). Heterogeneity impacts legal scrutiny too, as the division of labour between the two levels of governance of EU border controls has so far justified the absence of any findings of liability against Frontex. The law in the books, combined with extensive evidence drawn from the law in action, shows the inadequacy of the framework to ensure accountability and compliance with the rule of law.

## 6.5 Conclusions

Pathways to scrutiny in EU external border controls are characterized by structural heterogeneity. In part, this is explained by the overall heterogeneity of the legal framework uncovered in the previous chapters. The existence of such a multi-layered system of sources, decision-making centres, and addressees of control, as well as conditions and criteria for exercising controls imposed on the person concerned, is bound to result in a kaleidoscope of mechanisms to monitor constitutional compliance. Beyond those inherent and inescapable features of the law, however, there is a specific heterogeneity proper to the pathways to scrutiny themselves. When combined, these different types of heterogeneity produce a legal set-up dotted with holes in legal protection. Across the board, a panoply of sources underpinning controls (eg risk indicators, MoUs) and scrutiny (eg supervisory mechanisms on the use of force) result in a legal framework that undermines access to effective mechanisms of redress. The issues caused by the heterogeneity of levels of governance and actors making and implementing the law hinder administrative and legal scrutiny, where the division of

[274] Case T-136/22, *Alaa Hamoudi v European Border and Coast Guard Agency (Frontex)*, EU:T:2023:821. See J De Coninck, 'Shielding Frontex 2.0: The One with the Impossible Proof', VerfassungBlog, 30 January 2024.

tasks between the competent authorities is either unclear or interpreted in an excessively formalistic manner. The heterogeneity of objectives also contributes to the picture, as security grounds can restrict scrutiny of operational activities—restrictions which are, in turn, difficult if not impossible to challenge. Ultimately, it is the heterogeneity of persons concerned that receives the least recognition. In continuity with the discussion of sources and exercise of controls, over-prioritizing the prevention of entry weakens access to scrutiny and accountability for legitimate travel and vulnerable persons. In the light of the foregoing, and due to the lack of provision and deployment of effective mechanisms to address unfairness within the meaning of this book, the law of EU border controls fails to pass the test of constitutional compliance.

# PART III
# THE LAW OF EU INTERNAL BORDER CONTROLS

# 7
# Setting the Context

## 7.1 Introduction

In line with the analytical framework of this research, Part II of this book exposed the detrimental impact of heterogeneity on constitutional compliance. While the allocation of tasks complies with the principle of subsidiarity overall, the legal framework poses significant challenges to solidarity and fair treatment of addressees of control—mostly, third-country nationals (TCNs). With increasing reliance on non-transparent or ineffective sources, a body of law has emerged which is ripe with opportunities for interinstitutional tensions. Also, this law and its implementation over-pursue the prevention of migration and crime at the expense of the effective protection of vulnerable groups. Further, the law in the books and/or in practice opens deep pockets of impunity and a lack of accountability to the benefit of the authorities in charge.

After concluding Part II on EU external border controls, this chapter metaphorically takes us across the EU external frontiers into its territory. Internal and external border controls have always been inextricably linked. The European Integrated Border Management (EIBM) currently rests on a four-tier model, which includes, among its constituent components, measures within Schengen. An exploration of the approach to activities at the internal frontiers is, therefore, an indispensable stop in this journey through the constitutional compliance of EU border controls. Parts II and III follow a similar trail. This chapter sets the scene for the analysis developed in the next three chapters, which will focus respectively on: sources, exercise of controls, and pathways to scrutiny. To frame the discussion, this chapter is structured as follows. Firstly, we place the creation and development of an area without internal frontiers in its historical context. We look at the main policy drivers behind the lifting of controls as well as the main strands of measures applicable within Schengen that have been 'associated' with this initiative. This section introduces certain elements of heterogeneity concerning the governance of the borderless area, especially as regards the range of decision-making centres and overarching objectives. Against this background, we uncover the challenges to the proper functioning of Schengen that have emerged over the years, and the main coping mechanisms to deal with these challenges as identified by the EU institutions. As with the scene-setting chapter of Part II, these coping mechanisms correspond to certain components of the structured network of principles which makes EU law work—and particularly the components forming part of the test of constitutional compliance devised in this book (eg sincere cooperation, solidarity, mutual trust, and respect for essential state functions). In this context, we zoom in on a protagonist of this whole Part: internal border surveillance. As shown in this and the following chapters, the policy and legal debate about internal border surveillance lives at the intersection between the levels of analysis developed

*The Law of EU Border Controls*. Leandro Mancano, Oxford University Press. © Leandro Mancano 2025.
DOI: 10.1093/9780191966187.003.0008

in this book: allocation of task (including law-making), horizontal cooperation, and fair treatment of the persons concerned. Most fundamentally, the meaning and scope of internal border surveillance are testbeds for the state of Schengen as an area without internal border controls—and, therefore, for the nature of Schengen itself. Lastly, we set out and justify the materials discussed in this Part and assess the consistency of the objectives stated in those measures with those established in primary law.

## 7.2 An Area without Internal Frontiers

To properly grasp the 'spirit of Schengen', we must understand the main drivers behind the creation and preservation of the area without internal frontiers. A 'genetic' analysis must be followed by a diachronic assessment of how those policy goals have evolved over time, and how they have translated into the relevant legal provisions of primary and secondary EU law. While this chapter primarily pays heed to the objectives of this area, we must link them to the values and the principles that are more often being invoked in this context. Values, principles, and objectives are, after all, the three main building blocks of the EU legal order in the view espoused in this book.

As mentioned in Chapter 3, the borderless area and its flanking measures are like conjoined twins. The two projects concretely kicked off outwith the EU framework, through the intergovernmental Schengen Agreement[1] and its implementing Convention (CISA).[2] These developments occurred as similar initiatives were being taken by the EU, with both tracks progressing in parallel until Schengen was 'communitarized' by the Amsterdam Treaty at the end of the last century.[3] Conceptually, the idea of abolishing internal controls had been contemplated by the Union's institutions as early as 1962.[4] As decades passed by, however, the institutions grew increasingly conscious of the fact that founding a polity on free movement, as the EEC had been, while maintaining border checks between member states, was a contradiction in terms on several levels.

As the EU and certain member states decided to step up around the mid-1980s, the measures moving the controls at the external borders and enhancing cooperation within were presented as compensatory and accessory to—albeit inextricably linked with—the abolition of controls inside the Union. The epicentre of a seismic shift—the freedom to cross an internal border without being checked—was described

[1] Agreement between the Governments of the States of the Benelux Economic Union, the Federal Republic of Germany and the French Republic on the gradual abolition of checks at their common borders [2000] OJ L 239/13. The agreement was, in turn, based on the Saarbrücken Agreement, signed in July 1984 between France and Germany.

[2] Convention implementing the Schengen Agreement of 14 June 1985 between the Governments of the States of the Benelux Economic Union, the Federal Republic of Germany and the French Republic on the gradual abolition of checks at their common borders [2000] OJ L 239/19.

[3] By communitarization, we mean the integration of the Schengen acquis into the EU legal framework through a specific protocol attached to the EU Treaties. The Treaty of Lisbon confirms this process, by Protocol no 19 TFEU. For an overview, see S Peers, *EU Justice and Home Affairs Law* (Oxford University Press 2023), vol I 13 and onwards.

[4] As early as in 1962, the Commission argued that internal border checks prevented citizens from realizing the relevance of the European project. COM (62) 300 final.

by the Schengen Agreement as a means to strengthen the solidarity between EU nationals and an expression of their ever-closer union. Similarly, the EU-driven actions stemmed from the resolve to create a 'People's Europe', as apparent from the conclusions of the 1984 European Council of Fontainebleau,[5] the ad hoc committee established as a result thereof, and its ensuing reports,[6] as well as the 1985 Commission White Paper on the completion of the internal market.[7] Physical barriers to border crossing within the Union were described as 'the obvious manifestation of the continued division' to which 'ordinary citizens' are exposed, 'the outward sign of an arbitrary administrative power over individuals' and 'an affront' to free movement.[8] What is more, free movement was not seen purely as a matter for the workforce, but also as a way to help young people 'to think in European terms'.[9] It is not surprising, then, that one of the key practical elements of the project was the creation of a common passport.[10] If those statements hint at the pole star guiding the abolition of internal controls and all that came with it, the following quote from the Adonnino report conclusively reveals the deep-seated conviction behind it:

> The Committee has kept in mind that most of what has been achieved until now in Europe has been the work of those who experienced the horrors and destruction of war. Continuation of this venture rests on the assumption that future generations will also understand and appreciate one another across borders and will realize the benefits to be derived from closer cooperation and solidarity.[11]

The abolition of border controls between member states has primarily a poietic function. It creates a new reality, which in turn has implications on a symbolic level. The factual change brought about by the dismantling of material structures at border crossing points[12] generates a different type of territory and identity. The place of a community is key to the way the community understands itself,[13] and free movement leads to the emergence of the concept of EU territory as a physical, legal, and normative space.[14] Not dissimilar from EU citizenship, the EU territory adds to rather than replaces the member states' territory: it 'opens national territories and creates

[5] One of the conclusion's main headings was 'A People's Europe'.

[6] Adonnino Committee on a People's Europe. P Adonnino, *A People's Europe: Reports from the Ad Hoc Committee. Bulletin of the European Communities*, Supplement 7/85.

[7] White Paper from the Commission to the European Council, 'Complementing the Internal Market', COM(85) 310 final.

[8] COM(85) 310 final 8 and 14.

[9] COM(85) 310 final 25.

[10] See also COM (75) 322 final 7, where the Commission points to the importance of a common passport to develop a sense of belonging to the Community on the part of the member states' citizens.

[11] Adonnino, *A People's Europe* 18.

[12] Decision of the Executive Committee [1994] OJ L 239/1.

[13] H Lindahl, 'Finding a Place for Freedom, Security and Justice: The European Union's Claim to Territorial Unity' (2004) 29 European Law Review 461.

[14] N Nic Shuibhne, 'The "Territory of the Union" in EU Citizenship Law: Charting a Route from Parallel to Integrated Narratives' (2019) 38 Yearbook of European Law 267. As the author shows, there are several factors that have played over time into the development of an EU territory. This achievement is not all down to the abolition of border controls, but they have certainly facilitated it.

a transnational, mutually integrating, and yet bounded space'.[15] Thereby, free movement becomes a powerful 'vehicle for identity formation'.[16]

Doing justice to the conception of the borderless area and the noble aspirations of its founders need not, however, turn into a show of naivety. In a way, Schengen looks like the poster child of the liberal paradox,[17] which describes states' conflicting attitudes towards non-nationals[18] depending on what interest takes the driving seat: openness for the sake of economic advantage, and/or closure—or at least restrictiveness—induced by national identity and security concerns.[19] While the pursuit of the economic advantage is not all there is to the openness of Schengen, it is a fundamental part of the picture.

Turning to the other core policy driver of the creation of Schengen, identity-building was not necessarily based on a process of 'othering'—at least not at first and not that prominently. This is even more so when considering that the security concerns, at the time, did not focus on TCNs per se. Still to this day, the Treaties state that there should be no checks at the internal borders regardless of the person's nationality.[20] This being said, immigration was indeed described as one of the 'other relevant problems' to be dealt with, once barriers to movement were removed.[21] Remarkably, there and then the Commission already advocated for ways *to achieve comparable levels of protection* other than border checks, including via police checks and enhanced co-operation between national authorities.[22] It is undeniable, therefore, that security played a major role in the construction of the EU borderless area. Zaiotti observes that the symbiotic relationship between the absence of controls within and the stronger outer borders rested on the logic of the security deficit: 'the abolition of controls inevitably creates a vacuum that needs to be constantly filled'.[23] The use of the adverb *constantly* should be emphasized: an area of free movement is an achievement requiring never-ending maintenance, and can only survive by means suitable for addressing new challenges any time they arise.[24] Not dissimilarly, Bigo argues that the security

[15] J Weinzierl, 'Territoriality Beyond the State: The EU's Territorial Claims and the Search for Their Legitimacy' (2021) 22 German Law Journal 650.

[16] S Salomon and J Rijpma, 'A Europe Without Internal Frontiers: Challenging the Reintroduction of Border Controls in the Schengen Area in the Light of Union Citizenship' (2023) 24 German Law Journal 284; K Lenaerts, 'The Contribution of the European Court of Justice to the Area of Freedom, Security and Justice' (2010) 59 International and Comparative Law Quarterly 255.

[17] J Hollifield, *Immigrants, Markets, and States: The Political Economy of Postwar Europe* (Harvard University Press 1992).

[18] Or, in the case of the EU, TCNs. This is, of course, because of the principle of non-discrimination on grounds of nationality. As is very well known, the equality of treatment between a member state's citizen and other EU nationals has also limitations.

[19] It is also important to contextualize legal phenomena. It should not be assumed that in the mid-1980s TCNs were the main source of concern.

[20] The other view on this is that the equality of treatment is not a principled choice but an inevitable consequence of the 'check no one' choice. Once checks are lifted, there is no way to distinguish between EU and non-nationals. As shown in the following chapters, things are probably more nuanced than that.

[21] COM(85) 310 final 6. It is also known that much of the caution around the abolition of border controls was to do with France's fears of possible repercussions related to the Netherlands' tolerant drugs policy.

[22] COM(85) 310 final 9–10.

[23] R Zaiotti, *Cultures of Border Control: Schengen and the Evolution of European Frontiers* (University of Chicago Press 2011) 72.

[24] While security is an important element, it also and decisively links to the freedom-orientated objective of removing controls within the EU and the defence of an open society. Ad Hoc Working Group on Immigration, WGI (1) SN 3647/86.

deficit discourse was shaped by the ministries of the interior and national agencies.[25] Power and funding grabs alone can hardly explain the emphasis on security, however. Something more powerful than this has been at play, and is inextricably linked to the impact of lifting controls on national sovereignty.[26] In the era of the so-called migration state,[27] control over the movement of people is the last bastion of sovereignty.[28] The latter covers not only questions of identity, but also concerns of security related to the preservation of essential state functions.[29] The analysis of intra-EU bordering, therefore, revolves around ensuring free movement while guaranteeing security in a manner consistent with fundamental rights[30] and EU law more broadly. As this Part makes apparent, the uncertainty around whose security are we talking about stems from the dual—or ambiguous—nature of the EU territory mentioned above: the adjective 'internal' can have either an EU[31] or state[32] dimension; the security of a state can also be 'national'—most notably, under Article 4(2) TEU. In this regard, Zaiotti rightly argues that Schengen has caused a shift in the culture of border control: based on a new set of assumptions and related practices, the Westphalian/national framework has given way—at least to an extent—to a post-national and 'intensive trans-governmental' system.[33] This new culture of control aligns with the idea of the EU territory portrayed above, but also raises questions of where the authority lies. Who is competent to decide about the reintroduction of controls, and on what grounds? Who has the responsibility to protect citizens, and why? These questions have animated the life of the borderless area since its inception. What the EU institutions and the member states had not predicted, perhaps, is that the communitarization of Schengen would roughly coincide with decades of nearly uninterrupted crisis, starting with 9/11[34] and continuing through to—just to name a few–the refugee crisis,[35] the wave of terrorist attacks across several Western EU states,[36] the Covid-19 pandemic[37] and the

[25] D Bigo, 'Border Regimes, Police Cooperation and Security in an Enlarged European Union' in J Zielonka (ed), *Europe Unbound: Enlarging and Reshaping the Boundaries of the European Union* (Routledge 2002).

[26] D Thym and J Bornemann, 'Schengen and Free Movement Law During the First Phase of the Covid-19 Pandemic: Of Symbolism, Law and Politics' (2021) 5 European Papers 1143.

[27] J Hollifield, 'The Emerging Migration State' (2004) 38 International Migration Review 885. The author defines migration as a state 'where regulation of international migration is as important as providing for the security of the state and the economic well being of the citizenry'. This has been further compounded by the link made between control of migration to security concerns, as well as economic arguments from a protectionist perspective.

[28] C Dauvergne, 'Sovereignty, Migration and the Rule of Law in Global Times' (2004) 67 Modern Law Review 588.

[29] See, very clearly, Article 4(2) TEU.

[30] TFEU, Article 67(1).

[31] TFEU, Article 67(3).

[32] TFEU, Article 72.

[33] R Zaiotti, 'Revisiting Schengen: Europe and the Emergence of a new Culture of Border Control' (2007) 8 Perspectives on European Politics and Society 31.

[34] M Longo, 'A "21st Century Border"? Cooperative Border Controls in the US and EU after 9/11' (2016) 31 Journal of Borderlands Studies 187.

[35] H Kriesi and others, 'Debordering and Re-Bordering in the Refugee Crisis: A Case of 'Defensive Integration' (2021) 28 Journal of European Public Policy 331.

[36] E Evrard, B Nienaber, and A Sommaribas, 'The Temporary Reintroduction of Border Controls Inside the Schengen Area: Towards a Spatial Perspective' (2018) 35 Journal of Borderlands Studies 369.

[37] A Jacobs and M Kabata, 'Covid-19 and the Collective Securitisation of Schengen: An Analysis of EU and National Responses to Border Control' (2024) 32 Journal of Contemporary European Studies 1.

war in Ukraine.[38] This chain of events has significantly strained the EU space without internal frontiers, and has prompted EU institutions to protect Schengen from implosion.[39]

## 7.3 Why Protect Schengen? Diagnosing Dysfunctions, Drawing Boundaries

Openness and closure—embodied by the absence of control and their maintenance on security grounds—have characterized the debate about the birth and development of Schengen. This heterogeneity of policy drivers, together with the heterogeneity of decision-making centres and levels of governance and actors, has been compounded by a series of exogenous factors, such as those mentioned at the end of the last section. Particularly following the refugee crisis which started in 2015, member states have repeatedly reintroduced controls, often in an uncoordinated manner and outwith the limits and conditions established by the Schengen Borders Code.[40] While the motives behind this trend have changed over time, the dysfunctional control of the EU external borders and the ensuing concerns over secondary movement have played a major role in this regard. Part II showed this connection through the analysis of the existing legal framework, especially in connection with the lack of solidarity within the Common European Asylum System (CEAS).[41] Scholars have argued that the sustained reintroduction of control[42] is the epiphenomenon of something else—of what specifically, depends on the proposed account. While some authors see internal controls as a symptom of renationalization and associate them with a risk of disintegration,[43] others regard them as 'defensive integration'.[44] The single-handed and consistent reinstating of border checks has undoubtedly occurred in breach of important aspects of primary and secondary law, thus questioning the integrity of the area. In this context, the EU strategy on the preservation of Schengen has revolved around two main levers: arguments about the indispensable nature of the borderless area, and identification of causes of malfunctioning and corresponding counteractions. The

[38] W Opioła and others, 'War and Politics: The 2022 Russian Invasion of Ukraine and Refugee Crisis on the Eastern EU Border from the Perspective of Border Studies' (2022) 10 Border and Regional Studies 7.

[39] For a diachronic analysis, see E Guild, 'Schengen Borders and Multiple National States of Emergency: From Refugees to Terrorism to COVID-19' (2021) 23 European Journal of Migration and Law 385.

[40] Regulation (EU) 2016/399 establishing a Schengen Borders Code [2016] OJ L 77/1 (SBC).

[41] On this aspect and the lack of progress made by the 2024 asylum and migration pact, see D Thym, 'Secondary Movements: Lack of Progress as the Flipside of Meagre Solidarity', EU Immigration and Asylum Law and Policy, EU Migration Law Blog, 3 October 2024.

[42] Or, as it has also been described, the 'new' normal. F Gülzau, 'A "new normal" for the Schengen area: When, Where and Why Member States Reintroduce Temporary Border Controls' (2021) 38 Journal of Borderlands Studies 1.

[43] J P Brekke and A Staver, 'The Renationalisation of Migration Policies in Times of Crisis: The Case of Norway' (2018) 44 Journal of Ethnic and Migration Studies 2163; M Eilstrup-Sangiovanni, 'Re-bordering Europe? Collective Action Barriers to "Fortress Europe"' (2021) 28 Journal of European Public Policy 447.

[44] F Schimmelfennig, 'Rebordering Europe: External Boundaries and Integration in the European Union' (2021) 28 Journal of European Public Policy 311; and, for a more nuanced approach, J Pettersson Fürst, 'Defensive Integration Through Cooperative Re-bordering? How Member States Use Internal Border Controls in Schengen' (2024) 31 Journal of European Public Policy 478.

arguments adduced for the importance of protecting Schengen are both existential and economic.[45] The absence of internal border control constitutes the very essence of Schengen,[46] and one fundamental element 'of what citizens identify as the European idea'.[47] Free movement is 'a defining principle' of the EU, and 'the ability to move within the EU without facing border checks at internal borders is one of its most successful achievements'.[48] Free travel is 'the most cherished accomplishment' of the EU and 'one of the central achievements of integration and the construction of a shared European space'.[49] The notion of a European territory defined by the absence of control has remained, throughout the decades, *the* trademark of European identity in the eyes of its citizens. In this respect, the internal borders cause harm to 'the European way of life' in a Union where those citizens can travel freely across borders.[50] These costs would be reflected in border controls for commuters and long waits, which would in turn discourage movement further. The tourism industry would be lost, possibly compounded by a fragmented visa policy. Judicial and police cooperation, 'one of the key elements of added-value arising from the Schengen system', would also be jeopardized.[51] While the Commission places all these undesirable scenarios under the broader umbrella of the so-called 'cost of non-Schengen', it also envisages a snowball (or unravelling) effect that would result in the permanent reintroduction of border controls and, from there, the unravelling of the process of integration on the whole.

How can that scenario be prevented? In other words, what are the causes of the dysfunctions of the borderless area, and how can they be fixed? As observed by the foregoing diachronic analysis, the debate on the borderless area revolves around two main strands: the governance of the reintroduction of controls and the framework of security measures guaranteeing a level of protection comparable to that offered by border checks. In both scenarios, the emphasis of the EU policy and legal approach is on the three overarching themes developed in this book: allocation of task, interinstitutional cooperation, and treatment of the persons concerned. The structured network of relevant principles used in this research as parameters of constitutional compliance is the protagonist in all those interrelated levels of analysis. The heterogeneity of levels of governance and decision-making centres creates opportunities for dysfunction. Respect for subsidiarity and essential state functions has meant that member states have the last word on the reintroduction of checks at their internal borders. This has resulted in a 'patchwork' of unilateral decisions[52] which have

[45] The two are obviously connected, as the underlying concept underpinning the EU lies in the integration of states' economies to fend off the resurgence of nationalism.

[46] Communication from the Commission to the European Parliament and the Council on preserving and strengthening Schengen COM(2017) 570 final.

[47] European Parliament resolution of 8 July 2021 on the Annual Report on the Functioning of the Schengen Area (2019/2196(INI) 160.

[48] Communication from the Commission to the European Parliament, the Council, the European Economic and Social Committee and the Committee of the Regions, 'Schengen governance—strengthening the area without internal border control', COM(2011) 561 final 2.

[49] Communication from the Commission to the European Parliament, the European Council and the Council, 'Back to Schengen—A Roadmap', COM(2016) 120 final 4.

[50] Communication from the Commission, 'Towards a phased and coordinated approach for restoring freedom of movement and lifting internal border controls—COVID-19', 2020/C 169/03 30.

[51] COM(2016) 120 final 3.

[52] COM(2016) 120 final 1.

not been backed up by sound evidence of the actual existence of a serious threat.[53] However, free movement is based on a system which relies on the mutual trust that all states will be 'ready and able' to implement the relevant legal framework.[54] On the one hand, closer cooperation and coordination would foster mutual trust[55] and must exist among states as well as the EU institutions and agencies.[56] On the other hand, mutual trust also requires solidarity and security.[57] Cooperation and coordination, and security and solidarity, are not parallel lines that never intersect. To the contrary, coordination and cooperation are ways to operationalize solidarity and security. As for solidarity, this is apparent from the EP's criticisms of the lack of consideration given to the common European interest in maintaining Schengen as an area without internal border controls.[58] The Commission, for its part, has argued in favour of a 'coordinated, EU-based response [that] would allow all European interests to be taken into account'.[59] This would also apply in cases where controls are to be lifted. It presupposes information from the states concerned (mostly, neighbouring ones) and the 'fully objective basis' behind the decision.[60] The deceptively identical nature of these statements raises a thorny issue characterizing the use of solidarity as a procedural duty of taking into account. While the EP referred to the common *interest* (singular), the Commission mentioned *all the interests*; the latter approach clearly makes it harder to assess compliance with procedural solidarity.

As regards security, the next section addresses the role of enhanced law enforcement cooperation as a way of compensating for the absence of controls. Here, we must highlight the mirroring development of approaches to external border controls and measures within Schengen. In Part II, we have seen that external border controls are built on the idea that the outer member states act on behalf of the whole Union: their success or failure in implementing the law of EU external border controls is the success or failure of all member states. A comparable dynamic emerges internally. The existence of a shared space also entails the sharing of threats, which should be met by shared threat-countering: in an area without internal border controls, issues of public policy or internal security are a matter of common interest. Inside Schengen, shared threat-countering occurs mostly via the reintroduction of controls within the constitutional framework described above and cross-border law enforcement cooperation. Cross-border cooperation in these two areas should reduce the need for solo initiatives: pooled—as opposed to unilateral—sovereignty allows for preserving at once free movement *and* essential state functions. Yet, the pieces of this jigsaw are far from falling perfectly into place. Firstly, blurring the boundaries between the security

[53] A8-0160/2018 4.

[54] COM(2011) 561 final 3. See also the State of Schengen Report 2022, COM(2022) 301 final/2 5.

[55] Communication from the Commission to the European Parliament, the European Council and the Council, 'Managing Migration in All Its Aspects: Progress under the European Agenda on Migration', COM(2018) 798 final 6. See also 2019/2196(INI) 161.

[56] State of Schengen Report 2023, COM(2023) 274 final 3.

[57] A8-0160/2018 3-5. For an analysis of the role of trust and secondary movement, see D. Thym, 'Secondary Movements: Overcoming the Lack of Trust among the Member States?', EU Immigration and Asylum Law and Policy, EU Migration Law Blog, 29 October 2020.

[58] 2019/2196(INI) 161.

[59] COM(2011) 561 final 3.

[60] 2020/C 169/03 30.

internal to a member state or the whole Union increases the ambiguity as to the locus of responsibility for the protection of those interests. Secondly, the possible emergence of conflicting interests in situations touching upon a protected area of sovereignty can undermine the effectiveness of procedural solidarity. Thirdly, there is the position of the persons concerned. The trust of the citizens in the integration project is also key to the sustainability of Schengen.[61] Any measures taken must not disproportionately affect the free movement of persons and goods and respect fundamental rights (most notably, data protection, privacy, and non-discrimination).[62] Furthermore, transparency and accountability between member states and the European institutions must be ensured through proper mechanisms of scrutiny.[63] However, most TCNS enjoy no right to free movement, save for very limited cross-Schengen mobility rights.[64] The heterogeneity of addressees of control and the legal regimes applicable to them has resulted in the implementation of discriminatory practices both in the context of border policing[65] and the performance of checks proper.[66] The three main 'moments' that characterized the assessment of constitutional compliance of external border controls resurface within Schengen. Decision-making, implementation, and scrutiny of the law of internal border controls must unfold in a way that is appropriate as regards the level of governance, but also horizontal cooperation and the treatment of the persons concerned.

## 7.4 The Role of Surveillance: Retaining Controls in Schengen through Greater Integration

The Schengen area rests, inter alia, on the idea that internal controls are a last resort, and that ways of ensuring comparable protection should be prioritized. This being the maxim, two main questions arise: what are we protecting, and what are these alternative ways? The first question has consistently found an answer in the conceptual couple: public policy and internal security. As for the second question, the emphasis has been on interstate police cooperation.

The general premise is that 'the proper functioning of the Schengen area'[67] requires effective and efficient cross-border police cooperation to prevent the avoidance of law enforcement through the exploitation of free movement.[68] In discussing the lifting of controls at the internal frontiers of Bulgaria and Romania, the Commission pointed

[61] A8-0160/2018 3-5.

[62] Commission Recommendation (EU) 2017/820 on proportionate police checks and police cooperation in the Schengen area, OJ [2017] L 122/79.

[63] A8-0160/2018 6-7.

[64] I Goldner Lang, 'Freedom of Movement of EU Citizens and Mobility Rights of Third-Country Nationals: Where EU Free Movement and Migration Policies Intersect or Disconnect?' in L Tsourdi and P De Bruycker (eds), *Research Handbook on EU Migration and Asylum Law* (Edward Elgar 2022) 98.

[65] S Casella Colombeau, 'Policing the Internal Schengen borders—Managing the Double Bind Between Free Movement and Migration Control' (2017) 27 Policing and Society 482.

[66] J Pettersson Fürst, 'Defensive Integration Through Cooperative Re-bordering' 496–97.

[67] Commission Recommendation (EU) 2017/820 3.

[68] Council Recommendation (EU) 2022/915 on operational law enforcement cooperation, OJ [2022] L 158/53 53.

to the 'significant obligations and responsibilities that come with being in Schengen' ('integral part of the EU legal framework'), including efficient interstate law enforcement cooperation.[69]

The diagnosis is one that speaks the language of heterogeneity. Cross-border police cooperation is hindered by the coexistence, in many member states, of different police bodies,[70] by the fragmentation of the legislative framework and the ensuing flexibility for member states in implementing it.[71] This observation of the way member states organize their law enforcement structure is echoed by other statements of a similar nature. The absence of controls can endure as long as the Union acquis is applied uniformly, and member states use their responsibilities on law and order and internal security *in line with* the objectives of the Schengen acquis.[72] The overarching idea, capturing the road that lies ahead, is the 'moving towards a common Union law enforcement culture'.[73] Particularly over the last few years, a number of innovative initiatives have emerged involving interstate cooperation and border surveillance within the EU. Such measures include the performance of joint patrols, the creation of mixed brigades, or even the establishment of joint police stations.[74] Some of those joint patrols, set up by different member states around their shared borders, also aim to verify the regularity of the stay of the person. The Commission has not only shied away from chastising member states for these initiatives. It has, in fact, encouraged their further development,[75] by endorsing inter alia the use of technical means of surveillance such as helicopters and drones, as well as bilateral or trilateral agreements for readmission of irregular TCNs,[76] hot pursuit, and hot surveillance.[77] These experiences, as well as further systems and technologies, should be used to monitor traffic flows and contribute to the surveillance of the main European transport corridors.[78] On the back

[69] Communication from the Commission to the European Parliament and the Council, 'Making Schengen stronger with the full participation of Bulgaria, Romania and Croatia in the area without internal border controls', COM(2022) 636 final 1.

[70] Communication from the Commission to the European Parliament and the Council, 'Making Schengen stronger with the full participation of Bulgaria, Romania and Croatia in the area without internal border controls', COM(2022) 301 final/2 18.

[71] COM(2022) 301 final/2 19.

[72] Commission Recommendation (EU) 2017/820 1.

[73] Council Recommendation (EU) 2022/915 54. See also COM(2022) 301 final/2 5.

[74] A joint police station at the border between Sweden and Norway should become operational in 2025. The same applies to Poland and Germany. For a broader analysis of development in certain border regions integration, see J Dittel and others, 'The Covid-19 Pandemic as a Driver for Transformation Processes in European Border Regions? A Comparative Analysis of Franco-German and German-Polish Borderlands' in F Weber, O Kühne, and J Dittel (eds) *Transformation Processes in Europe and Beyond: Perspectives for Horizontal Geographies* (Springer 2024) 503.

[75] Unsurprisingly, not all the measures taken have been without controversy (especially if taken unilaterally). For example, in the case of the France–Spain border, Spanish authorities expressed the view that verification of the legality of the stay should not be part of the check. See SWD(2023) 388 final. The same document mentions an interesting figure worth highlighting: the Italian authorities were satisfied with the cross-border cooperation activities with France which, despite the 100% increase in disembarkations on the Italian coasts, led in 2023 only to a 10% increase in the number of refusals of entry.

[76] See also two recommendations on making returns more effective and on mutual recognition of return decisions in [2017] OJ L 66/15 and OJ [2023] L 86/58 respectively.

[77] Council Recommendation (EU) 2022/915 53.

[78] On the connection between mobility, technology, and identity, see C Binder, 'Making "Europe" Through Technologised Mobility Control: Schengen, R&D, and the Imagined Community of "Europe"' (2025) 30 Geopolitics 1.

of these examples, the Commission has observed that cross-border law enforcement cooperation has successfully enabled the vast majority of member states to avoid resorting to internal border controls.[79] In this regard, one of the key priorities to foster integration even further is the review of the bilateral and multilateral agreements between member states on police cooperation with the view to meeting the current operational needs.[80]

The emphasis on the importance of enhanced police cooperation—including the intensification of police checks—might be seen as an attempt to draw borders conceptually and legally (prohibited border checks versus allowed security checks) in order to tear them down physically. This emphasis, however, contributes to the criminalization of migration, as it sees those permissible police checks as potentially necessary and justified to also face the *risk* of secondary movement of persons who have irregularly crossed the external borders. This is consistent with the idea, espoused by the Commission, that the risk of breach of rules on residence might be higher in border areas.[81] More specifically, the policy framework set out above can also raise issues of constitutional compliance. Firstly, the idea that achieving the objectives of Schengen rests also on the member states' proper performance of essential state functions and responsibilities can be read in two ways. Either as an expression of the well-established principle that they must exercise their discretion in compliance with EU law, or that these objectives should steer member states' use of their protected space of sovereignty. The latter designs a different frame for the relationship between the EU and state levels of governance. Secondly, extensive reliance on border surveillance and use of technology poses challenges to individual rights of the persons concerned and, depending on how systematic the deployment of such technology is, to the nature of the border area more broadly. Thirdly, intra-EU agreements play a much more prominent role internally than they do at the external borders. As discussed in the next chapters, the maze of interstate arrangements on law enforcement and the conditions for control laid down therein increase the heterogeneity of the legal framework.

## 7.5 The Objectives of EU Internal Border Controls in the Legislative Framework

The previous pages have introduced the different forms of heterogeneity of actors, persons concerned, objectives, and sources characterizing the law of internal border controls. In an area of competence shared between the EU and the member states, which touches upon one of the most sensitive aspects of sovereignty and leaves

[79] COM(2023) 274 final 20. Differently, authors argue that the pandemic provided an opportunity to strengthen the Schengen area through reforms of the SBC and the Schengen governance more broadly. See S Montaldo, 'Internal Border Control in the Schengen Area and Health Threats: Any Lessons from the COVID-19 Pandemic?' (2021) 23 *European Journal of Migration and Law* 405.

[80] COM(2023) 274 final.

[81] Commission Recommendation (EU) 2017/820 2. On the link between these two issues, see among many, M Weissensteiner, 'Cross-Border Police Cooperation and "Secondary Movements": On Reconfigurations in Enforcing Differential Mobility Rights Within the Spatial-Legal Schengen Space' (2021) 17 Utrecht Law Review 73.

member states masters of their own destiny, the policy framework aims to keep the Schengen borders open while ensuring 'internal security'. There should be no checks on anyone, even though only EU citizens and specific categories of TCNs are entitled to free movement. There must be close law enforcement cooperation, and internal controls on strict conditions if strictly necessary. Respect for essential state functions, mutual trust and solidarity, protection of fundamental rights, transparency, and accountability are supposed to be the constitutional tools to manage this heterogeneity.

Primary and secondary EU law resonate with the policy approach. As regards the question of decision-making power, the EU has the competence to adopt measures to ensure the absence of any controls on persons, whatever their nationality, when crossing internal borders.[82] Nonetheless, the exercise of member states' responsibilities vis-à-vis the maintenance of law and order and the safeguarding of internal security remains unaffected by the EU competences.[83] Furthermore, member states can cooperate *as they deem appropriate* to safeguard national security.[84] While member states retain the final say when it comes to reintroducing controls in situations that might warrant such a decision, they must do so within the procedural framework of EU law, including the vertical dimension of solidarity and sincere cooperation.[85] In fact, the principle of solidarity and fair sharing of responsibility governs the whole of Chapter II of the TFEU Title on the Area of Freedom, Security and Justice, thus including areas that—directly or indirectly—relate to internal border controls.[86] As shown in the following chapters, the recent legislative reforms have embedded to a much greater extent solidarity and mutual trust into the law of EU internal border controls. Less clear is whether the principle of fairness towards TCNs would apply internally as well. The TFEU stipulates that this principle must inform the EU policy—also—on asylum and immigration,[87] and especially these two areas might be seen as covering the treatment of TCNs internally vis-à-vis border controls. As mentioned, a fundamental idiosyncrasy of Schengen lies in the commitment to free and secure movement for everyone,[88] albeit the right to free movement is only enjoyed by certain groups of people on the assumption that those with no such right will comply with the limits of their status. The principle of fairness as theorized in this book is applicable, with adaptations, to both categories of persons concerned. Similar to the approach taken in the context of external border controls, the parameters of fairness towards the latter group consist of principles and rights that apply regardless of the entitlement to free movement—particularly legal certainty, the right to liberty, or effective judicial protection.

[82] TFEU, Article 77.
[83] TFEU, Article 72.
[84] TFEU, Article 73.
[85] For example, the reintroduction of border controls and their implementation must be justified by, and adapt to, the level of the threat. This might entail resorting to police checks and cross-border law enforcement, rather than reinstating checks with neighbouring countries. See Commission Recommendation on the implementation of the provisions of the Schengen Borders Code on temporary reintroduction of border control at internal borders in the Schengen area C(2017) 6560 final 4–5.
[86] TFEU, Article 80.
[87] TFEU, Article 67.
[88] SBC, recital 18.

The structure of this Part mirrors that of Part II, and so do the reasons behind it.[89] Here, the discussion of sources (Chapter 8), exercise of controls (Chapter 9), and pathways to scrutiny (Chapter 10) revolve around sources falling within the two strands of activities composing the law of internal border controls: the framework on the absence of controls and the exception to that general rule, and the framework of transnational law enforcement cooperation. Both strands of instruments respond to the call of ensuring security in an area without internal frontiers. As to the framework on the absence of controls, the focus will mostly be on the reformed Schengen Borders Code and the extensive interpretation developed by the Court of Justice on the scope of the allowed exception to internal border checks. As for the framework of transnational law enforcement cooperation, we will analyse the instruments of EU law allowing or encouraging interstate cooperation at the internal borders, and especially:[90] the Convention Implementing the Schengen Agreement;[91] the Prüm Decision[92] and Implementing Decision;[93] the Joint Investigating Teams Framework Decision;[94] and three recommendations, issued by either the Commission or the Council between 2017 and 2024, on the use of police cooperation as a means to avoid the reintroduction of controls.[95] In both scenarios, we will also look into the relevant laws and practice of two member states: France and Norway. These case studies will provide valuable insight. They will reveal how those states' approaches to the reintroduction of control compound the legal challenges posed by the different forms of heterogeneity raised in this book. Furthermore, they will uncover another world of interstate agreements in security cooperation beneath the surface of EU law, which can undermine individual rights in different ways.

[89] The rationales underlying such a structure, explained in section 3.6 as regards external border controls, hold true for internal border controls as well.

[90] As shown by the list of measures, this Part does not cover the specific set of measures that involve the harnessing of technology to enact systematic controls on persons travelling across the internal borders of Schengen states, in particular Directive (EU) 2016/681 on the use of passenger name record (PNR) data for the prevention, detection, investigation and prosecution of terrorist offences and serious crime [2016] OJ L 119/132. While acknowledging the importance of such an aspect, the focus on transnational law enforcement at the internal borders is deemed to fit better with the analytical framework of this research. The PNR Directive is not part of the framework of interoperability. Furthermore, it is from transnational law enforcement that we see the impact of heterogeneity most prominently, particularly within a policy framework that encourages surveillance at the border but regards systematic border checks as incompatible with the SBC. For a commentary on a very important judgment on the PNR, see E Brouwer, 'Ligue des droits humains and the Validity of the PNR Directive: Balancing Individual Rights and State powers in Times of New Technologies' (2023) 60 Common Market Law Review 839.

[91] Convention implementing the Schengen Agreement of 14 June 1985 between the Governments of the States of the Benelux Economic Union, the Federal Republic of Germany and the French Republic on the gradual abolition of checks at their common borders [2000] OJ L 239/19.

[92] Council Decision 2008/615/JHA on the stepping up of cross-border cooperation, particularly in combating terrorism and cross-border crime [2008] OJ L 210/1 (Prüm Decision).

[93] Council Decision 2008/616/JHA on the implementation of Decision 2008/615/JHA on the stepping up of cross-border cooperation, particularly in combating terrorism and cross-border crime [2008] OJ L 210/12.

[94] Council Framework Decision on joint investigation teams 2002/465/JHA (JITs FD) [2002] OJ L 162/1.

[95] Council Recommendation 2022/915; Commission Recommendation (EU) 2017/820; Commission Recommendation (EU) 2024/268 on cooperation between the Member States with regard to serious threats to internal security and public policy in the area without internal border controls.

## 7.6 Conclusions

The fundamental objective of EU external border controls is to make the absence of controls within Schengen sustainable. A very strict selection of persons allowed to enter the EU applies, with a view to reducing the risks of overstay, irregular migration, and secondary movement. The story continues inside the Union, where two main levers offset the unintended consequences of free movement: controlled reintroduction of controls (pun intended) and transnational security cooperation. Inside Schengen also, the legal dilemma about task allocation, interinstitutional trust and solidarity, and fair treatment of the persons concerned are bound to arise as a result of the heterogeneity of the legal framework. The next three chapters discuss these dilemmas in detail. By assessing the constitutional compliance of the law of internal border controls, we will attempt to understand the necessary conditions for the legal sustainability of an area without internal frontiers.

# 8
# Preparing for the Absence of Controls

## 8.1 Introduction

The law of EU border controls is heterogeneous. As an area of shared competence, it involves different levels of governance.[1] EU legislative measures in this field establish common rules, while decision-making is normally decentralized and left to the member states. Inside Schengen, the aim is to check no one crossing the internal borders while guaranteeing a high level of internal security.[2] To this end, activities at such borders can still take place in the form of: checks reintroduced on an exceptional basis; transnational law enforcement, often governed by bilateral or multilateral agreements. Openness and security are intended to be complementary, but can inevitably pull in different directions. This is especially so in light of the heterogeneity of addressees of control, with most third-country nationals (TCNs) enjoying no right of free movement as such. In line with this divide between persons concerned, the EU institutions have emphasized the importance of a transparent and accountable governance of internal border controls to retain the trust of EU *citizens* in the European project. To be sure, actions around an internal frontier must still comply with universally applicable principles such as non-discrimination[3] and legal certainty.

These types of heterogeneity warrant an investigation into how border control-related tasks are allocated, how decision-making impacts interinstitutional cooperation, and what consequences the above can have in terms of the treatment of the persons concerned. Against this background, and consistent with the analytical framework of this book, in this Part we ask whether the law of internal border controls and its implementation are constitutionally compliant (or systemically appropriate). More specifically, we investigate whether legal heterogeneity, as described above, creates actual or potential issues of compatibility with a structured network of relevant principles of EU law (subsidiarity and respect for essential state functions,[4] mutual trust and solidarity,[5] and fairness[6]). For these purposes, we focus on conditions for controls and conditions imposed on the persons concerned. As principles ensure the

[1] Consolidated Version of the Treaty on the Functioning of the EU (TFEU) [2012] OJ C 326/47, Article 4(2)(j).

[2] Consolidated Version of the Treaty on EU (TEU) [2012] OJ C 326/13, Article 3(2) and TFEU, Article 67(2) and (3).

[3] Article 21(1) of the Charter of Fundamental Rights of the EU (CFR or the Charter) [2012] OJ C 326/391.

[4] TEU, Articles 5(3) and 4(2), respectively.

[5] TFEU, Article 80.

[6] TFEU, Article 67(2).

*The Law of EU Border Controls*. Leandro Mancano, Oxford University Press. 
DOI: 10.1093/9780191966187.003.0009

pursuit of the EU objective in line with Article 2 TEU, the assessment ultimately aims to identify the necessary conditions for an area without internal frontiers.[7]

The element figuratively embracing these overarching themes is the notion of internal border control itself, defined in the Schengen Borders Code (SBC) as 'the activity carried out at a border, in response exclusively to an intention to cross or the act of crossing that border, regardless of any other consideration, consisting of border checks and border surveillance'.[8] As with the corresponding chapter in Part II, the following pages deal with the system of sources of activities at the internal borders. The discussion is divided into two scenarios. Firstly, we consider the sources related to the absence of controls and the allowed exceptions to it laid down in the SBC. Secondly, we assess sources of law enforcement activities at the internal border, and particularly the Convention Implementing the Schengen Agreement (CISA),[9] the Framework Decision on Joint Investigation Teams (JITs FD),[10] the Prüm Decision,[11] and the Implementing Decision.[12] The chapter also presents two cross-cutting features. Particularly when it comes to interstate law enforcement, we point to the role played by informal and non-structured sources of EU law. Furthermore, the analysis in both scenarios is enriched by the discussion of the approaches taken by France and Norway. Overall, the chapter uncovers the heterogeneity of actors and the procedures relevant to the adoption of those sources, as well as of the sources themselves, and evaluates the implications of heterogeneity for task allocation, interstate cooperation, and treatment of the persons concerned.

## 8.2 Absence of Internal Border Controls and Its Exceptions

Within Schengen, border controls on any persons are prohibited.[13] This being the rule, the SBC also provides for a framework of exceptions, allowing checks to be reintroduced on a temporary and exceptional basis. The SBC establishes an articulate system of sources in this regard. This scenario revolves around four main types of such sources. Firstly, there are those related to the grounds for reintroducing checks. Secondly, we discuss sources relevant to the process of reintroduction. Thirdly, we explore the role played by national law (including interstate agreements) in the context of the SBC. Finally, we look at the laws and practices of France and Norway.

[7] See Chapter 1 for the discussion on the relationship among these three building blocks of the EU legal order.

[8] Regulation (EU) 2016/399 establishing a Schengen Borders Code [2016] OJ L 77/1 (SBC), Article 2.

[9] Convention implementing the Schengen Agreement of 14 June 1985 between the Governments of the States of the Benelux Economic Union, the Federal Republic of Germany and the French Republic on the gradual abolition of checks at their common borders [2000] OJ L 239/19.

[10] Council Framework Decision 2002/465/JHA on joint investigation teams [2002] OJ L 162/1 (JITs FD).

[11] Council Decision 2008/615/JHA on the stepping up of cross-border cooperation, particularly in combating terrorism and cross-border crime [2008] OJ L 210/1 (Prüm Decision).

[12] Council Decision 2008/616/JHA on the implementation of Decision 2008/615/JHA on the stepping up of cross-border cooperation, particularly in combating terrorism and cross-border crime [2008] OJ L 210/12, Article 17.

[13] SBC, Article 22.

### 8.2.1 Sources and Grounds for Reintroducing Checks

In Part II, we discussed the vague and/or non-transparent nature of the sources underpinning the decision to exercise controls at the external border controls. We observed a delicate balance of task allocation, where the centralization of certain aspects of law-making towards (mostly) the Commission goes hand in hand with a general decentralization of decision-making to the member states. Overall, this set-up seems in line with the principle of subsidiarity, but is also likely to create tensions in terms of interinstitutional solidarity and the fair treatment of addressees of control. These patterns also emerge from the law of internal border controls. In this context, we must distinguish between the sources justifying the decision that controls should be reintroduced and the sources whereby controls are reinstated.

The former originates primarily from the member states. Generally, a member state can reintroduce controls in the case of a serious threat to public policy or internal security. The possible sources of the threat include: incidents or threats posed by terrorism or serious organized crime;[14] large-scale or high-profile international events; and an exceptional situation, consisting of a sudden unauthorized secondary movement of TCNs on a large scale.[15] Following the Covid-19 pandemic, the SBC also added a discrete ground for reintroducing internal controls in reaction to large-scale public health emergencies affecting several member states and putting at risk the overall functioning of the Schengen area.[16] The 'in particular' preceding the list shows that the sources of threats enumerated therein are not a *numerus clausus*. Such a choice of legislative drafting is bizarre, especially considering how broad and flexible the existing grounds already are. They 'tick' the 'essential state functions' box, but doubts can be raised as to the appropriateness of this provision in overcoming the unilateralism of member states' reintroduction of checks. Furthermore, the reference to terrorism or organized crime is not linked to existing legislative instruments.[17] This

[14] For a critical assessment of the use of border controls for anti-terrorism purposes, see S Léonard, 'Border Controls as a Dimension of the European Union's Counter-Terrorism Policy: A Critical Assessment' (2015) 30 Intelligence and National Security 306.

[15] SBC, Article 25(1). Ceccorulli argues that the refugee crisis has triggered a collective securitization of the Schengen area. See M Ceccorulli, 'Back to Schengen: The Collective Securitisation of the EU Free-Border Area' (2019) 42 West European Politics 302.

[16] SBC, Article 28. That decision would have to provide for mitigating measures established at EU and national level, if those referred to in Articles 21a and 23 SBC were insufficient to address the emergency. Article 23 concerns measures in the territory and at the internal borders taken by member states which do not amount to border checks. Article 21a is a new article introduced by the reform and governs the restrictions on travel to the EU in the case of large-scale public health emergencies. More generally, on a legal account of the impact of Covid-19 on free movement, see D Thym and J Bornemann, 'Schengen and Free Movement Law During the First Phase of the Covid-19 Pandemic: Of Symbolism, Law and Politics' (2020) 5 European Papers 1143. For an application of the framework of collective securitization to Covid-driven border controls, see A Jacobs and M Kabata, 'Covid-19 and the Collective Securitisation of Schengen: An Analysis of EU and National Responses to Border Control' (2024) 32 Journal of Contemporary European Studies 1.

[17] Directive (EU) 2017/541 on combating terrorism and replacing Council Framework Decision 2002/475/JHA and amending Council Decision 2005/671/JHA [2017] OJ L 88/6; Council Framework Decision 2008/841/JHA on the fight against organised crime [2008] OJ L 300/42. On the importance of common definitions in the fight against transnational serious crime and especially terrorism, CC Cocq, *Mutual Trust in Regional and Interregional Cooperation on Counterterrorism: EU and ASEAN Approaches* (Springer 2024) 21.

is an example of the EU legislature not making the most of the heterogeneity of the sources of law—for example, by clarifying the meaning of these two areas of crime as defined in the two relevant Directives.[18] The ground for reintroducing checks concerning unauthorized secondary movement, for its part, requires that the strain on resources and capacities of well-prepared authorities be *likely to* put at risk the functioning of the Schengen area 'as evidenced by information analysis and all available data' (including from EU agencies). Two considerations are in order. As noted already in Part II, the law of EU border controls tends to link decision-making processes to an open-ended list of sources. This approach can not only result in contradictions between the sources themselves, but also make it harder to scrutinize the relevant processes and ensure that decisions are evidence-based. The threshold for the decision—a risk to the functioning of the Schengen area—compounds the uncertainty. What does that risk consist of, and how can it be measured?

With regard to the sources whereby controls are introduced, as a rule these originate from the member state too. States have the last word on such a decision, subject to a duty of information to certain EU institutions, which might in turn be followed by a consultation process.[19] This being said, the Council can recommend that a member state reintroduce controls, but only on the basis of a proposal from the Commission.[20] In neither case, however, does the SBC establish an obligation for the Commission or the Council to act. The circle is squared, so to speak, with the type of source that could be used by the Council if it did decide to follow through: the recommendation would not bind the member states.[21] Similarly, on duly justified grounds of urgency, the Commission can adopt a recommendation through an immediately applicable implementing act whereby controls would be *prolonged*.[22] The act must be followed by a recommendation to the Council within 14 days of the adoption of the recommendation. In this delicate balance, no actor seems to be under an obligation to do anything. This should not be taken to mean that the SBC is a dead letter, of course. In the situations described above, the principle of solidarity as a duty of taking into account the common interest can steer, or underpin an ex post review of, the conduct of the competent actor. In line with the solidarity test proposed in this book (see Figure 2.1), a number of factors must be taken into account. While it is true that we are looking at a derogation from a general rule (checks on no one at the internal borders), secondary law empowers certain bodies to take certain actions if the common interest so requires. For the Commission and the Council, the action consists of recommending the reintroduction of controls. Given that the two institutions are under no duty of doing so, the solidarity review could not be of particularly high intensity. A breach of such a principle could be found, however, if those institutions were in possession of

[18] We cannot help but noticing the adjective 'serious' next to 'organised crime'. Leaving aside for a moment the easy irony elicited by such a definition, a question arises in relation to the threshold required by this provision.

[19] In certain cases, a different procedure might apply. We are referring in particular to the reintroduction of controls in cases where deficiencies at the external borders might put at risk the overall functioning of the Schengen area. See SBC, Article 29.

[20] This proposal can also follow from a member state's request.

[21] We should also highlight that the recommendation must at least contain the information referred to in Article 27(1)(a). This list has been amended by the reform.

[22] SBC, Article 29(4).

evidence that a credible ground for the reintroduction of controls existed and they did not exercise their discretion. The member state concerned, for their part, has a duty to engage with this recommendation. If the state decides *not* to reintroduce controls, it must notify the Council of the reasons why it has decided against the recommendation.[23] This would, in turn, be followed by a Commission report to the EP and the Council assessing the reasons for the decision as well as the impact on the Schengen common interests.[24] Depending on the extent of evidence and threat behind the recommendation, the member state could ignore the proposed action and still 'pass' a solidarity review only if it had a relatively strong justification for doing so.[25]

### 8.2.2 Sources and the Process of Reintroduction

The reformed SBC has significantly strengthened the relevant procedures for the reintroduction of controls and built a prominent element of solidarity into them. This is apparent from certain sources related to the process of reintroduction of checks, and particularly the notification and opinion. In notifying the reintroduction or prolongation of checks to the Commission, the member state must refer to certain information. Such information includes, in particular, an assessment of the likely impact of the measure on the movement of persons within Schengen as well as on cross-border regions.[26] A notification can be submitted jointly by more than one member state, and according to a template adopted by the Commission via an implementing act.[27] The need for an impact assessment reveals that the choice to use checks should not be entirely unilateral.

An opinion can be issued on two distinct grounds. Firstly, the Commission must issue an opinion if,[28] without prejudice to Article 72 TFEU and based on the information contained in the notification about reintroduction or prolongation (including the risk assessment), it has concerns about the necessity and proportionality of the measure. The 'without prejudice' clause is particularly important. The final decision will lie with the member state, just as the responsibility for law and order and internal security does.[29] Furthermore, the obligation for the Commission arises only if it has

[23] For completeness, the member state concerned must also notify the other member states, the EP, and the Commission when it decides to reintroduce checks pursuant to the recommendation. Furthermore, while possible in the abstract, member states are more likely to reintroduce controls unilaterally. This is, at least, the practice that we have observed in recent years.

[24] For understandable reasons, the same procedure does not apply in cases where controls are reintroduced. The Commission and the Council would have already considered the impact on the general interest. Furthermore, the member state concerned must inform the other member states and the EP.

[25] Such justifications could include information questioning the evidence underlying the recommendation, or the fact that the damage caused by the reintroduction of controls would outweigh the risk in the circumstances under consideration.

[26] SBC, Article 27(1). This is a welcome amendment to the SBC. The other pieces of information included in the notification are identical to the previous version of the SBC and include the data related to the serious threat and scope of the reintroduction.

[27] SBC, Article 27(1) and (6).

[28] Any member state can as well.

[29] This is different from the scenario, hinted at in the previous chapter and developed further below, where the Commission encourages the member states to use these responsibilities and powers particularly with the view to avoiding the reintroduction of controls. Recommending to actively take certain measures (police checks) as opposed to refraining from doing so (in the case of border controls) might be seen as

concerns of the kind mentioned above.[30] Secondly, the Commission must issue an opinion every time it has been notified of the decision by a member state to prolong controls resulting in a total duration of 12 months.[31] This scenario presents significant differences from the previous one. The obligation arises by default—that is, simply because of the prolongation of controls. Furthermore, the SBC provides greater detail about the required content of the opinion. While the scope is pretty much identical to the first one and focuses on the necessity and proportionality of the controls,[32] it must also include a specific assessment of whether alternative measures to *remedy* the threat were *sufficiently explored*. This clause is consequential for two reasons. Firstly, there is no reference to Article 72 TFEU. This is no exemption for the Commission to respect essential state functions. However, its absence from this ground could be read as meaning that the provisions about prolongation of control already give expression to Article 72 TFEU, and that a member state might be unsuccessful in using this Article as a general 'get out of jail' clause. In addition, the scope of opinion covers the *sufficient exploration of alternative measures*. These two factors make the Commission's opinion resemble a solidarity review of the member states' conduct. The intensity of such a review is mitigated by the benchmark set in that provision, since the alternative measures must be capable of *remedying* the identified threat. This is not the only case where SBC uses the word 'remedy' in relation to a threat, but other expressions such as 'address' are sometimes preferred.[33] The remedial nature of the measure suggests the requirement of a higher threshold. Unlike the other terms, it conveys more forcefully the idea of an 'obligation of results' and therefore makes it easier for the member state to justify the prolongation of controls.

In the case of a positive assessment—that is, in favour of the member state prolonging controls—the opinion must contain recommendations *where appropriate* to improve cooperation between member states, with a view to limiting the impact of the controls and contributing to reducing the threat. In the end, the opinion on the prolongation will result in an obligation of taking into account. Once an opinion has been issued under either of the two grounds mentioned above, it must be discussed with the member states in the context of a consultation process that *must* be established by the Commission. It seems, therefore, that such a consultation *will* have to happen at least in the case of controls lasting for 12 months.[34] To be sure, the effectiveness of these

less intrusive vis-à-vis Article 4(2) TEU and 72 TFEU. This view, however, is probably misguided. They are inextricably linked, to the extent that the emphasis of alternative measures is indirectly a recommendation not to rely on checks at the internal border. In the end, both are instruments that could be used to pursue the protection of internal security, which is ultimately the responsibility of each member state.

[30] The Commission inevitably enjoys significant discretion in the assessment of 'concern'.

[31] See SBC, Article 25a(4).

[32] The relevant provision states that the opinion must include an assessment of whether the reintroduction or prolongation is necessary and proportionate. It is interesting that, in the opinion about prolongation, the mandatory opinion issued by the Commission must also focus on the merit of reintroduction of controls. We must assume that such an assessment would be carried out with the benefit of hindsight, as the decision about controls is made on the basis of the information available at the time. It is, most probably, the case that such a retrospective assessment will be used to learn lessons from past experience and potentially use them in future cases, bearing in mind that each situation will possess its own specific characteristics.

[33] See SBC, Articles 23(a), 26a(6), and 28(1).

[34] See SBC, Article 27a(4). This is a consultation process *in accordance with paragraph 1* of Article 27a. The latter provision stipulates that the Commission *may* establish a consultation process. The obligation

sources will be ultimately dependent upon the level of rigour of the Commission's scrutiny.

### 8.2.3 Interstate Cooperation and the Role of National Law

Similarly to what we observed in Part II, the role for member state-driven sources arises from two main scenarios: bilateral cooperation, and 'delegation' to member states made by EU law. As regards the former, the new procedure laid down in the SBC governing the transfer of a person apprehended at an internal border offers a particularly interesting example of interaction between different sources.[35] The need for more structured cooperation in this area is apparent from the several instances of systemic pushbacks at the internal frontiers and the issues of solidarity and fair treatment they raise.[36] Article 23a is the relevant provision in this regard and applies where a number of conditions are satisfied. Firstly, the TCN must have been apprehended in the context of checks involving authorities from both states 'within the framework of bilateral cooperation'. The other—cumulative—condition is that there are clear indications that the person has arrived directly from another member state, and it has been established that they have no right to stay in the state of arrival, on the basis of information immediately available to the apprehending authorities, including statements from the person concerned, documents on the person, or results of searches in national and Union databases.

If those conditions are fulfilled, the member state can immediately transfer the person to the state of departure, pursuant to the procedure stated in Annex XII SBC.[37] This would constitute a derogation from Article 6(1) Return Directive,[38] and should apply exceptionally.[39] The relevant provisions of the Return Directive would

arises only if a member state issues a request in this sense to the Commission. Both Articles 27a(2) and (3), to which Article 27a(4) refers, establish an obligation for the Commission to issue an opinion. The obligation to establish a consultation process to discuss the opinion must be thus read alongside the obligation to issue an opinion. It is important to remember, however, that under Article 27a(2) the Commission *must* issue the opinion only *if* there are concerns about the necessity and proportionality of the controls. Framing the establishment of the consultation process on its own initiative as a choice for the Commission, as stated by Article 27a(1), makes sense—symbolically, because it might be seen as establishing where the authority lies for the decision about the controls, and legally, because the member states will then implement and enforce the check in light of the content of the consultation, rather than pursuant to what they might have wanted to.

[35] SBC, Article 23a.

[36] The French–Italian border is one of the places most in the spotlight in this regard. See on this S Peracchi, 'Migration Crisis in the Local News: Evidence from the French-Italian Border', available at SSRN: https://ssrn.com/abstract = 4673997. Since Germany has reintroduced internal border controls, hundreds of pushbacks into the Netherlands have occurred too. See https://schengen.news/germany-has-turned-away-368-people-at-its-border-with-netherlands-since-internal-checks-began/.

[37] The Annex itself is a 'new entry' ensuing from the reform of the SBC. Transfer operating in derogation from the Directive 2008/115/EC [2008] OJ L 348/98 (Return Directive) must be issued through a standard form. The form should be handed to the TCN, and contain specific notes on whether the person has refused to sign it.

[38] Article 6(1) Return Directive stipulates that, as you would expect, a TCN found to be staying irregularly in the territory of a member state must be issued with a return decision.

[39] SBC, Article 23a(3a).

apply once the person has been transferred to the receiving member state, and this includes the exceptions to the obligation that a member state issue a return decision against a TCN found to be staying irregularly in their territory:[40] the person has a valid title of stay in another member state and can only be issued with a return decision if they do not return to that state or for reasons of public policy or national security; the person is taken back by another member state on the basis of a bilateral arrangement predating the entry into force of the Directive;[41] the member state where the person was found can issue a title to stay on other grounds (including compassionate or humanitarian);[42] or the procedures for the renewal of the title of stay are pending.[43] The SBC prescribes that certain elements be included in the bilateral framework of cooperation. This is especially the case where the apprehending member state opts for the internal transfer, rather than applying the Return Directive itself. The member states, in particular, must establish the 'practical modalities' of cooperation. Furthermore, when the transferring member state presumes that the person is a minor, it must inform the receiving member state and both must ensure that measures are taken in the best interest of the child 'in accordance with their respective national laws'. Such a procedure does not apply to applicants or beneficiaries of international protection.

This new procedure is a significant addition to the law of internal border controls, with relevant implications for constitutional compliance. In the previous two sections, the discussion has mostly revolved around the heterogeneity of sources caused by the heterogeneity of decision-making centres, in turn a product of the task-allocation set-up in this area. Here, the issue is slightly different. Arguably, Article 23a builds on the idea that each state should play its part to make the Schengen area function properly, which in turn is required by the principles of mutual trust and solidarity. If a TCN is already in the EU and enters another member state where they have no right to stay, the member state of departure might have to take charge. In other words, the member state where the person has entered will not have to be responsible for returning the person. There is an estoppel undertone to this provision: if a state has not prevented unauthorized movement from its own territory, it should not be allowed to free ride on other states' resources but must do its fair share to ensure internal security within Schengen. Such a procedure would not be imposed unilaterally, as it can apply only if member states have voluntarily agreed a framework of cooperation in this regard. This is clearly aimed at facilitating a more cooperative attitude between member states vis-à-vis secondary movement, with the hope of departing from the despicable practice of internal pushbacks. The system of sources on interstate cooperation on what is essentially a readmission mechanism is incapable of ensuring fair treatment of the persons concerned, however. The finding that the TCN has no right of entry into the second member state can be based on information drawn from databases. The concerns occasioned by the interoperability of

[40] Return Directive, Article 6(2)–(5).

[41] However, in this case the member state in which the person was found can still issue a return decision.

[42] In this case, the member state must not issue a return decision.

[43] The member state has an obligation to 'consider refraining from issuing a return decision' until the procedure comes to an end.

large-scale information systems discussed in Part II apply to this scenario as well.[44] This is so, even if Article 23a clearly governs interception occurring as a result of security—rather than immigration—checks, since EU law covers the interoperability between both categories of databases.[45] Secondly, beyond the bare bones of the SBC, member states are left with a free rein in establishing 'the practical modalities' of co-operation. The lack of input from EU law stands out. Compare it with the provisions of the VISA on the member states' use of external service providers in the context of visa applications. Granted, these two cases of 'delegation' are rather different, but the variance in the prescribed content of the readmission agreement is remarkable. This is particularly so in relation to two aspects. On the one hand, there is no indication of what kind of procedure would apply to applicants for international protection. On the other hand, the treatment of the situation of minors is particularly worrying. Except for the generic reference to the best interest of the child, there is clear potential for inconsistency, given the reference to the two different states' laws and the absence of any 'conflict rule' or 'dispute resolution' mechanism. Generally, the heterogeneity of sources caused by the plurality of bilateral agreements in the absence of a common framework works significantly to the detriment of legal certainty and legal protection for addressees of control.

Cross-border regions offer another interesting example of interstate cooperation. They represent a novelty in the context of the SBC and play an important part in the architecture thereof.[46] Communication about areas considered as cross-border regions figures among the information that must be notified by the member states to the Commission.[47] The member states cooperate closely to establish these regions, 'taking into account the strong social and economic ties between them'.[48] The SBC leaves member states 'procedural autonomy' as to how these regions should be identified and established. There is no specific method or form that should be followed in this regard, except for the duty of cooperation mentioned above. As shown further in the next chapter, they will play an important role in the decision about the lawful reintroduction of border checks.

Finally, member states-based sources matter especially in the context of non-border checks, which escape the general provision established by the SBC. Checks not amounting to border checks and performed in accordance with the powers conferred by national law to the competent authorities are allowed.[49] The next scenario analyses these provisions in detail. Before moving on to this, we will provide insight into source-related practices by France and Norway vis-à-vis internal border controls.

[44] H Aden, 'Interoperability Between EU Policing and Migration Databases: Risks for Privacy' (2020) 26 European Public Law 2693.

[45] Regulation (EU) 2019/817 on establishing a framework for interoperability between EU information systems in the field of borders and visa [2019] OJ L 135/27 and Regulation (EU) 2019/818 on establishing a framework for interoperability between EU information systems in the field of police and judicial cooperation, asylum and migration [2019] OJ L 135/85.

[46] See https://cor.europa.eu/en/our-work/cooperations-and-networks/european-cross-border-platform.

[47] SBC, Article 39(1)(h). These must be notified by member states with common internal borders within six months of the entry into force of the SBC.

[48] SBC, Article 42b.

[49] SBC, Article 23.

While these 'highlights' partly resonate with the spirit and the details of the foregoing framework, they also add a further layer of complexity to the discussion.

### 8.2.4 Tales from France and Norway

The reintroduction of border controls in French law is primarily governed by the *Code de l'entrée et du séjour des étrangers et du droit d'asile* (or *Code de l'entrée*), which lays down the definition of internal borders[50] and the conditions for temporarily reintroducing checks as provided for in the SBC.[51] The decision on the reintroduction of controls itself is taken by the Prime Minister, who exercises regulatory (executive) power.[52] The performance of controls is a prerogative of the French Border Police (*Direction nationale de la police aux frontières*, or DNPAF),[53] which comprises different departments and particularly 'la sous-direction des frontières'. Two key objectives of the latter are: to control borders and to secure (*sécurisation*) the railway lines and international transport corridors; to develop cross-border cooperation.[54] The General Directorate for customs and indirect taxes (*Direction générale des douanes et des droits indirects*) is in charge of cooperation with other European customs services.[55] French customs officers[56] are also involved in border controls, as per Article 67 of the *Code des douanes*.[57] They exercise controls by, for example, stopping and searching persons under certain conditions.[58] Within the framework of this research, three main aspects of legal interest are worth highlighting as regards the approach to sources of internal border controls in French law: the distinction between checks and surveillance; the type of evidence or motive underlying the reintroduction of control; clarity and accessibility of the source.

As regards the relation between sources on internal checks and surveillance, the latter is mostly governed by the Code of Criminal Procedure and the Customs Code. Those sources reflect the types of authorities empowered to perform

[50] Code de l'entrée, Article L331-1.

[51] Code de l'entrée, Article L331-3.

[52] Il exerce le 'pouvoir règlementaire', as per Article 21 of the French Constitution. This is generally the rule for subjects which are not under a legislative aspect are under a regulatory one. See also Article 37 of the French Constitution.

[53] Police aux frontières, PAF–Direction nationale de la police aux frontières (DNPAF) is a 'Direction nationale spécialisée en charge du contrôle aux frontières et de la lutte contre l'immigration irrégulière'. See Arrêté du 29 juin 2023 portant organisation de l'administration centrale de la direction générale de la police nationale, JOFR n°150 du 30 juin 2023: Article 29. As for the mission and the instrument governing it, see here and Décret n°2013-728 du 12 août 2013 portant organisation de l'administration centrale du ministère de l'intérieur et du ministère des outre-mer, JORF n°188 du 14 août 2013, Article 20.

[54] Arrêté du 29 juin 2023 portant organisation de l'administration centrale de la direction générale de la police nationale, JOFR n°150 du 30 juin 2023.

[55] Décret n°2007-1664 du 26 novembre 2007 relatif à la direction Générale des douanes et droits indirects, Article 2, 6 and Arrêté du 19 décembre 2019 portant organisation de l'administration centrale de la direction générale des douanes et droits indirects, JORF n°0301 du 28 décembre 2019.

[56] Douanes—Direction générale des douanes et des droits indirects, DGDDI—Ministère de l'économie, des finances et de la souveraineté industrielle et numérique.

[57] See the mission of DGDDI.

[58] Concerning the conditions for controls and their exercise, see Rules for controls: Articles 60 à 60-10 Code des douanes.

surveillance-related tasks at the internal borders: namely, police and customs officials. Importantly, the *Cour des comptes* uses 'controls' and 'surveillance' interchangeably. This is not an isolated episode or a slip. It is part of a consistent approach, where surveillance is regarded as aiming to make 'sure that crossing points are not bypassed'.[59] The next chapter discusses in more detail the kind of measures of surveillance that can be adopted by those authorities. The approach to such a concept in French law corroborates the overall argument, proposed in this book, that a definition of controls as checks-plus-surveillance should be applied to the EU external and internal borders. This, in turn, calls into question the brand of Schengen as an area without internal border controls.

Secondly, the existence of sources evidencing a certain threat and the related risk assessment are particularly important to a sound decision to reintroduce controls. In this regard, this research has shown no noticeable impact assessment or adoption of mitigating measures by France. However, the European Commission highlighted in its 2024 State of Schengen report that that French internal border controls were 'performed . . . in a non-systematic manner and the intensity [was] adapted based on the type of border (air, maritime, land) and relevant risk analysis carried out by the competent local authorities'. Most importantly, this risk analysis was performed by using the tools developed by Frontex (CIRAM 2.0), which has allowed for a more adaptable approach to controls and a more limited impact on cross-border movement. Spanish, Belgian, Italian, Luxembourgish, and Swiss authorities confirmed such a finding.[60] This seems, to all intents and purposes, a positive development. It also sheds some light on the kind of sources that might be used by member states for their risk assessment. The example also reveals, however, the extent to which Frontex can play a role inside the Schengen area, somehow bending the rule of the EBCG Regulation itself that this Agency 'shall not support any measures or be involved in any activities related to controls at internal borders'.[61]

Thirdly, the source behind the decision on resorting to checks understood as motive can also be particularly important for the assessment of constitutional compliance. While the grounds normally invoked refer to threats of different sorts—public health, security, public policy—the actual dynamic behind them must not be overlooked. In this regard, it is worth noting that France decided to lift internal controls in June 2020 with all its neighbouring states, except for Spain. This was due to the prolonged performance of checks operated by the latter. The instructions state no reasons for the decision beyond the fact that controls at the Spanish borders were kept in place.[62] Had the French government's stance been purely 'retaliatory' in nature, serious questions would have arisen about the compatibility of this position with the principle of solidarity. In a sense, this might be exactly the sort of situation which the new consultation process, discussed in this chapter, aims to address and prevent.

[59] '[S]'assurer du non contournement des points de passage'. Cour des comptes, *Les contrôles d'identité. Une pratique généralisée aux finalités à préciser*, Rapport public thématique, Décembre 2023, p. 76.

[60] See State of Schengen Report 2024 7.

[61] Regulation (EU) 2019/1896 on the European Border and Coast Guard and repealing Regulations (EU) No 1052/2013 and (EU) 2016/1624 [2019] OJ L 295/1 (EBCG Regulation), Article 7(4).

[62] Instruction from the Prime minister, 14 June 2020, n° 6180/SG 1.

Lastly, there are considerations of accessibility and clarity. France has repeatedly reintroduced controls at the internal borders since 2015,[63] almost without interruption.[64] Among those forms of controls adopted over time, there have been measures taken in reaction to the Covid-19 pandemic, such as border closures, internal border controls, and restrictions on entry. The last measure consisted mostly of instructions from the Prime Minister to the effect that entry had to be refused to people attempting to enter French territory who were not members of the EU, the Schengen area, or the UK, or who had no imperative reason to go to Europe and France. Such instructions provided for a series of exceptions to the general prohibition of entry.[65] The overall approach was upheld by the French Government as the pandemic progressed, but also saw the addition of further requirements (showing certificates[66]) or exceptions (for seasonal workers,[67] or relaxation of restrictions on travel for certain categories of people and coordination of border controls with other states[68]). In one particular example of litigation that ensued, the 'Juge des référés' of the French Conseil d'État (who rules in urgent cases) rejected the request of the *Ligue des droits de l'Homme* (LDH) to put an end to the violation of people's free movement (*libertés fondamentales*) caused by the lack of clear instructions for internal border controls.[69] The Conseil d'État found that the Prime Minister's instructions had set the position of the government as regards the applicable measures by the competent authorities to ensure the control of the frontiers in a sufficiently precise, clear, and intelligible manner. This was particularly so in consideration of a number of factors including: the level of risk at the moment the contested order had been adopted; the possibility of quickly pivoting to less restrictive measures of border management in the case of a positive evolution of the situation, and account being taken of the very important objectives of those measures. In conclusion, these measures were not deemed to pose a serious and manifestly illegal threat to the fundamental freedoms invoked by the complainant.[70] While we should be wary of drawing systemic conclusions from one ruling, we can safely say that an unprecedented—and in many ways unpredictable—new situation would leave the executive greater flexibility as to the form and substance of decisions related to the control of the internal frontiers. It should also be noted that the Juge des référés

[63] State of Schengen report 2023 15.

[64] See Full list of Member States' notifications of the temporary reintroduction of border control at internal borders pursuant to Article 25 et seq. of the Schengen Borders Code.

[65] Instruction from the Prime minister, 18 March 2020, n°6149/SG 1-3.

[66] Instruction from the Prime minister, 12 May 2020, n°6167/SG.

[67] Instruction from the Prime minister, 20 May 2020, n°6171/SG.

[68] Press release from the French government, 22 May 2020.

[69] See details of the measures applied in France, paras 7–9 and 23–24.

[70] '[C]ompte tenu du niveau de risque persistant à la date de la présente ordonnance et des possibilités d'adaptation des mesures de gestion des frontières en cas d'évolution favorable plus rapide, les instructions du Premier ministre des 18 mars, 15 avril, 12 et 20 mai 2020 ont fixé, de manière suffisamment précise, claire et intelligible, la position du Gouvernement français sur les mesures à appliquer par les services pour assurer les contrôles aux frontières en tenant compte de l'objectif de lutte contre la pandémie de covid-19 et du droit de l'Union auxquelles elles se réfèrent, ne portent pas aux libertés fondamentales invoquées, et notamment à celles de libre circulation garanties par le droit de l'Union européenne, une atteinte grave et manifestement illégale'. Conseil d'État, Juge des référés, 02/06/2020, 440449, para 24. For a comment on internal border controls and Covid-19, see A Bouveresse, 'La libre circulation des personnes à l'épreuve de la Covid-19: Extremis malis extrema remedia?' (2020) 3 Revue trimestrielle de droit européen 509.

simultaneously addressed several points made by the LDH, and did not engage directly with the *doléance* concerning the lack of clarity. In fact, the circumstances mentioned above that would have averted a risk of fundamental rights violation have very little to do with legal certainty itself.

The example of Norway shares a certain degree of similarity with that of France. As known, Norway joined the Schengen area through a specific agreement.[71] This is true, first and foremost, for the definition of border controls themselves. Beyond measures falling squarely within the notion of border checks, the approach to surveillance in Norwegian law brings the latter under the conceptual umbrella of border controls.[72] Just like border checks, surveillance is carried out by the Police and is defined as 'the monitoring of border crossing points and the borders on the stretches between border crossing points in order to prevent persons from circumventing border control'.[73] The Norwegian Border Act stipulates that an internal border may only be monitored sporadically *or* when border control has been temporarily reintroduced.[74] While the Act breaks the link of interdependence between border checks and surveillance, it also requires that the latter be non-systematic. This phrasing is consistent with the spirit of the SBC, but also semantically accurate. If surveillance is a form of control, a constant monitoring of the internal borders would not be entirely compatible with the prohibition under Article 22 SBC. Against this background, different legislative sources govern the reintroduction of controls at Norway's internal borders, and unsurprisingly they refer to the Schengen Borders Code as well.[75] The *Grenseloven* (Border Act) stipulates that controls are reintroduced by decision of the Ministry of Justice and Public Security.[76] More specific instructions on the implementation of internal border controls are provided by the Directorate of Police via a circular to police districts and other relevant authorities. The latest consulted version of such instructions is from 2024,[77] but it is only accessible with a login.[78] However, in a letter of 8 July 2023, the Ministry gave the National Police Directorate the authority to decide on the reintroduction of border control at internal Schengen borders for up to 10 days for situations that require *immediate measures* and issued further instructions for the exercise of this competence.[79] The National Police Directorate can, in turn, delegate decision-making authority to the Chief of Police for the reintroduction of border control at internal Schengen borders in its own police district for a period limited to *up to*

[71] Agreement concluded by the Council of the European Union and the Republic of Iceland and the Kingdom of Norway concerning the latters' association with the implementation, application and development of the Schengen acquis [1999] OJ L 176/36.

[72] Grenseloven, Article 1-1g.

[73] Grenseloven, Article 18.

[74] Grenseloven, Article 20.

[75] The SBC applies as Norwegian law according to Grenseloven (Border Act) § 8 (1) no 1.

[76] Grenseloven, Article 14. This is the Ministry responsible for the implementation of the Schengen rules, and is also given the power to further regulate cf. § 25 cf. delegation of the King.

[77] National Police Directorate—National guideline—RPOD-2024-9.

[78] This is the Lovdata Pro Subscription, which all law practitioners and students have access to, through their work, universities, etc. Most of the sources available at Lovdata (the Norwegian legal database) are available for the wider public, but circulars are good examples of sources where you need a login to gain access. In short this was very easy for me to access, but it requires a paid subscription.

[79] Letter 8. of June 2023 from the Ministry of Justice to the POD cf. RPOD-2024-9.

*72 hours*. This system of delegation and sub-delegation is remarkable, as it confers law enforcement authorities the power to make a decision affecting directly the exercise of free movement rights, if only for a relatively short period. When controls are reintroduced, the internal border may be crossed at border crossing points designated by the Ministry. The Police implement the controls,[80] although they also cooperate with other authorities[81] and especially the Customs Service.[82] The competent Ministry has expressly taken the view that effective border controls require more detailed rules, in the relevant regulations, as regards the interaction with other districts and authorities. While heterogeneity is seen as a potential strength—not least to achieve a more cost-effective utilization of existing equipment and instruments—there is also an acknowledgement of the need to combine this with clear task attribution.[83]

Another source-related similarity between France and Norway concerns the frequency of decisions made to reintroduce controls and the justifications behind them. In the period 2014–24, Norway notified the EU of its reintroduction of internal border control 36 times.[84] The reasons varied and included terrorism threats, migration (secondary movement), and the awarding of the Nobel Peace Prize and sports events.[85] When reintroducing or prolonging controls, the Ministry would have to assess their impact in line with the SBC. Such an assessment emerges from the notification letters sent to the European Commission, even though such letters are not always as detailed as one might expect.[86] In this regard, the approach of the government has been criticized, particularly for being very 'liberal' with the interpretation of public security grounds underpinning the prolonged checks at the internal borders.[87] Even more strikingly, the Norwegian Supreme Court explicitly espoused the expansive approach taken by the French Conseil d'État to the concept of a 'new threat' under the SBC, effectively granting the executive much larger room for manoeuvre in keeping controls in place for longer, albeit on a different ground.[88] The observation of law and practice

[80] Grenseloven, Article 4(1).

[81] Grenseloven, Article 4(2).

[82] Grenseloven, Article 7.

[83] Prop 161 L (2016–2017) 56. This source is a preparatory document for the legislative proposal that was then subsequently enacted by the Norwegian legislature.

[84] See https://home-affairs.ec.europa.eu/document/download/11934a69-6a45-4842-af94-18400fd274b7_en?filename=Full%20list%20of%20MS%20notifications_en.pdf. The individual notification letters contain more information on the reasons for the specific reintroductions.

[85] See the specified reasons for reintroduction in this https://home-affairs.ec.europa.eu/document/download/11934a69-6a45-4842-af94-18400fd274b7_en?filename=Full%20list%20of%20MS%20notifications_en_2.pdf.

[86] See https://www.regjeringen.no/contentassets/80197702ddb144e8a016a040e656751f/temporary-controls-at-the-norwegian-internal-borders_notifikasjon-til-eu.pdf of a notification from the Norwegian Ministry of Justice and Security of 16 April 2024.

[87] See https://www.aftenposten.no/verden/i/y4KExA/norge-bruker-omstridt-smutthull-for-aa-stenge-grensen-vi-er-ikke-alene-igjen-har-europa-sluttet-aa-gaa-i-takt (especially beneath the heading 'Norge fortsetter med grensekontroll') and https://www.nrk.no/norge/mener-norge-bryter-schengen-avtalen_-_-begrunnelsen-holder-ikke-1.12755811 on criticism regarding the condition of 'serious threat' not being met in all the cases of reintroduction of internal border control in Norway.

[88] This is further discussed in the next chapter. The Norwegian government, for its part, opined that controls could be kept in place beyond the limit, even if the same threat persisted. See the reaction to the EU Court of Justice's *NW* judgment at https://www.stortinget.no/no/Hva-skjer-pa-Stortinget/EU-EOS-informasjon/EU-EOS-nytt/2022/eueos-nytt---28.-april-2022/eu-domstolen-uttaler-seg-om-indre-grensekontroll/. The European Court of Justice rules on internal border control—stortinget.no.

of internal border controls in Norway also confirms how prone to litigation Covid-driven measures proved to be. Like many other Schengen states during the pandemic, Norway reintroduced controls at its internal borders several times in this period. The need for those controls was periodically assessed and adjusted based on the evolving situation, and various mitigating measures were introduced to minimize the impact on free movement while addressing public health concerns.[89] Different cases made their way up to the Norwegian Supreme Court, which ruled that the SBC and EEA law did not preclude the legislation under consideration.[90]

### 8.2.5 Interim Conclusions

The analysis of the sources of internal border controls has revealed the challenges of squaring the heterogeneity of the legal framework with constitutional compliance. The foregoing discussion has shown that, to a significant extent, the heterogeneity of sources is a result of the heterogeneity of levels of governance and actors, persons concerned, and objectives. In this context, doubts remain about the appropriateness of this system of sources for achieving its goals. Consistent with the findings of the research so far, the respect for subsidiarity and essential state functions is directly linked to the risk of tensions in terms of solidarity and fair treatment of the persons concerned. The sources relevant to the reintroduction of checks, be they related to the grounds for such reintroduction or the procedures for doing so, are either vague (the threat can be evidenced in any way) or 'soft' (ie non-binding). This being said, we have observed a much stronger solidarity-oriented system, as shown by the nature of the mandatory scope of the state's notification as well as the Commission's opinion. Ultimately, the correct implementation of the framework will presuppose a rigorous application of solidarity understood as a procedural duty of taking account of the common interest. The new rules on internal readmission following apprehension at the internal borders are also supposed to foster mutual trust and solidarity, with member states working together to counter secondary movement. However, the legal framework established by the SBC is extremely vague and provides next to no mandatory content for such bilateral cooperation. This creates serious issues of legal certainty, protection of asylum seekers, and the best interests of the child. The insight into the French and Norwegian laws and practices is consistent with said picture, while also adding further elements of interest to our discussion. As also proposed in this book, both countries approach internal border controls as checks-plus-surveillance. The heterogeneity of sources of law and decision-making actors characterizes these two legal systems as well, but in neither case has such a feature translated into successful legal challenges.

89 Such as health checks and quarantine requirements. See a report from a 'Corona Committee' submitted to the Prime Minister in June 2023 (NOU 2023: 16), which however focused on the response at all levels of society and does not specifically concern border control.

90 HR-2024-1109-A; HR-2024-1110-A; and HR-2024-1107-A. In the case HR-2024-1107-A, the Covid-related requirement to quarantine in a hotel was not assessed in relation to the Schengen rules.

## 8.3 Compensatory Measures

As the story goes, compensatory measures are a fundamental component of the borderless area, since they make the absence of controls sustainable politically and practically. Part II has shown how heterogeneous the range of measures governing the EU external borders is. That heterogeneity can also be observed with regard to measures applicable inside the Union's territory. Provisions concerning rules on residence[91] live alongside highly streamlined mechanisms of judicial and police cooperation. A comprehensive analysis of the whole spectrum of these rules would go beyond the scope of this research. Here, we focus on measures and activities that are more closely linked to internal border controls from a geographical and conceptual point of view. In the previous scenario, we introduced a distinction between prohibited border checks and the otherwise allowed police/security checks. The next chapter discusses in depth this dichotomy by also dissecting the Court of Justice's approach on the matter. Re-evoking this distinction in the context of compensatory measures is important for two main reasons. Firstly, we must emphasize that the vocabulary on the meaning of the borderless area is not always uniform. The adage is that the EU is an area without internal border *controls*,[92] the latter being defined in the SBC itself as checks-plus-surveillance.[93] This wider approach is flanked by a narrower ban on border *checks* and measures having an equivalent effect thereto (MEEs). Other types of checks, and particularly police and security checks, are not affected by this provision. While the SBC prohibits 'border checks' and MEEs, surveillance is otherwise absent from the part of the SBC that governs the measures at the internal borders. There is no hint at a distinction between police and border surveillance mirroring that between different types of checks. Furthermore, border surveillance can be performed without checks being in place, as the reformed SBC defines the former as aiming 'to prevent or detect unauthorised border crossings *or* the circumvention of border checks'. With this in mind, this Part espouses the definition of border controls as checks-plus-surveillance and applies it throughout the analysis of intra-Schengen measures. From the insight into national laws and practices discussed in the previous scenario, surveillance at the internal borders has already emerged as a relevant area of investigation for the purposes of this research.[94] The evaluation of compensatory measures, which will zero in on transnational initiatives taking place around the internal frontiers, will reinforce this impression.

This scenario is structured as follows. Firstly, we set out the relevant framework as established by EU law. We consider the role of member states' declarations and bilateral agreements in the context of hot pursuit, hot surveillance, and joint operations carried out around the internal borders. Thereafter, we get a glimpse of the system of

[91] Directive (EU) 2024/1233 on a single application procedure for a single permit for third-country nationals to reside and work in the territory of a Member State and on a common set of rights for third-country workers legally residing in a Member State (recast).

[92] SBC, recital 22.

[93] SBC, Article 2.

[94] See on this topic, with a case study on the Franco-Spanish border, I Barbero, 'The European Union Never Got Rid of Its Internal Controls: A Case Study of Detention and Readmission in the French-Spanish Border' (2018) 20 European Journal of Migration and Law 1.

operational sources that might be relevant to security checks or surveillance. Given its complexity, a comprehensive analysis of these sources would go beyond the scope of this chapter. Just as in Part II, it is nonetheless important to highlight the impact of these informal and non-structured sources on operational cooperation, particularly in terms of legal certainty and accessibility to the legal information—and, ultimately, on fair treatment of the persons concerned. Against this background, the second part of this scenario looks at relevant examples of laws and practices from France and Norway. This section uncovers the relevance of interstate arrangements in this area and the challenges they pose to individual protection.

### 8.3.1 Declarations and Bilateral Agreements

The main sources of EU law governing law enforcement activities around the internal border are the CISA, the Prüm Decision, and the JITs FD. They set out a very minimalistic legal framework for the performance of a number of activities, while referring to the member states for the establishment of the relevant details. The CISA features a series of provisions that are still applicable today, alone or in conjunction with other measures. Police and security activities are covered by Title III, and rest on the general obligation of mutual assistance, barring constraints in the legislation of the requested state.[95] The second general clause of relevance states that cooperation in border areas may be covered by arrangements between the states, and it does not preclude future agreements between states sharing a border.[96] Within this framework, two actions are relevant to our discussion: hot surveillance and hot pursuit. Member states can carry out hot surveillance, which consists of continuing surveillance of a person in another state, subject to the authorization of the requested state.[97] The provisions on hot surveillance contain no significant references to other types of sources, apart from: the request of authorization and notification, by the surveilling officers, that they have entered the state where surveillance is continuing; the document certifying this authorization to the surveilling officer has been granted, which must be carried by the officer at all times; and the report that must be provided by the surveilling officer to the competent authorities of the state of surveillance. States can extend bilaterally the scope of the relevant provisions of CISA, but no specific obligation of form is established for those purposes.[98] Hot pursuits, for their part, allow the pursuit of a person starting in one member state and continuing across the border of another member state by the same officers. Member states can issue a declaration for the following purposes: establishing whether the pursuing officer has the right to apprehend the person or not;[99] defining the applicable time and space limits of the hot

[95] For example, where the police authority is not competent to deal with the request, including the case where the judicial authorities must be involved. CISA, Article 39(1).

[96] CISA, Article 39(4) and (5).

[97] CISA, Article 40.

[98] CISA, Article 40(6).

[99] The apprehension is, any case, subject to the condition that the authorities of the state of pursuit cannot intervene 'quickly enough'. CISA, Article 40(2).

pursuit; and identifying the offences for which the measure can be carried out.[100] The declaration must follow consultation with all the states concerned—presumably the bordering ones—'with a view to obtaining equivalent arrangements on both sides of internal borders'.[101] Furthermore, as with hot surveillance, the states can bilaterally adopt 'additional provisions' in the implementation of Article 41.

The system of sources governing joint operations at the internal borders follows a similar pattern: (very) bare bones established in EU legislation, accompanied by references to interstate agreements and declarations. The Prüm Decision establishes rules on the stepping up of cross-border cooperation, particularly as regards the exchange of information in the following areas:[102] DNA profiles, vehicle registration data, major events, measures to prevent terrorist offences, and other forms of cooperation. The latter are the most interesting for our discussion, as they potentially cover activities at the internal borders.[103] The Prüm Decision, in turn, allows member states to introduce joint patrols and other joint operations with a view to maintaining public order and security and preventing criminal offences. Such measures would involve officers from one member state participating in an operation on the territory of another member state (the host state). The practical aspects of such a joint operation must be laid down in a declaration, as per Article 36 Prüm Decision.[104] A member state can also dispatch officers and supply equipment to another member state at the request of the latter, on the occasion of mass gatherings or other major events, to prevent criminal offences *and* maintain public order and security.[105] Member states must submit a declaration listing arms and equipment that can be used only in self-defence or defence of others,[106] as well as the details of the practical aspects of their use.[107] Such declarations must first be sent to the Council and the Commission, and then to the Council alone in the case of subsequent amendments.[108] The Council must draft and keep updated, in the form of a Council document, a manual 'comprising exclusively factual information provided by the Member States through' the declarations mentioned above.[109] While the declaration is a very important source in the framework of Prüm, the practice from certain member states shows that there has been little use of this—at best—in favour of bilateral agreements. In fact, member states can continue to apply or conclude new bilateral or multilateral agreements or arrangements on cross-border cooperation. Pre-existing agreements must be compatible with the

[100] More specifically, a state can declare that such offences are those listed in Article 41(4)(a) CISA, or that hot pursuit can be used for extraditable offences. These are the same as listed for hot surveillance, as per Article 40(7).

[101] CISA, Article 41(9).

[102] Prüm Decision.

[103] The Prüm Implementing Decision lays down detailed rules concerning technical aspects of the cooperation.

[104] Prüm Decision, Article 17.

[105] Prüm Decision, Article 18.

[106] The host state can prohibit seconded officers from carrying certain arms or equipment.

[107] Prüm Decision, Article 19. The host member state's officer in charge of the operation can allow the home state's officer to use arms and equipment beyond self-defence or defence of others. In general, the use of arms is governed by the law of the host state.

[108] The Council, in such a case, must inform the Commission and the member states. Prüm Decision, Article 36.

[109] Prüm Implementing Decision, Article 18(2).

Prüm Decision, whereas the new ones must extend or enlarge the objectives of the Decision.[110] Agreements of a different kind can also be necessary to set up a Joint Investigation Teams (JITs), at the initiative of two or more states for a specific purpose and limited period, in the cases of difficult investigations with links to other member states, or because the circumstances require a coordinated and concerted action.[111]

The scarcity of EU legislative sources on operational activities at the internal borders might lead us to think that the relevant framework raises no issue of heterogeneity or constitutional compliance. This impression would be erroneous. The minimalistic nature of the measures, combined with the significant deference to member states' initiative, respects the principle of subsidiarity and essential state functions. Likewise, the instruments show no obvious tension with the principle of solidarity. Law enforcement and security being a protected space, cooperation remains primarily a matter for the member states' sovereign choices, made on a case-by-case basis and on the back of the obligation of mutual legal assistance. A number of questions arise, however: Can the extensive reliance on interstate cooperation, and the fragmented system of sources potentially resulting from it, hinder the achievement of cooperation in an area without border controls? Can that system of sources affect legal certainty and accessibility to the relevant information for the persons concerned, therefore undermining the fairness of the legal framework? The first question will find an answer in the next chapter, where we will discuss initiatives taken by the Council and the Commission over the last few years, focused on fostering law enforcement cooperation. Here, it suffices to say that based on several examples of legal fragmentation, member states have been strongly encouraged to review and adjust their bilateral agreements and arrangements in this area.[112] Useful material to address the second question will be provided by the analysis of laws and practices in France and Norway, which will show how member states' experiences add an equally complex layer of stratification to the law and practice of police cooperation around the EU internal borders. Before delving into those case studies, we must catch a glimpse of the complex network of operational sources linked to law enforcement cooperation at the internal borders.

### 8.3.2 Structures and Networks of Cooperation

In recent years, the EU institutions have increasingly relied on recommendations to foster cross-border police cooperation and, ultimately, safeguard internal security without reintroducing checks within Schengen.[113] The content of these

[110] Prüm Decision, Article 35.

[111] JITs FD, Article 1.

[112] Commission Recommendation (EU) 2024/268 on cooperation between the Member States with regard to serious threats to internal security and public policy in the area without internal border controls, C(2023) 8139 final.

[113] In most cases, the legal basis used for these purposes has been Article 292 TFEU. Council Recommendation 2022/915 on operational law enforcement cooperation [2022] OJ L 158/53, however, refers to Article 87(3) or 89 TFEU, stating that it builds on, and constitutes a development of, the Schengen acquis (recitals 15 and 16). Article 87(3) TFEU lays down a special legislative procedure for the Council to establish 'measures concerning operational cooperation' between law enforcement authorities as defined in that Article. Article 89 TFEU allows the Council to establish conditions and limitations under which states'

recommendations, particularly as regards the modalities of cooperation, will be discussed in the next chapter. Here, we pay attention to three types of operational sources[114] invoked in direct connection with operations at the internal frontiers.

Firstly, increasing emphasis is being placed by the Commission and the Council on the creation of a Union law enforcement culture. Member states are encouraged to cooperate with the European Union Agency for Law Enforcement Training (CEPOL)[115] in the design of training courses on cross-border law enforcement and align their training to CEPOL's EU Strategic Training Need Assessments (EU-STNAs).[116] As a longer-term ambition, states should consider creating 'pan-European joint training'.[117] Secondly, there are sources of best practices and forums for sharing them. The 'Schengen catalogue'[118] (identifying best practices in the field of operational cross-border police cooperation) and the National Fact Sheets of the 'Manual on cross-border operations'[119] are mentioned as sources that must be considered in the context of strengthened transnational law enforcement. As we will see through the case studies, several of the best practices mentioned in the documents have been taken forward by the member states considered (such as the creation of joint police stations or multi-party structures in border areas). The Council's Law Enforcement Working Party (LEWP) is identified as the forum where discussions on the coordination of cross-border law enforcement activities and the source of good practices in member states could develop.[120] It must be noted that the information on the LEWP website is very scant, and while the dates and agendas of the meeting are recorded, the relevant documents are either equally laconic or not accessible. When it comes to best practices and sources, we must make a special mention of the Police and Customs Cooperation Centres (PCCCs), which member states are encouraged to set up and reinforce. The institutional and scholarly[121] debate on these Centres is limited, and no EU-wide framework exists in this regard, except for best practice guidelines issued by

competent authorities can operate in the territory of another member state. The reference to 'conditions and limitations'—rather than directives as per Article 83 TFEU—might be seen as an attempt to leave the door open to different kinds of legislative initiatives. Interestingly, Article 89 TFEU mentions more specifically the authorities referred to in Articles 87 and 82. While the former provision clearly concerns law enforcement authorities and attempts to define them, Article 82 TFEU offers no equivalent clause. The only reference is in Article 82(1)(d) TFEU, which grants the EU competence to establish rules to 'facilitate cooperation between judicial or equivalent authorities'.

[114] For the understanding of 'operational source' adopted in this book and the relevance to the subject of our investigation, see section 4.1.

[115] Regulation (EU) 2015/2219 on the European Union Agency for Law Enforcement Training (CEPOL) [2015] OJ L 319/1.

[116] Based on EU-STNAS last report, the training is linked to the training priorities of the EMPACT cycle mentioned below. See https://www.cepol.europa.eu/training-and-education/training-needs-analysis/strategic-training-needs-assessments.

[117] Council Recommendation 2022/915 54.

[118] Council Document 15785/3/10 Rev 3.

[119] Council Document 10505/4/09 Rev 4.

[120] Commission Recommendation (EU) 2024/268 5. See https://www.consilium.europa.eu/en/council-eu/preparatory-bodies/law-enforcement-working-party/. The mandate of the LEWP is available as Council document 8728/21.

[121] See A Gruszczak, 'Police and Customs Cooperation Centres and Their Role in EU Internal Security Governance' in R Bossong and H Carrapico (eds) *EU Borders and Shifting Internal Security: Technology, Externalization and Accountability* (Springer 2016) 157.

the Council.[122] As stated in response to a Parliamentary question, the establishment of a PCCC remains a matter of competence for the participating member states. The Council has no access to 'aggregated information on existing PCCCs and their exact location', and its discussions on this issue pertain to their nature or the exchange of relevant good practices.[123] Thirdly, some platforms should be relied on as a source of support to member states' actions, particularly those technology-related. It is recommended that operational cooperation in border areas (including targeted joint patrols) be taken in the context of the European Multidisciplinary Platform Against Criminal Threats (EMPACT)[124] and be supported by intelligence-led policing.[125] The European Innovation hub for internal security,[126] the European Network of Law Enforcement Technology Services (ENLETS),[127] and the BroadWay project[128] are also (some of the) instruments mentioned as potential sources of support. The Innovation Hub was established in 2020 by the Council's Standing Committee on Operational Cooperation on Internal Security (COSI)[129] and brings together expertise from a large range of EU agencies. ENLETS was created in 2008 as a sub-group of the Council LEWP and reports to COSI with the objective of establishing a stronger connection between law enforcement agencies and innovative technologies. Information on the BroadWay project is not extensive and, at the time of writing, the project's website was not available. Similarly to what we observed in respect of the systems of external border surveillance,[130] cooperation in internal frontier areas also rests on a complex web of bodies and their relationship is not always clear.

That operational cooperation around internal border areas is heavily reliant on operational sources is not an earth-shattering finding. We must, however, highlight the contrast between the complexity of these structures and networks and the bare bones of the EU legislative framework in this area. This structural feature ensues, at least partly, from the heterogeneity of levels of governance and actors in a field where national sovereignty has managed to rein in the advances of Union-wide legal integration. This brief taxonomy confirms how relevant questions of task allocation are to the lawful control of the internal borders. 'Lawful control' is here understood not only as being in line with the requirements laid down in the SBC, but also with the structured network of relevant principles of EU law meant to ensure constitutional compliance. Consistently throughout this research, we have seen that the respect of the legal

[122] 11770/2/10 REV 2.

[123] See the answer to a written question at https://www.europarl.europa.eu/doceo/document/E-9-2022-003850-ASW_EN.html.

[124] See https://www.europol.europa.eu/crime-areas-and-statistics/empact.

[125] Council conclusions on the permanent continuation of the EU Policy Cycle for organised and serious international crime, 7100/23.

[126] See https://www.europol.europa.eu/operations-services-innovation/innovation-lab/eu-innovation-hub-for-internal-security.

[127] See https://enlets.eu/about/.

[128] The most recent information available on the BroadWay project can be found in https://cordis.europa.eu/project/id/786912. See also the following response by Commissioner Johansson to a parliamentary question on the project: https://www.europarl.europa.eu/doceo/document/E-9-2022-001485-ASW_EN.html.

[129] Council Decision 2010/131 on setting up the Standing Committee on operational cooperation on internal security [2010] OJ L 52/50.

[130] See section 5.3.

framework for subsidiarity and essential state functions raises doubts of compatibility with other aspects of the structured network of principles. In this specific context, the question arises as to how the heterogeneity of levels of governance, and the heterogeneity of sources and structures stemming from it, can raise in terms of legal certainty and accessibility to legal information.

### 8.3.3 Tales from France and Norway

France has developed different strands of activities falling within the framework of the compensatory measures discussed in the previous sections.[131] As a preliminary observation, it is worth noting that the State of Schengen report 2024 revealed a satisfactory degree of cooperation between French authorities and their neighbours.[132] With this in mind, France has established a vast range of bilateral agreements on activities of control at the internal frontiers. It has a long-standing agreement with Belgium about the establishment of a PCCC,[133] as well as on the authorization for their respective customs services to exercise cross-border hot surveillance and hot pursuit as per Articles 40 and 41 CISA.[134] Such agreements are also in place with Luxembourg,[135] Germany,[136] Spain,[137] Italy,[138] and Switzerland.[139] An interesting trend has seen bilateral PCCCs evolving into multi-party centres. This is the case of the (initially) Franco-Luxembourgish PCCC, which now also involves Belgium and Germany.[140] Beyond the PCCCs, France has developed cooperation with its neighbouring countries in different ways. It has established a 'Comité stratégique franco-belge' (created by the agreement of Tournai in 2001)[141] and a 'Groupe de travail opérationnel spécial douane',[142] as well as an agreement with Belgium on joint patrols.[143] France and Belgium have also signed an agreement, based on Article 39 CISA, for the exchange of information and personal data relating to holders of vehicle registration certificates to penalize traffic offences.[144] France is working with Italy on the

[131] For an explanatory note issued by the French government on Articles 39 to 41 CISA, see Circulaire du 23 juin 1995 commentant les dispositions des articles 39, 40 et 41 de la convention signée à Schengen le 19 juin 1990, JORF n°152 du 1er juillet 1995.

[132] State of Schengen report 2024, pages 9 to 11. The Olympic Games have been a case where a member state (France) has mobilized multilateral police cooperation.

[133] Décret n°2005-258 du 14 mars 2005.

[134] Décret n°95-1181 du 7 novembre 1995.

[135] See Décret n°95-1182 du 7 novembre 1995 and https://www.senat.fr/leg/pjl11-664.pdf

[136] Décret n°2000-924 du 18 septembre 2000 and Décret n°95-1183 du 7 novembre 1995.

[137] Décret n°2003-915 du 19 septembre 2003 and Décret n°95-1184 du 7 novembre 1995.

[138] Décret n°2000-923 du 18 septembre 2000.

[139] Décret n°2000-1045 du 18 octobre 2000; n°2003-135 du 13 février 2003; and Décret n°2009-836 du 7 juillet 2009.

[140] Décret n°2016-1294 du 29 septembre 2016.

[141] See further information on the https://www.prefectures-regions.gouv.fr/hauts-de-france/Actualites/Transfrontalier-Comite-strategique-franco-belge#:~:text=Le%20comit%C3%A9%20strat%C3%A9gique%20franco%2Dbelge%20se%20r%C3%A9unit%20deux%20fois%20par,pour%20les%20mois%20%C3%A0%20venir.

[142] See https://www.prefectures-regions.gouv.fr/hauts-de-france/Actualites/Cooperation-transfrontaliere-franco-belge for further information on Franco-Belgian cooperation.

[143] Décret n°2015-1297 du 15 octobre 2015.

[144] Décret n°2011-1590 du 18 novembre 2011.

creation of a French–Italian operational unit,[145] and has created a mixed brigade with the same state in 2020.[146] Similarly, it has developed a joint action plan and cooperative arrangements—consisting particularly of joint patrols—with Luxembourg,[147] Switzerland[148] and Germany.[149] There are also cross-border cooperation agreements as regards missions of the police over the French–German part of the Rhine,[150] as well as on the employment of aerial cross-border surveillance.[151] This maze of bilateral cooperation unfolds against the bare bones of the supranational legal framework described above, and often adds little detail to this. In several cases, the primary source of cooperation is not accessible at all. Where access is possible, however, we note references to further important sources such as plans of various kinds, including for carrying out cross-border search operations in border areas.[152] This national case study confirms a suspicion formed on the basis of the previous analysis. The nature of this area has seen minimal intervention by the EU legislature and has left most of the action in the hands of the member states, which has in turn incentivized the emergence of a very fragmented landscape. This trend is compounded by the geographical focus on the internal borders, which inevitably leads to more agreements between the member states concerned. The most striking consequence of the EU subsidiarity-driven non-engagement is the absence of any duty of information of publication, embodied by the Council's lack of access to aggregate information on the number and sites of PCCCs.

As part of the Schengen package, Norway also applies measures on law enforcement cooperation.[153] The Norwegian Police Act allows foreign police officers to perform their policing duties in Norway if 'it follows from an agreement with a foreign state'.[154] The main instruments covered by such a provision are the second additional protocol to the European Convention on Mutual Assistance in Criminal Matters,[155] the CISA[156] and the Prüm Decision.[157] In this regard, Norway has issued a declaration not to limit, in time or space, hot pursuit and hot surveillance on its territory.[158] On a more general level, Norway (and Iceland) have signed an agreement with the EU

145 See the State of Schengen Report 2024 8.

146 See https://www.lemonde.fr/international/article/2020/08/01/immigration-darmanin-annonce-la-creation-par-la-france-et-l-italie-d-une-brigade-mixte-contre-les-passeurs-a-la-frontiere_6047866_3210.html.

147 See https://www.virgule.lu/granderegion/france-et-luxembourg-signent-un-plan-d-alerte/12567.html.

148 See https://www.sem.admin.ch/sem/fr/home/sem/medien/mm.msg-id-98380.html and Décret n°2000-1045 du 18 octobre 2000.

Décret n°2003-135 du 13 février 2003; Décret n°2009-836 du 7 juillet 2009.

149 See State of Schengen Report 2024 9 and https://www.gendarmerie.interieur.gouv.fr/gendinfo/actualites/2023/bapteme-de-l-unite-operationnelle-franco-allemande and https://www.diplomatie.gouv.fr/IMG/pdf/traite.aix-la-chapelle.22.01.2019_cle8d3c8e.pdf. See also https://www.interieur.gouv.fr/archives/actualites/communiques-de-presse/communique-de-presse-conjoint-a-lissue-du-conseil-des-ministres.

150 Décret n°2004-906 du 26 août 2004.

151 See Décret n°2018-893 du 16 octobre 2018

152 Decree n°2009-836 du 7 julliet 2009, Article 14.

153 Norway is connected to the Prüm cooperation through a separate agreement, ratified in 2020.

154 Police Act, Section 20a.

155 ETS No. 182, Articles 17–20.

156 CISA, Articles 40 and 41.

157 Prüm Decision, Articles 17 and 18.

158 See Innst. O. nr. 89 (1998-99) 23; St. mld. Nr. 18 34; Ot. Prop. Nr. 56 (1998-99), chapter 8.1.1.

on the application of the 2000 Convention on Mutual Assistance in Criminal Matters and its 2001 protocol,[159] as well as a surrender agreement modelled on the European Arrest Warrant.[160] While Norway has participated in many JITs, it has no specific national legislation on this subject matter.[161] Zooming in on the legal ecosystem of Norway and its neighbours, the Atlas Agreement is meant to strengthen cooperation between Norwegian and Swedish authorities in connection with the handling of crisis situations such as terrorism and serious crime.[162] Norway and Sweden are also proceeding with the creation of a joint police station at the border.[163] Looking more widely, Norway is part of the Nordic Arrest Warrant[164] and of the 1974 Nordic Police Cooperation Agreement. The latter, which includes Denmark, Finland, and Iceland, constitutes an administrative agreement among the countries' police directors and national police chiefs. In 2002, a trilateral agreement was concluded at the level of the police directors between Norway, Sweden, and Finland on the operationalization of Articles 40 and 41 CISA. A Circular issued by the Police Directorate in 2004 (Circular 2004/004) contains more information on the agreement, but the document itself is two pages long and provides very few details about the actual implementation of the cooperation. Uglevik noted that, based on consultation with Police authorities, 'the Norwegian police in the border regions seem to be unaware of [the agreement] existence . . .Their informal attitude towards [it], alongside the absence of restrictions, may signal a very high level of trust between the neighbouring states (or at least the police personnel in question)—so high, in fact, that a formal agreement is not perceived as necessary'.[165] Lack of transparency and accessibility to information characterize Norway's network of cooperation as well. There is a slightly different constitutional undertone to this case study, in comparison to that of France. France seems to act primarily in the context of its protected sovereign space carved out by the EU Treaties and respected by the Union's legislature, whereas the distinctive Nordic eco-system might operate on a level and understanding of mutual trust that is at odds with the one developed in EU law.[166] Assuming the correlation between informality and mutual trust is correct, the Nordic cooperation builds on an understanding of interstate relations that departs quite significantly from the one we have been used to in recent decades. The well-established approach of EU law to trust-driven cooperation in law

[159] See Agreement between Iceland, Norway and the European Union on the application of certain provisions of the Convention of 29-05-2000 on Mutual Assistance in Criminal Matters between the Member States of the European Union and the 2001 Protocol thereto [2004] OJ L 26/3.

[160] Agreement between the European Union and the Republic of Iceland and the Kingdom of Norway on the surrender procedure between the Member States of the European Union and Iceland and Norway [2006] OJ L 292/2.

[161] The only relevant provision refers to the activities of seconded members (Article 20a of the Police Act). See Guidelines on Joint Investigation Teams involving Third Countries 25.

[162] The agreement with Sweden entered into force on 2 April 2020 and is based on EU Council Decision 2008/617 by which Sweden is bound (the Atlas Decision). Norway has no agreement with the EU on adherence to this Council decision, nor has it entered into similar bilateral agreements with other countries.

[163] See Government press release 88-32 (27 August 2023) and press release 45-2024 (15 May 2024) in which the idea of the cooperation in explained. This project is still in progress.

[164] Konvensjon om overlevering for straffbare forhold mellom de nordiske land (Nordisk arrestordre).

[165] S Ugelvik, *Police Cooperation and Sovereignty in the EU: Norway's Lessons for Europe* (Routledge 2018) 148.

[166] See the discussion in section 2.5.2.

enforcement builds on the existence of legal proximity achieved through common rules among the cooperating parties. While this trust could be justified by close cooperation developed in practice over many years, it is likely to create challenges for legal certainty and individual protection.

### 8.3.4 Interim Conclusions

The structural heterogeneity of EU border controls has produced a fragmented legal framework for compensatory measures at the internal frontiers. Unlike the discussion of border checks, where most sources are referred to in the SBC, the landscape of sources of law enforcement cooperation is dispersed and composed of a plethora of bilateral or multilateral agreements. The EU approach is certainly compliant with respect for essential state functions, but is not conducive to making legal information accessible. Compensatory measures inside Schengen, and particularly interstate cooperation at the internal borders, are the epicentre of a constitutional dilemma. The EU tries to mitigate the distortions caused by heterogeneity through less intrusive fora of coordination and sharing of good practices. However, not only do these structures increase heterogeneity, but they have also proved so far ineffective in addressing some of the most pressing issues due to a lack of uniformity in a field which has a direct impact on the most cherished accomplishment of European integration.

## 8.4 Conclusions

Activities at the internal borders can take place in two main scenarios: the border checks proper, reintroduced as a last resort within the framework of conditions and procedures laid down in the SBC; all other forms of exercise of public powers, and especially transnational law enforcement, not amounting to measures equivalent to border checks. In a sense, the analysis of the controls inside Schengen has started where we left the discussion on the external borders: a system based on a heterogeneity of sources, produced by a heterogeneity of decision-making centres, heavily reliant on operational or non-structured forms of cooperation. Regularly, the delicate balance between centralization and subsidiarity poses challenges to interinstitutional solidarity and fair treatment of the persons concerned. The new rules adopted recently by the SBC have introduced more pronounced elements of procedural solidarity, which might contribute to reducing the uncertainty arising from the discretion left to the actor competent to act. The analysis of sources has also shown certain differences between external and internal controls, and particularly so in the area of law enforcement cooperation. The latter is characterized by a vast landscape of bilateral or multilateral agreements, which in turn are either not so accessible or refer to further sources without specification. In certain cases, this informality could be justified by the existence of a high level of mutual trust, understood in a way that sits at odds with its well-established meaning in EU law but seems difficult to challenge. This heterogeneity has developed against a common framework that is particularly minimalistic, which in turn can impact legal certainty and foreseeability of consequences for the persons caught by it.

# 9
# Exercising Controls in a Borderless Area

## 9.1 Introduction

The law of internal border controls is characterized by heterogeneity of sources, objectives, levels of governance and actors, and addressees of control. The pursuit of a high level of internal security must go hand in hand with the absence of systematic checks on persons upon crossing an internal frontier[1]—even though third-country nationals (TCNs) have no right to free movement in many cases (at least not beyond the 90 days in any 180-day period rule).[2] This law rests on two main pillars: the rules on the absence of controls and the systems of exceptions thereof; the set of compensatory measures, and specifically law enforcement cooperation taking place around the shared internal frontier. The cornerstone of the legal framework is a narrower approach to the concept of border controls themselves, as compared to that applied to the external borders. Within Schengen, 'border controls' and 'border checks' are used interchangeably by the EU institutions, leaving surveillance out of the equation. Conversely, we argue that a sound legal analysis requires the adoption of the general definition of controls as checks-plus-surveillance provided for in the Schengen Borders Code (SBC).[3] The discussion on the sources of this law, developed in the previous chapter, has cast doubts on their appropriateness for achieving the objective(s) of free movement and internal security inside Schengen. Consistent with the findings that have emerged throughout the book so far, constitutional compliance on one level (ie subsidiarity and task allocation) entails tensions in terms of solidarity and fair treatment. These tensions have structural reasons. The governance of the internal border intersects a legally protected space of sovereignty.[4] Despite the shared nature of this area of competence,[5] national authorities are left with the last word on the reintroduction of controls and on the performance of border surveillance. Relatedly, the duality of the territory created by the lifting of controls—a territory which is simultaneously the EU and the state's—causes ambiguities around the 'ownership' of *internal* security (internal to the Union or the state?), which has repercussions on the identification of the locus of political and legal authority for measures aimed to protect this interest. While the SBC has introduced enhanced mechanisms to reconcile the exercise of

[1] Consolidated Version of the Treaty on the Functioning of the EU (TFEU) [2012] OJ C 326/47, Article 67(1).

[2] See I Goldner Lang, 'Freedom of Movement of EU Citizens and Mobility Rights of Third-Country Nationals: Where EU Free Movement and Migration Policies Intersect or Disconnect?' in L Tsourdi and P De Bruycker (eds), *Research Handbook on EU Migration and Asylum Law* (Edward Elgar 2022) 98.

[3] Regulation (EU) 2016/399 establishing a Schengen Borders Code [2016] OJ L 77/1 (SBC).

[4] See Consolidated Version of the Treaty on EU (TEU) [2012] OJ C 326/13, Article 4(2) and TFEU, Article 72.

[5] TFEU, Article 4(2)(j).

*The Law of EU Border Controls*. Leandro Mancano, Oxford University Press. © Leandro Mancano 2025.
DOI: 10.1093/9780191966187.003.0010

this essential state function with the principles of mutual trust and solidarity, questions remain about the actual scope of enforceability of the solidarity principle. The heterogeneity of decision-making centres and sources has even more striking effects in cross-border law enforcement. The common framework is somehow suspended in time—mostly at the conclusion of the Convention Implementing the Schengen Agreement (CISA)[6]—while the action in the field has thrived on the basis of bilateral or multilateral cooperation. These initiatives are often based on non-accessible or minimalistic and flexible arrangements. Here, we develop the impressions sketched in the previous chapter. We follow the same structure, and we focus on the two main strands of the absence of controls and compensatory measures. Supported by the extensive case law of the Court of Justice, we discuss in detail the procedure and conditions for reintroducing controls, as well as the definition of allowed non-border checks. Secondly, we uncover the possible paradigm shift in cross-border law enforcement cooperation pursued by the Commission. In both scenarios, we explore how the approach of France and Norway on certain issues might support, align, or conflict with that taken at the EU level. In both scenarios, we try to weave together the different expressions of heterogeneity and assess their constitutional compliance in the sense espoused in this book.

## 9.2 Absence of Internal Border Controls and Exceptions

The SBC is the backbone of the law of EU internal border controls. At the forefront of the Code lies the idea of free movement as one of the main achievements of the European Union, accompanied by the statement that the Schengen area is based on trust and solidarity.[7] On the basis of the SBC and the Court's case law, we must distinguish between two sets of measures taken by member states at their internal borders. On the one hand, border checks and measures having an equivalent effect to border checks (MEEs) are normally prohibited,[8] except in the cases and according to the procedures established therein. On the other hand, checks performed pursuant to the powers conferred by national law to the competent authorities are left unaffected by the abovementioned prohibition.[9] In this regard, the SBC lays down the criteria to identify a measure as amounting to or not a border check or MEE. Firstly, we will focus on the legislative framework. Against this background, we consider two important aspects of the implementation of the Code as developed through the interpretation of the Court of Justice: the limits of the member states' power to extend checks at the borders; the permissible actions by the member states having reintroduced the checks in reaction to irregular border crossing. Secondly, we will analyse the concept of non-border checks as set out in the SBC and interpreted by the Court. Lastly, we look at the experiences from France and Norway.

[6] Convention implementing the Schengen Agreement of 14 June 1985 between the Governments of the States of the Benelux Economic Union, the Federal Republic of Germany and the French Republic on the gradual abolition of checks at their common borders [2000] OJ L 239/19.

[7] SBC, recital 1a.

[8] SBC, Article 22.

[9] SBC, Article 23.

### 9.2.1 Reintroducing Checks at the Internal Borders: The Legislative Framework

The SBC stipulates that internal borders can be crossed at any point without border checks, irrespective of the nationality of the border crosser.[10] This being the rule, the SBC also provides for a framework of exceptions, within which border controls—or, rather, checks—can be reintroduced on a temporary and exceptional basis. When controls are reintroduced, Title II applies insofar as is relevant.[11] The discussion of the legislative framework revolves around the following issues: types of threat justifying the reintroduction of checks; types of scenarios for reintroducing checks; relevance of passage of time; and solidarity-driven procedures.

#### 9.2.1.1 Types of threat

Broadly, a member state can reintroduce border checks in the case of a serious threat to public policy or internal security. The SBC enumerates in a non-exhaustive manner the types of threat that could justify the checks: incidents or threats posed by terrorism or serious organized crime; large-scale public health emergencies; large-scale or high-profile international events; an exceptional situation, consisting of sudden unauthorized secondary movement of TCNs on a large scale;[12] and public health emergency affecting several member states and putting the overall functioning of the Schengen area at risk.[13] The reformed SBC retains the idea that the reintroduction of internal border control should be a last resort, and that their scope and duration should not be disproportionate in relation to the threat.

Beyond what was discussed in the previous chapter, we must consider the appropriateness of the abovementioned list to achieving the objectives of the legal and policy framework, account being taken of the types of heterogeneity considered in this research. The ground related to unauthorized intra-EU movement is of particular interest. Based on the wording chosen by the Union's lawmakers, successfully invoking that threat might presuppose the fulfilment of a number of requirements. An exceptional situation, consisting of sudden and large-scale unauthorized movement of TCNs between member states, must put a substantial strain on the resources of well-prepared authorities. The reference to well-preparedness resonates with the wording of the Crisis Regulation,[14] and reminds us of the estoppel argument underpinning the direct effect of directives.[15] Member states cannot use their own failure to justify non-compliance with EU law. These two words might be easily overlooked, but they are rooted in the fundamental values of the EU legal order. They give effect to the principles of solidarity and mutual trust, mandating every state to do its part to make

[10] SBC, Article 22.
[11] SBC, Article 32.
[12] SBC, Article 25(1).
[13] SBC, Article 28.
[14] As a reminder, a member state can submit a request to the Commission when it faces a situation of (inter alia) crisis, in order to obtain solidarity measures or be granted leave to derogate from provisions of EU asylum law. In its request, the member state must show the strain on its well-prepared system. See Regulation (EU) 2024/1359 addressing situations of crisis and force majeure in the field of migration and asylum (Crisis Regulation), Article 1(4).
[15] See Case 148/78, *Ratti*, EU:C:1979:110, para 22.

the system work. The condition of well-preparedness ties a state's lawful reliance to one of its essential functions (safeguarding national security through internal border controls) to its compliance with its collective obligations. This provision gives effect to the principle of solidarity and attempts to manage the heterogeneity of decision-making centres inherent in the governance of internal border controls. At the same time, this 'managing' potential is mitigated by other circumstances. The strain is likely to put at risk the functioning of the Schengen area as evidenced by information analysis and all available data, including from the EU agency. The adjective 'likely' (without any further qualifiers) signals the requirement of a moderate risk. While this risk must be evidence-based, the subject of the evidence gathering is quite nebulous. Furthermore, the constraints set by this specific provision might not be particularly meaningful without a clearer idea of what constitutes a risk to the overall functioning of the Schengen area.

*9.2.1.1.1 Scenario #1: Unforeseeable and foreseeable events, public health emergencies*
Within the general framework, the SBC allows the reintroduction of checks in the following scenarios: on the basis of Articles 25a and 28, taking into account the criteria set in Article 26(1); or Article 29, in which case the criteria stated in Article 30 would apply.[16] Interestingly, and as regards the prolonging of the control, the SBC provides that the same threat 'should be considered to exist' where the reasons adduced by the member state for extending the duration of the control are the same as those invoked when reinstating them in the first place. Therefore, the provision seems to establish a presumption that a threat is lingering simply because a member state declared so.[17]

There are controls reintroduced in connection with unforeseeable or foreseeable events.[18] The unforeseeable situation refers to a public policy or internal security threat in a member state. It must require immediate action and allow the state to reintroduce controls immediately. As this happens, the state must also inform the Council, the EP, the Commission, and the other member states.[19] The controls can last for a maximum of a month initially, and three months in total after they have been prolonged.

The same provision allows member states to reintroduce controls in the case of foreseeable threats for a maximum duration of six months, which can be prolonged by subsequent six-month periods for a maximum total of two additional years. When controls have been in place for six months, however, any further extension must be accompanied by a risk assessment detailing the 'anticipated evolution' of the threat and containing information concerning coordination with the affected member states.[20] The peremptory nature of the two-year duration is relative, since the member state can extend checks by a further six months in the case of a 'major exceptional situation'.[21] The state must notify the relevant EU institutions and the affected member

[16] In the case where controls are prolonged, Article 26(2) applies too.
[17] SBC, Article 25(3).
[18] This ground, enshrined in Article 25a, has been inserted as an autonomous ground by the reform of the SBC.
[19] This is in accordance with Article 27(1) SBC.
[20] SBC, Article 27(2).
[21] SBC, Article 25(6a).

state(s) of its intention to rely on this provision. This last notification must take account of the Commission's opinion[22] and include a risk assessment containing the following elements:[23] evidence of the continuing threat and the reasons why other measures are considered or have proven ineffective to remedy; mitigating measures; and a plan for the lifting of the controls *where appropriate*. Upon receipt of the notification, the Commission can or must (if requested by a member state affected) establish a consultation process (see below). Within three months following the notification, the Commission must issue another opinion. Lo and behold, this is not the end of the road. In fact, the last subparagraph of Article 25a(6a) allows a further six-month-extension-of-the-extension-of-the-extension, in line with the risk assessment mentioned above and on the basis of a 'major exceptional' situation combined with the unavailability of sufficiently effective alternative measures to address the threat. The member state is only obliged to notify the Commission in this case, which must in turn adopt a recommendation stating it considers the compatibility of prolongation with Treaties and identify, *where appropriate*, compensatory measures to be implemented. The reformed SBC has also added a ground for reintroducing checks in reaction to large-scale public health emergencies that put at risk the overall functioning of the Schengen area.[24] Checks can be performed for an initial period of six months maximum and, upon proposal from the Commission, be prolonged by six months for each extension and for as long as the emergency persists.[25] Based on the evolution of the emergency and the impact of the measure, the Commission must regularly assess whether the controls are still justified. If member states decide to introduce the controls, they must immediately notify the Commission, the Council, the European Parliament, and the other member states. Member states remain free to take alternative measures to limit the scope of controls, with the Commission taking this into account in its review. A public health threat does not seem to be treated that differently from menaces caused by crime or terrorism, to the extent that the most the EU institutions can do is to authorize the reintroduction of controls. The framework established here is clearly distinct from those discussed above when it comes to its degree of specificity, which is rather difficult to explain.

The framework grants the states a wide margin for reintroducing and prolonging border checks. In the case of a foreseeable threat, the checks can last for as long as three years. When it comes to public health emergencies, there is no set limit for how protracted those checks can be. This is remarkable for a self-professed area without internal border controls. Combined with the heterogeneity of decision-making centres and sources justifying the checks, the SBC redefines the balance between the objectives of ensuring free movement and internal security in favour of the latter. In this new legal set-up, member states enjoy significantly broader powers to derogate from the prohibition of internal checks. Admittedly, the EU legislature has not disregarded constitutional compliance altogether. In this case too, the SBC attempts to manage

[22] The opinion is issued on the basis of Article 27a.
[23] SBC, Article 26(2).
[24] SBC, Article 28.
[25] Article 28(3) SBC also states that when member states reintroduce or prolong controls for such a reason, their decision must be based on the Council decision.

heterogeneity via a structured mechanism built on solidarity. The overview shows the existence of a system where the performance of checks is in principle subject to a set of requirements that becomes more stringent with each extension. The obligations of risk assessments and taking account of the Commission's opinion are clear expressions of the principle of solidarity and are welcome additions to the previous version of the SBC. It is also worth noting that, for the last extension, the member state must prove the ineffectiveness of alternative measures to address, rather than remedy, the threat. The former establishes a lower threshold, meaning that it would be harder for the member states to justify keeping checks in place. Consistent with the test proposed in this book (see Figure 2.1), the fact that the member states would be derogating from a general rule (no checks) and be subject to an express obligation of procedural solidarity means that they could keep checks in place and pass a solidarity review only in the presence of particularly robust evidence substantiating the alleged threat. The evidence should be even more robust when the decision on an extension of checks ignored a contrary opinion by the Commission or other member states.

When invoking one of the grounds discussed above, the member states must take into account certain criteria established by the SBC which are relevant to the assessment of necessity and proportionality. Firstly, the member state must consider the appropriateness of controls to remedy the threat, in light of its nature, and whether other measures might not be suitable for achieving the result. These are measures of police cooperation, and particularly non-border checks and intra-EU transfer, or common measures on temporary restrictions on travel.[26] Secondly, the likely impact of controls must be considered, as regards free movement of persons as well as the functioning of cross-border regions. Those elements also form part of the risk assessment behind the extension of controls mentioned above. Thirdly, where any time controls are reintroduced or prolonged, the member states are under an obligation to take *appropriate* measures to mitigate the impact on persons and on transport of goods, 'giving particular consideration to the strong social and economic ties between cross-border regions, and to persons undertaking essential travel'.[27] In a welcome amendment to the SBC, such an impact assessment must now be part of the notification by the member state that is going to reintroduce the controls.[28] The question is, of course, how to measure appropriateness. Arguably, the member state would have to show that, based on information in its possession, the mitigating measures adopted—if any—are the only or least intrusive ones compatible with the objective of dealing with the specific ground for reintroducing control. Once again, the small print of the SBC casts doubts on the capacity of these solidarity-based mechanisms for managing heterogeneity effectively. Let us consider the case of the reintroduction of checks due to large-scale unauthorized movements. Here, the necessity and proportionality assessment must include a risk assessment and information on those movements, which can include data analysis from information systems.[29] The vagueness of this last provision is a

[26] SBC, Article 21a(2).
[27] SBC, Article 26(3).
[28] SBC, Article 27(1). This in addition to other elements that must be covered in the notification. These are identical to those laid down in the previous version of the SBC and include the data related to the serious threat and scope of the reintroduction.
[29] SBC, Article 27(3).

conduit for increasing heterogeneity: of sources of data analysis, of the authorities providing it and/or relying on it, and of information systems. Within this framework, it is not entirely implausible that a member state will pick and choose the type of information corroborating the idea that controls are necessary. If requested by the Commission, the member state must provide *any* further information.[30] This information, as apparent from the wording of the provision, can be relevant to identify possible alternative and less intrusive measures to address the threat at stake. The obligation is not limitless, however. Member states can refuse on security grounds, taking into account the confidentiality of a pending investigation. The provision does not qualify the investigation as 'criminal' and therefore leaves the member state ample discretion.

#### *9.2.1.1.2 Scenario #2: Deficiencies at the external borders and risk to the functioning of Schengen*

The path to the reintroduction of checks set out in Articles 29 and 30 SBC has been left unaltered by the 2024 reform. Those two provisions relate to exceptional circumstances that could put the overall functioning of the Schengen area at risk, by reason of persistent serious deficiencies concerning external border controls.[31] Here, we address the same question as in the previous sections: do those Articles raise doubts of constitutional compliance, given the heterogeneity of internal border controls? To answer this question, we must once again look at the criteria and procedures for reintroducing checks. Other than being persistent and serious, the deficiencies must constitute a serious threat to public policy or internal security within the Schengen area.[32] Therefore, firstly we must identify the meaning of 'serious deficiencies' through a systemic interpretation. The Regulation on the Schengen Evaluation and Monitoring Mechanism (SEMM) comes in handy, as it defines them as 'a general assessment of the situation attributed to one or more non-compliant findings which concern the effective application of the Schengen acquis and which, individually or in combination, risk to constitute *a* violation of fundamental rights or which have, or risk to have over time, a significant negative impact on one or more Member States or on the functioning of the area without internal border control'.[33] This definition must be used with, and adjusted to, the additional condition provided in Article 29 SBC that the deficiencies be persistent—that is, being associated with a lingering situation of non-compliance. Secondly, the controls can be reintroduced if the functioning of

[30] SBC, Article 27(4).

[31] In this regard, the SBC cross-refers to Article 21. These deficiencies must have been established in an evaluation report, drawn up by the Commission on the basis of Council Regulation (EU) 2022/922 on the establishment and operation of an evaluation and monitoring mechanism to verify the application of the Schengen acquis, and repealing Regulation (EU) No 1053/2013 [2022] OJ L 160/1 (SEMM Regulation).

[32] More specifically, the provision stipulates that controls can be reintroduced 'In exceptional circumstances where the overall functioning . . . is put at risk [by] deficiencies relating to external border controls'. The meaning of the 'exceptional circumstances' clause is not entirely clear. It could be interpreted as meaning that those exceptional circumstances materialize every time serious deficiencies are found, which however could cast doubt on the need for this clause to exist. Or else, and more plausibly, it should be taken to mean that not all serious deficiencies are prone to resulting in a risk of the kind stated in Article 29, but only in exceptional circumstances.

[33] SEMM Regulation, Article 2.

the area without border controls is *at risk* due to the threat caused by the deficiencies at the external borders. What would this predictive assessment of dysfunctionality be focused on? How would that dysfunction manifest itself? The absence of permanent checks marks the temperature of its (dys)function. Either controls are reintroduced ex ante, to address a threat preventatively, or ex post, after the materialization of the threat has proven the absence of controls to be unsustainable, even if caused by the deficiencies at the external borders. In any case, regulated and temporary internal controls are a way to avoid their permanent reintroduction. The use of the adjective 'overall' suggests that the Schengen area as a whole could collapse: namely, that checks be reintroduced by one or more member states on a permanent basis, due to the actual or perceived impossibility to keep ensuring a high level of internal security while performing internal checks only on a temporary and exceptional basis. Checks under Article 29 SBC can last for a first period of a maximum of six months, possibly followed by a maximum of three extensions of up to six months each. In this case as well, the Council can act only on the basis of a proposal from the Commission. The Council's recommendation must come as a last resort as a way to 'protect the common interests' of the Schengen area, where other measures are ineffective in mitigating the threat.[34] Like with other grounds for reintroducing controls, the SBC establishes a number of criteria that must be relied on for these purposes.[35] In its assessment, the Council must consider the proportionality of internal control and the likelihood that it will adequately remedy the threat.[36] The factors that the Council must take into account include, but are not limited to, the likely impact of serious deficiencies at the external border or the likely impact of controls on the free movement of persons.

Similarly to the previous scenario, the framework of Article 29 SBC is meant to mitigate the impact of heterogeneity. Two main features of that framework undermine the effectiveness in achieving that objective. The heterogeneity of sources, criteria, and factors of assessment, as well as the absence of any hint at which one of them should be paid particular attention, leaves the Council in a situation of extremely wide discretion. Also, the Council should form its view on the basis of different 'benchmarks'; at different points, it is stated that other measures have been deemed ineffective in mitigating or remedying the threat, but these thresholds clearly entail different levels of severity. Further, as the analysis below shows, the heterogeneous governance of internal border controls has led to the emergence of different understandings of the notion of

[34] These measures include the deployment of European border guard teams, or the submission of strategic plans. The list of measures enumerated in Article 21, however, is not exhaustive. Considering that this version of Article 21 predates Regulation (EU) 2019/1896 on the European Border and Coast Guard and repealing Regulations (EU) No 1052/2013 and (EU) 2016/1624 (EBCG Regulation) [2019] OJ L 295/1, it might well be that the Commission would recommend stronger measures, which in turn might make the need for the Council's recommendation less pressing.

[35] SBC, Article 30.

[36] While the paragraph concerning the Commission stipulates that the Commission must take these actions 'before adopting the proposal', the Council must perform its assessment 'where [it] recommends . . . the temporary reintroduction of border control'. It would not make sense to imagine that the Council would make the assessment only after it has adopted the recommendation, or as it does so. The wording of the text suggests a certain contemporaneity between the assessment and the recommendation. This probably means that this assessment will form part—at least to an extent—of the recommendation itself, having already been carried out before the formal issuing thereof.

'threat', developed by certain states' highest jurisdiction, which has in turn led to the 'validation' of questionable uses of Article 29 SBC.

#### 9.2.1.2 Passage of time

The issue of passage of time is key to the reintroduction and prolongation of checks. In this regard, two interrelated factors are at play: the types of threat for which checks have been reintroduced and their continuity. As to the former, the non-identity of the threat is a decisive criterion in determining whether the maximum duration of allowed checks has been reached. As discussed in the previous sections, this varies in relation to the type of threat and ground invoked. The SBC refers to an overall maximum period of allowed checks only in situations where such checks have been prolonged. On this basis, we can assume that the relevance of that calculation presupposes that checks have been kept in place over different periods of time and in immediate succession. The prolongation on the same ground would require the identity of a threat. The SBC provides no direct answer to less linear scenarios. Different threats might underpin the reintroduction of border controls in succession. This seems easier to justify, as long as the relevant conditions and procedures laid down in the SBC are complied with. Less obvious is the answer in situations where controls have been reinstated at two or more points in time without continuity, on the basis of the same threat of a terrorist attack against the same target and on the part of the same actor/organization. When the ground is invoked at different points, and in relation to essentially the same threat, the question arises as to whether the clock starts ticking again, and whether there is a minimum amount of time or required circumstances that would break the continuity. For example, would a gap of only a few days fall under that circumstance?

#### 9.2.1.3 Strengthening procedural solidarity: Focus on the consultation procedure

The previous sections have shown the possible impact of heterogeneity of internal border controls, and of decision-making centres specifically, on constitutional compliance. We have also seen that the new SBC attempts to deal with the side effects of such heterogeneity through a series of solidarity-driven mechanisms. In this section, we look closely at the main example of such a mechanism: the consultation procedure.[37] The Commission *may* start this process, following the notification by a member state that they intend to reintroduce or prolong internal controls. The Commission *must* do so, if requested by a member state directly affected.[38] What this consultation entails, or what form it could take, is not exhaustively explained. There is a reference to joint meetings between the member states[39] and the relevant Union agencies.[40] The 2024

[37] SBC, Article 27a.

[38] It is most likely that the member states are those bordering with the country reinstating controls. The expression used by the Code, however, seems to be more flexible and allow for the involvement of other states that, while not in the immediate proximity where checks are being reintroducing, are nonetheless impacted by them.

[39] The provision, in fact, only mentions the other member states and especially those directly affected, but this should not be interpreted as restricting the range of states that could participate in the meeting.

[40] Even if the provision only refers to the member states and the relevant agencies in the context of the joint meeting, the reader should not be under the illusion that the wording rigidly restricts the types of authorities or bodies that could potentially be in the consultation process. The flexibly framing of the

Commission Recommendation on member states' cooperation on security threats might offer some useful elements in this regard.[41] Especially in cases of cross-border unauthorized movement within Schengen, the member states are encouraged to intensify police controls in the internal border areas[42] and give preference to targeted checks based on a data-driven approach. The decision on the reintroduction of controls should be discussed in advance with the neighbouring member state(s), and be based on a joint risk analysis.[43] When such controls are reintroduced, the member states concerned must organize bilateral meetings to monitor the evolution of the threat and examine the proportionality of the measure. Furthermore, they must provide all relevant information to the Schengen Coordinator if they so request—even though it is not clear what the role entails nor what are the tasks associated with it. While the Recommendation makes no express reference to the consultation procedure, it is not implausible that it will also cover some of the above-mentioned aspects.

Turning back to the SBC, the consultation procedure is not confined to a specific type of procedure for the reintroduction of control. Therefore, it could also take place when controls are reintroduced immediately, the notification being sent simultaneously with the adoption of such a measure.[44] The purpose of the consultation process is to examine *in particular* the threat, the necessity, and proportionality of controls, with account being taken of possible alternative measures, the impact of controls, and cooperation between member states. The member state must take into account the results of the consultation when making a decision on reintroducing or prolonging the controls, as well as when performing them. The practical relevance of this new procedure remains to be seen. The member state is under an obligation to *take into account* the consultation process—once again, an obligation of means rather than of results.[45] However, the scope of the obligation is not confined to the decision-making process, but also covers its implementation. This is significant because a member state might potentially be found in breach of EU law for having disproportionately resorted to checks *in practice*, while operating in a situation where their use was in principle justified.

consultation leaves significant discretion. Given the nature of the grounds that member states can invoke to reintroduce controls, it is very likely that the consultation would significantly rely on intelligence from law enforcement authorities. Furthermore, we should also expect an increasing role for Frontex and the Immigration Liaison Officer in the internal activities of the Union and the Schengen area.

[41] Commission Recommendation (EU) 2024/268 on cooperation between the Member States with regard to serious threats to internal security and public policy in the area without internal border controls C(2023) 8139 final.

[42] Commission Recommendation (EU) 2024/268 8.

[43] Commission Recommendation (EU) 2024/2689.

[44] One might argue that consultation is even more important in such a scenario, considering that the directly affected member states have had no time to adjust to the measure and might therefore feel the impact thereof to a greater extent than they would, had they been notified weeks in advance.

[45] While the provision of an obligation of results is implausible, and even of dubious legality, it is important to highlight the limits of an obligation of means too.

#### 9.2.1.4 Proper implementation of the SBC before the Court

The different expressions of heterogeneity considered in this book have an impact on the constitutional compliance of internal border controls. The absence of controls must go hand in hand with a high level of internal security. The inherent tension in that dual objective is compounded by the heterogeneity of actors and persons concerned. Opening the borders while differentiating between persons with and without a right to free movement warrants mechanisms to counter irregular movement within Schengen. While the governance of internal border controls is shared, the link between border-related decisions and security means that the member states remain the ultimate masters of their own destiny—if within a regulatory framework often inspired by mutual trust and solidarity. Beyond creating a heterogeneity of decision-making centres, the shared governance also produces ambiguities about the nature of security (internal to what?) and about the appropriate locus of political and legal authority empowered to defend it. When it comes to measures applicable within Schengen, the Commission's approach to the functioning of the borderless area rests on coordination, cooperation on measures alternative to controls, and proper implementation of the SBC. Starting in particular with the 2015 refugee crisis, we have witnessed a stark dissociation between heterogeneity and constitutional compliance in this regard. Member states have reintroduced checks at the internal borders in a way and to an extent difficult to reconcile with the letter of the SBC and solidarity more broadly. This has also had an effect on fair treatment, to the extent that the implementation of the 'practice' (the SBC) has been inconsistent with the objectives and the principles underlying it. While the Commission itself is supposed to act as the guardian of the Treaties, questions have been raised about how effectively it has played that role in this context. For example, despite the appeals to coordination and cooperation in its Communications, in none of its post-2015 annual reports on the application of EU law has the Commission mentioned once the persistence of internal border checks. Perhaps as a result of that lingering inertia in an era of perpetual prolongation of internal checks, in 2022 the Court for the first time ever ruled on member states' compliance with the relevant provisions of the Code.[46] The case originated from an action brought before an Austrian court by NW, who was subject to border checks when entering Austria from Slovenia by car. While the referring court acknowledged that those checks would in principle be prohibited by the SBC, it also recalled the two exceptions enshrined in the Regulation: a serious threat to public policy or internal security;[47] and, persistent serious deficiencies relating to external border controls, putting at risk the functioning of the area without internal border control.[48] Initially, the controls were based on Council recommendations or were otherwise consistent

[46] Joined Cases C-368/20 and C-369/20, *NW v Landespolizeidirektion Steiermark and Bezirkshauptmannschaft Leibnitz*, EU:C:2022:298. See the series of blogposts by Marta Morvillo and Pola Cebulak on the Verfassungblog: 'The Guardian is Absent: Legality of Border Controls within Schengen Before the European Court of Justice', 25 June 2021; 'The Writing is on the Wall: Proportionality of Border Controls Within the Schengen Area', 11 October 2021; 'Schengen Restored: The CJEU Sets Clear Limits to the Reintroduction of Internal Border Controls', 5 May 2022.

[47] SBC, former Article 25(1).

[48] SBC, Article 29(1).

with the time limit set in the SBC under Article 29 thereof—serious and persistent deficiencies at the external borders. However, from October 2017 to November 2021, and in the absence of further recommendations, Austria prolonged controls every six months on the basis of successive ministerial decrees by relying on Articles 25 and 27. Former Article 25(1) stipulated that member states could reintroduce controls for a period of a maximum of 30 days, possibly prolonged each time for an equal maximum duration for a total of no longer than six months, or two years in the case of serious and persistent deficiencies at the external borders. Therefore, the wording of the SBC left no room for misunderstanding, as far as the maximum duration of controls is concerned.

Two interrelated themes, relevant to the framework of this book, were developed by the Court: the relation between the heterogeneous objectives governed by the SBC, and the concept of 'threat' allowing for reintroduction or prolongation of controls. Pursuant to Articles 3 TEU and 67 TFEU, free movement of persons is ensured in conjunction with appropriate (compensatory) measures.[49] Those provisions, and the measures of secondary law giving effect to them, aim to strike a *fair* balance between free movement of persons and the safeguarding of public policy and internal security 'of the territory on which they move'.[50] The link between the territory (singular) and the exercise of free movement seems to give the former a Schengen-wide dimension (as opposed to national), and so it goes for the concept of internal security. This impression might be misplaced. The Court developed no clear understanding of fairness either, but rather focused on the crucial relation between the notion of 'threat' and passage of time.[51]

The starting assumption was that, in an area without internal borders, the reintroduction of controls must constitute the exception and be used as a measure of last resort.[52] Now, both reintroduction and prolongation of controls presuppose the existence of a new, or persisting, threat. Prolongation must take place on the basis of the same threat that justified the reintroduction in the first place. New elements can be taken into account in this regard, but they must be connected to this threat.[53] Given the wording and the spirit of Article 25 SBC, allowing the prolongation of controls beyond the maximum time limit established therein on the basis of the persistence of the threat

> even when assessed in the light of new elements, or of a reappraisal of the necessity and proportionality of the border control established to respond to it [would] in practice effectively allow the reintroduction of internal border control on account of the same threat for an unlimited period, thereby compromising the very principle that there is to be no internal border control, as enshrined in Article 3(2) TEU and reiterated in Article 67(2) TFEU.[54]

[49] Case C-341/18, *Staatssecretaris van Justitie en Veiligheid*, EU:C:2020:76, para 55 and case law cited.
[50] Joined Cases C-368/20 and C-369/20, *NW*, para 72.
[51] On the relevance of this relation to assess compliance with the SBC, see section 9.2.1.2.
[52] Joined Cases C-368/20 and C-369/20, *NW*, para 65.
[53] Joined Cases C-368/20 and C-369/20, *NW*, para 62.
[54] Joined Cases C-368/20 and C-369/20, *NW*, para 66.

Such an expansive interpretation of Article 25 would also render meaningless the distinction between this ground for reintroduction and Article 29. In the presence of a new serious threat, however, a member state could potentially reintroduce controls even directly after the end of a two-year period of internal controls under Article 29 SBC—and provided that the conditions established in the SBC are fulfilled.[55] Therefore, the existence of a new serious threat to public policy or internal security is a *condicio sine qua* for resetting the clock of internal controls. These maximum periods and conditions are an expression of the balance between free movement and the member states' interest—duly taken into account by the EU legislature—'in safeguarding the security of their territories'.[56] In the end, the Schengen territory is always the (heterogeneous) sum of the territories of all its states: the decision about reintroduction and prolongation of controls is theirs (within certain limits), and so is the internal nature of security interests underlying those decisions. Despite the potential relevance to the case at hand, the concept of 'new threat' was not addressed in detail by the Court. The Court did imply, however, that the newness—and so the resetting of the check's clock—requires a certain degree of distinction. As that concept might pave the way to long and consecutive periods of controls, it could emerge as one of the next interpretative battlegrounds of the SBC. This is shown in the analysis below, with the highest jurisdiction courts in France and Norway taking a clear stance on how the newness should be understood.[57]

#### 9.2.1.5 Irregular border crossing in an area with (temporary) internal controls

When it comes to member states' practices at the internal border in reaction to border crossing, the heterogeneity of internal border controls raises questions about the type of legal regime applicable to those borders. For the purposes of our assessment of constitutional compliance, we must distinguish between different scenarios. Firstly, there are the actions taken when checks have been lawfully reintroduced. The consistent pushbacks by several member states have sparked a debate about the permissible measures a member state can take against irregular border crossers.[58] Secondly, a similar debate has emerged where the internal border is formally being left open. The reformed SBC aims to deal with these scenarios via a framework of interstate cooperation.[59] Thirdly, a related yet different issue concerns the legality of interstate readmission agreement. These have also drawn the attention of institutions[60]

[55] This can also be inferred from Article 29(5) SBC, according to which that Article shall be without prejudice to measures that may be adopted by the Member States in the event of a serious threat to public policy or internal security under Articles 25, 27, and 28.

[56] Joined Cases C-368/20 and C-369/20, *NW*, para 76.

[57] See section 9.2.3 below.

[58] See, among many, A Kompatscher, 'Border Controls and Pushbacks as the New Normal? The Tension Between Freedom of Movement and Migration Management Under the Reformed Schengen Border Control Regulation' (2025) Quaderni AISDUE—Rivista quadrimestrale 1.

[59] It is submitted that Article 23a is not applicable where checks have been reinstated. This is apparent from the opening clause of that provision: '*Without prejudice to Article 22*, this Article lays down the procedure for the transfer of a third-country national apprehended in border areas as referred to in *Article 23*' (emphases added). Article 22 enshrines the prohibition of internal checks, whereas Article 23 concerns non-border checks within the member state's territory.

[60] See on one of such agreements, European Court of Human Rights, *HT v Germany and Greece*, judgment 15 October 2024, App no 13337/19.

and the literature.[61] Here, we focus on the member states' conduct where checks are formally back in place. This is the area where the Court's case law has developed to a greater extent, and its discussion can also help us answer the question about the legality of the other practices mentioned above.[62] According to the SBC, where checks at internal borders have been reintroduced, its relevant provisions on external border controls would apply *mutatis mutandis*.[63] Those provisions include the rule mandating member states to apprehend and return a TCN that has crossed the border illegally and has no right to stay in that member state *in accordance with the Return Directive*.[64] This being the case, the applicability of that Directive to apprehension at the internal borders must be considered.[65] We can distinguish between three different scenarios. The first situation can be called the *Affum* scenario, from the name of the first case on this issue ever addressed by the Court.[66] Ms Affum is a Ghanaian national who was subject to a check by French police officers at the point of entry into the Channel Tunnel, when she was on a bus from Belgium to the UK. French authorities took the view that she should be readmitted by Belgium. Therefore, this is a situation where a TCN without authorization to stay in the EU is intercepted at an internal Schengen border, as they are travelling through Schengen to reach a member state which is not in the area without internal border controls. The Court found that the Return Directive applies in such a situation, and member states cannot derogate from it on the basis of Article 2(2)(a) thereof. This provision allows member states not to apply the Return Directive to TCNs who: are subject to a refusal of entry in accordance with (former) Article 13 (now 14) SBC; or, are apprehended or intercepted by the competent authorities in connection with the irregular crossing by land, sea, or air of the external border of a member state and who have not subsequently obtained an authorization or a right to stay in that state. While Ms Affum's situation was clearly different from the former scenario, the Court considered that she fell outside the scope of the latter too. The reference to the fact that the interception or apprehension must have occurred in connection with the irregular crossing implies 'a direct temporal and spatial link with that crossing of the [external] border' and concerns persons apprehended or intercepted 'at the very time of the irregular crossing of the border or near that border after it has been so crossed'.[67] This seemed not to be the case in *Affum*. Furthermore, the second situation under Article 2(2)(a) concerns cases where those nationals have entered (or attempted to enter) the territory of the state concerned, rather than left (or sought to leave) the Schengen area.

[61] E Pistoia, 'Rule of Law Backsliding Within the EU: The Case of Informal Readmissions of Third-Country Nationals at Internal Border' (2024) 30 European Law Journal 60.

[62] For a comment, see I Barbero, 'A Ubiquitous Border for Migrants in Transit and Their Rights: Analysis and Consequences of the Reintroduction of Internal Borders in France' (2020) 22 European Journal of Migration and Law 366.

[63] SBC, Article 32.

[64] SBC, Article 13.

[65] Directive 2008/115/EC on common standards and procedures in Member States for returning illegally staying third-country nationals [2008] OJ L 348/98 (or Return Directive).

[66] Case C-47/15, *Sélina Affum v Préfet du Pas-de-Calais, Procureur général de la cour d'appel de Douai*, EU:C:2016:408. See for comment G Zaccaroni, 'The Pragmatism of the Court of Justice on the Detention of Irregular Migrants: Comment on Affum' (2017) 2 European Papers 449.

[67] Case C-47/15, *Affum*, para 72.

Therefore, the internal border and its crossing by an irregular TCN play no meaningful role in this context, either factually or legally.

We will name the second, more straightforward, situation as the *Arib* scenario. Here, we are dealing with the case of a TCN who had received a removal order from French authorities and had tried to re-enter the country via Spain. However, since France had reintroduced border controls, he was checked and apprehended in the vicinity of that border.[68] The Court reiterated the principle that member states can only derogate from the Return Directive where the apprehension or refusal of entry takes place at its external borders. As the derogation under Article 2(2)(a) should be interpreted strictly, member states cannot rely on that provision as regards the treatment of a person intercepted at the internal borders where controls have been re-introduced.[69] A third scenario concerning the application of the Return Directive to intra-Schengen border crossing was discussed in *ADDE*.[70] In this case as well, the preliminary ruling concerned the compatibility of French law with the Return Directive. Specifically, the relevant national provisions allowed state authorities, in the context of internal border checks, to refuse entry to a TCN on the basis of Article 14 SBC and without applying the Return Directive. The Court found that that provision of the SBC would certainly be applicable in those situations: a person who is trying to cross the border must be refused entry if they do not fulfil the conditions stated in the SBC.[71] This being said, a person found to be staying illegally on the territory of a member state—including that of first irregular entry—falls within the scope of the Return Directive and must be subject to the procedures established therein unless otherwise dictated by the specific circumstances.[72] This would be the case where the person has been apprehended at a border crossing where the crossing is in that state's territory.[73] In this regard, the Court provided an interesting example to explain its view on this matter. Specifically, it observed that a check performed on a train at the last station before leaving a state territory and entering into a state that has reintroduced internal controls, must be considered a check at a border crossing point of the second state, unless otherwise agreed by the two states involved.[74] Where the crossing point is in the member state that has reintroduced controls, this state must ensure that the application of Article 14 SBC does not lead to disregarding the standards and procedures set in the Return Directive.[75]

[68] Case C-444/17, *Préfet des Pyrénées-Orientales v Abdelaziz Arib, Procureur de la République près le tribunal de grande instance de Montpellier, Procureur général près la cour d'appel de Montpellier*, EU:C:2019:220. See S Bartolini, 'Return Directive or Criminal Law? The Next Episode of the Series is Called Arib', EU Migration Law Blog, 24 July 2019.

[69] Case C-444/17, *Arib*, paras 50 and 67.

[70] Case C-143/22, *ADDE and Others*, EU:C:2023:689.

[71] Case C-143/22, *ADDE and Others*, para 30.

[72] For example, if their stay has been regularized. Case C-143/22, *ADDE and Others*, paras 30–31. See C Raucea, 'Refusal of Entry or Return? The Court's Ambiguous Conclusions in ADDE and Others' (8 December 2023). Available at SSRN: https://ssrn.com/abstract = 4940274 or http://dx.doi.org/10.2139/ssrn.4940274

[73] In fact, a person can enter a state territory without crossing a crossing point. See Case C-341/18, *Staatssecretaris van Justitie en Veiligheid*, para 45.

[74] Case C-143/22, *ADDE and Others*, para 32.

[75] As the Court stated at para 40 of the judgment: 'The fact that this obligation on the Member State concerned is likely to render ineffective to a large extent any decision to refuse entry to a third-country national arriving at one of its internal borders is not such as to alter that finding'.

Through a rigorous interpretation of the relevant legal framework, the Court has attempted to mitigate the impact of heterogeneity on constitutional compliance. On a broader level, precluding member states from derogating from the common framework when checks at the internal borders have been reinstated is meant to pre-empt the risk of (further) fragmentation. As a result, it aims to reduce unilateralism and unfair treatment of the persons apprehended. In clarifying that the Return Directive remains applicable to apprehension in the context of internal border checks, the Court answers the question about the legality of pushbacks within Schengen. The answer is negative. The apprehending state is under an obligation to perform an individualized assessment and implement return procedures, unless they have a readmission agreement with another state.[76] As for people applying for international protection, the rules on the identification of the state responsible for examining the claim established in the Dublin Regulation would apply.[77] The same would go for apprehension and pushback where checks have not been formally reinstated. The Return Directive would still apply. Derogation from that Directive is now allowed under Article 23a SBC, but such a scenario presupposes the existence of a bilateral agreement and is not applicable to asylum seekers or beneficiaries of international protection.[78] Several such agreements have raised controversy, particularly as regards the treatment of asylum seekers.[79] To ensure fair treatment of the person concerned, the framework at the bilateral level must comply with the criteria concerning the identification of the state responsible for the examination of the asylum claim. Neither the Dublin Regulation[80] nor the new Asylum Regulation Procedure[81] enable bilateral agreements to derogate from these criteria. Furthermore, as these agreements fall clearly within the scope of EU law, their compatibility with this law could certainly be scrutinized by the Court of Justice. Their informal nature would not detract from the argument, as the Court could consider the compliance of member states' practices too—indirectly, of course, through an interpretation of EU law.

#### 9.2.1.6 Interim conclusions

As regards the impact of heterogeneity on constitutional compliance of internal border controls, the analysis by the SBC and the Court has hitherto painted a complex picture. The reform of the Code has marked a clear shift in a context where the ultimate decision on the reintroduction of checks is left to the member states. These states have seen their leeway increase significantly, if constrained by mechanisms, procedures, and conditions, giving effect to the principle of solidarity as a duty to take account of the common interest. While such mechanisms are meant to enhance constitutional compliance, two factors make us question their effectiveness in managing

[76] Return Directive, Article 6(3).

[77] See E Tsourdi, 'Not Only Legally Dubious But Also Ineffective', Verfassungsblog, 27 September 2024.

[78] SBC, Article 23a(1).

[79] Kompatscher, 'Border Controls and Pushbacks as the New Normal' 5 onwards.

[80] Regulation (EU) No 604/2013 establishing the criteria and mechanisms for determining the Member State responsible for examining an application for international protection lodged in one of the Member States by a third-country national or a stateless person (recast) [2013] OJ L 180/31, Article 36(1).

[81] Regulation (EU) 2024/1348 establishing a common procedure for international protection in the Union, Article 53(1).

heterogeneity. The first concerns their correct implementation by the member states and the EU institutions. Obvious as it is, the degree of constitutional compliance will depend on how seriously the Commission interprets its role as guardian of the Treaties. Also, a closer inspection of the fine print of the SBC limits (if not undermines) the constraining nature of these conditions and procedures. The heterogeneity of decision-making centres also implies, at least at the moment and in the Court's view, the heterogeneity of territories and internal security. In dealing with the heterogeneity of objectives of internal border controls, the CJ has shown us once again the role of structural principles in achieving constitutional compliance. The reference to a fair balance between such objectives has not been followed by a development of what that fairness would entail. The understanding of fairness proposed in this book would support this conceptual endeavour. The balance would be fair if non-arbitrary and consistent with the principles and spirit of the SBC. More specifically, reliable evidence should show that no other less restrictive measures would be capable of addressing/remedying the threat identified. As mentioned in the introduction to this scenario, the SBC builds on the distinction between prohibited and permissible checks. Having extensively discussed the former, the next sections assess the relation between heterogeneity and constitutional compliance in the latter, regard being had to the legislative framework and the Court's interpretation.

## 9.2.2 The Exercise of Public Powers and Non-Border Checks

### 9.2.2.1 The legislative framework

The prohibition of checks at the internal borders enshrines a deceptively simple idea, built on the assumption that the meaning and scope of such checks can be easily defined. The SBC itself, however, allows the exercise of police or other public powers at the borders within Schengen, as long as it does not result in measures having an equivalent effect to border checks. Such measures may include, where appropriate, monitoring and surveillance generally used in the territory to tackle threats to public security or public policy.[82] As the 'may include' suggests, the reference to surveillance is only an example of the type of measures that could be taken by national authorities. More generally, the SBC lays down a series of criteria (or indicators) which, if met, would render the measure in question different from an MEE and therefore compatible with EU law. Even in this case, however, the legal framework is rather flexible: as the SBC stipulates, 'the exercise by competent authorities of their powers shall not, *in particular*, be considered equivalent to the exercise of border checks *when the measures fulfil each of the following*' (emphasis added).

Let us take a closer look at each of these indicators. Firstly, the measure must not have border control as an objective. This is an interesting requirement since, based on the definition of border control provided in the SBC, the prevention of cross-border crime and irregular migration is *the* goal connected to the performance of that function. Secondly, the measures must be based on general police or public health

[82] SBC, Article 23.

information (depending on the threat) *and* competent authorities' experience on possible threats to public security or public policy. From the wording of the provision, it would seem that both the information and the experience must underlie the exercise of the powers. Thirdly, the measures must aim, *in particular*, to: combat cross-border crime, reduce illegal immigration, and contain the spread of a disease.[83] Apart from observing the introduction of yet another open requirement, this last clause seems to contradict fundamentally the first one (ie that such checks must not have border controls as an objective). Fourthly, they must be clearly distinct from the systematic checks as performed at the external borders.

The SBC carves out some further areas of lawful checks for the member states' benefit.[84] Member states can still perform security checks at transport hubs—including when performed by carriers—in accordance with their law and as long as they apply to intra-state journeys too.[85] In this case, the form is substance: formal equality of treatment in the law means that a measure would not have equivalent effect to border checks. Since the vocabulary is borrowed from the internal market, however, the question might be raised as to whether an assessment of the possible discrimination in practice would be warranted.[86]

The first type of check discussed above creates an opportunity for the heterogeneity of decision-making centres to grow at the expense of constitutional compliance. The provision leaves considerable discretion to the member states when it comes to the kinds of action that can be taken by their authorities in internal border areas. That discretion is, at least to an extent, constrained by the specific criteria that the measure must meet. However, the list itself is open-ended and relies on concepts that are far from straightforward. The reference to the need that the measure fulfils 'each' of the conditions hints at the cumulative nature of those criteria. However, the same provision is left open like a window on a hot night in Southern Italy: if the exercise of police powers shall not *in particular* be considered equivalent to the exercise of border checks when all those conditions are fulfilled, it still means that the member states might try to rely on other indicators to show that they are acting in compliance with the EU law. Depending on the nature of the non-border checks, their exercise might have a negative impact on constitutional in terms of solidarity, understood as a duty to take into account the common interest, and fair treatment of the persons concerned, regarded as consistency of a 'practice' (the area without internal border controls) with its spirit and principles behind it. In the next section, we discuss how the Court has

[83] The disease must have epidemic potential, as established by the European Centre for Disease Control.

[84] Member states can still impose an obligation to hold or carry 'papers and documents'. member states are still allowed to provide an obligation for TCNs to 'report their presence on its territory and the obligation for managers of establishments providing accommodation to see to it that third-country nationals complete and sign registration forms, with the exception of accompanying spouses or accompanying minors or members of travel groups, pursuant respectively to the provisions of Articles 22 and 45 CISA'.

[85] Presumably, these security checks amount to the type of checks that would apply in airports, for example. Obviously, airport security checks are quite specific in the sense that they are not normally required—not to the same extent at least—for train and coach journeys.

[86] It is not entirely clear whether the obligation would cover only identity documents or, depending on the individual situation, also documents proving the existence of a valid title of stay and movement. Possibly, the latter might seem more plausible.

dealt with said risks associated with the legal heterogeneity possibly caused by the legislative framework.

#### 9.2.2.2 Toeing the line: The definition of (non)border checks in the Court's case law

##### *9.2.2.2.1 Setting the scene: Introducing the key criteria*

The definition of what amounts to a border check, and what does not, has been substantially fleshed out by the Court of Justice over the years. This line of judgment has developed through the interpretation of the relevant provisions of the SBC set out above, within the framework of Article 67(1) TFEU, which states that the Union must ensure the absence of internal controls on any persons. Unsurprisingly, the Court's hermeneutic endeavour has mostly focused on the exercise of police powers in border areas and measures taken in the implementation thereof. As is apparent from the legislation, the application of measures throughout the territory can more easily exclude equivalence with border checks. In the absence of such a general application, the Court has interpreted the SBC in light of the requirement of legal certainty. On this basis, national law must provide the necessary framework to guide the discretion of the competent authorities and guarantee that the exercise of those powers in practice has no equivalent effect to border checks.[87] With this in mind, a number of criteria must be taken into account, regard being had to the type of authorities performing the checks, the area where they take place, their modalities, and the purposes. The idea is that where certain aspects of those checks make the equivalence more likely, such as their performance only in a border area, there must be counterbalancing factors.[88]

As reality always surpasses imagination, each national legislation on the exercise of police powers can have its own specific features. The border area, for example, is not a clearly defined concept. We can infer we are talking about a portion of a member state's territory that is marked, on one end, by its internal border with another Schengen country, but we have no criteria to determine how large this should—or should not—be in order to fall within or outwith that category. This is probably a context where the adage that size does not matter rings true. Regardless of how large or small the border area where police checks are performed, the mere fact that they apply specifically in a space contiguous to a frontier within Schengen—as opposed to anywhere in that state's territory—is enough to raise a red flag to the Court of Justice. The fact that state police authorities can exercise their powers within 30 rather than 20 km is likely to make little or no difference to the assessment of equivalence with border checks.[89]

[87] Joined Cases C-188/10 and C-189/10, *Aziz Melki and Sélim Abdeli*, EU:C:2010:363, paras 71–75. See, among many comments, G Cornelisse, 'What's Wrong With Schengen? Border Disputes and the Nature of Integration in the Area Without Internal Borders' (2014) 51 Common Market Law Review 761 onwards

[88] Case C-278/12 PPU, *Atiqullah Adil v Minister voor Immigratie, Integratie en Asiel*, EU:C:2012:508, para 75. In this specific case, the Court found that the objectives under consideration were different from those pursued through border checks. They were based on general police information and experience regarding illegal residence after the crossing of a border. They were executed in a non-systematic way. They could be carried out in border areas only for limited number of hours and not on all vehicles anyway. In practice, the checks were carried out on the basis of profiling or sample stops. The profiles depend on the information or data showing an increased risk of illegal residence or cross-border crime on certain routes, at certain times or on the basis of the type and other characteristics of the vehicles.

[89] This statement must be nuanced. In Case C-9/16, *A*, EU:C:2017:483, the Court hinted at the fact that the absence of limitations or more detailed rules seemed to play a role in the ECJ's assessment.

Other factors must be considered. While the Court leaves the verification of the compatibility of the national rules with EU law to the referring court, it provides guidance on whether certain measures might amount to MEEs. In the assessment of the Court, the law in the book and in action are inextricably linked. If the national legislation contains insufficiently detailed rules and limitations on the exercise of those powers, especially as regards their intensity, frequency, and selectivity, their practical exercise will be more likely to result in controls which have effects equivalent to border checks.[90]

*9.2.2.2.2 A catch-22 objective? Defining the goal of border controls*

We have observed that the test for distinguishing between border checks and other measures relies on a heterogeneous set of criteria. One of the main indicators, at once the most heterogeneous and deceptively simple, concerns the objectives of the measure under scrutiny. The wording of the SBC in this respect must be carefully considered. The Regulation stipulates that the exercise of public powers must not have border controls as an objective. The emphasis is on the objectives of the powers and their exercise, rather than the measures themselves. The difference in practice, however, might be immaterial. We can certainly imagine a situation where these powers are exercised in a way that is not entirely in line with the spirit of relevant legislation, including where this is the result of (mis)use of the discretion left to these authorities by state law. This is exactly why the rules on the exercise of the powers must be clearly defined, as stated by the Court.

Against this background, the assessment must focus on the legal framework and the objectives pursued by the measure through which the public powers can be exercised. Firstly, we must identify the objectives of border checks. Logic would suggest that we answer that question by looking at the relevant instruments of EU law. As already seen, one of the main narratives of this book lies precisely in the heterogeneity of these objectives, spanning from preventing unauthorized border crossing to identification of vulnerable people through to combating cross-border crime. We can draw a preliminary conclusion from this: the wider the net of those goals, the higher the chance that a measure will end up caught in it.[91] Secondly, we must identify the objectives of the national measures. In light of the above, the question we must ask is: for what reasons can public powers be exercised, pursuant to national law?[92] Thirdly, we must consider whether these reasons can be subsumed under the objectives of EU

[90] Case C-9/16, *A.*

[91] It is also important to remember that, according to the SBC, the checks can escape the prohibition if they meet *each* of the conditions established therein. Therefore, having border controls as an objective would be enough for those checks to be found in violation of EU law—regardless of the fact that they comply with all the other criteria set in Article 23 SBC. This is a very important change in the SBC introduced by the recent reform. Under the previous text of Article 23, 'the exercise of police powers may not, in particular, be considered equivalent to the exercise of border checks when the police measures [a list of criteria followed]'. The cumulative or alternative nature of these criteria was far from clear.

[92] Bearing in mind the requirement that national law governs precisely and in detail the exercise of these powers, the scenario where public authorities wrongly use the powers conferred upon them raises different questions. It would still be relevant under EU law. However, it would not have the same systemic consequences unless it was clear that the practice had been knowingly tolerated by state authorities which might have stopped them, à la *Spanish Strawberry*. This case concerned the conduct of private parties, however, so the two scenarios do not match perfectly.

border controls. This subsumption is perhaps the trickiest part of this hermeneutic exercise. In fact, EU law establishes macro-areas of objectives of controls, with the view to encompassing the largest number of measures that could be taken to prevent unauthorized entry into the Union. National law might be framed in different and more specific terms, and the issue of whether or not a more narrowly defined task can be considered as falling within one of these macro-areas might not always find a straightforward response. These reflections apply only to *one* of the criteria of equivalence established in the SBC; when considered together with each and every one of the others, we can see how complex the assessment can be. For example, would the exercise of public powers in a border area have border controls as an objective, when they aim to prevent or terminate unlawful entry into or residence in a member state, or prevent criminal offences undermining the security of the border or the implementation of border protection or which are committed in connection with the crossing of the border, irrespective of the behaviour of the person concerned and of the existence of specific circumstances, without there being any temporary reintroduction of border controls?[93] The Court acknowledged that the criteria enumerated by the SBC constituted no exhaustive list. It also observed that member states retain powers on preventing illegal migration and residence, as long as these powers are exercised in compliance with EU law.[94] Therefore, the fact that checks performed in a border area pursue the objectives mentioned above is not enough to bring them under the definition of border checks.

#### 9.2.2.2.3 *Modality of exercise*

Alongside the objectives, the modality of exercise seems to be one of the key factors to determine the equivalence between police and border checks. In this regard, the Court will consider a number of aspects. One aspect is the basis for the exercise of powers. If the checks are performed following certain police information, or relate to the personal behaviour or circumstances that could result in a risk to public order, they would be more likely to comply with EU law. In the absence of such specific 'triggers', checks are more likely to be carried out systematically than selectively, or in the form of spot checks.

Another aspect concerns the performance of checks on cross-border transport. We can have a situation where public authorities can check, on board trains and railway premises, the documents of any person, and briefly stop and question them in this connection. Such checks would be based on knowledge of the situation or border police experience, to the extent that the train or railway premises might have been used for unlawful entry into the territory of that member state. The ultimate objective of the measure would thus be the prevention and termination of unlawful entry into that member state. While these elements would mitigate in favour of a finding of non-equivalence, the question of whether they are executed in a manner clearly distinct from systematic checks is also crucial.

93 Case C-9/16, *A*, EU:C:2017:483.

94 More specifically, the Court refers here to Article 79(1) and (2)(c) TFEU.

#### 9.2.2.2.4 *The role of private carriers*

An important question concerns the imposition of a duty by national law to check on private parties, such as coach operators.[95] In *Touring Tours*, under scrutiny there was a German law establishing a twofold obligation: for all foreign nationals, to be in possession of an identity document and to submit to police checks when crossing a border; and for the carriers, on threat of punishment, to bring into the territory only those with a document or a residence permit. In particular, any coach transport undertakings providing cross-border service within Schengen were supposed to check the passports and residence permits of passengers before they crossed an internal border, with a view to preventing cross-border movement of TCNs without travel documents. The national legislation also allowed police authorities to enforce this obligation against said undertaking, by issuing an order prohibiting the transport and a recurring fine for the companies which had transported TCNs without travel documents into the territory. In principle, the Court has found that there was no equivalence in cases where the checks were not performed at borders or when the border was crossed, but in the territory of the member state.[96] This is only the starting point, however, since the assessment of the criteria established in the SBC requires a deeper examination. The outsourcing of checks to a private actor, in this sense, cannot work as a 'get out of jail' card: the checks which a company is obliged to perform might still fall within the scope of Article 23 SBC. Otherwise, that provision could easily be circumvented and its effectiveness compromised. As regards the territorial scope of those checks, their application throughout the state territory would make a finding of equivalence with border checks less likely. A difference in modality of exercise linked to the area of application would not make those checks automatically equivalent to those prohibited under Article 22 SBC, however. The Code imposes no requirement that the methods and purposes of police checks carried out in a border area be identical to those carried out throughout the national territory.[97]

The reform of the SBC could be particularly relevant to the assessment of equivalence between police and border checks. The questions raised in *Touring Tours* concerned the previous version of the SBC, which did not specify that police checks must meet *each* of the listed criteria. In this judgment, the Court found that 'if some of those indicators are present, the checks in question will be authorised only if they are carried out within a framework, in national legislation identifying those checks, which is governed by detailed rules and limitations, which are themselves sufficiently precise and detailed with regard to the intensity, frequency and selectivity of those checks'.[98] The idea behind the principle is clear: the more extensive the indicia reflected in that national legislation, in relation to the objective pursued by the checks carried out in a border area, the territorial scope of those checks and the existence of a distinction between the basis of those checks and that of the checks carried out in the remainder of the territory of the Member State concerned, the greater the need for those detailed

[95] Joined Cases C-412/17 and C-474/17, *Bundesrepublik Deutschland v Touring Tours und Travel GmbH, Sociedad de Transportes SA*, EU:C:2018:1005.

[96] Joined Cases C-188/10 and C-189/10, *Melki and Abdeli*, para 68.

[97] Joined Cases C-412/17 and C-474/17, *Touring Tours*, para 51.

[98] Joined Cases C-412/17 and C-474/17, *Touring Tours*, para 54.

rules and limitations to be strict and strictly observed.[99] This principle should apply even more rigorously, following the amendment of the SBC mentioned above.

The Court has also clarified that, in its view, border checks aim to ensure that persons may be authorized to enter or leave the territory of a member state, and prevent persons from circumventing border checks. If the checks aim to verify that the conditions for entry laid down in the SBC are satisfied—as was the case in *Touring Tours*—they can be seen as having border controls as an objective. With regard to the modality of exercise, while the systemic nature of police checks in a border area is not a cause of automatic equivalence,[100] the general nature of the obligation imposed on the coach transport undertaking is a possible symptom thereof.[101] In this regard, it was of little relevance that these checks were not performed by the carrier to the same depth as they would have been by the police, since they still systematically address all persons travelling on all cross-border services. The fact that the obligation of controls was triggered by the cross-border nature of the service only corroborated the finding of equivalence.[102] The combined operation of these factors and 'their relative weight', as well as the absence of limitations and rules in the national legislation, made those measures equivalent to border checks.[103] Another important aspect of the question concerned the lawfulness of the enforcement powers conferred upon the national authorities to police the compliance of the transport undertakings with that obligation incompatible with EU law. It seems safe to argue that, in light of the previous considerations, those powers would be precluded by the SBC.[104]

*9.2.2.2.5 Measures sui generis: Health-related checks during a pandemic*

As known, the Covid-19 pandemic constituted a health emergency that most—if not all—European countries were unprepared to confront. The resilience of Schengen was one of the areas where that unpreparedness showed most visibly, with member states introducing measures often difficult to square with EU law and without much coordination among themselves and the EU institutions. Despite the heterogeneity of such measures taken across Schengen, only one significant example of litigation reached the Court of Justice.[105] Under consideration was the compatibility of two measures taken by Belgium with the Citizenship Directive[106] and the SBC, respectively.

[99] Case C-9/16, *A*, paras 38–41.

[100] Case C-278/12 PPU, *Adil*, para 61.

[101] The obligation covered all cross-border services, irrespective of the conduct of the persons concerned or of circumstances giving rise to a risk to public order.

[102] This somehow resonates with the definition of a measure having equivalent effect to customs duties as a charge levied on a good for the mere fact that it crosses a border.

[103] Joined Cases C-412/17 and C-474/17, *Touring Tours*, para 73.

[104] Joined Cases C-412/17 and C-474/17, *Touring Tours*, para 73, the Court stated that the SBC precludes 'the provision [of the national legislation] in so far as it penalises an infringement of the general obligation to carry out checks . . . by way of an order prohibiting transport, together with a threat to impose a recurring fine. Such a penalty provision is not compatible with [former] Article 21(a) [of the SBC], inasmuch as it is imposed in order to ensure compliance with the obligation to carry out checks which itself does not comply with that provision'.

[105] Case C-128/22, *NORDIC INFO*, EU:C:2023:645. See VN Delhomme, 'The Legality of COVID-19 Travel Restrictions in an "Area Without Internal Frontiers": Court of Justice (Grand Chamber) 5 December 2023, Case C-128/22, "Nordic Info."' (2024) 20 European Constitutional Law Review 307.

[106] More specifically, Articles 27 and 29 of Directive 2004/38, read in conjunction with Articles 4 and 5 thereof.

The former constituted a legislation of general application which, on public health grounds, prohibited Union citizens and their family members from engaging in non-essential travel from Belgium to member states classified by the former as high-risk zones based on their epidemiological situation. It also required Union citizens who were not Belgian nationals to undergo screening tests and quarantine when entering the country from one of those high-risk states. These measures were regarded as compatible with the Citizenship Directive, as long as they complied with all the conditions and safeguards referred to in Articles 30 to 32 thereof and the Charter, and particularly the fundamental rights and principles enshrined in the Charter, such as non-discrimination and proportionality.[107]

The second set of measures consisted of random controls, performed by the national authorities to verify compliance with the ban mentioned above. Here, the 'terms of reference' for the assessment of compatibility with EU law were those established in the SBC. The question was whether those measures amounted to MEEs and, if so, could be justified under the Code. Once again, the analysis of the Court was objective-driven. The main objective, in this case, was limiting the spread of Covid-19 and monitoring travellers. The expression 'in particular', preceding the list of indicators that would make a measure a non-border check, reveals that this list is not exhaustive, neither with regard to the conditions which the measure must satisfy, nor the objectives which those measures must pursue. Public health matters can therefore fall within the scope of Article 23(a) SBC. Further, the measure must be based on 'general police information and experience' in the area concerned, and controls cannot be imposed based on a general prohibition, irrespective of the conduct of the persons concerned or of circumstances giving rise to a risk of harm in that area.[108] The Court acknowledged that the measures in question did not satisfy this requirement, but also observed that they were 'enacted in the context of a serious threat to public health'. With this in mind, it was sufficient that 'the controls were decided on and implemented in the light of circumstances objectively giving rise to a risk of grave and serious harm to public health and on the basis of the authorities' general knowledge of the areas of entry to and exit from the national territory through which a large number of travellers targeted by that prohibition were likely to transit'.[109] As regards the non-systematic nature of the checks, the Court noted that in the situation described above, 'it may be extremely difficult or even impossible to determine in advance which persons using various modes of transport come from Member States classified as high-risk zones or travel to such Member States'.[110] This being the case, the state concerned must be allowed some discretion in the intensity, frequency, and selectivity with which they implement those controls, as also justified by the precautionary principle. To be sure, the discretion must not be used in a way that would make those measures undistinguishable from systematic checks on persons at the EU external borders. Even if that were to be the case, in such circumstances a member state could lawfully rely on (former) Article 25(1) SBC to apply such measures, since a health threat posed by

[107] Case C-128/22, *NORDIC INFO*, para 98.
[108] Case C-128/22, *NORDIC INFO*, para 119.
[109] Case C-128/22, *NORDIC INFO*, para 120.
[110] Case C-128/22, *NORDIC INFO*, para 122.

the Covid-19 pandemic could fall within the scope of public policy and/or internal security.[111]

While the new SBC features a public health-based ground for reintroducing controls, the findings of this judgment are still relevant. This holds true particularly for the definition of non-border checks, which the Court has stretched to an extent that only the facts of the case might realistically justify. The sleight of hand played by the ECJ is remarkable, if rather visible. While the ultimate objective of the checks was public health-related, these checks were meant to enforce the ban on a prohibition of entry. As regards another key criterion—the modality of exercise—the ECJ was inclined to justify more intense checks for administrative convenience. With this in mind, one element above all seems to have played a decisive role: the random nature of the checks under consideration. Had they leaned more prominently towards the systematic end of the spectrum, it is difficult to imagine how they might have been regarded as non-border checks.[112] Incidentally, this is a case where the asymmetry of EU and Schengen membership shines through. EU membership, through the Citizenship Directive, governs restrictions on movement and entry, whereas the Schengen membership, pursuant to the SBC, homes in on the controls attached to that ban. Could either an EU-only or Schengen-only state be at a disadvantage because of their status? Probably not. Apart from the practical difficulty of targeting either persons of a certain nationality or coming from a certain country, the principle of non-discrimination would anyway require a very strong objective foundation for such a difference in treatment.

#### 9.2.2.3 Interim conclusions

The flexible framework on conditions for performing non-border checks, combined with the heterogeneity of the legal framework, poses a number of challenges to constitutional compliance. These are apparent from the extensive case law of the Court on the subject, and concern especially solidarity and fair treatment of the persons concerned. This is consistent with the discussion of other aspects of the legal framework. National measures resulting in systematic checks on an internal border breach the states' duty to consider the impact of their decisions on the common interest. Furthermore, they undermine the person's enjoyment of the prohibition of checks established by the SBC. The Court's approach has introduced additional constraints on member states' action, but it has also left heterogeneity considerable room for impact. The CJ relied on a heterogeneous and objective-driven set of criteria, which in turn makes the test even more challenging: not only do the objectives of controls themselves constitute a heterogeneous category, but they also seem to change depending on whether the focus is on the external or internal border. Furthermore, assuming that the approach to Covid checks was not entirely the product of the specific circumstances, the 'preferential treatment' accorded to public health might create further

[111] Case C-128/22, *NORDIC INFO*, paras 125–27. It could, in fact, affect one of the fundamental interests of society and the very survival of a part of the population. See, Case C-601/15 PPU, *JN*, EU:C:2016:84, paras 65–66 and the case law cited.

[112] Because the assessment of selectivity, frequency, and intensity develops over a spectrum rather than in a binary manner, it is difficult to define a clear-cut number or threshold beyond which a measure would turn into a MEE.

heterogeneity in an already multi-layered assessment of equivalence. These different forms of heterogeneity create very broad pockets of discretion, which in turn are detrimental to legal certainty and accountability and cast doubt on the capacity of the legal framework to achieve its objectives appropriately.

### 9.2.3 Tales from France and Norway

The analysis of French laws and practices on the reintroduction of border controls reveals the relevance of the heterogeneity of internal border controls to constitutional compliance. Three main areas are worth highlighting: the type of actors involved in the implementation of controls; the scope of the concept of control; and the regime applicable to TCNs at the internal borders when controls have been reintroduced. Firstly, concerning the actors of control, we have an example of (allegedly) positive heterogeneity. In a recent report, the *Cour des Comptes* has been critical of the government's approach to internal border controls, and particularly for the following reasons. These controls have morphed from exceptional to permanent. A strong mobilization of different national bodies or authorities has been followed by a gradual disengagement, mostly shouldered by the French border police and customs officers. The overall effectiveness of such controls is, furthermore, uncertain.[113] Beyond the unsurprising observation that border controls have been kept in place for way longer than they were allowed to, it is particularly interesting to see the *Cour* taking the view that the involvement of a plurality (heterogeneity) of authorities could in fact be conducive to more efficient implementation of the legal framework.

Secondly, the scope of permissible border controls under French law is wider than that allowed by the EU. The difference stems from the *Conseil d'État*'s interpretation of the concept of 'new threat'[114] and the legislative approach to the concept of surveillance. By building on the case law of the Court of Justice,[115] the *Conseil* has found that a threat would justify controls where it is new by its own nature (*par sa nature*),[116] or when the circumstances around an existing threat have changed in relation to its subject, breadth, or intensity, so that the actuality, scope, and extent of the threat itself have changed.[117] This flexible approach to the concept of a 'new threat' gives significantly wider margin to start anew the clock of lawful border controls. Unless applied very strictly, this approach could impact solidarity and fair treatment of the persons concerned. On the one hand, national authorities would have to rigorously consider the impact of such an approach on the common interest. On the other hand, a flexible implementation of this notion could undermine the right to free movement and contravene the spirit and principles underlying this 'practice'. The understanding of

[113] Cour des comptes, *La politique de lutte contre l'immigration irrégulière*, Rapport public thématique, Janvier 2024.

[114] See Conseil d'État, 28 décembre 2017, n°415291; Conseil d'État, 16 octobre 2019, n°425936; Conseil d'État, 27 juillet 2022, n°463850.

[115] See Conseil d'État, 27 juillet 2022, n°463850, para 5.

[116] In case of 'risques générés par le conflit ukrainien sur le territoire français en matière de criminalité organisée et de trafic d'êtres humains'.

[117] Conseil d'État, 27 juillet 2022, n°463850, para 6.

surveillance in French law also contributes to enlarging the meaning and scope of border controls. The rules on internal border surveillance are mostly provided in the Code of Criminal Procedure. Identity checks are key in this regard, and the Code identifies a series of areas where they can take place.[118] While such checks may only be carried out for 12 consecutive hours and cannot be systematic,[119] customs officers can generally inspect goods, transports, and persons at ports, airports, train and bus stations, and on motorways and trains at any time (*à toute heure*).[120] Importantly, these locations are exempt from the 12-hour restriction referred to above.[121] Furthermore, the scope of customs controls in other areas can be extended under certain conditions.[122] These measures must be distinguished by general immigration controls, governed by other provisions of national law. In this regard, any person can be asked to provide ID documents in the areas indicated in the Code of Criminal Procedure for the prevention and investigation of cross-border crime. Checks related to the obligation to hold, carry, and present documents are also governed by the *Code de l'entrée*. The *Code* itself establishes the obligation for foreigners, in Article L812-1, to carry those documents to prove they are allowed to move and reside in France and authorizes detention of persons where it appears they have no such right.[123] Against this backdrop, checks can be performed if, regardless of whether or not they follow identity checks under the Code of Criminal Procedure, objective elements deduced from circumstances external to the person concerned are such as to reveal their status as a foreigner. These measures can apply throughout the territory, which includes border areas. The French legal framework on border surveillance grants national authorities, and especially customs, a noticeable degree of flexibility. Based on the extensive discussion conducted in the previous sections, these powers are constrained by the criteria developed by the Court of Justice.

Thirdly, certain French bodies—in line with the Court of Justice's case law discussed below—have upheld the applicability of the Return Directive at the internal borders, and specifically where irregular TCNs have been intercepted at a frontier where checks have been formally reintroduced. In such a scenario, national authorities cannot refuse entry to a TCN in the context of those checks. This also entails that an application for international protection made at the internal border must be registered. In this regard, the French *Conseil d'État* annulled the second sentence of Article L332-3 of the *Code de l'entrée*, which extended the procedures for refusal of entry applicable at the external borders to the internal borders. Interestingly, the *Conseil* found that the provision was unlawful to the extent that its application was not limited to cases where entry was refused with a view to the readmission of the person

[118] More specifically, in the area between France's land border with the States party to the Schengen and a line drawn 20 kilometres beyond it, as well as in the areas accessible to the public of ports, airports, and railway or road stations open to international traffic and designated by decree, and in the vicinity of these stations.

[119] The *Code de procédure pénale* allows to proceed to ID check, and particularly Article 78-2 al.9 et 10. See also *Code des douanes*, Article 67 quater.

[120] *Code des douanes*, Article 60-1.

[121] *Code des douanes*, 60-5.

[122] *Code des douanes*, Article 60-2.

[123] *Code de l'entrée*, Article 813-1.

concerned by the member state from which the person came pursuant to an existing agreement or agreement.[124] This interpretation is not incompatible with the *ADDE* scenario. The latter allowed—rather than obliged—the member state to refuse entry at the internal border and reiterated the obligation for the member state to apply the Return Directive. In practice, therefore, the specific conclusions of the *Conseil d'État* align with those of the Court of Justice.

The experience in Norway echoes that of France, at least to an extent. As seen in the previous chapter, Norway can reintroduce border control at internal Schengen borders if there is a serious threat to public order or internal security. The *Grenseloven* (Border Act) empowers the Norwegian Police to perform border controls,[125] which must also be assisted by other authorities and especially the Customs Service.[126] As Norway is not part of the EU customs union, customs controls are carried out at both internal and external borders. The Norwegian Police 2019–2021 National Strategy for Comprehensive Border Management stated that performing controls at the internal borders is a resource-intensive measure, not least because it challenges a structure that in all other periods is not adapted for this exceptional situation.[127] The observation is of particular interest, since it challenges the assumption that national authorities would always be favourable to measures of this kind.

Surveillance of the border can be carried out only sporadically when it is not associated with the reintroduction of border controls. This is probably to be interpreted strictly, in geographical terms. Surveillance in the border area might be exempt from this condition, which presumably applies to the border proper. With this in mind, surveilling authorities can ask a person to provide an ID document and an explanation for their stay at the border if, during the performance of border surveillance, a need for identification arises.[128] It is also worth noting that Norwegian law also allows surveillance-related checks and general immigration checks in the territory (which may include border areas). Under the immigration checks, authorities can stop persons and require them to provide identification when there is reason to believe that they are foreign nationals, and the time, place, and situation justify such control.[129] Even though the constraints on the exercise of surveillance limit the frequency with which such control could be carried out at the border, the very broad discretion left to the authorities borders—pun intended—on arbitrariness. The problematic nature of this provision stands out even further when compared to its French equivalent, which requires, for the exercise of comparable powers, the existence of factors external to the person.

It is in the Covid-related litigation before the Norwegian Supreme Court that we can find important elements for our assessment of constitutional compliance. These findings are relevant despite the transient nature of the measures under scrutiny and

[124] See Conseil d'État, 2 février 2024, n°450285.

[125] Grenseloven, Article 15. See also Grenseforskriften, Article 1-4.

[126] Grenseloven, Articles 4 and 7.

[127] Nasjonal strategi for helhetlig grenseforvaltning (National strategy for integrated border management), p 22.

[128] Grenseloven, Article 21.

[129] See Immigration Act, Article 21 and Prop 161 L (2016–2017), p 52.

resonate with some of the themes discussed in relation to both French and EU law. Two main issues were discussed in this judicial saga: whether the requirement of a Covid test and the check thereof at the border constituted border checks or an MEE, within the meaning of the SBC; and whether the duration of the checks was justified by the 'newness' of the threat. On both counts, the Norwegian Supreme Court found in favour of the government.[130] For context, it must be mentioned that such checks on the test were associated with entry checks, which were acknowledged by both the Norwegian and the Swedish authorities as the type of measure normally prohibited under the SBC, but arguably allowed in these circumstances. By relying on the ECJ's *Nordic Info* ruling, the Supreme Court found that the test-related checks were not, in fact, MEEs. While the Supreme Court acknowledged the systematic nature of the checks and the potentially identical outcome in case of failure to comply with the measures (refusal of entry), it also highlighted the difference in intensity and selectivity of said checks.[131] On this basis, the Supreme Court concluded that the measure was not an MEE. On the second point, it espoused in full the position taken by the *Conseil d'État*, and found that the newness of a threat should be assessed not only in relation to its nature, but also in light of the concrete circumstances and its intensity. This point is important procedurally and substantively. The Norwegian government's notification to the European Commission in one of the contested cases was based on the legal basis governing prolongation—rather than reintroduction—of checks.[132] While the Supreme Court regarded the choice of the Government as incorrect, it considered that error inconsequential as the notification was 'clearly' based on the existence of a new threat and the letter met the requirements of former Article 27(1) SBC.[133] The implications are significant on a substantive level, too. The practical relevance of labelling those controls on a negative test as an MEE or not is shadowed by the circumstance that those checks constituted an extension of measures that were explicitly acknowledged as border checks. If the test-related controls applied autonomously (ie in the absence of border checks), they would have to comply with the constraints set in the case law of the Court of Justice. While potentially challenging, we can see how such a form of 'control' could in principle be squared with the prohibition of MEEs. Furthermore, the application of such a measure without checks or MEEs would lose intensity, especially for crossings by land, where more systematic monitoring would be particularly visible and raise more serious questions on a possible breach of the SBC. However, we also see a potential point of tension between the test of equivalence devised by the ECJ and the approach taken by the Norwegian Supreme Court. While the former specified in *Touring Tours* that the non-thorough nature of the checks does not make them less systematic, the latter clearly saw that circumstance as a very important factor to reach the opposite conclusion.

[130] Another case-HR-2024-1107-A (*Quarantine Hotel*) concerned border control and the requirement of an entry quarantine during the Covid-19 pandemic. The question for the court, however, was connected to the EEA free movement rules. The possible qualification of the quarantine as 'border control' was not discussed.

[131] The requirement only applied to people who came from an area with a duty to quarantine and exemptions were possible for certain categories of people.

[132] That is, pursuant to Article 25(3), as opposed to Article 25(1) SBC.

[133] HR-2024-1109-A (*Covid-test I*). See also another similar case, HR-2024-1110-A (*Covid-test II*).

## 9.3 Compensatory Measures

### 9.3.1 Origins and Development: From Schengen to Prüm

The so-called compensatory measures are essential to the preservation of an area without internal border checks. Over the last three decades, we have witnessed a remarkable advancement in legal integration through judicial cooperation in criminal matters.[134] Police cooperation has also progressed significantly, especially as regards the exchange of information.[135] When it comes to operational cooperation, however, the situation is rather different. This area is, for the most part, still governed by the Convention Implementing the Schengen Agreement. The CISA provides for a series of transnational policing activities to be carried out at or around the border between neighbouring member states.[136] The relevant provisions establish conditions and empower actors for these purposes. The main measures of interest in this research are hot surveillance and hot pursuit. Hot surveillance, as mentioned in the previous chapter, concerns the situation where an authority from a member state seeks to continue the surveillance of a person in the territory of another member state.[137] This is possible if a series of requirements are met. Fundamentally, the person must be presumed to have participated in an extraditable criminal offence. Now that extradition between EU states has been replaced by the European Arrest Warrant (EAW),[138] it is reasonable to assume that the hot surveillance would be applicable for offences whose level of severity is set in Article 2 of the European Arrest Warrant Framework Decision. On this basis, the law of the issuing state would be the one determining whether the offence at stake is one that meets the requirement of hot surveillance.[139] Hot surveillance must be authorized by the requested state, unless in particularly urgent cases and for certain offences,[140] with the 'surveillant' state under an obligation to immediately inform the

[134] Regulation (EU) 2023/1543 on European Production Orders and European Preservation Orders for electronic evidence in criminal proceedings and for the execution of custodial sentences following criminal proceedings [2023] OJ L 191/118 is the best example defining this trajectory towards the EU as a single space of cooperation in criminal matters. The Regulation allows authorities from one state to require that a private service provider in another member state transmit e-evidence without—in most cases—oversight from a judicial authority in the state of execution.

[135] Directive (EU) 2023/977 on the exchange of information between the law enforcement authorities of Member States [2023] OJ L 134/1, Article 1.

[136] This is not to say that the proximity to the border is a precondition or a specific feature of the measures discussed below. Their cross-border nature is, however, one of their distinctive characteristics and, as such, they can potentially *also* cover situations occurring at or around the border between two member states.

[137] CISA, Article 40.

[138] Council Framework Decision 2002/584/JHA on the European arrest warrant and the surrender procedures between Member States (EAW FD) [2002] OJ L 190/1.

[139] Specifically, the offence must be punishable by the law of the issuing state by a custodial sentence or a detention order for a maximum period of at least 12 months or, where a sentence has been passed or a detention order has been made, for sentences of at least four months. As known, the EAW FD has also dropped the double criminality requirement for a list of 32 areas of crime. When the person is suspected of, or has been convicted for, one of these crimes, Article 2(2) stipulates that the offence must be punishable by the law in the issuing state, by a custodial sentence or a detention order for a maximum period of at least three years and as they are defined by the law of the issuing Member State.

[140] The offences are: murder, manslaughter, rape, arson, forgery of money, aggravated burglary and robbery and receiving stolen goods, extortion, kidnapping and hostage taking, trafficking in human beings, illicit trafficking in narcotic drugs and psychotropic substances, breach of the laws on arms and explosives, wilful damage through the use of explosives, and illicit transportation of toxic and hazardous waste.

other state that the border has been crossed, and why. With or without prior authorization, hot surveillance must be carried out following a series of conditions.[141] In particular, the officer from the requesting state must obey the instruction of the competent authorities in the requested state. It can only use weapons for self-defence and cannot arrest or access non-public premises.

The other main cross-border activity that can take place around the border is hot pursuit.[142] This consists of the pursuit of a person caught in the fact of committing or participating in one of the offences listed in the CISA, which has started in one member state (pursuing state) and continues in the territory of another member state (state of pursuit).[143] The hot pursuit can be carried out without authorization in cases of particular urgency—as with hot surveillance—and in two further scenarios: when the authorities of the member state where the pursuit is continuing cannot get to the scene in time to take charge of the operation; and when the person has escaped custody or the penalty involving deprivation of liberty they were serving. The greater flexibility granted to the authorities continuing the operation in another jurisdiction is noteworthy but also explainable by the higher threshold set by the CISA in comparison to hot surveillance. The pursuing officer must inform the competent authority of the state of pursuit no later than when they cross the border and must stop the pursuit if the authorities of the state of pursuit so request. The pursuing officer cannot apprehend the person, but they can detain them if the competent authorities cannot intervene 'quickly enough' and until the state of pursuit officers can take over. In this case, the person can only undergo a security search, handcuffing and the seizing of objects they were carrying at the moment of the apprehension. Furthermore, the officer of the state of pursuit must challenge the person to establish their identity or arrest them if the pursuing officer so requests. The hot pursuit can be carried out either in a predefined area or period following the border crossing, or without such limitations. As mentioned in the last chapter, which of these two options applies depends on the declaration of the member state concerned. The hot pursuit is subject to certain conditions, which closely resemble those established for hot surveillance. It can happen only over land borders. Importantly, a person arrested by the pursuing state authorities in the context of the operation can be held for questioning, in accordance with the rules of national law which apply *mutatis mutandis*. The provision is not straightforward as to which state law should apply, and what the *mutatis mutandis* clause would entail in the circumstances.

The Prüm Decision, for its part, establishes the possibility of setting up joint operations, joint patrols, and cross-border assistance. The relevant provisions are rather laconic, however. They offer very little detail, other than enabling member states to establish these forms of cooperation. Member states are required to provide officers of member states that cross the border with the same protection and assistance they would to their own officers in the performance of those tasks or the discharge of the same duties.[144] The Prüm Implementing Decision lays down more specific rules

[141] CISA, Article 40(3).
[142] CISA, Article 41.
[143] The list is the same as that concerning hot surveillance.
[144] Council Decision 2008/615/JHA on the stepping up of cross-border cooperation, particularly in combating terrorism and cross-border crime [2008] OJ L 210/1 (Prüm Decision), Article 20.

concerning cross-border cooperation. It stipulates that, before the start of an operation, the member states concerned must make written or verbal arrangements that *may cover details such as* the purpose of the operation, the host state and the geographical area, the powers and equipment that the seconded officers can use in the host state. The same provision states that 'declarations, procedures and designations provided for in this Article shall be reproduced in the Manual'.[145] The framework leaves much to be desired, as it allows authorities to operate in a legal vacuum. Not only is there no obligation to set up the terms of the cooperation in writing, but also the Implementing Decision lays down no exhaustive list as regards the content of such arrangements. Once again, vagueness is a vector for potential heterogeneity and ensuing gaps in accessibility, legal certainty, and individual protection.

### 9.3.2 A New Era of Transnational Policing?

As regards compensatory measures materializing in activities around an internal border, we must discuss three recommendations adopted by either the Council or the Commission in the relatively recent past. While not legally binding, these recommendations are important to understand how the approach to certain forms of cooperation has evolved over the years and to uncover the heterogeneity of the EU understandings of internal and external border controls. The recommendations have implications for the relation between cross-border law enforcement and member states' reserved areas of action, for the principles of mutual trust and solidarity, and the treatment of the persons concerned.[146] The starting point is always the proper functioning of the area without border controls, which rests on two main pillars: the uniform application of the Union acquis, and the use of national competences on law and order and internal security in line with the objectives of Schengen. Against this background, the framework outlined by the recommendations revolves around three interrelated issues: the relevance of the border areas, the EU wide dimension of public policy and internal security, and the actions that member states should take.

Firstly, the member states' use of police powers internally and in border areas is as important as their management of their external borders. The focus is on threats to public policy and internal security that can arise from serious cross-border crime and risks of secondary movement. Such a vision builds on the blurring of boundaries between crime and migration, with public policy and security being treated as bywords for criminal conduct. This is apparent from the idea that border areas can be more exposed to offences committed in the whole territory, such as unauthorized secondary movement,[147] and suggests that certain offences are more likely to be perpetrated in

[145] Council Decision 2008/616/JHA on the implementation of Decision 2008/615/JHA on the stepping up of cross-border cooperation, particularly in combating terrorism and cross-border crime [2008] OJ L 210/12, Article 17.

[146] Commission Recommendation (EU) 2017/820 of 12 May 2017 on proportionate police checks and police cooperation in the Schengen area [2017] OJ L 122/79.

[147] Recommendation (EU) 2017/820 80. Part of the strategy to counter irregular secondary movement lies in the bilateral readmission agreement and arrangement between member states.

border areas.[148] Likewise, border areas might have a higher risk of breaches of a certain member state's rules on residence.[149] However, neither of these points is underpinned by any specific source or piece of evidence.[150]

Secondly, and relatedly, the recommendations blur the boundaries between the member state and the Schengen dimension of public policy and internal security.[151] This development mirrors closely the change of paradigm on the EU outer frontiers. Elevating a member state's concern to a matter of Union-wide interest has led, over the years, to increasing centralization. The same seems to be happening here: when dealing with issues of law and order and security within Schengen, each member state acts on behalf of the entire Union. To be sure, the prohibition of internal controls leaves member states' police powers unaffected, as long as measures taken on those grounds are not tantamount to border checks.[152] On the one hand, the Union's obligation under Article 4(2) TEU has a 'passive' nature: its action must not affect the state's exercise of its essential state function. On the other hand, the very strong encouragement to use those powers for the benefit of the whole Schengen area betrays a very different interpretation of that sovereign clause. This interpretation, jointly with the blurring of national and Union-wide understanding of security or public policy, might augur the EU legislature's attempt to make further inroads into this area. This approach is not uncontroversial. As the Court's case law has also shown, the ambiguity of the EU territory, combined with the shared nature of the competence in this area and the relevance of a state's borders to its essential functions, favours an interpretation of the concept of internal security linked to the state itself rather than the Union as a whole. This is another example of the possible tension between a conservative interpretation of the constitutional set-up as regards competences and responsibilities and procedural solidarity as a duty of taking into account the common interest.

How would this duty manifest in this area? Through the third feature of the framework set out in the recommendations—that is, the concrete actions that member states are encouraged to take. The wider appeal to police (as opposed to border) checks finds expression in concrete examples of how the threats to public policy and internal security should be addressed. In a further example of the role of free movement as a driver of identity formation, cross-border cooperation should develop within a framework of Union-wide law enforcement culture with a view to keeping the absence of controls sustainable.[153] The emphasis is on the use of modern technologies to allow the monitoring of traffic flows for law enforcement purposes, in line

[148] The Recommendation also states that 'border areas may have specific risks as regards cross-border crime'. Taken as it is, this sentence is a word salad. Even if we tried to reconstruct its meaning beyond the current juxtaposition of words, the statement is tautological at best. Cross-border crime presupposes the existence of a border, and we fail to see the point the recommendation is attempting to make.

[149] Recommendation (EU) 2017/820 80.

[150] This scarcely evidence-based approach informs other parts of the recommendation, eg when it is stated that 'As demonstrated by the recent migratory crisis, uncontrolled secondary movements of irregular migrants may pose a serious threat to public policy or internal security'.

[151] See also, for a similar approach, Commission Recommendation (EU) 2024/268 on cooperation between the Member States with regard to serious threats to internal security and public policy in the area without internal border controls 1.

[152] Recommendation (EU) 2017/820 79.

[153] Council Recommendation 2022/915 on operational law enforcement cooperation [2022] OJ L 158/53.

with the applicable rules concerning camera surveillance and data protection.[154] The ultimate goal is to foster surveillance of the main European transport corridor without impacting free movement. Attention is growing towards areas that are not yet governed by EU rules, such as the monitoring of the internal land borders in a manner that would not constitute border checks. The focus on road traffic and land borders is understandable but problematic in two main respects. It is understandable from the perspective of the Commission, considering that other forms of intra-EU border crossing, such as by plane, can already be monitored through the exchange of passenger name record (PNR).[155] It is also problematic because the encouragement to use intrusive means of surveillance in a legally grey area is prone to challenges and abuses. In this respect, the reference to the need to respect data protection is inconsequential, especially when coupled with the mention of the 'applicable framework' on camera surveillance. What would the applicable framework be? The logical answer would be Directive (EU) 2016/680 on data protection in the context of law enforcement.[156] This Directive, however, does not apply to activities falling outside the scope of EU law.[157] Would the recommendation be enough to bring cross-border surveillance, broadly understood, under the umbrella of EU law? The answer should be in the affirmative. Also, the question arises as to where the use of technology and surveillance could change the nature of Schengen as an area without internal border controls, particularly where those instruments could de facto enable systematic, if invisible, checks on border-crossings.

Furthermore, the recommendations set out a new framework for existing measures of cross-border cooperation, such as hot pursuit and hot surveillance. They should no longer require the minimum level of severity set in Articles 40 and 41 CISA. They should be allowed to take place also on river, lake, and air borders, and should be applied with no restriction in time or space. The recommendation also proposes to extend certain powers of the pursuing officer, and particularly the carrying and use of service weapons for the defence of others, and not only of themselves, as well as the use of traffic privileges in line with the law of the state of pursuit.[158] The scope of cross-border surveillance should also broaden. Some of the proposed changes mirror those related to hot pursuit,[159] whereas some differ.[160] In the context of joint operations, host states should allow seconded officers at least—and provided that the same applies to their own agents—to carry out identity checks and provisionally detain persons who try to avoid the checks. Member states that host or take part in PCCCs

[154] More specifically, there is mention of automatic number plate recognition.

[155] See Directive (EU) 2016/681 on the use of passenger name record (PNR) data for the prevention, detection, investigation, and prosecution of terrorist offences and serious crime [2016] OJ L 119/132. It should be noted, however, that the Directive primarily concerns flights entering and departing the EU. For intra-EU flights, member states are not obliged to collect and share such data.

[156] Directive (EU) 2016/680 on the protection of natural persons with regard to the processing of personal data by competent authorities for the purposes of the prevention, investigation, detection or prosecution of criminal offences or the execution of criminal penalties, and on the free movement of such data, and repealing Council Framework Decision 2008/977/JHA [2016] OJ L 119/89.

[157] Directive (EU) 2016/680, Article 2(3).

[158] Recommendation 2022/915 59.

[159] For example, this cross-border surveillance should be allowed across land, sea, river, lake, and air borders, and the surveillant officer should be allowed to carry and use weapons in defence of others.

[160] Needless to say, this would have to take place pursuant to the law of the host state.

should empower them to support operations in internal border areas, including investigation into crimes taking place in those areas. The picture that emerges from these recommended and non-legally binding changes to the existing rules governing cross-border pursuit and surveillance is significant. To be sure, the fact that member states are not obliged to implement the content of the recommendation is consequential. Putting these amendments into historical perspective adds a note of nuance to them. Almost 40 years have passed between the CISA and the recommendation. While legal integration in operational cooperation in the meantime has proceeded very slowly, we are perhaps witnessing a paradigm shift to cross-border law enforcement within the EU. The internal borders are, in one breath, acquiring and losing further relevance. On the one hand, relaxing the constraints of officers' action in another member state aims to reduce the importance of borders in legal terms, as a boundary that rigidly marks the distinction between different jurisdictions and the exercise of sovereign powers. On the other hand, that distinction will and should never fade completely. Member states will always have their own systems of substantive and procedural criminal law. This is, according to the EU narrative, one of the key drivers for cross-border criminality, and in turn for counter-measures such as hot pursuit and hot surveillance. As long as the internal border as a line distinguishing two different legal systems continues to exist, the EU will endeavour to make it a place that is simultaneously relevant and irrelevant. Irrelevant, insofar as it should constrain as little as possible the capacity for law enforcement action. Relevant, because this is where much of the focus of that action will be, for the reason stated above. These issues reveal a certain heterogeneity of purpose in the EU action. They certainly express the heterogeneous nature of the internal border as a place that should disappear and be very visible at the same time. Likewise, it is undeniable that the measures recommended by the Council and the Commission, and the broader vision they express, straddle different remits,[161] and test the limits of how far legal integration in this area can reconcile respect for essential state functions, interinstitutional solidarity, and fair treatment of the persons concerned.

### 9.3.3 Tales from France and Norway

The previous chapter uncovered the heterogeneous landscape of bilateral or multilateral cooperation in cross-border law enforcement, and particularly as regards activities taking place at the borders. Here, we look more closely at some of the substantive provisions governing those activities. Within the framework of the previous discussion, insight into state practices is revealing in three respects: the extensive nature of this network of interstate agreements beneath the surface of EU law, the impact this lack of visibility can have on fair treatment of addressees of control, and the contrast between integration in this area and for example judicial cooperation. Many

[161] If the Treaties avoid the use of the word 'competence' in Articles 4(2) TEU and 72 TFEU, it is best to do the same in this book, where the terms of the discussion go beyond the question of competence strictly speaking.

examples of strengthened cooperation—such as joint surveillance, joint patrol, joint intervention, and joint border exercises—identify border areas as their focal point (including with the view to intercepting and preventing irregular border crossing). This is not inconsequential. Looking at some of France's bilateral agreements, as a rule a designated officer from each state would take operational control during joint patrols, depending on where the operation is being carried out at any given moment. However, the patrol closest to the place in situations of emergency can intervene, regardless of its country of origin.[162] The fact that the border is often the centre of gravity of such activities increases the likelihood that such a scenario will materialize. Police and Customs Cooperation Centres are the perfect showcase for border-centred integration in law enforcement cooperation. The proper functioning of such centres is built on mutual trust,[163] with the view to preventing and investigating crime, in particular illegal immigration and threats to security and public order.[164] While such cooperation primarily takes the form of collection and exchange of information,[165] the centres are also supposed to support hot surveillance and hot pursuit in the cross-border area, and organize coordinated operations between the services responsible for combating illegal immigration, including, if necessary, preparing for the surrender of foreigners in an irregular situation.[166] In this regard, as mentioned, Article L621-1 *Code de l'entrée* provides for a general possibility of refusing entry to a person at the border, provided that it occurs within the framework of bilateral cooperation. In this regard, France has readmission agreements with many member states, including with neighbouring Germany,[167] Switzerland,[168]and Spain.[169] Within this maze of interstate agreement, the opportunity for unfair treatment of the persons concerned is always around the corner. This can not only occur as a result of implementation based on racial profiling,[170] but also due to the extreme flexibility of the legal framework itself. The French-Swiss cooperation agreement provides that, if the person was arrested in a state of which they are not a national, they must be released no later than six hours after the arrest unless the competent local authorities have received, before the expiry of that period, a notice announcing a request for provisional arrest for the purpose of extradition *in any form whatsoever*.[171]

Overall, these agreements reveal the border areas as a fertile ground for fostering cooperation between law enforcement authorities, through a host of measures falling within the broader scope of 'surveillance' and built on the assimilation of irregular migration into crime-related activity. This being said, certain features of the framework show a stark contrast with areas already subject to approximation at a Union level.

162 Décret n°2015-1297 du 15 octobre 2015, Article 14.
163 See, for example, Décret n°2016-1294 du 29 septembre 2016, Article 7.
164 Décret n°2016-1294, Article 4.
165 Décret n°2016-1294, Article 5.
166 Décret n°2016-1294, Article 6.
167 Décret n°2006-33 du 11 janvier 2006.
168 Décret n°2000-287 du 28 mars 2000.
169 Décret n°2004-226 du 9 mars 2004.
170 S Casella Colombeau, 'Policing the Internal Schengen Borders: Managing the Double Bind Between Free Movement and Migration Control' (2017) 27 *Policing and Society* 482.
171 Décret n°2009-836 du 7 juillet 2009, Article 13.

Two main examples can be provided in this regard. Without prejudice to the tasks and objectives of the PCCC, the parties can also establish direct cooperation with each other. Direct cooperation can materialize in coordinating the intervention of forces on both sides of the border, establishing joint operational and command centres, participating, on the basis of jointly established plans, in cross-border searches, and preparing and implementing joint crime prevention programmes. However, a state can refuse cooperation or make it subject to certain conditions, when it considers that it would harm the sovereignty, security, public order, rules of organization, or the functioning of the judicial authority or other essential interests of the state.[172] This wording evokes the concept of essential state function under Article 4(2) TEU. Conceptually speaking, this clause is not particularly enlightening, since it lists sovereignty as an essential interest of the state, rather than the product of several different functions and prerogatives. It is, however, worth noting that sovereignty is explicitly mentioned as a barrier to further cooperation, and that the organization of the judicial system and the relationship between different state powers fall within one of its essential interests. The second example is offered by the provisions of French law on Joint Investigation Teams (JITs).[173] Specific Articles of the Code of Criminal Procedure and the Customs Code of French law relate to the setting up of, or participation in, joint operations and joint investigation teams at the internal borders—albeit they do not refer specifically to this geographical area. The Code of Criminal Procedure stipulates that, with the prior agreement of the Minister of Justice and the consent of the other member state(s) concerned, the competent judicial authority may set up a JIT in certain situations.[174] In this context, foreign officials seconded by another state to a JIT may, within the limits of the powers attached to their status and under certain conditions,[175] perform a series of important tasks such as assisting French judicial police officers in the exercise of their duties, or carrying out surveillance (including by infiltration).[176] With the prior consent of the Minister of Justice, foreign customs officers may carry out undercover operations on French territory under the direction of French competent authorities. The agreement of the Minister of Justice may be subject to conditions,[177] and the operation must then be authorized by the public prosecutor at the Paris Judicial Court. While judicial authorities play an important role once cooperation has started, the power to trigger an operation lies with the executive. The role of a minister in this area reveals just how sensitive cooperation still is. It also suggests a correlation between the absence of approximation of the degree of legal integration.

[172] Décret n°2016-1294, Article 12.

[173] See Eurojust annual report 13.

[174] Either when it is necessary to carry out, in the context of a French procedure, complex investigations involving the mobilization of significant resources which concern other states, or when several states carry out investigations into offences requiring coordinated action.

[175] Specifically, they must act under the direction of the competent judicial authority, subject to the consent of the seconding state.

[176] *Code de Procedure Penale*, Article 695-2.

[177] The Minister of Justice may give his consent only if the foreign agents are assigned in their country to a specialized service and carry out tasks similar to those of the specially authorized national agents. See also *Code des douanes*, Article 67a.

### 9.3.4 Interim Conclusions

The discussion on compensatory measures taken around the internal border has shown another side to the impact of heterogeneity on constitutional compliance. This chapter has assessed the possible effects of the heterogeneity of sources, which ensues from the heterogeneity of levels of governance and actors in an area falling squarely within the remit of essential state functions. The conditions for transnational law enforcement deepen the challenges to constitutional compliance. On the one hand, the large network of interstate agreements has developed within an outdated framework of EU law which poses little constraint on member states' action. A closer inspection of the agreements compound that concern, due to a lack of accessibility, legal uncertainty or flexibility bordering on arbitrariness. On the other hand, the Commission and the Council have tried to reframe the constitutional conversation about law enforcement cooperation at the internal borders. Based on this approach, member states are encouraged to use border surveillance to an extent that might question the nature of Schengen as an area without internal border controls. Member states are also strongly invited to use their essential state functions in line with the objectives of Schengen. Far from understanding Article 4(2) TEU as a dam against the EU action, the Council and the Commission regard this sovereign clause as a lever to foster vertical solidarity and 'communitarize' the concept of internal security for the purposes of the common interest.

## 9.4 Conclusions

The analysis of conditions for controls and their exercise within the Schengen area has cast further light on the relationship between heterogeneity and constitutional compliance. The reformed SBC has made some progress in managing the heterogeneity of decision-makers and objectives, especially through clauses inspired by procedural solidarity. This reinforced structure, centred on the states' obligation of 'taking into account' the common interest, has not eliminated at all the risk of tensions generated by the heterogeneity of conditions and sources possibly underpinning the reinstating of checks. In a context where the ultimate decision about controls remains within states, and so does the concept of internal security, a rigorous application of the principle of solidarity can contribute to achieving a higher level of constitutional compliance. The impact of heterogeneity is equally apparent from the analysis of measures alternative to border checks. As regards the exercise of police powers and the established criteria to assess their possible equivalence to border checks, the objective-driven nature of this assessment reveals a stark contrast with the EU approach to the meaning of 'border controls' externally and internally. Inside the Schengen area, this function becomes much narrower vis-à-vis both its goals and definition. The role of border surveillance is the epitome of this conceptual heterogeneity, as the Commission attempts to herald a new era of law enforcement cooperation based on integration around border activities and frames the proper exercise of essential state functions as a fundamental precondition for a healthy Schengen. At the end of the day, however, the last word still lies with the member states, which have produced a complex ecosystem of agreements for these purposes. Against this background, heterogeneity in both scenarios creates pockets of discretion verging on arbitrariness. With vagueness and unstructured co-operation creating issues of legal certainty and possible gaps in individual protection, serious doubts arise about the capacity of the legal framework to achieve a fair balance between free movement and security within the meaning of this book.

# 10
# Controlling the Absence of Controls

## 10.1 Introduction

The law of internal border controls is characterized by heterogeneity of sources, actors, persons concerned, and objectives. The governance of this part of the Schengen acquis is shared between the EU and the member states, but is predicated upon the idea that member states remain the ultimate decision-makers in the control of their borders—where 'control' is understood as checks *and* surveillance activities, performed alone or in conjunction with other states. The degree of decentralization in this area is particularly visible in transnational law enforcement, where the minimalistic EU legal framework hides another world of interstate agreements and arrangements. The high level of internal security, which should be ensured alongside open borders, is still the security internal to the member states. The previous two chapters have highlighted the strain exerted by this set-up on terms of constitutional compliance, defined in this book as the consistency of EU and member state laws and practices with a structured network of relevant principles of Union law. While the law in the books and in actions has been shown to be overall in line with the principle of subsidiarity and the constitutional framework on task allocation, interinstitutional solidarity and fair treatment of the persons concerned have been seriously challenged. Within the meaning proposed in this research, legal fairness entails the non-arbitrary accommodation of claims in the designing and implementation of a 'practice'; the application of such a practice coherently with its objectives and underlying principles; and, particularly relevant to this chapter, the provision and deployment of effective mechanisms to react to unfairness, regarded as negation of both of the above.

Against this background, we hit the final milestone on our path by focusing on the mechanisms of scrutiny related to activities at the Schengen internal borders. As discussed in this context,[1] we see transparency as enabling scrutiny of EU or member state activities. Scrutiny is in turn necessary for accountability, this being an important vector of enforcement of EU values and constitutional compliance, we can distinguish mainly between legal, democratic, and administrative accountability. Legal accountability relates to 'the judicial enforcement of constitutional standards [and, above all] compliance with the rule of law'.[2] Democratic scrutiny materializes in a duty of explanation in a public forum,[3] whereas administrative scrutiny offers

[1] See section 6.1.

[2] TRS Allan, 'Accountability to Law' in N Bamforth and P Leyland (eds), *Accountability in the Contemporary Constitution* (Oxford University Press 2013) 77.

[3] V Schmidt and M Wood, 'Conceptualizing Throughput Legitimacy: Procedural Mechanisms of Accountability, Transparency, Inclusiveness and Openness in EU Governance' (2019) 97 Public Administration 730.

*The Law of EU Border Controls*. Leandro Mancano, Oxford University Press. © Leandro Mancano 2025.
DOI: 10.1093/9780191966187.003.0011

'post hoc answerability of administrators [and not only of elected officials] during the policy implementation' (as exemplified by the EU Ombudsman).[4] As in Chapter 6, we cluster the materials into individual-led scrutiny, and scrutiny at the level of the EU and the member state. Similarly, we must bear in mind the distinction between structural[5] and specific[6] mechanisms of scrutiny.

This being said, this chapter also presents as noticeably different from its homologue in Part II. The scope of the latter was much broader, which reflected the larger range of EU measures adopted as regards the governance of external border controls. The difference is also explained by the lesser degree of integration in this area and the extensive deference to member states' decision-making autonomy, which keeps much of the scrutiny activities within the member states themselves. Following the structure of the previous chapters, we consider pathways to scrutiny in relation to the absence of controls and their exceptions, and compensatory measures. Those are then followed by a discrete discussion of the Schengen Evaluation and Monitoring Mechanism (SEMM), which covers an administrative mechanism of scrutiny of the member states' actions in this area (and the Schengen acquis more broadly), and the analysis thereof links with several aspects discussed in the previous chapters. Overall, the chapter highlights the impact of heterogeneity on access to scrutiny and constitutional compliance.

## 10.2 Absence of Internal Border Controls and Exceptions

### 10.2.1 The Legal Framework at EU Level

In the previous chapters, we have seen that the ultimate decision about the reintroduction of controls lies with the member states. This is relevant not only to questions of solidarity and respect for essential functions, but also has consequences on the extent to which scrutiny can be exercised. In this scenario, we consider the different mechanisms of scrutiny accessible in situations related to the reintroduction of controls and situations associated with it. Firstly, we discuss the EU- or member state-driven scrutiny by the person concerned. Secondly, we look at the margin for individual scrutiny. This scenario uncovers the relevance of heterogeneity to access to scrutiny, particularly as regards the range of sources that could underpin a decision on the reintroduction of checks and the way tasks have been allocated.

In the context of the reintroduction of checks, and beyond the possibility for member states[7] or the Commission[8] to seize the Court of Justice 'directly',[9] the SBC

[4] P Kostadinova, 'Improving the Transparency and Accountability of EU Institutions: The Impact of the Office of the European Ombudsman' (2015) 53 Journal of Common Market Studies 1080.

[5] For example, Article 263 TFEU.

[6] See Council Regulation (EU) 2022/922 on the establishment and operation of an evaluation and monitoring mechanism to verify the application of the Schengen acquis, and repealing Regulation (EU) No 1053/2013 (SEMM Regulation) [2022] OJ L 160/1, or specific provisions of Regulation (EU) 2016/399 establishing a Schengen Borders Code [2016] OJ L 77/1 (SBC).

[7] TFEU, Article 259.

[8] TFEU, Article 258.

[9] The inverted commas are used here because, as the relevant provisions of the TFEU and the practice reveal, there would be preliminary steps to be taken by either the member states or the Commission before the action reaches Kirchberg.

established three main pathways to scrutiny for certain EU institutions and the member states. These materialize in obligations of information, reporting, and consultation. Firstly, the Commission and the member states are under an obligation to inform the EP of the arising of circumstances that might cause the reintroduction of internal border controls.[10] They must also inform the public of such decisions by indicating the start and end of the controls unless otherwise justified on security grounds.[11] Such communication need not possess any specific degree of detail, however. In other words, the Commission and the member states might be seen as having met their obligations by simply stating that certain circumstances have arisen which justify internal controls. Furthermore, the SBC allows member states to redact the notification concerning the introduction and prolongation of controls,[12] although the affected member states must be able to access that information through appropriate and secure channels. The European Parliament (EP) must receive the information contained in the notification on the basis of rules on the handling of classified information, but such information must not include the risk assessment.[13] Therefore, the degree of democratic scrutiny of such information is relatively limited.

Secondly, the reformed SBC provides a new system for specific reporting obligations. The Commission must report annually to the Council and the EP on the state of Schengen. The report must include information on the controls reintroduced during that year and the actions taken by the Commission in that regard. It must contain an assessment of the proportionality and necessity of those controls.[14] The state of Schengen report must also feature specific information on trends concerning the unauthorized movement of persons within the Schengen area. This aspect has always been at the forefront of the EU and member states' concerns since the coming into being of Schengen. The recent wave of legislative reforms, however, has given it much greater prominence in many different provisions of secondary law. One should hope that, at least, this will serve to enhance the level of transparency of the debate and decision-making related to concerns about unauthorized movement. One of the issues raised by the EP in the recent past, which also emerges from references in the legislation, concerns precisely the adoption of an 'impressionistic' approach to threats and controls at the expense of an evidence-based modus operandi.

Member states, for their part, must report on the reintroduction or prolongation of controls to the Council, the Commission, and the EP, on which the Commission may issue an opinion. Based on the evolution of the emergency and the impact of the measure, the Commission must regularly assess whether the controls are still justified. The member state's report must include a series of elements enabling said institutions to perform some form of scrutiny of the use of controls within the Schengen area.

[10] SBC, Article 31.
[11] SBC, Article 34.
[12] This would also include the risk assessment.
[13] SBC, Article 27(5).
[14] Here, presumably that assessment would be by the Commission. The questions raised above in the context of the member state's report remain, particularly considering the lack of public information underpinning the decision to reintroduce controls.

Unsurprisingly, the focus is on the initial follow-up, as well as ex-post assessment of proportionality and necessity, their effectiveness, and the impact on free movement of persons, especially in cross-border regions. The evaluation of the state's assessment should probably form an integral part of the ex-post scrutiny, but this could be a difficult exercise to engage with. Both the proportionality and effectiveness will have to be measured against the objectives of border controls, and the vocabulary of the SBC on this aspect is not always consistent. In a given situation, the results of this assessment might change, depending on whether the aim of the controls was to remedy the threat, or to address it. As mentioned, the two terms seem to set different thresholds, 'remedying' being clearly higher than 'addressing'. The difficulty is compounded by the reference to the ex-post investigation. It would be unreasonable to gauge the proportionality and necessity with the benefit of hindsight, as counterfactuals are notoriously very hard to prove. The nebulous nature of the goals of the controls would make that assessment even harder. It seems sounder to assume the ex-post part of the report to be forward-looking, with the view to learning lessons for the future. Importantly, the mandatory content of the report also includes a part on cooperation with neighbouring member states. As discussed in the previous two chapters, several provisions of the SBC give effect to a duty of solidarity and sincere cooperation, and these principles must guide the action of the member states wanting to reintroduce checks at their internal borders.

Thirdly, the consultation process might offer an indirect pathway to scrutiny.[15] Member states must take into account the outcome of this process. Flexible as it is, an obligation remains nonetheless—particularly if backed up by a rigorous interpretation of the principle of solidarity as proposed in this book.[16] The process aims to overcome unilateralism and embed solidarity into decision-making concerning the reintroduction of checks. The extent to which the process will be effective in achieving its objectives remains to be seen. One very practical issue is to do with the effectiveness of a scrutiny process where highly confidential and potentially classified information is involved. This is true for the administrative process of enforcement—for example, through an infringement procedure—and perhaps even more so should the Commission or another member state decide to take the member state reintroducing control before the Court of Justice. Also, on a more systemic level, this is a situation where the tension between different principles might emerge: namely, the respect for essential state functions, on the one hand, and mutual trust and solidarity, on the other. While the collision between the two is not *bound to* happen,[17] it is not entirely unlikely that it will. We have seen how obligations of solidarity can take a procedural form. While a breach of this principle will be found in the absence of evidence that the interests of other member states and the Union have been duly taken into account, we can expect that the threshold for finding a member state in breach of the obligation will be set quite high.

[15] SBC, Article 27a.

[16] See the discussion in section 2.5.1.

[17] Considering the Europeanization of the concept of internal security, and the emphasis placed by the Commission on the fact that each member state must play their part in defending the security of the Schengen area, it is possible that the collective interest and the protection of the essential state function will coincide, in certain situations.

Given the structural features of the law of internal border controls, the first point of contact for individual scrutiny would be at the national level. As shown in Chapter 9, private parties must first explore domestic remedies, especially as regards the exercise of controls that might be in breach of EU law, with the national court in turn referring a question to the EU Court of Justice. As regards individual scrutiny at the EU level, access to democratic scrutiny is underwhelming, as revealed by the member states' information and reporting duties discussed above. Administrative scrutiny is available via the possibility of lodging a complaint with the EU Ombudsman or the Commission. In this regard, we have seen that the Commission and the Council are protagonists in the process of reintroduction of control. However, the Commission in particular has been criticized for not fulfilling its role of guardian of the Treaties properly in situations where member states had kept controls in place beyond the limits of the SBC.[18] The question, therefore, arises as to whether those institutions could be the subject of an action for failure to act and/or an action for damages. The analysis of the Court's case law on the types of actions against Frontex tells us that a person's chances of succeeding are very slim for two main reasons.[19] As regards the failure to act, the Commission would be able to defuse the threat of infringement by defining its position. As to the action for annulment and damage related to the this decision, the Commission's discretion in initiating infringement proceedings against a member state would be seen as entailing at best an obligation to reconsider its decision not to act, which the Court would not consider to be an advantage capable of demonstrating the applicant's interest in bringing proceedings.[20]

### 10.2.2 Insight into France and Norway's Systems

Forms of scrutiny within member states vary, of course, depending on the features of their legal systems. In France, the decision on the reintroduction of controls can be challenged before the *Conseil d'État*.[21] Other independent bodies might offer a valuable pathway to scrutiny too. The Defender of Rights (DoR) is an independent constitutional authority,[22] which can receive complaints from any natural or legal persons considering that their rights or freedoms have been infringed by a public authority.[23] The *Contrôleur général des lieux de privation de liberté* is an independent administrative authority, responsible for monitoring the conditions of care and transfer of persons deprived of their liberty, in order to ensure that their fundamental rights are respected. For the same purposes, it supervises the execution by the administration of expulsion measures issued against aliens until they are handed over to the authorities

[18] P Cebulak and M Morvillo, *The Guardian Is Absent*, Verfassungsblog, 25 June 2021, https://verfassungsblog.de/the-guardian-is-absent/

[19] See Chapter 6, particularly section 6.3, 'In Transit'.

[20] See, by analogy, Case C-62/24 P, *ST v Frontex*, EU:C:2024:882, para 48.

[21] *Code de la justice administrative*, Article R311-1.

[22] See Article 71-1 Constitution.

[23] Loi organique n°2011-333 du 29 mars 2011, Article 5, which includes the right not to be subject to discrimination.

of the state of destination.[24] We must highlight that both these courts, as well as the DoR, have found practices related to the treatment of TCNs at the internal borders in violation of EU law, be it for detention ordered without an examination of the individual situation,[25] or where the illegality related to the systemic nature of the control that led to it.[26] These decisions are consistent with a bleak picture painted by other documents. In an official opinion from 2018 concerning the situation of TCNs at the Franco-Italian border, the *Commission nationale consultative des droits de l'homme* (CNCDH) raised several issues concerning the respect for the rights of the persons concerned. These related to the violations of the guarantee surrounding the non-admission procedure and of the rights of the persons concerned; violations of the rights and dignity of persons temporarily deprived of their liberty; specific situation of unaccompanied minors; and lack of identification and protection of victims of human trafficking at the Franco-Italian border.[27]

Similarly, the Norwegian Parliamentary Ombudsman (Sivilombudsmannen) serves as an independent institution overseeing the action of public bodies. The Ombudsman can investigate complaints about border control practices and compensatory measures, either through individual complaints or on its own initiative. The Ombudsman can issue recommendations to public authorities and highlight systemic issues. Although these recommendations are not legally binding, they carry significant moral and political weight. The Norwegian National Human Rights Institution (NIM) is tasked with promoting and protecting human rights in Norway. It monitors how border control measures impact human rights and can issue reports, make recommendations, and engage in advocacy to address any issues identified. Pathways to scrutiny for natural or legal persons mostly consist of access to documents and judicial challenges. Individuals have the right to access documents and information held by public authorities under the Freedom of Information Act (Offentleglova). They can also request access to personal data held by authorities under the Personal Data Act (personopplysningsloven), which implements the General Data Protection Regulation in Norway. This includes information processed during border control operations. Access to Police Directorate circulars is somewhat restricted. They can be accessed upon request but are not always available online. As for judicial challenges, decisions by border control authorities can be challenged in court. Individuals can bring cases to the ordinary courts, and ultimately to the Supreme Court if necessary. Courts can review the legality of administrative decisions and assess whether they comply with national and international law. It is worth bearing in mind, however, that Norway is not subject to the jurisdiction of the Court of Justice and that

[24] Loi n° 2007-1545 du 30 octobre 2007, Article 1.

[25] Decision of the Defender of the Rights n°2022-147, 30 June 2022, paras 25, 35, and 46 especially. The written observations were requested by the Court of Justice. See also Decision of the Defender of the Rights n°2024-008, 18 January 2024, paras 74 and 75. See T Fleury Graff and I Giauffret, 'Frontières de l'âge, frontières de l'État: retours choisis sur la jurisprudence 2022 en matière de migrations' (2023) 2 Revue critique de droit international privé 351.

[26] Cour d'appel de Paris, 1 May 2015, n°15/01621. See C Saas, 'Les contrôles d'identité "Schengen" viciés par l'absence d'aléa. Arrêt rendu par Cour d'appel de Paris' (2015) AJ Pénal 435.

[27] *Commission nationale consultative des droits de l'homme* (CNCDH), *Avis sur la situation des personnes migrantes à la frontière franco-italienne: missions dans les Hautes-Alpes et les Alpes-Maritimes*, mars-avril 2018 (adoption à l'unanimité), JORF n°150 du 1er juillet 2018.

an intergovernmental mixed committee deals with possible 'substantial differences' in the case law of the Court and the courts of Iceland or Norway, or in the application more broadly, of the provisions of the Schengen acquis.[28]

## 10.3 Compensatory Measures

As the previous two chapters have shown, we must distinguish between different types of compensatory measures that could be taken at or around an internal border. There are the older instruments such as the Convention Implementing the Schengen Agreement (CISA),[29] the Prüm, and the JITDecisions.[30] The exercise of police powers not amounting to measures equivalent to border checks, allowed under the SBC, falls under this category as well. Three more recent Recommendations have encouraged member states to take integration in cross-border policing a step further. Underneath this relatively thin layer of legislation, we have observed the labyrinth of interstate agreements. This section shows the relevance of heterogeneity to access to scrutiny in two main respects. Firstly, the heterogeneity of sources, levels of governance, and actors involved can seriously undermine a person's effective access to legal scrutiny. Given the impact of these measures on fundamental rights, this aspect is key to ensuring compliance with the rule of law. Secondly, we must consider the role of the heterogeneity of sources and levels of governance in relation to the Commission's exercise of administrative scrutiny, particularly as regards possible states' non-responsiveness to said Recommendations.

To start with the older instruments, the provisions of the CISA concerning the measures of interest to this research are still relevant. The recent 2022 Recommendation on operational police cooperation, which also covers said measures, stipulates that the definitions and guarantees contained therein must be based on and interpreted in line with applicable Union law, and particularly Articles 39 to 46 CISA.[31] It is, therefore, important to consider what are the mechanisms of control, broadly understood, of transnational policing occurring around the border between two member states. Consistent with the scope of this research, the main measures of such nature provided in the CISA are hot surveillance and hot pursuit. The previous chapters discussed conditions and limits of surveillance starting in one member state and continuing across the border into another one. We have also mentioned that, unless under the exceptional circumstances established in Article 40 CISA, hot surveillance can go ahead provided that authorization has been granted by the state in whose territory surveillance is continuing. The officers of the requesting state must at all times be able to prove that they are acting in an official capacity, and must carry a certification

[28] Agreement concluded by the Council of the European Union and the Republic of Iceland and the Kingdom of Norway concerning the latter's association with the implementation, application and development of the Schengen acquis [1999] OJ L 176/36, Article 10.

[29] Convention Implementing the Schengen Agreement (CISA) [2000] OJ L 239/19.

[30] Council Framework Decision 2002/465/JHA on joint investigation teams (JITs FD) [2002] OJ L 162/1.

[31] Council Recommendation 2022/915 on operational law enforcement cooperation [2022] OJ L 158/53.

showing that authorization has been granted.[32] All operations of this kind must be reported to the competent authorities of the requested state. If so requested by the state where the surveillance took place, the surveillant state must assist with the inquiry following the operation. The same provisions apply to the case of hot pursuit, as referred to in the previous two chapters, with a series of additional safeguards in all likelihood explained by the greater intrusiveness of this measure. The pursuing officer must report on their mission to the competent authorities of the state of pursuit. They must remain at those authorities' disposal until the circumstances of the pursuing officer's action have been sufficiently clarified.[33] Therefore, the legal framework is very much focused on interstate scrutiny, whereas the effective protection of the persons subject to those measures is left to national procedural autonomy. The rules on the liability of officers carrying out hot surveillance and hot pursuit are similar to those provided for in subsequent instruments. The party in which territory the damage occurred must make good the losses caused, but the state of the officer who caused the damage is liable and must reimburse the sums paid by the state where the measure took place.[34] Comparable rules apply to cross-border joint operations, including cases of cross-border assistance on mass gatherings or major events[35] and JITs.[36] As regards criminal liability for offences committed by or against them, and unless provided differently in an agreement, seconded officers must be treated as the host state's officers.[37]

As for intra-EU transfer post-apprehension in border areas, the person has the right to appeal in line with national law and must be provided with an effective remedy as per Article 47 CFR.[38] We must presume that the law in question is the law of the transferring state. For the purposes of the appeal, information about legal representations must be provided in writing and in a language that they can understand.[39] The appeal, however, must not have suspensive effect, which will significantly undermine the effectiveness of such pathway to scrutiny.

The second group of measures concerns the three Recommendations issued between 2017 and 2024. These actions taken by the EU in the area of compensatory measures at the internal borders raise questions in terms of scrutiny. Two, inextricably linked, issues arise. Is the content of the recommendation compatible with certain provisions of the Treaties, and particularly Article 4(2) TEU and 72 TFEU? Could the member states face consequences for non or incorrect implementation thereof? A decisive argument in support of a positive finding of compatibility of the recommendation with those provisions of primary law lies in their non-legally binding nature. In other words, those Articles would remain unaffected because of the absence of consequence for member states' inaction. If this is the case, a negative answer to the

[32] This specific requirement does not apply to hot surveillance without prior authorization.

[33] CISA, Article 41.

[34] CISA, Article 43.

[35] Council Decision 2008/615/JHA on the stepping up of cross-border cooperation, particularly in combating terrorism and cross-border crime [2008] OJ L 210/1 (Prüm Decision), Article 21.

[36] JITs FD, Articles 2 and 3.

[37] Prüm Decision, Article 22.

[38] SBC, Article 23a(2a).

[39] SBC, Article 23a(2a) refers more specifically to a language that they understand or 'are reasonably supposed to understand'. It is not difficult to see how this might lend itself to flexible interpretation by the competent authorities.

second question flows naturally and, in turn, creates issues of accountability. It is also worth considering to what extent the content of those measures would impinge upon the prerogatives protected by Articles 4(2) TEU and 72 TFEU, even if member states were to be held accountable somehow for their non-compliance. Especially in the case of hot pursuit and surveillance, the pursuing or surveillant officer—and by extension the member state to which they belong—would not be ensuring the territorial integrity of the host state, maintaining law and order and safeguarding its national security; nor would those measures affect the exercise of the host state's responsibilities on the maintenance of law and order and the safeguarding of internal security. The officer of the home state, in other words, would not act to replace or step in *au lieu de* the host state's authorities. Rather, they would *continue* the exercise of their own responsibilities across the border, under certain conditions, and due to the specific circumstances of the case.

## 10.4 The Schengen Evaluation and Monitoring Mechanism

The SEMM Regulation establishes a system of evaluation and monitoring of the application of the Schengen acquis. A series of preliminary observations are in order. Firstly, as the name suggests, the mechanism governs two types of activities which are rather different in nature: evaluation and monitoring. Secondly, the material scope of the Regulation coincides with the 'borders' of the Schengen acquis. Just like the physical borders of the Area of Freedom, Security and Justice, the metaphorical frontiers of the Schengen acquis are left open, as the Regulation applies to any current *and future* areas forming part of Schengen, and includes the absence of controls inside the EU, police and judicial cooperation in criminal matters, and judicial cooperation.[40] In terms of what specific measures compose the Schengen acquis, these are the provisions integrated into EU law via Protocol no 19, the acts that build on them, or that are *otherwise related to them.* The open nature of the Schengen acquis borders might not be inconsequential, especially considering that the SEMM Regulation would apply to such not-so-clearly identified groups of measures. Thirdly, the evaluation can take account of the functioning of the authorities that apply the Schengen acquis. This suggests that the method, the findings, or the consequences thereof might be adjusted to the characteristics of the relevant body.

### 10.4.1 Actors and Coordination

The Commission has a coordination role as regards the establishment of the annual and multiannual evaluation programmes. These documents are important insofar as they include the periodic and thematic evaluations (but not the unannounced ones). The multiannual evaluation programme, established by the Commission, covers a seven-year period. Such a programme must be adopted by an implementing act,

[40] SEMM Regulation, recital 6 and Article 1.

and must be transmitted to the Council and the European Parliament.[41] By the same source, the Commission also establishes an annual evaluation programme, which must be based *in particular* on risk analyses and the same information used for the multiannual programme.[42] As another example of the potential spillover impact of Frontex *into* the Schengen, the SEMM Regulation prescribes that Frontex submit risk analysis to the Commission, the Council, and the EP for the purposes of the annual evaluation programme, as well as a separate risk analysis with recommendations for unannounced evaluations.[43]

The Commission can enter into arrangements with other Union bodies participating in the implementation of the acquis.[44] It can use their 'relevant mechanisms and instruments' to prepare its activities under the SEMM, to improve awareness of the functioning of the borderless areas and avoid duplication of efforts and conflicting measures. The Commission can also use information from third parties (eg NGOs and independent authorities) to plan its activities, and must give the member state the opportunity to comment on the substance of this information.[45] The Commission must establish, with no specified form, guidelines on a number of aspects, including conducting visits, evaluation and monitoring activities, follow-up procedures, and synergies with other evaluation and monitoring mechanisms.[46] Its coordination role extends to the drafting of the questionnaires, the scheduling and conducting of visits, and the drafting of evaluation reports and recommendations. It also ensures that the follow-up and monitoring activities are carried out. It is rather unfortunate that no further detail is provided on an important aspect of the exercising of the very centralized coordination power by the Commission. This is particularly the case with regard to the involvement of other EU bodies, as well as the coordination with other monitoring mechanisms. Combined with the absence of a duty of information vis-à-vis the EP, this aspect of the SEMM leaves much to be desired in terms of democratic scrutiny.

More operationally, the evaluations (first-time, periodic, unannounced, or thematic) aim to verify the application of the acquis by a member state with a view to assessing its overall performance in that regard. They are carried out by teams consisting of experts from member states and the Commission. The two levels of governance are jointly responsible, and must cooperate fully—just as the Council and the Commission must—to ensure the effective implementation of the SEMM. The member states must take all measures to assist the Commission in this regard, including by allowing the latter access areas, documents, and persons as relevant. The Council, for its part, must carry out its political role by discussing the report and, more generally, the implementation and the proper functioning of the borderless area.[47] The relevant Union body may send observers, although they do not participate in the decision-making process of the team. The Commission appoints a lead expert

41 SEMM Regulation, Article 12.
42 SEMM Regulation, Article 13.
43 SEMM Regulation, Article 8(1) and (2).
44 SEMM Regulation, Article 7(1).
45 SEMM Regulation, Article 11.
46 SEMM Regulation, Article 26.
47 SEMM Regulation, Article 3.

and proposes a member state's lead expert, who is in turn appointed by the team members. The lead experts are responsible for carrying out the evaluation, coordinating the drafting of the report, the quality check, and follow-up, as well as monitoring activities *where appropriate*.[48] Remarkably, the SEMM Regulation does not seem to contemplate the hypothesis that there might be disagreement between the lead experts, despite the heterogeneity of levels of governance and actors involved. It only provides that the team shall endeavour to reach a compromise in case of disagreement.[49]

### 10.4.2 Forms of Evaluation and Monitoring

There are four forms of evaluations: first-time, periodic, unannounced, and thematic. Unannounced evaluations can be organized *in particular*: to evaluate the application of the acquis at the internal borders; where there are *emerging* or *systemic* problems with a potentially significant impact on the borderless area, including where this could give rise to a public policy or internal security threat *within that area*; and when there are grounds to consider that a member state is seriously neglecting its obligations.[50] The unannounced visits are particularly important for a number of reasons. Firstly, and more generally, the list of grounds on which they might be organized is left open. Here, we must note the absence of references to sources. The information from which the Commission has formed an opinion that might trigger an unannounced evaluation also remains entirely open. Secondly, each of the grounds is indicative of the direction of travel taken by the borderless area. The Commission can decide to evaluate the Schengen acquis applicable at the internal borders, potentially at any time it deems relevant. The reference to the acquis applicable at the internal borders must be read in the broader context of cross-border policing. As the member states are being strongly encouraged to step up integration in this area, including by joint patrols and surveillance at the internal borders, this provision might become an important tool for the Commission to 'gently nudge' member states to implement its recommendations in this sense. Furthermore, this ground confirms the barycentric role played by the borderless area in the Europeanization of the concept of internal security. However, as discussed in previous chapters, this specific role of the Commission vis-à-vis Schengen internal security might create tension with Article 4(2) TEU. Thirdly, the vocabulary is not consistent across the SEMM Regulation. The reference to emerging or systemic problems does not really match the concept of 'serious deficiency'. The question therefore arises as to whether the two are to be interpreted uniformly or not and, either way, what the consequences might be. Monitoring activities can include the review of action plans and follow-up reports submitted by the evaluated member states, revisits, or verification visits.[51] Visits also constitute an important instrument. They can reveal inter alia a deficiency constituting a serious threat to public policy or internal security within the borderless area, or a deficiency 'identified on the basis of the risk of

[48] SEMM Regulation, Article 18.
[49] SEMM Regulation, Article 20(1).
[50] SEMM Regulation, Article 4.
[51] SEMM Regulation, Article 5.

a systemic fundamental rights violation'.[52] Nonetheless, the SEMM Regulation offers little on when, and under which conditions, visits can or must take place. This is particularly so when it comes to unannounced visits at the internal borders, for which the Commission must not give prior notification.[53]

### 10.4.3 Outcome

The Commission adopts the evaluation report through an implementing act. The sources of this report are: replies to the questionnaire,[54] any information obtained from relevant Union bodies or third parties, and the findings of the evaluation activity. Interestingly, documentary or digital material can also be included, but there is no reference to the obligation to do so (not even in situations when that might be necessary). The report must list the deficiencies, areas of improvement, and best practices. The findings are categorized as 'best practice', 'improvement necessary', or 'non-compliant'. The Commission must inform the member state concerned and the Council that a serious deficiency was identified during an evaluation, as well as the relevant Union bodies which could provide assistance. The member state must take immediate remedial action, and inform the Commission and the other member states in this regard. Regrettably, neither the Commission nor the member state have an obligation to inform the European Parliament.[55]

The report must also contain recommendations, unless the member state concerned substantially contests the content of the draft report or the nature of the finding. In the case of contestation, the Commission must submit a separate proposal to the Council containing the recommendations. The Council will then adopt the recommendations by means of an implementing decision. Another case where the Council is tasked with the adoption of recommendations is where serious deficiencies have been identified.[56] For its part, the member state concerned must send the Commission and the Council an action plan on the implementation of the recommendations, and report regularly on it. If it does not do this, the Commission will inform the Council and the European Parliament.[57]

Specific provisions apply in the case where a report finds the existence of serious deficiencies. In the context of an evaluation and on duly justified imperative grounds of urgency, the Commission must adopt the report via an immediately applicable implementing act, send it to the EP and propose recommendations for remedial actions to the Council. The Council must adopt the recommendations and send them to the EP and the national parliaments. It must also set *proportionate*—different from reasonable, as defined in other cases—time limits for the implementation of the

[52] SEMM Regulation, Article 22(5).
[53] SEMM Regulation, Article 19.
[54] These are prepared by the Commission, which can consult relevant EU bodies for the purposes of drafting them. SEMM Regulation, Article 14.
[55] SEMM Regulation, Article 22(1) and (2).
[56] SEMM Regulation, Articles 3 Article 20(5).
[57] SEMM Regulation, Article 21.

recommendations. Similar provisions apply when such deficiencies are identified in the context of a visit. Therefore, it is the Commission that determines whether the violation(s) meet the threshold of seriousness—that is, a threat to public policy or internal security of the borderless area, or risk of systemic fundamental rights violation. However, it is the Council that formally adopts the recommendation. In the case of recommendations adopted following a visit, the SEMM states that they shall be without prejudice to Article 29 SBC or Article 42(1) EBCG Regulation.[58] It is important to coordinate the content of the SEMM with these provisions. As known, Article 29 SBC empowers the Council to recommend that a member state should reintroduce controls, where serious deficiencies at the external borders threaten the area of free movement. A similar power, in a nearly identical situation, is granted to the Council under Article 42(1) EBCG Regulation. The 'without prejudice' clause might mean that the SEMM scenario is a residual one, with either provisions under the SBC or the EBCG Regulation to be preferred. However, this idea is somehow undermined by the SEMM Regulation itself, which stipulates that the recommendations made under the Mechanism must be *complementary to* the vulnerability assessment under the EBCG Regulation.[59] In a showcase of heterogeneity and ensuing legal uncertainty, doubts remain as to the relationships between these different grounds for intervention, which essentially cover the same situation: namely, deficiencies at the external borders putting the survival of Schengen at risk.

### 10.4.4 Evaluations of the Evaluation

The Commission reviews the application of the SEMM and submits a report to the Council and the EP six months after the conclusion of the first multiannual evaluation programme.[60] The Commission must report annually and comprehensively to the EP and the Council on the evaluations carried out during the previous year. The report must be public. The information included in such a report must cover the evaluations, the conclusions drawn from them (rather than the content of the evaluations themselves, it seems), and the progress on the implementation of remedial actions. It must identify common issues, best practices, and solutions, and take account of synergies with other monitoring tools to 'increase awareness about the functioning' of the borderless area. The report must also be sent to the national parliaments. The Council must discuss the report, 'considering the contribution of the evaluations to the functioning of the area without internal border control'. The Commission must also inform the EP and the Council twice a year on the progress made with implementation of member states' action plans, particularly as regards the revisits and verification visits.[61]

[58] SEMM Regulation, Article 22(5).
[59] SEMM Regulation, Article 10(3).
[60] SEMM Regulation, Article 27.
[61] SEMM Regulation, Article 25.

## 10.5 Conclusions

The system of scrutiny inside the Schengen area is structurally similar to that of external border controls, to the extent that it rests on systemic and specific pathways. Those pathways can be taken by the EU, the member states, or the person concerned. This is as far as the analogy goes, however. Overall, the potential for individual-driven scrutiny is much less significant than it would be for activities related to external border controls. One of the key reasons lies in the role of member states as ultimate decision-makers, with regard to both the reintroduction of controls and transnational law enforcement cooperation. To be sure, remedies before national authorities remain available. In this regard, the insight into certain state practices shows that challenges to decisions on the reintroduction and prolongation of controls are unlikely to be successful. We must also note, in fairness, the view taken by some national bodies that the use of internal border controls has vastly exceeded the limits of the legislation. National procedural autonomy dominates individual scrutiny in the area of compensatory measures as well. The informal nature of the cooperation, and the wording of the agreements discussed in the previous chapter, might make it difficult for individuals to know effectively what pathways to scrutiny they have in the jurisdiction where the cross-border action is taken. In both strands, and subject to a future assessment based on the implementation, the recent reforms contain significant changes to EU and member state-led scrutiny. On the one hand, the reformed SBC grants member states more extensive leeway in terms of time limits to keep controls in place and grounds for doing so. On the other hand, it also constrains this increased discretion by introducing structured and solidarity-based mechanisms of consultation. In this context, the EP is not always in a particularly strong position. While several provisions establish an obligation to inform the EP, this is not the case on other important issues. Furthermore, even where such a duty exists, restrictions could apply based on reasons of confidentiality. Going forward, the use of the SEMM in relation to the actions recommended by the Commission on law enforcement cooperation might open new and interesting areas of development. This is particularly so in light of the Commission's approach to Article 4(2) TEU, and more broadly the idea that certain reserved competences should be used by the member states in line with the Schengen acquis and its objectives. In the background, those forms of heterogeneity build on the heterogeneity of membership of the Schengen area. Countries like Norway are not covered by the EU system of judicial remedies. The emergence of significant divergence between case laws is dealt with by an intergovernmental committee, which in turn can increase the heterogeneity of standards of protection inside the area without internal border controls.

# Conclusion

## Looking Back, Moving Forward: What Future for Heterogeneity and Borders in Europe?

This systemic assessment of the law of EU border controls started from three keywords: heterogeneity, systemic appropriateness, and conditions. The analytical umbrella of heterogeneity, understood as the quality or state of consisting of dissimilar or diverse elements, has been of significant heuristic value. We have focused on four expressions of heterogeneity: levels of governance and actors, sources, persons concerned, and objectives. Adopting these mutually interactive forms of heterogeneity has helped us answer certain fundamental questions on the making and implementation of the law: who, how, when, for/against whom, and why. The Treaties establish external and internal border controls as an area of shared competence, while carving out a protected space of sovereignty for the member states' essential state functions. The plurality of decision-making centres in this area, only compounded by the enhanced role entrusted to the EU's agencies over the years, has contributed to an existing trend of multiplication of sources underpinning the decision to exercise controls. In this context, at the outer frontiers of the EU as well as within it, border controls are meant to be omnipotent. Externally, they must facilitate regular travel, prevent illegal immigration and cross-border crime, and identify and protect the vulnerable. This diverse set of goals corresponds to a stereotyped range of addressees of control. Similarly, once inside the borderless area, the EU aims for a fair balance between protecting free movement and safeguarding internal security, particularly by measures meant to prevent the exploitation of the absence of internal border controls for the purposes of cross-border crime or irregular movement across Schengen. This mission is notoriously made more difficult by the coexistence of a general prohibition of checks on anyone and the lack of free movement rights for most categories of non-EU citizens.

This perspective has incentivized us to evaluate the implications of heterogeneity in three interrelated respects: the allocation of border-control related tasks as regards both law-making and implementation; the dynamic of interinstitutional cooperation; and the impact on the persons concerned. Combining those themes, we have addressed the overarching question as to whether the appropriate action is being taken at the appropriate level of governance, and by the appropriate actor, on the basis of the appropriate source, for the appropriate purpose, vis-à-vis the appropriate group of persons. Appropriateness, understood in a systemic sense beyond the more specific issue of proportionality, has entailed an assessment of constitutional compliance, regarded as the consistency of EU and national laws and practices with a structured network of relevant principles of EU law. This approach to appropriateness

*The Law of EU Border Controls*. Leandro Mancano, Oxford University Press. © Leandro Mancano 2025.
DOI: 10.1093/9780191966187.003.0012

as constitutional compliance has been built on a view of the EU's legal order resting on the interaction among three building blocks: values, principles, and objectives. In the EU constitutional architecture, principles ensure the pursuit of objectives in line with the Union's values. Both principles and objectives flow from the values, with these values informing the entire system by concretizing figures of variable degrees of specificity and being operationalized via rules and procedures. Against this background, the structured network of principles used in this book has consisted primarily of the following legal constructs, deemed most suitable to address the questions raised by heterogeneity: subsidiarity, solidarity, and fairness. Subsidiarity and respect for essential state functions are important tools to deal with issues of task allocation in an area of shared competence, which also constitutes the quintessential expression of national sovereignty. With member states retaining ultimate responsibility for most decisions related to the implementation of border controls, the principles of mutual trust and solidarity are key to coordinating the plethora of decision-making centres involved. A relatively narrow understanding of solidarity has been applied in this book, as a procedural obligation for the competent actor to take into account the interest of the Union and of other member states. As border controls entail the exercise of authority over individuals, the Treaties require that the law and practice be fair to the persons concerned. Fairness as theorized in this book requires three main elements: non-arbitrary accommodation of claims in the designing and implementation of a 'practice'; compliance, in designing and implementing a practice, with the intentions of a practice and the mutually accepted principles behind it; and provision and deployment of effective mechanisms to react to legal unfairness. While the EU and its member states enjoy a sovereign right to decide who can access their territory, they have also accepted certain constraints on that right: inter alia, non-refoulement, non-discrimination, the right to liberty, the right to access asylum procedures, and effective judicial protection. To make the most of the concepts of heterogeneity and constitutional compliance as defined in this book, the three axes of interaction must be considered together in an integrated analysis with a focus on conditions for control, on the persons concerned, and the associated or mandated conducts associated with both. In light of the EU's constitutional edifice, systemic appropriateness is an imperative requirement for the law of EU border controls. An assessment thereof in the sense described above illuminates the legal conditions *for* the EU as an area without internal frontiers.

Against this background, the law of EU border controls has shown serious issues of constitutional compliance. The objectives of the relevant measures broadly align with those stated in the Treaties' Articles. However, the provisions on conditions and their combined operation are either inappropriate to achieve those goals or might prove to be as such if not supported by a rigorous application of certain fundamental principles of EU law. The principle of subsidiarity and the respect for essential state functions have generally emerged intact from the assessment. On the one hand, EU border controls have undergone a remarkable process of centralization over the past two decades, expressed primarily via legal approximation or greater powers conferred to EU agencies such as Frontex. On this basis, the EU institutions (mostly the Council and the Commission) and Frontex have taken initiatives in a number of important areas such as retaliation on third countries in the context of the common visa policy, establishment of risk indicators steering decisions on visas and travel authorizations, and co-optation of third countries in the management of the Union's external borders. These actions have widened and deepened the scope of the law of EU border controls, through reliance on sources going way beyond those set in Article 288 TFEU—for example, delegated acts, status agreements, working arrangements, memoranda of understanding, and administrative decisions internal to the agency. This centralization has been mitigated by three structural features of the legal framework: a decentralized system of implementation (eg in the processing of visa, travel authorization, or asylum applications); reliance on 'innocuous' sources, such as recommendations or guidance, in areas where concerns of national sovereignty have been voiced most prominently (such as criminalization of humanitarian assistance and NGO-driven search and rescue at sea); and self-restraint from legislating in favour of interstate co-operation, as shown by the maze of bi- and multi-lateral agreements characterizing transnational law enforcement around the internal borders.

This set-up, jointly with the conditions for controls and on the addressees of control, poses several challenges to interinstitutional solidarity and fair treatment of the persons concerned. Often, these two have proved to be inextricably linked. Issues of solidarity have emerged particularly from situations where a certain actor is allowed to act (or not) at their discretion, but their formally lawful (in)action might jeopardize the achievement of the objectives of the law. The law of external and internal border controls is dotted with such examples: from a state's possibility of revoking a short-term visa issued by another member state, to the state's right not to authorize other states or Frontex to take action in its territorial water where not taking part in a joint surveillance operation, through to the state refusal to request Frontex's assistance in cases of pressure at its external borders, or its decision to introduce/prolong checks at the internal borders despite the Commission's or other states' recommendations or opinion. In these circumstances, an application of a duty of procedural solidarity could orient the conduct of the actor in question, even though the issue of allocation of responsibility has already been resolved by the legislature. Two dilemmas arise from such an application of solidarity: what to do if the states and the common interests are not aligned, and to what extent can a case law-based duty stretch a system of task allocation established by the Union's legislature? To put the latter question differently, would procedural solidarity enhance or reduce constitutional compliance? We have devised a test for those purposes which does justice to the shared nature of this area of competence and builds on a number of criteria: is the power associated with a derogation from a rule of EU law? Are the relevant provisions giving effect to an express duty of taking into account the states' or the EU's interest? What is/was the impact of the competent actor's conduct, regard being had to the objectives of the law and its underlying principles? While a state's refusal to allow certain actions in its territorial waters constitutes no derogation from a rule of EU law, that state might be in breach of solidarity where its decision has no justifications in circumstances that have led to the loss of lives at sea. By the same token, a state's power to reinstate or prolong checks at the internal borders must be an exception, but departure from the Commission's or other states' views might be underpinned by reliable evidence substantiating the reasons for doing so.

While heterogeneity impacts solidarity, particularly in the implementation of the framework, the law in the books *and* in action have failed to live up to their proclaimed aspirations of fair treatment. This failure emerges from all three parameters of fairness proposed in this book. Firstly, the non-arbitrary accommodation of competing claims is undermined by the major role played by large information systems in making border-control related decisions—from the country of departure through to inside the Schengen area. The wide range of statistics and correlation shape a process bound to move away from an individualized assessment and raise serious concerns in terms of non-discrimination.

Secondly, and relatedly, the law and its implementation are often inconsistent with the objectives and underlying principles of border controls. Given the heterogeneity of objectives pursued by EU border controls, the overemphasis on preventing entry without the appropriate counterweights can occur at the expense of facilitating regular travel or identifying and protecting vulnerable persons. The degree of the imbalance takes this issue beyond the legitimate realm of policy discretion and breaches the principle of effectiveness. The imbalance in the pursuit of the manifold objectives of the legal framework is only part of the story. As the flip side of the coin, the law is inappropriate for dealing with the heterogeneity of persons concerned it intends to address. This is exemplified by the system of border procedures introduced by the asylum and migration pact, which can seriously hinder access to fair asylum procedures and enable years of detention at the borders. The same holds true for the framework applicable within Schengen, in spite of—or perhaps even more so because of—one crucial distinction: the understanding of border controls itself. While the presiding over the external frontiers is built upon the blending of crime prevention and migration management, with checks and surveillance joined at the hip, the opposite can be said for internal border controls. Within Schengen, the EU keeps the illusion of an area without internal border controls alive through a formally rigid distinction between checks and surveillance: the former prohibited, the latter encouraged and given effect to by an ecosystem of interstate agreements.

Thirdly, the persons' access to effective mechanisms to challenge unfairness is restricted by a number of factors. In this case too, heterogeneity visibly affects the fairness of the framework. The heterogeneity of sources across the board in the law of EU border controls results in low standards of legal certainty and curtails avenues for redress. The heterogeneity of objectives can make it hard to pursue transparency and accountability of the competent bodies, with the legal framework allowing them to shield themselves behind confidentiality and security. The heterogeneity of levels of governance and actors creates a situation of 'divide and conquer', where many bodies and officers are empowered with monitoring functions, but nobody bears responsibility.

At the end of this rocky journey, the time has come to lay our eyes on the road ahead and put our two cents on possible good news. The EU overhauled the asylum and migration system in 2024 through a very controversial reform, which has already been scrutinized by several commentators. As we move forward, close observation of the implementation of those measures will be key to the accountability of the EU and member states in what promises to significantly worsen the state of constitutional compliance of border controls. Relatedly, and beyond the specifics of the reform, member states' laws and practices can prove to be a particularly fruitful strand of investigation. The existing scholarship has demonstrated this to be the case not only as regards examples of non-compliance, as revealed by the studies on the reaction by certain Eastern European countries to the Russian invasion of Ukraine. Gaining insight into national approaches can also bring good practices to the fore, with a view to improving the rule of law across the Union. This is apparent from the example of the Italian Supreme Court, which has used Italy's obligations under international law—and the non-refoulement specifically—to hold private parties accountable for illegal pushbacks at sea *and* to exempt from criminal liability TCNs at risk of inhumane treatment. More broadly, research in member states' legal regimes can shed light on the different ways the law of border controls is operationalized across the Union, and thus advance the knowledge of the field. This can be seen, for example, in the law of internal border controls. The expansive interpretation of the concept of 'new threat', elaborated by the French *Conseil d'État* and endorsed by the Norwegian Supreme Court, could legalize extensive and consecutive periods of border controls at the internal borders. The fragmented framework(s) of transnational policing around the internal borders is an area of extreme interest too, especially considering the misalignment between their relevance and their relatively underexplored nature. Issues of heterogeneity and constitutional compliance are here to stay, above and beyond the specific subject matter of this research. This book hopes to make a contribution to the debate on border controls and EU constitutional law more broadly that will survive the test of time.

# Index

*For the benefit of digital users, indexed terms that span two pages (e.g., 52–53) may, on occasion, appear on only one of those pages.*